# SOCIAL SECURITY LEGIS
## SUPPLEMENT 2013

General Editor
**Nick Wikeley, M.A. (Cantab)**

Commentary by
**David Bonner, LL.B., LL.M.**
*Emeritus Professor of Law, University of Leicester*
*Formerly Member, Social Security Appeal Tribunals*

**Ian Hooker, LL.B.**
*Formerly Lecturer in Law, University of Nottingham*
*Formerly Chairman, Social Security Appeal Tribunals*

**Richard Poynter B.C.L., M.A. (Oxon)**
*District Tribunal Judge,*
*Judge of the Upper Tribunal*

**Mark Rowland, LL.B.**
*Judge of the Upper Tribunal*

**Robin White, M.A., LL.M.**
*Emeritus Professor of Law, University of Leicester,*
*Judge of the Upper Tribunal*

**Nick Wikeley, M.A. (Cantab)**
*Judge of the Upper Tribunal,*
*Emeritus Professor of Law,*
*University of Southampton*

**David W. Williams, LL.M., Ph.D., C.T.A.**
*Judge of the Upper Tribunal,*
*Honorary Professor of Tax Law,*
*Queen Mary College, London*

**Penny Wood, LL.B., M.Sc.**
*District Tribunal Judge*

Consultant to Vol.II
**John Mesher, B.A., B.C.L., LL.M.**
*Judge of the Upper Tribunal,*
*Professor Associate of Law,*
*University of Sheffield*

Consultant Editor
**Child Poverty Action Group**

**SWEET & MAXWELL**  **THOMSON REUTERS**

Published in 2014 by
Sweet & Maxwell, 100 Avenue Road, London NW3 3PF
Part of Thomson Reuters (Professional) UK Limited
(Registered in England & Wales, Company No 1679046.
Registered Office and address for service:
Aldgate House, 33 Aldgate High Street,
London EC3N 1DL)

Typeset by Interactive Sciences Ltd, Gloucester
Printed and bound in Great Britain by
Ashford Colour Press, Gosport, Hants

For further information on our products and services,
visit www.sweetandmaxwell.co.uk

No natural forests were destroyed to make this product.
Only farmed timber was used and re-planted.

A CIP catalogue record for this book is
available from the British Library

ISBN 978–0–414–03390–0

# PREFACE

This is the combined Supplement to the 2013/14 edition of the four volume work, *Social Security Legislation*, which was published in September 2013. However, this Supplement does *not* include the primary and secondary legislation governing the new universal credit and associated commentary. This will appear in a separate new Vol.V of this series, *Universal Credit*, to be published shortly.

Part I of this Supplement contains other new legislation (Acts and Regulations), presented in the same format as the main volumes. This will enable readers to note very quickly relevant new sets of legislation. The most significant additions are the Jobseeker's Allowance Regulations 2013 (SI 2013/378) and the Employment and Support Allowance Regulations 2013 (SI 2013/379). These do not replace their 1996 and 2008 predecessors, but provide for a purely contribution-based benefit (new-style JSA and new-style ESA respectively) to run alongside universal credit in the "Pathfinder" areas. There are also important new Regulations reflecting the accession of Croatia to the EU.

Parts II, III, IV and V contain the standard updating material—a separate Part for each volume of the main work—which amends the legislative text and key aspects of the commentary, drawing attention to important recent case law, so as to be up to date as at January 1, 2014. Part VI, the final section of the Supplement, gives some notice of changes forthcoming between that date and the date to which the main work (2014/15 edition) will be up to date (mid-April) and some indication of the April 2014 benefit rates, and takes account of changes known to us as at January 1, 2014.

Among the many changes, particularly noteworthy are those with respect to:

- The amendments to existing legislation consequential upon the introduction of universal credit in "Pathfinder" areas;
- Developments in Upper Tribunal case law relating to both disability living allowance (DLA) and the descriptors for employment and support allowance (ESA);
- Further changes impacting on right to reside;
- New powers relating to civil penalties as an alternative to prosecution in cases of benefit fraud or other breaches.

As always we welcome comments from those who use this Supplement. Please address these to the General Editor, Nick Wikeley, c/o School of Law, The University of Southampton, Highfield, Southampton SO17 1BJ (njw@soton.ac.uk).

David Bonner
Ian Hooker
John Mesher
Richard Poynter
Mark Rowland

Robin White
Nick Wikeley
David Williams
Penny Wood
January 16, 2014

# CONTENTS

# USING THE UPDATING MATERIAL IN THIS SUPPLEMENT

The amendments and updating contained in Parts II–V of this Supplement are keyed in to the page numbers of the relevant main volume of *Social Security Legislation 2013/14*. Where there have been a significant number of changes to a provision, the whole section, subsection, paragraph or regulation, as amended, will tend to be reproduced. Other changes may be noted by an instruction to insert or substitute new material or to delete part of the existing text. The date the change takes effect is also noted. Where explanation is needed of the change, or there is updating to do to existing annotations but no change to the legislation, you will also find commentary in this Supplement. The updating material explains new statutory material, takes on board Upper Tribunal or court decisions, or gives prominence to points which now seem to warrant more detailed attention.

This Supplement amends the text of the main volumes of *Social Security Legislation 2013/14* to be up to date as at January 1, 2014.

Nick Wikeley
General Editor

# PAGES OF MAIN VOLUMES AFFECTED BY MATERIAL IN THIS SUPPLEMENT

*Pages of Main Volumes Affected by Material in this Supplement*

# VOLUME 2

# VOLUME 3

*Pages of Main Volumes Affected by Material in this Supplement*

# VOLUME 4

*Pages of Main Volumes Affected by Material in this Supplement*

# TABLE OF ABBREVIATIONS USED IN THIS SERIES

| | |
|---|---|
| 1978 Act | Employment Protection (Consolidation) Act 1978 |
| 1979 Act | Pneumoconiosis (Workers' Compensation) Act 1979 |
| 1995 Regulations | Social Security (Incapacity for Work) (General) Regulations 1995 |
| 1998 Act | Social Security Act 1998 |
| 1999 Regulations | Social Security and Child Support (Decisions and Appeals) Regulations 1999 |
| 2002 Act | Tax Credits Act 2002 |
| 2004 Act | Child Trust Funds Act 2004 |
| (No.2) Regulations | Statutory Paternity Pay (Adoption) and Statutory Adoption Pay (Adoptions from Overseas) (No.2) Regulations 2003 |
| A1P1 | First Protocol, art.1 to the European Convention on Human Rights |
| AA | Attendance Allowance |
| AA 1992 | Attendance Allowance Act 1992 |
| AA Regulations | Social Security (Attendance Allowance) Regulations 1991 |
| AAC | Administrative Appeal Chamber |
| AACR | Administrative Appeals Chamber Reports |
| AAW | Algemene Arbeidsongeschiktheidswet (Dutch General Act on Incapacity for Work) |
| A.C. | Law Reports Appeal Cases |
| A.C.D. | Administrative Court Digest |
| ADHD | Attention Deficit Hyperactivity Disorder |
| Adjudication Regs | Social Security (Adjudication) Regulations 1986 |
| Admin | Administrative Court |
| Admin L.R. | Administrative Law Reports |
| Administration Act | Social Security Administration Act 1992 |
| AIDS | Acquired Immune Deficiency Syndrome |
| AIIS | Analogous Industrial Injuries Scheme |
| AIP | assessed income period |
| All E.R. | All England Reports |
| All E.R. (E.C.) | All England Reports (European Cases) |
| AMA | American Medical Association |
| Amendment Regulations | Social Security Benefit (Dependency) Amendment Regulations 1992 |

| | |
|---|---|
| ANW | Algemene Nabestaandenwet (Dutch general law on insurance for surviving dependants) |
| AO | Adjudication Officer |
| AO | Authorised Officer |
| AOG | *Adjudication Officers Guide* |
| AOW | Algemene Ouderdomswet (Dutch legislation on general old-age insurance) |
| APG | Austrian General Pensions Act of 18 November 2004 |
| art. | article |
| Art. | Article |
| ASPP | Additional Statutory Paternity Pay |
| ASVG | Allgemeines Sozialversicherungsgesetz (Austrian General Social Security Act) |
| A.T.C. | Annotated Tax Cases |
| Attendance Allowance Regulations | Social Security (Attendance Allowance) Regulations 1991 |
| AWT | All Work Test |
| BA | Benefits Agency |
| BAMS | Benefits Agency Medical Service |
| B.C.L.C. | Butterworths Company Law Cases |
| Benefits Act | Social Security Contributions and Benefits Act 1992 |
| B.H.R.C. | Butterworths Human Rights Cases |
| B.L.G.R. | Butterworths Local Government Reports |
| Blue Books | *The Law Relating to Social Security*, Vols 1–11 |
| BMI | body mass index |
| B.M.L.R. | Butterworths Medico Legal Reports |
| B.P.I.R. | Bankruptcy and Personal Insolvency Reports |
| BSVG | Bauern-Sozialversicherungsgesetz (Austrian Social Security Act for Farmers) |
| B.T.C. | British Tax Cases |
| BTEC | Business and Technology Education Council |
| B.V.C. | British Value Added Tax Reporter |
| B.W.C.C. | Butterworths Workmen's Compensation Cases |
| C | Commissioner's decision |
| c. | chapter |
| C&BA 1992 | Social Security Contributions and Benefits Act 1992 |
| CAA 2001 | Capital Allowances Act 2001 |
| CAB | Citizens Advice Bureau |

| | |
|---|---|
| CAO | Chief Adjudication Officer |
| CBA 1975 | Child Benefit Act 1975 |
| CBJSA | Contribution-Based Jobseeker's Allowance |
| C.C.L. Rep. | Community Care Law Reports |
| CCM | HMRC New Tax Credits Claimant Compliance Manual |
| CCN | New Tax Credits Claimant Compliance Manual |
| CCTV | closed circuit television |
| C.E.C. | European Community Cases |
| CERA | cortical evoked response audiogram |
| CESA | Contribution-based Employment and Support Allowance |
| CFS | chronic fatigue syndrome |
| Ch. | Chancery Division Law Reports |
| Child Benefit Regulations | Child Benefit (General) Regulations 2006 |
| CIR | Commissioners of Inland Revenue |
| Citizenship Directive | Directive 2004/38 |
| Claims and Payments Regulations | Social Security (Claims and Payments) Regulations 1987 |
| Claims and Payments Regulations 1979 | Social Security (Claims and Payments) Regulations 1979 |
| CMA | Chief Medical Adviser |
| CMEC | Child Maintenance and Enforcement Commission |
| C.M.L.R. | Common Market Law Reports |
| C.O.D. | Crown Office Digest |
| Com. L.R. | Commercial Law Reports |
| Commissioners Procedure Regulations | Social Security Commissioners (Procedure) Regulations 1999 |
| Community treaties | EU treaties |
| Community institution | EU institution |
| Community instrument | EU instrument |
| Community law | EU law |
| Community legislation | EU legislation |
| Community obligation | EU obligation |
| Community provision | EU provision |
| Computation of Earnings Regulations | Social Security Benefit (Computation of Earnings) Regulations 1978 |
| Computation of Earnings Regulations 1996 | Social Security Benefit (Computation of Earnings) Regulations 1996 |
| Con. L.R. | Construction Law Reports |
| Consequential Provisions Act | Social Security (Consequential Provisions) Act 1992 |
| Const. L.J. | Construction Law Journal |

## Table of Abbreviations used in this Series

| | |
|---|---|
| Contributions and Benefits Act | Social Security Contributions and Benefits Act 1992 |
| Convention | Human Rights Convention |
| Council Tax Benefit Regulations | Council Tax Benefit (General) Regulations 1992 (SI 1992/1814) |
| CP | Carer Premium |
| CP | Chamber President |
| CPAG | Child Poverty Action Group |
| C.P.L.R. | Civil Practice Law Reports |
| CPR | Civil Procedure Rules |
| C.P. Rep. | Civil Procedure Reports |
| Cr. App. R. | Criminal Appeal Reports |
| Cr. App. R. (S.) | Criminal Appeal Reports (Sentencing) |
| CRCA 2005 | Commissioners for Revenue and Customs Act 2005 |
| Credits Regulations 1974 | Social Security (Credits) Regulations 1974 |
| Credits Regulations 1975 | Social Security (Credits) Regulations 1975 |
| Crim. L.R. | Criminal Law Review |
| CRU | Compensation Recovery Unit |
| CSA 1995 | Child Support Act 1995 |
| CSIH | Inner House of the Court of Session |
| CSOH | Outer House of the Court of Session |
| CS(NI)O | Child Support (Northern Ireland) Order 1995 |
| CSO | Child Support Officer Act 2000 |
| CSPSSA 2000 | Child Support, Pensions and Social Security Act 2000 |
| CTA | Common Travel Area |
| CTB | Council Tax Benefit |
| CTC | Child Tax Credit |
| CTC Regulations | Child Tax Credit Regulations 2002 |
| CTF | child trust fund |
| CTS | Carpal Tunnel Syndrome |
| CV | curriculum vitae |
| DAT | Disability Appeal Tribunal |
| DCA | Department for Constitutional Affairs |
| DCP | Disabled Child Premium |
| Decisions and Appeals Regulations 1999 | Social Security Contributions (Decisions and Appeals) Regulations 1999 |
| Dependency Regulations | Social Security Benefit (Dependency) Regulations 1977 |
| DfEE | Department for Education and Employment |

| | |
|---|---|
| DHSS | Department of Health and Social Security |
| DIY | do it yourself |
| Disability Living Allowance Regulations | Social Security (Disability Living Allowance) Regulations |
| DLA | Disability Living Allowance |
| DLA Regulations | Social Security (Disability Living Allowance) Regulations 1991 |
| DLAAB | Disability Living Allowance Advisory Board |
| DLAAB Regs | Disability Living Allowance Advisory Board Regulations 1991 |
| DLADWAA 1991 | Disability Living Allowance and Disability Working Allowance Act 1991 |
| DM | Decision Maker |
| DMA | Decision-making and Appeals |
| DMG | Decision Makers' Guidance |
| DMP | Delegated Medical Practitioner |
| DP | Disability Premium |
| DPTC | Disabled Person's Tax Credit |
| D.R. | European Commission of Human Rights Decisions and Reports |
| DRO | Debt Relief Order |
| DSD | Department for Social Development (Northern Ireland) |
| DSDNI | Department for Social Development, Northern Ireland |
| DSS | Department of Social Security |
| DTI | Department of Trade and Industry |
| DWA | Disability Working Allowance |
| DWP | Department of Work and Pensions |
| DWPMS | Department for Work and Pensions Medical Service |
| EAA | Extrinsic Allergic Alveolitis |
| EAT | Employment Appeal Tribunal |
| EC | Treaty establishing the European Economic Community |
| ECHR | European Convention on Human Rights |
| ECHR rights | European Convention on Human Rights |
| ECJ | European Court of Justice |
| ECSMA Agreement | European Convention on Social and Medical Assistance |
| E.C.R. | European Court Report |
| ECtHR | European Court of Human Rights |
| Ed.C.R. | Education Case Reports |
| EEA | European Economic Area |

## Table of Abbreviations used in this Series

| | |
|---|---|
| EEA Regulations | Immigration (European Economic Area) Regulations 2006 |
| EEC | European Economic Community |
| EESSI | Electronic Exchange of Social Security Information |
| E.G. | Estates Gazette |
| E.G.L.R. | Estates Gazette Law Reports |
| EHIC | European Health Insurance Card |
| E.H.R.L.R. | European Human Rights Law Review |
| E.H.R.R. | European Human Rights Reports |
| E.L.R. | Education Law Reports |
| EMA | Education Maintenance Allowance |
| EMO | Examining Medical Officer |
| EMP | Examining Medical Practitioner |
| Employment and Support Allowance Regulations | Employment and Support Allowance Regulations 2008 |
| Enforceable Community right | Enforceable EU right |
| English Regulations (eligible children) | Care Planning, Placement and Case Review (England) Regulations 2010 |
| English Regulations (relevant children) | Care Leavers (England) Regulations 2010 |
| Eq. L.R. | Equality Law Reports |
| ERA | Employment, Retention and Advancement Scheme |
| ERA | Evoked Response Audiometry |
| ERA 1996 | Employment Rights Act 1996 |
| ER(NI)O | Employers Rights (Northern Ireland) Order 1996 |
| ES | Employment Service |
| ESA | Employment and Support Allowance |
| ESA Regulations | Employment and Support Allowance Regulations 2008 |
| ESA WCAt | Employment and Support Allowance Work Capability Assessment |
| ETA 1973 | Employment and Training Act 1973 |
| ETA(NI) 1950 | Employment and Training Act (Northern Ireland) 1950 |
| EU | European Union |
| Eu.L.R. | European Law Reports |
| European Coal and Steel Communities | European Union |
| European Community | European Union |
| European Community law | EU law |
| European Community legislation | EU legislation |
| European Community provision | EU provision |
| European Communities | European Union |

| | |
|---|---|
| EWCA Civ | Civil Division of the Court of Appeal in England and Wales |
| EWHC Admin | Administrative Court division of the High Court (England and Wales) |
| F(No.2)A 2005 | Finance (No.2) Act 2005 |
| FA 1990 | Finance Act 1990 |
| FA 1993 | Finance Act 1993 |
| FA 1996 | Finance Act 1996 |
| FA 2000 | Finance Act 2000 |
| FA 2004 | Finance Act 2004 |
| Fam. Law | Family Law |
| FAS | Financial Assistance Scheme |
| F.C.R. | Family Court Reporter |
| FIS | Family Income Supplement |
| FISMA 2000 | Financial Services and Markets Act 2000 |
| Fixing and Adjustment of Rates Regulations 1976 | Child Benefit and Social Security (Fixing and Adjustment of Rates) Regulations 1976 |
| F.L.R. | Family Law Reports |
| Former Regulations | Employment and Support Allowance (Transitional Provisions, Housing Benefit and Council Tax Benefit) (Existing Awards) Regulations 2010 |
| FME | further medical evidence |
| FOTRA | Free of Tax to Residents Abroad |
| FRAA | flat rate accrual amount |
| FSCS | Financial Services Compensation Scheme |
| FSMA 2000 | Financial Services and Markets Act 2000 |
| FSVG | Bundesgestez über die Sozialversicherung freiberuflich selbständig Erwerbstätiger (Austrian Federal Act of 30 November 1978 on social insurance for the self-employed in the liberal professions) |
| FTT | First-tier Tribunal |
| GA | Guardians Allowance |
| GA Regulations | Social Security (Guardian's Allowance) Regulations 1975 |
| General Benefit Regulations 1982 | Social Security (General Benefit) Regulations 1982 |
| General Regulations | Statutory Maternity Pay (General) Regulations 1986 |
| GMP | Guaranteed Minimum Pension |
| G.P. | General Practitioner |
| GRA | Gender Recognition Act |
| GRB | Graduated Retirement Benefit |
| GRP | Graduated Retirement Pension |

| | |
|---|---|
| GSVG | Gewerbliches Sozialversicherungsgesetz (Austrian Federal Act on Social Insurance for Persons engaged in Trade and Commerce) |
| G.W.D. | Greens Weekly Digest |
| HASSASSA | Health and Social Services and Social Security Adjudication Act 1983 |
| HB | Housing Benefit |
| HCD | House of Commons Debates |
| HCP | health care professional |
| HCWA | House of Commons Written Answer |
| HESC | Health, Education and Social Care |
| HIV | Human Immunodeficiency Virus |
| H.L.R. | Housing Law Reports |
| HMIT | Her Majesty's Inspector of Taxes |
| HMRC | Her Majesty's Revenue and Customs |
| HMSO | Her Majesty's Stationery Office |
| HNCIP | (Housewives') Non-Contributory Invalidity Pension |
| Hospital In-Patients Regulations 1975 | Social Security (Hospital In-Patients) Regulations 1975 |
| Housing Benefit Regulations | Housing Benefit (General) Regulations 1987 |
| HP | Health Professional |
| HPP | Higher Pensioner Premium |
| HRA 1998 | Human Rights Act 1998 |
| H.R.L.R. | Human Rights Law Reports–UK Cases |
| HSE | Health and Safety Executive |
| IAC | Immigration and Asylum Chamber |
| IAP | Intensive Activity Period |
| IB | Invalidity Benefit |
| IB/IS/SDA | Incapacity Benefits' Regime |
| IBJSA | Incapacity Benefit Job Seekers Allowance |
| IBJSA | Income-Based Jobseeker's Allowance |
| IB PCA | Incapacity Benefit Personal Capability Assessment |
| IB Regs | Social Security (Incapacity Benefit) Regulations 1994 |
| IB Regulations | Social Security (Incapacity Benefit) Regulations 1994 |
| IBS | Irritable Bowel Syndrome |
| ICA | Invalid Care Allowance |
| ICA Regulations | Social Security (Invalid Care Allowance) Regulations 1976 |
| ICA Unit | Invalid Care Allowance Unit |
| I.C.R. | Industrial Cases Reports |

# Table of Abbreviations used in this Series

| | |
|---|---|
| ICTA 1988 | Income and Corporation Taxes Act 1988 |
| I(EEA) Regulations | Immigration (European Economic Area) Regulations 2006 |
| IFW Regulations | Incapacity for Work (General) Regulations 1995 |
| I.I. | Industrial Injuries |
| IIAC | Industrial Injuries Advisory Council |
| IIDB | Industrial Injuries Disablement Benefit |
| ILO | International Labour Organization |
| ILO Convention | International Labour Organization Convention |
| Imm. A.R. | Immigration Appeal Reports |
| Immigration and Asylum Regulations | Social Security (Immigration and Asylum) Consequential Amendments Regulations 2000 |
| Incapacity for Work Regulations | Social Security (Incapacity for Work) (General) Regulations 1995 |
| Income Support General Regulations | Income Support (General) Regulations 1987 |
| Income Support Regulations | Income Support (General) Regulations 1987 |
| Increases for Dependants Regulations | Social Security Benefit (Dependency) Regulations 1977 |
| IND | Immigration and Nationality Directorate of the Home Office |
| I.N.L.R. | Immigration and Nationality Law Reports |
| IO | Information Officer |
| I.O. | Insurance Officer |
| IPPR | Institute of Public Policy Research |
| IRC | Inland Revenue Commissioners |
| IRESA | Income-Related Employment and Support Allowance |
| I.R.L.R. | Industrial Relations Law Reports |
| IS | Income Support |
| IS Regs | Income Support Regulations |
| IS Regulations | Income Support (General) Regulations 1987 |
| IS | Income Support |
| ISA | Individual Savings Account |
| ITA 2007 | Income Tax Act 2007 |
| ITEPA | Income Tax (Earnings and Pensions) Act 2003 |
| ITEPA 2003 | Income Tax, Earnings and Pensions Act 2003 |
| I.T.L. Rep. | International Tax Law Reports |
| ITS | Independent Tribunal Service |

| | |
|---|---|
| ITTOIA | Income Tax (Trading and Other Income) Act 2005 |
| ITTOIA 2005 | Income Tax (Trading and Other Income) Act 2005 |
| IVB | Invalidity Benefit |
| IWA 1994 | Social Security (Incapacity for Work) Act 1994 |
| IW | Incapacity for Work |
| IW (Dependants) Regs | Social Security (Incapacity for Work) (Dependants) Regulations |
| IW (General) Regs | Social Security (Incapacity for Work) (General) Regulations 1995 |
| IW (Transitional) Regs | Incapacity for Work (Transitional) Regulations |
| JD(NI)O 1995 | Jobseekers (Northern Ireland) Order 1995 |
| Jobseeker's Allowance Regulations | Jobseekers Allowance Regulations 1996 |
| Jobseeker's Regulations 1996 | Jobseekers Allowance Regulations 1996 |
| J.P. | Justice of the Peace Reports |
| J.P.L. | Journal of Public Law |
| JSA | Job Seekers Allowance |
| JSA 1995 | Jobseekers Act 1995 |
| JSA (NI) Regulations | Jobseeker's Allowance (Northern Ireland) Regulations 1996 |
| JSA (Transitional) Regulations | Jobseeker's Allowance (Transitional) Regulations 1996 |
| JSA Regs 1996 | Jobseekers Allowance Regulations 1996 |
| JSA Regulations 1996 | Jobseekers Allowance Regulations 1996 |
| JSA Regulations | Jobseeker's Allowance Regulations 1996 |
| JS(NI)O 1995 | Jobseekers (Northern Ireland) Order 1995 |
| J.S.S.L. | Journal of Social Security Law |
| J.S.W.F.L. | Journal of Social Welfare and Family Law |
| J.S.W.L. | Journal of Social Welfare Law |
| K.B. | Law Reports, King's Bench |
| K.I.R. | Knight's Industrial Law Reports |
| L.& T.R. | Landlord and Tenant Reports |
| LCW | limited capability for work |
| LCWA | Limited Capability for Work Assessment |
| LCWRA | Limited Capability for Work-Related Activity |
| LEA | local education authority |
| LEL | Lower Earnings Limit |
| LET | low earnings threshold |
| L.G.R. | Local Government Law Reports |
| L.G. Rev. | Local Government Review |
| L.J.R. | Law Journal Reports |

| | |
|---|---|
| Ll.L.Rep | Lloyd's List Law Report |
| Lloyd's Rep. | Lloyd's Law Reports |
| LRP | liable relative payment |
| L.S.G. | Law Society Gazette |
| LTAHAW | Living Together as Husband and Wife |
| Luxembourg Court | Court of Justice of the European Communities (also referred to as ECJ) |
| MA | Maternity Allowance |
| MAF | Medical Assessment Framework |
| MAT | Medical Appeal Tribunal |
| Maternity Allowance Regulations | Social Security (Maternity Allowance) Regulations 1987 |
| Maternity Benefit Regulations | Social Security (Maternity Benefit) Regulations 1975 |
| ME | myalgic encephalomyelitis |
| Medical Evidence Regulations | Social Security (Medical Evidence) Regulations 1976 |
| Mesher and Wood | *Income Support, the Social Fund and Family Credit: the Legislation* |
| M.H.L.R. | Mental Health Law Reports |
| MHP | mental health problems |
| MIG | minimum income guarantee |
| Migration Regulations | Employment and Support Allowance (Transitional Provisions, Housing Benefit and Council Tax Benefit (Existing Awards) (No.2) Regulations 2010 |
| MIRAS | mortgage interest relief at source |
| MRI | Magnetic resonance imaging |
| MRSA | methicillin-resistant Staphylococcus aureus |
| MS | Medical Services |
| NACRO | National Association for the Care and Resettlement of Offenders |
| NCB | National Coal Board |
| NDPD | Notes on the Diagnosis of Prescribed Diseases |
| NHS | National Health Service |
| NI | National Insurance |
| N.I. | Northern Ireland Law Reports |
| NI Com | Northern Ireland Commissioner |
| NI | National Insurance |
| NICA | Northern Ireland Court of Appeal |
| NICs | National Insurance Contributions |
| NICom | Northern Ireland Commissioner |
| NINO | National Insurance Number |

| | |
|---|---|
| NIQB | Northern Ireland, Queen's Bench Division |
| NIRS 2 | National Insurance Recording System |
| N.L.J. | New Law Journal |
| NMC | Nursing and Midwifery Council |
| Northern Ireland Contributions and Benefits Act | Social Security Contributions and Benefits (Northern Ireland) Act 1992 |
| N.P.C. | New Property Cases |
| NTC Manual | Clerical procedures manual on tax credits |
| NUM | National Union of Mineworkers |
| OA | Osteoarthritis |
| OCD | Obsessive Compulsive Disorder |
| OGA | Agricultural Insurance Organisation |
| *Ogus, Barendt and Wikeley* | A. Ogus, E. Barendt and N. Wikeley, *The Law of Social Security* (4th edn, Butterworths, 1995) |
| O.J. | Official Journal |
| Old Cases Act | Industrial Injuries and Diseases (Old Cases) Act 1975 |
| OPA | Overseas Pensions Act 1973 |
| OPB | One Parent Benefit |
| O.P.L.R. | Occupational Pensions Law Reports |
| OPSSAT | Office of the President of Social Security Appeal Tribunals |
| Overlapping Benefits Regulations | Social Security (Overlapping Benefits) Regulations 1979 |
| Overpayments Regulations | Social Security (Payments on account, Overpayments and Recovery) Regulations |
| P | retirement pension |
| P. & C.R. | Property and Compensation Reports |
| pa | per annum |
| para. | paragraph |
| PAYE | Pay As You Earn |
| Payments on Account Regulations | Social Security (Payments on account, Overpayments and Recovery) Regulations |
| PCA | Personal Capability Assessment |
| PD | prescribed disease |
| P.D. | Practice Direction |
| Pens. L.R. | Pensions Law Reports |
| Persons Abroad Regulations | Social Security Benefit (Persons Abroad) Regulations 1975 |
| Persons Residing Together Regulations | Social Security Benefit (Persons Residing Together) Regulations 1977 |
| PIE | Period of Interruption of Employment |
| PILON | pay in lieu of notice |
| P.I.Q.R. | Personal Injuries and Quantum Reports |

| | |
|---|---|
| PIW | Period of Incapacity for Work |
| P.I.W.R. | Personal Injury and Quantum Reports |
| P.L.R. | Estates Gazette Planning Law Reports |
| Polygamous Marriages Regulations | Social Security and Family Allowances (Polygamous Marriages) Regulations 1975 |
| PPF | Pension Protection Fund |
| PPU | ECJ urgent preliminary ruling procedure |
| Prescribed Diseases Regulations | Social Security (Industrial Injuries) (Prescribed Diseases) Regulations 1985 |
| Present Regulations | Employment and Support Allowance (Transitional Provisions, Housing Benefit and Council Tax Benefit) (Existing Awards) (No.2) Regulations 2010 |
| PSCS | Pension Service Computer System |
| Pt | Part |
| PTA | pure tone audiometry |
| P.T.S.R. | Public and Third Sector Law Reports |
| PTWR 2000 | Part-time Workers (Prevention of Less Favourable Treatment) Regulations 2000 |
| PVC | polyvinyl chloride |
| PVS | private or voluntary sectors |
| pw | per week |
| Q.B. | Queen's Bench Law Reports |
| QBD (NI) | Queen's Bench Division (Northern Ireland) |
| QEF | qualifying earnings factor |
| QYP | qualifying young person |
| R | Reported Decision |
| r. | rule |
| RC | Rules of the Court of Session |
| REA | Reduced Earnings Allowance |
| Recoupment Regulations | Social Security (Recoupment) Regulations 1990 |
| reg. | regulation |
| RIPA | Regulation of Investigatory Powers Act 2000 |
| RMO | Responsible Medical Officer |
| rr. | rules |
| R.T.R. | Road Traffic Reports |
| S | Scottish Decision |
| s. | section |
| SAP | Statutory Adoption Pay |
| SAYE | Save As You Earn |
| SB | Supplementary Benefit |
| SBAT | Supplementary Benefit Appeal Tribunal |

| | |
|---|---|
| SBC | Supplementary Benefits Commission |
| S.C. | Session Cases |
| S.C. (H.L.) | Session Cases (House of Lords) |
| S.C. (P.C.) | Session Cases (Privy Council) |
| S.C.C.R. | Scottish Criminal Case Reports |
| S.C.L.R. | Scottish Civil Law Reports |
| Sch. | Schedule |
| SDA | Severe Disablement Allowance |
| SDP | Severe Disability Premium |
| SEC | Social Entitlement Chamber |
| SERPS | State Earnings Related Pension Scheme |
| Severe Disablement Allowance Regulations | Social Security (Severe Disablement Regulations Allowance) Regulations 1984 |
| SI | Statutory Instrument |
| SIP | Share Incentive Plan |
| S.J. | Solicitors Journal |
| S.J.L.B. | Solicitors Journal Law Brief |
| S.L.T. | Scots Law Times |
| SMP | Statutory Maternity Pay |
| SMP (General) Regulations 1986 | Statutory Maternity Pay (General) Regulations 1986 |
| SP | Senior President |
| SPC | State Pension Credit |
| SPC Regulations | State Pension Credit Regulations 2002 |
| SPCA | State Pension Credit Act 2002 |
| SPCA 2002 | State Pension Credit Act 2002 |
| SPCA(NI) 2002 | State Pension Credit Act (Northern Ireland) 2002 |
| SPP | Statutory Paternity Pay |
| SPP and SAP (Administration) Regs 2002 | Statutory Paternity Pay and Statutory Adoption Pay (Administration) Regulations 2002 |
| SPP and SAP (General) Regulations 2002 | Statutory Paternity Pay and Statutory Adoption Pay (General) Regulations 2002 |
| SPP and SAP (National Health Service) | Statutory Paternity Pay and Statutory Adoption Pay (National Health Service Employees) Regulations 2002 |
| SPP and SAP (Weekly Rates) Regulations | Statutory Paternity Pay and Statutory Adoption Pay (Weekly Rates) Regulations 2002 |
| SS(MP)A 1977 | Social Security (Miscellaneous Provisions) Act 1977 |
| ss. | sections |
| SSA 1975 | Social Security Act 1975 |
| SSA 1977 | Social Security Act 1977 |
| SSA 1978 | Social Security Act 1978 |

## Table of Abbreviations used in this Series

| | |
|---|---|
| SSA 1979 | Social Security Act 1979 |
| SSA 1981 | Social Security Act 1981 |
| SSA 1986 | Social Security Act 1986 |
| SSA 1988 | Social Security Act 1988 |
| SSA 1989 | Social Security Act 1989 |
| SSA 1990 | Social Security Act 1990 |
| SSA 1998 | Social Security Act 1998 |
| SSAA 1992 | Social Security Administration Act 1992* |
| SSAC | Social Security Advisory Committee |
| SSAT | Social Security Appeal Tribunal |
| SSCB(NI)A | Social Security Contributions and Benefits (Northern Ireland) Act 1992 |
| SSCBA 1992 | Social Security Contributions and Benefits Act 1992* |
| SSCPA 1992 | Social Security (Consequential Provisions) Act 1992 |
| SSHBA 1982 | Social Security and Housing Benefits Act 1982 |
| SSHD | Secretary of State for the Home Department |
| SS(MP) A 1977 | Social Security (Miscellaneous Provisions) Act 1977 |
| SS (No.2) A 1980 | Social Security (No.2) Act 1980 |
| SSP | Statutory Sick Pay |
| SSP (General) Regulations | Statutory Sick Pay (General) Regulations 1982 |
| SSPA 1975 | Social Security Pensions Act 1975 |
| SSWP | Secretary of State for Work and Pensions |
| State Pension Credit Regulations | State Pension Credit Regulations 2002 |
| S.T.C. | Simon's Tax Cases |
| S.T.C. (S.C.D.) | Simon's Tax Cases: Special Commissioners Decisions |
| S.T.I. | Simon's Tax Intelligence |
| STIB | Short-Term Incapacity Benefit |
| Strasbourg Court | European Court of Human Rights |
| Students Directive | Directive 93/96/EEC |
| subpara. | subparagraph |
| subs. | subsection |
| T | Tribunal of Commissioners' Decision |
| Taxes Act | Income and Corporation Taxes Act 1988 |
| (TC) | Tax and Chancery |
| T.C. | Tax Cases |
| TC (Claims and Notifications) Regs 2002 | Tax Credits (Claims and Notifications) Regulations 2002 |
| TCA | Tax Credits Act |

| | |
|---|---|
| TCA 1999 | Tax Credits Act 1999 |
| TCA 2002 | Tax Credits Act 2002 |
| TCEA 2007 | Tribunals, Courts and Enforcement Act 2007 |
| TCGA | Taxation of Chargeable Gains Act 1992 |
| TCGA 1992 | Taxation of Chargeable Gains Act 2002 |
| TCTM | Tax Credits Technical Manual |
| TEC | Treaty Establishing the European Community |
| TEU | Treaty on European Union |
| TFEU | Treaty on the Functioning of the European Union |
| The Board | Commissioners for Revenue and Customs |
| The Community | European Union |
| The EC | European Union |
| This Act | Tax Credits Act 2002 |
| TIOPA 2010 | Taxation (International and Other Provisions) Act 2010 |
| TMA 1970 | Taxes Management Act 1970 |
| T.R. | Taxation Reports |
| Transfer of Functions Act | Social Security Contributions (Transfer of Functions etc.) Act 1999 |
| Transitional Provisions Regulations | Employment and Support Allowance (Transitional Provisions Regulations 2008 |
| Treaty | Rome Treaty |
| Tribunal Procedure Rules | Tribunal Procedure (First-tier Tribunal)(Social Entitlement Chamber) Rules 2008 |
| UB | Unemployment Benefit |
| UC | Universal Credit |
| UCITS | Undertakings for Collective Investments in Transferable Securities |
| UKAIT | UK Asylum and Immigration Tribunal |
| UKBA | UK Border Agency of the Home Office |
| UKCC | United Kingdom Central Council for Nursing, Midwifery and Health Visiting |
| UKFTT | United Kingdom First-tier Tribunal Tax Chamber |
| UKHL | United Kingdom House of Lords |
| U.K.H.R.R. | United Kingdom Human Rights Reports |
| UKSC | United Kingdom Supreme Court |
| UKUT | United Kingdom Upper Tribunal |
| Unemployment, Sickness and Invalidity Benefit Regs | Social Security (Unemployment, Sickness and Invalidity Benefit) Regulations 1983 |
| URL | uniform resource locator |

| | |
|---|---|
| USI Regs | Social Security (Unemployment, Sickness and Invalidity Benefit) Regulations 1983 |
| UT | Upper Tribunal |
| VAMS | Veterans Agency Medical Service |
| VAT | Value Added Tax |
| VCM | vinyl chloride monomer |
| VERA 1992 | Vehicle Excise and Registration Act 1992 |
| VWF | Vibration White Finger |
| W | Welsh Decision |
| WAO | Wet op arbeidsongeschiktheidsverzekering (Dutch Act on Incapacity for Work) |
| WAZ | Wet arbeidsongeschiktheidsverzekering (Dutch Act on Self-employed Persons' Incapacity for Work) |
| WCA/WCAt | Work Capability Assessment |
| Welsh Regulations | Children (Leaving Care) (Wales) Regulations 2001 (SI 2001/2189) |
| WFHRAt | Work-Focused Health-Related Assessment |
| WFI | work-focused Interview |
| WFTC | Working Families Tax Credit |
| WIA | Wet Werk en inkomen naar arbeidsvermogen (Dutch Act on Work and Income according to Labour Capacity) |
| Widow's Benefit and Retirement Pensions Regs | Social Security (Widow's Benefit and Retirement Pensions) Regulations 1979 |
| *Wikeley, Annotations* | N. Wikeley, "Annotations to Jobseekers Act 1995 (c.18)" in *Current Law Statutes Annotated* (1995) |
| *Wikeley, Ogus and Barendt* | Wikeley, Ogus and Barendt, *The Law of Social Security* (5th ed., Butterworths, 2002) |
| W.L.R. | Weekly Law Reports |
| Workmen's Compensation Acts | Workmen's Compensation Acts 1925 to 1945 |
| WPS | War Pensions Scheme |
| WRA 2007 | Welfare Reform Act 2007 |
| WRA 2009 | Welfare Reform Act 2009 |
| WRA 2012 | Welfare Reform Act 2012 |
| WRAAt | Work-Related Activity Assessment |
| WRPA 1999 | Welfare Reform and Pensions Act 1999 |
| WRP(NI)O 1999 | Welfare Reform and Pensions (Northern Ireland) Order |
| WTC | Working Tax Credit |
| WTC (Entitlement and Maximum Rate) Regulations 2002 | Working Tax Credit (Entitlement and Maximum Rate) Regulations 2002 |

| | |
|---|---|
| WTC Regulations | Working Tax Credit (Entitlement and Maximum Rate) Regulations 2002 |
| W.T.L.R. | Wills & Trusts Law Reports |

\* Where the context makes it seem more appropriate, these could also be referred to as Contributions and Benefits Act 1992, Administration Act 1992.

# TABLE OF CASES

# TABLE OF COMMISSIONERS' DECISIONS 1948–2009

# TABLE OF EUROPEAN MATERIALS

# TABLE OF STATUTES

# TABLE OF STATUTORY INSTRUMENTS

# PART I

# NEW LEGISLATION

# NEW STATUTES

## Welfare Reform Act 2012

(2012 c.5)

33. Abolition of benefits                                                          1.001

## Abolition of benefits

**33.**—(1) The following benefits are abolished—                                   1.002
  (a) income-based jobseeker's allowance under the Jobseekers Act
      1995;
  (b) income-related employment and support allowance under Part 1
      of the Welfare Reform Act 2007;
  (c)  . . . ;
  (d)  . . . ;
  (e)  . . . ;
  (f)  . . . .
  (2) In subsection (1)—
  (a) "income-based jobseeker's allowance" has the same meaning as in
      the Jobseekers Act 1995;
  (b) "income-related employment and support allowance" means an
      employment and support allowance entitlement to which is based
      on section 1(2)(b) of the Welfare Reform Act 2007.

GENERAL NOTE

   See further the initial General Note to the Jobseeker's Allowance Regulations   1.003
2013 (SI 2013/378), below, and that to the Employment and Support Allowance
Regulations 2013 (SI 2013/379), below.

# Welfare Benefits Up-rating Act 2013

(2013 c.16)

CONTENTS

An Act to make provision relating to the up-rating of certain social security benefits and tax credits. [26th March 2013]

GENERAL NOTE

1.005     This Act, which entered into force on October 1, 2013 (see the Welfare Benefits Up-rating Act 2013 (Commencement) Order 2013 (SI 2013/2317)), is part of the implementation of the Government's plan to reduce welfare expenditure. Under the Social Security Administration Act 1992, the Secretary of State is required to review the value of benefits in the light of changes in prices and to make annual uprating orders, subject to Parliamentary approval, in the light of those changes. The Treasury is under a similar obligation under the Tax Credits Act 2002.

    The Act provides that working age benefits will be uprated by 1 per cent in 2014–15 and 2015–16. Working age benefits are the main rates of income support, jobseeker's allowance, employment and support allowance, and housing benefit, the work-related activity group component of employment and support allowance, maternity allowance, and statutory adoption, maternity, paternity and sick pay. Corresponding payments under universal credit are also covered. In addition, increases in the couple element and lone parent element of working tax credit, and the child element of tax credit, are also limited to 1 per cent. Rounding the resulting sums will be done to the nearest five pence.

## Up-rating of certain social security benefits for tax years 2014–15 and 2015–16

1.006     **1.**—(1) The Secretary of State must, in each of the tax years ending with 5 April 2014 and 5 April 2015, make an order by statutory instrument increasing each of the relevant sums by 1%.

For the meaning of the "relevant sums" see paragraph 1 of the Schedule.

(2) An order under this section must be framed so as to bring the variations to which it relates into force—

     (a) in the week beginning with the first Monday in the tax year following that in which the order is made, or

     (b) on an earlier date in April specified in the order;

and the provision that may be made under this subsection includes provision bringing the variation in a particular sum into force on different dates for different purposes.

(3) The Secretary of State may, in providing for an increase under subsection (1), adjust the amount of the increase so as to round any sum up or down to the extent the Secretary of State thinks appropriate.

(4) After making an order under this section, the Secretary of State must lay before Parliament a copy of a report by the Government Actuary or the Deputy Government Actuary giving that Actuary's opinion on the likely effect on the National Insurance Fund of the parts of the order that relate to sums payable out of the Fund.

(5) Subsection (1) does not apply in relation to a tax year if, on the review in that tax year under section 150(1) of the Social Security Administration Act 1992, the Secretary of State determines that the general level of prices in Great Britain has not increased, or has increased by less than 1%, over the period under review.

(6) Where subsection (1) applies in relation to a tax year, the draft of any up-rating order laid before Parliament by virtue of the review in that tax year under section 150(1) of the Social Security Administration Act 1992 must not include provision increasing any of the relevant sums.

(7) In this section a reference to the Secretary of State, in relation to the sums mentioned in section 150(1)(i) of the Social Security Administration Act 1992, is a reference to the Treasury.

(8) A reference in any enactment, other than this Act and sections 189 and 190 of the Social Security Administration Act 1992, to an order under section 150 of that Act includes a reference to an order under this section.

(9) Nothing in section 166 of the Social Security Administration (Northern Ireland) Act 1992 applies in relation to an order made by the Treasury under section 132 of that Act which corresponds to an order made under this section.

### Up-rating of tax credits for tax years 2014–15 and 2015–16

**2.**—(1) The Treasury must, in each of the tax years ending with 5 April 2014 and 5 April 2015, make an order by statutory instrument increasing each of the relevant amounts by 1%.     **1.007**

For the meaning of the "relevant amounts" see paragraph 2 of the Schedule.

(2) An order under this section must be framed so that it has effect in relation to awards of tax credits for the tax year following that in which the order is made.

(3) The Treasury may, in providing for an increase under subsection (1), adjust the amount of the increase so as to round any amount up or down to the extent the Treasury think appropriate.

(4) Subsection (1) does not apply in relation to a tax year if, on the review in that tax year under section 41 of the Tax Credits Act 2002, the Treasury determine that the general level of prices in the United Kingdom has not increased, or has increased by less than 1%, over the period under review.

(5) Where subsection (1) applies in relation to a tax year, the Treasury must not exercise any other power to vary any of the relevant amounts if

that variation would take effect in relation to awards of tax credits for the tax year following that in which the order is made.

### Short title, interpretation, commencement and extent

1.008   **3.**—(1) This Act may be cited as the Welfare Benefits Up-rating Act 2013.

(2) In this Act "tax year" means a period beginning with 6 April in one year and ending with 5 April in the next.

(3) This section comes into force on the day on which this Act is passed.

(4) The other provisions of this Act come into force on such day as the Secretary of State or the Treasury may by order made by statutory instrument appoint; and different days may be appointed for different purposes.

(5) Section 1(1) to (7) and paragraph 1 of the Schedule extend to England and Wales and Scotland only.

(6) Section 1(9) extends to Northern Ireland only.

(7) The other provisions of this Act extend to England and Wales, Scotland and Northern Ireland.

SCHEDULE Sections 1 and 2

MEANING OF THE "RELEVANT SUMS" AND THE "RELEVANT AMOUNTS"

*The "relevant sums" for the purposes of section 1*

1.009   1. The "relevant sums" for the purposes of section 1 are the sums—

  (a) specified in paragraph 1 of Schedule 2 to the Income Support (General) Regulations 1987 (S.I. 1987/1967);

  (b) specified in paragraph 1 of Schedule 3 to the Housing Benefit Regulations 2006 (S.I. 2006/213);

  (c) mentioned in section 150(1)(i) and (j) of the Social Security Administration Act 1992;

  (d) specified in regulations under section 4(2) of the Jobseekers Act 1995;

  (e) specified in paragraph 1 of Schedule 1 to the Jobseeker's Allowance Regulations 1996;

  (f) specified in regulations under section 2(1)(a) of the Welfare Reform Act 2007;

  (g) specified in regulations under section 2(4)(c) of the Welfare Reform Act 2007, so far as relating to the component under section 2(3) of that Act;

  (h) specified in paragraph 1 of Schedule 4 to the Employment and Support Allowance Regulations 2008;

  (i) specified in regulations under section 4(6)(c) of the Welfare Reform Act 2007, so far as relating to the component under section 4(5) of that Act;

  (j) specified in regulations under section 9(2) of the Welfare Reform Act 2012;

  (k) specified in regulations under section 10(3) of the Welfare Reform Act 2012 in respect of an amount to be included under section 10(2) of that Act (but where more than one sum is so specified, only the smaller or smallest of those sums is a "relevant sum");

  (l) specified in regulations under section 12(3) of the Welfare Reform Act 2012 in respect of needs or circumstances of a claimant prescribed by virtue of section 12(2)(a) of that Act (but not in respect of needs or circumstances prescribed by virtue of section 12(2)(b)).

*The "relevant amounts" for the purposes of section 2*

2. The "relevant amounts" for the purposes of section 2 are the monetary amounts—

(a) specified in Schedule 2 to the Working Tax Credit (Entitlement and Maximum Rate) Regulations 2002 for the basic element, the 30 hour element, the second adult element and the lone parent element;

(b) specified in regulation 7(4)(c) and (f) of the Child Tax Credit Regulations 2002.

# NEW REGULATIONS AND ORDERS

## The Social Security (Civil Penalties) Regulations 2012

(SI 2012/1990)

In force October 1, 2012

ARRANGEMENT OF REGULATIONS

The Secretary of State for Work and Pensions makes the following Regulations in exercise of the powers conferred by sections 115C(2), 115D(1) and (2), 189(1) and 191 of the Social Security Administration Act 1992.

In accordance with section 190(1) of that Act, a draft of this instrument was laid before Parliament and approved by a resolution of each House of Parliament.

This instrument contains only regulations made by virtue of section 116(1) of the Welfare Reform Act 2012 and is made before the end of the period of 6 months beginning with the coming into force of that section.

In so far as these Regulations relate to housing benefit and council tax benefit, in accordance with section 176(1) of the Social Security Administration Act 1992, consultation has taken place with organisations appearing to the Secretary of State to be representative of the authorities concerned.

## Citation, commencement and interpretation

1.011    1.—(1) These Regulations may be cited as the Social Security (Civil Penalties) Regulations 2012 and come into force on 1st October 2012.

(2) In these Regulations, "the Act" means the Social Security Administration Act 1992.

8

## Prescribed amount of penalty: section 115C of the Act

**2.** The prescribed amount of the penalty for the purpose of section 115C(2) of the Act (incorrect statements etc.) is £50.

1.012

## Prescribed amount of penalty: section 115D(1) of the Act

**3.** The prescribed amount of the penalty for the purpose of section 115D(1) of the Act (failure to provide information) is £50.

1.013

## Prescribed amount of penalty: section 115D(2) of the Act

**4.** The prescribed amount of the penalty for the purpose of section 115D(2) of the Act (failure to notify appropriate authority of a relevant change of circumstances) is £50.

1.014

# The Jobseeker's Allowance Regulations 2013

(SI 2013/378) (*as amended*)

In force April 29, 2013

ARRANGEMENT OF REGULATIONS

## PART 1

### GENERAL

## PART 2

### CLAIMANT RESPONSIBILITIES

## PART 3

### SANCTIONS

PART 4

INFORMATION AND EVIDENCE

PART 5

CONDITIONS OF ENTITLEMENT

PART 6

AMOUNTS OF A JOBSEEKER'S ALLOWANCE

PART 7

EARNINGS

PART 8

PART WEEKS

PART 9

SHARE FISHERMEN

PART 10

MODIFICATION OF THE ACT

SCHEDULE—Sums to be disregarded in the calculation of earnings

The Secretary of State for Work and Pensions makes the following Regulations in exercise   **1.016**
of the powers conferred by sections 2(1)(c), (2A) and (3B)(a), 4(1)(b), (2) and (4), 5(3),
6A(5), 6B(2), 6D(4), 6E(3) and (5), 6F(1), 6H(1)(a), (5) and (6), 6I, 6J(2)(a), (5) and
(7), 6K(4), (5) and (9), 12(1) to (4)(a) and (b), 35(1) and (3) and 36(2) to (4) of, and
Schedule 1 to, the Jobseekers Act 1995, sections 5(1)(i) and (j) and (1A), 189(4), (5) and
(6) and 191 of the Social Security Administration Act 1992, sections 171D, 171G(2) and
175(3) to (5) of the Social Security Contributions and Benefits Act 1992 and paragraphs
2(3) and 3 of Schedule 5 to the Welfare Reform Act 2012.

The Social Security Advisory Committee has agreed that the proposals in respect of
these Regulations should not be referred to it.

A draft of these Regulations has been laid before Parliament in accordance with section
37(2) of the Jobseekers Act 1995 and approved by a resolution of each House of Parliament.

GENERAL NOTE

These regulations govern eligibility for "new style JSA". This is a wholly   **1.017**
contribution-based benefit for those who are out of work and are seeking
employment. Those entitled to it whose "resources" are insufficient to meet
"needs" will have to seek a top-up through Universal Credit (UC). In the longer
term, when the UC scheme is fully rolled out the result will be a simpler system,
since there will then be only one income-related benefit—UC—for persons of
working age, rather than the current system of several income-related benefits
each for different categories of claimant and administered by different authorities: IS, IBJSA and IRESA (by DWP/JobCentres), tax credits (by HMRC) and
housing benefit (by local authorities). But until the UC scheme is fully rolled
out, UC is an additional benefit rather than a benefit replacing all those other
income related benefits. The roll-out of UC is slow and complicated. As the
commentators to Vol.V in this series, *Universal Credit*, put it:

"it is inherent in the design of UC that it overlaps with each of the older
benefits it is eventually intended to replace. That overlap means that, in
addition to the complication of the old and new systems existing side-by-side
(including having two different and mutually exclusive benefits both called
JSA and two different and mutually exclusive benefits each called ESA), it is
also necessary to have legislation defining which set of rules applies to any
particular claimant at any given time. That legislation is to be found first, in
the Universal Credit (Transitional Provisions) Regulations ('the Transitional
Provisions Regulations') which create a 'Pathfinder Group' of claimants who,
depending on where they live, may have to claim UC rather than one of the
'legacy' benefits and, second, in a series of Commencement Orders that, even
by the high standards set by past social security legislation, are bewilderingly
complex."

The areas in which, and within them, the cases to which, "new style JSA" and
these Regulations apply—the "Pathfinder" pilots—is set by reg.1(2), (3), read
with the Transitional Provisions Regulations and the various Welfare Reform Act
2012 Commencement Orders noted in the annotation to reg.1(2), (3), and the
subject of fuller commentary in Part 4 of the new Vol.V, *Universal Credit*.

In respect of areas and cases in relation to which IBJSA has yet to be abolished
(i.e. those outside the 'Pathfinder' pilots), entitlement to "old style JSA" (either
or both CBSA and IBJSA) remain governed by the Jobseekers Act 1995 and the
JSA Regulations 1996 as set out in Vol.II (2013/14 edn) and amended by the
provisions (other than "Pathfinder" amendments) noted in the pertinent updates
in Part III of this Supplement.

These 2013 Regulations are both a consolidation of and a rewrite of the
already existing JSA Regulations 1996 (as amended so as somewhat to align a

"new style JSA" claimant commitments and sanctions' regime with those applicable to "new style ESA and UC".

Most of the key rules on "new style JSA" remain the same in terms of effect as those applicable to CBJSA in the ESA Regulations 2008, but the DWP considers that in drawing up the JSA Regulations 2013 "opportunities have been taken to make simplifications and improvements". In addition, the regulations specific to IBJSA are not carried into the 2013 Regulations. This means that material may be differently distributed within the same-numbered regulation in these JSA Regulations 2013 as compared to the JSA Regs 1996, or be found in a differently numbered one. In addition, in the JSA Regulations 2013, there is a regime of claimant commitments and sanctions analogous in some respects to those applicable to UC and "new style ESA", some of which were foreshadowed in earlier amendments to the sanctions regime for "old style JSA".

## PART 1

## GENERAL

### Citation, commencement and application

1.018    **1.**—(1) These Regulations may be cited as the Jobseeker's Allowance Regulations 2013.

(2) They come into force on 29th April 2013.

(3) They apply in relation to a particular case on any day on which section 33(1)(a) of the Welfare Reform Act 2012 (abolition of income-based jobseeker's allowance) is in force and applies in relation to that case.

GENERAL NOTE

1.019    Although these regulations entered into force on April 29, 2013, they do not as yet apply throughout the country. They will only do so once there has been a full-rolling out of Universal Credit and consequent total abolition of IBJSA.

Instead, they are applicable only in those "Pathfinder" areas where IBJSA has been abolished and only as regards certain types of case ("in a particular case . . . on any day on which section 33(1)(a) of the Welfare Reform Act 2012 (abolition of income-based jobseeker's allowance) is in force and applies in relation to that case"). Areas and types of case will expand as the system moves to full roll out of Universal Credit and abolition of CBJSA and IRESA in 2017. See further, Part 1 of Vol.V, *Universal Credit*.

As at January 1, 2014, areas and types of case were those covered by provisions in each of the Welfare Reform Act 2012 Commencement Nos 9, 11, 13 and 14 Orders (see Part 4 of Vol.V in this series, *Universal Credit*).

As regards "Pathfinder" postcode areas of application, the "relevant districts" are set out in each Commencement Order. Briefly, Commencement No. 9 Order covered four postcode districts in Manchester, Oldham and Stockport as from April 29, 2013; Commencement No. 11 Order embraced certain postcodes in Wigan ("the No. 2 relevant districts") and Manchester, Oldham and Warrington ("the No. 3 relevant districts") as from July 1, 2013); the Commencement No. 13 Order brought in certain postcodes in West London, Manchester and Wigan ("the No. 4 relevant districts") as from October 28, 2013; and the Commencement No. 14 Order embraced certain postcodes in Rugby, Inverness and Perth ("the No. 5 relevant districts") as from November 25, 2013.

As regards cases to which "new style JSA" applies, this is from each of the dates noted above governed centrally by art.4 of each Commencement Order (annotated more fully in Part 4 of Vol.V, *Universal Credit*) covering six classes of case. In relation to each, a key requisite is that the claimant has met the criteria for being in the "Pathfinder Group". These are set out in regs 5–12 of the Universal Credit (Transitional) Regulations 2013 (SI 2013/000) (see Part 4 of Vol.V, *Universal Credit*), reading them as if any reference to making a claim for universal credit included a reference to making a claim for a jobseeker's allowance.

The initial groups in the Pathfinder pilots have been single persons without children, new claimants who would otherwise have claimed old style JSA, whether CBJSA alone, IBJSA alone or a combination of the two. Thus these JSA Regulations 2013 are among the first used in "Pathfinder" areas and cases.

## General interpretation

**2.**—(1) For the purposes of the Act and of these Regulations—     1.020
"employed earner" has the meaning it has in Part 1 of the Benefits Act by virtue of section 2(1)(a) of that Act;
"employment" includes any trade, business, profession, office or vocation, except in section 14 of the Act, where it means employed earner's employment within the meaning in the Benefits Act;
"jobseeking period" means the period described in regulation 37;
"pensionable age" has the meaning it has in Parts 1 to 6 of the Benefits Act by virtue of section 122(1) of that Act.
(2) In these Regulations—
"the Act" means the Jobseekers Act 1995;
"adoption leave" means a period of absence from work on ordinary or additional adoption leave by virtue of section 75A or 75B of the Employment Rights Act 1996;
"attendance allowance" means—
    (a) an attendance allowance under section 64 of the Benefits Act;
    (b) an increase of disablement pension under section 104 or 105 of the Benefits Act;
    (c) a payment by virtue of article 14, 15, 16, 43 or 44 of the Personal Injuries (Civilians) Scheme 1983 or any analogous payment;
    (d) any payment based on the need for attendance which is paid as an addition to a war disablement pension (which means any retired pay or pension or allowance payable in respect of disablement under an instrument specified in section 639(2) of the Income Tax (Earnings and Pensions) Act 2003);
"basic rate" has the same meaning as in the Income Tax Act 2007;
"benefit week" means a period of seven days ending with the end day unless, in any particular case or class of case, the Secretary of State arranges otherwise, and for these purposes "end day" means the day in column (2) which corresponds to the series of numbers in column (1) which includes the last two digits of the person's national insurance number—

| (1) | (2) |
|---|---|
| 00 to 19 | Monday |
| 20 to 39 | Tuesday |
| 40 to 59 | Wednesday |
| 60 to 79 | Thursday |
| 80 to 99 | Friday; |

"Claims and Payments Regulations 2013" means the Universal Credit, Personal Independence Payment, Jobseeker's Allowance and Employment and Support Allowance (Claims and Payments) Regulations 2013;

"close relative" means a parent, parent-in-law, son, son-in-law, daughter, daughter-in-law, step-parent, step-son, step-daughter, brother, sister or, if any of the preceding persons is one member of a couple, the other member of that couple;

"date of claim" means the date on which the claimant makes, or is treated as making, a claim for a jobseeker's allowance for the purposes of—

    (a) regulation 6 of the Social Security (Claims and Payments) Regulations 1987; or

    (b) regulation 20, 22 or 24 of the Claims and Payments Regulations 2013;

"earnings", for the purposes of section 35(3) of the Act, has the meaning specified—

    (a) in the case of an employed earner, in regulation 58; or

    (b) in the case of a self-employed earner, in regulation 60;

"Health Service Act" means the National Health Service Act 2006;

"Health Service (Wales) Act" means the National Health Service (Wales) Act 2006;

"maternity leave" means a period during which a woman is absent from work because she is pregnant or has given birth to a child, and at the end of which she has a right to return to work either under the terms of her contract of employment or under Part 8 of the Employment Rights Act 1996;

"net earnings" means such earnings as are calculated in accordance with regulation 59;

"net profit" means such profit as is calculated in accordance with regulation 61;

"occupational pension" means any pension or other periodical payment under an occupational pension scheme but does not include any discretionary payment out of a fund established for relieving hardship in particular cases;

"partner" means, where a claimant—

(a) is a member of a couple, the other member of that couple;

(b) is married polygamously to two or more members of the claimant's household, any such member;

"paternity leave" means a period of absence from work on leave by virtue of section 80A or 80B of the Employment Rights Act 1996;

"payment" includes a part of a payment;

"remunerative work" has the meaning prescribed in regulation 42(1);

"self-employed earner" is to be construed in accordance with section 2(1)(b) of the Benefits Act;

"sports award" means an award made by one of the Sports Councils named in section 23(2) of the National Lottery etc. Act 1993 out of sums allocated to it for distribution under that section;

"training allowance" means an allowance (whether by way of periodical grants or otherwise) payable—

(a) out of public funds by a Government department or by or on behalf of the Secretary of State, Skills Development Scotland, Scottish Enterprise, Highlands and Islands Enterprise, the Chief Executive of Skills Funding or the Welsh Ministers;

(b) to a person for their maintenance or in respect of the maintenance of a member of their family; and

(c) for the period, or part of the period, during which the person is following a course of training or instruction provided by, or in pursuance of arrangements made with, that department or approved by that department in relation to them or provided or approved by or on behalf of the Secretary of State, Skills Development Scotland, Scottish Enterprise, Highlands and Islands Enterprise or the Welsh Ministers,

but it does not include an allowance paid by any Government department to or in respect of a person by reason of the fact that the person is following a course of full-time education, other than under arrangements made under section 2 of the Employment and Training Act 1973 or section 2 of the Enterprise and New Towns (Scotland) Act 1990, or the person is training as a teacher;

"voluntary organisation" means a body, other than a public or local authority, the activities of which are carried on otherwise than for profit;

"voluntary work" means work other than for a member of the claimant's family, where no payment is received by the claimant or the only payment due to be made to the claimant by virtue of being so engaged is a payment in respect of any expenses reasonably incurred by the claimant in the course of being so engaged;

"week" means, in the definition of "Work Experience" and in Parts 5, 6, 7, 9 and 10, a period of seven days;

"Work Experience" means a programme which consists of work experience, job search skills and job skills (and which is not employment), provided in pursuance of arrangements made by or on behalf of the Secretary of State under section 2 of the Employment and Training Act 1973, and which—

(a) subject to paragraph (b), is of between two and eight weeks duration; or

(b) is of between two and 12 weeks duration where, during the first eight weeks of the claimant's participation in Work Experience, and as a result of that participation, the claimant is offered and accepts an apprenticeship made under government arrangements made respectively for England, Wales or Scotland;

"young person" means a person who falls within the definition of "qualifying young person" in section 142 of the Benefits Act (child and qualifying young person).

GENERAL NOTE

**1.021**     This sets out key definitions for the application of these Regulations. It is, not, however, the sole provider of relevant definitions. Aside from s.35 of the Jobseekers Act 1995, important definitions are also to be found in regs 3, 4, 17, 67 and occasionally within other regulations, in this last case generally defining a term used solely in that regulation.

## Further interpretation

**1.022**     **3.**—(1) Any reference to the claimant's family or, as the case may be, to a member of the claimant's family, is to be construed for the purposes of these Regulations as if it included, in relation to a polygamous marriage, a reference to any partner and to any child or young person who is treated by the Secretary of State as the responsibility of the claimant or their partner, where that child or young person is a member of the claimant's household.

(2) In such cases and subject to such conditions or requirements as the Secretary of State may specify by means of a direction, any requirement imposed under these Regulations for a signature may be satisfied by means of an electronic signature (within the meaning given in section 7(2) of the Electronic Communications Act 2000).

(3) A person of a prescribed description for the purposes of the definition of "family" in section 35(1) of the Act is a young person.

(4) For the purposes of paragraph (d) of the definition of "couple" in section 35(1) of the Act, two persons of the same sex are to be regarded as living together as if they were civil partners only if they would be regarded as living together as husband and wife were they instead two persons of the opposite sex.

(5) In this regulation, "polygamous marriage" means any marriage during the subsistence of which a party to it is married to more than one person and the ceremony of marriage took place under the law of a country which permits polygamy.

(6) References in these Regulations to a person participating as a service user are to the person—

  (a) a person who is being consulted by or on behalf of—
      (i) a body which has a statutory duty to provide services in the field of health, social care or social housing; or
      (ii) a body which conducts research or undertakes monitoring for the purpose of planning or improving such services, in the person's capacity as a user, potential user, carer of a user or person otherwise affected by the provision of those services; or
  (b) the carer of a person consulted under sub-paragraph (a).

(7) In these Regulations, references to obtaining paid work includes obtaining more paid work or obtaining better-paid work.

DEFINITIONS

  "the Act"—see reg.2(2).
  "child"—see Jobseekers Act 1995, s.35(1).
  "claimant"—see Jobseekers Act 1995, s.35(1).
  "couple"—see Jobseekers Act 1995, s.35(1).
  "partner"—see reg.2(2).
  "young person"—see reg.2(2).

GENERAL NOTE

This provides further definitions in addition to those in reg.2.      **1.023**

## PART 2

## CLAIMANT RESPONSIBILITIES

GENERAL NOTE

  "Claimant responsibilities" in "new style JSA" cover similar issues as the   **1.024** "labour market" conditions" (entering into a jobseeker's agreement; availability for and actively seeking employment) in old style JSA".

For "new style JSA" these responsibilities are set by Jobseekers Act 1995 ss.6–6L inserted by the Welfare Reform Act 2012 s.49 (see "Pathfinder" amendment, update to pp.58–74 in Part III of this Supplement). These responsibilities—not all of which are imposed on all claimants—are called "work-related requirements" and will be set out in the "claimant commitment" (s.6A) which will be required of all JSA claimants, other than those exempted by reg.8, as a condition of a valid JSA claim. They embrace a work-focused interview requirement (s.6B); a work preparation requirement (s.6C); a work search requirement (s.6D); and a work availability requirement (s.6E). Connected requirements, such as participation in an interview to verify and assist claimants' compliance with their claimant commitment, can also be imposed (ss.6G, 6H). Sanctions can be imposed for non-compliance with the imposed "work-related requirements" (ss.6H-6J) and there is provision for delegating and contracting out certain of these functions (those embraced by ss.6-6I, so not including the imposition of sanctions (ss.6J, 6K)).

## Interpretation

  **4.**—(1) In this Part—      **1.025**
  "relevant carer" means—

    (a) a parent of a child who is not the responsible carer, but has caring responsibilities for the child; or

    (b) a person who has caring responsibilities for a person who has a physical or mental impairment which makes those caring responsibilities necessary;

"responsible carer", in relation to a child, means—

    (a) a person who is the only person responsible for the child; or

    (b) a person who is a member of a couple where—

        (i) both members of the couple are responsible for the child; and

        (ii) the person has been nominated by the couple jointly as responsible for the child;

"responsible foster parent", in relation to a child, means—

    (a) a person who is the only foster parent in relation to the child; or

    (b) a person who is a member of a couple where—

        (i) both members of the couple are foster parents in relation to the child; and

        (ii) the person has been nominated by the couple jointly as the responsible foster parent;

"voluntary work preparation" means particular action taken by a claimant and agreed by the Secretary of State for the purpose of making it more likely that the claimant will obtain paid work, but which is not specified by the Secretary of State as a work preparation requirement under section 6C of the Act.

(2) The nomination of a responsible carer or responsible foster parent for the purposes of paragraph (1) may be changed—

    (a) once in a 12 month period, beginning with the date of the previous nomination; or

    (b) on any occasion where the Secretary of State considers that there has been a change of circumstances which is relevant to the nomination.

(3) Only one person may be nominated as a responsible carer or a responsible foster parent.

(4) The nomination applies to all of the children for whom the claimant is responsible.

DEFINITIONS

"child"—see Jobseekers Act 1995, s.35(1).
"claimant"—see Jobseekers Act 1995, s.35(1).
"couple"—see Jobseekers Act 1995, s.35(1); reg.3(4).

GENERAL NOTE

1.026    In addition to terms already defined in regs 2 and 3, this provides for purposes of this Part (Part 2 Claimant responsibilities) a number of important definitions: "relevant carer"; "responsible foster parent"; "responsible carer"; "voluntary work preparation".

## Application of regulations where there is dual entitlement

**5.**—(1) This regulation applies where a person is entitled to universal credit and a jobseeker's allowance.　1.027

(2) The work-related requirements under sections 6B to 6I of the Act and regulations 9 to 16 of these Regulations do not apply to such a person.

(3) Reductions relating to the award of a jobseeker's allowance under section 6J or 6K of the Act and regulations 17 to 29 of these Regulations do not apply to such a person.

GENERAL NOTE

This provides that where a person is entitled to UC and JSA, the work-related requirements and sanctions regime applicable to JSA does not apply. The person will instead be subject to the comparable UC regime. See Universal Credit Regulations 2013 regs 84–114.　1.028

## Sanction ceases to apply to jobseeker's allowance

**6.**—(1) This regulation applies where—　1.029
(a) a person is entitled to a jobseeker's allowance;
(b) there is a reduction relating to the person's award of a jobseeker's allowance under section 6J or 6K of the Act;
(c) the person becomes entitled to universal credit; and
(d) the person remains entitled to a jobseeker's allowance.

(2) Any reduction relating to the person's award of the jobseeker's allowance is to cease being applied to the award of the jobseeker's allowance.

GENERAL NOTE

Where a JSA reduction is in place and the person then becomes entitled to UC as well as JSA, the JSA reduction ceases to apply. The person will instead be dealt with under the UC regime. See Universal Credit Regulations 2013 regs 112 and Sch.11.　1.030

## Claimant commitment—date and method of acceptance

**7.**—(1) For the purposes of section 1(2)(b) of the Act, a claimant who has accepted a claimant commitment within such period after making a claim for a jobseeker's allowance as the Secretary of State specifies is to be treated as having accepted that claimant commitment on the first day of the period in respect of which the claim is made.　1.031

(2) The Secretary of State may extend the period within which a claimant is required to accept a claimant commitment or an updated claimant commitment where the claimant requests that the Secretary of State review—
(a) any action proposed as a work search requirement or a work availability requirement; or
(b) whether any limitation should apply to those requirements,
and the Secretary of State considers that the request is reasonable.

(3) A claimant must accept a claimant commitment by one of the following methods, as specified by the Secretary of State—
(a) electronically;

(b) by telephone; or
(c) in writing.

DEFINITIONS

"the Act"—see reg.2(2).
"claimant"—see Jobseekers Act 1995, s.35(1).
"claimant commitment"—see Jobseekers Act 1995, s.6A.

GENERAL NOTE

1.032     This provides for a claimant commitment accepted within a period after the claim to be backdated to the first day of the claim period (para.(1)). A period can be extended by the Secretary of State where the claimant reasonably requests an extension (para.(2)). The commitment must be accepted electronically, in writing or by telephone, whichever is specified by the Secretary of State (para.(3)).

## Claimant commitment—exceptions

1.033     **8.**—A claimant may be entitled to a jobseeker's allowance without having accepted a claimant commitment if the Secretary of State considers—

(a) the claimant cannot accept a claimant commitment because they lack capacity to do so; or

(b) there are exceptional circumstances in which it would be unreasonable to expect the person to accept a claimant commitment.

DEFINITIONS

"claimant"—see Jobseekers Act 1995, s.35(1).
"claimant commitment"—see Jobseekers Act 1995, s.6A.

GENERAL NOTE

1.034     This allows the Secretary of State to release the claimant from the requirement to accept a claimant commitment as a condition of receiving JSA where the Secretary of State considers that exceptional circumstances pertain in which it would be unreasonable to expect acceptance, or where the claimant lacks capacity to accept a claimant commitment.

## Expected hours

1.035     **9.**—(1) The expected number of hours per week in relation to a claimant for the purposes of determining any limitations on work search or work availability requirements is 35 unless some lesser number of hours applies in the claimant's case under paragraph (2).

(2) The lesser number of hours referred to in paragraph (1) is—

(a) where—

(i) the claimant is a relevant carer, a responsible carer or a responsible foster parent; and

(ii) the Secretary of State is satisfied that the claimant has reasonable prospects of obtaining paid work, the number of hours,

being less than 35, that the Secretary of State considers is compatible with those caring responsibilities;
(b) where the claimant is a responsible carer or a responsible foster carer for a child under the age of 13, the number of hours that the Secretary of State considers is compatible with their caring responsibilities for the child during the child's normal school hours (including the normal time it takes the child to travel to and from school); or
(c) where the claimant has a physical or mental impairment, the number of hours that the Secretary of State considers is reasonable in light of the impairment.

DEFINTIONS

"child"—see Jobseekers Act 1995, s.35(1).
"claimant"—see Jobseekers Act 1995, s.35(1).
"relevant carer"—see reg.4(1).
"responsible carer"—see reg.4(1).
"responsible foster carer"—see reg.4(1).

GENERAL NOTE

Paragraph (1) sets 35 hours as the usual requisite for determining any limita- **1.036** tions on work search or work availability requirements. Paragraph (2) gives an exhaustive list of situations in which a lesser number of hours is acceptable.

Under para.(2)(a), for a person with caring responsibilities as a "relevant carer", "responsible carer", or "responsible foster parent" (on all of which see reg.4(1)) the Secretary of State, so long as satisfied that the person has reasonable prospects of obtaining paid work, is to accept such number of hours less than 35 as he considers compatible with that person's caring responsibilities.

Paragraph (2)(b) means that the Secretary of State must accept such lesser number of hours than 35 as he considers compatible with the caring responsibilities of a "responsible carer" or "responsible foster carer" (on each of which see reg.4(1)) for a child under 13 during that child's normal school hours (including the child's requisite travel time).

Paragraph (2)(c), like JSA Regulations 1996 reg.6(1) (availability for 40 hours per week) and reg.13(3) on restrictions on availability, sets the lesser number of hours than 35 as the number considered reasonable in light of the person's physical or mental impairment.

## Purposes of a work-focused interview

**10.**—The purposes of a work-focused interview are any or all of the **1.037** following—
(a) assessing the claimant's prospects for remaining in or obtaining work;
(b) assisting or encouraging the claimant to remain in or obtain work;
(c) identifying activities that the claimant may undertake that will make remaining in or obtaining work more likely;
(d) identifying training, educational or rehabilitation opportunities for the claimant which may make it more likely that the claimant will remain in or obtain work or be able to do so;

(e) identifying current or future work opportunities for the claimant that are relevant to the claimant's needs and abilities.

DEFINITIONS

"claimant"—see Jobseekers Act 1995, s.35(1).

GENERAL NOTE

1.038    This sets out the purposes of a work-focused interview. Compare ESA Regulations 2008 reg.55 and Universal Credit Regulations 2013 reg.93.

## Work search requirement: interviews

1.039    **11.**—A claimant is to be treated as not having complied with a work search requirement to apply for a particular vacancy for paid work where the claimant fails to participate in an interview offered to the claimant in connection with the vacancy.

DEFINITIONS

"claimant"—see Jobseekers Act 1995, s.35(1).

GENERAL NOTE

1.040    Jobseekers Act 1995 s.6D (see update to pp.58–74 in Part III of this Supplement) defines making applications for paid work as one work-search requirement that can be stipulated as one the claimant must undertake. This regulation provides that failure to participate in an interview offered to the claimant in connection with a particular vacancy for paid work must result in the claimant being treated as not complying with a work-search requirement to apply for that vacancy.

## Work search requirement: all reasonable action

1.041    **12.**—(1) A claimant is to be treated as not having complied with a work search requirement to take all reasonable action for the purpose of obtaining paid work in any week unless—
    (a) either—
        (i) for the purpose of obtaining paid work, the claimant takes action for the claimant's expected hours per week minus any relevant deductions; or
        (ii) the Secretary of State is satisfied that the claimant has taken all reasonable action for the purpose of obtaining paid work despite the number of hours that the claimant spends taking such action being lower than the expected number of hours per week; and
    (b) that action gives the claimant the best prospects of obtaining work.
    (2) In this regulation "relevant deductions" means the total of any time agreed by the Secretary of State—
    (a) for the claimant to carry out paid work in that week;
    (b) for the claimant to carry out voluntary work in that week;
    (c) for the claimant to carry out a work preparation requirement, or voluntary work preparation, in that week; or

(d) for the claimant to deal with temporary child care responsibilities, a domestic emergency, funeral arrangements or other temporary circumstances.

(3) For the purpose of paragraph (2)(b) the time agreed by the Secretary of State for the claimant to carry out voluntary work must not exceed 50% of the claimant's expected number of hours per week.

DEFINITIONS

"claimant"—see Jobseekers Act 1995, s.35(1).
"relevant deductions"—see para.(2).

GENERAL NOTE

In "old style ESA", the claimant had to be "actively seeking work". For "new  1.042
style JSA", this has become the obligation to comply with a "work search requirement". This is dealt with in the Jobseekers Act 1995 ss.6, 6D (see update to pp.58–74 in Part III of this Supplement). These enable the Secretary of State to require a claimant to take all reasonable action or any particular action for the purpose of obtaining paid work, more paid work or better-paid work. JSA thus recognises that not all claimants will be wholly unemployed, but may be doing some part-time paid work or voluntary work. The aim is to try to move persons from benefit into work, better paid work, work for more hours (whether with one job or more than one job), work being the best way out of poverty, welfare through work.

This regulation means that to comply with the obligation the claimant must take action which gives the claimant the best prospects of obtaining work and must do so for his number of expected hours (set pursuant to reg.9—generally 35 but less for cases within reg.9(2)) minus "relevant deductions".

These deductions, reducing the expected number of hours for "work search", consist of such of the total of any time agreed by the Secretary of State as enabling the claimant to undertake in a particular week or weeks one or more of the activities set out in para.(2) (the list is exhaustive): for example, doing some paid work or voluntary work (the latter being limited to half or less of the claimant's expected hours set under reg.9); or dealing with temporary child care responsibilities, a domestic emergency, funeral arrangements or other temporary circumstances.

## Work availability requirement: able and willing immediately to take up paid work

**13.**—(1) Subject to paragraph (2), a claimant is to be treated as not  1.043
having complied with a work availability requirement if the claimant is—

(a) not able and willing immediately to attend an interview offered to the claimant in connection with obtaining paid work;

(b) a prisoner on temporary release in accordance with the provisions of the Prison Act 1952 or rules made under section 39(6) of the Prisons (Scotland) Act 1989.

(2) A claimant is to be treated as having complied with a work availability requirement despite not being able immediately to take up paid work, if paragraph (3), (4) or (5) applies.

(3) This paragraph applies where—

(a) a claimant is a responsible carer or a relevant carer;

(b) the Secretary of State is satisfied that as a consequence the claimant needs a period of up to one month to take up paid work, or up to 48 hours to attend an interview in connection with obtaining paid work, taking into account alternative care arrangements; and

(c) the claimant is able and willing to take up paid work, or attend such an interview, on being given notice for that period.

(4) This paragraph applies where—

(a) a claimant is carrying out voluntary work;

(b) the Secretary of State is satisfied that as a consequence the claimant needs a period of up to one week to take up paid work, or up to 48 hours to attend an interview in connection with obtaining paid work; and

(c) the claimant is able and willing to take up paid work, or attend such an interview, on being given notice for that period.

(5) This paragraph applies where a claimant is—

(a) employed under a contract of service;

(b) required by section 86 of the Employment Rights Act 1996, or by the contract of service, to give notice to terminate the contract;

(c) able and willing to take up paid work once the notice period has expired; and

(d) able and willing to attend an interview in connection with obtaining paid work on being given 48 hours notice.

DEFINITIONS

"claimant"—see Jobseekers Act 1995, s.35(1).
"relevant carer"—see reg.4(1).
"responsible carer"—see reg.4(1).

GENERAL NOTE

1.044   With respect to "old style JSA", Jobseekers Act 1995 s.6 stipulated that a claimant was available for work if willing and able to take up immediately any employed earners' employment and the JSA Regulations 1996 provided some exemptions from the "immediately" requirement (reg.5) and enabled limitations to be placed on availability (regs 6–13A)

As regards "new style JSA", work availability requirements are set by the Jobseekers Act 1995 ss.6, 6E (see update to pp.58–74 in Part III of this Supplement). They require the claimant to be available for work, that is, able and willing immediately to take up paid work, more paid work or better paid work. They also enable limitations to be placed on availability via regulations or by specification by the Secretary of State in any particular case.

Paragraph (1) of this regulation specifies that a prisoner on temporary release is to be treated as not available. More generally it provides a claimant is not available for work if not able and willing *immediately* to attend an interview offered to the claimant in connection with paid work, unless (as provided in para.(2)) one of the exemptions from the "immediately" requirement set out in paras (3), (4) or (5) apply.

A responsible carer or relevant carer is exempt from the "immediately" requirement (whether to take up paid work or attend an interview in respect of such work) if the Secretary of State considers that in consequence and taking into account alternative care arrangements, the claimant needs a period of up to a month to take up paid work or a period of up to 48 hours with respect to an interview, so long as the claimant is willing to take up paid work or attend for an interview on being given notice for that period (para.(3)).

Someone carrying out voluntary work is exempt from the "immediately" requirement (whether to take up paid work or attend an interview in respect of such work) if the Secretary of State considers that in consequence the claimant needs a period of up to one week to take up paid work, or up to 48 hours to attend an interview in connection with obtaining paid work, so long as the claimant is willing to take up paid work or attend for an interview on being given notice for that period (para.(4)).

Similarly someone employed under a contract of service and required to give notice to terminate it (whether by the contract or Employment Rights Act 1986 s.86) will be available if able and willing to attend an interview on being given 48 hours notice and able and willing to take up paid employment once the notice period has expired (para.(5)).

### Work search requirement and work availability requirement: limitations

**14.**—(1) Paragraphs (2) to (5) set out the limitations on a work search requirement and a work availability requirement. 

1.045

(2) A work search requirement and a work availability requirement must be limited to work that is in a location which would normally take the claimant—

    (a) a maximum of one hour and 30 minutes to travel from home to the location; and

    (b) a maximum of one hour and 30 minutes to travel from the location to home.

(3) Where a claimant has previously carried out work of a particular nature, or at a particular level of remuneration, a work search requirement and a work availability requirement must be limited to work of a similar nature, or level of remuneration, for such period as the Secretary of State considers appropriate; but

    (a) only if the Secretary of State is satisfied that the claimant will have reasonable prospects of obtaining paid work in spite of such limitation; and

    (b) the limitation is to apply for no more than three months beginning on the date of claim.

(4) Where a claimant has a physical or mental impairment that has a substantial adverse effect on the claimant's ability to carry out work of a particular nature, or in particular locations, a work search requirement or work availability requirement must not relate to work of such a nature or in such locations.

(5) In the case of a claimant who is a relevant carer or a responsible carer or has a physical or mental impairment, a work search and work availability requirement must be limited to the number of hours that is determined to be the claimant's expected number of hours per week in accordance with regulation 9(2).

DEFINITIONS

    "claimant"—see Jobseekers Act 1995, s.35(1).
    "date of claim"—see reg.2(2).
    "relevant carer"—see reg.4(1).

"responsible carer"—see reg.4(1).
"week"—see Jobseekers Act 1995, s.35(1); reg.2(2).

GENERAL NOTE

1.046    For "new style JSA", Jobseekers Act 1995 ss.6, 6D and 6E (see update to pp.58–74 in Part III of this Supplement), which deal with work search and work availability requirements, also enable limitations to be placed on availability via regulations or by specification by the Secretary of State in any particular case. This regulation sets out the limitations permitted by regulations.

Paragraph (2) deals with travel time to and from work requiring work-search and work availability requirements to be limited to a maximum of one and a half hours journey time each way.

Where a claimant has previously carried out work of a particular nature or at a particular level of remuneration, para.(3) (comparable to JSA Regulations 1996 reg.15) requires work search and work availability to be limited to that work or level of remuneration for such period up to three months from the date of claim as the Secretary of State thinks appropriate so long as the Secretary of State is satisfied that the claimant will, despite the limitation, have reasonable prospects of obtaining paid work.

For claimants with physical or mental impairments having a substantial adverse effect on their ability to do particular types of work or to work in particular locations, work search and availability requirements cannot relate to such work or such locations (para.(4)).

For relevant carers, responsible carers and those with a physical or mental impairment, work search and availability requirements have to be confined to their expected number of hours a week as determined by reg.9(2).

## Victims of domestic violence

1.047    **15.**—(1) Where a claimant has recently been a victim of domestic violence and the circumstances set out in paragraph (3) apply—

(a)  a requirement imposed on that claimant under sections 6 to 6G of the Act ceases to have effect for a period of 13 consecutive weeks starting on the date of the notification referred to in paragraph (3)(a); and

(b)  the Secretary of State must not impose any other such requirement on that claimant during that period.

(2) A person has recently been a victim of domestic violence if a period of six months has not expired since the violence was inflicted or threatened.

(3) The circumstances are that—

(a)  the claimant notifies the Secretary of State, in such manner as the Secretary of State specifies, that domestic violence has been inflicted on or threatened against the claimant by a person specified in paragraph (4) during the period of six months ending on the date of the notification;

(b)  this regulation has not applied to the claimant for a period of 12 months before the date of the notification;

(c)  on the date of the notification the claimant is not living at the same address as the person who inflicted or threatened the domestic violence; and

(d) as soon as possible, and no later than one month, after the date of the notification the claimant provides evidence from a person acting in an official capacity which demonstrates that—

    (i) the claimant's circumstances are consistent with those of a person who has had domestic violence inflicted on or threatened against them during the period of six months ending on the date of the notification; and

    (ii) the claimant has made contact with the person acting in an official capacity in relation to such an incident, which occurred during that period.

(4) A person is specified in this paragraph if the person is—

(a) where the claimant is, or was, a member of a couple, the other member of the couple;

(b) the claimant's grandparent, grandchild, parent, parent-in-law, son, son-in-law, daughter, daughter-in-law, step-parent, step-son, step-daughter, brother, step-brother, brother-in-law, sister, step-sister or sister-in-law; or

(c) where any of the persons listed in sub-paragraph (b) is a member of a couple, the other member of that couple.

(5) In this regulation—

[[1]"coercive behaviour" means an act of assault, humiliation or intimidation or other abuse that is used to harm, punish or frighten the victim;

"controlling behaviour" means an act designed to make a person subordinate or dependent by isolating them from sources of support, exploiting their resources and capacities for personal gain, depriving them of the means needed for independence, resistance or escape or regulating their everyday behaviour;

"domestic violence" means any incident, or pattern of incidents, of controlling behaviour, coercive behaviour, violence or abuse, including but not limited to—

    (a) psychological abuse;

    (b) physical abuse;

    (c) sexual abuse;

    (d) emotional abuse;

    (e) financial abuse,

regardless of the gender or sexuality of the victim;]

"health care professional" means a person who is a member of a profession regulated by a body mentioned in section 25(3) of the National Health Service Reform and Health Care Professions Act 2002;

"person acting in an official capacity" means a health care professional, a police officer, a registered social worker, the claimant's employer, a representative of the claimant's trade union or any public, voluntary or charitable body which has had direct contact with the claimant in connection with domestic violence;

"registered social worker" means a person registered as a social worker in a register maintained by—

    (a) the General Social Care Council;

    (b) the Care Council for Wales;

    (c) the Scottish Social Services Council; or

    (d) the Northern Ireland Social Care Council.

AMENDMENT

1. Social Security (Miscellaneous Amendments) (No. 2) Regulations 2013 (SI 2013/1508), reg.4(1), (2) (October 29, 2013).

DEFINITIONS

"claimant"—see Jobseekers Act 1995, s.35(1).
"coercive behaviour"—see para.(5).
"controlling behaviour"—see para.(5).
"domestic violence"—see para.(5).
"health care professional"—see para.(5).
"person acting in an official capacity"—see para.(5).
"recently been a victim of domestic violence"—see Jobseekers Act 1995, s.6H(6)(b); para.(2).
"registered social worker"—see para.(5).
"victim of domestic violence"—see Jobseekers Act 1995, s.6H(6)(b).

GENERAL NOTE

1.048    For "new style JSA", Jobseekers Act 1995 s.6H (see update to pp.58–74 in Part III of this Supplement) mandates that regulations must be made to give a person who has recently been a victim of domestic violence (V) a 13-week period of respite from work requirements already imposed and in which no further requirements can be added. It also states that "domestic violence" is to have a meaning prescribed in regulations. This regulation is the result. Compare Universal Credit Regulations 2013 reg.98 and JSA Regulations 1996 reg.14A.

Domestic violence is defined in para.(5). The regulation covers both its infliction and it being threatened. Recently means in the last six months. V can obtain this 13-week period of respite commencing with V's notification to the Secretary of State so long as V provides within one month of the notification evidence from a person acting in an official capacity confirming that the claimant is indeed such a victim in the last six months and has been in contact with that person about an incident of domestic violence. The claimant must not be living on the date of notification at the same address as the person who inflicted or threatened the domestic violence. The person inflicting or threatening the domestic violence must be someone specified in para.(4) (covering a very wide range of "family" members or relatives). There can only be one respite period in any 12 months (para.(3)(b)).

## Circumstances in which requirements must not be imposed

1.049    **16.**—(1) Where paragraph (3), (4) or (5) applies—

    (a) the Secretary of State must not impose a work search requirement on a claimant; and

    (b) "able and willing immediately to take up work" under a work availability requirement means able and willing to take up paid work, or attend an interview, immediately once the circumstances set out in paragraph (3), (4) or (5) no longer apply.

(2) A work search requirement previously applying to the claimant ceases to have effect from the date on which the circumstances set out in paragraph (3), (4) or (5) apply.

(3) This paragraph applies where—

(a) the claimant is attending a court or tribunal as a party to any proceedings or as a witness;

(b) the claimant is temporarily absent from Great Britain because they are—

    (i) taking their child outside Great Britain for medical treatment;

    (ii) attending a job interview outside Great Britain; or

    (iii) receiving medical treatment outside Great Britain;

(c) it is within six months of the death of—

    (i) where the claimant is a member of a couple, the other member;

    (ii) a child for whom the claimant or, where the claimant is a member of a couple, the other member, is responsible; or

    (iii) a child, where the claimant is the child's parent;

(d) the claimant is receiving and participating in a structured, recovery-orientated, course of alcohol or drug dependency treatment, for a period of up to six months (where the course is for more than six months, this sub-paragraph only applies for the first six months);

(e) the claimant is a person for whom arrangements have been made by a protection provider under section 82 of the Serious Organised Crime and Police Act 2005, for a period of up to three months (where the arrangements are for more than three months, this sub-paragraph only applies for the first three months).

(4) This paragraph applies where the Secretary of State is satisfied that it would be unreasonable to require the claimant to comply with a work search requirement, including if such a requirement were limited in accordance with section 6D(4) of the Act, because the claimant—

(a) has temporary child care responsibilities;

(b) is subject to temporary circumstances;

(c) is carrying out a public duty; or

(d) is carrying out a work preparation requirement or voluntary work preparation.

(5) This paragraph applies where the claimant—

(a) is unfit for work—

    (i) for a maximum of 14 consecutive days after the date on which the evidence referred to in sub-paragraph (b) is provided; and

    (ii) on no more than two such periods in any period of 12 months; and

(b) provides to the Secretary of State the following evidence—

    (i) for the first seven days when they are unfit for work, a declaration made by the claimant in such manner and form as the Secretary of State approves that the claimant is unfit for work; and

    (ii) for any further days when they are unfit for work, a statement given by a doctor in accordance with the rules set out in Part 1 of Schedule 1 to the Social Security (Medical Evidence) Regulations 1976 which advises that the person is not fit for work.

(6) In this regulation, "tribunal" means any tribunal listed in Schedule 1 to the Tribunal and Inquiries Act 1992.

DEFINITIONS

"claimant"—see Jobseekers Act 1995, s.35(1).
"tribunal"—see para.(6).

GENERAL NOTE

1.050 This regulation gives persons in specified circumstances temporary relief from work search requirements. None can be imposed until those circumstances cease to pertain, and, during that period of relief, the "able and willing immediately to take up work" requirement means able and willing to take up paid work, or attend an interview, immediately once the circumstances no longer apply. In addition, where work search requirements are already in place they must cease once the circumstances arise, but can be re-imposed once they end.

The circumstances are set out in paras (3)–(5). They are generally self-explanatory. One requires a little elucidation. Paragraph (3)(e) deals with s.86 of the Serious and Organised Crime and Police Act 2005 which makes provision for the protection of witnesses and certain other persons (jurors, accomplices given immunity, judges) involved in investigations or legal proceedings. Arrangements for protection are made by protection providers (e.g. Chief Constables, any of the Commissioners for Her Majesty's Revenue and Customs).

PART 3

SANCTIONS

## Interpretation

1.051 17.—For the purposes of this Part—

"ESA sanctionable failure" means a failure by a claimant which is sanctionable under section 11J of the Welfare Reform Act 2007;

"higher-level sanction" means a reduction of a jobseeker's allowance in accordance with section 6J of the Act;

"low-level sanction" means a reduction of a jobseeker's allowance in accordance with section 6K of the Act for a sanctionable failure by the claimant to comply with—

(a) a work-focused interview requirement under section 6B(1) of the Act;

(b) a work preparation requirement under section 6C(1) of the Act;

(c) a work search requirement under section 6D(1)(b) of the Act (requirement to take action specified by the Secretary of State to obtain work); or

(d) a requirement under section 6G of the Act (connected requirements);

"medium-level sanction" means a reduction of a jobseeker's allowance in accordance with section 6K of the Act for a sanctionable failure by the claimant to comply with—

(a) a work search requirement under section 6D(1)(a) of the Act (requirement to take all reasonable action to obtain paid work); or

(b) a work availability requirement under section 6E(1) of the Act (requirement to be available for work);

"pre-claim failure" means a sanctionable failure listed in section 6J(3) of the Act;

"reduction period" means the number of days for which a reduction in the amount of an award of a jobseeker's allowance is to have effect;

"sanctionable failure" means a failure by a claimant which is sanctionable under section 6J or 6K of the Act;

"total outstanding reduction period" means the total number of days for which no reduction has yet been applied for all of the claimant's higher-level sanctions, medium-level sanctions, low-level sanctions and reductions to which regulation 30 applies;

"UC sanctionable failure" means a failure by a claimant which is sanctionable under section 26 or 27 of the Welfare Reform Act 2012.

GENERAL NOTE

This provides definitions of various terms for the purposes of this Part (Part 3: Sanctions) of these regulations.

**1.052**

## General principles for calculating reduction periods

**18.**—(1) Subject to paragraphs (3) and (4), the reduction period is to be determined in relation to each sanctionable failure in accordance with regulations 19, 20 and 21.

**1.053**

(2) Reduction periods are to run consecutively.

(3) Where the reduction period calculated in relation to a sanctionable failure in accordance with regulation 19, 20 or 21 would result in the total outstanding reduction period exceeding 1095 days, the number of days in the reduction period in relation to that failure is to be adjusted so that 1095 days is not exceeded.

(4) In determining the reduction period in relation to a sanctionable failure, a previous sanctionable failure, UC sanctionable failure or ESA sanctionable failure is to be disregarded if it—

(a) occurred in the 14 days immediately preceding the failure in question; and

(b) gave rise to a reduction under these Regulations, the Universal Credit Regulations 2013 or the Employment and Support Allowance Regulations 2013.

DEFINITIONS

"ESA sanctionable failure"—see reg.17.
"reduction period"—see reg.17.
"sanctionable failure"—see reg.17.
"total outstanding reduction period"—see reg.17.
"UC sanctionable failure"—see reg.17.

1.054     This deals with the general principles applicable to sanctionable failures with respect to work-related requirements as regards JSA under s.6J or 6K of the Jobseekers Act 1995 (see update to pp.58–74 in Part III of this Supplement). Section 6J deals with higher-level sanctions. Section 6K deals with other sanctions (medium-level or low-level). Sanctions consist of periods for which JSA is reduced. The reduction period is to be set in accordance with regs 19 (higher-level sanctions), 20 (medium-level sanctions) and 21 (low-level sanctions), below (para.(1)). Reduction periods run consecutively (para.(2)). That is subject to the general overall three-year limit in para.(3): a reduction in accordance with regs 19, 20 or 21 cannot take over three years (1,095 days) in length the total outstanding reduction period for all the claimant's higher level or other sanctions. This drafting is somewhat opaque. The idea appears to be that if adding a new reduction period to the end of what is likely to be a chain of reduction periods would take the total days in the chain over 1,095 days the new reduction period must be adjusted (reduced) to make the total 1,095 days in all.

Paragraph (4) stipulates when previous sanctionable failures or ones sanctionable under UC and ESA are to be ignored. It is unclear whether para.(4) also qualifies para.(3) to allow a total outstanding reduction period to exceed 1,095 days.

## Higher-level sanction

1.055     **19.**—(1) Where the sanctionable failure is not a pre-claim failure, the reduction period for a higher-level sanction is—

(a) 91 days, if sub-paragraphs (b) and (c) do not apply;

(b) 182 days, if in the 365 days preceding the failure in question there was—

    (i) another sanctionable failure giving rise to a higher-level sanction for which a 91 day reduction period applies; or

    (ii) a UC sanctionable failure giving rise to a higher-level sanction under regulation 102(2) of the Universal Credit Regulations 2013 for which a 91 day reduction period applies; or

(c) 1095 days, if in that period of 365 days there was—

    (i) another sanctionable failure giving rise to a higher-level sanction for which a 182 day or 1095 day reduction period applies; or

    (ii) a UC sanctionable failure giving rise to a higher-level sanction under regulation 102(2) of the Universal Credit Regulations 2013 for which a 182 day or 1095 day reduction period applies.

(2) But where—

(a) the other sanctionable failure referred to in paragraph (1) was a pre-claim failure; or

(b) the UC sanctionable failure referred to in paragraph (1) was a pre-claim failure under regulation 102(4) of the Universal Credit Regulations 2013,

it is to be disregarded in determining the reduction period in accordance with paragraph (1).

(3) Where the sanctionable failure for which a reduction period is to be determined is a pre-claim failure, the reduction period is the lesser of—

(a) the period which would be applicable to the claimant under paragraph (1) if it were not a pre-claim failure; or

(b) where the sanctionable failure relates to paid work that was due to last for a limited period, the period beginning with the day after the date of the sanctionable failure and ending with the last day of the limited period,

minus the number of days beginning with the day after the date of the sanctionable failure and ending with the day before the date of claim.

DEFINITIONS

"date of claim"—see reg.2(2).
"pre-claim failure"—see reg.17.
"reduction period"—see reg.17.
"sanctionable failure"—see reg.17.
"UC sanctionable failure"—see reg.17.

GENERAL NOTE

As regards "new style JSA", sanctions involve imposition of a period of **1.056** reduction of JSA, the period varying according to the type of sanction: higher-level, medium-level and low-level. Section 6J of the Jobseekers Act 1995 (see update to pp.58–74 in Part III of this Supplement) sets out the circumstances in which higher-level sanctions are to be imposed. This regulation stipulates the period to be imposed.

Section 6J—which has affinities with Jobseekers Act 1995 s.19 as applicable to "old style ESA"—covers both failures after the claim and ones before the claim. The former are covered by subs.(2):

- Failure for no good reason to comply with a work preparation requirement to undertake a work placement of a prescribed description.
- Failure for no good reason to comply with a work preparation requirement to apply for a particular vacancy for paid work.
- Failure for no good reason to comply with a work availability requirement by not taking up an offer of paid work.
- Ceasing paid work or losing pay by reason of misconduct.
- Voluntarily and without good reason ceasing paid work or losing pay.

Pre claim failures are dealt with in subs.(3): it is a sanctionable failure where prior to making the claim by reference to which the JSA award was made, the claimant

- failed for no good reason to take up an offer of paid work.
- ceased paid work or lost pay by reason of misconduct.
- voluntarily and without good reason ceased paid work or lost pay.

For the meaning of "misconduct", "voluntarily leaving", "failing to apply", "failing to take up an offer" and "good reason", see the annotations to Jobseekers Act 1995 s.19(2), now directly applicable only to "old style JSA".

With respect to failures during the claim: basically, looking at things over the 365 days preceding the failure in question, the period of reduction is 91 days for a first higher level "sanctionable failure", 182 days for a second where a previous one (whether under JSA or UC) had attracted 91 days, and 1,095 days (three years) for a third or subsequent failure where the previous one (whether under JSA or UC) had attracted 182 days or 1,095 days. If there is less than two weeks between the previous failure attracting a reduction (whether under JSA or UC) and a subsequent one, that previous failure must be disregarded (reg.18(4)). If the previous sanctionable failures were pre-claim failures whether under JSA or UC, they must be disregarded in determining the reduction period (para.(2)).

The period of reduction for pre-claim failures is set by the rather confusingly drafted para.(3). Where the failure to be penalised is a pre-claim failure under s.6J(3) (but not one in relation to work due to last only for a limited period), the period of reduction is that which would have applied had it occurred during the claim is to reduced by the number of days of no-claim for JSA since that sanctionable failure.

If the pre-claim failure is in respect of work due to last for a limited period, the period of reduction is the lesser of (i) that which would have applied had it occurred during the claim minus the number of days of no-claim for JSA since that sanctionable failure or (ii) the period beginning with the day after the sanctionable failure and ending with the last day of the limited period minus the number of days between that failure and the date of claim (para.(3)).

## Medium-level sanctions

1.057     **20.**—The reduction period for a medium-level sanction is—
    (a) 28 days, if paragraph (b) does not apply; or
    (b) 91 days, if in the 365 days preceding the failure in question there was—
        (i) another sanctionable failure giving rise to a medium-level sanction for which a 28 day or 91 day reduction period applies; or
        (ii) a UC sanctionable failure giving rise to a medium-level sanction under regulation 103 of the Universal Credit Regulations 2013 for which a 28 day or 91 day reduction period applies.

DEFINITIONS

"medium-level sanction"—see reg.17.
"sanctionable failure"—see reg.17.
"UC sanctionable failure"—see reg.17.
"reduction period"—see reg.17.

GENERAL NOTE

1.058     A medium level sanction is reduction of JSA under Jobseekers Act 1995 s.6K (see update to pp.58–74 in Part III of this Supplement) for a sanctionable failure by the claimant to comply with—
    (a) a work search requirement under section 6D(1)(a) of the Act (requirement to take all reasonable action to obtain paid work); or
    (b) a work availability requirement under section 6E(1) of the Act (requirement to be available for work).
This regulation sets the period of reduction at 28 days if there have been no other medium-level sanctionable failures in the previous 365 days, and at 91 days if there have been one or more such failures (whether JSA or UC) in that period. That is subject to the disregard in reg.18(4) of any sanctionable failures attracting reduction under JSA or UC in the 14 days before the sanctionable failure in question.

## Low-level sanctions

1.059     **21.**—(1) The reduction period for a low-level sanction is the total of the number of days referred to in paragraphs (2) and (3).

(2) The number of days beginning with the date of the sanctionable failure and ending with—

(a) the day before the day on which the claimant meets a compliance condition specified by the Secretary of State;

(b) the day before the day on which the claimant is no longer required to take a particular action specified as a work preparation requirement by the Secretary of State under section 6C(1) of the Act; or

(c) the day on which the award of a jobseeker's allowance is terminated,

whichever is soonest.

(3) Whichever of the following number of days is applicable in the claimant's case—

(a) seven days, if sub-paragraphs (b) and (c) do not apply;

(b) 14 days, if in the 365 days preceding the failure in question there was—

(i) another sanctionable failure giving rise to a low-level sanction for which a seven day reduction period applies;

(ii) a UC sanctionable failure giving rise to a low-level sanction under regulation 104 of the Universal Credit Regulations 2013 for which a seven day reduction period applies; or

(iii) an ESA sanctionable failure giving rise to a low-level sanction under regulation 52 of the Employment and Support Allowance Regulations 2013 for which a seven day reduction period applies; or

(c) 28 days, if in the 365 days preceding the failure in question there was—

(i) another sanctionable failure giving rise to a low-level sanction for which a 14 day or 28 day reduction period applies;

(ii) a UC sanctionable failure giving rise to a low-level sanction under regulation 104 of the Universal Credit Regulations 2013 for which a 14 day or 28 day reduction period applies; or

(iii) an ESA sanctionable failure giving rise to a low-level sanction under regulation 52 of the Employment and Support Allowance Regulations 2013 for which a 14 day or 28 day reduction period applies.

## Definitions

"ESA sanctionable failure"—see reg.17.
"low-level sanction"—see reg.17.
"sanctionable failure"—see reg.17.
"UC sanctionable failure"—see reg.17.

## General Note

A "low-level sanction" is a reduction of JSA under Jobseekers Act 1995 s.6K **1.060** (see update to pp.58–74 in Part III of this Supplement) in respect of a sanctionable failure by the claimant to comply with—

(a) a work-focused interview requirement under section 6B(1) of the Act;

(b) a work preparation requirement under section 6C(1) of the Act;

(c) a work search requirement under section 6D(1)(b) of the Act (requirement to take action specified by the Secretary of State to obtain work); or

(d) a requirement under section 6G of the Act (connected requirements).

This regulation sets the period of reduction as the sum of two periods. Under para.(2) the first period begins on the day of the sanctionable failure and ends on whichever is the earliest of the days identified in sub-paras (a)–(c) which apply in the particular case. Sub-paragraph (a) sets the end of the first period as the day before the one on which the claimant does what the Secretary of State wants in terms of the relevant work-related requirements or connected requirements (remedies the failure). Sub-paragraph (b) sets the end of this first period where the claimant is no longer required to take a particular action as a work preparation requirement under s.6C(1) of the Jobseekers Act 1995 (see update to pp.58–74 in Part III of this Supplement). Finally, sub-paragraph (c) sees the end of the first period as the day on which the JSA award is terminated.

Paragraph (3) sets the second period at varying lengths (7, 14 or 28 days) depending on whether the failure was a first, second or subsequent one (whether with respect to ESA, JSA or UC) in the 365 days preceding the failure in question. Note, however, that sanctionable failures attracting a JSA, ESA or UC reduction occurring in the 14 days before the sanctionable failure in question are to be disregarded (reg.18(4)).

### Start of the reduction

1.061      **22.**—A reduction period determined in relation to a sanctionable failure takes effect from—

(a) where the claimant has not been paid a jobseeker's allowance for the benefit week in which the sanctionable failure occurred, the first day of that benefit week;

(b) where the claimant has been paid a jobseeker's allowance for the benefit week referred to in paragraph (a), the first day of the first benefit week for which the claimant has not been paid a jobseeker's allowance; or

(c) where the amount of the award of the jobseeker's allowance for the benefit week referred to in paragraph (a) or (b) is already subject to a reduction because of a previous sanctionable failure, the first day of the first benefit week in respect of which the amount of the award is no longer subject to that reduction.

DEFINITIONS

"benefit week"—see reg.2(2).
"reduction period"—see reg.17.
"sanctionable failure"—see reg.17.

GENERAL NOTE

1.062      This stipulates in which benefit week the relevant period of reduction appropriate to the sanctionable failure actually takes effect in relation to an award of JSA.

### Reduction period to continue where award of jobseeker's allowance terminates

1.063      **23.**—(1) Where an award of a jobseeker's allowance terminates while there is an outstanding reduction period—

(a) the period continues to run as if a daily reduction were being applied; and

(b) if the claimant becomes entitled to a new award of a jobseeker's allowance before the period expires, that new award is subject to a reduction for the remainder of the total outstanding reduction period.

(2) Paragraph (3) applies where—

(a) an award of a jobseeker's allowance terminates before the Secretary of State determines that the amount of the award is to be reduced in accordance with section 6J or 6K of the Act in relation to a sanctionable failure; and

(b) that determination is made after the claimant becomes entitled to a new award of a jobseeker's allowance.

(3) Where this paragraph applies—

(a) the reduction period in relation to the sanctionable failure referred to in paragraph (2) is to be treated as having taken effect on the day before the previous award terminated;

(b) that reduction period is treated as having continued to run as if a daily reduction were being applied; and

(c) if the new award referred to in paragraph (2)(b) begins before that reduction period expires, that new award is subject to a reduction for the remainder of the total outstanding reduction period.

DEFINITIONS

"reduction period"—see reg.17.
"sanctionable failure"—see reg.17.
"total outstanding reduction period"—see reg.17.

GENERAL NOTE

If an award of JSA terminates while there is an outstanding reduction period, **1.064** subsequent days count as if an actual reduction of benefit were being applied (thus reducing the days outstanding in the period), so that on any further claim for JSA the claimant is subject to the reduction only for the remainder of the period, if any (para.(1)). If an award of JSA terminates before the Secretary of State has made a decision about a reduction for a sanctionable failure, but a new award is in place by the time the decision is made, the reduction period starts as if the decision had been made on the day before the previous award terminated, so that the new award of ESA will be reduced for the remainder of the total outstanding reduction period (paras (2), (3).

## Suspension of a reduction where a fraud sanction applies

**24.**—(1) A reduction in the amount of an award of a jobseeker's **1.065** allowance in accordance with section 6J or 6K of the Act is to be suspended for any period during which section 6B or 7 of the Social Security Fraud Act 2001(39) applies to the award.

(2) The reduction ceases to have effect on the day on which that period begins and has effect again on the day after that period ends.

DEFINITION

"the Act"—see reg.2(2).

### Termination of a reduction

1.066    **25.**—(1) A reduction in the amount of an award of a jobseeker's allowance in accordance with section 6J or 6K of the Act is to be terminated where, since the date of the most recent sanctionable failure which gave rise to such a reduction, the claimant has been in paid work—

(a) for a period of at least 26 weeks; or

(b) for more than one period where the total of those periods amounts to at least 26 weeks.

(2) The termination of the reduction has effect—

(a) where the date on which paragraph (1) is satisfied falls within a period of entitlement to a jobseeker's allowance, from the beginning of the benefit week in which that date falls; or

(b) where that date falls outside a period of entitlement to a jobseeker's allowance, from the beginning of the first benefit week in relation to any subsequent award of a jobseeker's allowance.

(3) The claimant is in paid work for the purposes of paragraph (1) where their weekly earnings are at least equal to their expected number of hours per week calculated under regulation 9 multiplied by the national minimum wage which would apply for a person of the claimant's age under the National Minimum Wage Regulations 1999.

DEFINITIONS

"the Act"—see reg.2(2).
"benefit week"—see reg.2(2).
"in paid work"—see para.(3).
"sanctionable failure"—see reg.17.

GENERAL NOTE

1.067    Any reduction for any level of sanction or sanctions terminates where since the date of the most recent sanctionable failure the claimant has been in paid work for at least 26 weeks, not necessarily consecutive, with weekly earnings at least equal to their expected number of hours per week (see reg.9) multiplied by the national minimum wage applicable to a person of the claimant's age under the National Minimum Wage Regulations 1999 (paras (1), (3)). Paragraph (2) sets out the time the termination takes effect dependent on whether or not the day the 26-week period is up falls within or outside a period of entitlement to JSA. If within, termination takes effect from the beginning of the benefit week in which there fell the completion of the 26-week period. If outside, it takes effect from the beginning of the first benefit week of any subsequent JSA award.

### Amount of reduction for each benefit week

1.068    **26.** Where it has been determined that an award of a jobseeker's allowance is to be reduced in accordance with section 6J or 6K of the Act, the amount of the reduction for each benefit week in respect of which a reduction has effect is to be calculated as follows.

Step 1

Take the number of days—

(a) in the benefit week; or

(b) if lower, in the total outstanding reduction period,

and deduct any days in that benefit week or total outstanding reduction period for which the reduction is suspended in accordance with regulation 24.

Step 2

Multiply the number of days produced by step 1 by the daily reduction rate.

Step 3

Deduct the amount produced by step 2 from the amount of the award of jobseeker's allowance for the benefit week.

DEFINITIONS

"benefit week"—see reg.2(2).
"daily reduction rate"—see reg.27.
"total outstanding reduction period"—see reg.17.

GENERAL NOTE

This provides the means of calculating for each benefit week the amount of reduction.    **1.069**

## Daily reduction rate

**27.**—(1) The daily reduction rate for the purposes of regulation 26 is    **1.070** the amount applicable to the claimant under regulation 49 multiplied by 52 and divided by 365.

(2) The amount of the rate in paragraph (1) is to be rounded down to the nearest 10 pence.

## Failures for which no reduction is applied

**28.**—(1) No reduction is to be made in accordance with section 6J of    **1.071** the Act for a sanctionable failure where—
  (a) the sanctionable failure is listed in section 6J(2)(b) or (c) of the Act (failure to apply for a vacancy for paid work or failure to take up an offer of paid work) and the vacancy has arisen because of a strike arising from a trade dispute;
  (b) the sanctionable failure is listed in section 6J(2)(d) of the Act (ceases paid work or loses pay) and the following circumstances apply—
      (i) the claimant's work search and work availability requirements are subject to limitations under sections 6D(4) and 6E(3) of the Act in respect of work available for a certain number of hours;
      (ii) the claimant takes up paid work that is for a greater number of hours; and
      (iii) the claimant voluntarily ceases that paid work, or loses pay, within a trial period;
  (c) the sanctionable failure is listed in section 6J(3) of the Act (failures that occur before a claim is made) and the period of the reduction that would otherwise apply under regulation 19 is the same as or shorter than the number of days beginning with the day after the

date of the sanctionable failure and ending with the day before the date of that claim;

(d) the sanctionable failure is that the claimant voluntarily ceases paid work, or loses pay, because of a strike arising from a trade dispute;

(e) the sanctionable failure is that the claimant voluntarily ceases paid work as a member of the regular forces or the reserve forces (within the meanings in section 374 of the Armed Forces Act 2006, or loses pay in that capacity; or

(f) the sanctionable failure is that the claimant voluntarily ceases paid work in one of the following circumstances—

   (i) the claimant has been dismissed because of redundancy after volunteering or agreeing to be dismissed;

  (ii) the claimant has ceased work on an agreed date without being dismissed in pursuance of an agreement relating to voluntary redundancy; or

 (iii) the claimant has been laid-off or kept on short-time to the extent specified in section 148 of the Employment Rights Act 1996, and has complied with the requirements of that section.

(2) In this regulation—

"redundancy" has the same meaning as in section 139(1) of the Employment Rights Act 1996;

"strike" has the same meaning as in section 246 of the Trade Union and Labour Relations (Consolidation) Act 1992;

"trade dispute" has the same meaning as in section 244 of that Act.

DEFINITIONS

    "the Act"—see reg.2(2).
    "claimant"—see reg.2(2).
    "redundancy"—see para.(2)
    "sanctionable failure"—see reg.17.
    "strike"—see para.(2).
    "trade dispute"—see para.(2).

GENERAL NOTE

1.072    This provides that no reduction is to be made as regards higher level sanctions under Jobseekers Act 1995 s.6J in the situations set out in para.(1), several of which correspond to or are variations on exemptions set out as regards "old style JSA" in Jobseekers Act 1995 s.20 and, indeed in legislation governing its predecessor, unemployment benefit.

*Para. (1) (a)*

This maintains the traditional "neutral" approach to trade disputes taken in social security law. A claimant is not required to be a strike-breaker and so will not be sanctioned for refusing work that is vacant because of a trade dispute. No reduction is to be imposed in respect of failure to apply for a vacancy for paid work or failure to take up an offer of paid work if the vacancy has arisen because of a strike arising from a trade dispute. For the meaning of "strike", see s.246 of the Trade Union and Labour Relations (Consolidation) Act 1992 which provides:

"'strike' means any concerted stoppage of work;".

For that of "trade dispute", see s.244 of that Act which provides:

"(1) In this Part a "trade dispute" means a dispute between workers and their employer which relates wholly or mainly to one or more of the following—
  (a) terms and conditions of employment, or the physical conditions in which any workers are required to work;
  (b) engagement or non-engagement, or termination or suspension of employment or the duties of employment, of one or more workers;
  (c) allocation of work or the duties of employment between workers or groups of workers;
  (d) matters of discipline;
  (e) a worker's membership or non-membership of a trade union;
  (f) facilities for officials of trade unions; and
  (g) machinery for negotiation or consultation, and other procedures, relating to any of the above matters, including the recognition by employers or employers' associations of the right of a trade union to represent workers in such negotiation or consultation or in the carrying out of such procedures.
(2) A dispute between a Minister of the Crown and any workers shall, notwithstanding that he is not the employer of those workers, be treated as a dispute between those workers and their employer if the dispute relates to matters which—
  (a) have been referred for consideration by a joint body on which, by virtue of provision made by or under any enactment, he is represented, or
  (b) cannot be settled without him exercising a power conferred on him by or under an enactment.
(3) There is a trade dispute even though it relates to matters occurring outside the United Kingdom, so long as the person or persons whose actions in the United Kingdom are said to be in contemplation or furtherance of a trade dispute relating to matters occurring outside the United Kingdom are likely to be affected in respect of one or more of the matters specified in subsection (1) by the outcome of the dispute.
(4) An act, threat or demand done or made by one person or organisation against another which, if resisted, would have led to a trade dispute with that other, shall be treated as being done or made in contemplation of a trade dispute with that other, notwithstanding that because that other submits to the act or threat or accedes to the demand no dispute arises.
(5) In this section—
"employment" includes any relationship whereby one person personally does work or performs services for another; and
"worker", in relation to a dispute with an employer, means—
  (a) a worker employed by that employer; or
  (b) a person who has ceased to be so employed if his employment was terminated in connection with the dispute or if the termination of his employment was one of the circumstances giving rise to the dispute."

Note that this is narrower than that applicable to "old style JSA" in s.35(1) of the Jobseekers Act 1995 which also embraces disputes between employees.

*Para. (1)(b)*

A claimant can legitimately have his work search and work availability requirements limited in respect of work for a certain number of hours. Paragraph (1)(b) provides that where that has happened and the claimant has taken up paid work for more than those hours, the claimant is not to be penalised through reduction of JSA for a sanctionable failure if, during a trial period, s/he voluntarily ceases that paid work or loses pay. "Trial period" appears not to be defined in the legislation.

*Para. (1) (c)*

Where there is a pre-claim sanctionable failure and the reduction period normally applicable would expire on or before the date of the relevant JSA claim, there is to be no reduction. It may be that the same result is achieved by reg.19(3).

*Para. (1) (d)*

This affords the same protection as under para.(1)(a) to someone voluntarily ceasing paid work or losing pay because of a strike arising from a trade dispute.

*Para. (1) (e)*

Members of the armed forces who voluntarily cease paid work as such or lose pay, cannot in any circumstances suffer a reduction on that ground. The protection covers both regular and reserve forces.

*Para. (1) (f)*

This provides protection in the same circumstances as prescribed in reg.71 of the JSA Regulations 1996 applicable now only to "old style JSA" except that there the claimant is deemed not to have left employment voluntarily and so not subject to any sanction. Here the claimant is merely protected from having a reduction of benefit imposed, although it may be arguable under general principles that there was a good reason for voluntarily ceasing work, and thus no sanctionable failure.

## Sanctionable failures under section 6J of the Act: work placements

1.073     [¹29.—(1) A placement on the Mandatory Work Activity Scheme is a prescribed placement for the purpose of section 6J(2)(a) of the Act (sanctionable failure not to comply with a work placement).

(2) In paragraph (1) "the Mandatory Work Activity Scheme" means a scheme provided pursuant to arrangements made by the Secretary of State and known by that name that is designed to provide work or work-related activity for up to 30 hours per week over a period of 4 consecutive weeks with a view to assisting claimants to improve their prospects of obtaining employment.]

AMENDMENT

1. Universal Credit (Consequential, Supplementary, Incidental and Miscellaneous Provisions) Regulations 2013 (SI 2013/630) reg.39 (April 29, 2013).

## Sanctions where universal credit ends and the person is entitled to a jobseeker's allowance

1.074     **30.**—(1) This regulation applies where—
(a)  a person ceases to be entitled to universal credit;

(b) there is a reduction relating to the person's award of universal credit under section 26 or 27 of the Welfare Reform Act 2012; and

(c) the person is entitled to a jobseeker's allowance.

(2) Any reduction relating to the award of the universal credit is to be applied to the award of the jobseeker's allowance.

(3) The period for which the reduction relating to the award of the jobseeker's allowance is to have effect is the number of days which apply to the person under regulation 102, 103, 104 or 105 of the Universal Credit Regulations 2013 minus any such days which—

(a) have already resulted in a reduction in the amount of universal credit; or

(b) fall after the date the award of universal credit was terminated and before the date on which the award of a jobseeker's allowance starts.

(4) The daily reduction rate for the reduction relating to the award of the jobseeker's allowance is the amount of the claimant's jobseeker's allowance multiplied by 52 and divided by 365.

(5) The claimant's award of a jobseeker's allowance is to be reduced by the daily reduction amount referred to in paragraph (4) for each day of the period referred to in paragraph (3).

GENERAL NOTE

Where someone subject to one or more UC sanctions ceases to be entitled to UC and becomes entitled to JSA, the remaining reduction period applicable to the UC award carries over to reduce the JSA award. The remaining reduction period is calculated by deducting from the period imposed as regards UC (i) the days for which UC has been in consequence reduced and (ii) the days between the cessation of entitlement to UC and the beginning of entitlement to ESA. The JSA award must be reduced for each day of the remaining reduction period by the daily reduction amount set out in para.(4) (para.(5)). 1.075

PART 4

INFORMATION AND EVIDENCE

## Provision of information and evidence

**31.**—(1) A claimant must supply such information in connection with the claim for a jobseeker's allowance, or any question arising out of it, as may be required by the Secretary of State. 1.076

(2) A claimant must furnish such certificates, documents and other evidence as may be required by the Secretary of State for the determination of the claim.

(3) A claimant must furnish such certificates, documents and other evidence affecting their continuing entitlement to a jobseeker's allowance, whether that allowance is payable to them and, if so, in what amount, as the Secretary of State may require.

(4) A claimant must notify the Secretary of State—

(a) of any change of circumstances which has occurred which the claimant might reasonably be expected to know might affect their entitlement to a jobseeker's allowance or the payability or amount of such an allowance; and

(b) of any such change of circumstances which the claimant is aware is likely to occur.

(5) The notification referred to in paragraph (4) must be given as soon as reasonably practicable after the occurrence or, as the case may be, after the claimant becomes so aware, by giving notice of the change to an office of the Department for Work and Pensions specified by the Secretary of State—

(a) in writing or by telephone (unless the Secretary of State determines in any particular case that notice must be given in writing or may be given otherwise than in writing or by telephone); or

(b) in writing if in any particular case the Secretary of State requires written notice (unless the Secretary of State determines in any particular case to accept notice given otherwise than in writing).

(6) Where, pursuant to paragraph (1), a claimant is required to supply information, they must do so when they participate in a work-focused interview under section 6B of the Act, if so required by the Secretary of State, or within such period as the Secretary of State may require.

(7) Where, pursuant to paragraph (2) or (3), a claimant is required to provide certificates, documents or other evidence they must do so within seven days of being so required or such longer period as the Secretary of State may consider reasonable.

## Alternative means of notifying changes of circumstances

1.077    **32.**—(1) In such cases and subject to such conditions as the Secretary of State may specify, the duty in regulation 31(4) to notify a change of circumstances may be discharged by notifying the Secretary of State as soon as reasonably practicable—

(a) where the change of circumstances is a birth or death, through a local authority, or a county council in England, by personal attendance at an office specified by that authority or county council, provided the Secretary of State has agreed with that authority or county council for it to facilitate such notification; or

(b) where the change of circumstances is a death, by telephone to a telephone number specified for that purpose by the Secretary of State.

(2) In this regulation "local authority" has the same meaning as in section 191 of the Administration Act.

## Information given electronically

1.078    **33.**—(1) A person may give any certificate, notice, information or evidence required to be given and in particular may give notice of a change of circumstances required to be notified under regulation 31 by means of an electronic communication, in accordance with the provisions set out in Schedule 2 to the Claims and Payments Regulations 2013.

(2) In this regulation, "electronic communication" has the meaning given in section 15(1) of the Electronic Communications Act 2000.

PART 5

CONDITIONS OF ENTITLEMENT

## The conditions and relevant earnings

**34.**—(1) A claimant's relevant earnings for the purposes of section 2(2)(b) of the Act are the total amount of the claimant's earnings equal to the lower earnings limit for the base year.    1.079

(2) For the purposes of paragraph (1), earnings which exceed the lower earnings limit are to be disregarded.

GENERAL NOTE

This replicates JSA Regulations 1996 reg.47A now directly applicable only to "old style JSA". See the annotations to that regulation.    1.080

## Relaxation of the first set of conditions

**35.**—(1) A claimant who satisfies the condition in paragraph (2) is to be taken to satisfy the first set of conditions if the claimant has—    1.081

(a) paid Class 1 contributions before the relevant benefit week in respect of any one tax year; and

(b) earnings equal to the lower earnings limit in that tax year on which primary Class 1 contributions have been paid or treated as paid which in total, and disregarding any earnings which exceed the lower earnings limit for that year, are not less than that limit multiplied by 26.

(2) The condition referred to in paragraph (1) is that the claimant, in respect of any week during the last complete tax year preceding the relevant benefit year, is entitled to be credited with earnings in accordance with regulation 9E of the Social Security (Credits) Regulations 1975 (credits for certain spouses and civil partners of members of Her Majesty's forces).

(3) In this regulation, "relevant benefit week" means the week in relation to which the question of entitlement to a jobseeker's allowance is being considered.

DEFINITIONS

"relevant benefit week"—see para.(3).

GENERAL NOTE

See the annotations to JSA Regulations 1996 reg.45B.    1.082

## Waiting Days

1.083    **36.**—(1) Paragraph 4 of Schedule 1 to the Act does not apply in a case where a person's entitlement to a jobseeker's allowance commences within 12 weeks of an entitlement of theirs to income support, incapacity benefit, employment and support allowance or carer's allowance coming to an end.

(2) In the case of a person to whom paragraph 4 of Schedule 1 to the Act applies, the number of days is three.

DEFINITIONS

"the Act"—see reg.2(2).
"week"—see reg.2(2).

GENERAL NOTE

1.084    Unemployment benefit was a daily benefit payable in respect of a six-day week. JSA is a weekly benefit. Nonetheless, through para.4 of Sch.1 to the Jobseekers Act 1995, as amplified by this regulation, it deploys the concept of "waiting days". There is no entitlement to it for a number of days (currently three (see para.(2)) but alterable by regulations) at the start of a jobseeking period. On "jobseeking period" and the effect of "linking", see notes to regs 37 and 38, below. Note further that the "waiting days" rule does not apply where the claimant's entitlement to JSA begins within 12 weeks of the ending of his entitlement to income support, incapacity benefit, employment and support allowance or carer's allowance.

## Jobseeking Period

1.085    **37.**—(1) For the purposes of the Act, but subject to paragraph (2), the "jobseeking period" means any period throughout which the claimant satisfies or is treated as satisfying the conditions specified in section 1(2)(b) and (e) to (i) of the Act (conditions of entitlement to a jobseeker's allowance).

(2) The following periods are not to be, or to be part of, a jobseeking period—

(a) any period in respect of which no claim for a jobseeker's allowance has been made or treated as made;

(b) such period as falls before the day on which a claim for a jobseeker's allowance is made or treated as made;

(c) where a claim for a jobseeker's allowance has been made or treated as made but no entitlement to benefit arises in respect of a period before the date of claim by virtue of section 1(2) of the Administration Act (limits for backdating entitlement), that period;

(d) any week in which a claimant is not entitled to a jobseeker's allowance in accordance with section 14 of the Act (trade disputes); or

(e) any period in respect of which a claimant is not entitled to a jobseeker's allowance because section 1(1A) of the Administration Act (requirement to state national insurance number) applies.

(3) For the purposes of section 5 of the Act (duration of a jobseeker's allowance), a day must be treated as if it was a day in respect of which the claimant was entitled to a jobseeker's allowance where that day—

48

(a) falls within a jobseeking period; and
(b) is a day—
    (i) on which the claimant satisfies the conditions specified in section 2 of the Act (the contribution-based conditions) other than the conditions specified in section 2(1)(c) and (d) of the Act; and
    (ii) on which a jobseeker's allowance is not payable to the claimant by virtue of sections 6J or 6K of the Act or by virtue of a restriction imposed pursuant to section 6B, 7, 8 or 9 of the Social Security Fraud Act 2001 (loss of benefit provisions).

DEFINITIONS

"the Act"—see reg.2(2).
"claimant"—see reg.2(2).
"jobseeking period"—see para.(1).

GENERAL NOTE

This regulation, read with reg.38, below and para.3 of Sch.1 to the Jobseekers **1.086** Act 1995, makes provision which benefits those whose unemployment is intermittent, interspersed with, say, periods of employment, of incapacity for work, of training for work or periods when pregnant, by providing, somewhat after the fashion of unemployment benefit and its notion of "period of interruption of employment" ("PIE"), for the concept of "linking" and "linked periods" whereby apparently separate jobseeking periods are fused into one and certain periods ("linked periods") do not "break" a jobseeking period.

A "jobseeking period" is, basically, any period throughout which the claimant satisfies (or is treated as satisfying) the conditions of entitlement to JSA set out in Jobseekers Act 1995 s.1(2)(b) and (e)–(i): accepted a claimant commitment not in remunerative work; does not have limited capability for work; not receiving relevant education; under pensionable age; and in Great Britain (para.(1)) (note that reg.39, below, treats certain days as ones meeting those conditions in respect of persons approaching retirement).

None of the periods listed in para.(2) can constitute or form any part of, a jobseeking period.

A day which otherwise falls within a jobseeking period but on which someone satisfying the two contribution conditions (Jobseekers Act 1995 s.2(2)(a), (b)) is subject to a JSA sanction or a fraud sanction so that JSA is not payable, is nonetheless to be treated as a day of entitlement to JSA (para.(3)).

## Jobseeking periods: periods of interruption of employment

**38.**—(1) For the purposes of section 2(4)(b)(i) of the Act and for **1.087** determining any waiting days—
(a) where a linked period commenced before 7th October 1996, any days of unemployment which form part of a period of interruption of employment where the last day of unemployment in that period of interruption of employment was no more than eight weeks before the date upon which that linked period commenced;
(b) where a jobseeking period or a linked period commences on 7th October 1996, any period of interruption of employment ending within the eight weeks preceding that date; or

49

(c) where a jobseeking period or a linked period commences after 7th October 1996, any period of interruption of employment ending within the 12 weeks preceding the day the jobseeking period or linked period commenced,

must be treated as a jobseeking period and, for the purposes of sub-paragraph (a), a day must be treated as being, or not being, a day of unemployment in accordance with section 25A of the Benefits Act (determination of days for which unemployment benefit is payable) and with any regulations made under that section, as in force on 6th October 1996.

(2) In this regulation—

"period of interruption of employment" in relation to a period prior to 7th October 1996 has the same meaning as it had in the Benefits Act by virtue of section 25A of that Act as in force on 6th October 1996;

"waiting day" means a day—

    (a) at the beginning of a jobseeking period; and

    (b) in respect of which a person is not entitled to a jobseeker's allowance.

DEFINITIONS

"the Act"—see reg.2(2).
"the Benefits Act"—see Jobseekers Act 1995, s.35(1).
"jobseeking period"—see reg.7.
"linked period"—see reg.39(2).
"period of interruption of employment"—see para.(2).
"waiting day"—see para.(2).

GENERAL NOTE

1.088    Some spells of unemployment are continuous, others intermittent. A jobseeking period can consist of a long chain of such spells, interspersed with spells of work or entitlement to certain other benefits. This regulation enables such a chain to go back to the benefits regime before October 7, 1996 when JSA was introduced. Then the relevant concept was "period of interruption of employment" (PIE) and the regime worked on an eight-week linking rule where two or more ostensibly separate PIEs were fused into a single one where they were not more than eight weeks apart. JSA works on a 12-week linking period (see reg.39(1)). Regulation 39(2) sets out the periods which can be used as linked periods so as to fuse into a single jobseeking period two ostensibly separate jobseeking periods. These concepts are crucial in terms of benefit entitlement for those intermittently unemployed, for the application of the waiting days rule which only has to be served once in a jobseeking period, and for determining the relevant tax years for applying the two contribution conditions (Jobseekers Act 1995 s.2(2)(a), (b))).

## Linking Periods

1.089    **39.**—(1) For the purposes of the Act, two or more jobseeking periods must be treated as one jobseeking period where they are separated by a period comprising only—

    (a) any period of not more than 12 weeks;

    (b) a linked period;

    (c) any period of not more than 12 weeks falling between—

(i) any two linked periods; or

(ii) a jobseeking period and a linked period; or

(d) a period in respect of which the claimant is summoned for jury service and is required to attend court.

(2) Linked periods for the purposes of the Act are any of the following periods—

(a) to the extent specified in paragraph (4), any period throughout which the claimant is entitled to a carer's allowance under section 70 of the Benefits Act;

(b) any period throughout which the claimant is incapable of work, or is treated as incapable of work, in accordance with Part 12A of the Benefits Act;

(c) any period throughout which the claimant has, or is treated as having, limited capability for work for the purposes of Part 1 of the Welfare Reform Act 2007;

(d) any period throughout which the claimant was entitled to a maternity allowance under section 35 of the Benefits Act;

(e) any period throughout which the claimant was engaged in training for which a training allowance is payable;

(f) a period which includes 6th October 1996 during which the claimant attends court in response to a summons for jury service and which was immediately preceded by a period of entitlement to unemployment benefit.

(3) A period is a linked period for the purposes of section 2(4)(b)(ii) of the Act only where it ends within 12 weeks or less of the commencement of a jobseeking period or of some other linked period.

(4) A period of entitlement to carer's allowance is a linked period only where it enables the claimant to satisfy contribution conditions for entitlement to a jobseeker's allowance which the claimant would otherwise be unable to satisfy.

DEFINITIONS

"the Act"—see reg.2(2).
"claimant"—see reg.2(2).
"the Benefits Act"—see Jobseekers Act 1995, s.35(1).
"jobseeking period"—see reg.37.
"linked period"—see para.(2) as qualified by paras (3) and (4).
"training allowance"—see reg.2(2).
"week"—see reg.2(2).

GENERAL NOTE

Two or more jobseeking periods as defined in reg.37 must be fused into a 1.090 single jobseeking period where separated by no more than 12 weeks, by a linked period, by any period of not more than 12 weeks falling between any two linked periods or a jobseeking period and a linked period, or by a period in respect of which the claimant is summoned for jury service and is required to attend court. Thus are the intermittently unemployed protected, while oscillating between unemployment and work or training, or unemployment and sickness/disability related inability to work, or unemployment and maternity or performing jury service, or caring, or any combination of these. See the list of "linked periods" in para.(2), noting that not all linked periods count as such for all purposes.

Thus, a period of entitlement to a carer's allowance (para.(2)(a)) counts only to enable the JSA claimant to satisfy the JSA contribution conditions (Jobseekers Act 1995, s.2(2)(a), (b)) s/he would otherwise be unable to satisfy (para.(4)). Similarly, to rank for purposes of Jobseekers Act 1995 s.2(4)(b)(ii) (identifying the "relevant benefit year" for contributions conditions purposes as earlier than the start of the benefit year in which the JSA claim is made) if it ended within 12 weeks of a jobseeking period or another linked period (para.(3)).

## Persons approaching retirement and the jobseeking period

1.091    **40.**—(1) The provisions of this regulation apply only to days—

(a) which fall after 6th October 1996 and within a tax year in which the claimant has attained the qualifying age for state pension credit (which is, in the case of a woman, pensionable age and in the case of a man, the age which is pensionable age in the case of a woman born on the same day as the man) but is under pensionable age; and

(b) in respect of which a jobseeker's allowance is not payable because the decision of the determining authority is that the claimant—

(i) has exhausted their entitlement to a jobseeker's allowance;

(ii) fails to satisfy one or both of the contribution conditions specified in section 2(1)(a) and (b) of the Act; or

(iii) is entitled to a jobseeker's allowance but the amount payable is reduced to nil by virtue of deductions made in accordance with regulation 51 for pension payments.

(2) For the purposes of regulation 37(1) (jobseeking period) but subject to paragraphs (3), (4) and (5), any days to which paragraph (1) applies and in respect of which the person does not satisfy the condition specified in section 1(2)(b) of the Act (conditions of entitlement to a jobseeker's allowance), are to be days on which the person is treated as satisfying the condition in section 1(2)(b) and (e) to (i) of the Act.

(3) Where a person is employed as an employed earner or a self-employed earner for a period of more than 12 weeks, then no day which falls within or follows that period is to be a day on which the person is treated as satisfying those conditions, but this paragraph is not to prevent paragraph (2) from again applying to a person who makes a claim for a jobseeker's allowance after that period.

(4) Any day which is, for the purposes of section 30C of the Benefits Act, a day of incapacity for work falling within a period of incapacity for work is not to be a day on which the person is treated as satisfying the conditions referred to in paragraph (2).

(5) Any day which, for the purposes of Part 1 of the Welfare Reform Act 2007, is a day where the person has limited capability for work falling within a period of limited capability for work is not to be a day on which the person is treated as satisfying the conditions referred to in paragraph (2).

### DEFINITIONS

"the Act"—see reg.2(2).
"employed earner"—see reg.2(1).
"pensionable age"—see reg.2(1).

"self-employed earner"—see reg.2(2).
"tax year"—see Jobseekers Act 1995, s.35(1).
"week"—see reg.2(2).

GENERAL NOTE

This benefits persons for some days falling after October 6, 1996 during the    1.092
tax year in which they reach the qualifying age for SPC. The days are ones in that
tax year prior to actual attainment of pensionable age on which JSA is not
payable because of exhaustion of entitlement, failure to satisfy one or both
contribution conditions (ss.2(1)(a), (b), Jobseekers Act 1995), or because the
JSA amount has been reduced to nil under reg.51 because of pension payments.
Any such days (other than those excluded by any of paras (3)–(5)) are to be days
in a jobseeking period notwithstanding that there is no claimant commitment.

Days which were ones of incapacity for work within a period of incapacity for
work cannot form part of a jobseeking period in this way (para.(4)). Nor can
ones of limited capability for work forming part of a period of limited capability
for work (para.(5)). But both such situations rank as linked periods under
reg.38(2)(b). Further, where someone works in employment or self-employment
for more than 12 weeks, no day within or after that period can be treated as part
of a jobseeking period in this way, but the protection afforded by paras (1) and
(2) of the regulation can apply again after such a period when the person makes
a claim for JSA (para.(3)).

**Persons temporarily absent from Great Britain**

**41.**—(1) For the purposes of the Act, a claimant must be treated as    1.093
being in Great Britain during any period of temporary absence from
Great Britain—

 (a) not exceeding four weeks in the circumstances specified in para-
     graph (2);
 (b) not exceeding eight weeks in the circumstances specified in para-
     graph (3).

(2) The circumstances specified in this paragraph are that—

 (a) the claimant is in Northern Ireland and satisfies the conditions of
     entitlement to a jobseeker's allowance;
 (b) immediately preceding the period of absence from Great Britain,
     the claimant was entitled to a jobseeker's allowance; and
 (c) the period of absence is unlikely to exceed 52 weeks.

(3) The circumstances specified in this paragraph are that—

 (a) immediately preceding the period of absence from Great Britain,
     the claimant was entitled to a jobseeker's allowance;
 (b) the period of absence is unlikely to exceed 52 weeks;
 (c) the claimant continues to satisfy or be treated as satisfying the
     other conditions of entitlement to a jobseeker's allowance;
 (d) the claimant is, or the claimant and any other member of their
     family are, accompanying a member of the claimant's family who
     is a child or young person solely in connection with arrangements
     made for the treatment of that child or young person for a disease
     or bodily or mental disablement; and
 (e) those arrangements relate to treatment—
     (i) outside Great Britain;

    (ii) during the period whilst the claimant is, or the claimant and any member of their family are, temporarily absent from Great Britain; and

    (iii) by, or under the supervision of, a person appropriately qualified to carry out that treatment.

(4) A person must also be treated, for the purposes of the Act, as being in Great Britain during any period of temporary absence from Great Britain where—

  (a) the absence is for the purpose of attending an interview for employment;

  (b) the absence is for seven consecutive days or less;

  (c) notice of the proposed absence is given to the Secretary of State before departure, and is given in writing if so required by the Secretary of State; and

  (d) on their return to Great Britain the person satisfies the Secretary of State that they attended for the interview in accordance with their notice.

(5) For the purposes of the Act a claimant must be treated as being in Great Britain during any period of temporary absence from Great Britain if—

  (a) the claimant was entitled to a jobseeker's allowance immediately before the beginning of that period of temporary absence; and

  (b) that period of temporary absence is for the purpose of the claimant receiving treatment at a hospital or other institution outside Great Britain where the treatment is being provided—

    (i) under section 6(2) of the Health Service Act (performance of functions outside England) or section 6(2) of the Health Service (Wales) Act (performance of functions outside Wales);

    (ii) pursuant to arrangements made under section 12(1) of the Health Service Act (Secretary of State's arrangements with other bodies), section 10(1) of the Health Service (Wales) Act (Welsh Minister's arrangements with other bodies), paragraph 18 of Schedule 4 to the Health Service Act (joint exercise of functions) or paragraph 18 of Schedule 3 to the Health Service (Wales) Act (joint exercise of functions); or

    (iii) under any equivalent provision in Scotland or pursuant to arrangements made under such provision.

(6) For the purposes of the Act, a person must be treated as being in Great Britain during any period of temporary absence from Great Britain not exceeding 15 days where—

  (a) the absence is for the purpose of taking part in annual continuous training as a member of any territorial or reserve force prescribed in Part 1 of Schedule 6 to the Social Security (Contributions) Regulations 2001; and

  (b) the person was entitled to a jobseeker's allowance immediately before the period of absence.

(7) In this regulation, "appropriately qualified" means qualified to provide medical treatment, physiotherapy or a form of treatment which is similar to, or related to, either of those forms of treatment.

DEFINITIONS

"the Act"—see reg.2(2).
"appropriately qualified"—see para.(7).
"child"—see Jobseekers Act 1995, s.35(1).
"claimant"—see Jobseekers Act 1995, s.35(1).
"family"—see Jobseekers Act 1995, s.35(1).
"week"—see reg.2(2).
"young person"—see reg.2(2).

GENERAL NOTE

This is much the same as JSA Regulations 1996 reg.50. See the annotations to **1.094** that provision, ignoring those on joint-claim couples and on para.(3). Note also the protection in reg.41(6) in respect of absences for annual continuous training as a member of any territorial or reserve force. This is not in reg.50 of the JSA Regulations 1996.

## Remunerative work

**42.**—(1) For the purposes of the Act, "remunerative work" means **1.095** work—
  (a) for which payment is made or which is done in expectation of payment; and
  (b) in which a claimant is—
      (i) engaged for 16 or more hours per week; or
      (ii) where their hours of work fluctuate, engaged on average for 16 or more hours per week.
(2) For the purposes of paragraph (1), the number of hours in which a claimant is engaged in work is to be determined—
  (a) where no recognisable cycle has been established in respect of a person's work, by reference to the number of hours or, where those hours are likely to fluctuate, the average of the hours, which they are expected to work in a week;
  (b) where the number of hours for which they are engaged fluctuate, by reference to the average of hours worked over—
      (i) if there is a recognisable cycle of work, the period of one complete cycle (including, where the cycle involves periods in which the person does not work, those periods but disregarding any other absences);
      (ii) in any other case, the period of five weeks immediately before the date of claim or the date of supersession, or such other length of time as may, in the particular case, enable the person's average hours of work to be determined more accurately.
(3) In determining in accordance with this regulation the number of hours for which a person is engaged in remunerative work—
  (a) that number must include any time allowed to that person by their employer for a meal or for refreshments, but only where the person is, or expects to be, paid earnings in respect of that time;
  (b) no account must be taken of any hours in which the person is engaged in an employment or scheme to which any one of sub-

paragraphs (a) to (e) of regulation 44(1) (person treated as not engaged in remunerative work) applies;

(c) no account must be taken of any hours in which the person is engaged otherwise than in an employment as an earner in caring for—

    (i) a person who is in receipt of attendance allowance, the care component or the daily living component;

    (ii) a person who has claimed an attendance allowance, a disability living allowance or personal independence payment, but only for the period beginning with the date of claim and ending on the date on which the claim is determined or, if earlier, on the expiration of the period of 26 weeks from the date of claim;

    (iii) another person and is in receipt of a carer's allowance under section 70 of the Benefits Act; or

    (iv) a person who has claimed either an attendance allowance, a disability living allowance or personal independence payment and has an award of attendance allowance, the care component or the daily living component for a period commencing after the date on which that claim was made.

(4) In this regulation—

"disability living allowance" means a disability living allowance under section 71 of the Benefits Act;

"care component" means the care component of disability living allowance at the highest or middle rate prescribed under section 72(3) of the Benefits Act;

"daily living component" means the daily living component of personal independence payment at the standard or enhanced rate referred to in section 78 of the Welfare Reform Act 2012;

"personal independence payment" means an allowance under Part 4 of the Welfare Reform Act 2012.

DEFINITIONS

"the Act"—see reg.2(2).
"the Benefits Act"—see Jobseekers Act 1995, s.35(1).
"care component"—see para.(4).
"claimant"—see reg.2(2).
"daily living component"—see para.(4).
"disability living allowance"—see para.(4).
"personal independence payment"—see para.(4).
"remunerative work"—see para.(1).

GENERAL NOTE

1.096    This is much the same as JSA Regulations reg.51. See the annotations to that provision, ignoring those with respect to the claimant's partner, non-dependant, child or young person (relevant only for IBJSA).

## Persons treated as engaged in remunerative work

1.097    **43.**—(1) Except in the case of a person on maternity leave, paternity leave, adoption leave or absent from work through illness, a person is to be treated as engaged in remunerative work during any period for which they are absent from work referred to in regulation 42(1) (remunerative work) where the absence is either without good cause or by reason of a recognised, customary or other holiday.

(2) Subject to paragraph (3), a person who was, or was treated as being, engaged in remunerative work and in respect of that work earnings to which regulation 58(1)(c) (earnings of employed earners) applies are paid, is to be treated as engaged in remunerative work for the period for which those earnings are taken into account in accordance with Part 7.

(3) Paragraph (2) does not apply to earnings disregarded under paragraph 1 of the Schedule to these Regulations.

DEFINITIONS

"adoption leave"—see reg.2(2).
"maternity leave"—see reg.2(2).
"paternity leave"—see reg.2(2).
"remunerative work"—see reg.42(1).

GENERAL NOTE

This is similar to JSA Regulations 1996 reg.52. See the annotations to para.(1) **1.098** of that provision, thus ignoring provisions applicable in respect the claimant's partner and trade disputes (relevant only for IBJSA).

## Persons treated as not engaged in remunerative work

**44.**—(1) A person is to be treated as not engaged in remunerative work **1.099** in so far as they are—

(a) engaged by a charity or a voluntary organisation or are a volunteer where the only payment received by them or due to be paid to them is a payment in respect of any expenses incurred, or to be incurred, if they otherwise derive no remuneration or profit from the employment;

(b) engaged on a scheme for which a training allowance is being paid;

(c) engaged in employment as—
    [[1](i) a part-time fire-fighter employed by a fire and rescue authority under the Fire and Rescue Services Act 2004 or by the Scottish Fire and Rescue Service established under section 1A of the Fire (Scotland) Act 2005];
    (ii) [[1]*omitted*]
    (iii) an auxiliary coastguard in respect of coastal rescue activities;
    (iv) a person engaged part-time in the manning or launching of a lifeboat;
    (v) a member of any territorial or reserve force prescribed in Part 1 of Schedule 6 to the Social Security (Contributions) Regulations 2001;

(d) performing their duties as a councillor, and for this purpose "councillor" has the same meaning as in section 171F(2) of the Benefits Act;

    (e) engaged in caring for a person who is accommodated with them by virtue of arrangements made under any of the provisions referred to in regulation 60(2)(b) or (c), and are in receipt of any payment specified in regulation 60(2)(b) or (c);

    (f) engaged in an activity in respect of which—

       (i) a sports award had been made, or is to be made, to them; and

       (ii) no other payment is made or is expected to be made to them;

    (g) engaged in the programme known as Work Experience.

(2) In this regulation, "volunteer" means a person who is engaged in voluntary work, otherwise than for a close relative, grand-parent, grand-child, uncle, aunt, nephew or niece, where the only payment received, or due to be paid to the person by virtue of being so engaged, is in respect of any expenses reasonably incurred by the person in connection with that work.

AMENDMENT

1. Social Security (Miscellaneous Amendments) (No. 2) Regulations 2013 (SI 2013/1508) reg.4(1), (3) (July 29, 2013).

DEFINITIONS

"the Benefits Act"—see Jobseekers Act 1995, s.35(1).
"close relative"—see reg.2(2).
"sports award"—see reg.2(2).
"training allowance"—see reg.2(2).
"voluntary organisation"—see reg.2(2).
"voluntary work"—see reg.2(2).
"volunteer"—see para.(2).
"Work Experience"—see reg.2(2).

GENERAL NOTE

1.100    This is similar to JSA Regulations 1996 reg.53 and thus to the Income Support (General) Regulations reg.6. See the annotations to those provisions ignoring any dealing with the claimant's partner or joint-claim couples (relevant only to IBJSA).

## Relevant education

1.101    **45.**—(1) For the purposes of the Act—

    (a) a person is to be treated as receiving relevant education if they are a qualifying young person; and

    (b) the following are to be treated as relevant education—

       (i) undertaking a full-time course of advanced education; and

       (ii) undertaking any other full-time course of study or training at an educational establishment for which a student loan, grant or bursary is provided for the person's maintenance or would be available if the person applied for it.

(2) In paragraph (1)(b)(i), "course of advanced education" means—

    (a) a course of study leading to—

       (i) a postgraduate degree or comparable qualification;

(ii) a first degree or comparable qualification;

(iii) a diploma of higher education;

(iv) a higher national diploma; or

(b) any other course of study which is of a standard above advanced GNVQ or equivalent, including a course which is of a standard above a general certificate of education (advanced level), or above a Scottish national qualification (higher or advanced higher).

(3) A claimant who is not a qualifying young person and is not undertaking a course described in paragraph (1)(b) is nevertheless to be treated as receiving relevant education if the claimant is undertaking a course of study or training that is not compatible with any work-related requirement imposed on the claimant by the Secretary of State.

(4) For the purposes of paragraph (1)(b), a person is to be regarded as undertaking a course—

(a) throughout the period beginning on the date on which the person starts undertaking the course and ending on the last day of the course or on such earlier date (if any) as the person finally abandons it or is dismissed from it; or

(b) where a person is undertaking a part of a modular course, for the period beginning on the day on which that part of the course starts and ending—

(i) on the last day on which the person is registered with the provider of the course, or part of the course, as undertaking that part; or

(ii) on such earlier date (if any) as the person finally abandons the course or is dismissed from it.

(5) The period referred to in paragraph (4)(b) includes—

(a) where a person has failed examinations or has failed to complete successfully a module relating to a period when the person was undertaking a part of the course, any period in respect of which the person undertakes the course for the purpose of retaking those examinations or that module; and

(b) any period of vacation within the period specified in paragraph (4)(b) or immediately following that period except where the person has registered with the provider of the course, or part of the course, to attend or undertake the final module in the course and the vacation immediately follows the last day on which the person is to attend or undertake the course.

(6) A person is not to be regarded as undertaking a course by virtue of this regulation for any part of the period mentioned in paragraph (4) during which the following conditions are met—

(a) the person has, with the consent of the relevant educational establishment, ceased to attend or undertake the course because they are ill or caring for another person;

(b) the person has recovered from that illness or ceased caring for that person within the past year, but not yet resumed the course; and

(c) the person is not eligible for a grant or student loan.

(7) In this regulation, except where paragraph (8) applies, "qualifying young person" means a person who has reached the age of 16 but not the age of 20—

(a) up to, but not including, the 1st September following their 16th birthday; and

(b) up to, but not including, the 1st September following their 19th birthday, if they are enrolled in, or accepted for, approved training or a course of education—

(i) which is not a course of advanced education;

(ii) which is provided at a school or college or provided elsewhere but approved by the Secretary of State; and

(iii) where the average time spent during term time (excluding meal breaks) in receiving tuition, engaging in practical work, or supervised study, or taking examinations exceeds 12 hours per week.

(8) A person is not a "qualifying young person" within the meaning in paragraph (7) where they—

(a) are aged 19 and have not started the education or training or been enrolled or accepted for it before reaching the age of 19;

(b) fall within paragraph (7)(b) and their education or training is provided by means of a contract of employment; or

(c) are receiving universal credit, an employment or support allowance or a jobseeker's allowance.

(9) In this regulation—

"approved training" means training in pursuance of arrangements made under section 2(1) of the Employment and Training Act 1973 or section 2(3) of the Enterprise and New Towns (Scotland) Act 1990 which is approved by the Secretary of State for the purposes of this regulation;

"modular course" means a course which consists of two or more modules, the successful completion of a specified number of which is required before a person is considered by the educational establishment to have completed the course;

"student loan" means a loan towards a student's maintenance pursuant to any regulations made under section 22 of the Teaching and Higher Education Act 1998, section 73 of the Education (Scotland) Act 1980 or Article 3 of the Education (Student Support) (Northern Ireland) Order 1998, including in Scotland a young student's bursary paid under regulation 4(1)(c) of the Student's Allowances (Scotland) Regulations 2007.

DEFINITIONS

"the Act"—see reg.2(2).
"approved training"—see para.(9).
"course of advanced education"—see para.(2).
"modular course"—see para.(9).
"qualifying young person"—see paras (7), (8).
"student loan"—see para.(9).
"undertaking a course"—see paras (4)–(6).

GENERAL NOTE

A claimant cannot be entitled to JSA if he is receiving relevant education    1.102
(Jobseekers Act 1995 s.1(1)(g)). This regulation stipulates who is to be treated as
receiving it. The regulation combines in one place elements of exclusionary rules
on children and young persons and students which were split between JSA
Regulations 1996 regs 1(3), 54 (relevant education) and Chap.IX: students.

Paragraph (1)(a) is comparable with JSA Regulations 1996 reg.54 and reg.12
of the Income Support Regulations in that a child or qualifying young person
(QYP) is generally to be treated as receiving it, and thus excluded from JSA. A
child is someone under 16. A QYP is aged 16–19 meeting all of the criteria set
out in para.(7), but excluding those within one of the exempt "heads" in
para.(8).

Anyone undertaking a full-time course of "advanced education" (as defined in
para.(2)) is receiving relevant education and excluded from JSA (s.1(1)(g) read
with para.(1)(b)(i)). When a person is regarded as undertaking a course varies
according to the type of course, whether it is modular or not.

For a non-modular course, a person is regarded as undertaking a course from
when he starts the course until the last day of the course, or where the person has
been dismissed from it or finally abandoned it, from the date of dismissal or
abandonment (para.(4)(a)).

For a modular course, a person is regarded as undertaking part of a modular
course from when that part of the course starts until the last date on which he is
registered with the course provider or the provider of that part for that part of the
modular course, or where the person has been dismissed from it or finally
abandoned it, from the date of dismissal or abandonment. With modular
courses, the person is regarded as undertaking it during vacations other than the
vacation following completion of the final module and covers undertaking the
course for purposes of retaking failed examinations (para.(4)(b), (5)).

Whether the course of advanced education is modular or non-modular, someone who has taken time out of his course with the consent of his educational
establishment because of illness or caring responsibilities (not defined), and who
has now recovered or whose caring responsibilities have ended, can claim JSA
until the earlier of the day before he rejoins his course or the date the relevant
educational establishment has agreed that he can rejoin (subject to a maximum
of one year). This does not apply if the person is eligible for a grant or student
loan during this period (para.(6)).

Anyone aged 20 or over undertaking a course of study or training which is not
one of full-time advanced education must be treated as receiving relevant education if undertaking it is not compatible with the work-related requirements
imposed on them by the Secretary of State (para.(3)).

## Short periods of sickness

**46.**—(1) Subject to the following provisions of this regulation, a per-    1.103
son who—
  (a) satisfies the requirements for entitlement to a jobseeker's allow-
      ance or has been awarded a jobseeker's allowance, or is a person
      to whom any of the circumstances mentioned in section 6J(2) or
      (3) or 6K(2) of the Act apply;
  (b) proves to the satisfaction of the Secretary of State that they are
      unable to work on account of some specific disease or disable-
      ment; and
  (c) but for their disease or disablement, would satisfy the require-
      ments for entitlement to a jobseeker's allowance other than those

61

specified in section 1(2)(f) of the Act (capable of work or not having limited capability for work),

is to be treated for a period of not more than two weeks, beginning on the day on which sub-paragraphs (a) to (c) are met, as capable of work or as not having limited capability for work, except where the claimant states in writing that for the period of their disease or disablement they propose to claim or have claimed employment and support allowance.

(2) The evidence which is required for the purposes of paragraph (1)(b) is a declaration made by the claimant in writing, in a form approved for the purposes by the Secretary of State, that they have been unfit for work from a date or for a period specified in the declaration.

(3) The preceding provisions of this regulation do not apply to a claimant on more than two occasions in any one jobseeking period or, where a jobseeking period exceeds 12 months, in each successive 12 months within that period; and for the purposes of calculating any period of 12 months, the first 12 months in the jobseeking period commences on the first day of the jobseeking period.

(4) The preceding provisions of this regulation do not apply to any person where the first day in respect of which they are unable to work falls within eight weeks after the day the person ceased to be entitled to statutory sick pay.

(5) The preceding provisions of this regulation do not apply to a claimant who is temporarily absent from Great Britain in the circumstances prescribed by regulation 41(5).

GENERAL NOTE

1.104    It is a condition of entitlement to JSA that the claimant not have limited capability for work (Jobseekers Act 1995 s.1(2)(f)). This regulation permits persons unable to work on account of some specific disease or disablement to be entitled to JSA for up to two weeks in any 12-month period by treating them as capable of work or not having limited capability for work, unless they in writing inform the Secretary of State that they have claimed or propose to claim ESA. This regulation is much the same as JSA Regulations 1996 reg.55. See further the annotations to that provision, ignoring references to income support and SDA.

## Periods of sickness and persons receiving treatment outside Great Britain

1.105    **47.**—(1) A person—

(a) who has been awarded a jobseeker's allowance, or is a person to whom any of the circumstances mentioned in section 6J(2) or (3) or 6K(2) of the Act apply;

(b) who is temporarily absent from Great Britain in the circumstances prescribed by regulation 41(5);

(c) who proves to the satisfaction of the Secretary of State that they are unable to work on account of some specific disease or disablement; and

(d) but for their disease or disablement, would satisfy the requirements for entitlement to a jobseeker's allowance other than those specified in section 1(2)(f) of the Act (capable of work or not having limited capability for work),

is to be treated during that period of temporary absence abroad as capable of work or as not having limited capability for work, except where that person has stated in writing before that period of temporary absence abroad begins that immediately before the beginning of the period of that temporary absence abroad they have claimed employment and support allowance.

(2) The evidence which is required for the purposes of paragraph (1)(c) is a declaration made by that person in writing, in a form approved for the purposes by the Secretary of State, that they are unfit for work from a date or for a period specified in the declaration.

GENERAL NOTE

This is much the same as JSA Regulations 1996 reg.55A. See the annotation to that provision, ignoring references to joint-claim couple.   **1.106**

## Prescribed amount of earnings

**48.** The prescribed amount of earnings for the purposes of section 2(1)(c) of the Act (the contribution-based conditions) is to be calculated by applying the formula—   **1.107**

$$(A+D) - £0.01$$

where—

A is the age-related amount applicable to the claimant for the purposes of section 4(1)(a) of the Act; and D is any amount disregarded from the claimant's earnings in accordance with the Schedule to these Regulations and either regulation 59(2) (calculation of net earnings of employed earners) or regulation 61(2) (calculation of net profit of self-employed earners).

DEFINITIONS

"the Act"—see reg.2(2).
"claimant"—see reg.2(2).
"earnings"—see reg.2(2).
"employed earner"—see reg.2(2).
"net earnings"—see regs 2(2) and 59.
"net profit"—see regs 2(2) and 61.
"self-employed earner"—see reg.2(2).

GENERAL NOTE

It is a condition of entitlement to JSA that the claimant not have earnings in excess of the prescribed amount (Jobseekers Act 1995 s.2(1)(c)). This regulation gives the set formula for determining that prescribed amount, which amount is not the same for everyone. The prescribed amount is a level equal to the total of the claimant's personal age-related rate JSA (determined in accordance with Jobseekers Act 1995 s.4 and reg.49) (A in the formula) and the appropriate disregards from his earnings (D in the formula), minus one penny.   **1.108**

PART 6

AMOUNTS OF A JOBSEEKER'S ALLOWANCE

## Weekly amounts of jobseeker's allowance

1.109    **49.**—(1) In the case of a jobseeker's allowance, the age-related amount applicable to a claimant for the purposes of section 4(1)(a) of the Act is—

    (a) in the case of a person who has not attained the age of 25, £56.80 per week;

    (b) in the case of a person who has attained the age of 25, £71.70 per week.

    (2) Where the amount of any jobseeker's allowance would, but for this paragraph, include a fraction of one penny, that fraction is to be treated as one penny.

GENERAL NOTE

1.110    See the annotations to the similar JSA Regulations 1996 reg.79.

## Deductions in respect of earnings

1.111    **50.** The deduction in respect of earnings which falls to be made in accordance with section 4(1)(b) of the Act is an amount equal to the weekly amount of the claimant's earnings calculated in accordance with Part 7.

GENERAL NOTE

1.112    This is very much like JSA Regulations 1996 reg.80. See the annotations to that provision.

## Payments by way of pensions

1.113    **51.**—(1) The deduction in respect of pension payments, PPF payments or FAS payments which fall to be made in accordance with section 4(1)(b) of the Act is a sum equal to the amount by which that payment exceeds or, as the case may be, the aggregate of those payments exceed £50 per week.

    (2) Where pension payments, PPF payments or FAS payments first begin to be made to a person for a period starting other than on the first day of a benefit week, the deduction referred to in paragraph (1) has effect from the beginning of that benefit week.

    (3) Where pension payments, PPF payments or FAS payments are already in payment to a person and a change in the rate of payment takes effect in a week other than at the beginning of the benefit week, the

deduction referred to in paragraph (1) has effect from the first day of that benefit week.

(4) In determining the amount of any pension payments, PPF payments or FAS payments for the purposes of paragraphs (1) and (5), there are to be disregarded—

(a) any payments from a personal pension scheme, an occupational pension scheme or a public service pension scheme which are payable to the claimant and which arose in accordance with the terms of such a scheme on the death of a person who was a member of the scheme in question; and

(b) any PPF payments or FAS payments which—

(i) are payable to the claimant; and

(ii) arose on the death of a person who had an entitlement to such payments.

(5) Where a pension payment, PPF payment or FAS payment, or an aggregate of such payments, as the case may be, is paid to a person for a period other than a week, such payments are to be treated as being made to that person by way of weekly pension payments, weekly PPF payments or weekly FAS payments and the weekly amount is to be determined—

(a) where payment is made for a year, by dividing the total by 52;

(b) where payment is made for three months, by dividing the total by 13;

(c) where payment is made for a month, by multiplying the total by 12 and dividing the product by 52;

(d) where payment is made for two or more months, otherwise than for a year or for three months, by dividing the total by the number of months, multiplying the result by 12 and dividing the product by 52; or

(e) in any other case, by dividing the amount of the payment by the number of days in the period for which it is made and multiplying the result by seven.

DEFINITIONS

"the Act"—see reg.2(2).
"claimant"—see reg.2(2).
"FAS payments"—see Jobseekers Act 1995, s.35(1).
"payment"—see reg.2(2).
"pension payments"—see Jobseekers Act 1995, s.35(1).
"PPF payments"—see Jobseekers Act 1995, s.35(1).

GENERAL NOTE

See the annotations to the similar JSA Regulations 1996 reg.81.                1.114

## Minimum amount of a jobseeker's allowance

**52.** Where the amount of a jobseeker's allowance is less than 10 pence   1.115
a week that allowance is not payable.

PART 7

EARNINGS

## Rounding of fractions

1.116     **53.** Where any calculation under this Part results in a fraction of a penny that fraction must, if it would be to the claimant's advantage, be treated as a penny, but otherwise it must be disregarded.

## Calculation of earnings derived from employed earner's employment

1.117     **54.**—(1) Earnings derived from employment as an employed earner are to be taken into account over a period determined in accordance with the following paragraphs and at a weekly amount determined in accordance with regulation 57 (calculation of weekly amount of earnings).

(2) Subject to the following provisions of this regulation, the period over which a payment is to be taken into account is to be—

(a) where the payment is monthly, a period equal to the number of weeks beginning with the date on which the payment is treated as paid under regulation 56 and ending with the date immediately before the date on which the next monthly payment would have been so treated as paid whether or not the next monthly payment is actually paid;

(b) where the payment is in respect of a period which is not monthly, a period equal to the length of the period for which payment is made; or

(c) in any other case, a period equal to such number of weeks as is equal to the number obtained (see paragraph (13)) by applying the formula—

$$\frac{E}{J+D}$$

where—

E is the net earnings;

J is the amount of jobseeker's allowance which would be payable had the payment not been made;

D is an amount equal to the total of the sums which would fall to be disregarded from that payment under the Schedule to these Regulations (sums to be disregarded in the calculation of earnings), as is appropriate in the claimant's case,

and that period is to begin on the date on which the payment is treated as paid under regulation 56.

(3) Earnings derived by a claimant as a member of any territorial or reserve force prescribed in Part 1 of Schedule 6 to the Social Security (Contributions) Regulations 2001 in respect of a period of annual continuous training, whether paid to the claimant alone or together with

other earnings derived from the same source, are to be taken into account for a maximum of 15 days in any calendar year—

    (a) in the case of a period of training exceeding 14 days, over a period of 14 days; or

    (b) in any other case, over a period which is equal to the duration of the training period.

(4) The period referred to in paragraph (3) over which earnings are to be taken into account is to begin on the date on which they are treated as paid under regulation 56.

(5) Where earnings are derived from the same source but are not of the same kind and the periods in respect of which those earnings would, but for this paragraph, fall to be taken into account, overlap wholly or partly—

    (a) those earnings are to be taken into account over a period equal to the aggregate length of those periods; and

    (b) that period is to begin with the earliest date on which any part of those earnings would otherwise be treated as paid under regulation 56 (date on which earnings are treated as paid).

(6) In a case to which paragraph (5) applies, earnings falling within regulation 58 (earnings of employed earners) are to be taken into account in the following order of priority—

    (a) earnings normally derived from the employment;

    (b) any compensation payment;

    (c) any holiday pay.

(7) Where earnings to which regulation 58(1)(b) or (c) (earnings of employed earners) applies are paid in respect of part of a day, those earnings are to be taken into account over a period equal to a day.

(8) Subject to paragraph (9), the period over which a compensation payment is to be taken into account is to be the period beginning on the date on which the payment is treated as paid under regulation 56 (date on which earnings are treated as paid) and ending—

    (a) subject to sub-paragraph (b), where the person who made the payment represents that it, or part of it, was paid in lieu of notice of termination of employment or on account of the early termination of a contract of employment for a term certain, on the expiry date;

    (b) in a case where the person who made the payment represents that it, or part of it, was paid in lieu of consultation under section 188 of the Trade Union and Labour Relations (Consolidation) Act 1992(73), on the latest of—

        (i) the date on which the consultation period under that section would have ended;

        (ii) in a case where sub-paragraph (a) also applies, the expiry date; or

        (iii) the standard date; or

    (c) in any other case, on the standard date.

(9) The maximum period over which a compensation payment may be taken into account under paragraph (8) is 52 weeks from the date on which the payment is treated as paid under regulation 56.

(10) In this regulation—

"compensation payment" means any payment to which regulation 58(4) (earnings of employed earners) applies;

"the expiry date" means in relation to the termination of a person's employment—

(a) the date on which any period of notice (which means the period of notice of termination of employment to which a person is entitled by statute or by contract, whichever is the longer, or, if they are not entitled to such notice, the period of notice which is customary in the employment in question) applicable to the person was due to expire, or would have expired had it not been waived;

(b) subject to paragraph (11), where the person who made the payment represents that the period in respect of which that payment is made is longer than the period of notice referred to in paragraph (a), the date on which that longer period is due to expire; or

(c) where the person had a contract of employment for a term certain, the date on which it was due to expire;

"the standard date" means the earlier of—

(a) the expiry date; and

(b) the last day of the period determined by dividing the amount of the compensation payment by the maximum weekly amount which, on the date on which the payment is treated as paid under regulation 56, is specified in section 227(1) of the Employment Rights Act 1996, and treating the result (less any fraction of a whole number) as a number of weeks.

(11) For the purposes of paragraph (10), if it appears to the Secretary of State in a case to which paragraph (b) of the definition of "expiry date" applies that, having regard to the amount of the compensation payment and the level of remuneration normally received by the claimant when they were engaged in the employment in respect of which the compensation payment was made, it is unreasonable to take the payment into account until the date specified in that paragraph (b), the expiry date is to be the date specified in paragraph (a) of that definition.

(12) For the purposes of this regulation the claimant's earnings are to be calculated in accordance with regulations 58, 59 and 63.

(13) For the purposes of the number obtained as mentioned in paragraph (2)(c), any fraction is to be treated as a corresponding fraction of a week.

DEFINITIONS

"claimant"—see reg.2(2).
"compensation payment"—see para.(10).
"employed earner"—see reg.2(1).
"the expiry date"—see para.(10).
"the standard date"—see para.(10).
"week"—see reg.2(2).

GENERAL NOTE

*Paras (1)–(7)*

See also the notes to paras (1)–(4A) of reg.29 of the Income Support Regula-    **1.118**
tions, ignoring references to disregards.

This regulation specifies how earnings from employed earner's employment
are to be taken into account, over what period(s) and at a weekly amount
determined in accordance with reg.57.

The general rules on "what period" are found in para.(2). Different rules,
however, apply for earnings from annual continuous training as a member of a
territorial or reserve force (paras (3), (4)). Furthermore, where earnings from
the same source but of a different kind overlap, the general rules are first applied
to each kind and then that set by para.(5) is applied, so that they are to be taken
into account over a period equal to the aggregate length of the periods determined for each under the general rules, beginning on the earliest date on which
any of these earnings would be treated as paid in accordance with reg.56, with
para.(6) setting an order of priority. Where compensation payments or holiday
pay ("earnings to which regulation 58(1)(b) or (c)" apply) are paid in respect of
part of a day they are to be treated as applicable to a day (para.7).

*Paras (8) to (11)*

These provisions define the length of the period for which a "compensation
payment" (defined in para.(10)) is to be taken into account. There is no equivalent to reg.29(4C) of the Income Support Regulations so it seems that a compensation payment made on the termination of such part-time employment will
be taken into account as earnings for the period covered by the payment. The
"maximum weekly amount" referred to in para.(8)(c)(ii) is the amount specified
at the relevant time as the amount to be used in calculating the basic award for
unfair dismissal and redundancy payments. The figure in effect from February 1,
2013 is £450.

Note *CJSA 5529/1997* in which the effect of para.(6) of the JSA Regulations
1996 reg.94 (now para.(8) of this regulation) was that the period to which the
claimant's compensation payment was to be attributed ended before it started.
On October 1, 1996 the claimant agreed with her employer that her employment
would end on December 31, 1996 by way of voluntary redundancy. She was to
receive a payment of £41,500 on January 4, 1997, which would not include any
sum in lieu of notice. She claimed JSA with effect from January 1, 1997. The
Commissioner states that the period for which the compensation period was to
be taken into account under para.(6) (now para.8) ended on the "standard
date". Under para.(8)(c) (now para.(10)) the standard date was the earlier of the
"expiry date" and what might be termed the "apportionment date". The expiry
date in this case was no later than December 31, 1996 because the claimant was
entitled to 12 weeks' (or three months') notice and the agreement for redundancy had been made on October 1, 1996 (see para.(8)(b)(i) (now para.(a) of
the definition of "expiry date" in para.(10)). The result was that there was no
period in respect of which the compensation payment was to be taken into
account and thus no period during which she was to be treated as in remunerative work after December 31, 1996.

## Calculation of earnings of self-employed earners

**55.**—(1) Except where paragraph (2) applies, where a claimant's    **1.119**
income consists of earnings from employment as a self-employed earner
the weekly amount of their earnings is to be determined by reference to
their average weekly earnings from that employment—

(a) over a period of one year; or

(b) where the claimant has recently become engaged in that employment or there has been a change which is likely to affect the normal pattern of business, over such other period as may, in any particular case, enable the weekly amount of their earnings to be determined more accurately.

(2) Where the claimant's earnings consist of any items to which paragraph (3) applies, those earnings are to be taken into account over a period equal to such number of weeks as is equal to the number obtained (see paragraph (5)) by applying the formula—

$$\frac{E}{J+D}$$

where—

E is the earnings;

J is the amount of jobseeker's allowance which would be payable had the payment not been made;

D is an amount equal to the total of the sums which would fall to be disregarded from the payment under the Schedule to these Regulations (earnings to be disregarded) as is appropriate in the claimant's case.

(3) This paragraph applies to—

(a) royalties or other sums paid as a consideration for the use of, or the right to use, any copyright, design, patent or trade mark; or

(b) any payment in respect of any—

    (i) book registered under the Public Lending Right Scheme 1982; or

    (ii) work made under any international public lending right scheme that is analogous to the Public Lending Right Scheme 1982,

where the claimant is the first owner of the copyright, design, patent or trade mark, or an original contributor to the book or work concerned.

(4) For the purposes of this regulation the claimant's earnings are to be calculated in accordance with regulations 60 to 62.

(5) For the purposes of the number obtained as mentioned in paragraph (2), any fraction is to be treated as a corresponding fraction of a week.

DEFINITIONS

"claimant"—see reg.2(2).
"self-employed earner"—see reg.2(2).

GENERAL NOTE

1.120    See the notes to reg.30 of the Income Support Regulations. Note the more general exception to the rule in para.(1)(a) that is hidden in reg.61(10) which allows the amount of any item of income or expenditure to be calculated over a different period if that will produce a more accurate figure.

## Date on which earnings are treated as paid

**56.** A payment of earnings to which regulation 54 (calculation of 1.121
earnings derived from employed earner's employment) applies is to be
treated as paid—
  (a) in the case of a payment which is due to be paid before the first
      benefit week pursuant to the claim, on the date on which it is due
      to be paid; or
  (b) in any other case, on the first day of the benefit week in which it
      is due to be paid or the first succeeding benefit week in which it is
      practicable to take it into account.

DEFINITIONS

"benefit week"—see reg.2(2).
"payment"—see reg.2(2).

GENERAL NOTE

See the annotations to reg.31(1) of the Income Support Regulations insofar as 1.122
they deal with earnings rather than with other income.

## Calculation of weekly amount of earnings

**57.**—(1) For the purposes of regulation 54 (calculation of earnings 1.123
derived from employed earner's employment), subject to paragraphs (2)
to (5), where the period in respect of which a payment of earnings is
made—
  (a) does not exceed a week, the weekly amount is to be the amount of
      that payment;
  (b) exceeds a week, the weekly amount is to be determined—
      (i) in a case where that period is a month, by multiplying the
          amount of the payment by 12 and dividing the product by
          52;
      (ii) in a case where that period is three months, by multiplying
           the amount of the payment by four and dividing the product
           by 52;
      (iii) in a case where that period is a year, by dividing the amount
            of the payment by 52;
      (iv) in any other case, by multiplying the amount of the payment
           by seven and dividing the product by the number equal to the
           number of days in the period in respect of which it is
           made.
  (2) Where a payment for a period not exceeding a week is treated
under regulation 56(a) (date on which earnings are treated as paid) as
paid before the first benefit week and a part is to be taken into account
for some days only in that week ("the relevant days"), the amount to be
taken into account for the relevant days is to be calculated by multiplying
the amount of the payment by the number of relevant days and dividing
the product by the number of days in the period in respect of which it is
made.
  (3) Where a payment is in respect of a period equal to or in excess of
a week and a part is to be taken into account for some days only in a

benefit week ("the relevant days"), the amount to be taken into account for the relevant days is, except where paragraph (4) applies, to be calculated by multiplying the amount of the payment by the number of relevant days and dividing the product by the number of days in the period in respect of which it is made.

(4) Except in the case of a payment which it has not been practicable to treat under regulation 56(b) as paid on the first day of the benefit week in which it is due to be paid, where a payment of income from a particular source is or has been paid regularly and that payment falls to be taken into account in the same benefit week as a payment of the same kind and from the same source, the amount of that income to be taken into account in any one benefit week is not to exceed the weekly amount determined under paragraph (1)(a) or (b), as the case may be, of the payment which under regulation 56(b) (date on which earnings are treated as paid) is treated as paid first.

(5) Where the amount of the claimant's earnings fluctuates and has changed more than once, or a claimant's regular pattern of work is such that they do not work every week, paragraphs (1) to (4) may be modified so that the weekly amount of their earnings is determined by reference to their average weekly earnings—

(a) if there is a recognisable cycle of work, over the period of one complete cycle (including, where the cycle involves periods in which the claimant does no work, those periods but disregarding any other absences);

(b) in any other case, over a period of five weeks or such other period as may, in the particular case, enable the claimant's average weekly earnings to be determined more accurately.

DEFINITIONS

"benefit week"—see reg.2(2).
"claimant"—see reg.2(2).
"the relevant days"—see paras (2) and (3).
"week"—see reg.2(2).

GENERAL NOTE

1.124    See the annotations to JSA Regulations 1996 reg.94 and also to reg.32(1)–(6) of the Income Support Regulations insofar as they deal with earnings rather than with other income.

**Earnings of employed earners**

1.125    **58.**—(1) Subject to paragraphs (2) and (4), "earnings" means in the case of employment as an employed earner, any remuneration or profit derived from that employment and includes—

(a) any bonus or commission;

(b) any compensation payment;

(c) any holiday pay except any payable more than four weeks after the termination or interruption of employment but this exception does not apply to a person who is, or would be, prevented from being entitled to a jobseeker's allowance by section 14 of the Act (trade disputes);

72

(d) any payment by way of a retainer;

(e) any payment made by the claimant's employer in respect of expenses not wholly, exclusively and necessarily incurred in the performance of the duties of the employment, including any payment made by the claimant's employer in respect of—

    (i) travelling expenses incurred by the claimant between their home and place of employment;

    (ii) expenses incurred by the claimant under arrangements made for the care of a member of their family owing to the claimant's absence from home;

(f) any payment or award of compensation made under section 112(4), 113, 117(3)(a), 128, 131 or 132 of the Employment Rights Act 1996 (the remedies: orders and compensation, the orders, enforcement of order and compensation, interim relief);

(g) any payment made or remuneration paid under section 28, 34, 64, 68 or 70 of the Employment Rights Act 1996 (right to guarantee payments, remuneration on suspension on medical or maternity grounds, complaints to employment tribunals);

(h) any award of compensation made under section 156, 161 to 166, 189 or 192 of the Trade Union and Labour Relations (Consolidation) Act 1992 (compensation for unfair dismissal or redundancy on grounds of involvement in trade union activities, and protective awards);

(i) the amount of any payment by way of a non-cash voucher which has been taken into account in the computation of a person's earnings in accordance with Part 5 of Schedule 3 to the Social Security (Contributions) Regulations 2001.

(2) "Earnings" does not include—

(a) subject to paragraph (3), any payment in kind;

(b) any periodic sum paid to a claimant on account of the termination of their employment by reason of redundancy;

(c) any remuneration paid by or on behalf of an employer to the claimant in respect of a period throughout which the claimant is on maternity leave, paternity leave or adoption leave or is absent from work because they are ill;

(d) any payment in respect of expenses wholly, exclusively and necessarily incurred in the performance of the duties of the employment;

(e) any occupational pension;

(f) any redundancy payment within the meaning of section 135(1) of the Employment Rights Act 1996;

(g) any lump sum payment made under the Iron and Steel Re-adaptation Benefits Scheme;

(h) any payment in respect of expenses arising out of the claimant's participation as a service user.

(3) Paragraph (2)(a) does not apply in respect of any non-cash voucher referred to in paragraph (1)(i).

(4) In this regulation, "compensation payment" means any payment made in respect of the termination of employment other than—

(a) any remuneration or emolument (whether in money or in kind) which accrued in the period before the termination;
(b) any holiday pay;
(c) any payment specified in paragraphs (1)(f), (g), or (h) or (2);
(d) any refund of contributions to which the person was entitled under an occupational pension scheme.

DEFINITIONS

"compensation payment"—see para.(4).
"employed earner"—see reg.2(1).
"employment"—see reg.2(1).
"occupational pension scheme"—see Jobseekers Act 1995, s.35(1).

GENERAL NOTE

1.126    See the annotations to the similarly worded JSA Regulations 1996 reg.98 and to reg.35 of the Income Support Regulations, ignoring references to things not ranking as earnings being treated as income or capital, matters relevant only to income-related benefits.

## Calculation of net earnings of employed earners

1.127    **59.**—(1) For the purposes of regulation 54 (calculation of earnings of employed earners), the earnings of a claimant derived from employment as an employed earner to be taken into account are to be, subject to paragraph (2), their net earnings.

(2) There is to be disregarded from a claimant's net earnings, any sum, where applicable, specified in the Schedule to these Regulations.

(3) For the purposes of paragraph (1) net earnings are to be calculated by taking into account the gross earnings of the claimant from that employment less—

(a) any amount deducted from those earnings by way of—
   (i) income tax;
   (ii) primary Class 1 contributions payable under the Benefits Act; and
(b) half of any sum paid by the claimant in respect of a pay period (the period in respect of which a claimant is, or expects to be, normally paid by their employer, being a week, a fortnight, four weeks, a month or other longer or shorter period as the case may be) by way of a contribution towards an occupational or personal pension scheme.

DEFINITIONS

"claimant"—see reg.2(2).
"employed earner"—see reg.2(1).
"employment"—see reg.2(1).
"net earnings"—see reg.2(2) and para.(3).
"occupational pension scheme"—see Jobseekers Act 1995, s.35(1).
"personal pension scheme"—see Jobseekers Act 1995, s.35(1).

GENERAL NOTE

1.128    See the annotations to reg.36 of the Income Support Regulations.

**Earnings of self-employed earners**

**60.**—(1) Subject to paragraph (2), "earnings", in the case of employ-   1.129
ment as a self-employed earner, means the gross receipts of the
employment.

(2) "Earnings" does not include—

(a) where a claimant is involved in providing board and lodging
accommodation for which a charge is payable, any payment by
way of such a charge;

(b) any payment made to the claimant with whom a person is accommodated by virtue of arrangements made—

    (i) under section 22C(2), (3), (5) or (6)(a) or (b) of the Chil-
dren Act 1989 (provision of accommodation and maintenance for a child whom the local authority is looking
after);

    (ii) by a local authority under section 26 of the Children (Scot-
land) Act 1995 (manner of provision of accommodation to
child looked after by local authority); or

    (iii) by a local authority under regulation 33 or 51 of the Looked
After Children (Scotland) Regulations 2009 (fostering and
kinship care allowances and fostering allowances); or

    (iv) by a voluntary organisation under section 59(1)(a) of the
Children Act 1989 (provision of accommodation by voluntary organisations);

(c) any payment made to the claimant for a person ("the person
concerned"), who is not normally a member of the claimant's
household but is temporarily in the claimant's care, by—

    (i) the National Health Service Commissioning Board;

    (ii) a local authority but excluding payments of housing benefit
made in respect of the person concerned;

    (iii) a voluntary organisation;

    (iv) the person concerned pursuant to section 26(3A) of the
National Assistance Act 1948;

    (v) a clinical commissioning group established under section
14D of the Health Service Act; or

    (vi) a Local Health Board established by an order made under
section 11 of the Health Service (Wales) Act;

(d) any sports award.

(3) In this regulation, "board and lodging accommodation"
means—

(a) accommodation provided to a person or, if they are a member of
a family, to them or any other member of their family, for a charge
which is inclusive of—

    (i) the provision of that accommodation; and

    (ii) at least some cooked or prepared meals which are cooked or
prepared (by a person other than the person to whom the
accommodation is provided or a member of their family) and
consumed in that accommodation or associated premises;
or

(b) accommodation provided to a person in a hotel, guest house, lodging house or some similar establishment,

except accommodation provided by a close relative of theirs or of any other member of their family, or other than on a commercial basis.

DEFINITIONS

"claimant"—see reg.2(2).
"close relative"—see reg.2(2).
"employment"—see reg.2(1).
"family"—see Jobseekers Act 1995, s.35(1); reg.3(1).
"member of their family"—see reg.3(1).
"the person concerned"—see para.(2)(c).
"self-employed earner"—see reg.2(2).
"sports award"—see reg.2(2).
"voluntary organisation"—see reg.2(2).

GENERAL NOTE

1.130    See annotations to the similar JSA Regulations 1996 reg.100, ignoring references to payments being treated as other income, something relevant only to IBJSA, now abolished in cases and areas within the "Pathfinder" pilot.

## Calculation of net profit of self-employed earners

1.131    **61.**—(1) For the purposes of regulation 55 (calculation of earnings of self-employed earners), the earnings of a claimant to be taken into account are—

(a) in the case of a self-employed earner who is engaged in employment on their own account, the net profit derived from that employment;

(b) in the case of a self-employed earner whose employment is carried on in partnership, or is that of a share fisherman within the meaning of regulation 67, the claimant's share of the net profit derived from that employment less—

(i) an amount in respect of income tax and of national insurance contributions payable under the Benefits Act calculated in accordance with regulation 62 (deduction of tax and contributions for self-employed earners); and

(ii) half of any premium paid in the period that is relevant under regulation 55 in respect of a personal pension scheme.

(2) There is to be disregarded from a claimant's net profit any sum, where applicable, specified in paragraphs 1 to 11 of the Schedule to these Regulations.

(3) For the purposes of paragraph (1)(a) the net profit of the employment is, except where paragraph (9) applies, to be calculated by taking into account the earnings of the employment over the period determined under regulation 55 (calculation of earnings of self-employed earners) less—

(a) subject to paragraphs (5) to (7), any expenses wholly and exclusively incurred in that period for the purposes of that employment;

   (b) an amount in respect of—
      (i) income tax; and
      (ii) national insurance contributions payable under the Benefits
          Act, calculated in accordance with regulation 62 (deductions
          of tax and contributions for self-employed earners); and
   (c) half of any premium paid in the period determined under regula-
      tion 55 in respect of a personal pension scheme.

(4) For the purposes of paragraph (1)(b), the net profit of the employment is to be calculated by taking into account the earnings of the
employment over the period determined under regulation 55 less, subject to paragraphs (5) to (7), any expenses wholly and exclusively
incurred in that period for the purposes of that employment.

(5) Subject to paragraph (6), no deduction is to be made under
paragraph (3)(a) or (4) in respect of—
   (a) any capital expenditure;
   (b) the depreciation of any capital asset;
   (c) any sum employed or intended to be employed in the setting up or
      expansion of the employment;
   (d) any loss incurred before the beginning of the period determined
      under regulation 55;
   (e) the repayment of capital on any loan taken out for the purposes of
      the employment;
   (f) any expenses incurred in providing business entertainment.

(6) A deduction is to be made under paragraph (3)(a) or (4) in respect
of the repayment of capital on any loan used for—
   (a) the replacement in the course of business of equipment or
      machinery; and
   (b) the repair of an existing business asset except to the extent that any
      sum is payable under an insurance policy for its repair.

(7) The Secretary of State must not make a deduction under paragraph (3)(a) or (4) in respect of any expenses where the Secretary of
State is not satisfied that the expense has been incurred or, having regard
to the nature of the expense and its amount, that it has been reasonably
incurred.

(8) A deduction under paragraph (3)(a) or (4)—
   (a) must not be made in respect of any sum unless it has been
      incurred for the purposes of the business;
   (b) must be made in respect of—
      (i) the excess of any Value Added Tax paid over Value Added
         Tax received in the period determined under regulation 55;
      (ii) any income expended in the repair of an existing asset except
         to the extent that any sum is payable under an insurance
         policy for its repair;
      (iii) any payment of interest on a loan taken out for the purposes
         of the employment.

(9) Where a claimant is engaged in employment as a child-minder the
net profit of the employment is to be one-third of the earnings of that
employment, less—
   (a) an amount in respect of—
      (i) income tax; and

      (ii) national insurance contributions payable under the Benefits Act, calculated in accordance with regulation 62 (deductions of tax and contributions for self-employed earners); and

   (b) half of any premium paid in the period determined under regulation 55 in respect of a personal pension scheme.

(10) Notwithstanding regulation 55 and paragraphs (1) to (9), the Secretary of State may assess any item of a claimant's income or expenditure over a period other than that determined under regulation 55 provided that the other period may, in the particular case, enable the weekly amount of that item of income or expenditure to be determined more accurately.

(11) Where a claimant is engaged in employment as a self-employed earner and they are engaged in one or more other employments as a self-employed or employed earner, any loss incurred in any one of their employments is not to be offset against their earnings in any other of their employments.

DEFINITIONS

   "claimant"—see reg.2(2).
   "employed earner"—see reg.2(1).
   "personal pension scheme"—see Jobseekers Act 1995, s.35(1).
   "self-employed earner"—see reg.2(2).
   "share fisherman"—see reg.67.

GENERAL NOTE

1.132    See the annotations to reg.38 of the Income Support Regulations. Note the width of para.(10). See annotation to reg.55, above.

## Deduction of tax and contributions for self-employed earners

1.133    **62.**—(1) Subject to paragraph (2), the amount to be deducted in respect of income tax under regulation 61(1)(b)(i), (3)(b)(i) or (9)(a)(i) (calculation of net profit of self-employed earners) is to be calculated—

   (a) on the basis of the amount of chargeable income; and

   (b) as if that income were assessable to income tax at the basic rate of tax less only the personal allowance to which the claimant is entitled sections 35 and 38 to 40 of the Income Tax Act 2007 (personal reliefs) as is appropriate to their circumstances.

(2) If the period determined under regulation 55 is less than a year, the earnings to which the basic rate of tax is to be applied and the amount of the personal allowance deductible under paragraph (1) is to be calculated on a pro rata basis.

(3) Subject to paragraph (4), the amount to be deducted in respect of national insurance contributions under regulation 61(1)(b)(i), (3)(b)(ii) or (9)(a)(ii) is to be the total of—

   (a) the amount of Class 2 contributions payable under section 11(1) or, as the case may be, 11(3) of the Benefits Act at the rate applicable at the date of claim except where the claimant's chargeable income is less than the amount specified in section 11(4) of that Act (small earnings exception) for the tax year in which the date of claim falls; and

(b) the amount of Class 4 contributions (if any) which would be payable under section 15 of that Act (Class 4 contributions recoverable under the Income Tax Acts) at the percentage rate applicable at the date of claim on so much of the chargeable income as exceeds the lower limit but does not exceed the upper limit of profits and gains applicable for the tax year in which the date of claim falls.

(4) If the period determined under regulation 55 is less than a year—

(a) the amount specified for the tax year referred to in paragraph (3)(a) is to be reduced pro rata; and

(b) the limits referred to in paragraph (3)(b) are to be reduced pro rata.

(5) In this regulation "chargeable income" means—

(a) except where sub-paragraph (b) applies, the earnings derived from the employment less any expenses deducted under regulation 61(3)(a) or, as the case may be, (4);

(b) in the case of employment as a child minder, one-third of the earnings of that employment.

DEFINITIONS

"basic rate"—see reg.2(2).
"chargeable income"—see para.(5).
"employment"—see reg.2(1).
"tax year"—see Jobseekers Act 1995, s.35(1).

GENERAL NOTE

See the annotations to reg.39 of the Income Support Regulations.        **1.134**

## Notional earnings

**63.**—(1) Subject to paragraph (2), any earnings which are due to be    **1.135**
paid to the claimant but have not been paid to the claimant, are to be
treated as possessed by the claimant.

(2) Paragraph (1) does not apply to any earnings which are due to an
employed earner on the termination of their employment by reason of
redundancy but which have not been paid to them.

(3) Where a claimant's earnings are not ascertainable at the time of the
determination of the claim or of any revision or supersession, the Secretary of State must treat the claimant as possessing such earnings as is
reasonable in the circumstances of the case having regard to the number
of hours worked and the earnings paid for comparable employment in
the area.

(4) Subject to paragraph (5), where—

(a) a claimant performs a service for another person; and

(b) that person makes no payment of earnings or pays less than that
paid for a comparable employment in the area,

the Secretary of State must treat the claimant as possessing such earnings (if any) as is reasonable for that employment unless the claimant satisfies the Secretary of State that the means of that person are insufficient for that person to pay or to pay more for the service.

(5) Paragraph (4) does not apply—

(a) to a claimant who is engaged by a charity or voluntary organisation or who is a volunteer if the Secretary of State is satisfied in any of those cases that it is reasonable for the claimant to provide those services free of charge;

(b) to a claimant who is participating in a work placement approved by the Secretary of State (or a person providing services to the Secretary of State) before the placement starts.

(6) Where a claimant is treated as possessing any earnings under paragraphs (1) or (2), regulations 54 to 62 apply for the purposes of calculating the amount of those earnings as if a payment had actually been made and as if it were actual earnings which the claimant does possess.

(7) Where a claimant is treated as possessing any earnings under paragraphs (3) or (4), regulations 54 to 62 apply for the purposes of calculating the amount of those earnings as if a payment had actually been made and as if they were actual earnings which the claimant does possess, except that—

(a) regulation 59(3) does not apply; and

(b) the claimant's net earnings are to be calculated by taking into account the earnings which the claimant is treated as possessing less the amounts referred to in paragraph (8).

(8) The amounts mentioned in paragraph (7)(b) are—

(a) where the period over which the earnings which the claimant is treated as possessing are to be taken into account is—

(i) a year or more, an amount in respect of income tax equivalent to an amount calculated in accordance with paragraph (11);

(ii) less than a year, the earnings to which the starting rate of tax is to be applied and the amount of the personal allowance deductible under this paragraph are to be calculated on a pro rata basis;

(b) where the weekly amount of the earnings which the claimant is treated as possessing is not less than the lower earnings limit, an amount representing primary Class 1 contributions under the Benefits Act, calculated by applying to those earnings the initial and main primary percentages in accordance with section 8(1)(a) and (b) of that Act; and

(c) half of any sum payable by the claimant in respect of a pay period by way of a contribution towards an occupational or personal pension scheme.

(9) Paragraphs (1), (3) and (4) do not apply in respect of any amount of earnings derived from employment as an employed earner, arising out of the claimant's participation as a service user.

(10) In this regulation, "work placement" means practical work experience which is not undertaken in expectation of payment.

(11) For the purposes of paragraph (8)(a)(i), the amount is calculated by applying to those earnings—

(a) the starting rate of tax in the year of assessment; or as the case may be

(b) the starting rate and the basic rate of tax in the year of assessment,

less only the personal allowance to which the claimant is entitled under sections 35 and 38 to 40 of the Income Tax Act 2007 (personal reliefs) as is appropriate to the claimant's circumstances.

DEFINITIONS

"basic rate"—see reg.2(2).
"employment"—see reg.2(1).
"employed earner"—see reg.2(1).
"occupational pension scheme"—see Jobseekers Act 1995, s.35(1).
"personal pension scheme"—see Jobseekers Act 1995, s.35(1).
"voluntary organisation"—see reg.2(2).
"work placement"—see para.(10).

GENERAL NOTE

The concept of notional income and capital is familiar from "old style JSA" **1.136** and income support. It is also carried forward into UC (see Universal Credit Regulations 2013 reg.60). The concept is that in certain circumstances the benefits regime treats someone as possessing income or capital they do not actually have. This regulation applies that concept to earnings. Note that under para.(9) none of this regulation's "notional earnings" rules applies to any amount of earnings derived from employment as an employed earner, arising out of the claimant's participation as a service user.

*Paras (1), (2), (6),*

Earnings due, but not yet paid, to the claimant are treated as being possessed by the claimant, unless they are earnings not yet paid but due to the claimant (an employed earner) on the termination of their employment by reason of redundancy. They are to be calculated under regs 54–62 as if actually paid to and possessed by the claimant.

*Para. (3)*

Where the claimant's earnings are not ascertainable at the time of the relevant decision, revision or supersession, the decision maker must treat the claimant as possessing such earnings as is reasonable in the circumstances of the case having regard to the number of hours worked and the earnings paid for comparable employment in the area. This is a very general discretion. The decision-maker (or tribunal) must have regard to the number of hours worked and the going rate locally for comparable employment in deciding what is reasonable, but is not prevented from considering all relevant circumstances (*R(SB) 25/83, R(SB) 15/86, R(SB) 6/88*). Paragraphs (7), (8) and (11) govern their calculation. Note that reg.59(3) does not apply.

*Paras (4), (5)*

See the annotations to reg.42(6), (6A) of the Income Support Regulations. Note the definition of work placement in para.(10) of this JSA regulation.

PART 8

PART WEEKS

## Amount of a jobseeker's allowance payable

1.137    **64.**—(1) Subject to the following provisions of this Part, the amount payable by way of a jobseeker's allowance in respect of a part-week is to be calculated by applying the formula—

$$( N \times X ) / 7$$

where—

X is the personal rate determined in accordance with section 4(1) of the Act;

N is the number of days in the part-week.

(2) In this Part—

"part-week" means any period of less than a week in respect of which there is an entitlement to a jobseeker's allowance;

"relevant week" means the period of seven days determined in accordance with regulation 65.

DEFINITIONS

"claimant"—see reg.2(2).
"part-week"—see para.(2).
"relevant week"—see para.(2).

## Relevant week

1.138    **65.**—(1) Where the part-week—

(a) is the whole period for which a jobseeker's allowance is payable or occurs at the beginning of an award, the relevant week is the period of seven days ending on the last day of that part-week;

(b) occurs at the end of an award, the relevant week is the period of seven days beginning on the first day of the part-week; or

(c) occurs because a jobseeker's allowance is not payable for any period in accordance with sections 6J or 7K of the Act (circumstances in which a jobseeker's allowance is not payable), the relevant week is the seven days ending immediately before the start of the next benefit week to commence for that claimant.

(2) Where a person has an award of a jobseeker's allowance and their benefit week changes, for the purpose of calculating the amounts of a jobseeker's allowance payable for the part-week beginning on the day after their last complete benefit week before the change and ending immediately before the change, the relevant week is the period of seven days beginning on the day after the last complete benefit week.

## Modification in the calculation of income

1.139    **66.** For the purposes of regulation 64 (amount of jobseeker's allowance payable for part-weeks), a claimant's income is to be calculated in accordance with Part 7 subject to the following changes—

82

(a) any income which is due to be paid in the relevant week is to be treated as paid on the first day of that week;

(b) where the part-week occurs at the end of the claim, any income or any change in the amount of income of the same kind which is first payable within the relevant week but not on any day in the part-week is to be disregarded;

(c) where the part-week occurs immediately after a period in which a person was treated as engaged in remunerative work under regulation 43 (persons treated as engaged in remunerative work) any earnings which are taken into account for the purposes of determining that period are to be disregarded;

(d) where only part of the weekly amount of income is taken into account in the relevant week, the balance is to be disregarded.


PART 9


SHARE FISHERMEN


GENERAL NOTE

This Part of these Regulations modifies the usual rules so as to deal with "share fishermen" (defined in reg.67, below). Regulation 68, below, provides: **1.140**

"The Act and above provisions of these Regulations have effect in relation to share fishermen subject to the provisions of this Part."

Share Fishermen are paid by way of a share of the catch or the gross profits of the fishing boat. For contributions purposes they are treated as a special form of self-employed earner and pay a special Class 2 contribution. Normally, of course, those liable to pay Class 2 (self-employed earner's contributions) rather than Class 1 contributions (employed earner's contributions) would not be entitled to JSA where fulfillment of the key contribution conditions depends on paid and/or credited Class 1 contributions (Jobseekers Act 1995 s.2). Regulations 69, below, modifies s.2 to take in for purposes of qualifying for "new style JSA" the special Class 2 contributions paid by share fishermen at the rate applicable in accordance with reg.125(c) of the Social Security (Contributions) Regulations 2001 (SI 2001/1004).

Regulation 70 modifies the definition of "trade dispute" in Jobseekers Act 1995 s.35(1). Regulation 71(1) sets an additional condition with respect to the payment of a jobseeker's allowance to a share fisherman in respect of any benefit week: where in any benefit week claimants have not worked as a share fisherman (partly defined in reg.71(2)), they must prove that they have not neglected to avail themselves of a reasonable opportunity of employment as a share fisherman. Regulation 71(3) sets an additional condition that where claimants are master or a member of the crew of a fishing boat of which either the master or any member of the crew is the owner or part owner, they must also prove that in respect of any period in that benefit week when they were not working as a share fisherman, the fishing boat did not put to sea with a view to fishing for one of the reasons specified in reg.71(3)(a) to (c) or that "any other good cause necessitated abstention from fishing" (reg.71(3)(d)). Hours of engagement in work as a share fisherman are not to be counted "in determining the number of hours in which a person is engaged in remunerative work for the purposes of establishing entitlement to a jobseeker's allowance" (reg.72). Regulation 73 deals with calculation of the earnings of share fishermen, effecting modifications to the wording of standard rules in these Regsulations, enabling them to be applied differently in the case of share fishermen. Regulation 74 provides that the amount of JSA payable is to be determined under its provisions and not those in Part 8, above. For this purpose it also affords a different definition of "benefit week" (reg.74(3)).

### Interpretation

1.141    **67.** In this Part—

"fishing boat" means a fishing vessel as defined by section 313 of the Merchant Shipping Act 1995;

"owner" has the same meaning as in the Social Security (Mariners' Benefits) Regulations 1975;

"share fisherman" means any person who—

   (a) is ordinarily employed in the fishing industry otherwise than under a contract of service, as a master or member of the crew of any fishing boat manned by more than one person, and is remunerated in respect of that employment in whole or in part by a share of the profits or gross earnings of the fishing boat; or

   (b) has ordinarily been so employed, but who by reason of age or infirmity permanently ceases to be so employed and becomes ordinarily engaged in employment ashore in Great Britain, otherwise than under a contract of service, making or mending any gear relevant to a fishing boat or performing other services ancillary to or in connection with that boat and is remunerated in respect of that employment in whole or in part by a share of the profits or gross earnings of that boat and has not ceased to be ordinarily engaged in such employment.

### Special provisions in respect of share fishermen

1.142    **68.** The Act and above provisions of these Regulations have effect in relation to share fishermen subject to the provisions of this Part.

### Modifications of section 2

1.143    **69.**—(1) Section 2 of the Act (the contribution-based conditions) applies to share fishermen with the modifications set out in the following provisions of this regulation.

(2) After the words "Class 1 contributions" in each place where they appear there is to be inserted the words "or special Class 2 contributions".

(3) In subsection (4) after the definition of "the relevant benefit year" there is to be inserted the following definition—

"'special Class 2 contributions' means any Class 2 contributions paid by a share fisherman at the rate applicable to share fishermen in accordance with regulation 125(c) of the Social Security (Contributions) Regulations 2001.".

### Modification of section 35

**70.**—(1) The definition of "trade dispute" in section 35(1) of the Act    1.144
(interpretation) applies to share fishermen with the effect that the owner
(or managing owner if there is more than one owner) of a fishing boat is
to be treated as the employer of any share fisherman (other than themselves) ordinarily employed as master or member of the crew of, or
making or mending any gear relevant to, or performing other services
ancillary to or in connection with, that fishing boat, and any such share
fisherman is to be treated as their employee.

(2) In this regulation, "managing owner" means that the owner of any
ship or vessel who, where there is more than one such owner, is responsible for the control and management of that ship or vessel.

### Additional conditions for payment of a jobseeker's allowance

**71.**—(1) It is to be an additional condition with respect to the payment    1.145
of a jobseeker's allowance to a share fisherman in respect of any benefit
week, that in respect of any period in that benefit week when they have
not worked as a share fisherman, they prove that they have not neglected
to avail themselves of a reasonable opportunity of employment as a share
fisherman.

(2) The following provisions apply for the purposes of the application
of paragraph (1)—
  (a)  work as a share fisherman within the meaning of paragraph (1)
       includes any of the work specified in sub-paragraph (b) which—
       (i)  at the time of its performance is necessary for the safety or
            reasonable efficiency of the fishing boat, or is likely to
            become so necessary in the near future; and
       (ii) it is the duty of the share fisherman (whether by agreement,
            custom, practice or otherwise) to undertake without remu-
            neration other than by way of a share in the profits or gross
            earnings of the fishing boat, but any other work done to the
            fishing boat or its nets or gear is to be disregarded; and
  (b)  the work so included by sub-paragraph (a) is any work done to the
       fishing boat or its nets or gear by way of repairs (including running
       repairs) or maintenance, or in connection with the laying up of the
       boat and its nets and gear at the end of a fishing season or their
       preparation for a season's fishing.

(3) It is to be a further additional condition with respect to the
payment of a jobseeker's allowance to a share fisherman in respect of any
benefit week that, where they are master or a member of the crew of a
fishing boat of which either the master or any member of the crew is the
owner or part owner, they must also prove that in respect of any period
in that benefit week when they were not working as a share fisherman,
the fishing boat did not put to sea with a view to fishing, for the reason
that—
  (a)  on account of the state of the weather the fishing boat could not
       reasonably have put to sea with a view to fishing;
  (b)  the fishing boat was undergoing repairs or maintenance, not being
       repairs or maintenance to which paragraph (2) relates;

(c) there was an absence of fish from any waters in which the fishing boat could reasonably be expected to operate; or

(d) any other good cause necessitated abstention from fishing.

(4) In this regulation, "benefit week" in relation to a jobseeker's allowance has the meaning it has in regulation 74 (share fisherman: amount payable).

## Remunerative work

1.146     **72.** In determining the number of hours in which a person is engaged in remunerative work for the purposes of establishing entitlement to a jobseeker's allowance, no account is to be taken of any hours in which a person is engaged in work as a share fisherman.

## Calculation of earnings

1.147     **73.**—(1) In the calculation of earnings derived from work as a share fisherman for the purposes of establishing entitlement to a jobseeker's allowance, the provisions of Part 7 apply subject to the following provisions of this regulation.

(2) Regulation 55 (calculation of earnings of self-employed earners) is to be omitted.

(3) For regulation 61 (calculation of net profit of self-employed earners) there is to be substituted the following regulation—

### "Calculation of earnings derived from work as a share fisherman

61.—(1) Earnings derived from work as a share fisherman within the meaning of regulation 67 (interpretation) are to be calculated in accordance with the following provisions of this regulation.

(2) Any such earnings are to be treated as paid in the benefit week in respect of which they are earned.

(3) The amount of earnings to be taken into account in respect of any benefit week are to be the claimant's share of the net profit derived from the work as a share fisherman less—

(a) an amount in respect of income tax and national insurance contributions under the Benefits Act calculated in accordance with regulation 62 (deduction of tax and contributions for self-employed earners); and

(b) half of any premium paid in respect of a personal pension scheme.

(4) Subject to paragraph (5), there is to be disregarded from a claimant's share of the weekly net profit—

(a) £20; and

(b) the amount of any earnings specified in paragraphs 4 and 10 of the Schedule to these Regulations, if applicable.

(5) Where a share fisherman has earnings from work other than work as a share fisherman, and an amount is disregarded from those earnings in accordance with paragraph 5, 6 or 7 of the Schedule—

(a) if the amount so disregarded is £20, paragraph (4)(a) does not apply;

(b) if the amount so disregarded is less than £20, the amount disregarded under paragraph (4)(a) must not exceed the difference between the amount disregarded from those other earnings and [¹£20].

(6) For the purposes of paragraph (3), the net profit is to be calculated by taking into account the earnings less, subject to paragraphs (7) to (9), any expenses relevant to that benefit week which were wholly, exclusively and necessarily incurred for the purposes of the employment.

(7) Subject to paragraph (8), no deduction is to be made under paragraph (6) in respect of—

(a) any capital expenditure;

(b) the depreciation of any capital asset;

(c) any sum employed or intended to be employed in the setting up or expansion of the employment;

(d) the repayment of capital on any loan taken out for the purposes of the employment;

(e) any expenses incurred in providing business entertainment.

(8) A deduction is to be made under paragraph (6) in respect of the repayment of capital on any loan used for—

(a) the replacement in the course of business of equipment or machinery; and

(b) the repair of an existing business asset except to the extent that any sum is payable under an insurance policy for its repair.

(9) No reduction is to be made under paragraph (6) in respect of any expenses where the Secretary of State is not satisfied that the expense has been incurred or, having regard to the nature of the expense and its amount, that it has been reasonably incurred.

(10) A deduction under paragraph (6)—

(a) must not be made in respect of any sum unless it has been incurred for the purposes of the business;

(b) must be made in respect of—

(i) the excess of any Value Added Tax paid over Value Added Tax received in the benefit week;

(ii) any expense incurred in the repair of an existing asset except to the extent that any sum is payable under an insurance policy for its repair;

(iii) any payment of interest on a loan taken out for the purposes of the employment.

(11) Notwithstanding paragraphs (1) to (10), the Secretary of State may calculate earnings or expenditure over a period other than the benefit week if the Secretary of State considers it is reasonable to do so having regard to all the facts of the case and in particular whether the earnings earned or expenditure incurred in respect of a benefit week are unusually high or low.

(12) In this regulation "benefit week" has the same meaning as in regulation 74 (share fishermen: amount payable).".

(4) In regulation 62 (deduction of tax and contributions for self-employed earners)—

(a) in paragraphs (1) and (3), for the words "regulation 61(1)(b)(i)" there is to be substituted the words "regulation 61(3)(a)";

(b) paragraphs (2) and (4) are to be omitted;

(c) in paragraph (5)(a) for the words "regulation 61(3)(a) or, as the case may be, (4)" there is to be substituted the words "regulation 61(6)";

(d) at the end of the regulation there is to be added the following paragraph—

"(6) For the purposes of paragraphs (1) and (3) the earnings to which the basic rate of tax is to be applied and the amount of personal relief deductible, the amount specified in section 11(4) of the Benefits Act, and the upper limit of profits and gains referred to in paragraph (3)(b), are to be apportioned pro rata according to the period over which the earnings are assessed in accordance with regulation 61.".

AMENDMENT

1. Social Security (Miscellaneous Amendments) (No. 2) Regulations 2013 (SI 2013/1508) reg.4(1), (4) (July 29, 2013).

## Amount payable

1.148      **74.**—(1) The amount payable to a share fisherman by way of a jobseeker's allowance is to be calculated in accordance with regulations 49 to 51 (weekly amounts of jobseeker's allowance, deductions in respect of earnings and payments by way of pensions) and this regulation, and Part 8 does not apply.

(2) Regulations 49 to 51 apply in respect of share fishermen so that the amount payable is calculated by reference to earnings earned and pension payments received in the benefit week.

(3) In this regulation "benefit week" means—

(a) in respect of the week in which the claim is made, the period of seven days beginning with the date of claim; and

(b) in respect of any subsequent week, the period of seven days beginning with the day after the last day of the previous benefit week.

PART 10

MODIFICATION OF THE ACT

## Modification of section 2 of the Act

1.149      **75.** Section 2 of the Act (the contribution-based conditions) applies with the modifications that after the words "Class 1 contributions" in each place where they appear there is to be inserted the words "or Class 2 contributions under Case G of Part 9 of the Social Security (Contributions) Regulations 2001".

GENERAL NOTE

This modifies s.2 (already modified by reg.69, above, in relation to making **1.150** count the class 2 contributions paid by share fishermen), so as to make count for JSA entitlement "Class 2 contributions under Case G of Part 9 of the Social Security (Contributions) Regulations 2001". These cover a "volunteer development worker": someone who is ordinarily resident in Great Britain or Northern Ireland (as the case may be); but employed outsider Great Britain who has been allowed to pay Class 2 contributions in respect of whom the Board has certified that it is consistent with the proper administration of the Act that, subject to the satisfaction of the conditions in para.(2), that person should be entitled to pay Class 2 contributions under reg.151.

SCHEDULE       Regulations 59(2) and 61(2)

*Sums to be disregarded in the calculation of earnings*

**1.**—(1) In the case of a claimant who has been engaged in remunerative work as an **1.151** employed earner or, had the employment been in Great Britain, would have been so engaged—

    (a) any earnings, other than items to which sub-paragraph (2) applies, paid or due to be paid from the employment which was terminated before the first day of entitlement to a jobseeker's allowance;

    (b) any earnings, other than a payment of the nature described in sub-paragraph (2)(a) or (b)(ii), paid or due to be paid from the employment which has not been terminated where the claimant is not—

        (i) engaged in remunerative work; or

        (ii) suspended from their employment.

    (2) This sub-paragraph applies to—

    (a) any payment of the nature described in—

        (i) regulation 58(1)(d); or

        (ii) section 28, 64 or 68 of the Employment Rights Act 1996 (guarantee payments, suspension from work on medical or maternity grounds); and

    (b) any award, sum or payment of the nature described in—

        (i) regulation 58(1)(f) or (h); or

        (ii) section 34 or 70 of the Employment Rights Act 1996 (guarantee payments and suspension from work: complaints to employment tribunals), including any payment made following the settlement of a complaint to an employment tribunal or of court proceedings.

**2.**—(1) In the case of a claimant to whom this paragraph applies, any earnings (other than items to which paragraph 1(2) applies) which relate to employment which ceased before the first day of entitlement to a jobseeker's allowance whether or not that employment has been terminated.

    (2) This paragraph—

    (a) applies to a claimant who has been engaged in part-time employment as an employed earner or, had the employment been in Great Britain, would have been so engaged;

    (b) does not apply to a claimant who has been suspended from their employment.

**3.** Any payment to which regulation 58(1)(f) applies—

    (a) which is due to be paid more than 52 weeks after the date of termination of the employment in respect of which the payment is made; or

    (b) which is a compensatory award within the meaning of section 118(1)(b) of the Employment Rights Act 1996 for so long as such an award remains unpaid and the employer is insolvent within the meaning of section 127 of that Act.

**4.** In the case of a claimant who has been engaged in remunerative work or part-time employment as a self-employed earner or, had the employment been in Great Britain, would have been so engaged and who has ceased to be so engaged, from the date of the cessation of their employment any earnings derived from that employment except earnings to which regulation 55(2) (royalties etc) applies.

89

**5.** In a case to which neither of paragraphs 6 and 7 applies to the claimant, £5.

**6.** £20 of the total earnings derived from one or more employments as—

[¹(a)a part-time fire-fighter employed by a fire and rescue authority under the Fire and Rescue Services Act 2004 or by the Scottish Fire and Rescue Service established under section 1A of the Fire (Scotland) Act 2005];

(b) [¹ . . . .];

(c) an auxiliary coastguard in respect of coast rescue activities;

(d) a person engaged part-time in the manning or launching of a lifeboat;

(e) a member of any territorial or reserve force prescribed in Part I of Schedule 6 to the Social Security (Contributions) Regulations 2001.

**7.** Where the claimant is engaged in one or more employments specified in paragraph 6 but their earnings derived from such employments are less than £20 in any week and they are also engaged in any other part-time employment, so much of their earnings from that other employment up to £5 as would not in aggregate with the amount of their earnings disregarded under paragraph 6 exceed £20.

**8.** Notwithstanding paragraphs 1 to 7 of this Schedule, where two or more payments of the same kind and from the same source are to be taken into account in the same benefit week, because it has not been practicable to treat the payments under regulation 56(b) (date on which earnings are treated as paid) as paid on the first day of the benefit week in which they were due to be paid, there is to be disregarded from each payment the sum that would have been disregarded if the payment had been taken into account on the date on which it was due to be paid.

**9.** Any earnings derived from employment which are payable in a country outside the United Kingdom for such period during which there is a prohibition against the transfer to the United Kingdom of those earnings.

**10.** Where a payment of earnings is made in a currency other than sterling, any banking charge or commission payable in converting that payment into sterling.

**11.** Any earnings which are due to be paid before the date of claim and which would otherwise fall to be taken into account in the same benefit week as a payment of the same kind and from the same source.

**12.**—(1) Where by reason of earnings to which sub-paragraph (2) applies (in aggregate with the claimant's other earnings (if any) calculated in accordance with this Part) the claimant would (apart from this paragraph) have a personal rate of less than 10 pence, the amount of such earnings but only to the extent that that amount exceeds the claimant's personal rate less 10 pence.

(2) This sub-paragraph applies to earnings, in so far as they exceed the amount disregarded under paragraph 6, derived by the claimant from employment as a member of any territorial or reserve force prescribed in Part 1 of Schedule 6 to the Social Security (Contributions) Regulations 2001 in respect of a period of annual continuous training for a maximum of 15 days in any calendar year.

(3) In sub-paragraph (1), "personal rate" means the rate for the claimant calculated as specified in section 4(1) of the Act.

**13.** In this Schedule "part-time employment" means employment in which the person is not to be treated as engaged in remunerative work under regulation 43 or 44 (persons treated as engaged, or not engaged, in remunerative work).

AMENDMENT

1. Social Security (Miscellaneous Amendments) (No. 2) Regulations 2013 (SI 2013/1508) reg.4(1), (5) (July 29, 2013).

DEFINITIONS

"benefit week"—see reg.2(2).

"claimant"—see reg.2(2).

"part-time employment"—see para.13.

"personal rate"—see para.12(3).

GENERAL NOTE

This sets out—for the purposes of regs 59 and 62, dealing respectively with the 1.152 calculation of earnings of employed earners and self-employed earners—a range of payments which are wholly or to a degree to be disregarded in calculating those earnings.

# The Employment and Support Allowance Regulations 2013

(SI 2013/379) (*as amended*)

ARRANGEMENT OF REGULATIONS

PART 1

*General*

PART 2

*The assessment phase*

PART 3

*Conditions of entitlement*

PART 4

*Limited Capability for Work*

PART 5

*Limited Capability for Work-related Activity*

PART 6

*Effect of work on entitlement to an Employment and Support Allowance*

PART 7

*Claimant responsibilities*

PART 8

*Sanctions*

PART 9

*Amounts of Allowance*

PART 10

*Income and earnings*

PART 11

*Supplementary provisions*

PART 12

*Disqualification*

PART 13

*Periods of less than a week*

The Secretary of State for Work and Pensions makes the following Regulations in exercise of the powers conferred by sections 2(1)(a) and (c) and (4)(a) and (c), 3(1)(c), (2)(b) and (d) and (3), 8(1) to (3), (4)(a) and (b), (5) and (6), 9(1) to (3) and (4)(a) and (b), 11A(5), 11B(2) and (3), 11D(2)(d), 11E(1), 11H(5) and (6), 11J(3), (4) and (8), 17(1), (2) and (3)(a) and (b), 18(1), (2) and (4), 20(2)to (7), 24(1), (2)(b) and (3) and 25(2) to (5) of, and paragraphs 1(3) and (4), 3(2) and 4(1)(a) and (c), (3) and (4) of Schedule 1 and paragraphs 1 to 4A, 5, 6, 9 and 10 of Schedule 2 to, the Welfare Reform Act 2007, sections 5(1A), 189(4) to (6) and 191 of the Social Security Administration Act 1992, section 21(1)(a) of the Social Security Act 1998 and paragraphs 2(3) and 3 of Schedule 5 to the Welfare Reform Act 2012.

The Social Security Advisory Committee has agreed that the proposals in respect of these Regulations should not be referred to it.

A draft of these Regulations has been laid before Parliament in accordance with section 26(1) of the Welfare Reform Act 2007 and approved by a resolution of each House of Parliament.

GENERAL NOTE

1.154     These regulations govern eligibility for "new style ESA". This is a wholly contribution-based benefit for those who have a health condition or disability which limits their capability for work. Those entitled to it whose "resources" are insufficient to meet "needs" will have to seek a top-up through Universal Credit (UC). In the longer term, when the UC scheme is fully rolled out the result will be a simpler system, since there will then be only one income-related benefit—UC—for persons of working age, rather than the current system of several income-related benefits each for different categories of claimant and administered by different authorities: IS, IBJSA and IRESA (by DWP/JobCentres), tax credits (by HMRC) and housing benefit (by local authorities). But until the UC scheme is fully rolled out, UC is an additional benefit rather than a benefit replacing all those other income-related benefits. The roll-out of UC is slow and complicated. As the commentators to Vol.V in this series, *Universal Credit*, put it:

> "it is inherent in the design of UC that it overlaps with each of the older benefits it is eventually intended to replace. That overlap means that, in addition to the complication of the old and new systems existing side-by-side (including having two different and mutually exclusive benefits both called JSA and two called ESA), it is also necessary to have legislation defining which set of rules applies to any particular claimant at any given time. That legislation is to be found first, in the Universal Credit (Transitional Provisions) Regulations ("the Transitional Provisions Regulations") which create a "Pathfinder Group" of claimants who, depending on where they live, may have to claim UC rather than one of the "legacy" benefits and, second, in a series of Commencement Orders that, even by the high standards set by past social security legislation, are bewilderingly complex."

The areas in which, and within them, the cases to which, "new style ESA" and these Regulations apply—the "Pathfinder" pilots—is set by reg.1(2), (3), read with the those Transitional Provisions Regulations and the various Welfare Reform Act 2012 Commencement Orders noted in the annotation to reg.1(2), (3), and the subject of fuller commentary in Part 4 of the new Vol.V, *Universal Credit*.

In respect of areas and cases in relation to which IRESA has yet to be abolished (i.e. those outside the 'Pathfinder' pilots), entitlement to "old style ESA" (either or both CESA and IRESA) remain governed by the WRA 2007 and the ESA Regulations 2008 as set out in Vol.I (2013/14 edn) and amended by the provisions (other than "Pathfinder" amendments) noted in the pertinent updates in Part II of this Supplement.

These 2013 Regulations are both a consolidation of and a rewrite of the already existing ESA Regulations 2008 as amended to correct some unintended textual errors and to provide greater alignment with these 2013 Regulations (see pertinent updates (not "Pathfinder" amendments) in Part II of this Supplement) and so as somewhat to align a "new style ESA" claimant commitments and sanctions' regime with those applicable to new style JSA and UC.

Most of the key rules on "new style ESA" remain the same in terms of effect as those applicable to CESA in the ESA Regulations 2008, but the DWP considers that in drawing up the ESA Regulations 2013 "opportunities have been taken to make simplifications and improvements". In addition, the regulations specific to IRESA are not carried into the 2013 Regulations. This means that material may be differently distributed within the same-numbered regulation in these ESA Regulations 2013 as compared to the ESA Regulations 2008, or be found in a differently numbered one. In addition, in the ESA Regulations 2013, there is a regime of claimant commitments and sanctions analogous in some respects to those applicable to UC and "new style JSA".

PART 1

*General*

## Citation, commencement and application

1.155     **1.**—(1) These Regulations may be cited as the Employment and Support Allowance Regulations 2013.

(2) They come into force on 29th April 2013.

(3) They apply in relation to a particular case on any day on which section 33(1)(b) of the Welfare Reform Act 2012 (abolition of income-related employment and support allowance) is in force and applies in relation to that case.

GENERAL NOTE

*Paras 2, 3.*

1.156     Although these regulations entered into force on April 29, 2013, they do not as yet apply throughout the country. They will only do so once there has been a full-rolling out of Universal Credit and consequent total abolition of IRESA.

Instead, they are applicable only in those "Pathfinder" areas where IRESA has been abolished and only as regards certain types of case ("in a particular case . . . on any day on which section 33(1)(b) of the Welfare Reform Act 2012 (abolition of income-related employment and support allowance) is in force and applies in relation to that case"). Areas and types of case will expand as the system moves to full roll out of Universal Credit and abolition of CBJSA and IRESA in 2017. See further, Part 1 of Vol.V, *Universal Credit*. As at January 1, 2014, areas and types of case were those covered by provisions in each of the Welfare Reform Act 2012 Commencement Nos 9, 11, 13 and 14 Orders (subject to fuller commentary and analysis in Part 4 of Vol.V in this series *Universal Credit*).

As regards "Pathfinder" postcode areas of application, the "relevant districts" are set out in each Commencement Order. Briefly, Commencement No. 9 Order covered four postcode districts in Manchester, Oldham and Stockport as from April 29, 2013; Commencement No. 11 Order embraced certain postcodes in Wigan ("the No. 2 relevant districts") and Manchester, Oldham and Warrington ("the No. 3 relevant districts") as from July 1, 2013; the Commencement No. 13 Order brought in certain postcodes in West London, Manchester and Wigan ("the No. 4 relevant districts") as from October 28, 2013; and the Commencement No. 14 Order embraced certain postcodes in Rugby, Inverness and Perth ("the No. 5 relevant districts") as from November 25, 2013.

As regards cases to which "new style ESA" applies, this is from each of the dates noted above governed centrally by art.4 of each Commencement Order (annotated more fully in Part 4 of Vol.V, *Universal Credit*) covering six classes of case. Principally—there are exceptions with regard to newly formed couples and couples recently split up—a key requisite is that the claimant meets the criteria for being in the "Pathfinder Group". These are set out in regs 5–12 of the Universal Credit (Transitional) Regulations 2013 (SI 2013/000) (see Part 4 of Vol.V, *Universal Credit*), reading them as if any reference to making a claim for universal credit included a reference to making a claim for an employment and support allowance. To date, however, these ESA Regulations 2013 remain of limited applicability even to Pathfinder cases in the "relevant areas" since, as the commentators to Vol.V, *Universal Credit* note:

"fitness for work is an essential requirement for membership of the Pathfinder Group. However, perhaps counter-intuitively, fitness for work is not judged by whether or not someone has limited capability for work for the purposes of ESA. For the purposes of universal credit, the following are regarded as being unfit for work (and so ineligible for the Pathfinder Group): (a) those with a doctor's note (unless they have since actually scored less than 15 points); (b) those who have applied for a doctor's note; (c) those who have self-declared themselves as unfit for work (see also reg.4(2)); and (d) those who are subject to a current ruling that they have limited capability for work. The intention, it seems, is to keep out of the Pathfinder Group anyone with as much as a hint of incapacity, whether or not they have scored 15 points under the work capability assessment."

However, once claimants have gone on to UC or new style JSA, if they thereafter become incapable for work, their claim will be for "new style ESA" (alone or topped up by UC) rather than for "old style ESA" (CESA topped up by IRESA). This is because the general principle (colloquially known as the "lobster pot" principle—see Part 1 of Vol.V, *Universal Credit*) is that once in the new scheme one remains in it, even if one no longer lives in a relevant district or one's circumstances change so as to be incompatible with membership of the Pathfinder Group. One cannot go back to the old style benefits because they cease to exist once one makes a valid claim for, or is actually awarded, UC, new style JSA or new style ESA.

While these ESA Regulations 2013 will eventually apply to all new claimants in relation to limited capability for work, it would seem that existing "old style ESA" claimants will not be migrated until at least 2017.

## Interpretation

**2.**—In these Regulations—                                                          1.157
"the Act" means the Welfare Reform Act 2007;
"advanced education" means education for the purposes of—

(a) a course in preparation for a degree, a diploma of higher education, a higher national diploma, a higher national diploma of the Business and Technology Education Council or the Scottish Qualifications Authority, or a teaching qualification; or

(b) any other course which is of a standard above ordinary national diploma, a diploma of the Business and Technology Education Council or a higher or advanced higher national certificate of the Scottish Qualifications Authority or a general certificate of education (advanced level);

"benefit week" means a period of seven days ending on such day as the Secretary of State may direct, but for the purposes of calculating any payment of income "benefit week" means the period of seven days ending on—

(a) the day before the first day of the first period of seven days which—

(i) ends on such day as the Secretary of State may direct; and

(ii) follows the date of claim for an employment and support allowance; or

(b) the last day on which an employment and support allowance is paid if it is in payment for less than a week;

"carer's allowance" means an allowance under section 70 of the Contributions and Benefits Act;

"child" means a person under the age of 16;

"Claims and Payments Regulations 2013" means the Universal Credit, Personal Independence Payment, Jobseeker's Allowance and Employment and Support Allowance (Claims and Payments) Regulations 2013;

"close relative" means a parent, parent-in-law, son, son-in-law, daughter, daughter-in-law, step-parent, step-son, step-daughter, brother, sister or, if any of the preceding persons is one member of a couple, the other member of that couple;

"confinement" has the meaning given to it by section 171(1) of the Contributions and Benefits Act;

"councillor" means—

    (a) in relation to England and Wales, a member of a London borough council, a county council, a county borough council, a district council, a parish or community council, the Common Council of the City of London or the Council of the Isles of Scilly; and

    (b) in relation to Scotland, a member of a council constituted under section 2 of the Local Government etc. (Scotland) Act 1994;

"councillor's allowance" means—

    (a) in England, an allowance under or by virtue of—

        (i) section 173 or 177 of the Local Government Act 1972; or

        (ii) a scheme made by virtue of section 18 of the Local Government and Housing Act 1989,

other than such an allowance as is mentioned in section 173(4) of the Local Government Act 1972;

    (b) in Wales, an allowance under or by virtue of a scheme made by virtue of section 18 of the Local Government and Housing Act 1989 other than such an allowance as is mentioned in section 173(4) of the Local Government Act 1972; or

    (c) in Scotland, an allowance or remuneration under or by virtue of—

        (i) a scheme made by virtue of section 18 of the Local Government and Housing Act 1989; or

        (ii) section 11 of the Local Governance (Scotland) Act 2004;

"couple" means—

    (a) a man and woman who are married to each other and are members of the same household;

    (b) a man and woman who are not married to each other but are living together as husband and wife;

    (c) two people of the same sex who are civil partners of each other and are members of the same household; or

(d) two people of the same sex who are not civil partners of each other but are living together as if they were civil partners,

and for the purposes of paragraph (d), two people of the same sex are to be regarded as living together as if they were civil partners only if they would be regarded as living together as husband and wife were they instead two people of the opposite sex;

"Decisions and Appeals Regulations 1999" means the Social Security and Child Support (Decisions and Appeals) Regulations 1999;

"Decisions and Appeals Regulations 2013" means the Universal Credit, Personal Independence Payment, Jobseeker's Allowance and Employment and Support Allowance (Decisions and Appeals) Regulations 2013;

"descriptor" means, in relation to an activity specified in column (1) of Schedule 2, a descriptor in column (2) of that Schedule which describes a person's ability to perform that activity;

"employed earner" is to be construed in accordance with section 2(1)(a) of the Contributions and Benefits Act;

"employment" includes any trade, business, profession, office or vocation; and "employed" has a corresponding meaning;

"enactment" includes an enactment comprised in, or in an instrument made under, an Act of the Scottish Parliament or the National Assembly of Wales;

"family" means—

    (a) a couple;

    (b) a couple and a member of the same household for whom one of them is or both are responsible and who is a child or a young person;

    (c) a person who is not a member of a couple and a member of the same household for whom that person is responsible and who is a child or a young person;

"first contribution condition" means the condition set out in paragraph 1(1) of Schedule 1 to the Act;

"First-tier Tribunal" has the meaning given by section 3(1) of the Tribunals, Courts and Enforcement Act 2007;

"health care professional" means—

    (a) a registered medical practitioner;

    (b) a registered nurse; or

    (c) an occupational therapist or physiotherapist registered with a regulatory body established by an Order in Council under section 60 of the Health Act 1999;

"Health Service Act" means the National Health Service Act 2006;

"Health Service (Wales) Act" means the National Health Service (Wales) Act 2006;

"Income Support Regulations" means the Income Support (General) Regulations 1987;

"limited capability for work assessment" means the assessment described in regulation 15(2) and in Schedule 2;

"Medical Evidence Regulations" means the Social Security (Medical Evidence) Regulations 1976;

"medical treatment" means medical, surgical or rehabilitative treatment (including any course or diet or other regimen), and references to a person receiving or submitting to medical treatment are to be construed accordingly;

"member of Her Majesty's forces" means a person, other than one mentioned in Part 2 of Schedule 1, who is—

(a) over 16 years of age; and

(b) a member of an establishment or organisation specified in Part 1 of that Schedule,

but does not include any such person while absent on desertion;

"National Minimum Wage" means the rate of the national minimum wage specified in regulation 11 of the National Minimum Wage Regulations 1999 (rate of the national minimum wage);

"net earnings" means such earnings as are calculated in accordance with regulation 81;

"occupational pension scheme" has the meaning given by section 1 of the Pension Schemes Act 1993;

"part-time employment" means, if the claimant were entitled to income support, employment in which the claimant is not to be treated as engaged in remunerative work under regulation 5 or 6(1) and (4) of the Income Support Regulations (persons treated, or not treated, as engaged in remunerative work);

"partner" means—

(a) where a claimant is a member of a couple, the other member of that couple; or

(b) where a claimant is a husband or wife by virtue of a polygamous marriage, the other party to the marriage or any spouse additional to either party to the marriage;

"payment" includes a part of a payment;

"pay period" means the period in respect of which a claimant is, or expects to be, normally paid by the claimant's employer, being a week, a fortnight, four weeks, a month or other shorter or longer period as the case may be;

"period of limited capability for work" means, except in regulation 3(2), a period throughout which a person has, or is treated as having, limited capability for work under these Regulations, and does not include a period which is outside the prescribed time for claiming as specified in regulation 28 of the Claims and Payments Regulations 2013;

"permanent health insurance payment" means any periodical payment arranged by an employer under an insurance policy providing benefits in connection with physical or mental illness or disability, in relation to a former employee on the termination of that person's employment;

"personal pension scheme" means—

(a) a personal pension scheme as defined by section 1 of the Pension Schemes Act 1993;

(b) an annuity contract, trust scheme or substituted contract which is treated as having become a registered pension scheme by virtue of paragraph 1(1)(f) of Schedule 36 to the Finance Act 2004;

(c) a personal pension scheme which is treated as having become a registered pension scheme by virtue of paragraph 1(1)(g) of Schedule 36 to the Finance Act 2004;

"polygamous marriage" means any marriage entered into under a law which permits polygamy where—

(a) either party has for the time being any spouse additional to the other party; and

(b) the claimant, the other party to the marriage and the additional spouse are members of the same household;

"qualifying young person" has the meaning given by section 142 of the Contributions and Benefits Act (child and qualifying young person);

"relative" means close relative, grand-parent, grand-child, uncle, aunt, nephew or niece;

"second contribution condition" means the condition set out in paragraph 2(1) of Schedule 1 to the Act;

"self-employed earner" is to be construed in accordance with section 2(1)(b) of the Contributions and Benefits Act;

"state pension credit" means a state pension credit under the State Pension Credit Act 2002;

"Tax Credits Act" means the Tax Credits Act 2002;

"terminally ill", in relation to a claimant, means the claimant is suffering from a progressive disease and death in consequence of that disease can reasonably be expected within six months;

"training" means—

(a) training in pursuance of arrangements made under section 2(1) of the Employment and Training Act 1973 or section 2(3) of the Enterprise and New Towns (Scotland) Act 1990; or

(b) any training received on a course which a person attends for 16 hours or more a week, the primary purpose of which is the teaching of occupational or vocational skills;

"training allowance" means an allowance (whether by way of periodical grants or otherwise) payable—

(a) out of public funds by a Government department or by or on behalf of the Secretary of State, Skills Development Scotland, Scottish Enterprise, Highlands and Islands Enterprise, the Chief Executive of Skills Funding or the Welsh Ministers;

(b) to a person for that person's maintenance or in respect of a member of that person's family; and

(c) for the period, or part of the period, during which the person is following a course of training or instruction provided by, or in pursuance of arrangements made with, that department or approved by that department in relation to that person or provided or approved by or on behalf of the Secretary of State, Skills Development Scotland, Scottish

Enterprise, Highlands and Islands Enterprise, or the Welsh Ministers,

but does not include an allowance paid by any Government department to or in respect of a person by reason of the fact that that person is following a course of full-time education, other than under arrangements made under section 2 of the Employment and Training Act 1973 or section 2 of the Enterprise and New Towns (Scotland) Act 1990, or is training as a teacher;

"voluntary organisation" means a body, other than a public or local authority, the activities of which are carried on otherwise than for profit;

"week" means a period of seven days except in relation to regulation 22;

"working tax credit" means a working tax credit under section 10 of the Tax Credits Act;

"young person" is a person who, except where section 6 of the Children (Leaving Care) Act 2000 (exclusion from benefits) applies, falls within the definition of qualifying young person in section 142 of the Contributions and Benefits Act (child and qualifying young person).

### Further interpretation

1.158     **3.**—(1) In these Regulations, any reference to the claimant's family is to be construed as if it included in relation to a polygamous marriage a reference to any partner and any child or young person who is a member of the claimant's household.

(2) For the purposes of paragraph 4 of Schedule 1 to the Act (condition relating to youth),

"period of limited capability for work" means a period throughout which a person has, or is treated as having, limited capability for work.

(3) For the purposes of paragraph 5 of Schedule 1 to the Act, "week" means a period of seven days.

DEFINITIONS

"child"—see reg.2.
"partner"—see reg.2.
"period of limited capability for work"—see para.(2).
"week"—see para.(3).
"young person"—see reg.2.

### Rounding of fractions

1.159     **4.**—For the purposes of these Regulations—

(a) where any calculation under these Regulations results in a fraction of a penny, that fraction is, if it would be to the claimant's advantage, to be treated as a penny, but otherwise it must be disregarded;

(b) where an employment and support allowance is awarded for a period which is not a complete benefit week and the applicable amount in respect of the period results in an amount which includes a fraction of a penny, that fraction is to be treated as a penny.

DEFINITIONS

"benefit week"—see reg.2.

GENERAL NOTE

As with ESA Regulations 2008 reg.3, fractions are always rounded in favour of   **1.160**
the claimant.


PART 2


THE ASSESSMENT PHASE


## The end of the assessment phase

**5.**—(1) Subject to paragraphs (2) and (3) and regulation 6, the assess-   **1.161**
ment phase in relation to a claimant ends on the last day of a period of 13 weeks beginning on the first day of the assessment phase as determined under section 24(2)(a) of the Act.

(2) Where paragraph (3) applies, the assessment phase is to end when it is determined whether the claimant has limited capability for work.

(3) This paragraph applies where, at the end of the 13 week period referred to in paragraph (1)—

(a) the claimant has not been assessed in accordance with a limited capability for work assessment; and

(b) the claimant has not been treated as having limited capability for work in accordance with regulation 16, 21, 22 or 25.

DEFINITIONS

"the assessment phase"—see WRA 2007, s.24(2).
"claimant"—see WRA 2007, s.24(1).
"limited capability for work"—see WRA 2007, s.1(4).
"limited capability for work assessment"—see reg.2(1).
"week"—see reg.2(1).

GENERAL NOTE

This has the same effect as ESA Regulations 2008 reg.4 (as amended by the   **1.162**
updates in Part II of this Supplement). In para.(3)(b), the renumbered regulations compare with equivalent ones in the ESA Regulations 2008 as follows:

| 2013 Regs | 2008 Regs | Coverage |
|:---:|:---:|:---:|
| 16 | 20 | Certain claimants to be treated as having limited capability for work |
| 21 | 25 | Hospital patients |
| 22 | 26 | Claimants receiving certain treatment |
| 25 | 29 | Exceptional circumstances |

There is no equivalent in the ESA Regulations 2013 of ESA Regulations reg.33(2) which dealt with ability to treat as having limited capability with respect only to IRESA, a benefit abolished in the cases and areas in which these 2013 Regulations apply.

### The assessment phase—previous claimants

1.163    **6.**—(1) Where the circumstances in paragraph (2) apply in relation to a claimant, the assessment phase—

(a) begins on the first day of the period for which the claimant was previously entitled to an employment and support allowance; and

(b) subject to paragraphs (3), (4) and (5), ends on the day when the sum of the period for which the claimant was previously entitled to an employment and support allowance and the period for which the claimant is currently entitled to such an allowance is 13 weeks.

(2) The circumstances are that—

(a) all of the following apply—

(i) the claimant's current period of limited capability for work is to be treated as a continuation of an earlier period of limited capability for work under regulation 86;

(ii) the claimant was entitled to an employment and support allowance in the earlier period of limited capability for work;

(iii) the assessment phase had not ended in the previous period for which the claimant was entitled to an employment and support allowance; and

(iv) the period for which the claimant was previously entitled was no more than 13 weeks;

(b) all of the following apply—

(i) the claimant's current period of limited capability for work is to be treated as a continuation of an earlier period of limited capability for work under regulation 86;

(ii) the claimant was entitled to an employment and support allowance in the earlier period of limited capability for work;

(iii) the previous period of limited capability for work was terminated by virtue of a determination that the claimant did not have limited capability for work;

(iv) the period for which the claimant was previously entitled was no more than 13 weeks; and

(v) a determination is made in relation to the current period of limited capability for work that the claimant has or is treated, other than under regulation 26, as having limited capability for work; or

(c) all of the following apply—

(i) the claimant's current period of limited capability for work is to be treated as a continuation of an earlier period of limited capability for work under regulation 86;

(ii) the claimant was entitled to an employment and support allowance in the earlier period of limited capability for work;

(iii) in relation to the previous award of an employment and support allowance, a determination was made that the claimant had limited capability for work or was treated, other than under regulation 26, as having limited capability for work; and

(iv) the period for which the claimant was previously entitled was no more than 13 weeks.

(3) Where paragraph (4) applies, the assessment phase is to end when it is determined whether the claimant has limited capability for work.

(4) This paragraph applies where, on the day referred to in paragraph (1)(b)—

(a) the claimant has not been assessed in accordance with a limited capability for work assessment; and

(b) the claimant has not been treated as having limited capability for work in accordance with regulation 16, 21, 22 or 25.

(5) Where a person has made and is pursuing an appeal against a decision of the Secretary of State that embodies a determination that the claimant does not have limited capability for work—

(a) paragraphs (3) and (4) do not apply; and

(b) paragraph (1) does not apply to any period of limited capability for work to which regulation 87(2) applies until a determination of limited capability for work has been made following the determination of the appeal by the First-tier Tribunal.

DEFINITIONS

"the assessment phase"—see WRA 2007, s.24(2).
"claimant"—see WRA 2007, s.24(1).
"limited capability for work"—see WRA 2007, s.1(4).
"limited capability for work assessment"—see reg.2(1).
"week"—see reg.2(1).

GENERAL NOTE

This is the equivalent of ESA Regulations 2008 reg.5. On the 2008 equivalents **1.164** of the renumbered regs in para.(4)(b), see the Table in the annotations to reg.6, above. Regulation 86 referred to in para.(2)(a)(i), (b)(i) and (c)(i) is the equivalent of reg.145(1) of the ESA Regulations 2008. Regulation 26 referred to in para.(2)(b)(v) is the equivalent of reg.30 of the ESA Regulations 2008. Regulation 87(2) in para.(5)(b) corresponds to reg.147A(2) of the ESA Regulations 2008.

### Circumstances where the condition that the assessment phase has ended before entitlement to the support component or the work-related activity component arises does not apply

1.165  **7.**—(1) Subject to paragraph (4), section 2(2)(a) and (3)(a) of the Act does not apply where—

(a) a claimant is terminally ill and has either—

   (i) made a claim expressly on the ground of being terminally ill; or

   (ii) made an application for supersession or revision in accordance with the Decisions and Appeals Regulations 1999 or the Decisions and Appeals Regulations 2013 which contains an express statement that the claimant is terminally ill;

(b) the case is a relevant linked case;

(c) the case is one where—

   (i) the claimant's entitlement to an employment and support allowance commences within 12 weeks of the claimant's entitlement to income support coming to an end;

   (ii) in relation to that entitlement to income support, immediately before it ended, the claimant's applicable amount included the disability premium by virtue of their satisfying the conditions in paragraphs 11 and 12 of Schedule 2 to the Income Support Regulations; and

   (iii) that entitlement to income support ended only by virtue of the coming into force, in relation to the claimant, of the Social Security (Lone Parents and Miscellaneous Amendments) Regulations 2008; or

(d) a claimant is entitled to an employment and support allowance by virtue of section 1B of the Act (further entitlement after time-limiting).

(2) For the purposes of paragraph (1)(b) a relevant linked case is a case mentioned in paragraph (3) where a period of limited capability for work is to be treated as a continuation of an earlier period of limited capability for work under regulation 86.

(3) For the purposes of paragraph (2), the cases are as follows—

(a) case 1 is where—

   (i) the claimant was entitled to an employment and support allowance (including entitlement to a component under section 2(2) or (3) of the Act) in the earlier period of limited capability for work; and

   (ii) the previous period for which the claimant was entitled to an employment and support allowance was terminated other than by virtue of a determination that the claimant did not have limited capability for work;

(b) case 2 is where—

108

(i) the claimant was entitled to an employment and support allowance in the earlier period of limited capability for work;

(ii) the previous period for which the claimant was entitled to an employment and support allowance was 13 weeks or longer;

(iii) the previous period for which the claimant was entitled to an employment and support allowance was terminated by virtue of a determination that the claimant did not have, or was treated as not having, limited capability for work; and

(iv) it is determined in relation to the current period of limited capability for work that the claimant has limited capability for work or is treated, other than under regulation 26, as having limited capability for work;

(c) case 3 is where—

(i) the claimant was entitled to an employment and support allowance in the earlier period of limited capability for work;

(ii) the previous period for which the claimant was entitled to an employment and support allowance was 13 weeks or longer;

(iii) the previous period for which the claimant was entitled to an employment and support allowance was terminated before it could be determined whether the claimant had limited capability for work or was treated, other than under regulation 26, as having limited capability for work; and

(iv) it is determined in relation to the current period of limited capability for work that the claimant has limited capability for work or is treated, other than under regulation 26, as having limited capability for work; and

(d) case 4 is where—

(i) the claimant was entitled to an employment and support allowance (including entitlement to a component under section 2(2) or (3) of the Act) in the earlier period of limited capability for work;

(ii) the previous period for which the claimant was entitled to an employment and support allowance was terminated because it was determined that the claimant did not have limited capability for work or was treated as not having limited capability for work; and

(iii) it is determined in relation to the current period of limited capability for work that the claimant has limited capability for work or is treated, other than under regulation 26, as having limited capability for work.

(4) Paragraph (1)(b) does not apply to any period of limited capability for work to which regulation 87(2) applies until the determination of limited capability for work has been made following the determination of the appeal by the First-tier Tribunal.

DEFINITIONS

"claimant"—see WRA 2007, s.24(1).
"entitled"—see WRA 2007, s.24(1).
"limited capability for work"—see WRA 2007, s.1(4).
"period of limited capability for work"—see reg.2(1).
"relevant linked case"—see paras (2)(b), (3).
"terminally ill"—see reg.2(1).
"the assessment phase"—see WRA 2007, s.24(2).

GENERAL NOTE

1.166    This is the equivalent of reg.7 of the ESA Regulations 2008. Regulation 86 referred to in para.(2) is the equivalent of reg.145(1) of the ESA Regulations 2008. Regulation 26 referred to in para.(3)(b), (c) and (d) is the equivalent of reg.30 of the ESA Regulations 2008. Regulation 87(2) in para.(4) corresponds to reg.147A(2) of the ESA Regulation 2008.

PART 3

*Conditions of Entitlement*

## Conditions relating to national insurance and relevant earnings

1.167    **8.**—(1) A claimant's relevant earnings for the purposes of paragraph 1(2)(a) of Schedule 1 to the Act (employment and support allowance: conditions relating to national insurance) are the total amount of the claimant's earnings equal to the lower earnings limit for the base tax year.

(2) For the purposes of paragraph (1), earnings which exceed the lower earnings limit are to be disregarded.

GENERAL NOTE

1.168    See reg.7A of the ESA Regulations 2008.

## Relaxation of the first contribution condition

1.169    **9.**—(1) A claimant who satisfies any of the conditions in paragraph (2) is to be taken to satisfy the first contribution condition if—
    (a) the claimant paid Class 1 or Class 2 contributions before the relevant benefit week in respect of any one tax year; and
    (b) the claimant has—
        (i) earnings equal to the lower earnings limit in that tax year on which primary Class 1 contributions have been paid or treated as paid which in total, and disregarding any earnings which exceed the lower earnings limit for that year, are not less than that limit multiplied by 26; or
        (ii) earnings factors in that tax year derived from Class 2 contributions multiplied by 26.

110

(2) The conditions referred to in paragraph (1) are that the claimant—

(a) was entitled to a carer's allowance in the last complete tax year immediately preceding the relevant benefit year;

(b) had been—

   (i) engaged in qualifying remunerative work (which has the meaning given by Part 1 of the Tax Credits Act) for a period of more than two years immediately before the first day of the period of limited capability for work; and

   (ii) entitled to working tax credit where the disability element or the severe disability element of working tax credit specified in regulation 20(1)(b) or (f) of the Working Tax Credit (Entitlement and Maximum Rate) Regulations 2002 was included inthe award;

(c) in respect of any week in any tax year preceding the relevant benefit year—

   (i) is entitled to be credited with earnings or contributions in accordance with regulation 9D of the Social Security (Credits) Regulations 1975 (credits for certain periods of imprisonment or detention in legal custody); or

   (ii) would have been so entitled had an application to the Secretary of State been made for the purpose of that regulation; or

(d) in respect of any week in the last complete tax year preceding the relevant benefit year, is entitled to be credited with earnings in accordance with regulation 9E of the Social Security (Credits) Regulations 1975 (credits for certain spouses and civil partners of members of Her Majesty's forces).

DEFINITIONS

"benefit week"—see reg.2(1).
"carer's allowance"—see reg.2(1).
"claimant"—see WRA 2007, s.24(1).
"Class 1 contributions"—see WRA 2007, s.1, Sch.1, Pt 1, para.3(1)(b).
"Class 2 contributions—see WRA 2007, s.1, Sch.1, Pt 1, para.3(1)(b).
"earnings"—see WRA 2007, s.1, Sch.1, Pt 1, para.3(1)(c).
"earnings factor"—see WRA 2007, s.1, Sch.1, Pt 1, para.3(1)(d).
"first contribution condition"—see reg.2(1); WRA 2007, Sch.1, para.1(1).
"lower earnings limit"—see WRA 2007, s.1, Sch.1, Pt 1, para.3(1)(e).
"period of limited capability for work,"—see reg.2(1).
"primary Class 1 contributions"—see WRA 2007, s.1, Sch.1, Pt 1, para.3(1)(b).
"relevant benefit year"—see WRA 2007, s.1, Sch.1, Pt 1, para.3(1)(f).
"tax year"—see WRA 2007, s.1, Sch.1, Pt 1, para.3(1)(g).
"week"—see reg.2(1).

GENERAL NOTE

See reg.8 of the ESA Regulations 2008.

1.170

## Condition relating to youth—claimants aged 20 or over but under 25

1.171     **10.**—(1) For the purposes of paragraph 4(1)(a) of Schedule 1 to the Act, a claimant who satisfies the conditions specified in paragraph (2) falls within a prescribed case.

(2) The conditions are that the claimant—

(a) registered on a course of—
    (i) full-time advanced or secondary education; or
    (ii) training,
    at least three months before attaining the age of 20; and

(b) not more than one academic term immediately after registration attended one or more such courses in respect of a period referred to in paragraph (3).

(3) The period mentioned in paragraph (2)(b) is a period which—

(a) began on or before a day at least three months before the day the claimant attained the age of 20; and

(b) ended no earlier than the beginning of the last two complete tax years before the relevant benefit year which would have applied if the claimant was entitled to an employment and support allowance having satisfied the first contribution condition and the second contribution condition.

(4) For the purposes of this regulation a claimant is to be treated as attending a course on any day on which the course is interrupted by an illness or domestic emergency.

(5) In this regulation—

"full-time" includes part-time where the person's disability prevents attendance at a full-time course;

"secondary education" means a course of education below a course of advanced education by attendance—

    (a) at an establishment recognised by the Secretary of State—
        (i) as being a university, college or school; or
        (ii) as comparable to a university, college or school;

    (b) at an establishment that is not mentioned in paragraph (a) where the Secretary of State is satisfied that the education is equivalent to that given in an establishment recognised—
        (i) as being a university, college or school; or
        (ii) as comparable to a university, college or school.

(6) A claimant is to be treated as not having limited capability for work on a day which is not, for the purposes of paragraph 4(1)(d)(ii) of Schedule 1 to the Act (period of 196 consecutive days preceding the relevant period of limited capability for work), part of a period of consecutive days of limited capability for work.

DEFINTIONS

"advanced education"—see reg.2(1).
"claimant"—see WRA 2007, s.24(1).
"first contribution condition"—see reg.2(1); WRA 2007, Sch.1, para.1(1).

"full-time"—see para.(5).
"relevant benefit year"—see WRA 2007, s.1, Sch.1, Pt 1, para.3(1)(f).
"secondary education"—see para.(5).
"second contribution condition"—see reg.2(1); WRA 2007, Sch.1,
    para.2(1).
"tax year"—see WRA 2007, s.1, Sch.1, Pt 1, para.3(1)(g).
"training"—see reg.2(1).

GENERAL NOTE

This is the same as ESA Regulations 2008 reg.9.                    1.172

## Condition relating to youth—previous claimants

**11.**—(1) Paragraph 4(1)(a) of Schedule 1 to the Act does not apply to    1.173
a claimant—
  (a) who has previously ceased to be entitled to an employment and
      support allowance to which the claimant was entitled by virtue of
      satisfying the condition set out in paragraph 4(1) of Schedule 1 to
      the Act;
  (b) whose previous entitlement had not been ended by a decision
      which embodied a determination (other than a determination in
      the circumstances applicable to a claimant under paragraph
      (2)(a)) that the claimant did not have limited capability for
      work;
  (c) in relation to whom regulation 86 (linking rules) does not
      apply;
  (d) who is aged 20 or over or, where regulation 10 would otherwise
      apply to the person, aged 25 or over; and
  (e) to whom paragraph (2) applies.
  (2) This paragraph applies to a claimant—
  (a) whose previous entitlement to an employment and support allow-
      ance ended only with a view to that person taking up employment
      or training;
  (b) whose earnings factor from an employment or series of employ-
      ments pursued in the period from the end of the previous entitle-
      ment to the beginning of the period of limited capability for work,
      was below the lower earnings limit multiplied by 25 in any of the
      last three complete tax years before the beginning of the relevant
      benefit year; and
  (c) who—
      (i) in respect of the last two complete tax years before the
          beginning of the relevant benefit year has either paid or been
          credited with earnings equivalent in each of those years to the
          year's lower earnings limit multiplied by 50, of which at least
          one such payment or credit, in the last complete tax year, was
          in respect of the disability element or severe disability ele-
          ment of working tax credit; or
      (ii) makes a claim for an employment and support allowance
          within the period of 12 weeks after the day on which the last
          employment referred to in sub-paragraph (b) ceased.

DEFINITIONS

"claimant"—see WRA 2007, s.24(1).
"earnings factor"—see WRA 2007, s.1, Sch.1, Pt 1, para.3(1)(d).
"employment"—see reg.2(1).
"limited capability for work"—see WRA 2007, s.1(4).
"lower earnings limit"—see WRA 2007, s.1, Sch.1, Pt 1, para.3(1)(e).
"period of limited capability for work"—see reg.2(1).
"relevant benefit year"—see WRA 2007, s.1, Sch.1, Pt 1, para.3(1)(f).
"tax year"—see WRA 2007, s.1, Sch.1, Pt 1, para.3(1)(g).
"training"—see reg.2(1).
"week"—see reg.2(1).
"working tax credit"—see reg.2(1).

GENERAL NOTE

1.174    This is the same as ESA Regulations 2008 reg.10. The equivalent in the 2008 Regulations of reg.86 (linking rules) referred to in para.(1) is reg.145.

## Condition relating to youth—residence or presence

1.175    **12.**—(1) The conditions prescribed for the purposes of paragraph 4(1)(c) of Schedule 1 to the Act as to residence and presence in Great Britain are that the claimant—

(a) is ordinarily resident in Great Britain;
(b) is not a person subject to immigration control within the meaning of section 115(9) of the Immigration and Asylum Act 1999 or is a person to whom paragraph (3) applies;
(c) is present in Great Britain; and
(d) has been present in Great Britain for a period of, or for periods amounting in aggregate to, not less than 26 weeks in the 52 weeks immediately preceding the relevant benefit week.

(2) For the purposes of paragraph (1), a claimant is to be treated as being resident and present in Great Britain where the claimant is absent from Great Britain by reason only of being—

(a) the spouse, civil partner, son, daughter, father, father-in-law, mother or mother-in-law of, and living with, a member of Her Majesty's forces who is abroad in that capacity;
(b) in employment prescribed for the purposes of paragraph 7(1)(c) of Schedule 2 to the Act in connection with continental shelf operations; or
(c) abroad in the capacity of being an aircraft worker or mariner.

(3) This paragraph applies where a person is—

(a) a member of a family of a national of an European Economic Area state;
(b) a person who is lawfully working in Great Britain and is a national of a State with which the European Union has concluded an agreement under Article 217 of the Treaty on the Functioning of the European Union providing, in the field of social security, for the equal treatment of workers who are nationals of the signatory State and their families;
(c) a person who is a member of a family of, and living with, a person specified in subparagraph (b); or

(d) a person who has been given leave to enter, or remain in, the United Kingdom by the Secretary of State upon an undertaking by another person or persons pursuant to the immigration rules within the meaning of the Immigration Act 1971 to be responsible for that person's maintenance and accommodation.

(4) A person is to be treated as having satisfied the residence or presence conditions in paragraph (1) throughout a period of limited capability for work where those conditions are satisfied on the first day of that period of limited capability for work.

(5) In this regulation—

"aircraft worker" means a person who is, or has been, employed under a contract of service either as a pilot, commander, navigator or other member of the crew of any aircraft, or in any other capacity on board any aircraft where—

(a) the employment in that other capacity is for the purposes of the aircraft or its crew or of any passengers or cargo or mail carried on that aircraft; and

(b) the contract is entered into in the United Kingdom with a view to its performance (in whole or in part) while the aircraft is in flight,

but does not include a person who is in employment as a member of Her Majesty's forces;

"mariner" means a person who is, or has been, in employment under a contract of service either as a master or other member of the crew of any ship or vessel, or in any other capacity on board any ship or vessel where—

(a) the employment in that other capacity is for the purposes of that ship or vessel or its crew or any passengers or cargo or mail carried by the ship or vessel; and

(b) the contract is entered into in the United Kingdom with a view to its performance (in whole or in part) while the ship or vessel is on its voyage,

but does not include a person who is in employment as a member of Her Majesty's forces.

(6) In the definition of "mariner" in paragraph (5), "passenger" means any person carried on a ship or vessel except—

(a) a person employed or engaged in any capacity on board the ship or vessel on the business of the ship or vessel; or

(b) a person on board the ship or vessel either in pursuance of an obligation to carry shipwrecked, distressed or other persons, or by reason of any circumstance that neither the master nor the owner nor the charterer (if any) could have prevented or forestalled.

DEFINITIONS

"aircraft worker"—see para.(5)).
"benefit week"—see reg.2(1).
"claimant"—see WRA 2007, s.24(1).
"continental shelf operations"—see WRA 2007, s.22, Sch.2, para.7(3).
"employment"—see reg.2(1).
"family"—see reg.2(1).

"member of Her Majesty's forces"—see reg.2(1).
"mariner"—see para.(5).
"passenger"—see para.(5).
"period of limited capability for work"—see reg.2(1).
"prescribed"—see WRA 2007, s.24(1).
"week"—see reg.2(1).

GENERAL NOTE

1.176    This is the same as ESA Regulations 2008 reg.11.

## Condition relating to youth—full-time education

1.177    **13.**—(1) For the purposes of paragraph 4(1)(b) of Schedule 1 to the Act, a claimant is to be treated as receiving full-time education for any period during which the claimant—

(a) is at least 16 years old but under the age of 19; and
(b) attends a course of education for 21 hours or more a week.

(2) For the purposes of paragraph (1)(b), in calculating the number of hours a week during which a claimant attends a course, no account is to be taken of any instruction or tuition which is, in the opinion of the Secretary of State, not suitable for persons of the same age who do not have a disability.

(3) In determining the duration of a period of full-time education under paragraph (1) any temporary interruption of that education may be disregarded.

(4) A claimant who is 19 years of age or over is not to be treated for the purposes of paragraph 4(1)(b) of Schedule 1 to the Act as receiving full-time education.

DEFINITIONS

"claimant"—see WRA 2007, s.24(1).
"week"—see reg.2(1).

GENERAL NOTE

1.178    This is exactly the same as ESA Regulations 2008 reg.12.

## Modification of the relevant benefit year

1.179    **14.**—(1) Where paragraph (2) applies, paragraph 3(1)(f) of Schedule 1 to the Act has effect as if the "relevant benefit year" were any benefit year which includes all or part of the period of limited capability for work which includes the relevant benefit week.

(2) This paragraph applies where a claimant has made a claim for employment and support allowance but does not satisfy—

(a) the first contribution condition;
(b) the second contribution condition; or
(c) either contribution condition,

but would satisfy both of those conditions if the modified definition of "relevant benefit year" provided in paragraph (1) applied.

DEFINITIONS

"claimant"—see WRA 2007, s.24(1).
"first contribution condition"—see reg.2(1); WRA 2007, s.1, Sch.1, para.1(1).
"period of limited capability for work"—see reg.2(1).
"relevant benefit year"—see para.(1).
"second contribution condition"—see reg.2(1); WRA 2007, s.1, Sch.1, para.2(1).

GENERAL NOTE

This is exactly the same as ESA Regulations 2008 reg.13.                    **1.180**

PART 4

LIMITED CAPABILITY FOR WORK

## Determination of limited capability for work

**15.**—(1) For the purposes of Part 1 of the Act, whether a claimant's    **1.181**
capability for work is limited by the claimant's physical or mental condition and, if it is, whether the limitation is such that it is not reasonable to require the claimant to work is to be determined on the basis of a limited capability for work assessment of the claimant in accordance with this Part.

(2) The limited capability for work assessment is an assessment of the extent to which a claimant who has some specific disease or bodily or mental disablement is capable of performing the activities prescribed in Schedule 2 or is incapable by reason of such disease or bodily or mental disablement of performing those activities.

(3) Subject to paragraph (6), for the purposes of Part 1 of the Act a claimant has limited capability for work if, by adding the points listed in column (3) of Schedule 2 against each descriptor listed in that Schedule which applies in the claimant's case, the claimant obtains a total score of at least—

(a) 15 points whether singly or by a combination of descriptors specified in Part 1 of that Schedule;

(b) 15 points whether singly or by a combination of descriptors specified in Part 2 of that Schedule; or

(c) 15 points by a combination of descriptors specified in Parts 1 and 2 of that Schedule.

(4) In assessing the extent of a claimant's capability to perform any activity listed in Part 1 of Schedule 2, the claimant is to be assessed as if—

(a) fitted with or wearing any prosthesis with which the claimant is normally fitted or normally wears; or, as the case may be,

(b) wearing or using any aid or appliance which is normally, or could reasonably be expected to be, worn or used.

(5) In assessing the extent of a claimant's capability to perform any activity listed in Schedule 2, it is a condition that the claimant's incapability to perform the activity arises—

    (a) in respect of any descriptor listed in Part 1 of Schedule 2, from a specific bodily disease or disablement;

    (b) in respect of any descriptor listed in Part 2 of Schedule 2, from a specific mental illness or disablement; or

    (c) in respect of any descriptor or descriptors listed in—

        (i) Part 1 of Schedule 2, as a direct result of treatment provided by a registered medical practitioner for a specific physical disease or disablement; or

        (ii) Part 2 of Schedule 2, as a direct result of treatment provided by a registered medical practitioner for a specific mental illness or disablement.

(6) Where more than one descriptor specified for an activity applies to a claimant, only the descriptor with the highest score in respect of each activity which applies is to be counted.

(7) Where a claimant—

    (a) has been determined to have limited capability for work; or

    (b) is to be treated as having limited capability for work under regulation 16, 21, 22 or 25,

the Secretary of State may, if paragraph (8) applies, determine afresh whether the claimant has or is to be treated as having limited capability for work.

(8) This paragraph applies where—

    (a) the Secretary of State wishes to determine whether there has been a relevant change of circumstances in relation to the claimant's physical or mental condition;

    (b) the Secretary of State wishes to determine whether the previous determination of limited capability for work or that the claimant is to be treated as having limited capability for work, was made in ignorance of, or was based on a mistake as to, some material fact; or

    (c) at least three months have passed since the date on which the claimant was determined to have limited capability for work or to be treated as having limited capability for work.

DEFINITIONS

"claimant"—see WRA 2007, s.24(1).
"descriptor"—see reg.2(1).
"limited capability for work"—see WRA 2007, s.1(4).
"limited capability for work assessment"—see para.(2).

GENERAL NOTE

**1.182**    This replicates ESA Regulations 2008 reg.19. In para.(7)(b), the renumbered regulations compare with equivalent ones in the ESA Regulations 2008 as follows:

| 2013 Regs | 2008 Regs | Subject Matter |
|:---:|:---:|:---:|
| 16 | 20 | Certain claimants to be treated as having limited capability for work |
| 21 | 25 | Hospital patients |
| 22 | 26 | Claimants receiving certain treatment |
| 25 | 29 | Exceptional circumstances |

There is no equivalent in the ESA Regulations 2013 of ESA Regulations 2008 reg.33(2) which dealt with ability to treat as having limited capability with respect only to IRESA, a benefit abolished in the cases and areas in which these 2013 Regulations apply.

### Certain claimants to be treated as having limited capability for work

**16.**—(1) A claimant is to be treated as having limited capability for work if—   1.183
(a) the claimant is terminally ill;
(b) the claimant is—
  (i) receiving treatment for cancer by way of chemotherapy or radiotherapy;
  (ii) likely to receive such treatment within six months after the date of the determination of capability for work; or
  (iii) recovering from such treatment,
and the Secretary of State is satisfied that the claimant should be treated as having limited capability for work;
(c) the claimant is—
  (i) excluded or abstains from work pursuant to a request or notice in writing lawfully made or given under an enactment; or
  (ii) otherwise prevented from working pursuant to an enactment,
  by reason of it being known or reasonably suspected that the claimant is infected or contaminated by, or has been in contact with a case of, a relevant infection or contamination;
(d) in the case of a pregnant woman, there is a serious risk of damage to her health or to the health of her unborn child if she does not refrain from work;
(e) in the case of a pregnant woman, she—
  (i) is within the maternity allowance period (which has the meaning it has in section 35(2) of the Contributions and Benefits Act); and
  (ii) is entitled to a maternity allowance under section 35(1) of the Contributions and Benefits Act;
(f) in the case of a pregnant woman whose expected or actual date of confinement has been certified in accordance with the Medical Evidence Regulations, on any day in the period—

119

    (i) beginning with the first date of the 6th week before the expected week of her confinement or the actual date of her confinement, whichever is earlier; and

    (ii) ending on the 14th day after the actual date of her confinement,

if she would have no entitlement to a maternity allowance or statutory maternity pay were she to make a claim in respect of that period;

(g) the claimant meets any of the descriptors at paragraph 15 or 16 of Schedule 3 in accordance with regulation 30(2), (3) and (6) where applicable; or

(h) the claimant is entitled to universal credit and it has previously been determined that the claimant has limited capability for work on the basis of an assessment under Part 5 of the Universal Credit Regulations 2013.

(2) In this regulation, "relevant infection or contamination" means—

(a) in England and Wales—

    (i) any incidence or spread of infection or contamination, within the meaning of section 45A(3) of the Public Health (Control of Disease) Act 1984 in respect of which regulations are made under Part 2A of that Act (public health protection) for the purpose of preventing, protecting against, controlling or providing a public health response to, such incidence or spread; or

    (ii) tuberculosis or any infectious disease to which regulation 9 of the Public Health (Aircraft) Regulations 1979 (powers in respect of persons leaving aircraft) applies or to which regulation 10 of the Public Health (Ships) Regulations 1979 (powers in respect of certain persons on ships) applies; and

(b) in Scotland, any—

    (i) infectious disease within the meaning of section 1(5) of the Public Health etc (Scotland) Act 2008, or exposure to an organism causing that disease; or

    (ii) contamination within the meaning of section 1(5) of that Act, or exposure to a contaminant, to which sections 56 to 58 of that Act (compensation) apply.

DEFINITIONS

"claimant"—see WRA 2007, s.24(1).
"confinement"—see reg.2(1).
"Contributions and Benefits Act"—see WRA 2007, s.65.
"limited capability for work"—see WRA 2007, s.1(4).
"maternity allowance period"—see para.(1)(e)(i).
"Medical Evidence Regulations"—see reg.2(1).
"relevant infection or contamination"—see para.(2).
"terminally ill"—see reg.2(1).
"week"—see reg.2(1).

GENERAL NOTE

This is much the same as ESA Regulations 2008 reg.20.                    1.184

## Information required for determining capability for work

**17.**—(1) Subject to paragraphs (2) and (3), the information or evi-    1.185
dence required to determine whether a claimant has limited capability
for work is—
(a) evidence of limited capability for work in accordance with the
    Medical Evidence Regulations (which prescribe the form of doc-
    tor's statement or other evidence required in each case);
(b) any information relating to a claimant's capability to perform the
    activities referred to in Schedule 2 as may be requested in the form
    of a questionnaire; and
(c) any such additional information as may be requested.
(2) Where the Secretary of State is satisfied that there is sufficient
information to determine whether a claimant has limited capability for
work without the information specified in paragraph (1)(b), that information must not be required for the purposes of making the determination.
(3) Paragraph (1) does not apply in relation to a determination
whether a claimant is to be treated as having limited capability for work
under any of regulations 16 (certain claimants to be treated as having
limited capability for work), 21 (hospital in-patients) and 22 (claimants
receiving certain treatment).

DEFINITIONS

"claimant"—see WRA 2007, s.24(1).
"limited capability for work"—see WRA 2007, s.1(4).
"Medical Evidence Regulations"—see reg.2(1).

GENERAL NOTE

This corresponds to ESA Regulations 2008 reg.21.                         1.186

## Failure to provide information in relation to limited capability for work

**18.**—(1) Where a claimant fails without good cause to comply with the   1.187
request referred to in regulation 17(1)(b), that claimant is, subject to
paragraph (2), to be treated as not having limited capability for work.
(2) Paragraph (1) does not apply unless—
(a) the claimant was sent a further request at least three weeks after
    the date of the first request; and
(b) at least one week has passed since the further request was sent.

DEFINITIONS

"claimant"—see WRA 2007, s.24(1).
"limited capability for work"—see WRA 2007, s.1(4).
"week"—see reg.2(1).

GENERAL NOTE

**1.188**      This is the same as ESA Regulations 2008 reg.22.

**Claimant may be called for a medical examination to determine whether the claimant has limited capability for work**

**1.189**      **19.**—(1) Where it falls to be determined whether a claimant has limited capability for work, that claimant may be called by or on behalf of a health care professional approved by the Secretary of State to attend for a medical examination.

(2) Subject to paragraph (3), where a claimant fails without good cause to attend for or to submit to an examination mentioned in paragraph (1), the claimant is to be treated as not having limited capability for work.

(3) Paragraph (2) does not apply unless—

   (a) written notice of the date, time and place for the examination was sent to the claimant at least seven days in advance; or

   (b) that claimant agreed to accept a shorter period of notice whether given in writing or otherwise.

DEFINITIONS

   "claimant"—see WRA 2007, s.24(1).
   "health care professional"—see reg.2(1).
   "limited capability for work"—see WRA 2007, s.1(4).

GENERAL NOTE

**1.190**      This is the same as ESA Regulations 2008 reg.23.

**Matters to be taken into account in determining good cause in relation to regulations 18 or 19**

**1.191**      **20.** The matters to be taken into account in determining whether a claimant has good cause under regulation 18 (failure to provide information in relation to limited capability for work) or 19 (failure to attend a medical examination to determine limited capability for work) include—

   (a) whether the claimant was outside Great Britain at the relevant time;

   (b) the claimant's state of health at the relevant time; and

   (c) the nature of any disability the claimant has.

DEFINITION

   "claimant"—see WRA 2007, s.24(1).

GENERAL NOTE

**1.192**      This corresponds to ESA Regulations 2008 reg.24.

**Hospital patients**

**1.193**      **21.**—(1) A claimant is to be treated as having limited capability for work on any day on which that claimant is undergoing medical or other treatment as a patient in a hospital or similar institution [¹on any day], or which is a day of recovery from that treatment.

(2) The circumstances in which a claimant is to be regarded as undergoing treatment falling within paragraph (1) include where the claimant is attending a residential programme of rehabilitation for the treatment of drug or alcohol addiction.

(3) For the purposes of this regulation, a claimant is to be regarded as undergoing treatment as a patient in a hospital or similar institution only if that claimant has been advised by a health care professional to stay [¹for a period of 24 hours or longer] following medical or other treatment.

(4) For the purposes of this regulation, "day of recovery" means a day on which a claimant is recovering from treatment as a patient in a hospital or similar institution as referred to in paragraph (1) and the Secretary of State is satisfied that the claimant should be treated as having limited capability for work on that day.

AMENDMENT

1. Social Security (Miscellaneous Amendments) (No. 2) Regulations 2013 (SI 2013/1508) reg.5(1), (2) (July 29, 2013).

DEFINITIONS

"claimant"—see WRA 2007, s.24(1).
"day of recovery"—see para.(4).
"limited capability for work"—see WRA 2007, s.1(4).
"medical treatment"—see reg.2(1).

GENERAL NOTE

This is the same as ESA Regulations 2008 reg.25.                    1.194

## Claimants receiving certain treatment

22.—(1) Subject to paragraph (2), a claimant receiving—          1.195
  (a) regular weekly treatment by way of haemodialysis for chronic renal failure;
  (b) treatment by way of plasmapheresis; or
  (c) regular weekly treatment by way of total parenteral nutrition for gross impairment of enteric function,
is to be treated as having limited capability for work during any week in which that claimant is engaged in receiving that treatment or has a day of recovery from that treatment.

(2) A claimant who receives the treatment referred to in paragraph (1) is only to be treated as having limited capability for work from the first week of treatment in which the claimant undergoes no fewer than—
  (a) two days of treatment;
  (b) two days of recovery from any of the forms of treatment listed in paragraph (1)(a) to (c); or
  (c) one day of treatment and one day of recovery from that treatment,

but the days of treatment or recovery from that treatment or both need not be consecutive.

(3) For the purpose of this regulation "day of recovery" means a day on which a claimant is recovering from any of the forms of treatment listed in paragraph (1)(a) to (c) and the Secretary of State is satisfied that the claimant should be treated as having limited capability for work on that day.

DEFINITIONS

"claimant"—see WRA 2007, s.24(1).
"day of recovery"—see para.(3).
"limited capability for work"—see WRA 2007, s.1(4).
"week"—see reg.2(1).

GENERAL NOTE

1.196    This replicates ESA Regulations 2008 reg.26.

## Claimant to be treated as having limited capability for work throughout a day

1.197    **23.** A claimant who, at the commencement of any day has, or after that develops, limited capability for work as determined in accordance with the limited capability for work assessment is to be treated as having limited capability for work on that day.

DEFINITIONS

"claimant"—see WRA 2007, s.24(1).
"limited capability for work"—see WRA 2007, s.1(4).
"limited capability for work assessment"—see reg.2(1).

GENERAL NOTE

1.198    This is identical to ESA Regulations 2008 reg.27.

## Night workers

1.199    **24.**—(1) Where a claimant works for a continuous period which extends over midnight into the following day, that claimant is to be treated as having limited capability for work on the day on which the lesser part of that period falls if that claimant had limited capability for work for the remainder of that day.

(2) Where, in relation to a period referred to in paragraph (1), the number of hours worked before and after midnight is equal—

(a) if the days in question fall at the beginning of a period of limited capability for work, the claimant is to be treated as having limited capability on the second day; and

(b) if the days in question fall at the end of a period of limited capability for work, the claimant is to be treated as having limited capability for work on the first day.

124

DEFINITIONS

"claimant"—see WRA 2007, s.24(1).
"limited capability for work"—see WRA 2007, s.1(4).
"period of limited capability for work"—see reg.2(1).

GENERAL NOTE

This replicates ESA Regulations 2008 reg.28.                          1.200

## Exceptional circumstances

**25.**—(1) A claimant who does not have limited capability for work as   1.201
determined in accordance with the limited capability for work assessment is to be treated as having limited capability for work if paragraph
(2) applies to the claimant.
  (2) Subject to paragraph (3), this paragraph applies if—
  (a)  the claimant is suffering from a life-threatening disease in relation
       to which—
        (i)  there is medical evidence that the disease is uncontrollable,
             or uncontrolled, by a recognised therapeutic procedure;
             and
       (ii)  in the case of a disease that is uncontrolled, there is a reason-
             able cause for it not to be controlled by a recognised ther-
             apeutic procedure; or
  (b)  the claimant suffers from some specific disease or bodily or mental
       disablement and, by reason of such disease or disablement, there
       would be a substantial risk to the mental or physical health of any
       person if the claimant were found not to have limited capability for
       work.
  (3) Paragraph (2)(b) does not apply where the risk could be reduced
by a significant amount by—
  (a)  reasonable adjustments being made in the claimant's workplace;
       or
  (b)  the claimant taking medication to manage the claimant's condi-
       tion where such medication has been prescribed for the claimant
       by a registered medical practitioner treating the claimant.
  (4) In this regulation "medical evidence" means—
  (a)  evidence from a health care professional approved by the Secre-
       tary of State; and
  (b)  evidence (if any) from any health care professional or a hospital or
       similar institution, or such part of such evidence as constitutes the
       most reliable evidence available in the circumstances.

DEFINITIONS

"claimant"—see WRA 2007, s.24(1).
"limited capability for work"—see WRA 2007, s.1(4).
"limited capability for work assessment"—see reg.2(1).
"medical evidence"—see para.(4).

GENERAL NOTE

This replicates ESA Regulations 2008 reg.29.                          1.202

## Conditions for treating a claimant as having limited capability for work until a determination about limited capability for work has been made

1.203    **26.**—(1) A claimant is, if the conditions set out in paragraph (2) are met, to be treated as having limited capability for work until such time as it is determined—

(a) whether or not the claimant has limited capability for work;

(b) whether or not the claimant is to be treated as having limited capability for work otherwise than in accordance with this regulation; or

(c) whether the claimant falls to be treated as not having limited capability for work in accordance with regulation 18 (failure to provide information in relation to limited capability for work) or 19 (failure to attend a medical examination to determine limited capability for work).

(2) The conditions are—

(a) that the claimant provides evidence of limited capability for work in accordance with the Medical Evidence Regulations; and

(b) that it has not, within the six months preceding the date of claim for employment and support allowance, been determined, in relation to the claimant's entitlement to any benefit, allowance or advantage which is dependent on the claimant having limited capability for work, that the claimant does not have limited capability for work or is to be treated as not having limited capability for work under regulation 18 or 19 unless paragraph (4) applies.

(3) Paragraph (2)(b) does not apply where a claimant has made and is pursuing an appeal against a decision that embodies a determination that the claimant does not have limited capability for work and that appeal has not yet been determined by the First-tier Tribunal.

(4) This paragraph applies where—

(a) the claimant is suffering from some specific disease or bodily or mental disablement from which the claimant was not suffering at the time of that determination;

(b) a disease or bodily or mental disablement from which the claimant was suffering at the time of that determination has significantly worsened; or

(c) in the case of a claimant who was treated as not having limited capability for work under regulation 18 (failure to provide information), the claimant has since provided the information requested under that regulation.

DEFINITIONS

"claimant"—see WRA 2007, s.24(1).
"limited capability for work"—see WRA 2007, s.1(4).
"Medical Evidence Regulations"—see reg.2(1).

GENERAL NOTE

1.204    This corresponds to ESA Regulations 2008 reg.30.

### Certain claimants to be treated as not having limited capability for work

**27.**—(1) A claimant who is or has been a member of Her Majesty's     1.205
forces is to be treated as not having limited capability for work on any day
which is recorded by the Secretary of State as a day of sickness absence
from duty.

(2) A claimant is to be treated as not having limited capability for work
on any day on which the claimant attends a training course in respect of
which the claimant is paid a training allowance or premium pursuant to
arrangements made under section 2 of the Employment and Training
Act 1973 or section 2(3) of the Enterprise and New Towns (Scotland)
Act 1990.

(3) Paragraph (2) is not to apply—

(a) for the purposes of any claim to an employment and support
   allowance for a period commencing after the claimant ceased
   attending the training course in question; or

(b) where any training allowance or premium paid to the claimant is
   paid for the sole purpose of travelling or meal expenses incurred or
   to be incurred under the arrangements made under section 2 of
   the Employment and Training Act 1973 or section 2(3) of the
   Enterprise and New Towns (Scotland) Act 1990.

(4) A claimant is to be treated as not having limited capability for work
where—

(a) it has previously been determined, within the six months preceding the date of claim for employment and support allowance, on
   the basis of an assessment under Part 5 of the Universal Credit
   Regulations 2013, that the claimant does not have limited capability for work; and

(b) it appears to the Secretary of State that—

   (i) the determination was not based on ignorance of, or mistake
      as to, a material fact; and

   (ii) there has been no relevant change of circumstances in rela-
      tion to the claimant's physical or mental condition since the
      determination.

DEFINITIONS

"claimant"—see WRA 2007, s.24(1).
"limited capability for work"—see WRA 2007, s.1(4).

GENERAL NOTE

This is much the same as ESA Regulations 2008 reg.32.     1.206

### Claimants to be treated as not having limited capability for work at the end of the period covered by medical evidence

**28.**—(1) Where the Secretary of State is satisfied that it is appropriate     1.207
in the circumstances of the case, a claimant may be treated as not having
limited capability for work if—

(a) the claimant has supplied medical evidence;

(b) the period for which medical evidence was supplied has ended;

    (c) the Secretary of State has requested further medical evidence; and

    (d) the claimant has not, before whichever is the later of either the end of the period of six weeks beginning with the date of the Secretary of State's request or the end of six weeks beginning with the day after the end of the period for which medical evidence was supplied—

        (i) supplied further medical evidence; or

        (ii) otherwise made contact with the Secretary of State to indicate that they wish to have the question of limited capability for work determined.

(2) In this regulation "medical evidence" means evidence provided under regulation 2 or 5 of the Medical Evidence Regulations.

DEFINITIONS

    "claimant"—see WRA 2007, s.24(1).
    "limited capability for work"—see WRA 2007, s.1(4).
    "Medical Evidence Regulations"—see sub-para.(2).

GENERAL NOTE

1.208    This is the same as ESA Regulations 2008 reg.32A.

### Additional circumstances where claimants are to be treated as having limited capability for work

1.209    **29.** For the purposes of paragraph 4(1)(d)(ii) of Schedule 1 to the Act, a claimant is to be treated as having limited capability for work on any day in respect of which that claimant is entitled to statutory sick pay.

GENERAL NOTE

1.210    This is exactly the same as ESA Regulations 2008 reg.33(1).

PART 5

*Limited Capability for Work-related Activity*

### Determination of limited capability for work-related activity

1.211    **30.**—(1) For the purposes of Part 1 of the Act, where, by reason of a claimant's physical or mental condition, at least one of the descriptors set out in Schedule 3 applies to the claimant, the claimant has limited capability for work-related activity and the limitation must be such that it is not reasonable to require that claimant to undertake such activity.

(2) A descriptor applies to a claimant if that descriptor applies to the claimant for the majority of the time or, as the case may be, on the majority of the occasions on which the claimant undertakes or attempts to undertake the activity described by that descriptor.

(3) In determining whether a descriptor applies to a claimant, the claimant is to be assessed as if—

(a) the claimant were fitted with or wearing any prosthesis with which the claimant is normally fitted or normally wears; or, as the case may be

(b) wearing or using any aid or appliance which is normally, or could reasonably be expected to be, worn or used.

(4) Where a determination has been made about whether a claimant—

(a) has limited capability for work-related activity;

(b) is to be treated as having limited capability for work-related activity; or

(c) is to be treated as not having limited capability for work-related activity,

the Secretary of State may, if paragraph (5) applies, determine afresh whether the claimant has or is to be treated as having limited capability for work-related activity.

(5) This paragraph applies where—

(a) the Secretary of State wishes to determine whether there has been a relevant change of circumstances in relation to the claimant's physical or mental condition;

(b) the Secretary of State wishes to determine whether the previous determination about limited capability for work-related activity or about treating the claimant as having or as not having limited capability for work-related activity, was made in ignorance of, or was based on a mistake as to, some material fact; or

(c) at least three months have passed since the date of the previous determination about limited capability for work-related activity or about treating the claimant as having or as not having limited capability for work-related activity.

(6) In assessing the extent of a claimant's capability to perform any activity listed in Schedule 3, it is a condition that the claimant's incapability to perform the activity arises—

(a) in respect of descriptors 1 to 8, 15(a), 15(b), 16(a) and 16(b)—

(i) from a specific bodily disease or disablement; or

(ii) as a direct result of treatment provided by a registered medical practitioner for a specific physical disease or disablement; or

(b) in respect of descriptors 9 to 14, 15(c), 15(d), 16(c) and 16(d)—

(i) from a specific mental illness or disablement; or

(ii) as a direct result of treatment provided by a registered medical practitioner for a specific mental illness or disablement.

DEFINITIONS

"the Act"—see reg.2(1).
"claimant"—see WRA 2007, s.24(1).
"descriptor"—see reg.2(1).
"limited capability for work-related activity"—see WRA 2007, s.2(5).
"work-related activity"—see WRA 2007, ss. 24(1), 13(7).

1.212   This corresponds to ESA Regulations 2008 reg.34.

## Certain claimants to be treated as having, or not having, limited capability for work-related activity

1.213   **31.**—(1) A claimant is to be treated as having limited capability for work-related activity if—

(a) the claimant is terminally ill;

(b) the claimant is—

    (i) receiving treatment for cancer by way of chemotherapy or radiotherapy;

    (ii) likely to receive such treatment within six months after the date of the determination of capability for work-related activity; or

    (iii) recovering from such treatment,

    and the Secretary of State is satisfied that the claimant should be treated as having limited capability for work-related activity;

(c) in the case of a woman, she is pregnant and there is a serious risk of damage to her health or to the health of her unborn child if she does not refrain from work-related activity; or

(d) the claimant is entitled to universal credit and it has previously been determined that the claimant has limited capability for work and work-related activity on the basis of an assessment under Part 5 of the Universal Credit Regulations 2013.

(2) A claimant who does not have limited capability for work-related activity as determined in accordance with regulation 30(1) is to be treated as having limited capability for work-related activity if—

(a) the claimant suffers from some specific disease or bodily or mental disablement; and

(b) by reason of such disease or disablement, there would be a substantial risk to the mental or physical health of any person if the claimant were found not to have limited capability for work-related activity.

(3) A claimant is to be treated as not having limited capability for work-related activity where—

(a) it has previously been determined, within the six months preceding the date of claim for employment and support allowance, on the basis of an assessment under Part 5 of the Universal Credit Regulations 2013, that the claimant does not have limited capability for work and work-related activity; and

(b) it appears to the Secretary of State that—

    (i) the determination was not based on ignorance of, or mistake as to, a material fact; and

    (ii) there has been no relevant change of circumstances in relation to the claimant's physical or mental condition.

DEFINITIONS

"claimant"—see WRA 2007, s.24(1).
"limited capability for work-related activity"—see WRA 2007, s.2(5).

"terminally ill"—see reg.2(1).
"work-related activity"—see WRA 2007, ss.24(1), 13(7).

GENERAL NOTE

This is the same as ESA Regulations 2008 reg.35.                    1.214

## Relevant linked cases—limited capability for work-related activity

**32.** A claimant is to be treated as having limited capability for work-    1.215
related activity where—
  (a) they fall within case 1, as defined in regulation 7(3)(a); and
  (b) in respect of the earlier period of limited capability for work
      referred to in regulation 7(3)(a)(i), they had been entitled to a
      support component under section 2(2) of the Act.

GENERAL NOTE

This corresponds to ESA Regulations 2008 reg.35A.                  1.216

## Information required for determining capability for work-related activity

**33.**—(1) Subject to paragraph (2), the information or evidence    1.217
required to determine whether a claimant has limited capability for
work-related activity is—
  (a) any information relating to the descriptors set out in Schedule 3 as
      may be requested in the form of a questionnaire; and
  (b) any such additional information as may be requested.
  (2) Where the Secretary of State is satisfied that there is sufficient
information to determine whether a claimant has limited capability for
work-related activity without the information specified in paragraph
(1)(a), that information must not be required for the purposes of making
the determination.

DEFINITIONS

"claimant"—see WRA 2007, s.24(1).
"limited capability for work-related activity"—see WRA 2007, s.2(5).
"work-related activity"—see WRA 2007, ss.24(1), 13(7).

GENERAL NOTE

This is the same as ESA Regulations 2008 reg.36.                   1.218

## Failure to provide information in relation to work-related activity

**34.**—(1) Where a claimant fails without good cause to comply with the    1.219
request referred to in regulation 33(1)(a), the claimant is, subject to
paragraph (2), to be treated as not having limited capability for work-
related activity.
  (2) Paragraph (1) does not apply unless—
  (a) the claimant was sent a further request at least three weeks after
      the date of the first request; and

(b) at least one week has passed since the further request was sent.

DEFINITIONS

"claimant"—see WRA 2007, s.24(1).
"limited capability for work-related activity"—see WRA 2007, s.2(5).
"week"—see reg.2(1).
"work-related activity"—see WRA 2007, ss.24(1), 13(7).

GENERAL NOTE

1.220   This corresponds to ESA Regulations 2008 reg.37.

## Claimant may be called for a medical examination to determine whether the claimant has limited capability for work-related activity

1.221   **35.**—(1) Where it falls to be determined whether a claimant has limited capability for work-related activity, that claimant may be called by or on behalf of a health care professional approved by the Secretary of State to attend for a medical examination.

(2) Subject to paragraph (3), where a claimant fails without good cause to attend for or to submit to an examination mentioned in paragraph (1), the claimant is to be treated as not having limited capability for work-related activity.

(3) Paragraph (2) does not apply unless—

(a) written notice of the date, time and place for the examination was sent to the claimant at least seven days in advance; or

(b) the claimant agreed to accept a shorter period of notice whether given in writing or otherwise.

DEFINITIONS

"claimant"—see WRA 2007, s.24(1).
"health care professional"—see reg.2(1).
"limited capability for work-related activity"—see WRA 2007, s.2(5).
"work-related activity"—see WRA 2007, ss.24(1), 13(7).

GENERAL NOTE

1.222   This is the same as ESA Regulations 2008 reg.38.

## Matters to be taken into account in determining good cause in relation to regulations 34 or 35

1.223   **36.** The matters to be taken into account in determining whether a claimant has good cause under regulation 34 (failure to provide information in relation to work-related activity) or 35 (failure to attend a medical examination to determine limited capability for work-related activity) include—

(a) whether the claimant was outside Great Britain at the relevant time;

(b) the claimant's state of health at the relevant time; and

(c) the nature of any disability the claimant has.

132

DEFINITION

"claimant"—see WRA 2007, s.24(1).

GENERAL NOTE

This corresponds to ESA Regulations 2008 reg.39.                    1.224

PART 6

*Effect of work on entitlement to an Employment and Support Allowance*

## A claimant who works to be treated as not entitled to an employment and support allowance

**37.**—(1) Subject to the following paragraphs, a claimant is to be   1.225
treated as not entitled to an employment and support allowance in any
week in which that claimant does work.

(2) Paragraph (1) does not apply to—

(a) work as a councillor;

(b) duties undertaken on either one full day or two half-days a week as
a member of the First-tier Tribunal where the member is eligible
for appointment to be such a member in accordance with article
2(3) of the Qualifications for Appointment of Members to the
First-tier Tribunal and Upper Tribunal Order 2008;

(c) domestic tasks carried out in the claimant's own home or the care
of a relative;

(d) duties undertaken in caring for another person who is accommodated with the claimant by virtue of arrangements made under
any of the provisions referred to in paragraph (7) or where the
claimant is in receipt of any payment specified in that paragraph;

(e) any activity the claimant undertakes during an emergency to
protect another person or to prevent serious damage to property
or livestock; or

(f) any of the categories of work set out in regulation 39(1) (exempt
work).

(3) This regulation is subject to regulation 40 (effect of work on
entitlement to an employment and support allowance where claimant is
receiving certain treatment).

(4) A claimant who does work to which this regulation applies in a
week which is—

(a) the week in which the claimant first becomes entitled to a benefit,
allowance or advantage on account of the claimant's limited capability for work in any period; or

(b) the last week in any period in which the claimant has limited
capability for work or is treated as having limited capability for
work,

is to be treated as not entitled to an employment and support allowance by virtue of paragraph (1) only on the actual day or days in that week on which the claimant does that work.

(5) Regulation 86 (linking rules) does not apply for the purposes of calculating the beginning or end of any period of limited capability for work under paragraph (4).

(6) The day or days in a week on which a night worker works, for the purposes of paragraph (4), are to be calculated by reference to regulation 24 (night workers).

(7) The payments and provisions mentioned in paragraph (2)(d) are—

   (a) any payment made to the claimant with whom a person is accommodated by virtue of arrangements made—

      (i) by a local authority under section 22C(2), (3), (5) or (6)(a) or (b) of the Children Act 1989 (provision of accommodation and maintenance for a child whom the local authority is looking after);

      (ii) by a local authority under section 26 of the Children (Scotland) Act 1995 (manner of provision of accommodation to child looked after by local authority);

      (iii) by a local authority under regulations 33 or 51 of the Looked After Children (Scotland) Regulations 2009 (fostering and kinship care allowances and fostering allowances); or

      (iv) by a voluntary organisation under section 59(1)(a) of the 1989 Act (provision of accommodation by voluntary organisations);

   (b) any payment made to the claimant or the claimant's partner for a person ("the person concerned"), who is not normally a member of the claimant's household but is temporarily in the claimant's care, by—

      (i) the National Health Service Commissioning Board;

      (ii) a local authority but excluding payments of housing benefit made in respect of the person concerned;

      (iii) a voluntary organisation;

      (iv) the person concerned pursuant to section 26(3A) of the National Assistance Act 1948;

      (v) a clinical commissioning group established under section 14D of the Health Service Act; or

      (vi) a Local Health Board established by an order made under section 11 of the Health Service (Wales) Act.

(8) In this regulation—

"week" means a week in respect of which a claimant is entitled to an employment and support allowance;

"work" means any work which a claimant does, whether or not that claimant undertakes it in expectation of payment;

"work as a councillor" includes any work which a claimant undertakes as a member of any of the bodies referred to in section 177(1) of the Local Government Act 1972 or section 49(1) or (1A) of the Local Government (Scotland) Act 1973, of which the claimant is a member by reason of being a councillor.

DEFINITIONS

"claimant"—see WRA 2007, s.24(1).
"entitled"—see WRA 2007, s.24(1).
"relative"—see reg.2(1).
"week"—see para.(8) and reg.2(1).
"work"—see para.(8).
"work as a councillor"—see para.(8).

GENERAL NOTE

This has much the same effect as ESA Regulations 2008 reg.40.          1.226

## Claimants who are treated as not entitled to any allowance at all by reason of regulation 37(1) are to be treated as not having limited capability for work

**38.**—(1) Where a claimant is treated as not entitled to an employment   1.227
and support allowance by reason of regulation 37(1), the claimant is to
be treated as not having limited capability for work.
   (2) Paragraph (1) applies even if—
   (a) it has been determined that the claimant has or is to be treated as
       having, under any of regulations 16 (certain claimants to be
       treated as having limited capability for work), 21 (hospital in-pa-
       tients), 22 (claimants undergoing certain treatment) and 25
       (exceptional circumstances), limited capability for work; or
   (b) the claimant meets the conditions set out in regulation 26(2) for
       being treated as having limited capability for work until a determi-
       nation is made in accordance with the limited capability for work
       assessment.

GENERAL NOTE

This is much the same as ESA Regulations 2008 reg.44.          1.228

## Exempt work

**39.**—(1) The categories of work referred to in regulation 37(2)(f)   1.229
are—
   (a) work for which the total earnings in any week does not exceed
       £20;
   (b) work for which the total earnings in any week does not exceed 16
       multiplied by the National Minimum Wage, subject to paragraph
       (4), and which—
       (i) is part of the claimant's treatment programme and is done
           under medical supervision while the claimant is an in-pa-
           tient, or is regularly attending as an out-patient, of a hospital
           or similar institution; or
       (ii) is supervised by a person employed by a public or local
            authority or by a voluntary organisation or community inter-
            est company engaged in the provision or procurement of
            work for persons who have disabilities;
   (c) work which is done for less than 16 hours a week, for which total
       earnings in any week does not exceed 16 multiplied by the

National Minimum Wage, subject to paragraph (4), and which is done—

   (i) during a work period, provided that paragraph (7) applies; or

   (ii) by a claimant who has or is treated as having limited capability for work-related activity;

(d) work done in the course of receiving assistance in pursuing self-employed earner's employment whilst participating in a programme provided, or in other arrangements made, under section 2 of the Employment and Training Act 1973 (functions of the Secretary of State) or section 2 of the Enterprise and New Towns (Scotland) Act 1990 (functions in relation to training for employment etc);

(e) work done where the claimant receives no payment of earnings and where the claimant is—

   (i) engaged by a charity or voluntary organisation; or

   (ii) a volunteer,

and where the Secretary of State is satisfied in either of those cases that it is reasonable for the claimant to do the work free of charge;

(f) work done in the course of participating in a work placement approved in writing by the Secretary of State before the placement starts.

(2) The number of hours for which a claimant is engaged in work is to be determined—

(a) where no recognisable cycle has been established in respect of a claimant's work, by reference to the number of hours or, where those hours are likely to fluctuate, the average of the hours, which the claimant is expected to work in a week;

(b) where the number of hours for which the claimant is engaged fluctuate, by reference to the average of hours worked over—

   (i) if there is a recognisable cycle of work, the period of one complete cycle (including, where the cycle involves periods in which the claimant does no work, those periods but disregarding any other absences);

   (ii) in any other case, the period of five weeks immediately before the date of claim or the date on which a superseding decision is made under section 10 of the Social Security Act 1998 (decisions superseding earlier decisions)(a), or such other length of time as may, in the particular case, enable the claimant's average hours of work to be determined more accurately.

(3) For the purposes of determining the number of hours for which a claimant is engaged in work, that number is to include any time allowed to that claimant by the claimant's employer for a meal or for refreshment, but only where that claimant is, or expects to be, paid earnings in respect of that time.

(4) Where the amount determined by the calculation in paragraph (1)(b) or (c) would, but for this paragraph, include an amount of—

(a) less than 50p, that amount is to be rounded up to the nearest 50p; or

(b) less than £1 but more than 50p, that amount is to be rounded up to the nearest £1.

(5) Part 10 applies for the purposes of calculating any income which consists of earnings under this regulation.

(6) In this regulation—

"relevant benefit" means—

    (a) an employment and support allowance; or

    (b) credits under regulations made under section 22(5) of the Contributions and Benefits Act, in respect of which the question of the claimant's limited capability for work arises under the Act;

"volunteer" means a person who is engaged in voluntary work otherwise than for a relative, where the only payment received or due to be paid to the person by virtue of being so engaged is in respect of any expenses reasonably incurred by the person in connection with that work;

"work period" means a period which begins on the first day on which any work referred to in paragraph (1)(c) is undertaken and continues for a period of 52 weeks, whether or not any further work referred to in paragraph (1)(c) is undertaken during that period;

"work placement" means practical work experience with an employer, which is neither paid nor undertaken in expectation of payment.

(7) This paragraph applies where—

(a) the claimant has not previously done any work under paragraph (1)(c);

(b) since the beginning of the last work period, the claimant has ceased to be entitled to a relevant benefit for a continuous period exceeding 12 weeks; or

(c) not less than 52 weeks have elapsed since the last work period.

DEFINITIONS

"the Act"—see reg.2(1).
"claimant"—see WRA 2007, s.24(1).
"Contributions and Benefits Act"—see WRA 2007, s.65.
"employment"—see reg.2(1).
"relevant benefit"—see para.(6).
"self-employed earner"—see reg.2(1).
"voluntary organisation"—see reg.2(1).
"volunteer"—see para.(6).
"week"—see reg.2(1).
"work period"—see para.(6).
"work placement"—see para.(6).

GENERAL NOTE

This corresponds to ESA Regulations 2008 reg.45.

**1.230**

### Effect of work on entitlement to an employment and support allowance where claimant is receiving certain treatment

1.231    **40.** Where a claimant who is entitled to an employment and support allowance and is treated as having limited capability for work by virtue of regulation 22 works on any day during a week when the claimant is receiving certain treatment mentioned in regulation 22 or recovering from that treatment, that work is to have no effect on the claimant's entitlement to the employment and support allowance.

DEFINITIONS

"claimant"—see WRA 2007, s.24(1).
"entitled"—see WRA 2007, s.24(1).
"limited capability for work"—see WRA 2007, s.24(1).
"week"—see reg.2(1), WRA 2007, s.24(1).

GENERAL NOTE

1.232    This is the same as ESA Regulations 2008 reg.46.

PART 7

*Claimant responsibilities*

### Interpretation

1.233    **41.**—(1) In this Part—
"responsible carer", in relation to a child, means—
    (a) a person who is the only person responsible for the child; or
    (b) a person who is a member of a couple where—
        (i) both members of the couple are responsible for the child; and
        (ii) the person has been nominated by the couple jointly as responsible for the child;
"responsible foster parent", in relation to a child, means—
    (a) a person who is the only foster parent in relation to the child; or
    (b) a person who is a member of a couple where—
        (i) both members of the couple are foster parents in relation to the child; and
        (ii) the person has been nominated by the couple jointly as the responsible foster parent.
(2) The nomination of a responsible carer or responsible foster parent for the purposes of paragraph (1) may be changed—
    (a) once in a 12 month period, beginning with the date of the previous nomination; or
    (b) on any occasion where the Secretary of State considers that there has been a change of circumstances which is relevant to the nomination.

138

(3) Only one person may be nominated as a responsible carer or a responsible foster parent.

(4) The nomination applies to all of the children for whom the claimant is responsible.

DEFINITIONS

"child"—see reg.2(1).
"claimant" see WRA 2007, s.24(1).
"couple"—see reg.2(1).
"responsible carer"—see para.(1).
"responsible foster parent"—see para.(1).

GENERAL NOTE

Compare Universal Credit Regulations 2013 regs 85, 86.    **1.234**

## Application of regulations where there is dual entitlement

**42.**—(1) This regulation applies where a person is entitled to universal    **1.235**
credit and an employment and support allowance.

(2) The work-related requirements under sections 11B to 11I of the Act and regulations 46 to 49 of these Regulations do not apply to such a person.

(3) Reductions relating to the award of an employment and support allowance under section 11J of the Act and regulations 50 to 60 of these Regulations do not apply to such a person.

GENERAL NOTE

This provides that where a person is entitled to UC and ESA, the work-related    **1.236**
requirements and sanctions regime applicable to ESA does not apply. The person will instead be subject to the comparable UC regime. See Universal Credit Regulations 2013 regs 84–114.

## Sanction ceases to apply to employment and support allowance

**43.**—(1) This regulation applies where—    **1.237**
(a) a person is entitled to an employment and support allowance;
(b) there is a reduction relating to the award of the employment and support allowance under section 11J of the Act;
(c) the person becomes entitled to universal credit; and
(d) the person remains entitled to an employment and support allowance.

(2) Any reduction relating to the award of the employment and support allowance is to cease being applied to the award of the employment and support allowance.

GENERAL NOTE

Where an ESA reduction is in place and the person then becomes entitled to    **1.238**
UC as well as ESA, the ESA reduction ceases to apply. The person will instead be dealt with under the UC regime. See Universal Credit Regulations 2013 reg.112 and Sch.11.

## Claimant commitment—date and method of acceptance

1.239　　**44.**—(1) For the purposes of section 1(3)(aa) of the Act, a claimant who has accepted a claimant commitment within such period after making a claim for an employment and support allowance as the Secretary of State specifies is to be treated as having accepted that claimant commitment on the first day of the period in respect of which the claim is made.

(2) In a case where an award of an employment and support allowance may be made without a claim, a claimant who accepts a claimant commitment within such period as the Secretary of State specifies is to be treated as having accepted a claimant commitment on the day that would be the first day of the first benefit week in relation to the award.

(3) The Secretary of State may extend the period within which a claimant is required to accept a claimant commitment or an updated claimant commitment where the claimant requests an extension and the Secretary of State considers that the request is reasonable.

(4) A claimant must accept a claimant commitment by one of the following methods, as specified by the Secretary of State—

(a) electronically;

(b) by telephone; or

(c) in writing.

DEFINITIONS

"benefit week"—see reg.2(1).

GENERAL NOTE

1.240　　This provides for a claimant commitment accepted within a period after the claim to be backdated to the first day of the claim period (para.(1)). As regards an award of ESA without a claim, acceptance of a claimant commitment within a specified period can be attributed to the first day of the first benefit week of the award (para.(2)). A period can be extended by the Secretary of State where the claimant reasonably requests an extension (para.(3)). The commitment must be accepted electronically, in writing or by telephone, whichever is specified by the Secretary of State (para.(4)).

## Claimant commitment—exceptions

1.241　　**45.** A claimant may be entitled to an employment and support allowance without having accepted a claimant commitment if the Secretary of State considers that—

(a) the claimant cannot accept a claimant commitment because they lack capacity to do so; or

(b) there are exceptional circumstances in which it would be unreasonable to expect the person to accept a claimant commitment.

GENERAL NOTE

1.242　　This allows the Secretary of State to release the claimant from the requirement to accept a claimant commitment as a condition of receiving ESA where the Secretary of State considers that exceptional circumstances pertain in which it would be unreasonable to expect acceptance or where the claimant lacks capacity to accept a claimant commitment.

## Purposes of a work-focused interview

**46.** The purposes of a work-focused interview are any or all of the following—    1.243
  (a) assessing the claimant's prospects for remaining in or obtaining work;
  (b) assisting or encouraging the claimant to remain in or obtain work;
  (c) identifying activities that the claimant may undertake that will make remaining in or obtaining work more likely;
  (d) identifying training, educational or rehabilitation opportunities for the claimant which may make it more likely that the claimant will remain in or obtain work or be able to do so;
  (e) identifying current or future work opportunities for the claimant that are relevant to the claimant's needs and abilities.

General Note

This sets out the purposes of a work-focused interview. Compare ESA Regula-    1.244
tions 2008 reg.55 and Universal Credit Regulations 2013 reg.93.

## Claimants subject to no work-related requirements

**47.**—(1) A claimant falls within section 11D of the Act (persons    1.245
subject to no work-related requirements) if they are a claimant who—
  (a) has caring responsibilities for one or more severely disabled persons for at least 35 hours a week but does not meet the conditions of entitlement to a carer's allowance;
  (b) is the responsible foster parent of a child under the age of one;
  (c) is an adopter and it is 52 weeks or less since—
      (i) the date on which the child was placed with the claimant; or
      (ii) if the claimant requested that the 52 weeks should run from a date within 14 days before the child was expected to be placed, that date;
  (d) has been enrolled on, been accepted for or is undertaking, a full-time course of study or training which is not a course of advanced education and—
      (i) is under the age of 21, or is 21 and reached that age whilst undertaking the course; and
      (ii) is without parental support;
  (e) is entitled to an employment and support allowance which is payable at a nil rate;
  (f) is pregnant and it is 11 weeks or less before her expected week of confinement; or
  (g) was pregnant and it is 15 weeks or less since the date of her confinement.

(2) Subject to paragraph (3), for the purposes of section 11D of the Act, a person has regular and substantial caring responsibilities for a severely disabled person if the person—

(a) satisfies the conditions for entitlement to a carer's allowance; or

(b) would satisfy those conditions but for the fact that their earnings have exceeded the limit prescribed for the purposes of that allowance.

(3) A person does not have regular and substantial caring responsibilities for a severely disabled person if the person derives earnings from those caring responsibilities.

(4) Paragraph (2) applies whether or not the person has made a claim for a carer's allowance.

(5) In this regulation—

"adopter" means a person who has been matched with a child for adoption and who is, or is intended to be, the responsible carer for the child, but excluding a person who is a foster parent or close relative of the child;

"matched with a child for adoption" means an adoption agency has decided that the person would be a suitable adoptive parent for the child;

"severely disabled" has the meaning in section 70 of the Contributions and Benefits Act;

"without parental support" means the person is not being looked after by a local authority and—

(a) has no parent (in this definition, "parent" includes any person acting in the place of a parent);

(b) cannot live with their parents because the person is estranged from them or there is a serious risk—

(i) to the person's physical or mental health; or

(ii) that the person would suffer significant harm if the person lived with them; or

(c) is living away from their parents, and neither parent is able to support the person financially because that parent—

(i) has a physical or mental impairment;

(ii) is detained in custody pending trial or sentence upon conviction or under a sentence imposed by a court; or

(iii) is prohibited from entering or re-entering Great Britain.

DEFINITIONS

"adopter"—see para.(5).

"carer's allowance—see reg.2(1).

"close relative"—see reg.2(1).

"matched with a child for adoption"—see para.(5).

"parent"—see para.(5).

"severely disabled"—see para.(5).

"without parental support"—see para.(5).

This specified the person who under s.11D of the WRA 2012 (see update to  1.246
pp.367–379) in Part II of this Supplement) are not subject to any work-related
requirements. Compare Universal Credits Regulations 2013 reg.89.

## Claimants subject to work-focused interview requirement only

**48.**—(1) For the purposes of section 11E(1)(a) of the Act (claimant is  1.247
the responsible carer for a child aged at least one and under a prescribed
age) the prescribed age is five.

(2) A claimant falls within section 11E of the Act (claimants subject to
work-focused interview requirement only) if—

(a) the claimant is the responsible foster parent in relation to a child
aged at least one;

(b) the claimant is the responsible foster parent in relation to a qualifying young person and the Secretary of State is satisfied that the
qualifying young person has care needs which would make it
unreasonable to require the claimant to comply with a work
preparation requirement;

(c) the claimant is a foster parent, but not the responsible foster
parent, in relation to a child or qualifying young person and the
Secretary of State is satisfied that the child or qualifying young
person has care needs which would make it unreasonable to
require the claimant to comply with a work preparation requirement;

(d) the claimant is a foster parent who—

(i) does not have a child or qualifying young person placed with
them, but intends to; and

(ii) fell within sub-paragraph (a) within the past eight weeks;
or

(e) the claimant has become a friend or family carer in relation to a
child within the past 12 months and is also the responsible carer
in relation to that child.

(3) In paragraph (2)(e), "friend or family carer" means a person who
is responsible for a child, but is not the child's parent or step-parent, and
has undertaken the care of the child in the following circumstances—

(a) the child has no parent or has parents who are unable to care for
the child; or

(b) it is likely that the child would otherwise be looked after by a local
authority because of concerns in relation to the child's welfare.

DEFINITIONS

"child"—see reg.2(1).
"friend or family carer"—see para.(3).
"qualifying young person"—see reg.2(1).

GENERAL NOTE

This lists for the purposes of s.11E of the WRA 2007 (see update to  1.248
pp.367–379 in Part II of this Supplement) the persons who are to be subject only
to a work-focused interview requirement. Compare Universal Credit Regulations 2013 reg.91.

## Victims of domestic violence

1.249    **49.**—(1) Where a claimant has recently been a victim of domestic violence and the circumstances set out in paragraph (3) apply—

(a) a requirement imposed on that claimant under sections 11 to 11G of the Act ceases to have effect for a period of 13 consecutive weeks starting on the date of the notification referred to in paragraph (3)(a); and

(b) the Secretary of State must not impose any other such requirement on that claimant during that period.

(2) A person has recently been a victim of domestic violence if a period of six months has not expired since the violence was inflicted or threatened.

(3) The circumstances are that—

(a) the claimant notifies the Secretary of State, in such manner as the Secretary of State specifies, that domestic violence has been inflicted on or threatened against the claimant by a person specified in paragraph (4) during the period of six months ending on the date of the notification;

(b) this regulation has not applied to the claimant for a period of 12 months before the date of the notification;

(c) on the date of the notification the claimant is not living at the same address as the person who inflicted or threatened the domestic violence; and

(d) as soon as possible, and no later than one month, after the date of the notification the claimant provides evidence from a person acting in an official capacity which demonstrates that—

(i) the claimant's circumstances are consistent with those of a person who has had domestic violence inflicted on or threatened against them during the period of six months ending on the date of the notification; and

(ii) the claimant has made contact with the person acting in an official capacity in relation to such an incident, which occurred during that period.

(4) A person is specified in this paragraph if the person is—

(a) where the claimant is, or was, a member of a couple, the other member of the couple;

(b) the claimant's grandparent, grandchild, parent, parent-in-law, son, son-in-law, daughter, daughter-in-law, step-parent, step-son, step-daughter, brother, step-brother, brother-in-law, sister, step-sister or sister-in-law; or

(c) where any of the persons listed in sub-paragraph (b) is a member of a couple, the other member of that couple.

(5) In this regulation—

[¹"coercive behaviour" means an act of assault, humiliation or intimidation or other abuse that is used to harm, punish or frighten the victim;

"controlling behaviour" means an act designed to make a person subordinate or dependent by isolating them from sources of support, exploiting their resources and capacities for personal gain,

depriving them of the means needed for independence, resistance or escape or regulating their everyday behaviour;
"domestic violence" means any incident, or pattern of incidents, of controlling behaviour, coercive behaviour, violence or abuse, including but not limited to—

(a) psychological abuse;
(b) physical abuse;
(c) sexual abuse;
(d) emotional abuse;
(e) financial abuse,

regardless of the gender of sexuality of the victim;]
"person acting in an official capacity" means a person who is a member of a profession regulated by a body mentioned in section 25(3) of the National Health Service Reform and Health Care Professions Act 2002, a police officer, a registered social worker, the claimant's employer, a representative of the claimant's trade union or any public, voluntary or charitable body which has had direct contact with the claimant in connection with domestic violence;
"registered social worker" means a person registered as a social worker in a register maintained by—

(a) the General Social Care Council;
(b) the Care Council for Wales;
(c) the Scottish Social Services Council; or
(d) the Northern Ireland Social Care Council.

AMENDMENT

1. Social Security (Miscellaneous Amendments) (No. 2) Regulations 2013 (SI 2013/1508) reg.5(1), (3) (October 29, 2013).

DEFINITIONS

"coercive behaviour"—see para.5.
"controlling behaviour"—see para.5.
"couple"—see reg.2(1).
"domestic violence"—see para.5.
"person acting in an official capacity"—see para.5.
"registered social worker"—see para.5.

GENERAL NOTE

This enables recent victims (V) of domestic violence to obtain a "breathing space" during which work-related requirement already imposed are lifted and others can not be imposed. Compare Universal Credit Regulations 2013 reg.98 and JSA Regulations 1996 reg.14A.     **1.250**

Domestic violence is defined in para.(5). The regulation covers both its infliction and it being threatened. V is a recent victim if no more than six months have elapsed since domestic violence was inflicted or threatened (para.(2)).

V can obtain this 13-week period of respite commencing with V's notification to the Secretary of State so long as V provides within one month of the notification evidence from a person acting in an official capacity confirming that the claimant is indeed such a victim in the last six months and has been in contact with that person about an incident of domestic violence. The claimant must not be living on the date of notification at the same address as the person who inflicted or threatened the domestic violence. The person inflicting or threatening the domestic violence must be someone specified in para.(4) (covering a very wide range of "family" members or relatives). There can only be one respite period in any 12 months (para.(3)(b)).

PART 8

*Sanctions*

### Interpretation

1.251     **50.** For the purposes of this Part—
     "JSA sanctionable failure" means a failure by a claimant which is sanctionable under section 6K of the Jobseekers Act 1995;
     "low-level sanction" means a reduction of an employment and support allowance in accordance with section 11J of the Act for a sanctionable failure by the claimant to comply with—
         (a) a work-focused interview requirement imposed under section 11F(2) of the Act (persons subject to work preparation requirement and work-focused interview requirement);
         (b) a work preparation requirement imposed under section 11F(2) of the Act; or
         (c) a requirement under section 11G of the Act (connected requirements);
     "lowest-level sanction" means a reduction of an employment and support allowance in accordance with section 11J of the Act for a sanctionable failure by the claimant to comply with a requirement imposed under section 11E(2) of the Act (persons subject to work-focused interview requirement only);
     "reduction period" means the number of days for which a reduction in the amount of an award of an employment and support allowance is to have effect;
     "sanctionable failure" means a failure which is sanctionable under section 11J of the Act;
     "total outstanding reduction period" means the total number of days for which no reduction has yet been applied for all of the claimant's low-level sanctions, lowest-level sanctions and reductions to which regulation 61 applies;
     "UC sanctionable failure" means a failure by a claimant which is sanctionable under section 26 or 27 of the Welfare Reform Act 2012.

### General principles for calculating reduction periods

1.252     **51.**—(1) Subject to paragraphs (3) and (4), the reduction period is to be determined in relation to each sanctionable failure in accordance with regulations 52 and 53.
     (2) Reduction periods are to run consecutively.

146

(3) Where the reduction period calculated in relation to a sanctionable failure in accordance with regulation 52 or 53 would result in the total outstanding reduction period exceeding 1095 days, the number of days in the reduction period in relation to that failure is to be adjusted so that 1095 days is not exceeded.

(4) In determining the reduction period in relation to a sanctionable failure, a previous sanctionable failure, UC sanctionable failure or JSA sanctionable failure is to be disregarded if it—

(a) occurred in the 14 days immediately preceding the failure in question; and

(b) gave rise to a reduction under these Regulations, the Universal Credit Regulations 2013 or the Jobseeker's Allowance Regulations 2013.

DEFINITIONS

"JSA sanctionable failure"—see reg.50.
"reduction period"—see reg.50.
"sanctionable failure"—see reg.50.
"total outstanding reduction period"—see reg.50.
"UC sanctionable failure"—see reg.50.

GENERAL NOTE

This deals with the general principles applicable to sanctionable failures with     **1.253**
respect to work-related requirements as regards ESA under s.11J of the WRA 2007 (see update to pp.367–379 in Part II of this Supplement). Sanctions consist of periods for which ESA is reduced. The reduction period is to be set in accordance with regs 52, 53, below (para.(1)). Reduction periods run consecutively (para.(2)). That is subject to the general overall three-year limit in para.(3): a reduction in accordance with regs 52 and 53 cannot take over three years (1,095 days) in length the total outstanding reduction period for all the claimants low-level or lowest level sanctions (whether under ESA, JSA or UC) and those under reg.61. This drafting is somewhat opaque. The idea appears to be that if adding a new reduction period to the end of what is likely to be a chain of reduction periods would take the total days in the chain over 1,095 days the new reduction period must be adjusted to make the total 1,095 days in all.

Paragraph (4) stipulates when previous sanctionable failures or ones sanctionable under UC and JSA are to be ignored.

## Low-level sanction

52. The reduction period for a low-level sanction is the total of—     **1.254**

(a) the number of days beginning with the date of the sanctionable failure and ending with—

(i) the day before the date on which the claimant meets a compliance condition specified by the Secretary of State;

(ii) the day before the date on which the claimant falls within section 11D of the Act;

(iii) the day before the date on which the claimant is no longer required to take a particular action specified as a work preparation requirement by the Secretary of State under section 11C(1) or 11F(2) of the Act; or

        (iv) the day on which the award of an employment and support allowance is terminated,

    whichever is soonest; and

(b) whichever of the following number of days is applicable in the claimant's case—

    (i) seven days, if sub-paragraphs (ii) and (iii) do not apply;

    (ii) 14 days, if in the 365 days preceding the failure in question there was another sanctionable failure giving rise to a low-level sanction for which a seven day reduction period applies;

    (iii) 14 days, if in the 365 days preceding the failure in question there was a UC sanctionable failure giving rise to a low-level sanction under regulation 104 of the Universal Credit Regulations 2013 for which a seven day reduction period applies;

    (iv) 14 days, if in the 365 days preceding the failure in question there was a JSA sanctionable failure giving rise to a low-level sanction under regulation 21 of the Jobseeker's Allowance Regulations 2013 for which a seven day reduction period applies;

    (v) 28 days, if in the 365 days preceding the failure in question there was another sanctionable failure giving rise to a low-level sanction for which a 14 day or 28 day reduction period applies;

    (vi) 28 days, if in the 365 days preceding the failure in question there was a UC sanctionable failure giving rise to a low-level sanction under regulation 104 of the Universal Credit Regulations 2013 for which a 14 day or 28 day reduction period applies; or

    (vii) 28 days, if in the 365 days preceding the failure in question there was a JSA sanctionable failure giving rise to a low-level sanction under regulation 21 of the Jobseeker's Allowance Regulations 2013 for which a 14 day or 28 day reduction period applies.

DEFINITIONS

"compliance condition"—see WRA 2007, s.11J(5).
"JSA sanctionable failure"—see reg.50.
"low-level sanction"—see reg.50.
"reduction period"—see reg.50.
"sanctionable failure"—see reg.50.
"UC sanctionable failure"—see reg.50.

GENERAL NOTE

**1.255** This regulation deals with the period of reduction of ESA in respect of a low-level sanction. See also reg.54 on when the period takes effect.

This regulation specifies the reduction period as the sum of two periods. Under para.(a) the first period begins on the day of the sanctionable failure and ends on whichever is the earliest of the days identified in para.(a)(i)–(iv) which apply in the particular case. Sub-paragraph (i) in effect means the day before the one on which the claimant does what the Secretary of State wants in terms of work-related requirements (remedies the failure). Sub-paragraph (ii) sets the end of this first period as the day before that on which the claimant becomes exempt from work-related requirements under s.11D of the WRA 2007 (see update to pp.367–379 in Part II of this Supplement) read with reg.47, above. Sub-paragraph (iii) envisages this first period ending where the claimant is no longer required to take a particular action as a work preparation requirement under s.11C(1) of 11F(2) of the WRA 2007 (see update to pp.367–379 in Part II of this Supplement). Finally, sub-para.(iv) sees the end of the first period as the day on which an ESA award is terminated.

Paragraph (b) sets the second period at varying lengths (7, 14 or 28 days) depending on whether the failure was a first, second or subsequent offence (whether with respect to ESA, JSA or UC) in the 365 days preceding the failure in question. Note, however, that sanctionable failures attracting a JSA, ESA or UC reduction occurring in the 14 days before the sanctionable failure in question are to be disregarded (reg.51(4)).

## Lowest-level sanction

**53.** The reduction period for a lowest-level sanction is the number of days beginning with the date of the sanctionable failure and ending with—    **1.256**

    (a) the day before the date on which the claimant meets a compliance condition specified by the Secretary of State;

    (b) the day before the date on which the claimant falls within section 11D of the Act; or

    (c) the day on which the claimant's award of an employment and support allowance is terminated,

whichever is soonest.

DEFINITIONS

    "compliance condition"—see WRA 2007, s.11J(5).
    "lowest-level sanction"—see reg.50.
    "sanctionable failure"—see reg.50.

GENERAL NOTE

This deals with the reduction period in respect of a lowest-level sanction. Such a sanction is in respect of a failure by the claimant to comply with a requirement imposed under s.11E(2) of the Act (persons subject to work-focused interview requirement only) (see update to pp.367–379 in Part II of this Supplement). The period ends on whichever is the earliest of the days specified in paras (a), (b) or (c) as is applicable to the particular case. Paragraph (a) specifies this as the day before that on which the claimant complies with the condition. Paragraph (b) sets it as the day before that on which the claimant becomes exempt from work-related requirements under s.11D of the WRA 2007 (see update to pp.367–379 in Part II of this Supplement) read with reg.47, above. Paragraph (c) deals with the case where an award of ESA is terminated.    **1.257**

## Start of the reduction

**54.** A reduction period determined in relation to a sanctionable failure takes effect from—    **1.258**

(a) where the claimant has not been paid an employment and support allowance for the benefit week in which the Secretary of State determines that the amount of the award of employment and support allowance is to be reduced under section 11J of the Act, the first day of that benefit week;

(b) where the claimant has been paid an employment and support allowance for the benefit week referred to in paragraph (a), the first day of the first benefit week for which the claimant has not been paid an employment and support allowance; or

(c) where the amount of the award of the employment and support allowance for the benefit week referred to in paragraph (a) or (b) is already subject to a reduction because of a previous sanctionable failure, the first day in respect of which the amount of the award is no longer subject to that reduction.

DEFINITIONS

"benefit week"—see reg.2.
"reduction period"—see reg.50.
"sanctionable failure"—see reg.50.

GENERAL NOTE

1.259     This regulation deals with the matter of when a reduction period is to be given effect.

## Reduction period to continue where award of employment and support allowance terminates

1.260     **55.**—(1) Where an award of an employment and support allowance terminates while there is an outstanding reduction period—

(a) the period continues to run as if a daily reduction were being applied; and

(b) if the claimant becomes entitled to a new award of an employment and support allowance before the period expires, that new award is subject to a reduction for the remainder of the total outstanding reduction period.

(2) Paragraph (3) applies where—

(a) an award of an employment and support allowance terminates before the Secretary of State determines that the amount of the award is to be reduced under section 11J of the Act in relation to a sanctionable failure; and

(b) that determination is made after the claimant becomes entitled to a new award of an employment and support allowance.

(3) Where this paragraph applies—

(a) the reduction period in relation to the sanctionable failure referred to in paragraph (2) is to be treated as having taken effect on the day before the previous award terminated;

(b) that reduction period is treated as having continued to run as if a daily reduction were being applied; and

   (c) if the new award referred to in paragraph (2)(b) begins before that reduction period expires, that new award is subject to a reduction for the remainder of the total outstanding reduction period.

DEFINITIONS

   "reduction period"—see reg.50.
   "sanctionable failure"—see reg.50.
   "total outstanding reduction period"—see reg.50.

GENERAL NOTE

   If an award of ESA terminates while there is an outstanding reduction period, **1.261** subsequent days count as if an actual reduction of benefit were being applied (thus reducing the days outstanding in the period), so that on any further claim for ESA the claimant is subject to the reduction only for the remainder of the period, if any (para.(1)). If an award of ESA terminates before the Secretary of State has made a decision about a reduction for a sanctionable failure, but a new award is in place by the time the decision is made, the reduction period starts as if the decision had been made on the day before the previous award terminated, so that the new award of ESA will be reduced for the remainder of the total outstanding reduction period (paras (2), (3)).

## Suspension of a reduction where a fraud sanction applies

   **56.**—(1) A reduction in the amount of an award of an employment **1.262** and support allowance in accordance with section 11J of the Act is to be suspended for any period during which section 6B or 7 of the Social Security Fraud Act 2001 applies to the award.

   (2) The reduction ceases to have effect on the day on which that period begins and has effect again on the day after that period ends.

## Termination of a reduction

   **57.**—(1) A reduction in the amount of an award of an employment **1.263** and support allowance under section 11J of the Act is to be terminated where, since the date of the most recent sanctionable failure which gave rise to such a reduction, the claimant has been in paid work—
   (a) for a period of at least 26 weeks; or
   (b) for more than one period where the total of those periods amounts to at least 26 weeks.
   (2) The termination of the reduction has effect—
   (a) where the date on which paragraph (1) is satisfied falls within a period of entitlement to an employment and support allowance, from the beginning of the benefit week in which that date falls; or
   (b) where that date falls outside a period of entitlement to an employment and support allowance, from the beginning of the first benefit week in relation to any subsequent award of an employment and support allowance.
   (3) The claimant is in paid work for the purposes of paragraph (1) where their weekly earnings are at least equal to 16 multiplied by the national minimum wage which would apply for a person of the claimant's age under the National Minimum Wage Regulations 1999.

DEFINITIONS

    "benefit week"—see reg.2.
    "in paid work"—see para.(3).
    "sanctionable failure"—see reg.50.

GENERAL NOTE

1.264    Any reduction for any level of sanction or sanctions terminates where since the date of the most recent sanctionable failure the claimant has been in paid work for at least 26 weeks, not necessarily consecutive, with weekly earnings at least equal to 16 multiplied by the national minimum wage applicable to a person of the claimant's age under the National Minimum Wage Regulations 1999 (paras (1), (3)). Paragraph (2) sets out the time the termination takes effect dependent on whether or not the day the 26-week period is up falls within or outside a period of entitlement to ESA. If within, termination takes effect from the beginning of the benefit week in which there fell the completion of the 26-week period. If outside, it takes effect from the beginning of the first benefit week of any subsequent ESA award.

## Amount of reduction for each benefit week

1.265    **58.** Where it has been determined that an award of an employment and support allowance is to be reduced in accordance with section 11J of the Act, the amount of the reduction for each benefit week in respect of which a reduction has effect is to be calculated as follows.

Step 1

    Take the number of days—
    (a)  in the benefit week; or
    (b)  if lower, in the total outstanding reduction period,
and deduct any days in that benefit week or total outstanding reduction period for which the reduction is suspended in accordance with regulation 56.

Step 2

Multiply the number of days produced by step 1 by the daily reduction rate.

Step 3

Deduct the amount produced by step 2 from the amount of the award of employment and support allowance for the benefit week.

DEFINITIONS

    "benefit week"—see reg.2.
    "daily reduction rate"—see regs 59(1), 60.
    "total outstanding reduction period"—see reg.50.

GENERAL NOTE

1.266    This provides the means of calculating for each benefit week the amount of reduction depending on whether the claimant's case fits within reg.58(1) (daily reduction rate) or reg.60 (lower daily reduction rate).

## Daily reduction rate

**59.**—(1) The daily reduction rate for the purposes of regulation 58 is, unless regulation 60 applies, the amount prescribed for the claimant under regulation 62(1) or, where applicable, regulation 63(2), multiplied by 52 and divided by 365.

(2) The amount of the daily reduction rate is to be rounded down to the nearest 10 pence.

1.267

GENERAL NOTE

Unless the lower daily reduction rate in reg.60 applies, the daily reduction rate is the weekly prescribed amount appropriate for the particular claimant under reg.62, or if the claimant is a special case within reg.62, the weekly amount there prescribed. The pertinent prescribed amount is then multiplied by 52 and divided by 365 to produce the daily reduction rate. The daily rate must be rounded down to the nearest 10 pence.

1.268

## Lower daily reduction rate

**60.**—(1) The daily reduction rate is 40% of the rate applicable under regulation 59(1) if, at the end of the benefit week, the claimant falls within—

(a) section 11E of the Act;

(b) section 11D(2)(c) of the Act; or

(c) regulation 47(1)(b), (c), (f) or (g).

(2) The daily reduction rate is nil if, at the end of the benefit week, claimant falls within section 11D(2)(a) of the Act.

1.269

DEFINITIONS

"benefit week"—see reg.2.

GENERAL NOTE

If at the end of the benefit week the claimant falls within s.11E (person subject only to work-focused interview requirement) or s.11D(2)(c) (someone subject to no work-related requirements as a single person responsible for a child aged less than one) of the Welfare Reform Act 2007 (see update to pp.367–379 in Part II of this Supplement), the daily reduction rate is instead 40 per cent of the daily reduction rate determined under reg.59(1). Similarly if at the end of the benefit week the claimant falls with reg.47(1)(b) (responsible foster parent of a child aged under one), (1)(c) (an adopter in the first year of the adoption), (1)(f) (pregnant with 11 weeks or less to confinement), or (1)(g) (was pregnant and it is 15 weeks or less since confinement). If, however, the claimant falls within s.11D(2)(a) of the 2007 Act (as someone with limited capability for work and work related activity—a member of the support group) the reduction rate is nil.

1.270

## Sanctions where universal credit ends and the person is entitled to an employment and support allowance

**61.**—(1) This regulation applies where—

(a) a person ceases to be entitled to universal credit;

1.271

(b) there is a reduction relating to the person's award of universal credit under section 26 or 27 of the Welfare Reform Act 2012; and

(c) the person is entitled to an employment and support allowance.

(2) Any reduction relating to the award of the universal credit is to be applied to the award of the employment and support allowance.

(3) The period for which the reduction relating to the award of employment and support allowance is to have effect is the number of days which apply to the person under regulation 102, 103, 104 or 105 of the Universal Credit Regulations 2013 minus any such days which—

(a) have already resulted in a reduction in the amount of universal credit; or

(b) fall after the date on which the person ceases to be entitled to universal credit and before the date on which the person becomes entitled to an employment and support allowance.

(4) The daily reduction rate for the reduction relating to the award of employment and support allowance is—

(a) the amount referred to in regulation 60(1) where, on the date the claimant becomes entitled to an employment and support allowance, the claimant falls within—

(i) section 11E of the Act;

(ii) section 11D(2)(c) of the Act; or

(iii) regulation 47(1)(b), (c), (f) or (g);

(b) zero where the claimant falls within section 11D(2)(a) of the Act; or

(c) the amount referred to in regulation 59(1) in all other cases.

(5) The amount of the reduction of the claimant's award of an employment and support allowance is the number of days arrived at under paragraph (3) multiplied by the daily reduction rate referred to in paragraph (4).

GENERAL NOTE

1.272    Where someone subject to a UC sanction ceases to be entitled to UC and becomes entitled to ESA, the remaining reduction period applicable to the UC award carries over to reduce the ESA award. The remaining reduction period is calculated by deducting from the period imposed as regards UC (i) the days for which UC has been in consequence reduced and (ii) the days between the cessation of entitlement to UC and the beginning of entitlement to ESA. Paragraph (4) identifies the appropriate daily reduction rate according to whether the claimant falls within reg.61 (paras (4)(a) and (b)) or reg.59(1) (para.(4)(c)).

PART 9

*Amounts of Allowance*

## Prescribed amounts

1.273    **62.**—(1) Subject to regulation 63 (special cases) the amount prescribed for the purposes of the calculation of the amount of a claimant's employment and support allowance under section 2(1)(a) of the Act is—

    (a) where the claimant satisfies the conditions set out in section 2(2) or (3) of the Act, £71.70; or

    (b) where the claimant does not satisfy the conditions set out in section 2(2) or (3) of the Act—

        (i) where the claimant is aged not less than 25, £71.70; or

        (ii) where the claimant is aged less than 25, £56.80.

    (2) Subject to regulation 63, the amount of—

    (a) the work-related activity component is £28.45; and

    (b) the support component is £34.80.

GENERAL NOTE

    This sets the prescribed amounts of ESA, for claimants who are not special **1.274** cases under reg.63. Where the assessment phase has ended, the weekly rate is £71.70, to which will be added either a further £34.80 support component if the claimant has limited capability for work and work-related activity (members of the support group), or a further £28.45 work-related activity component for those who have limited capability for work but not for work-related activity (members of the work-related activity group).

    Where the assessment phase has not yet ended for the claimant, the rate of basic ESA depends on age: £71.70 for those aged 25 or over; £56.80 for those under 25.

## Special cases

    **63.**—(1) The amount prescribed for the purposes of the calculation of **1.275** the amount of a claimant's employment and support allowance under section 2(1)(a) of the Act in respect of a claimant who—

    (a) satisfies either of the conditions in paragraphs (3) or (4); or

    (b) has been a patient for a continuous period of more than 52 weeks,

is the amount applicable under regulation 62(1) and the amount of nil under regulation 62(2).

    (2) The amount prescribed for those purposes in respect of a claimant who is a person in hardship, is the amount to which the claimant is entitled—

    (a) under regulation 62(1) reduced by 20%; and

    (b) under regulation 62(2).

    (3) The first condition mentioned in paragraph (1)(a) is that—

    (a) the claimant is being detained under section 45A or 47 of the Mental Health Act 1983 (power of higher courts to direct hospital admission; removal to hospital of persons serving sentences of imprisonment etc); and

    (b) in any case where there is in relation to the claimant a release date within the meaning of section 50(3) of that Act, the claimant is being detained on or before the day which the Secretary of State certifies to be that release date.

    (4) The second condition mentioned in paragraph (1)(a) is that the claimant is being detained under—

(a) section 59A of the Criminal Procedure (Scotland) Act 1995 (hospital direction); or

(b) section 136 of the Mental Health (Care and Treatment) (Scotland) Act 2003 (transfer of prisoners for treatment of mental disorder).

(5) In this regulation—

"patient" means a person (other than a prisoner) who is regarded as receiving free in-patient treatment within the meaning of regulation 2(4) and (5) of the Social Security (Hospital In- Patients) Regulations 2005;

"prisoner" means a person who—

(a) is detained in custody pending trial or sentence on conviction or under a sentence imposed by a court; or

(b) is on temporary release in accordance with the provisions of the Prison Act 1952 or the Prisons (Scotland) Act 1989,

other than a person who is detained in hospital under the provisions of the Mental Health Act 1983 or, in Scotland, under the provisions of the Mental Health (Care and Treatment) (Scotland) Act 2003 or the Criminal Procedure (Scotland) Act 1995.

(6) For the purposes of this regulation—

(a) except where sub-paragraph (b) applies, a person is a "person in hardship" if they satisfy regulation 94; and

(b) where a person satisfies regulation 94 for more than six weeks, they are a "person in hardship" only for the first six weeks.

DEFINITIONS

"patient"—see para.(5).
"person in hardship"—see para.(5).
"prisoner"—see para.(5).

GENERAL NOTE

1.276  This sets the prescribed amounts of ESA awards for claimants who are special cases either as patients, certain persons detained under specified provisions of the applicable mental health legislation, persons in hardship and some remand prisoners or ones on temporary release.

## Permanent health insurance

1.277  **64.** For the purposes of sections 2(1)(c) and 3(3) of the Act (deductions from an employment and support allowance) "pension payment" is to include a permanent health insurance payment.

DEFINITIONS

"pension payment"—see WRA 2007, s.3(3).
"permanent health insurance payment"—see reg.2.

GENERAL NOTE

1.278  This is the same as ESA Regulations 2008 reg.72(1).

### Financial Assistance Scheme

**65.**—(1) For the purposes of sections 2(1)(c) and 3(3) of the Act (deductions from an employment and support allowance) "pension payment" is to include a Financial Assistance Scheme payment.

1.279

(2) In this regulation "Financial Assistance Scheme payment" means a payment made under the Financial Assistance Scheme Regulations 2005.

DEFINITIONS

"Financial Assistance Scheme payment"—see para.(2).
"pension payment"—see WRA 2007, s.3(3).

GENERAL NOTE

This replicates ESA Regulations 2008 reg.72A.

1.280

### Councillor's allowance

**66.** For the purposes of section 3(1)(c) of the Act—

1.281

(a) a councillor's allowance is a payment of a prescribed description; and
(b) the prescribed bodies carrying out public or local functions are—
   (i) in relation to England and Wales, a London borough council, a county council, a county borough council, a district council, a parish or community council, the Common Council of the City of London or the Council of the Isles of Scilly; and
   (ii) in relation to Scotland, a council constituted under section 2 of the Local Government etc. (Scotland) Act 1994.

DEFINITIONS

"councillor"—see reg.2.
"councillor's allowance"—see reg.2.

GENERAL NOTE

This is the same as ESA Regulations 2008 reg.73.

1.282

### Deductions for pension payment and PPF payment

**67.**—(1) Where—

1.283

(a) a claimant is entitled to an employment and support allowance in respect of any period of a week or part of a week;
(b) there is—
   (i) a pension payment;
   (ii) a PPF periodic payment; or
   (iii) both of the payments specified in paragraphs (i) and (ii),
   payable to that person in respect of that period (or a period which forms part of that period or includes that period or part of it); and
(c) the amount of the payment, or payments when taken together, exceeds—

     (i)  if the period in question is a week, £85; or

    (ii)  if that period is not a week, such proportion of £85 as falls to be calculated in accordance with regulation 79(1) or (5) (calculation of weekly amount of income),

the amount of that allowance is to be reduced by an amount equal to 50% of the excess.

(2) For the purposes of regulations 67 to 72 "payment" means a payment or payments, as the case may be, referred to in paragraph (1)(b).

DEFINITIONS

"claimant"—see WRA 2007, s.24(1).
"payment"—see para.(2).
"pension payment"—see WRA 2007, s.3(3); regs 64, 65.
"PPF periodic payment"—see WRA 2007, s.3(3).

GENERAL NOTE

1.284    This is the same as ESA Regulations 2008 reg.74.

## Payments treated as not being payments to which section 3 applies

1.285    **68.** The following payments are to be treated as not being payments to which section 3 of the Act applies—

(a) any pension payment made to a claimant as a beneficiary on the death of a member of any pension scheme;

(b) any PPF periodic payment made to a claimant as a beneficiary on the death of a person entitled to such a payment;

(c) where a pension scheme is in deficit or has insufficient resources to meet the full pension payment, the extent of the shortfall;

(d) any pension payment made under an instrument specified in section 639(2) of the Income Tax (Earnings and Pensions) Act 2003;

(e) any guaranteed income payment (which means a payment made under article 15(1)(a) or 29(1)(a) of the Armed Forces and Reserved Forces (Compensation Schemes) Order 2011);

(f) any permanent health insurance payment in respect of which the employee had contributed to the premium to the extent of more than 50%.

DEFINITIONS

"claimant"—see WRA 2007, s.24(1).
"guaranteed income payment"—see para.(e).
"pension payment"—see WRA 2007, s.3(3); regs 64, 65.
"permanent health insurance payment"—see reg.2.
"PPF periodic payment"—see WRA 2007, s.3(3).

GENERAL NOTE

1.286    This is much the same as ESA Regulations 2008 reg.75.

### Deductions for councillor's allowance

**69.**—(1) Where the net amount of councillor's allowance to which a claimant is entitled in respect of any week exceeds 16 multiplied by the National Minimum Wage, subject to paragraph (3), an amount equal to the excess is to be deducted from the amount of an employment and support allowance to which that claimant is entitled in respect of that week, and only the balance remaining (if any) is to be payable.

(2) In paragraph (1) "net amount", in relation to any councillor's allowance to which a claimant is entitled, means the aggregate amount of the councillor's allowance or allowances, or remuneration to which that claimant is entitled for the week in question, reduced by the amount of any payment in respect of expenses wholly, exclusively and necessarily incurred by that claimant, in that week, in the performance of the duties of a councillor.

(3) Where the amount determined by the calculation in paragraph (1) would, but for this paragraph, include an amount of—

(a) less than 50p, that amount is to be rounded up to the nearest 50p; or

(b) less than £1 but more than 50p, that amount is to be rounded up to the nearest £1.

1.287

DEFINITIONS

"councillor's allowance"—see reg.2.
"net amount"—see para.(2).

GENERAL NOTE

This is the same as ESA Regulations 2008 reg.76.

1.288

### Date from which payments are to be taken into account

**70.** Where regulation 67(1) or 69(1) applies, a deduction must have effect, calculated where appropriate in accordance with regulation 79(1) or (5), from the first day of the benefit week in which the payment or councillor's allowance is paid to a claimant who is entitled to an employment and support allowance in that week.

1.289

DEFINITIONS

"benefit week"—see reg.2.
"claimant"—see WRA 2007, s.24(1).
"councillor's allowance"—see reg.2.
"payment—see reg.67(2).

GENERAL NOTE

This corresponds to ESA Regulations 2008 reg.77. The annotation there refers to reg.94(1) and (6) of those Regulations. The equivalent provisions in these 2013 Regulations are reg.79(1), (5).

1.290

### Date from which a change in the rate of the payment takes effect

**71.** Where a payment or councillor's allowance is already being made to a claimant and the rate of that payment or that allowance changes, the

1.291

deduction at the new rate must take effect, calculated where appropriate in accordance with regulation 79(1) or (5), from the first day of the benefit week in which the new rate of the payment or councillor's allowance is paid.

DEFINITIONS

"benefit week"—see reg.2.
"claimant"—see WRA 2007, s.24(1).
"councillor's allowance"—see reg.2.
"payment—see reg.67(2).

GENERAL NOTE

1.292    This is the equivalent of ESA Regulations 2008 reg.78. The annotation there refers to reg.94(1) and (6) of those Regulations. The equivalent provisions in these 2013 Regulations are reg.79(1), (5).

## Calculation of payment made other than weekly

1.293    **72.**—(1) Where the period in respect of which a payment or councillor's allowance is paid is otherwise than weekly, an amount calculated or estimated in accordance with regulation 79(1) or (5) is to be regarded as the weekly amount of that payment or allowance.

(2) In determining the weekly payment, where two or more payments are payable to a claimant, each payment is to be calculated separately in accordance with regulation 79(1) or (5) before aggregating the sum of those payments for the purposes of the reduction of an employment and support allowance in accordance with regulation 67.

DEFINITIONS

"benefit week"—see reg.2.
"claimant"—see WRA 2007, s.24(1).
"councillor's allowance"—see reg.2.
"payment—see reg.67(2).

GENERAL NOTE

1.294    This is the equivalent of ESA Regulations 2008 reg.79. The annotation there refers to reg.94(1) and (6) of those Regulations. The equivalent provisions in these 2013 Regulations are reg.79(1), (5). The deduction rule (then in reg.74) is now in reg.67.

## Effect of statutory maternity pay on an employment and support allowance

1.295    **73.**—(1) This regulation applies where—
(a) a woman is entitled to statutory maternity pay and, on the day immediately preceding the first day in the maternity pay period, she—
    (i) is in a period of limited capability for work; and
    (ii) satisfies the conditions of entitlement to an employment and support allowance in accordance with section 1(2)(a) of the Act; and
(b) on any day during the maternity pay period—

160

    (i) she is in a period of limited capability for work; and

    (ii) that day is not a day where she is treated as not having limited capability for work.

(2) Where this regulation applies, notwithstanding section 20(2) of the Act, a woman who is entitled to statutory maternity pay is to be entitled to an employment and support allowance in respect of any day that falls within the maternity pay period.

(3) Where by virtue of paragraph (2) a woman is entitled to an employment and support allowance for any week (including part of a week), the total amount of employment and support allowance payable to her for that week is to be reduced by an amount equivalent to any statutory maternity pay to which she is entitled in accordance with Part 12 of the Contributions and Benefits Act for the same week (or equivalent part of a week where entitlement to an employment and support allowance is for part of a week), and only the balance, if any, of the employment and support allowance is to be payable to her.

DEFINITIONS

"the Act"—see reg.2.
"Contributions and Benefits Act"—see WRA 2007, s.65.
"maternity pay period"—see WRA 2007, s.20(8); SSCBA 1992, s.165(1).
"week"—see reg.2.

GENERAL NOTE

This is the same as ESA Regulations 2008 reg.80.        1.296

### Effect of statutory adoption pay on an employment and support allowance

**74.**—(1) This regulation applies where—        1.297

(a) a claimant is entitled to statutory adoption pay and, on the day immediately preceding the first day in the adoption pay period, she—

    (i) is in a period of limited capability for work; and

    (ii) satisfies the conditions of entitlement to an employment and support allowance in accordance with section 1(2)(a) of the Act; and

(b) on any day during the adoption pay period—

    (i) that claimant is in a period of limited capability for work; and

    (ii) that day is not a day where that claimant is treated as not having limited capability for work.

(2) Where this regulation applies, notwithstanding section 20(4) of the Act, a claimant who is entitled to statutory adoption pay is to be entitled to an employment and support allowance in respect of any day that falls within the adoption pay period.

(3) Where by virtue of paragraph (2) a claimant is entitled to an employment and support allowance for any week (including part of a week), the total amount of employment and support allowance payable to that claimant for that week is to be reduced by an amount equivalent

to any statutory adoption pay to which that claimant is entitled in accordance with Part 12ZB of the Contributions and Benefits Act for the same week (or equivalent part of a week where entitlement to an employment and support allowance is for part of a week), and only the balance, if any, of the employment and support allowance is to be payable to that claimant.

DEFINITIONS

> "the Act"—see reg.2.
> "adoption pay period"—see WRA 2007, s.20(8).
> "claimant"—see WRA 2007, s.24(1).
> "Contributions and Benefits Act"—see WRA 2007, s.65.
> "week"—see reg.2.

GENERAL NOTE

1.298    This replicates ESA Regulations 2008 reg.81 but, presumably mistakenly, deploys "she" in referring to the claimant, rather than the gender neutral language of that regulation.

## Effect of additional statutory paternity pay on an employment and support allowance

1.299    **75.**—(1) This regulation applies where—
(a) a claimant is entitled to additional statutory paternity pay and, on the day immediately preceding the first day in the additional paternity pay period, she—
  (i) is in a period of limited capability for work; and
  (ii) satisfies the conditions of entitlement to an employment and support allowance in accordance with section 1(2)(a) of the Act; and
(b) on any day during the additional statutory paternity pay period—
  (i) that claimant is in a period of limited capability for work; and
  (ii) that day is not a day where that claimant is treated as not having limited capability for work.

(2) Where this regulation applies, notwithstanding section 20(6) of the Act, a claimant who is entitled to additional statutory paternity pay is to be entitled to an employment and support allowance in respect of any day that falls within the additional paternity pay period.

(3) Where by virtue of paragraph (2) a person is entitled to an employment and support allowance for any week (including part of a week), the total amount of employment and support allowance payable to that claimant for that week is to be reduced by an amount equivalent to any additional statutory paternity pay to which that claimant is entitled in accordance with Part 12ZA of the Contributions and Benefits Act for the same week (or equivalent part of a week where entitlement to an employment and support allowance is for part of a week), and only the balance, if any, of the employment and support allowance is to be payable to that claimant.

DEFINITIONS

"the Act"—see reg.2.
"additional paternity pay period"—see WRA 2007, s.20(8).
"claimant"—see WRA 2007, s.24(1).
"Contributions and Benefits Act"—see WRA 2007, s.65.
"week"—see reg.2.

GENERAL NOTE

This is the same as ESA Regulations 2008 reg.82 but presumably mistakenly **1.300** (especially since SPP is paid to the father) uses 'she' in relation to the claimant rather than the gender neutral language in that regulation.

PART 10

*Income and earnings*

## Calculation of earnings derived from employed earner's employment and income other than earnings

**76.**—(1) Earnings derived from employment as an employed earner **1.301** and income which does not consist of earnings are to be taken into account over a period determined in accordance with the following provisions of this regulation and at a weekly amount determined in accordance with regulation 79 (calculation of weekly amount of income).

(2) Subject to the following provisions of this regulation, the period over which a payment is to be taken into account is to be—

(a) where the payment is monthly, a period equal to the number of weeks beginning with the date on which the payment is treated as paid and ending with the date immediately before the date on which the next monthly payment would have been treated as paid whether or not the next monthly payment is actually paid;

(b) where the payment is in respect of a period which is not monthly, a period equal to the length of the period for which payment is made;

(c) in any other case, a period equal to such number of weeks as is equal to the number obtained (see paragraph (9)) by applying the formula—

$$\frac{E}{J}$$

where—
E is the net earnings;
J is the amount of an employment and support allowance which would be payable had the payment not been made;

163

and that period is to begin on the date on which the payment is treated as paid under regulation 78 (date on which income is treated as paid).

(3) Where—

(a) earnings are derived from the same source but are not of the same kind; and

(b) but for this paragraph, the periods in respect of which those earnings would fall to be taken into account overlap, wholly or partly, those earnings are to be taken into account over a period equal to the aggregate length of those periods, and that period is to begin with the earliest date on which any part of those earnings would be treated as paid under regulation 78.

(4) In a case to which paragraph (5) applies, earnings under regulation 80 (earnings of employed earners) are to be taken into account in the following order of priority—

(a) earnings normally derived from the employment;

(b) any payment to which paragraph (1)(b) or (c) of that regulation applies;

(c) any payment to which paragraph (1)(j) of that regulation applies;

(d) any payment to which paragraph (1)(d) of that regulation applies.

(5) Where earnings to which regulation 80(1)(b) to (d) applies are paid in respect of part of a day, those earnings are to be taken into account over a period equal to a day.

(6) Any earnings to which regulation 80(1)(j) applies which are paid in respect of, or on the termination of, part-time employment, are to be taken into account over a period of one week.

(7) For the purposes of this regulation the claimant's earnings are to be calculated in accordance with regulations 80 and 81.

(8) For the purposes of paragraph 10 of Schedule 2 to the Act (effect of work), the income which consists of earnings of a claimant is to be calculated on a weekly basis by determining the weekly amount of those earnings in accordance with regulations 77 to 84.

(9) For the purposes of the number obtained as mentioned in paragraph (2)(c), any fraction is to be treated as a corresponding fraction of a week.

DEFINITIONS

"the Act"—see reg.2.
"claimant"—see WRA 2007, s.24(1).
"employed earner"—see reg.2.
"employment"—see reg.2.
"net earnings"—see reg.2.
"week"—see reg.2.

GENERAL NOTE

1.302     This has affinities with ESA Regulations 2008 reg.91, save with respect to the formula in para.(2)(c) of this regulation.

## Calculation of earnings of self-employed earners

**77.**—(1) Where a claimant's income consists of earnings from employment as a self-employed earner, the weekly amount of the claimant's earnings is to be determined by reference to the claimant's average weekly earnings from that employment—

    (a) over a period of one year; or

    (b) where the claimant has recently become engaged in that employment or there has been a change which is likely to affect the normal pattern of business, over such other period as may, in any particular case, enable the weekly amount of the claimant's earnings to be determined more accurately.

(2) For the purposes of this regulation the claimant's earnings are to be calculated in accordance with regulations 82 to 84.

1.303

DEFINITIONS

"claimant"—see WRA 2007, s.24(1).
"self-employed earner"—see reg.2.

GENERAL NOTE

This is much the same as ESA Regulations 2008 reg.92(1), (3).

1.304

## Date on which income is treated as paid

**78.** A payment of income to which regulation 76 (calculation of earnings derived from employed earner's employment and income other than earnings) applies is to be treated as paid—

    (a) in the case of a payment which is due to be paid before the first benefit week pursuant to the claim, on the date on which it is due to be paid;

    (b) in any other case, on the first day of the benefit week in which it is due to be paid or the first succeeding benefit week in which it is practicable to take it into account.

1.305

DEFINITIONS

"benefit week"—see reg.2.
"claimant"—see WRA 2007, s.24(1).
"employed earner"—see reg.2.
"employment"—see reg.2.

GENERAL NOTE

This is the equivalent of ESA Regulations 2008 reg.93(1).

1.306

## Calculation of weekly amount of income

**79.**—(1) For the purposes of regulation 76 (calculation of earnings derived from employed earner's employment and income other than earnings) and regulations 64 to 72 (deductions from employment and support allowance), subject to paragraphs (2) to (5), where the period in respect of which a payment is made—

    (a) does not exceed a week, the weekly amount is to be the amount of that payment;

1.307

(b) exceeds a week, the weekly amount is to be determined—

 (i) in a case where that period is a month, by multiplying the amount of the payment by 12 and dividing the product by 52;

 (ii) in a case where that period is three months, by multiplying the amount of the payment by four and dividing the product by 52;

 (iii) in a case where that period is a year and the payment is income, by dividing the amount of the payment by 52;

 (iv) in any other case, by multiplying the amount of the payment by seven and dividing the product by the number equal to the number of days in the period in respect of which it is made.

(2) Where a payment for a period not exceeding a week is treated under regulation 78(a) (date on which income is treated as paid) as paid before the first benefit week and a part is to be taken into account for some days only in that week (the relevant days), the amount to be taken into account for the relevant days is to be calculated by multiplying the amount of the payment by the number of relevant days and dividing the product by the number of days in the period in respect of which it is made.

(3) Where a payment is in respect of a period equal to or in excess of a week and a part thereof is to be taken into account for some days only in a benefit week (the relevant days), the amount to be taken into account for the relevant days is to be calculated by multiplying the amount of the payment by the number of relevant days and dividing the product by the number of days in the period in respect of which it is made.

(4) Except in the case of a payment which it has not been practicable to treat under regulation 78(b) (date on which income is treated as paid) as paid on the first day of the benefit week in which it is due to be paid, where a payment of income from a particular source is or has been paid regularly and that payment falls to be taken into account in the same benefit week as a payment of the same kind and from the same source, the amount of that income to be taken into account in any one benefit week is not to exceed the weekly amount determined under paragraph (1)(a) or (b) of the payment which under regulation 78(b) is treated as paid first.

(5) Where the amount of the claimant's income fluctuates and has changed more than once, or a claimant's regular pattern of work is such that the claimant does not work every week, the foregoing paragraphs may be modified so that the weekly amount of the claimant's income is determined by reference to the claimant's average weekly income—

(a) if there is a recognisable cycle of work, over the period of one complete cycle (including, where the cycle involves periods in which the claimant does no work, those periods but disregarding any other absences);

(b) in any other case, over a period of five weeks or such other period as may, in the particular case, enable the claimant's average weekly income to be determined more accurately.

DEFINITIONS

"benefit week"—see reg.2.
"claimant"—see WRA 2007, s.24(1).

GENERAL NOTE

This equates to ESA Regulations 2008 reg.94(1)–(3), (5), (6).          **1.308**

## Earnings of employed earners

**80.**—(1) Subject to paragraphs (2) and (3), "earnings" means, in the     **1.309**
case of employment as an employed earner, any remuneration or profit
derived from that employment and includes—
  (a) any bonus or commission;
  (b) any payment in lieu of remuneration except any periodic sum paid
      to a claimant on account of the termination of the claimant's
      employment by reason of redundancy;
  (c) any payment in lieu of notice;
  (d) any holiday pay except any payable more than four weeks after the
      termination or interruption of employment;
  (e) any payment by way of a retainer;
  (f) any payment made by the claimant's employer in respect of
      expenses not wholly, exclusively and necessarily incurred in the
      performance of the duties of the employment, including any pay-
      ment made by the claimant's employer in respect of—
      (i) travelling expenses incurred by the claimant between the
          claimant's home and place of employment;
      (ii) expenses incurred by the claimant under arrangements made
           for the care of a member of the claimant's family owing to the
           claimant's absence from home;
  (g) any award of compensation made under section 112(4) or
      117(3)(a) of the Employment Rights Act 1996 (the remedies:
      orders and compensation, enforcement of order and compensa-
      tion);
  (h) any payment made or remuneration paid under sections 28, 34,
      64, 68 and 70 of the Employment Rights Act 1996 (right to
      guarantee payments, remuneration on suspension on medical or
      maternity grounds, complaints to employment tribunals);
  (i) any such sum as is referred to in section 112(3) of the Contribu-
      tions and Benefits Act (certain sums to be earnings for social
      security purposes);
  (j) where a payment of compensation is made in respect of employ-
      ment which is part-time employment, the amount of the com-
      pensation;
  (k) the amount of any payment by way of a non-cash voucher which
      has been taken into account in the computation of a person's
      earnings in accordance with Part 5 of Schedule 3 to the Social
      Security (Contributions) Regulations 2001.
(2) "Earnings" are not to include—
  (a) subject to paragraph (3), any payment in kind;

(b) any remuneration paid by or on behalf of an employer to the claimant in respect of a period throughout which the claimant is on maternity leave, paternity leave or adoption leave (which means a period of absence from work on ordinary or additional adoption leave under section 75A or 75B of the Employment Rights Act 1996) or is absent from work because the claimant is ill;

(c) any payment in respect of expenses wholly, exclusively and necessarily incurred in the performance of the duties of the employment;

(d) any occupational pension (which means any pension or other periodical payment under an occupational pension scheme but does not include any discretionary payment out of a fund established for relieving hardship in particular cases);

(e) any lump sum payment made under the Iron and Steel Re-adaptation Benefits Scheme;

(f) any payment in respect of expenses arising out of the claimant participating as a service user.

(3) Paragraph (2)(a) is not to apply in respect of any non-cash voucher referred to in paragraph (1)(k).

(4) In this regulation—

"compensation" means any payment made in respect of, or on the termination of, employment in a case where a claimant has not received or received only part of a payment in lieu of notice due or which would have been due to the claimant had that claimant not waived the right to receive it, other than—

(a) any payment specified in paragraph (1)(a) to (i);

(b) any payment specified in paragraph (2)(a) to (f);

(c) any redundancy payment within the meaning of section 135(1) of the Employment Rights Act 1996;

(d) any refund of contributions to which that person was entitled under an occupational pension scheme; and

(e) any compensation payable by virtue of section 173 of the Education Reform Act 1988;

"paternity leave" means a period of absence from work on ordinary paternity leave by virtue of section 80A or 80B of the Employment Rights Act 1996 or on additional paternity leave by virtue of section 80AA or 80BB of that Act.

(5) The reference in paragraph (2)(f) to a person participating as a service user is to—

(a) a person who is being consulted by or on behalf of—

(i) a body which has a statutory duty to provide services in the field of health, social care or social housing; or

(ii) a body which conducts research or undertakes monitoring for the purpose of planning or improving such services,

in the person's capacity as a user, potential user, carer of a user or person otherwise affected by the provision of those services; or

(b) the carer of a person consulted under sub-paragraph (a).

DEFINITIONS

"claimant"—see WRA 2007, s.24(1).
"compensation"—see para.(4).
"employed earner"—see reg.2.
"employment"—see reg.2.
"part-time employment"—see reg.2.
"paternity leave"—see para.(4).
"person participating as a service user"—see para.(5).

GENERAL NOTE

This is much the same as ESA Regulations 2008 reg.95.                    **1.310**

## Calculation of net earnings of employed earners

**81.**—(1) For the purposes of regulation 76 (calculation of earnings  **1.311**
derived from employed earner's employment and income other than
earnings) the earnings of a claimant derived from employment as an
employed earner to be taken into account are the claimant's net earnings.

(2) For the purposes of paragraph (1) net earnings are to be calculated
by taking into account the gross earnings of the claimant from that
employment less—
  (a) any amount deducted from those earnings by way of—
      (i) income tax;
      (ii) primary Class 1 contributions under section 6(1)(a) of the
           Contributions and Benefits Act;
  (b) one-half of any sum paid by the claimant in respect of a pay period
      by way of a contribution towards an occupational or personal
      pension scheme.

DEFINITIONS

"claimant"—see WRA 2007, s.24(1).
"employed earner"—see reg.2.
"occupational pension scheme"—see reg.2.
"pay period"—see reg.2.
"personal pension scheme"—see reg.2.

GENERAL NOTE

Compare ESA Regulations 2008 reg.96(1), (3).                    **1.312**

## Earnings of self-employed earners

**82.**—(1) Subject to paragraph (2), "earnings", in the case of employ-  **1.313**
ment as a self-employed earner, means the gross receipts of the employment and include any allowance paid under section 2 of the Employment
and Training Act 1973 or section 2 of the Enterprise and New Towns
(Scotland) Act 1990 to the claimant for the purpose of assisting the
claimant in carrying on the claimant's business.

(2) "Earnings" do not include—
  (a) where a claimant is involved in providing board and lodging
      accommodation for which a charge is payable, any payment by
      way of such a charge;

169

(b) any award made by one of the Sports Councils named in section 23(2) of the National Lottery etc Act 1993 out of sums allocated to it for distribution under that section.

(3) In this regulation, "board and lodging" means—

(a) accommodation provided to a person or, if the person is a member of a family, to that person or any other member of that person's family, for a charge which is inclusive of the provision of that accommodation and at least some cooked or prepared meals which both are cooked or prepared (by a person other than the person to whom the accommodation is provided or a member of that person's family) and are consumed in that accommodation or associated premises; or

(b) accommodation provided to a person in a hotel, guest house, lodging house or some similar establishment,

except accommodation provided by a close relative of the person or any other member of the person's family, or other than on a commercial basis.

DEFINITIONS

"board and lodging"—see para.(3).
"claimant"—see WRA 2007, s.24(1).
"self-employed earner"—see reg.2.

GENERAL NOTE

1.314　　This is the same as ESA Regulations 2008 reg.97.

## Calculation of net profit of self-employed earners

1.315　　**83.**—(1) For the purposes of regulation 77 (calculation of earnings of self-employed earners), the earnings of a claimant to be taken into account are to be—

(a) in the case of a self-employed earner who is engaged in employment on that self-employed earner's own account, the net profit derived from that employment;

(b) in the case of a self-employed earner whose employment is carried on in partnership or is that of a share fisherman within the meaning of the Social Security (Mariners' Benefits) Regulations 1975, that self-employed earner's share of the net profit derived from that employment less—

(i) an amount in respect of income tax and of National Insurance contributions payable under the Contributions and Benefits Act calculated in accordance with regulation 84 (deduction of tax and contributions for self-employed earners); and

(ii) one half of any contribution paid in the period that is relevant under regulation 77 (calculation of earnings of self-employed earners) in respect of a personal pension scheme.

(2) For the purposes of paragraph (1)(a) the net profit of the employment, except where paragraph (8) applies, is to be calculated by taking into account the earnings of the employment over the period determined under regulation 77 less—

(a) subject to paragraphs (4) to (6), any expenses wholly and exclusively defrayed in that period for the purposes of that employment;

(b) an amount in respect of—
  (i) income tax; and
  (ii) National Insurance contributions payable under the Contributions and Benefits Act, calculated in accordance with regulation 84 (deduction of tax and contributions for self-employed earners); and

(c) one half of any contribution paid in the period that is relevant under regulation 77 in respect of a personal pension scheme.

(3) For the purposes of paragraph (1)(b), the net profit of the employment is to be calculated by taking into account the earnings of the employment over the period determined under regulation 77 less, subject to paragraphs (4) to (6), any expenses wholly and exclusively defrayed in that period for the purpose of that employment.

(4) Subject to paragraph (5), a deduction is not to be made under paragraph (2)(a) or (3) in respect of—

(a) any capital expenditure;

(b) the depreciation of any capital asset;

(c) any sum employed or intended to be employed in the setting up or expansion of the employment;

(d) any loss incurred before the beginning of the period determined under regulation 77 (calculation of earnings of self-employed earners);

(e) the repayment of capital on any loan taken out for the purposes of the employment;

(f) any expenses incurred in providing business entertainment.

(5) A deduction is to be made under paragraph (2)(a) or (3) in respect of the repayment of capital on any loan used for—

(a) the replacement in the course of business of equipment or machinery; and

(b) the repair of an existing business asset except to the extent that any sum is payable under an insurance policy for its repair.

(6) The Secretary of State must refuse to make a deduction in respect of any expenses under paragraph (2)(a) or (3) where the Secretary of State is not satisfied that the expense has been defrayed or, having regard to the nature of the expense and its amount, that it has been reasonably incurred.

(7) A deduction—

(a) is not to be made under paragraph (2)(a) or (3) in respect of any sum unless it has been expended for the purposes of the business;

(b) is to be made under paragraph (2)(a) or (3) in respect of—
  (i) the excess of any Value Added Tax paid over Value Added Tax received in the period determined under regulation 77;
  (ii) any income expended in the repair of an existing asset except to the extent that any sum is payable under an insurance policy for its repair;

    (iii) any payment of interest on a loan taken out for the purposes of the employment.

(8) Where a claimant is engaged in employment as a child minder the net profit of the employment is to be one-third of the earnings of that employment, less—

    (a) an amount in respect of—

       (i) income tax; and

      (ii) National Insurance contributions payable under the Contributions and Benefits Act, calculated in accordance with regulation 84 (deduction of tax and contributions for self-employed earners); and

    (b) one half of any contribution paid in respect of a personal pension scheme.

(9) Notwithstanding regulation 77 (calculation of earnings of self-employed earners) and the foregoing paragraphs, the Secretary of State may assess any item of a claimant's income or expenditure over a period other than that determined under regulation 77 as may, in the particular case, enable the weekly amount of that item of income or expenditure to be determined more accurately.

(10) Where a claimant is engaged in employment as a self-employed earner and that claimant is also engaged in one or more other employments as a self-employed or employed earner, any loss incurred in any one of the claimant's employments is not to be offset against the claimant's earnings in any other of the claimant's employments.

DEFINITIONS

    "claimant"—see WRA 2007, s.24(1).
    "employment"—see reg.2.
    "personal pension scheme"—see reg.2.
    "self-employed earner"—see reg.2.

GENERAL NOTE

1.316    This is much the same as ESA Regulations 2008 reg.98.

## Deduction of tax and contributions for self-employed earners

1.317    **84.**—(1) Subject to paragraph (2), the amount to be deducted in respect of income tax under regulation 83(1)(b)(i), (2)(b)(i) or (8)(a)(i) (calculation of net profit of self-employed earners) is to be calculated on the basis of the amount of chargeable income and as if that income were assessable to income tax at the basic rate of tax less only the personal allowance to which the claimant is entitled under sections 35 and 38 to 40 of the Income Tax Act 2007 (personal reliefs) as is appropriate to the claimant's circumstances.

(2) If the period determined under regulation 77 is less than a year, the earnings to which the basic rate of tax is to be applied and the amount of the personal reliefs deductible under paragraph (1) are to be calculated on a pro rata basis.

(3) The amount to be deducted in respect of National Insurance contributions under regulation 83(1)(b)(i), (2)(b)(ii) or (8)(a)(ii) is to be the total of—

(a) the amount of Class 2 contributions payable under section 11(1) or, as the case may be, (3) of the Contributions and Benefits Act at the rate applicable at the date of claim except where the claimant's chargeable income is less than the amount specified in section 11(4) of that Act (small earnings exception) for the tax year in which the date of claim falls; but if the assessment period is less than a year, the amount specified for that tax year is to be reduced pro rata; and

(b) the amount of Class 4 contributions (if any) which would be payable under section 15 of that Act (Class 4 contributions recoverable under the Income Tax Acts) at the percentage rate applicable at the date of claim on so much of the chargeable income as exceeds the lower limit but does not exceed the upper limit of profits applicable for the tax year in which the date of claim falls; but if the assessment period is less than a year, those limits are to be reduced pro rata.

(4) In this regulation—

"assessment period" means the period mentioned in regulation 77 over which the weekly amount of the claimant's earnings is to be determined;

"basic rate" has the same meaning as in the Income Tax Act 2007 (see section 989 of that Act);

"chargeable income" means—

    (a) except where paragraph (b) applies, the earnings derived from the employment less any expenses deducted under paragraph (2)(a) or, as the case may be, (3) of regulation 83;

    (b) in the case of employment as a child minder, one-third of the earnings of that employment.

DEFINITIONS

"claimant"—see WRA 2007, s.24(1).
"Contributions and Benefits Act"—see WRA 2007, s.65.

GENERAL NOTE

This is much the same as ESA Regulations 2008 reg.99.     1.318

PART 11

*Supplementary provisions*

**Waiting days**

85.—(1) The number of days prescribed for the purposes of paragraph   1.319
2 of Schedule 2 to the Act (days during which a person is not entitled to an employment and support allowance at the beginning of a period of limited capability for work) is three.

(2) Paragraph 2 of Schedule 2 to the Act does not apply where—

   (a) the claimant's entitlement to an employment and support allowance commences within 12 weeks of the claimant's entitlement to income support, incapacity benefit, severe disablement allowance, state pension credit, a jobseeker's allowance, a carer's allowance, statutory sick pay or a maternity allowance coming to an end;

   (b) the claimant is terminally ill and has—

     (i) made a claim expressly on the ground of being terminally ill; or

     (ii) made an application for supersession or revision in accordance with the Decisions and Appeals Regulations 1999 or the Decisions and Appeals Regulations 2013 which contains an express statement that the claimant is terminally ill;

   (c) the claimant has been discharged from being a member of Her Majesty's forces and three or more days immediately before that discharge were days of sickness absence from duty, which are recorded by the Secretary of State; or

   (d) the claimant is entitled to an employment and support allowance by virtue of section 1B of the Act (further entitlement after time-limiting).

DEFINITIONS

"claimant"—see WRA 2007, s.24(1).
"a member of Her Majesty's forces"—see reg.2(1).
"terminally ill"—see reg.2(1).

GENERAL NOTE

1.320    This is the same as ESA Regulations 2008 reg.144.

## Linking period

1.321    **86.** Any period of limited capability for work which is separated from another such period by not more than 12 weeks is to be treated as a continuation of the earlier period.

DEFINITIONS

"claimant"—see WRA 2007, s.24(1).
"week"—see reg.2.

GENERAL NOTE

1.322    This is the same as ESA Regulations 2008 reg.145.

## Claimants appealing a decision

1.323    **87.**—(1) This regulation applies where a claimant has made and is pursuing an appeal against a decision of the Secretary of State that embodies a determination that the claimant does not have limited capability for work under these Regulations.

(2) Subject to paragraph (3), where this regulation applies, a determination of limited capability for work by the Secretary of State under regulation 15 must not be made until the appeal is determined by the First-tier Tribunal.

174

(3) Paragraph (2) does not apply where either—

(a) the claimant suffers from some specific disease or bodily or mental disablement from which the claimant was not suffering when entitlement began; or

(b) a disease or bodily or mental disablement from which the claimant was suffering when entitlement began has significantly worsened.

(4) Where this regulation applies and the Secretary of State makes a determination—

(a) in a case to which paragraph (3) applies (including where the determination is not the first such determination) that the claimant does not have or, by virtue of regulation 18 or 19, is to be treated as not having limited capability for work; or

(b) subsequent to a determination that the claimant is to be treated as having limited capability for work by virtue of a provision of these Regulations other than regulation 26, that the claimant is no longer to be so treated,

this regulation and regulation 26 have effect as if that determination had not been made.

(5) Where this regulation applies and—

(a) the claimant is entitled to an employment and support allowance by virtue of being treated as having limited capability for work in accordance with regulation 26;

(b) neither of the circumstances in paragraph (3) applies, or, subsequent to the application of either of those circumstances, the claimant has been determined not to have limited capability for work; and

(c) the claimant's appeal is dismissed, withdrawn or struck out,

the claimant is to be treated as not having limited capability for work with effect from the day specified in paragraph (6).

(6) The day specified for the purposes of paragraph (5) is the first day of the benefit week following the date on which the Secretary of State receives the First-tier Tribunal's notification that the appeal is dismissed, withdrawn or struck out.

(7) Where a claimant's appeal is successful, subject to paragraph (8), any finding of fact or other determination embodied in or necessary to the decision of the First-tier Tribunal or on which the First-tier Tribunal's decision is based is to be conclusive for the purposes of the decision of the Secretary of State, in relation to an award made in a case to which this regulation applies, as to whether the claimant has limited capability for work or limited capability for work-related activity.

(8) Paragraph (7) does not apply where, due to a change of circumstances after entitlement began, the Secretary of State is satisfied that it is no longer appropriate to rely on such finding or determination.

DEFINITIONS

"claimant"—see WRA 2007, s.24(1).
"First-tier Tribunal"—see reg.2.

GENERAL NOTE

1.324　This is essentially the same as ESA Regulations 2008 reg.147A.

## Absence from Great Britain

1.325　**88.**—(1) A claimant who is entitled to an employment and support allowance is to continue to be so entitled during a period of temporary absence from Great Britain only in accordance with regulations 89 to 92.

(2) A claimant who continues to be entitled to an employment and support allowance during a period of temporary absence is not disqualified for receiving that allowance during that period under section 18(4) of the Act.

DEFINITIONS

"claimant"—see WRA 2007 s.24(1).

GENERAL NOTE

1.326　This is identical to ESA Regulations 2008 reg.151.

## Short absence

1.327　**89.** A claimant is to continue to be entitled to an employment and support allowance during the first four weeks of a temporary absence from Great Britain if—
　　(a) the period of absence is unlikely to exceed 52 weeks; and
　　(b) while absent from Great Britain, the claimant continues to satisfy the other conditions of entitlement to that employment and support allowance.

DEFINITIONS

"claimant"—see WRA 2007, s.24(1).
"week"—see reg.2.

GENERAL NOTE

1.328　This is identical to ESA Regulations 2008 reg.152.

## Absence to receive medical treatment

1.329　**90.**—(1) A claimant is to continue to be entitled to an employment and support allowance during the first 26 weeks of a temporary absence from Great Britain if—
　　(a) the period of absence is unlikely to exceed 52 weeks;
　　(b) while absent from Great Britain, the claimant continues to satisfy the other conditions of entitlement to that employment and support allowance;
　　(c) the claimant is absent from Great Britain only—
　　　　(i) in connection with arrangements made for the treatment of the claimant for a disease or bodily or mental disablement directly related to the claimant's limited capability for work which commenced before leaving Great Britain; or

(ii) because the claimant is accompanying a dependent child (which means any child or qualifying young person who is treated as the responsibility of the claimant or the claimant's partner, where that child or young person is a member of the claimant's household) in connection with arrangements made for the treatment of that child for a disease or bodily or mental disablement; and

(d) those arrangements relate to treatment—

    (i) outside Great Britain;

    (ii) during the period whilst the claimant is temporarily absent from Great Britain; and

    (iii) by, or under the supervision of, a person appropriately qualified to carry out that treatment.

(2) In this regulation, "appropriately qualified" means qualified to provide medical treatment, physiotherapy or a form of treatment which is similar to, or related to, either of those forms of treatment.

DEFINITIONS

"appropriately qualified"—see para.(2).
"child"—see reg.2.
"claimant"—see WRA 2007, s.24(1)
"dependent child"—see para.(1)(c)(ii).
"partner"—see reg.2.
"qualifying young person"—see reg.2.

GENERAL NOTE

This is the same as ESA Regulations 2008 reg.153.                     **1.330**

## Absence in order to receive NHS treatment

**91.** A claimant is to continue to be entitled to an employment and    **1.331**
support allowance during any period of temporary absence from Great
Britain if—

(a) while absent from Great Britain, the claimant continues to satisfy the other conditions of entitlement to that employment and support allowance; and

(b) that period of temporary absence is for the purpose of the claimant receiving treatment at a hospital or other institution outside Great Britain where the treatment is being provided—

    (i) under section 6(2) of the Health Service Act (Performance of functions outside England) or section 6(2) of the Health Service (Wales) Act (Performance of functions outside Wales);

    (ii) pursuant to arrangements made under section 12(1) of the Health Service Act (Secretary of State's arrangements with other bodies), section 10(1) of the Health Service (Wales) Act (Welsh Ministers' arrangements with other bodies), paragraph 18 of Schedule 4 to the Health Service Act (joint exercise of functions) or paragraph 18 of Schedule 3 to the Health Service (Wales) Act (joint exercise of functions); or

      (iii) under any equivalent provision in Scotland or pursuant to arrangements made under such provision.

<small>DEFINITIONS</small>

    "claimant"—see WRA 2007, s.24(1).

<small>GENERAL NOTE</small>

**1.332**    This is the same as ESA Regulations 2008 reg.154.

### Absence of member of family of member of Her Majesty's forces

**1.333**    **92.**—(1) A claimant is to continue to be entitled to an employment and support allowance during any period of temporary absence from Great Britain if the claimant is a member of the family of a member of Her Majesty's forces and temporarily absent from Great Britain by reason only of the fact that the claimant is living with that member.

    (2) In this regulation "member of the family of a member of Her Majesty's forces" means the spouse, civil partner, son, daughter, step-son, step-daughter, father, father-in-law, step-father, mother, mother-in-law or step-mother of such a member.

<small>DEFINITIONS</small>

    "claimant"—see WRA 2007 s.24(1).
    "member of Her Majesty's forces"—see reg.(2) and Sch.1.
    "member of the family of a member of Her Majesty's forces"—see para.(2).

<small>GENERAL NOTE</small>

**1.334**    This corresponds to ESA Regulations 2008 reg.155.

PART 12

*Disqualification*

### Disqualification for misconduct etc

**1.335**    **93.**—(1) Subject to paragraph (3), paragraph (2) applies where a claimant—

    (a) has limited capability for work by reason of the claimant's own misconduct, except in a case where the limited capability is due to a sexually transmitted disease;

    (b) fails without good cause to attend for or submit to medical or other treatment (excluding vaccination, inoculation or surgery which the Secretary of State considers is major) recommended by a doctor with whom, or a hospital or similar institution with which, the claimant is undergoing medical treatment, which would be likely to remove the limitation on the claimant's capability for work;

(c) fails without good cause to refrain from behaviour calculated to retard the claimant's recovery to health; or

(d) is, without good cause, absent from the claimant's place of residence without informing the Secretary of State where the claimant may be found.

(2) A claimant referred to in paragraph (1) is to be disqualified for receiving an employment and support allowance for such period not exceeding six weeks as the Secretary of State may determine in accordance with Chapter 2 of Part 1 of the Social Security Act 1998.

(3) Paragraph (2) does not apply where the claimant—

(a) is disqualified for receiving an employment and support allowance by virtue of regulations made under section 6B or 7 of the Social Security Fraud Act 2001; or

(b) is a person in hardship.

(4) In this regulation, "doctor" means a registered medical practitioner, or in the case of a medical practitioner practising outside the United Kingdom, a person registered or recognised as such in the country in which the person undertakes medical practice.

DEFINITIONS

"claimant"—see WRA 2007, s.24(1).
"doctor"—see para.(4).
"medical treatment"—see reg.2.
"person in hardship"—see reg.94.
"week"—see reg.2.

GENERAL NOTE

This has the same effect as ESA Regulations 2008 reg.157.                    **1.336**

## Meaning of "person in hardship"

**94.**—(1) A claimant is a "person in hardship" if the claimant—          **1.337**

(a) has informed the Secretary of State of the circumstances on which the claimant relies to establish that fact; and

(b) falls within paragraph (2), (3) or (5).

(2) A claimant falls within this paragraph if—

(a) she is pregnant;

(b) a member of the claimant's family is pregnant;

(c) the claimant is single and aged less than 18; or

(d) the claimant is a member of a couple and both members are aged less than 18.

(3) Subject to paragraph (4), the claimant falls within this paragraph if the claimant or the claimant's partner—

(a) has been awarded an attendance allowance, the care component or the daily living component;

(b) has claimed attendance allowance, disability living allowance or personal independence payment and the claim has not been determined;

(c) devotes what the Secretary of State considers is a considerable portion of each week to caring for another person who—

     (i) has been awarded an attendance allowance, the care component or the daily living component; or

    (ii) has claimed attendance allowance, disability living allowance or personal independence payment and the claim has not been determined; or

(d) has attained the qualifying age for state pension credit, which has the meaning given in section 1(6) of the State Pension Credit Act 2002.

(4) A claimant to whom paragraph (3)(b) or (3)(c)(ii) applies is a person in hardship only for 26 weeks from the date of the claim unless the claimant is a person in hardship under another provision of this regulation.

(5) The claimant falls within this paragraph where the Secretary of State is satisfied, having regard to all the circumstances and, in particular, the matters set out in paragraph (6), that unless an employment and support allowance is paid, the claimant, or a member of the claimant's family, will suffer hardship.

(6) The matters referred to in paragraph (5) are—

(a) the resources which are likely to be available to the claimant and the claimant's family and the length of time for which they might be available; and

(b) whether there is a substantial risk that essential items, including food, clothing and heating, will cease to be available to the claimant or a member of the claimant's family, or will be available at considerably reduced levels and the length of time for which this might be so.

(7) In this regulation—

"attendance allowance" means—

    (a) an attendance allowance under section 64 of the Contributions and Benefits Act;

    (b) an increase of disablement pension under section 104 or 105 of that Act;

    (c) [¹*omitted*]

    (d) [¹*omitted*];

    (e) a payment by virtue of article 14, 15, 16, 43 or 44 of the Personal Injuries (Civilians) Scheme 1983 or any analogous payment;

    (f) any payment based on the need for attendance which is paid as an addition to a war disablement pension (which means any retired pay or pension or allowance payable in respect of disablement under an instrument specified in section 639(2) of the Income Tax (Earnings and Pensions) Act 2003);

"care component" means the care component of disability living allowance at the highest or middle rate prescribed under section 72(3) of the Contributions and Benefits Act;

"daily living component" means the daily living component of personal independence payment at the standard or enhanced rate referred to in section 78 of the Welfare Reform Act 2012;

"disability living allowance" means a disability living allowance under section 71 of the Contributions and Benefits Act;
"personal independence payment" means an allowance under Part 4 of the Welfare Reform Act 2012.

AMENDMENT

1. Social Security (Miscellaneous Amendments) (No. 2) Regulations 2013 (SI 2013/1508) reg.5(1), (4) (October 29, 2013).

DEFINITIONS

"attendance allowance"—see para.(7).
"care component"—see para.(7).
"claimant"—see WRA 2007, s.24(1).
"Contributions and Benefits Act"—see WRA 2007, s.65.
"daily living component"—see para.(7).
"disability living allowance"—see para.(7).
"family"—see reg.2.
"person in hardship"—see para.(1).
"personal independence payment"—see para.(7).

GENERAL NOTE

This has the same effect as ESA Regulations 2008 reg.158.                    1.338

## Treating a claimant as not having limited capability for work

**95.** The claimant is to be treated as not having limited capability for      1.339
work if the claimant is disqualified for receiving an employment and
support allowance during a period of imprisonment or detention in legal
custody if that disqualification is for more than six weeks.

DEFINITIONS

"claimant"—see WRA 2007, s.24(1).
"week"—see reg.2.

GENERAL NOTE

This has the same effect as ESA Regulations 2008 reg.159(1).                 1.340

## Exceptions from disqualification for imprisonment

**96.**—(1) Notwithstanding section 18(4)(b) of the Act, a claimant is        1.341
not disqualified for receiving an employment and support allowance for
any period during which that claimant is undergoing imprisonment or
detention in legal custody—
  (a) in connection with a charge brought or intended to be brought
      against the claimant in criminal proceedings;
  (b) pursuant to any sentence of a court in criminal proceedings; or
  (c) pursuant to any order for detention made by a court in criminal
      proceedings,
unless paragraph (2) applies.
  (2) This paragraph applies where—
  (a) a penalty is imposed on the claimant at the conclusion of the
      proceedings referred to in paragraph (1); or

(b) in the case of default of payment of a sum adjudged to be paid on conviction, a penalty is imposed in respect of such default.

(3) Notwithstanding section 18(4)(b) of the Act, a claimant ("C") is not to be disqualified for receiving an employment and support allowance, for any period during which C is undergoing detention in legal custody after the conclusion of criminal proceedings if it is a period during which C is detained in a hospital or similar institution in Great Britain as a person suffering from mental disorder unless C satisfies either of the following conditions.

(4) The first condition is that—

(a) C is being detained under section 45A or 47 of the Mental Health Act 1983 (power of higher courts to direct hospital admission; removal to hospital of persons serving sentences of imprisonment etc); and

(b) in any case where there is in relation to C a release date within the meaning of section 50(3) of that Act, C is being detained on or before the day which the Secretary of State certifies to be that release date.

(5) The second condition is that C is being detained under—

(a) section 59A of the Criminal Procedure (Scotland) Act 1995 (hospital direction); or

(b) section 136 of the Mental Health (Care and Treatment) (Scotland) Act 2003 (transfer of prisoners for treatment of mental disorder).

(6) For the purposes of this regulation—

(a) "court" means any court in the United Kingdom, the Channel Islands or the Isle of Man or in any place to which the Colonial Prisoners Removal Act 1884 applies or any naval court-martial, army court-martial or air force court-martial within the meaning of the Courts-Martial (Appeals) Act 1968 or the Courts-Martial Appeal Court;

(b) "hospital or similar institution" means any place (not being a prison, a young offender institution, a secure training centre, secure accommodation in a children's home or a remand centre, and not being at or in any such place) in which persons suffering from mental disorder are or may be received for care or treatment;

(c) "penalty" means a sentence of imprisonment or detention under section 90 or 91 of the Powers of Criminal Courts (Sentencing) Act 2000, a detention and training order under section 100 of that Act, a sentence of detention for public protection under section 226 of the Criminal Justice Act 2003 or an extended sentence under section 228 of that Act or, in Scotland, under section 205, 207 or 208 of the Criminal Procedure (Scotland) Act 1995;

(d) in relation to a person who is liable to be detained in Great Britain as a result of any order made under the Colonial Prisoners Removal Act 1884, references to a prison must be construed as including references to a prison within the meaning of that Act;

(e) criminal proceedings against any person must be deemed to be concluded upon that person being found insane in those proceedings so that the person cannot be tried or that person's trial cannot proceed.

(7) Where a claimant outside Great Britain is undergoing imprisonment or detention in legal custody and, in similar circumstances in Great Britain, the claimant would, by virtue of this regulation, not have been disqualified for receiving an employment and support allowance, the claimant is not disqualified for receiving that allowance by reason only of the imprisonment or detention.

DEFINITIONS

"claimant"—see WRA 2007, s.24(1).
"court"—see para.(6)(a).
"hospital or similar institution"—see para.(6)(b).
"penalty"—see para.(6)(c).
"prison"—see para.(6)(d).

GENERAL NOTE

This has the same effect as ESA Regulations 2008 reg.160.          1.342

## Suspension of payment of an employment and support allowance during imprisonment

**97.**—(1) Subject to the following provisions of this regulation, the   1.343
payment of an employment and support allowance to any claimant—
 (a) which is excepted from the operation of section 18(4)(b) of the Act by virtue of the provisions of regulation 96(1), (3) or (7); or
 (b) which is payable otherwise than in respect of a period during which the claimant is undergoing imprisonment or detention in legal custody,
is suspended while that claimant is undergoing imprisonment or detention in legal custody.

(2) An employment and support allowance is not to be suspended while the claimant is liable to be detained in a hospital or similar institution, as defined in regulation 96(6), during a period for which in the claimant's case, the allowance is or would be excepted from the operation of section 18(4)(b) by virtue of the provisions of regulation 96(3).

(3) Where, by virtue of this regulation, payment of an employment and support allowance is suspended for any period, the period of suspension is not to be taken into account in calculating any period under the provisions of regulation 55 of the Claims and Payments Regulations 2013 (extinguishment of right to payment if payment is not obtained within the prescribed time).

DEFINITIONS

"claimant"—see WRA 2007, s.24(1).
"hospital or similar institution"—see reg.96(6).

**1.344**    This has the same effect as ESA Regulations 2008 reg.161.

PART 13

*Periods of less than a week*

## Entitlement for less than a week—amount of an employment and support allowance payable

**1.345**    **98.**—(1) This regulation applies where the claimant is entitled to an employment and support allowance for a part-week and this regulation is subject to the following provisions of this Part.

(2) The amount payable by way of an employment and support allowance in respect of a part-week is to be calculated by applying the formula—

$$(N \times X) \; / \; 7$$

where—

X is the amount calculated in accordance with section 2(1) of the Act;

N is the number of days in the part-week.

(3) In this Part—

"part-week" means an entitlement to an employment and support allowance in respect of any period of less than a week; and

"relevant week" means the period of seven days determined in accordance with regulation 99.

DEFINITIONS

"claimant"—see WRA 2007, s.24(1).
"part-week"—see para.(3).
"relevant week" "—see para.(3).

GENERAL NOTE

**1.346**    This has much the same effect as ESA Regulations 2008 reg.165.

## Relevant week

**1.347**    **99.**—(1) Where a part-week—

(a) is the whole period for which an employment and support allowance is payable, or occurs at the beginning of an award, the relevant week is the period of seven days ending on the last day of that part-week; or

(b) occurs at the end of an award, the relevant week is the period of seven days beginning on the first day of the part-week.

(2) Where a claimant has an award of an employment and support allowance and that claimant's benefit week changes, for the purpose of

calculating the amounts of an employment and support allowance payable for the part-week beginning on the day after the last complete benefit week before the change and ending immediately before the change, the relevant week is the period of seven days beginning on the day after the last complete benefit week.

DEFINITIONS

"benefit week"—see reg.2.
"claimant"—see WRA 2007, s.24(1).
"part-week"—see reg.98(3).
"relevant week"—see reg.98(3).

GENERAL NOTE

This has the same effect as ESA Regulations 2008 reg.166.                    **1.348**

## Modification in the calculation of income

**100.** For the purposes of regulation 98 (entitlement for less than a    **1.349**
week—amount of an employment and support allowance payable), a
claimant's income is to be calculated in accordance with regulations 76
to 84 subject to the following changes—
  (a) any income which is due to be paid in the relevant week is to be
      treated as paid on the first day of that week;
  (b) any widow's benefit, training allowance, widowed parent's allow-
      ance, bereavement allowance, carer's allowance and any increase
      in disablement pension payable in accordance with Part 1 of
      Schedule 7 to the Contributions and Benefits Act (unemploy-
      ability supplement) which is payable in the relevant week but not
      in respect of any day in the part-week is to be disregarded;
  (c) where the part-week occurs at the end of the claim—
        (i) any income; or
        (ii) any change in the amount of income of the same kind,
      which is first payable within the relevant week but not on any day
      in the part-week is to be disregarded;
  (d) where only part of the weekly balance of income is taken into
      account in the relevant week, the balance is to be disregarded.

DEFINITIONS

"carer's allowance"—see reg.2.
"claimant"—see WRA 2007, s.24(1).
"training allowance"—see reg.2.
"part-week"—see reg.98(3).
"relevant week"—see reg.98(3).
"week"—see reg.2.

GENERAL NOTE

This has the same effect as ESA Regulations 2008 reg.167.                    **1.350**

## Reduction in certain cases

**101.**—(1) Where a disqualification is to be made in accordance with    **1.351**
regulation 93 in respect of a part-week, the amount referred to in

paragraph (2) is to be payable by way of an employment and support allowance in respect of that part-week.

(2) The amount mentioned in paragraph (1) is—

(a) one seventh of the employment and support allowance which would have been paid for the part-week if—

   (i) there was no disqualification under regulation 93; and

   (ii) it was not a part-week; multiplied by

(b) the number of days in the part-week in respect of which no disqualification is to be made in accordance with regulation 93.

DEFINITIONS

"claimant"—see WRA 2007, s.24(1).
"part-week"—see reg.98(3).
"relevant week"—see reg.98(3).

GENERAL NOTE

1.352    This has the same effect as ESA Regulations 2008 reg.168.

## Payment of an employment and support allowance for days of certain treatment

1.353    **102.**—(1) Where a claimant is entitled to an employment and support allowance as a result of being treated as having limited capability for work in accordance with regulation 22, the amount payable is to be equal to one seventh of the amount of the employment and support allowance which would be payable in respect of a week in accordance with section 2(1) of the Act multiplied by N.

(2) In paragraph (1), N is the number of days in that week on which the claimant was receiving treatment referred to in regulation 22 or recovering from that treatment, but does not include any day during which the claimant does work.

SCHEDULE 1                                      **Regulation 2**

HER MAJESTY'S FORCES

PART 1

PRESCRIBED ESTABLISHMENTS AND ORGANISATIONS

1.354    **1.** Any of the regular naval, military or air forces of the Crown.
**2.** Royal Fleet Reserve.
**3.** Royal Navy Reserve.
**4.** Royal Marines Reserve.
**5.** Army Reserve.
**6.** Territorial Army.
**7.** Royal Air Force Reserve.
**8.** Royal Auxiliary Air Force.
**9.** The Royal Irish Regiment, to the extent that its members are not members of any force falling within paragraph 1.

Part 2

Establishments and Organisations of Which Her Majesty's Forces Do Not Consist

**10.** Her Majesty's forces are not to be taken to consist of any of the establishments or organisations specified in Part 1 of this Schedule by virtue only of the employment in such establishment or organisation of the following persons—

(a) any person who is serving as a member of any naval force of Her Majesty's forces and who (not having been an insured person under the National Insurance Act 1965 and not having been a contributor under the Social Security Act 1975 or not being a contributor under the Contributions and Benefits Act) locally entered that force at an overseas base;

(b) any person who is serving as a member of any military force of Her Majesty's forces and who entered that force, or was recruited for that force outside the United Kingdom, and the depot of whose unit is situated outside the United Kingdom;

(c) any person who is serving as a member of any air force of Her Majesty's forces and who entered that force, or was recruited for that force, outside the United Kingdom, and is liable under the terms of engagement to serve only in a specified part of the world outside the United Kingdom.

General Note

This is the same as ESA Regulations 2008 Sch.1.

**1.355**

SCHEDULE 2  **Regulation 15(2) and (3)**

*Assessment of Whether a Claimant has Limited Capability for Work*

Part 1

*Physical Disabilities*

**1.356**

| (1) Activity | (2) Descriptors | (3) Points |
|---|---|---|
| 1. Mobilising unaided by another person with or without a walking stick, manual wheelchair or other aid if such aid is normally or could reasonably be worn or used. | 1(a) Cannot, unaided by another person, either:<br>(i) mobilise more than 50 metres on level ground without stopping in order to avoid significant discomfort or exhaustion; or<br><br>(ii) repeatedly mobilise 50 metres within a reasonable timescale because of significant discomfort or exhaustion. | 15 |
| | (b) Cannot, unaided by another person, mount or descend two steps even with the support of a handrail. | 9 |
| | (c) Cannot, unaided by another person, either:<br><br>(i) mobilise more than 100 metres on level ground without stopping in order to avoid significant discomfort or exhaustion; or | 9 |

| (1) Activity | (2) Descriptors | (3) Points |
|---|---|---|
| | (ii) repeatedly mobilise 100 metres within a reasonable timescale because of significant discomfort or exhaustion. | |
| | (d) Cannot, unaided by another person, either: | 6 |
| | (i) mobilise more than 200 metres on level ground without stopping in order to avoid significant discomfort or exhaustion; or | |
| | (ii) repeatedly mobilise 200 metres within a reasonable timescale because of significant discomfort or exhaustion. | |
| | (e) None of the above applies. | 0 |
| 2. Standing and sitting. | 2(a) Cannot move between one seated position and another seated position which are located next to one another without receiving physical assistance from another person. | 15 |
| | (b) Cannot, for the majority of the time, remain at a work station: | 9 |
| | (i) standing unassisted by another person (even if free to move around); | |
| | (ii) sitting (even in an adjustable chair); or | |
| | (iii) a combination of paragraphs (i) and (ii), | |
| | for more than 30 minutes, before needing to move away in order to avoid significant discomfort or exhaustion. | |
| | (c) Cannot, for the majority of the time, remain at a work station: | 6 |
| | (i) standing unassisted by another person (even if free to move around); | |
| | (ii) sitting (even in an adjustable chair); or | |
| | (iii) a combination of paragraphs (i) and (ii), | |

| (1) Activity | (2) Descriptors | (3) Points |
|---|---|---|
| | for more than an hour before needing to move away in order to avoid significant discomfort or exhaustion. | |
| | (d) None of the above applies. | 0 |
| 3. Reaching. | 3(a) Cannot raise either arm as if to put something in the top pocket of a coat or jacket. | 15 |
| | (b) Cannot raise either arm to top of head as if to put on a hat. | 9 |
| | (c) Cannot raise either arm above head height as if to reach for something. | 6 |
| | (d) None of the above applies. | 0 |
| 4. Picking up and moving or transferring by the use of the upper body and arms. | 4(a) Cannot pick up and move a 0.5 litre carton full of liquid. | 15 |
| | (b) Cannot pick up and move a one litre carton full of liquid. | 9 |
| | (c) Cannot transfer a light but bulky object such as an empty cardboard box. | 6 |
| | (d) None of the above applies. | 0 |
| 5. Manual dexterity. | 5(a) Cannot press a button (such as a telephone keypad) with either hand or cannot turn the pages of a book with either hand. | 15 |
| | (b) Cannot pick up a £1 coin or equivalent with either hand. | 15 |
| | (c) Cannot use a pen or pencil to make a meaningful mark with either hand. | 9 |
| | (d) Cannot single-handedly use a suitable keyboard or mouse. | 9 |
| | (e) None of the above applies. | 0 |
| 6. Making self understood through speaking, writing, typing, or other means which are normally or could reasonably be used, unaided by another person, to strangers. | 6(a) Cannot convey a simple message, such as the presence of a hazard. | 15 |
| | (b) Has significant difficulty conveying a simple message | 15 |
| | (c) Has some difficulty conveying a simple message to strangers. | 6 |

| (1) Activity | (2) Descriptors | (3) Points |
|---|---|---|
| | (d) None of the above applies. | 0 |
| 7. Understanding communication by:<br><br>    (i) verbal means (such as hearing or lip reading) alone;<br><br>    (ii) non-verbal means (such as reading 16 point print or Braille) alone; or<br><br>    (iii) a combination of sub-paragraphs (i) and (ii),<br><br>using any aid that is normally or could reasonably be used, unaided by another person. | 7(a) Cannot understand a simple message, such as the location of a fire escape, due to sensory impairment. | 15 |
| | (b) Has significant difficulty understanding a simple message from a stranger due to sensory impairment. | 15 |
| | (c) Has some difficulty understanding a simple message from a stranger due to sensory impairment. | 6 |
| | (d) None of the above applies. | 0 |
| 8. Navigation and maintaining safety using a guide dog or other aid if either or both are normally used or could reasonably be used. | 8(a) Unable to navigate around familiar surroundings, without being accompanied by another person, due to sensory impairment. | 15 |
| | (b) Cannot safely complete a potentially hazardous task such as crossing the road, without being accompanied by another person, due to sensory impairment. | 15 |
| | (c) Unable to navigate around unfamiliar surroundings, without being accompanied by another person, due to sensory impairment. | 9 |
| | (d) None of the above applies. | 0 |
| 9. Absence or loss of control whilst conscious leading to extensive evacuation of the bowel and/or bladder, other than enuresis (bedwetting), despite the wearing or use of any aids or adaptations which are normally or could reasonably be worn or used. | 9(a) At least once a month experiences:<br><br>    (i) loss of control leading to extensive evacuation of the bowel and/or voiding of the bladder; or<br><br>    (ii) substantial leakage of the contents of a collecting device,<br><br>sufficient to require cleaning and a change in clothing. | 15 |

| (1) Activity | (2) Descriptors | (3) Points |
|---|---|---|
| | (b) The majority of the time is at risk of loss of control leading to extensive evacuation of the bowel and/or voiding of the bladder, sufficient to require cleaning and a change in clothing, if not able to reach a toilet quickly. | 6 |
| | (c) Neither of the above applies. | 0 |
| 10. Consciousness during waking moments. | 10(a) At least once a week, has an involuntary episode of lost or altered consciousness resulting in significantly disrupted awareness or concentration. | 15 |
| | (b) At least once a month, has an involuntary episode of lost or altered consciousness resulting in significantly disrupted awareness or concentration. | 6 |
| | (c) Neither of the above applies. | 0 |

PART 2

*Mental, cognitive and intellectual function assessment*

| (1) Activity | (2) Descriptors | (3) Points |
|---|---|---|
| 11. Learning tasks. | 11(a) Cannot learn how to complete a simple task, such as setting an alarm clock. | 15 |
| | (b) Cannot learn anything beyond a simple task, such as setting an alarm clock. | 9 |
| | (c) Cannot learn anything beyond a moderately complex task, such as the steps involved in operating a washing machine to clean clothes. | 6 |
| | (d) None of the above applies. | 0 |
| 12. Awareness of everyday hazards (such as boiling water or sharp objects). | 12(a) Reduced awareness of everyday hazards leads to a significant risk of: <br><br> (i) injury to self or others; or <br><br> (ii) damage to property or possessions, <br><br> such that the claimant requires supervision for the majority of the time to maintain safety. | 15 |

| (1) Activity | (2) Descriptors | (3) Points |
|---|---|---|
| | (b) Reduced awareness of everyday hazards leads to a significant risk of:<br><br>    (i) injury to self or others; or<br><br>    (ii) damage to property or possessions,<br><br>such that the claimant frequently requires supervision to maintain safety. | 9 |
| | (c) Reduced awareness of everyday hazards leads to a significant risk of:<br><br>    (i) injury to self or others; or<br><br>    (ii) damage to property or possessions,<br><br>such that the claimant occasionally requires supervision to maintain safety. | 6 |
| | (d) None of the above applies. | 0 |
| 13. Initiating and completing personal action (which means planning, organisation, problem solving, prioritising or switching tasks). | 13(a) Cannot, due to impaired mental function, reliably initiate or complete at least two sequential personal actions. | 15 |
| | (b) Cannot, due to impaired mental function, reliably initiate or complete at least two sequential personal actions for the majority of the time. | 9 |
| | (c) Frequently cannot, due to impaired mental function, reliably initiate or complete at least two sequential personal actions. | 6 |
| | (d) None of the above applies. | 0 |
| 14. Coping with change. | 14(a) Cannot cope with any change to the extent that day to day life cannot be managed. | 15 |
| | (b) Cannot cope with minor planned change (such as a prearranged change to the routine time scheduled for a lunch break), to the extent that, overall, day to day life is made significantly more difficult. | 9 |

| (1) Activity | (2) Descriptors | (3) Points |
|---|---|---|
| | (c) Cannot cope with minor unplanned change (such as the timing of an appointment on the day it is due to occur), to the extent that, overall, day to day life is made significantly more difficult. | 6 |
| | (d) None of the above applies | 0 |
| 15. Getting about. | 15(a) Cannot get to any place outside the claimant's home with which the claimant is familiar. | 15 |
| | (b) Is unable to get to a specified place with which the claimant is familiar, without being accompanied by another person. | 9 |
| | (c) Is unable to get to a specified place with which the claimant is unfamiliar without being accompanied by another person. | 6 |
| | (d) None of the above applies. | 0 |
| 16. Coping with social engagement due to cognitive impairment or mental disorder. | 16(a) Engagement in social contact is always precluded due to difficulty relating to others or significant distress experienced by the claimant. | 15 |
| | (b) Engagement in social contact with someone unfamiliar to the claimant is always precluded due to difficulty relating to others or significant distress experienced by the claimant. | 9 |
| | (c) Engagement in social contact with someone unfamiliar to the claimant is not possible for the majority of the time due to difficulty relating to others or significant distress experienced by the claimant. | 6 |
| | (d) None of the above applies. | 0 |
| 17. Appropriateness of behaviour with other people, due to cognitive impairment or mental disorder. | 17(a) Has, on a daily basis, uncontrollable episodes of aggressive or disinhibited behaviour that would be unreasonable in any workplace. | 15 |
| | (b) Frequently has uncontrollable episodes of aggressive or disinhibited behaviour that would be unreasonable in any workplace. | 15 |

| (1) Activity | (2) Descriptors | (3) Points |
|---|---|---|
| | (c) Occasionally has uncontrollable episodes of aggressive or disinhibited behaviour that would be unreasonable in any workplace. | 9 |
| | (d) None of the above applies. | 0 |

GENERAL NOTE

**1.357**     This Schedule is the same as ESA Regulations 2008 Sch.2, as amended by the updates to it in Part II of this Supplement.

SCHEDULE 3                    **Regulation 30(1)**

*Assessment of whether a claimant has limited capability for work-related activity*

**1.358**

| Activity | Descriptors |
|---|---|
| 1. Mobilising unaided by another person with or without a walking stick, manual wheelchair or other aid if such aid is normally or could reasonably be worn or used. | 1. Cannot either: <br><br>(a) mobilise more than 50 metres on level ground without stopping in order to avoid significant discomfort or exhaustion; or <br><br>(b) repeatedly mobilise 50 metres within a reasonable timescale because of significant discomfort or exhaustion. |
| 2. Transferring from one seated position to another. | 2 Cannot move between one seated position and another seated position located next to one another without receiving physical assistance from another person. |
| 3. Reaching. | 3 Cannot raise either arm as if to put something in the top pocket of a coat or jacket. |
| 4. Picking up and moving or transferring by the use of the upper body and arms (excluding standing, sitting, bending or kneeling and all other activities specified in this Schedule). | 4 Cannot pick up and move a 0.5 litre carton full of liquid. |
| 5. Manual dexterity. | 5 Cannot press a button (such as a telephone keypad) with either hand or cannot turn the pages of a book with either hand. |
| 6. Making self understood through speaking, writing, typing, or other means which are normally, or could reasonably be, used unaided by another person. | 6 Cannot convey a simple message, such as the presence of a hazard. |

| Activity | Descriptors |
|---|---|
| 7. Understanding communication by:<br><br>(i) verbal means (such as hearing or lip reading) alone;<br><br>(ii) non-verbal means (such as reading 16 point print or Braille) alone; or<br><br>(iii) a combination of subparagraphs (i) and (ii),<br><br>using any aid that is normally, or could reasonably, be used unaided by another person. | 7 Cannot understand a simple message, such as the location of a fire escape, due to sensory impairment. |
| 8. Absence or loss of control whilst conscious leading to extensive evacuation of the bowel and/or voiding of the bladder, other than enuresis (bed-wetting), despite the wearing or use of any aids or adaptations which are normally or could reasonably be worn or used. | 8 At least once a week experiences:<br><br>(a) loss of control leading to extensive evacuation of the bowel and/or voiding of the bladder; or<br><br>(b) substantial leakage of the contents of a collecting device sufficient to require the individual to clean themselves and change clothing. |
| 9. Learning tasks. | 9 Cannot learn how to complete a simple task, such as setting an alarm clock, due to cognitive impairment or mental disorder. |
| 10. Awareness of hazard. | 10 Reduced awareness of everyday hazards, due to cognitive impairment or mental disorder, leads to a significant risk of:<br><br>(a) injury to self or others; or<br><br>(b) damage to property or possessions,<br><br>such that the claimant requires supervision for the majority of the time to maintain safety. |
| 11. Initiating and completing personal action (which means planning, organisation, problem solving, prioritising or switching tasks). | 11 Cannot, due to impaired mental function, reliably initiate or complete at least two sequential personal actions. |
| 12. Coping with change. | 12 Cannot cope with any change, due to cognitive impairment or mental disorder, to the extent that day to day life cannot be managed. |
| 13. Coping with social engagement, due to cognitive impairment or mental disorder. | 13 Engagement in social contact is always precluded due to difficulty relating to others or significant distress experienced by the claimant. |
| 14. Appropriateness of behaviour with other people, due to cognitive impairment or mental disorder. | 14 Has, on a daily basis, uncontrollable episodes of aggressive or disinhibited behaviour that would be unreasonable in any workplace. |

| Activity | Descriptors |
|---|---|
| 15. Conveying food or drink to the mouth. | 15(a) Cannot convey food or drink to the claimant's own mouth without receiving physical assistance from someone else; |
| | (b) Cannot convey food or drink to the claimant's own mouth without repeatedly stopping or experiencing breathlessness or severe discomfort; |
| | (c) Cannot convey food or drink to the claimant's own mouth without receiving regular prompting given by someone else in the claimant's presence; or |
| | (d) Owing to a severe disorder of mood or behaviour, fails to convey food or drink to the claimant's own mouth without receiving: |
| | (i) physical assistance from someone else; or |
| | (ii) regular prompting given by someone else in the claimant's presence. |
| 16. Chewing or swallowing food or drink. | 16(a) Cannot chew or swallow food or drink; |
| | (b) Cannot chew or swallow food or drink without repeatedly stopping or experiencing breathlessness or severe discomfort; |
| | (c) Cannot chew or swallow food or drink without repeatedly receiving regular prompting given by someone else in the claimant's presence; or |
| | (d) Owing to a severe disorder of mood or behaviour, fails to: |
| | (i) chew or swallow food or drink; or |
| | (ii) chew or swallow food or drink without regular prompting given by someone else in the claimant's presence. |

GENERAL NOTE

1.359    This Schedule is the same as ESA Regulations 2008 Sch.3, as amended by the updates to it in Part II of this Supplement.

# The Accession of Croatia (Immigration and Worker Authorisation) Regulations 2013

(SI 2013/1460)

In force July 1, 2013

ARRANGEMENT OF REGULATIONS

The Secretary of State makes the following Regulations in exercise of the powers conferred by section 4 of the European Union (Croatian Accession and Irish Protocol) Act 2013.

In accordance with section 5(1) of that Act, a draft of this instrument was laid before Parliament and approved by resolution of each House of Parliament.

GENERAL NOTE

Croatia acceded to the European Union on July 1, 2013 by virtue of the treaty    **1.361**
concerning the accession of the Republic of Croatia to the European Union,

signed at Brussels on December 9, 2011, to which effect is given in UK domestic law by ss.1 and 3 of the European Union (Croatian Accession and Irish Protocol) Act 2013. Section 4 of that Act empowers the Secretary of State to make provision for "the entitlement of a Croatian national to enter or reside in the United Kingdom as a worker, and . . . any matter ancillary to that entitlement". That power has been exercised to make these Regulations, which provide that during a transitional period of five years, a Croatian national who is an "accession State national subject to worker authorisation" (i.e. any Croatian national who does not fall within the exceptions listed in reg.2(2)–(20)) does not have a right of residence of the United Kingdom as a "jobseeker" and only has a right to reside as a worker during a period in which s/he "holds an accession worker authorisation document and is working in accordance with the conditions set out in that document".

The structure of the scheme is similar to that which applied to nationals of Bulgaria and Romania before January 1, 2014 under the Accession (Immigration and Worker Authorisation) Regulations 2006 (see pp.816–830 of Vol.II of the main work). It requires that the employment of accession State national subject to worker authorisation should be authorised in advance in order to be lawful. It therefore differs from the scheme of registration that applied to nationals of the A8 states between May 1, 2004 and April 30, 2011.

See further the commentary to reg.21AA of the Income Support Regulations in Vol.II of the main work as updated below.

PART 1

INTERPRETATION ETC

### Citation, commencement, interpretation and consequential amendments

1.362     **1.**—(1) These Regulations may be cited as the Accession of Croatia (Immigration and Worker Authorisation) Regulations 2013 and come into force on 1st July 2013.

(2) In these Regulations—

"the 1971 Act" means the Immigration Act 1971;

"the 2006 Act" means the Immigration, Asylum and Nationality Act 2006;

"accession period" means the period beginning with 1st July 2013 and ending with 30th June 2018;

"accession State national subject to worker authorisation" has the meaning given in regulation 2;

"accession worker authorisation document" has the meaning given in regulation 8(2);

"authorised category of employment" means—

    (a) employment for which the applicant has been issued by a sponsor with a valid certificate of sponsorship under Tier 2 or Tier 5 of the Points-Based System; or

    (b) employment as—

        (i) a representative of an overseas business;

(ii) a postgraduate doctor or dentist; or

(iii) a domestic worker in a private household;

"certificate of sponsorship" has the meaning given in paragraph 6 of the immigration rules, except that the reference to an application or potential application for entry clearance or leave to enter or remain as a Tier 2 migrant or a Tier 5 migrant is to be read as including a reference to an application or potential application for a worker authorisation registration certificate;

"certificate of sponsorship checking service" has the meaning given in paragraph 6 of the immigration rules, except that the reference to an application or potential application for entry clearance or leave to enter or remain as a Tier 2 migrant or a Tier 5 migrant is to be read as including a reference to an application or potential application for a worker authorisation registration certificate;

"civil partner" does not include a party to a civil partnership of convenience;

"EEA registration certificate" means a certificate issued in accordance with regulation 16 of the EEA Regulations;

"the EEA Regulations" means the Immigration (European Economic Area) Regulations 2006;

"EEA State" excludes the United Kingdom and includes Switzerland;

"employer" means, in relation to a worker, the person who directly pays the wage or salary of that worker, and "employ", "employment" and "employs" shall be construed accordingly;

"the EU2 Regulations" means the Accession (Immigration and Worker Authorisation) Regulations 2006;

"extended family member" has the meaning given in regulation 8 of the EEA Regulations;

"family member" has the meaning given in regulation 7 of the EEA Regulations;

"highly skilled person" has the meaning given in regulation 3;

"immigration rules" means the rules laid down as mentioned in section 3(2) of the 1971 Act applying (except for in the definition of "relevant requirements") on 1st July 2013;

"Points-Based System" means the system established under Part 6A of the immigration rules;

"relevant requirements" means, in relation to an authorised category of employment, the requirements which, subject to any necessary modifications, a person in that category of employment was obliged to meet under the immigration rules in force on 9th December 2011 in order to obtain entry clearance or leave to enter or remain in the United Kingdom and which are set out in the relevant statement;

"relevant statement" means the statement entitled "the Statement of relevant requirements" dated May 2013 and published by the Secretary of State;

"right to reside" shall be interpreted in accordance with the EEA Regulations and "entitled to reside" and "right of residence" shall be construed accordingly;

"sponsor" means the holder of a sponsor licence;

"sponsor licence" has the meaning given in paragraph 6 of the immigration rules;

"spouse" does not include a party to a marriage of convenience;

"student" has the meaning given in regulation 4(1)(d) of the EEA Regulations;

"Tier 2" and "Tier 5" shall be construed in accordance in paragraph 6 of the immigration rules, except that the reference to the grant of leave is to be read as including a reference to the issuing of a worker authorisation registration certificate;

"unmarried or same sex partner" means a person who is in a durable relationship with another person;

"work" and "working" shall be construed in accordance with the meaning of "worker"; and

"worker authorisation registration certificate" means a certificate issued in accordance with regulation 10 of these Regulations.

(3) The Schedule (consequential amendments) shall have effect.

### "Accession State national subject to worker authorisation"

1.363   **2.**—(1) Subject to the following paragraphs of this regulation, other than where these Regulations expressly refer to an accession State national subject to worker authorisation within the meaning of regulation 2 of the EU2 Regulations, in these Regulations "accession State national subject to worker authorisation" means a Croatian national.

(2) A Croatian national is not an accession State national subject to worker authorisation if, on 30th June 2013, he had leave to enter or remain in the United Kingdom under the 1971 Act that was not subject to any condition restricting his employment, or he is given such leave after that date.

(3) A Croatian national is not an accession State national subject to worker authorisation if he was legally working in the United Kingdom on 30th June 2013 and had been legally working in the United Kingdom without interruption throughout the preceding period of 12 months ending on that date.

(4) A Croatian national who legally works in the United Kingdom without interruption for a period of 12 months falling partly or wholly after 30th June 2013 ceases to be an accession State national subject to worker authorisation at the end of that period of 12 months.

(5) For the purposes of paragraphs (3) and (4) of this regulation—

(a) a person working in the United Kingdom during a period falling before 1st July 2013 was legally working in the United Kingdom during that period if—

　(i) he had leave to enter or remain in the United Kingdom under the 1971 Act for that period, that leave allowed him to work in the United Kingdom, and he was working in accordance with any condition of that leave restricting his employment;

　(ii) he was exempt from the provisions of the 1971 Act by virtue of section 8(2) or (3) of that Act (persons exempted by order or membership of diplomatic mission); or

    (iii) he was entitled to reside in the United Kingdom for that period under the EEA Regulations without the requirement for such leave;

  (b) a person working in the United Kingdom on or after 1st July 2013 is legally working in the United Kingdom during any period in which he—

    (i) falls within any of paragraphs (6) to (16) or (18); or

    (ii) holds an accession worker authorisation document and is working in accordance with the conditions set out in that document; and

  (c) a person shall be treated as having worked in the United Kingdom without interruption for a period of 12 months if—

    (i) he was legally working in the United Kingdom at the beginning and end of that period; and

    (ii) during that period of 12 months, if his work in the United Kingdom was interrupted, any intervening periods of interruption did not exceed 30 days in total.

(6) Other than during any period in which he is also an accession State national subject to worker authorisation within the meaning of regulation 2 of the EU2 Regulations, a Croatian national is not an accession State national subject to worker authorisation during any period in which he is also a national of—

  (a) the United Kingdom; or

  (b) an EEA State, other than Croatia.

(7) A Croatian national is not an accession State national subject to worker authorisation during any period in which he is also an accession State national subject to worker authorisation within the meaning of regulation 2 of the EU2 Regulations and is working in accordance with those Regulations.

(8) A Croatian national is not an accession State national subject to worker authorisation during any period in which he is the spouse, civil partner, unmarried or same sex partner, or child under 18 of a person who has leave to enter or remain in the United Kingdom under the 1971 Act and that leave allows him to work in the United Kingdom.

(9) A Croatian national is not an accession State national subject to worker authorisation during any period in which he is the spouse, civil partner, unmarried or same sex partner of—

  (a) a national of the United Kingdom; or

  (b) a person that is settled in the United Kingdom in accordance with the meaning given in section 33(2A) (interpretation—meaning of "settled") of the 1971 Act.

(10) A Croatian national is not an accession State national subject to worker authorisation during any period in which he is a member of a mission or other person mentioned in section 8(3) (member of a diplomatic mission, the family member of such a person, or a person otherwise entitled to diplomatic immunity) of the 1971 Act, other than a person who, under section 8(3A) (conditions of membership of a mission) of that Act, does not count as a member of a mission for the purposes of section 8(3).

(11) A Croatian national is not an accession State national subject to worker authorisation during any period in which he is a person who is exempt from all or any of the provisions of the 1971 Act by virtue of an order made under section 8(2) (exemption for persons specified by order) of that Act.

(12) A Croatian national is not an accession State national subject to worker authorisation during any period in which he has a permanent right of residence under regulation 15 of the EEA Regulations.

(13) Subject to paragraph (14), a Croatian national is not an accession State national subject to worker authorisation during any period in which he is a family member (X) of an EEA national (Y) who has a right to reside in the United Kingdom.

(14) Where Y is an accession State national subject to worker authorisation under these Regulations or an accession State national subject to worker authorisation within the meaning of regulation 2 of the EU2 Regulations, paragraph (13) only applies where X is the—

(a) spouse or civil partner of Y;

(b) unmarried or same sex partner of Y; or

(c) a direct descendant of Y, Y's spouse or Y's civil partner who is—

(i) under 21; or

(ii) dependant of Y, Y's spouse or Y's civil partner.

(15) A Croatian national is not an accession State national subject to worker authorisation during any period in which he is a highly skilled person and holds an EEA registration certificate issued in accordance with regulation 7 that includes a statement that he has unconditional access to the United Kingdom labour market.

(16) A Croatian national is not an accession State national subject to worker authorisation during any period in which he is in the United Kingdom as a student and either—

(a) holds an EEA registration certificate that includes a statement that he is a student who may work in the United Kingdom whilst a student in accordance with the condition set out in paragraph (17) and complies with that condition; or

(b) has leave to enter or remain under the 1971 Act as a student and is working in accordance with any conditions attached to that leave.

(17) The condition referred to in paragraph (16)(a) is that the student shall not work for more than 20 hours a week unless—

(a) he is following a course of vocational training and is working as part of that training; or

(b) he is working during his vacation.

(18) A Croatian national who ceases to be a student at the end of his course of study is not an accession State national subject to worker authorisation during the period of four months beginning with the date on which his course ends provided he holds an EEA registration certificate that was issued to him before the end of the course that includes a statement that he may work during that period.

(19) A Croatian national is not an accession State national subject to worker authorisation during any period in which he is a posted worker.

(20) In paragraph (19), "posted worker" means a worker who is posted to the United Kingdom, within the meaning of Article 1(3) of the Council Directive 96/71/EC of the European Parliament and of the Council of 16 December 1996 concerning the posting of workers in the framework of the provision of services, by an undertaking established in an EEA State.

**"Highly skilled person"**

**3.** (1) In these Regulations "highly skilled person" means a person who— **1.364**

(a) meets the requirements specified by the Secretary of State for the purpose of paragraph 245BB(c) (requirements for entry clearance as a Tier 1 (Exceptional Talent) migrant) of the immigration rules; or

(b) has been awarded one of the following qualifications and applies for an EEA registration certificate within 12 months of being awarded the qualification—

(i) a recognised bachelor, masters or doctoral degree;

(ii) a postgraduate certificate in education or professional graduate diploma of education; or

(iii) a higher national diploma awarded by a Scottish higher education institution.

(2) For the purposes of paragraph (1)(b), the qualification must have been awarded by a higher education institution which, on the date of the award, is a UK recognised body or an institution that is not a UK recognised body but which provides full courses that lead to the award of a degree by a UK recognised body.

(3) For the purposes of paragraph (1)(b)(iii), to qualify as a higher national diploma from a Scottish institution, a qualification must be at level 8 on the Scottish credit and qualifications framework.

(4) In this regulation, a "UK recognised body" means an institution that has been granted degree awarding powers by a Royal Charter, an Act of Parliament or the Privy Council.

PART 2

APPLICATION OF THE EEA REGULATIONS AND OTHER INSTRUMENTS

**Derogation from provisions of European Union law relating to workers**

**4.** Pursuant to Annex V of the treaty concerning the accession of the **1.365** Republic of Croatia to the European Union, signed at Brussels on 9

December 2011, Regulations 5 and 7 to 10 derogate during the accession period from Article 45 of the Treaty on the Functioning of the European Union, Articles 1 to 6 of Regulation (EEC) No. 1612/68 of the Council of 15 October 1968 on freedom of movement for workers within the Community and Directive 2004/38/EC of the European Parliament and of the Council of 29 April 2004 on the right of citizens of the Union and their family members to move and reside freely within the territory of the member States, amending Regulation (EEC) No. 1612/68, and repealing Directives 64/221/EEC, 68/360/EEC, 72/194/EEC, 73/148/EEC, 75/34/EEC, 75/35/EEC, 90/364/EEC, 90/365/EEC and 93/96/EEC(14).

### Right of residence of an accession State national subject to worker authorisation

1.366    **5.**—(1) During the accession period, an accession State national subject to worker authorisation who is seeking employment in the United Kingdom shall not be treated as a jobseeker for the purposes of the definition of "qualified person" in regulation 6(1) of the EEA Regulations, and such a person shall be treated as a worker for the purposes of that definition only during a period in which he holds an accession worker authorisation document and is working in accordance with the conditions set out in that document.

(2) Regulation 6(2) of the EEA Regulations shall not apply to an accession State national subject to worker authorisation who ceases to work.

### Transitional provisions to take account of the application of the EEA Regulations to Croatian nationals and their family members on 1st July 2013

1.367    **6.**—(1) Where, before 1st July 2013, any direction has been given for the removal of a Croatian national or the family member of such a national under paragraphs 8 to 10A of Schedule 2 (removal of persons refused leave to enter and illegal entrants) to the 1971 Act, section 10 (removal of certain persons unlawfully in the United Kingdom) of the 1999 Act or section 47 (removal: persons with statutorily extended leave) of the 2006 Act, that direction shall cease to have effect on that date.

(2) Where before 1st July 2013 the Secretary of State has made a deportation order against a Croatian national or the family member of such a national under section 5(1) (deportation orders) of the 1971 Act—

(a) that order shall, on and after 1st July 2013, be treated as if it were a decision under regulation 19(3)(b) of the EEA Regulations; and

(b) any appeal against that order, or against the refusal of the Secretary of State to revoke the deportation order, made before 1st July 2013 under section 63 (deportation orders) of the 1999 Act, or under section 82(2)(j) or (k) (right of appeal: general) of the 2002

Act shall, on or after that date, be treated as if it had been made under regulation 26 of the EEA Regulations.

(3) In this regulation—

(a) "the 1999 Act" means the Immigration and Asylum Act 1999;

(b) "the 2002 Act" means the Nationality, Immigration and Asylum Act 2002; and

(c) any reference to the family member of a Croatian national is, in addition to the definition set out in regulation 1(2), a reference to a person who on 1st July 2013 acquires a right to reside in the United Kingdom under the EEA Regulations as the family member of a Croatian national.

### Issuing EEA registration certificates and residence cards

7.—(1) During the accession period, regulation 6 of the EEA Regulations has effect as if, in paragraph (1), after "EEA national", there were inserted ", except an accession State national subject to worker authorisation within the meaning of regulation 2 of the Croatian Regulations," and after paragraph (1), there were inserted—

1.368

"(1A) In these Regulations, a "qualified person" also means a person who is an accession State national subject to worker authorisation within the meaning of regulation 2 of the Croatian Regulations and in the United Kingdom as—

(a) a self-employed person;

(b) a self-sufficient person;

(c) a student; or

(d) a highly skilled person who is seeking employment or is employed in the United Kingdom.

(1B) In regulation 16(5), a "qualified person" includes an accession State national subject to worker authorisation within the meaning of regulation 2 of the Croatian Regulations.

(1C) In these Regulations—

(a) "the Croatian Regulations" means the Accession of Croatia (Immigration and Worker Authorisation) Regulations 2013; and

(b) "highly skilled worker" has the meaning given in regulation 1 of the Croatian Regulations."

(2) Subject to paragraph (6), an EEA registration certificate issued to a Croatian national during the accession period shall include a statement that the holder of the certificate has unconditional access to the United Kingdom labour market, unless that person is not an accession State national subject to worker authorisation solely by virtue of falling within paragraph (16) or (18) of regulation 2.

(3) A Croatian national who holds an EEA registration certificate that does not include a statement that he has unconditional access to the United Kingdom labour market may, during the accession period, submit the certificate to the Secretary of State for the inclusion of such a statement.

(4) The Secretary of State must re-issue a EEA certificate submitted to her under paragraph (3) with the inclusion of a statement that the

holder has unconditional access to the United Kingdom labour market if she is satisfied that the holder—

> (a) is a qualified person within the meaning of paragraph (1A) of regulation 6 of the EEA Regulations as applied by paragraph (1); or
>
> (b) has ceased to be an accession State national subject to worker authorisation other than solely by virtue of falling within paragraph (16) or (18) of regulation 2.

(5) An EEA registration certificate issued to a Croatian national who is a student during the accession period shall include a statement that the holder of the certificate is a student who may work in the United Kingdom whilst a student in accordance with the condition set out in paragraph (17) of regulation 2 and who, on ceasing to be a student, may work during the period referred to in paragraph (18) of regulation 2, unless it includes a statement under paragraph (2) or (4) that the holder has unconditional access to the United Kingdom labour market.

(6) Where under paragraph (5) of regulation 16 of the EEA Regulations an EEA registration certificate is issued to a Croatian national extended family member of an accession State national subject to worker authorisation, the certificate must include a statement that the certificate does not confer a permission to work.

PART 3

ACCESSION STATE WORKER AUTHORISATION AND ASSOCIATED DOCUMENTATION

**Requirement for an accession State national subject to worker authorisation to be authorised to work**

1.369    **8.**—(1) An accession State national subject to worker authorisation shall only be authorised to work in the United Kingdom during the accession period if he holds an accession worker authorisation document and is working in accordance with the conditions set out in that document.

(2) For the purpose of these Regulations, an accession worker authorisation document means—

> (a) a passport or other travel document endorsed before 1st July 2013 to show that the holder has leave to enter or remain in the United Kingdom under the 1971 Act, subject to a condition restricting his employment in the United Kingdom to a particular employer or category of employment; or
>
> (b) a worker authorisation registration certificate endorsed with a condition restricting the holder's employment to a particular employer and authorised category of employment.

(3) In the case of a document mentioned in paragraph (2)(a), the document ceases to be a valid accession worker authorisation document at the point at which—

(a) the period of leave to enter or remain expires; or

(b) the document holder ceases working for the employer, or in the employment, specified in the document for a period of time that exceeds 30 days in total.

(4) In the case of a document mentioned in paragraph (2)(b), the document ceases to be a valid accession worker authorisation document at the point at which—

(a) the document expires;

(b) the document holder ceases working for the employer, or in the authorised category of employment, specified in the document for a period of time that exceeds 30 days in total; or

(c) the document is revoked.

(5) For the purposes of this regulation, and regulations 9 and 11, the reference to a travel document other than a passport is a reference to a document which relates to a Croatian national and which can serve the same purpose as a passport.

## Application for a worker authorisation registration certificate as an accession worker authorisation document

**9.**—(1) An application for a worker authorisation registration certifi-   1.370
cate may be made by an accession State national subject to worker authorisation who wishes to work for an employer in the United Kingdom if the employment concerned falls within an authorised category of employment.

(2) The application shall be in writing and shall be made to the Secretary of State.

(3) The application shall state—

(a) the name, address in the United Kingdom or in Croatia, and date of birth, of the applicant;

(b) the name and address of the employer for whom the applicant wishes to work; and

(c) the authorised category of employment covered by the application.

(4) The application shall be accompanied by—

(a) proof of the applicant's identity in the form of—

   (i) a national identity card;

   (ii) a passport; or

   (iii) other travel document as defined by regulation 8(5);

(b) two passport size photographs of the applicant;

(c) where the relevant requirements require the applicant to hold a certificate of sponsorship, the certificate of sponsorship reference number;

(d) where sub-paragraph (c) does not apply, a letter from the employer specified in the application confirming that the applicant has an offer of employment with the employer; and

(e) a fee of £55.

(5) In this regulation "address" means, in relation to an employer which is a body corporate or partnership, the head or main office of that employer.

**Issuing and revoking a worker authorisation registration certificate**

1.371    **10.**—(1) Subject to paragraph (3), the Secretary of State shall issue a worker authorisation registration certificate pursuant to an application made in accordance with the provisions of regulation 9 if the Secretary of State is satisfied that the applicant is an accession State national subject to worker authorisation who meets the relevant requirements.

(2) A worker authorisation registration certificate shall include—

(a) a condition restricting the employment of the document holder to the employer and the authorised category of employment specified in the application;

(b) a statement that the document holder has a right of residence in the United Kingdom as a worker whilst working in accordance with any conditions specified in the certificate;

(c) where the authorised category of employment specified in the application is one for which a certificate of sponsorship is required, a statement that the holder of the document has a right to engage in supplementary employment; and

(d) where the period of authorised employment is less than 12 months, a statement specifying the date on which the worker authorisation registration certificate expires.

(3) The Secretary of State may—

(a) refuse to issue, revoke or refuse to renew a worker authorisation registration certificate if the refusal or revocation is justified on grounds of public policy, public security or public health,

(b) refuse the application where the Secretary of State is not satisfied that regulation 9 or this regulation has been complied with or satisfied, or

(c) revoke a worker authorisation registration certificate where—

(i) the document holder ceases working for the employer, or in the employment, specified in the document for a period of time that exceeds 30 days in total,

(ii) deception was used in order to obtain the document, or

(iii) the document was obtained on the basis of sponsorship by a sponsor whose licence has been withdrawn,

and where the Secretary of State has refused to issue, revoked or refused to renew a worker authorisation registration certificate, she shall issue a notice setting out the reasons.

(4) A worker authorisation registration certificate or notice of refusal or revocation issued under this regulation shall be sent to the applicant by post together with the identity card or passport that accompanied the application.

(5) Subject to paragraph (6), in this regulation, "supplementary employment" means—

(a) employment in a job which appears on the shortage occupation list in Appendix K of the immigration rules; or

(b) employment in the same profession and at the same professional level as the employment for which the applicant has been issued with a certificate of sponsorship.

(6) "Supplementary employment" is subject to the condition that—
  (i) the applicant remains working for the sponsor in the employment that the certificate of sponsorship checking service records that the applicant has been sponsored to do; and
  (ii) the supplementary employment does not exceed 20 hours per week and takes place outside of the hours when the applicant is contracted to work for the sponsor in the employment the applicant is being sponsored to do.

(7) The Secretary of State shall ensure that the relevant statement is available to the public through her website and the library of the Home Office.

# PART 4

PENALTIES AND OFFENCES

**Unauthorised employment of accession State national—penalty for employer**

11.—(1) It is contrary to this regulation to employ an accession State    1.372
national subject to worker authorisation during the accession period if that person is not the holder of a valid accession worker authorisation document or, where that person holds such a document, the person would be in breach of a condition of that document in undertaking the employment.

(2) The Secretary of State may give an employer who acts contrary to this regulation a notice requiring him to pay a penalty of a specified amount not exceeding £5,000.

(3) The Secretary of State may give a penalty notice without having established whether the employer is excused under paragraph (5).

(4) A penalty notice must—
  (a) state why the Secretary of State thinks the employer is liable to the penalty;
  (b) state the amount of the penalty;
  (c) specify a date, at least 28 days after the date specified in the notice as the date on which it is given, before which the penalty must be paid;
  (d) specify how the penalty must be paid;
  (e) provide a reference number;
  (f) explain how the employer may object to the penalty; and
  (g) explain how the Secretary of State may enforce the penalty.

(5) Subject to paragraph (7), an employer is excused from paying a penalty under this regulation if—
  (a) before the commencement of the employment, the employee or prospective employee produces to the employer any of the following documents—

(i) an accession worker authorisation document that authorises the employee or prospective employee to take the employment in question;

(ii) an EEA registration certificate which includes a statement that the holder has unconditional access to the United Kingdom labour market; or

(iii) one of the following documents confirming that the document holder is not an accession State national subject to worker authorisation by virtue of regulation 2(6)—

(aa) a passport;

(bb) a national identity card; or

(cc) other travel document as defined by regulation 8(5); and

(b) the employer complies with the requirements set out in paragraph (6) of this regulation.

(6) The requirements are that—

(a) the employer takes all reasonable steps to check the validity of the document;

(b) the employer has satisfied himself that the photograph on the document is of the employee or prospective employee;

(c) the employer has satisfied himself that the date of birth on the document is consistent with the appearance of the employee or prospective employee;

(d) the employer takes all other reasonable steps to check that the employee or prospective employee is the rightful holder of the document; and

(e) the employer securely retains a dated copy of the whole of the document in a format which cannot be subsequently altered for a period of not less than two years after the employment has come to an end.

(7) An employer is not excused from paying a penalty if the employer knew, at any time during the period of the employment, that the employment was contrary to this regulation.

(8) Nothing in these regulations permits an employer to retain documents produced by an employee or prospective employee for the purposes of paragraph (5) for any period longer than is necessary for the purposes of ensuring compliance with paragraph (6).

(9) The Secretary of State may issue a code of practice specifying factors to be considered by her in determining the amount of a penalty imposed under paragraph (2) of this regulation.

(10) The Secretary of State shall lay a code issued under paragraph (9) before Parliament and publish it.

(11) The Secretary of State may from time to time review the code and may revoke, or revise and re-issue it, following a review; and a reference in this section to the code includes a reference to the code as revised.

**Unauthorised employment of accession State national—penalty for employer—objection**

1.373    **12.** *[Omitted]*

### Unauthorised employment of accession State national—penalty for employer—appeal

**13.** *[Omitted]* 1.374

### Unauthorised employment of accession State national—penalty for employer—enforcement

**14.** *[Omitted]* 1.375

### Unauthorised employment of accession State national—employer offence

**15.** A person commits an offence if he employs another ("the 1.376 employee") knowing that the employee is an accession State national subject to worker authorisation and that—

(a) the employee is not the holder of a valid accession worker authorisation document; or

(b) the employee is prohibited from undertaking the employment because of a condition in his accession worker authorisation document.

(2) A person guilty of an offence under this section shall be liable on summary conviction—

(a) to imprisonment for a term not exceeding 51 weeks in England and Wales or 6 months in Scotland or Northern Ireland;

(b) to a fine not exceeding level 5 on the standard scale; or

(c) to both.

(3) An offence under this regulation shall be treated as—

(a) a relevant offence for the purpose of sections 28B (search and arrest by warrant) and 28D (entry and search of premises) of the 1971 Act; and

(b) an offence under Part 3 of that Act (criminal proceedings) for the purposes of sections 28E (entry and search of premises following arrest), 28G (searching arrested persons) and 28H (searching persons in police custody).

(4) In relation to an offence committed before the commencement of section 281(5) (alteration of penalties for other summary offences) of the Criminal Justice Act 2003, the reference to 51 weeks in paragraph (2)(a) shall be read as a reference to 6 months.

(5) For the purposes of paragraph (1), a body (whether corporate or not) shall be treated as knowing a fact about an employee if a person who has responsibility within the body for an aspect of the employment knows the fact.

### Unauthorised working by accession State national—employee offence and penalty

**16.**—(1) Subject to paragraph (2), an accession State national subject 1.377 to worker authorisation who works in the United Kingdom during the accession period shall be guilty of an offence if he does not hold a valid accession worker authorisation document.

(2) A person guilty of an offence under this regulation shall be liable on summary conviction—

(a) to imprisonment for a term not exceeding more than three months;

(b) to a fine not exceeding level 5 on the standard scale; or

(c) to both.

(3) A constable or immigration officer who has reason to believe that a person has committed an offence under this regulation may give that person a notice offering him the opportunity of discharging any liability to conviction for that offence by payment of a penalty of £1000 in accordance with the notice.

(4) Where a person is given a notice under paragraph (3) in respect of an offence under this regulation—

(a) no proceedings may be instituted for that offence before the expiration of the period of 21 days beginning with the day after the date of the notice; and

(b) he may not be convicted of that offence if, before the expiration of that period, he pays the penalty in accordance with the notice.

(5) A notice under paragraph (3) must give such particulars of the circumstances alleged to constitute the offence as are necessary for giving reasonable information of the offence.

(6) A notice under paragraph (3) must also state—

(a) the period during which, by virtue of paragraph (4), proceedings will not be instituted for the offence;

(b) the amount of the penalty; and

(c) that the penalty is payable to the Secretary of State at the address specified in the notice.

(7) Without prejudice to payment by any other method, payment of a penalty in pursuance of a notice under paragraph (3) may be made by pre-paying and posting a letter by registered post or the recorded delivery service containing the amount of the penalty (in cash or otherwise) to the Secretary of State at the address specified in the notice.

(8) Where a letter is sent in accordance with paragraph (7) payment is to be regarded as having been made at the time at which that letter would be delivered in the ordinary course of registered post or the recorded delivery service.

(9) A constable or immigration officer may withdraw a penalty notice given under paragraph (3) if the constable or immigration officer decides that—

(a) the notice was issued in error;

(b) the notice contains material errors; or

(c) he has reasonable grounds to believe that the employee has committed an offence under regulation 17.

(10) A penalty notice may be withdrawn—

(a) whether or not the period specified in paragraph (4)(a) has expired;

(b) under paragraph (9)(a) and (b), whether or not the penalty has been paid; and

(c) under paragraph (9)(c), only where the penalty has not yet been paid.

(11) Where a penalty notice has been withdrawn under paragraph (9)—

(a) notice of the withdrawal must be given to the recipient; and
(b) any amount paid by way of penalty in pursuance of that notice must be repaid to the person who paid it.

(12) Subject to paragraph (13), proceedings shall not be continued or instituted against an employee for an offence under paragraph (1) in connection with which a withdrawal notice was issued.

(13) Proceedings may be continued or instituted for an offence in connection with which a withdrawal notice was issued if—

(a) where the withdrawal notice was withdrawn pursuant to paragraph (9)(b)—
    (i) a further penalty notice in respect of the offence was issued at the same time as the penalty notice was withdrawn; and
    (ii) the penalty has not been paid pursuant to that further penalty notice in accordance with paragraph (4)(a); or
(b) the withdrawal notice was withdrawn pursuant to paragraph (9)(c).

## Deception—employee offence

17. *[Omitted]*                                                    1.378

## Offences under regulations 16 and 17—search, entry and arrest

18. *[Omitted]*                                                    1.379

### SCHEDULE
*Consequential amendments*

*[Omitted]*                                                        1.380

## The Social Security (Persons Required to Provide Information) Regulations 2013

(SI 2013/1510)

In force October 1, 2013

ARRANGEMENT OF REGULATIONS

The Secretary of State for Work and Pensions makes the following Regulations in exercise of the powers conferred by sections 109B(2)(ia), 189(1) and (5) and 191 of the Social Security Administration Act 1992.

In accordance with section 176(1) of that Act, the Secretary of State has consulted with organisations appearing to him to be representative of the authorities concerned.

This instrument has not been referred to the Social Security Advisory Committee because it contains only regulations made by virtue of section 110 of the Welfare Reform Act 2012 and is made before the end of the period of 6 months beginning with the coming into force of that section.

### Citation and commencement

1.382    **1.**—(1) These Regulations may be cited as the Social Security (Persons Required to Provide Information) Regulations 2013.

(2) They come into force on 1st October 2013.

### Persons required to provide information

1.383    **2.**—(1) The following are prescribed as descriptions of persons for the purpose of section 109B(2)(ia) of the Social Security Administration Act 1992 (power of authorised officers to require information)—

(a) a person who provides relevant childcare;

(b) a person to whom a person in receipt of universal credit ("C") is liable to make rent payments in respect of accommodation which C occupies, or purports to occupy, as their home where C's award of universal credit includes an amount in respect of such payments;

(c) a rent officer to the extent that the information required relates to the rent officer's functions under section 122 of the Housing Act 1996;

(d) a local authority which administers a council tax reduction scheme to the extent that the information required relates to such a scheme.

(2) In this regulation—

(a) "UC Regulations" means the Universal Credit Regulations 2013(5);
(b) "council tax reduction scheme"—
    (i) in England and Wales, has the meaning given in section 13A(9) of the Local Government Finance Act 1992 and includes a default scheme within the meaning of paragraph 4 of Schedule 1A (or in Wales paragraph 6(1)(e) of Schedule 1B) to that Act; and
    (ii) in Scotland, means a means-tested reduction to an individual's council tax liability in accordance with the Council Tax Reduction (Scotland) Regulations 2012 or the Council Tax Reduction (State Pension Credit) (Scotland) Regulations 2012;
(c) "relevant childcare" has the meaning given in regulation 35 of the UC Regulations;
(d) "rent payments" has the meaning given in paragraph 2 of Schedule 1 to the UC Regulations;
(e) "universal credit" means universal credit under Part 1 of the Welfare Reform Act 2012.

## The Industrial Injuries Benefit (Employment Training Schemes and Courses) Regulations 2013

(SI 2013/2540)

In force October 31, 2013

ARRANGEMENT OF REGULATIONS

The Secretary of State for Work and Pensions makes the following Regulations in exercise of the powers conferred by sections 95A, 122(1) and 175(1), (3), (4) and (5) of the Social Security Contributions and Benefits Act 1992 and section 66(3) of the Welfare Reform Act 2012.

In accordance with section 172(2) of the Social Security Administration Act 1992 reference has been made to the Industrial Injuries Advisory Council.

### Citation, commencement and interpretation

1.385    **1.**—(1) These Regulations may be cited as the Industrial Injuries Benefit (Employment Training Schemes and Courses) Regulations 2013.

(2) They come into force on 31st October 2013.

(3) In these Regulations—

"the Employment and Training Act" means the Employment and Training Act 1973;

"the Contributions and Benefits Act" means the Social Security Contributions and Benefits Act 1992;

"the Jobseekers Act" means the Jobseekers Act 1995.

### Employment training scheme and employment training course

1.386    **2.** The following descriptions of employment training scheme and employment training course are prescribed for the purposes of section 95A(1) of the Contributions and Benefits Act—

(a) an employment training scheme or employment training course provided pursuant to arrangements made by or on behalf of the Secretary of State or the Scottish or Welsh Ministers under section 2 of the Employment and Training Act (arrangements for the purpose of assisting persons to select, train for, obtain and retain employment);

(b) an employment training scheme or employment training course which constitutes, or participation in which forms part of, a

216

scheme of a description prescribed under section 17A of the Jobseekers Act (schemes for assisting persons to obtain employment: "work for your benefit" schemes etc.);

(c) an employment training scheme or employment training course in which a person participates pursuant to—

   (i) a requirement to undertake work-related activity imposed under regulations under section 13 of the Welfare Reform Act 2007; or

   (ii) a work preparation requirement within the meaning of section 6C of the Jobseekers Act, section 11C of the Welfare Reform Act 2007 or section 16 of the Welfare Reform Act 2012.

## Employer

**3.** The persons prescribed for the purposes of section 95A(2) of the Contributions and Benefits Act are any persons providing an employment training scheme or employment training course of a description prescribed under regulation 2 above.      1.387

## Payment of industrial injuries benefit where payments were previously payable under section 11(3) of the Employment and Training Act

**4.** Where, before section 66 of the Welfare Reform Act 2012 (trainees)      1.388
came into force for all purposes, payments were payable to a person in consequence of an injury or disease under section 11(3) of the Employment and Training Act (power to make payments in respect of trainees equivalent to social security benefits in respect of employees), that person is entitled to equivalent payments of industrial injuries benefit.

## Outstanding claims

**5.** Any claim for payments in consequence of an injury or disease      1.389
under section 11(3) of the Employment and Training Act, which was made but not determined before section 66 of the Welfare Reform Act 2012 came into force for all purposes, is to be treated as a claim for industrial injuries benefit.

# PART II

# UPDATING MATERIAL
## VOLUME I

# NON MEANS TESTED BENEFITS AND EMPLOYMENT AND SUPPORT ALLOWANCE

Commentary by

**David Bonner**

**Ian Hooker**

**Richard Poynter**

**Robin White**

**Nick Wikeley**

**Penny Wood**

---

**Important preliminary note**

In this Part, "'Pathfinder' amendment" or "'Pathfinder' repeal" means one that applies only to those cases and areas in which "Pathfinder" pilots are operational. On this see the new Vol.V, *Universal Credit*, Part 4 dealing with transition and the key Welfare Reform Act 2012 Commencement Orders. These make the amendments operational from various dates on or after April 29, 2013.

**p.xxxiii,** *Table of Cases*

The reference to *KM v SSWP* [2013] UKUT (AAC) should be to number 159.     2.001

**pp.8–9,** *amendments to the Vaccine Damage Payments Act 1979 s.4 (appeals to appeal tribunals)*

With effect from February 25, 2013, s.102(6) and Sch.11, paras 1, 2     2.002 of the Welfare Reform Act 2012 amended s.4. The draftsman's numbering within the subsection is awry. Section 4 now reads as follows:

### "Appeals to appeal tribunals

**4.**—(1) The claimant may appeal to the First-tier Tribunal against any decision of the Secretary of State under section 3 or 3A above.

[(1B) If the claimant's address is not in Northern Ireland, regulations may provide that, in such cases or circumstances as may be prescribed, there is a right of appeal only if the Secretary of State has considered whether to reverse the decision under section 3A.

(1C) The regulations may in particular provide that that condition is met only where—

(a) the consideration by the Secretary of State was on an application,

(b) the Secretary of State considered issues of a specified description, or

(c) the consideration by the Secretary of State satisfied any other condition specified in the regulations.]

(2) Regulations may make—

(a) provision as to the manner in which, and the time within which, appeals are to be brought; . . .

[(c) provision that, where in accordance with regulations under subsection (1B) there is no right of appeal against a decision, any purported appeal may be treated as an application to reverse the decision under section 3A.]

(3) The regulations may in particular make any provision of a kind mentioned in Schedule 5 to the Social Security Act 1998.

(4) In deciding an appeal under this section, an appeal tribunal shall consider all the circumstances of the case (including any not obtaining at the time when the decision appealed against was made)."

**p.11,** *amendment to the Vaccine Damage Payments Act 1979 s.8 (regulations)*

With effect from February 25, 2013, s.102(6) and Sch.11, paras 1, 2     2.003 of the Welfare Reform Act 2012 amended s.8 in several ways.

First, by deleting words so that subs.(2)(a) reads:

"(2) Any power of the Secretary of State under this Act to make regulations—

(a) shall be exercisable by statutory instrument [ . . . ];".

Secondly, by inserting after subs.(2) new subs.(2A) to read:

"(2A) A statutory instrument containing regulations made by the Secretary of State under this Act—

    (a) except in the case of an instrument containing regulations under section 4(1B), is subject to annulment in pursuance of a resolution of either House of Parliament;

    (b) in the case of an instrument containing regulations under section 4(1B), may not be made unless a draft of the instrument has been laid before and approved by a resolution of each House of Parliament."

Finally by inserting after subs.(3) (the draftsman's numbering is awry), a new subs.(5) to read:

"(5) The power to make regulations under section 4(1B) may be exercised—

    (a) in relation to all cases to which it extends, in relation to those cases but subject to specified exceptions or in relation to any specified cases or classes of case;

    (b) so as to make, as respects the cases in relation to which it is exercised—

        (i) the full provision to which it extends or any lesser provision (whether by way of exception or otherwise);

        (ii) the same provision for all cases, different provision for different cases or classes of case or different provision as respects the same case or class of case but for different purposes of this Act;

        (iii) provision which is either unconditional or is subject to any specified condition."

**p.75,** *annotation to Social Security Contributions and Benefits Act 1992 s.44 (Retirement pension change of sex-claimant remaining married)*

2.004    The position as set out in the main volume has been confirmed in *MB v SSWP* [2013] UKUT 290 (AAC). There, the claimant had made a male to female gender reassignment, but like the claimant in *Timbrell*, remained married to her wife from an earlier marriage. She reached the age of 60 in 2008 (well after the Gender Recognition Act (GRA) had come into force) and made her claim for her pension soon after that. The claim was refused on the ground that she did not have a full GRC because she could not satisfy s.4 of the Act, requiring that she be not married. In the UT an argument was advanced on the basis of *Timbrell* that she should be entitled to rely on the direct effect of EC Directive 79/7. This argument was rejected by Judge Wright on the ground that *Timbrell* (and the direct effect) applied only to a person reaching retirement age before the GRA came into force; there being then no means by which a claimant could effectively change her gender. The claimant's argument became, in effect, an attack upon the GRA as having not fulfilled the UK obligations under the Directive. Judge Wright held that this was not so; in his view both the ECJ in *Richards* and the CA in *Timbrell* had accepted the terms of the GRA, when in force, as fulfilling that obligation. The claimant could not, therefore, rely upon the direct effect of EC 97/7.

The judge dealt with two further arguments. He found that neither the terms of GRA nor those of the SSCBA 1992 were invalidated by the Equality Act 2010 because that Act makes specific provision in Sch.22 to exempt action taken under statute (or a statutory instrument). Secondly, he affirmed the decision of the ECtHR in *Parry v UK* (Application No. 42971/05) to the effect that s.4 of the GRA, requiring that the applicant be not married, was not in breach of the ECHR. But, finally, he noted too that he was advised by counsel for the DWP that the terms of the Marriage (Same Sex Couples) Bill, then before Parliament, (now the Marriage (Same Sex Couples) Act 2013, see Sch.5) would enable a claimant to obtain a full GRC notwithstanding that they remained a married person. (To do otherwise would have created discrimination between a woman by gender reassignment who remained married, and a natural woman who, under the terms of the new Act, was married.)

**p.95,** *correction to the layout of the Social Security Contributions and Benefits Act 1992 s.55(3) (Pension increase etc.)*

The correct layout is as follows: 2.005

"(3) For the purposes of this Act a person's entitlement to a Category A or Category B retirement pension is deferred if and so long as that person—
  (a) does not become entitled to that pension by reason only of not satisfying the conditions of section 1 of the Administration Act (entitlement to benefit dependent on claim), or
  (b) in consequence of an election under section 54(1), falls to be treated as not having become entitled to that pension,
and, in relation to any such pension, "period of deferment" shall be construed accordingly."

**p.127,** *annotation to Social Security Contributions and Benefits Act 1992 s.72 (Disability living allowance)*

The reference to *KM v SSWP* [2013] UKUT (AAC) should be to 2.006 number 159.

**p.133,** *annotation to Social Security Contributions and Benefits Act 1992 s.72 (Disability living allowance—attention and supervision)*

The reference to *KM v SSWP* [2013] UKUT (AAC) should be to 2.007 number 159.

**p.141,** *annotation to Social Security Contributions and Benefits Act 1992 s.72 (Disability living allowance—cooking test)*

The meaning of "preparing" a main meal has been explored further in 2.008 *HJ v SSWP* [2013] UKUT 613 (AAC). The claimant suffered from several conditions, one of which prevented her from peeling and cutting root vegetables. The question that arose (amongst other points) was whether this meant that she was incapable of cooking a main meal. On behalf of the Secretary of State it was argued that modern habits of retailing fresh vegetables included the presentation of ready prepared vegetables which could be used by the claimant. Presumably this argument sought to equate ready prepared vegetables with the minced meat mentioned in *R/DLA 2/95,* rather than a packet of frozen peas. However, Judge Jupp rejected it on the basis that to adopt the change in modern marketing methods as a sufficient explanation could open the door to a whole range of ready prepared meals that would require only to be heated before eating. Instead, the judge sidestepped this argument by holding (a) that not all meals need involve the use of root vegetables —what is required is a reasonable variety of wholesome foods—and (b) that, in any case, root vegetables could be cooked first, in their skins, and cut up afterwards when they were softened by the cooking process. The case was returned to the FTT for a new decision on this and other points.

**p.144,** *annotation to Social Security Contributions and Benefits Act 1992 s.72 (Disability living allowance—cooking test)*

2.009    In *DG v SSWP* [2013] UKUT 351 (AAC) the claimant suffered from several conditions, one of which was chronic fatigue syndrome (CFS). The claimant was in work but it was unclear where he worked; it is possible that he worked at home. The claim under this heading was based upon the fact that although the claimant was capable of cooking a main meal, that by the time he had completed his work, he lacked the energy to do so. The FTT held that he was not incapable of cooking. In its view he should have prioritised his life so that he took care of himself first and devoted time and energy to his work afterwards. As the UT judge pointed out this came close to deciding that it was unreasonable for this claimant to work. The appeal was allowed and returned to a new FTT for rehearing. The judge accepted the argument advanced on behalf of the Secretary of State that the claimant might be expected to moderate his working effort to conserve energy for self care and that the new FTT would have to explore the nature and extent of the claimant's working arrangements, before deciding what was a proper work/care balance for him. Note that this is another case that demonstrates that although the cooking test is a test only of the claimant's hypothetical ability to cook, this means only that his willingness and his need to cook can be ignored; it remains necessary to show that it is reasonable for that claimant, in his circumstances, to undertake the tasks of cooking.

**p.150,** *annotation to Social Security Contributions and Benefits Act 1992 s.72 (Disability living allowance)*

2.010    The reference to *KM v SSWP* [2013] UKUT (AAC) should be to number 159.

**p.158,** *annotation to Social Security Contributions and Benefits Act 1992 s.73(1)(a) (Mobility component—physical disablement)*

In *KS v SSWP* [2013] UKUT 390 (AAC) it was argued that the    2.011
limitation of the higher rate of the mobility component to those conditions having a physical cause was overruled by the provisions of the
Equality Act 2010, as being discriminatory on the grounds of mental
disablement. The argument failed because the terms of that Act specify
that nothing is unlawful if that action is required by the terms of legislation (see Sch.22 para.(1) of that Act).

**p.163,** *Social Security Contributions and Benefits Act 1992 s.73(1)(d) (Mobility component—unable to walk outside without guidance or supervision most of the time)*

In *AR v SSWP* [2013] UKUT 463 (AAC) the claimant suffered from    2.012
hyperacusis—an extreme intolerance to noise. In his claim form he said
that exposure to noise made him anxious and aggressive. He had been
arrested on several occasions as a result of confrontational behaviour
resulting from this medical condition. He claimed the lower rate of the
mobility component on the ground that he needed someone to accom-
pany him to provide reassurance and supervision when walking outside
most of the time. The FTT that heard his appeal against refusal of
benefit held, in a carefully reasoned decision, that a person accompanying him would not be providing "guidance or supervision" and that any
guidance or supervision that was available would, in any case, make no
difference to him. In the UT Judge Wikeley expressed his sympathy with
the FTT in dealing with a difficult and novel case only on the paper
record before them. However, he held that on both these points there
was an error of law and directed that the case be reheard before a fresh
tribunal. The representative of the Secretary of State had supported the
appeal on both grounds, though she argued too, that mobility allowance
could not be awarded if the purpose of supervision were to prevent or
dissuade the claimant from engaging in criminal activity. Judge Wikeley
says this proposition must be approached with caution in the light of
cases referred to above. It is possible that benefit might be available, he
suggests, if the supervision is needed to prevent a person with a psychiat-
ric condition engaging in criminal or at least anti-social behaviour.

**pp.205–206,** *correction in relation to the Social Security Contributions and Benefits Act 1992 s.95A (employment training schemes etc.)*

This section was inserted in error. Section 66 of the Welfare Reform    2.013
Act 2012 had been brought into force only for the purpose of making
regulations. Section 66(1), (2) inserting s.95A into the SSCBA 1992
were only brought into force on October 31, 2013. See update to p.423,
below. See also the Industrial Injuries Benefit (Employment Training
Schemes and Courses) Regulations 2013 (SI 2013/2540) in the "New
Legislation" section of this Supplement. The "employers" for industrial
injuries benefit purposes are persons providing an employment training

scheme or employment training course of a description prescribed in reg.2 of those Regulations (see reg.3).

**p.298,** *annotation to the Social Security Contributions and Benefits Act 1992 Sch.7: Part IV (Reduced Earnings Allowance)*

2.014    In *JR v Secretary of State for Work and Pensions (II)* [2013] UKUT 0317 (AAC), Judge Mesher considered the effect of the October 1994 amendment to para.11(1):

"and a person shall not be entitled to reduced earnings allowance—

. . .

  (ii) in relation to a disease prescribed before 10th October 1994 whose prescription is extended on or after that date under section 108(2) above but only in so far as the prescription has been so extended]."

He held that since the

"prescription process under section 108 can only be regarded as covering the definition of both diseases and occupational groups. [there was] nothing in the fact that the reference in paragraph 11(1) of Schedule 7 is to section 108(2) to suggest that extension of the prescription is limited to the definition of occupational groups covered. . . . the identification of those groups of employed earners for whom a disease ought to be treated as a risk of their occupation is directed just as much (if not more so in the light of paragraph (b)) at the identification and definition of the disease concerned as at the identification of the appropriate occupational groups" (para.20).

**pp.346–347,** *additions to the Welfare Reform Act 2007: Arrangement of Sections*

2.015    The following should be added in the appropriate location in the Arrangement of Sections:

  1A      Duration of contributory allowance
  1B      Further entitlement after time-limiting
  15A     Persons dependent on drugs etc.
  Sch1A  Persons dependent on drugs etc.

**p.348,** *"Pathfinder" amendment to the Welfare Reform Act 2007 s.1 (employment and support allowance): insertion of new subs.(3)(aa)*

2.016    With effect from various dates on or after April 29, 2013 (see art.7 of Commencement Order No. 9 (SI 2013/983)), s.54(1), (2) of the Welfare Reform Act 2012, inserted after subs.(3)(a) a new subs.(3)(aa) to read:

"(aa) has accepted a claimant commitment,".

**p.348,** *amendment to the Welfare Reform Act 2007 s.1 (employment and support allowance): insertion of new subs.(6A)*

With effect from May 8, 2012, s.50(1) of the Welfare Reform Act 2012, inserted after subs.(6) a new subs.(6A) to read: 2.017

"(6A) In subsection (3)(f), in relation to a contributory allowance, the reference to a couple entitled to a joint-claim jobseeker's allowance does not include a couple so entitled by virtue of regulations under paragraph 8A of Schedule 1 to the Jobseekers Act 1995."

Note also that s.50(2) gives this new subsection retrospective effect where to do so would benefit a claimant. It provides:

"(2) In a case where—
(a) an award of an employment and support allowance is made to a person in respect of any period of time before the coming into force of subsection (1), and
(b) the person was not entitled to an employment and support allowance in relation to that period but would have been had subsection (1) been in force in relation to that period,
subsection (1) shall be regarded as having been in force in relation to that period."

**p.348,** *"Pathfinder" amendment to the Welfare Reform Act 2007 s.1 (employment and support allowance)*

With effect from various dates on or after April 29, 2013 (see art.4 of Commencement Order No. 9 (SI 2013/983)), s.33(3), Sch.3, para.23, s.147 and Sch.14, Pt 1 together amended s.1 to read: 2.018

"**Employment and support allowance**

**1.**—(1) An allowance, to be known as an employment and support allowance, shall be payable in accordance with the provisions of this Part.

(2) Subject to the provisions of this Part, a claimant is entitled to an employment and support allowance if he satisfies the basic conditions and
[ . . . ]—
(a) the first and the second conditions set out in [ . . . ] Schedule 1 (conditions relating to national insurance) or the third condition set out in [ . . . ] that Schedule (condition relating to youth), [ . . . ]
[ . . . ].
(3) The basic conditions are that the claimant—
(a)   has limited capability for work,
(aa) has accepted a claimant commitment,
(b)   is at least 16 years old,
(c)   has not reached pensionable age,
(d)   is in Great Britain, [and]
(e)   is not entitled to income support, and

227

(f)    is not entitled to a jobseeker's allowance [ . . . ].

(3A) After the coming into force of this subsection no claim may be made for an employment and support allowance by virtue of the third condition set out in [ . . . ] Schedule 1 (youth).

(4) For the purposes of this Part, a person has limited capability for work if—

(a) his capability for work is limited by his physical or mental condition, and

(b) the limitation is such that it is not reasonable to require him to work.

(5) An employment and support allowance is payable in respect of a week.

(6) In subsection (3)—

[ . . . ];

"pensionable age" has the meaning given by the rules in paragraph 1 of Schedule 4 to the Pensions Act 1995.

[ . . . ].

(6A) [ . . . ].

(7) [ . . . ]."

**p.351,** *annotation to the Welfare Reform Act 2007 s.1 (employment and support allowance)*

2.019    In line 22, replace "public purpose" with "public purse".

**pp.353–354,** *"Pathfinder" amendment to Welfare Reform Act 2007 s.1A (duration of contributory allowance)*

2.020    With effect from various dates on or after April 29, 2013 (see art.4 of Commencement Order No. 9 (SI 2013/983)), s.33(3) and Sch.3 para. 26(a), s.147 and Sch.14, Pt 1 together amended s.1A to read:

**"Duration of [ . . . ] allowance**

**1A.**—(1) The period for which a person is entitled to [an employment and support allowance] by virtue of the first and second conditions set out in [ . . . ] Schedule 1 shall not exceed, in the aggregate, the relevant maximum number of days in any period for which his entitlement is established by reference (under the second condition set out in [ . . . ] Schedule 1) to the same two tax years.

(2) In subsection (1) the "relevant maximum number of days" is—

(a) 365 days, or

(b) if the Secretary of State by order specifies a greater number of days, that number of days.

(3) The fact that a person's entitlement to [an employment and support allowance] has ceased as a result of subsection (1) does not prevent his being entitled to a further such allowance if—

(a) he satisfies the first and second conditions set out in [ . . . ] Schedule 1, and

(b) the two tax years by reference to which he satisfies the second condition include at least one year which is later than the second of the two years by reference to which (under the second condition) his previous entitlement was established.

(4) The period for which a person is entitled to [an employment and support allowance] by virtue of the third condition set out in [ . . . ] Schedule 1 (youth) shall not exceed—

(a) 365 days, or

(b) if the Secretary of State by order specifies a greater number of days, that number of days.

(5) In calculating for the purposes of subsection (1) or (4) the length of the period for which a person is entitled to [an employment and support allowance], the following are not to be counted—

(a) days in which the person is a member of the support group,

(b) days not falling within paragraph (a) in respect of which the person is entitled to the support component referred to in section 2(1)(b), and

(c) days in the assessment phase, where the days immediately following that phase fall within paragraph (a) or (b).

(6) In calculating for the purposes of subsection (1) or (4) the length of the period for which a person is entitled to [an employment and support allowance], days occurring before the coming into force of this section are to be counted (as well as those occurring afterwards)."

**p.355,** *"Pathfinder" amendment to Welfare Reform Act 2007 s.1B (further entitlement after time-limiting)*

With effect from various dates on or after April 29, 2013 (see art.4 of Commencement Order No. 9 (SI 2013/983)), s.147 and Sch.14, Pt 1 of the Welfare Reform Act 2012 amended s.1B by repealing subs.(2). In addition, from that same date, s.33(3) and Sch.3, para.26(b) of the Welfare Reform Act 2012 amended subs.(1) to read:  2.021

**"Further entitlement after time-limiting**

**1B.**—(1) Where a person's entitlement to [an employment and support allowance] has ceased as a result of section 1A(1) or (4) but—

(a) the person has not at any subsequent time ceased to have (or to be treated as having) limited capability for work,

(b) the person satisfies the basic conditions, and

(c) the person has (or is treated as having) limited capability for work-related activity,

the claimant is entitled to an employment and support allowance by virtue of this section."

**p.355,** *"Pathfinder" amendment to Welfare Reform Act 2007 s.2(1) (amount of contributory allowance)*

With effect from various dates on or after April 29, 2013 (see art.4 of Commencement Order No. 9 (SI 2013/983)), s.33(3) and Sch.3 para.  2.022

26(a), s.147 and Sch.14, Pt 1 together amended both the heading to s.2 and s.2(1) to read:

"**Amount of [ . . . ] allowance**

**2.**—(1) [The amount payable by way of an employment and support allowance] in respect of a claimant shall be calculated by—
(a) taking such amount as may be prescribed;
(b) if in his case the conditions of entitlement to the support component or the work-related activity component are satisfied, adding the amount of that component; and
(c) making prescribed deductions in respect of any payments to which section 3 applies."

**p.358,** *"Pathfinder" amendment to Welfare Reform Act 2007 s.3 (deductions from contributory allowance: supplementary)*

2.023      With effect from various dates on or after April 29, 2013 (see art.4 of Commencement Order No. 9 (SI 2013/983)), s.147 and Sch.14, Pt 1 amended the heading to s.3 to read:

"**Deductions from [ . . . ] allowance: supplementary**".

In addition, from that same date, s.33(3) and Sch.3, para.26(c) of the Welfare Reform Act 2012 amended s.3(2)(d) by substituting "an employment and support allowance" for "a contributory allowance".

**pp.360–361,** *"Pathfinder" amendment to the Welfare Reform Act 2007 s.4 (Amount of income-related allowance)*

2.023A      With effect from various dates on or after April 29, 2013 s.147 and Sch.14, Pt 1 of the Welfare Reform Act 2012 repealed s.4.

**pp.362–363,** *"Pathfinder" amendment to the Welfare Reform Act 2007 s.5 (Advance award of income-related allowance)*

2.023B      With effect from various dates on or after April 29, 2013 s.147 and Sch.14, Pt 1 of the Welfare Reform Act 2012 repealed s.5.

**p.363,** *"Pathfinder" amendment to the Welfare Reform Act 2007 s.6 (Amount payable where claimant entitled to both forms of allowance)*

2.023C      With effect from various dates on or after April 29, 2013 s.147 and Sch.14, Pt 1 of the Welfare Reform Act 2012 repealed s.6.

**pp.367–379,** *"Pathfinder" amendment to the Welfare Reform Act 2007 ss.11–16 (Conditionality): substitution of new ss.11–11k (work-related requirements)*

2.024      With effect from various dates on or after April 29, 2013 (see art.7 of Commencement Order No. 9 (SI 2013/983)), s.57(1), (2) substituted for ss.11–16 (and the italic heading preceding s.11) new ss.11–11K to read:

"*Work-related requirements*

## Work-related requirements

**11.**—(1)The following provisions of this Part provide for the Secretary of State to impose work-related requirements with which persons entitled to an employment and support allowance must comply for the purposes of this Part.

(2) In this Part "work-related requirement" means—

(a) a work-focused interview requirement (see section 11B);

(b) a work preparation requirement (see section 11C).

(3)The work-related requirements which may be imposed on a person depend on which of the following groups the person falls into—

(a) persons subject to no work-related requirements (see section 11D);

(b) persons subject to work-focused interview requirement only (see section 11E);

(c) persons subject to work-focused interview and work preparation requirements (see section 11F).

## Claimant commitment

**11A.**—(1) A claimant commitment is a record of the responsibilities of a person entitled to an employment and support allowance in relation to the award of the allowance.

(2) A claimant commitment is to be prepared by the Secretary of State and may be reviewed and updated as the Secretary of State thinks fit.

(3) A claimant commitment is to be in such form as the Secretary of State thinks fit.

(4) A claimant commitment is to include—

(a) a record of the requirements that the person must comply with under this Part (or such of them as the Secretary of State considers it appropriate to include),

(b) any prescribed information, and

(c) any other information the Secretary of State considers it appropriate to include.

(5) For the purposes of this Part a person accepts a claimant commitment if, and only if, the claimant accepts the most up-to-date version of it in such manner as may be prescribed.

## Work-focused interview requirement

**11B.**—(1) In this Part a "work-focused interview requirement" is a requirement that a person participate in one or more work-focused interviews as specified by the Secretary of State.

(2) A work-focused interview is an interview for prescribed purposes relating to work or work preparation.

(3) The purposes which may be prescribed under subsection (2) include in particular that of making it more likely in the opinion of the Secretary of State that the person will obtain paid work (or more paid work or better-paid work).

(4) The Secretary of State may specify how, when and where a work-focused interview is to take place.

**Work preparation requirement**

**11C.**—(1) In this Part a "work preparation requirement" is a requirement that a person take particular action specified by the Secretary of State for the purpose of making it more likely in the opinion of the Secretary of State that the person will obtain paid work (or more paid work or better-paid work).

(2) The Secretary of State may under subsection (1) specify the time to be devoted to any particular action.

(3) Action which may be specified under subsection (1) includes in particular—

(a) attending a skills assessment;
(b) improving personal presentation;
(c) participating in training;
(d) participating in an employment programme;
(e) undertaking work experience or a work placement;
(f) developing a business plan;
(g) any action prescribed for the purpose in subsection (1).

(4) The action which may be specified under subsection (1) includes taking part in a work-focused health-related assessment.

(5) In subsection (4) "work-focused health-related assessment" means an assessment by a health care professional approved by the Secretary of State which is carried out for the purpose of assessing—

(a) the extent to which the person's capability for work may be improved by taking steps in relation to their physical or mental condition, and
(b) such other matters relating to their physical or mental condition and the likelihood of their obtaining or remaining in work or being able to do so as may be prescribed.

(6) In subsection (5) "health care professional" means—

(a) a registered medical practitioner,
(b) a registered nurse,
(c) an occupational therapist or physiotherapist registered with a regulatory body established by an Order in Council under section 60 of the Health Act 1999, or
(d) a member of such other profession regulated by a body mentioned in section 25(3) of the National Health Service Reform and Health Care Professions Act 2002 as may be prescribed.

**Persons subject to no work-related requirements**

**11D.**—(1)The Secretary of State may not impose any work-related requirement on a person falling within this section.

(2) A person falls within this section if—
(a) the person has limited capability for work and work-related activity,
(b) the person has regular and substantial caring responsibilities for a severely disabled person,
(c) the person is a single person responsible for a child under the age of 1,
(d) the person is of a prescribed description.

(3) Where a person falls within this section, any work-related requirement previously applying to the person ceases to have effect.

(4) In this section—
"regular and substantial caring responsibilities" has such meaning as may be prescribed;
"severely disabled" has such meaning as may be prescribed.

## Persons subject to work-focused interview requirement only

**11E.**—(1) A person falls within this section if—
(a) the person is a single person responsible for a child who is aged at least 1 and is under a prescribed age (which may not be less than 3), or
(b) the person is of a prescribed description.

(2) The Secretary of State may, subject to this Part, impose a work-focused interview requirement on a person entitled to an employment and support allowance who falls within this section.

(3) The Secretary of State may not impose a work preparation requirement on a person falling within this section (and, where a person falls within this section, a work preparation requirement previously applying to the person ceases to have effect).

## Persons subject to work preparation and work-focused interview requirement

**11F.**—(1) A person who does not fall within section 11D or 11E falls within this section.

(2) The Secretary of State may, subject to this Part, impose a work preparation requirement or work-focused interview requirement on a person entitled to an employment and support allowance who falls within this section.

## Connected requirements

**11G.**—(1)The Secretary of State may require a person entitled to an employment and support allowance to participate in an interview for any purpose relating to—
(a) the imposition of a work-related requirement on the person;
(b) verifying the person's compliance with a work-related requirement;
(c) assisting the person to comply with a work-related requirement.

(2) The Secretary of State may specify how, when and where such an interview is to take place.

(3) The Secretary of State may, for the purpose of verifying a person's compliance with a work-related requirement, require the person to—

(a) provide to the Secretary of State information and evidence specified by the Secretary of State in a manner so specified;

(b) confirm compliance in a manner so specified.

(4) The Secretary of State may require a person to report to the Secretary of State any specified changes in their circumstances which are relevant to—

(a) the imposition of work-related requirements on the person;

(b) the person's compliance with a work-related requirement.

### Imposition of requirements

**11H.**—(1) Regulations may make provision—

(a) where the Secretary of State may impose a requirement under this Part, as to when the requirement must or must not be imposed;

(b) where the Secretary of State may specify any action to be taken in relation to a requirement under this Part, as to what action must or must not be specified;

(c) where the Secretary of State may specify any other matter in relation to a requirement under this Part, as to what must or must not be specified in respect of that matter.

(2) Where the Secretary of State may impose a work-focused interview requirement, or specify a particular action under section 11C(1), the Secretary of State must have regard to such matters as may be prescribed.

(3) Where the Secretary of State may impose a requirement under this Part, or specify any action to be taken in relation to such a requirement, the Secretary of State may revoke or change what has been imposed or specified.

(4) Notification of a requirement imposed under this Part (or any change to or revocation of such a requirement) is, if not included in the claimant commitment, to be in such manner as the Secretary of State may determine.

(5) Regulations must make provision to secure that, in prescribed circumstances, where a person has recently been a victim of domestic violence—

(a) a requirement imposed on that person under this Part ceases to have effect for a period of 13 weeks, and

(b) the Secretary of State may not impose any other requirement on that person during that period.

(6) For the purposes of subsection (5)—

(a) "domestic violence" has such meaning as may be prescribed;

(b) "victim of domestic violence" means a person on or against whom domestic violence is inflicted or threatened (and regulations under subsection (5) may prescribe circumstances in which a person is to be treated as being or not being a victim of domestic violence);

(c) a person has recently been a victim of domestic violence if a prescribed period has not expired since the violence was inflicted or threatened.

## Compliance with requirements

**11I.**—Regulations may make provision as to circumstances in which a person is to be treated as having—
- (a) complied with or not complied with any requirement imposed under this Part or any aspect of such a requirement, or
- (b) taken or not taken any particular action specified by the Secretary of State in relation to such a requirement.

## Sanctions

**11J.**—(1) The amount of an award of an employment and support allowance is to be reduced in accordance with this section in the event of a failure by a person which is sanctionable under this section.

(2) It is a failure sanctionable under this section if a person—
- (a) fails for no good reason to comply with a work-related requirement;
- (b) fails for no good reason to comply with a requirement under section 11G.

(3) Regulations are to specify—
- (a) the amount of a reduction under this section, and
- (b) the period for which such a reduction has effect.

(4) Regulations under subsection (3)(b) may provide that a reduction under this section in relation to any failure is to have effect for—
- (a) a period continuing until the person meets a compliance condition specified by the Secretary of State,
- (b) a fixed period not exceeding 26 weeks which is—
  - (i) specified in the regulations, or
  - (ii) determined in any case by the Secretary of State, or
- (c) a combination of both.

(5) In subsection (4)(a) "compliance condition" means—
- (a) a condition that the failure ceases, or
- (b) a condition relating to future compliance with a work-related requirement or a requirement under section 11G.

(6) A compliance condition specified under subsection (4)(a) may be—
- (a) revoked or varied by the Secretary of State;
- (b) notified to the person in such manner as the Secretary of State may determine.

(7) A period fixed under subsection (4)(b) may in particular depend on either or both the following—
- (a) the number of failures by the person sanctionable under this section;

(b) the period between such failures.

(8) Regulations may provide—

(a) for cases in which no reduction is to be made under this section;

(b) for a reduction under this section made in relation to an award that is terminated to be applied to any new award made within a prescribed period of the termination;

(c) for the termination or suspension of a reduction under this section.

## Delegation and contracting out

**11K.**—(1) The functions of the Secretary of State under sections 11 to 11I may be exercised by, or by the employees of, such person as the Secretary of State may authorise for the purpose (an "authorised person").

(2) An authorisation given by virtue of this section may authorise the exercise of a function—

(a) wholly or to a limited extent;

(b) generally or in particular cases or areas;

(c) unconditionally or subject to conditions.

(3) An authorisation under this section—

(a) may specify its duration;

(b) may be varied or revoked at any time by the Secretary of State;

(c) does not prevent the Secretary of State or another person from exercising the function to which the authorisation relates.

(4) Anything done or omitted to be done by or in relation to an authorised person (or an employee of that person) in, or in connection with, the exercise or purported exercise of the function concerned is to be treated for all purposes as done or omitted to be done by or in relation to the Secretary of State or (as the case may be) an officer of the Secretary of State.

(5) Subsection (4) does not apply—

(a) for the purposes of so much of any contract made between the authorised person and the Secretary of State as relates to the exercise of the function, or

(b) for the purposes of any criminal proceedings brought in respect of anything done or omitted to be done by the authorised person (or an employee of that person).

(6) Where—

(a) the authorisation of an authorised person is revoked, and

(b) at the time of the revocation so much of any contract made between the authorised person and the Secretary of State as relates to the exercise of the function is subsisting,

the authorised person is entitled to treat the contract as repudiated by the Secretary of State (and not as frustrated by reason of the revocation)."

**p.379,** *"Pathfinder" repeal of the Welfare Reform Act 2007 s.16A (hardship payments)*

With effect from various dates on or after April 29, 2013, s.147 and Sch.14, Pt 5 of the Welfare Reform Act 2012 repealed s.16A.  **2.025**

**p.380,** *"Pathfinder" amendment to the Welfare Reform Act 2007 s.18 (disqualification)*

With effect from various dates on or after April 29, 2013 (see art.4 of Commencement Order No. 9 (SI 2013/983)), s.33(3) and Sch.3, para. 26(c) of the Welfare Reform Act 2012 amended s.18(4) by substituting "an employment and support allowance" for "a contributory allowance".  **2.026**

**p.384,** *"Pathfinder" amendment to the Welfare Reform Act 2007 s.23 (Recovery of sums in respect of maintenance)*

With effect from various dates on or after April 29, 2013, s.147 of, and Sch.14, Part I to, the Welfare Reform Act 2012 repealed s.23.  **2.026A**

**p.387,** *"Pathfinder" amendment to the Welfare Reform Act 2007 s.26 (Parliamentary control)*

With effect from various dates on or after April 29, 2013 s.147 and Sch.14, Pt 1 of the Welfare Reform Act 2012 amended s.26 by repealing the words from "or 4(4)(c) or 5(c)" in subs.(1)(a).  **2.026B**

**p.387,** *"Pathfinder" amendment to the Welfare Reform Act 2007 s.27 (Financial provisions relating to Part 1)*

With effect from various dates on or after April 29, 2013 s.147 and Sch.14, Pt 1 of the Welfare Reform Act 2012 amended s.27 by repealing subss.(2)(a) and (4).  **2.026C**

**p.392,** *amendment to the Welfare Reform Act 2007 Sch.1 (Employment and support allowance: additional conditions) para.1(5) (conditions relating to national insurance)*

With effect from April 29, 2013, s.31 and Sch.2, para.65, of the Welfare Reform Act 2012 amended para.1(5) by inserting, before sub-para.(a), a new sub-para.(za) to read:  **2.027**

"(za) universal credit,".

**pp.392–393,** *"Pathfinder" amendment to the Welfare Reform Act 2007 Sch.1 (Employment and support allowance: additional conditions)*

With effect from various dates on or after April 29, 2013 (see art.4 of Commencement Order No. 9 (SI 2013/983)), s.147 and Sch.14, Pt 1 of  **2.028** the Welfare Reform Act 2012 amended Sch.1 by deleting the following:

## "PART 1
### CONTRIBUTORY ALLOWANCE"

From that same date, s.33(3) and Sch.3, para.26(f) amended both para.1(5)(d) and para.3(2)(a) by substituting in each "an employment and support allowance" for "a contributory allowance".

**pp.396–398,** *"Pathfinder" amendment to the Welfare Reform Act 2007, Sch.1, Part 2 (Income-related Allowance)*

2.028A    With effect from various dates on or after April 29, 2013, s.147 of, and Sch.14, Part I to, the Welfare Reform Act 2012 repealed Sch.1, Part 2.

**p.399,** *amendment to the Welfare Reform Act 2007 Sch.2 (Employment and Support Allowance: Supplementary Provisions): insertion of a new para.4A (exemption)*

2.029    With effect from February 25, 2013, s.54(6) of the Welfare Reform Act 2012 inserted between paras 4 and 5 a new para.4A to read:

### "Exemption

**4A.** Regulations may prescribe circumstances in which a person may be entitled to employment and support allowance without having accepted a claimant commitment."

**p.399,** *"Pathfinder" amendments to the Welfare Reform Act 2007 Sch.2 (employment and support allowance: supplementary provisions)*

2.030    With effect from various dates on or after April 29, 2013 (see art.4 of Commencement Order No. 9 (SI 2013/983)), s.147 and Sch.14, Pt 1 of the Welfare Reform Act 2012 amended Sch.2 in several ways:
- deleting "Contributory allowance" from the headings to paras 6 and 7;
- repealing para.8;
- repealing para.11(b) and (c); and
- repealing para.12.

From that same date, s.33(3) and Sch.3, para.26(g) of the Welfare Reform Act 2012 amended both para.6 and para.7(2)(d) by replacing "a contributory allowance" in each with "an employment and support allowance".

**p.423,** *amendment to the Welfare Reform Act 2012 s.66 (Trainees)*

2.031    Note that s.66(1), (2) inserting a new s.95A into the SSCBA 1992 were brought into force on October 31, 2013. See update to pp.205–206, above.

**pp.453–455,** *amendment to the Social Security (Credits) Regulations 1975 (SI 1975/556) reg.8A (credits for unemployment)*

With effect from October 29, 2013, reg.3 of the Social Security 2.032 (Miscellaneous Amendments)(No. 3) Regulations 2013 (SI 2013/2536) amended reg.8A by omitting para.(4).

**p.476,** *amendment to the Social Security (Benefit) (Married Women and Widows Special Provisions) Regulations 1974 (SI 1974/2010) reg.3(1) (modification in relation to widows, etc.)*

With effect from April 29, 2013, reg.20(1), (3) of the Universal Credit 2.033 (Consequential, Supplementary, Incidental and Miscellaneous Provisions) Regulations 2013 (SI 2013/630) amended reg.3(1) to read:

**"Modifications, in relation to widows, of provisions with respect to . . . short-term incapacity benefit, [ . . . ] employment and support allowance, maternity allowance, and Category A retirement pension**

**3.**—(1) Subject to the following provisions of this regulation, where, otherwise than by reason of remarriage or cohabitation with a man as his wife, a woman ceases to be entitled either to a widow's allowance or to a widowed mother's allowance—

    (a) she shall be deemed to have satisfied the first contribution condition for short-term incapacity benefit or maternity allowance referred to in paragraph 1 or 3, as the case may be, of Schedule 3 to the Act or, in relation to [ . . . ] employment and support allowance, she shall be deemed to have satisfied the first condition referred to in paragraph 1(1) of Schedule 1 to the Welfare Reform Act;

    (b) for the purpose only of enabling her to satisfy the second contribution condition for unemployment and short-term incapacity Benefit or maternity allowance referred to in paragraph 1 or 3, as the case may be, of Schedule 3 to the Act or, in relation to [ . . . ] employment and support allowance, she shall be deemed to have satisfied the second condition referred to in paragraph 2(1) of Schedule 1 to the Welfare Reform Act, there shall be credited to her such Class 1 contributions (if any) for every year up to and including that in which she ceased to be entitled as aforesaid as are required to enable her to satisfy that condition; and

    (c) . . . ."

**p.497,** *amendment to the Social Security (Computation of Earnings) Regulations 1996 reg.2(1)*

With effect from April 1, 2013, art.11 of, and para.32(2) of Part 1 of 2.034 Sch.2 to, the National Treatment Agency (Abolition) and the Health and

Social Care Act 2012 (Consequential, Transitional and Saving Provisions) Order 2013 (SI 2013/235) inserted the following new definition after "claimant":

""clinical commissioning group" means a body established under section 14D of the National Health Service Act 2006;"

and omitted the definition of "Primary Care Trust".

**p.521,** *amendment to the Social Security (Computation of Earnings) Regulations 1996 Sch.1 (Sums to be disregarded in the calculation of earnings)*

2.035    With effect from April 1, 2013, art.11 of, and para.32(3) of Part 1 of Sch.2 to, the National Treatment Agency (Abolition) and the Health and Social Care Act 2012 (Consequential, Transitional and Saving Provisions) Order 2013 (SI 2013/235) substituted "a clinical commissioning group, the National Health Service Commissioning Board, a local authority or a voluntary organisation" for "or Primary Care Trust, local authority or voluntary organisation" in Sch.1, para.7.

With effect from October 29, 2013, reg.7 of the Social Security (Miscellaneous Amendments) (No. 3) Regulations 2013 (SI 2013/2536) amended Sch.1, para.9 as follows:

(a) by omitting sub-paras (a), (aa) and (ab)

(b) by inserting the following text before sub-para.(b):

"(a) a part-time fire-fighter employed by a fire and rescue authority under the Fire and Rescue Services Act 2004 or by the Scottish Fire and Rescue Service established under section 1A of the Fire (Scotland) Act 2005;"

**p.553,** *amendments to the Social Security (Overlapping Benefits) Regulations 1979 reg.2 (Interpretation)*

2.036    With effect from April 29, 2013, reg.25 of the Universal Credit (Consequential Supplementary, Incidental and Miscellaneous Provisions) Regulations 2013 (SI 2013/630), amended reg.2 as follows:

(a) by inserting the following definition after the definition of "child benefit";

""contribution-based jobseeker's allowance" means an allowance under the Jobseekers Act as amended by the provisions of Part 1 of Schedule 14 to the 2012 Act that remove references to an income-based allowance, and a contribution-based allowance under the Jobseekers Act as that Act has effect apart from those provisions;"

(b) by inserting the following definition after the definition of "contributory benefit":

""contributory employment and support allowance" means an allowance under Part 1 of the Welfare Reform Act as amended by the provisions of Schedule 3, and Part 1 of Schedule 14, to the 2012 Act that remove references to an income-related allowance, and a contributory allowance under Part 1 of the Welfare Reform Act as that Part has effect apart from those provisions;"

(c) by inserting the following definitions after the definition of "disablement pension":

""income-based jobseeker's allowance" means an income-based allowance under the Jobseekers Act;

"income-related employment and support allowance" means an income-related allowance under Part 1 of the Welfare Reform Act;"

(d) by inserting in the definition of "personal benefit" the words "or universal credit under Part 1 of the Welfare Reform Act" after the words "dependency benefit".

**p.573,** *amendments to the Social Security (Persons Abroad) Regulations 1975 reg.1 (Citation, commencement and interpretation)*

With effect from April 29, 2013, the Universal Credit (Consequential Supplementary, Incidental and Miscellaneous Provisions) Regulations 2013 (SI 2013/630), reg.23(2) amended reg.1(2) by inserting the following definition after the definition of "the Industrial Injuries Employment Regulations":  **2.037**

""jobseeker's allowance" means an allowance under the Jobseekers Act 1995 as amended by the provisions of Part 1 of Schedule 14 to the Welfare Reform Act 2012 that remove references to an income-based allowance, and a contribution-based allowance under the Jobseekers Act 1995 as that Act has effect apart from those provisions;"

**p.593,** *amendments to the Social Security (Persons Abroad) Regulations 1975 (SI 1975/563) reg.11 (Modification of the Act in relation to employment on the Continental Shelf)*

With effect from April 29, 2013, the Universal Credit (Consequential Supplementary, Incidental and Miscellaneous Provisions) Regulations 2013 (SI 2013/630), reg.23(3) amended reg.11(1A) by omitting the words "contribution-based" in both places where it occurs.  **2.038**

**p.634,** *annotation to Social Security (Disability Living Allowance) Regulations 1991 (SI 1991/2890) reg.8 (Hospitalisation)*

The further complications involved in administering this provision (and regs 9 and 12A) are demonstrated in *SSWP v TR (DLA)* [2013] UKUT 622 (AAC). The claimant was accommodated in a home for which the health authority and the local authority had agreed to share the costs on a 50/50 basis. The claimant was subjected to a statutory charge which he paid to the local authority. In the home, 31 per cent of the staff were qualified nurses, there was as well a "physio team", and the home was registered to provide care with nursing and rehabilitation services. The question to be determined was whether the claimant, in  **2.039** these circumstances, was being "maintained free of charge while undergoing medical or other treatment as an in-patient in a hospital or similar institution". The judge in the UT, Judge Fordham QC, found that he was not. He would have found that the home was a "hospital or similar institution" and he would have found too, that the claimant was "receiving medical treatment as an in-patient" there, but he did not find that the claimant was being "maintained free of charge" in the home. This was not because the claimant was paying a contribution towards his costs —that would have been the effect of giving this phrase its natural and ordinary meaning, but the phrase has a restricted meaning in reg.8(2) (and in reg.12A(2)). The effect of that definition is that a claimant can only be said to be "not being maintained in the hospital free of charge" if they are there entirely as a private patient; thus for someone in the claimant's position although he was being charged a contribution, he could still be regarded as being there free of charge! The judge's decision turns upon what is meant by being "maintained" and the interpretation given to that word in the earlier cases of *R (DLA) 2/06* and *CDLA/ 509/2009* which followed it. Those cases establish that a claimant is to be regarded as maintained in the hospital or other institution only as long as the health authority has a duty to do so under the relevant National Health Service Act. Correspondingly he cannot be maintained by the local authority while that is so, and he can be maintained by the local authority only when they have a duty to do so under Part III of the National Assistance Act 1948. In this case it appeared that the local authority took the view that they were obliged to maintain under Part III and it followed that the health authority were not, therefore "maintaining" him. This meant that the claimant was entitled to be paid DLA under both reg.8 and reg.12A. But he was not entitled to payment of the care component of DLA because under reg.9 (see below) at least some part of the cost of his accommodation and care was met from public funds. This a complex area of law that seems to be encumbered by provisions derived from past practices and badly in need of updating.

**p.635,** *Social Security (Disability Living Allowance) Regulations 1991 (SI 1991/2890) reg.8 (Hospitalisation)*

2.040     The meaning of the phrases "undergoing medical or other treatment as an in-patient" and "in a hospital or similar institution" has been considered again by Judge Turnbull in *JP v SSWP* [2013] UKUT 524 (AAC). There the claimant was a young man who suffered from a serious form of epilepsy. Until 2007 he had lived at home with his parents, but then it had been necessary to move him from his home to a place run by a charity that provided accommodation and specialist services for persons with conditions of that kind. The premises extended over a campus-like arrangement that included accommodation units, medical and other services and a GP surgery. The claimant lived in an accommodation unit that was staffed only by non-medically qualified persons, but the charity had engaged a number of other medically qualified staff including nurses, a doctor (other than the GP), psychologists and consultants who came to the campus to provide their services.

On behalf of the claimant, it was argued that where he lived was staffed only by care staff and that the medical services that he received were no more than would have been available from a local hospital, etc. had he been living still at his parents' home. Judge Turnbull, however, decided that the charity's premises should be regarded as a collective unit that, although clearly not a hospital, could fall within the description of a "similar institution". Furthermore, in his view, the treatment that the claimant received on the premises (though not that from the GP surgery) constituted "medical or other treatment as an in patient". Consequently the appeal against refusal of both the living component (under reg.8) and the mobility component (under reg.12A) was dismissed.

**p.642,** *annotation to Social Security (Disability Living Allowance) Regulations 1991 (SI 1991/2890) reg.10C (Prescribed circumstances for entitlement to the care component)*

There is an interesting example of the application of this argument **2.041** shown in the case of *HP v SSWP* [2013] UKUT 248 (AAC). There the claimant was suffering from depressive mental illness. Although she was living on her own she was able to function to a reasonable extent in managing her own daily care, but only if she received frequent attention in the form of encouragement and reminders from members of her family. At first this was provided chiefly by her sister who did that in person, but her sister moved to live in the USA. Thereafter, the attention was provided by means of a visual telephonic communication system ("Skype"). Evidence was given by the claimant that, without that support, she would not be able to function normally at all. Unfortunately, the FTT that heard her appeal against a refusal of benefit did not refer to this evidence at all; nor did they refer to reg.10C. They simply found that the claimant was self caring and therefore refused the appeal. In the UT Judge Fordham QC found that the decision was deficient in providing reasons for reaching the conclusion that they did. He holds that the only question is whether the claimant needs (requires) such attention and that evidence of attention given in the manner above can be evidence of such need. The reasons given by the FTT did not explain whether they rejected that evidence as untrue, or as irrelevant, or whether they had failed to notice it at all. Judge Fordham suggests, as an example of where telephonic assistance might succeed in showing such need, the case of a carer who formerly assisted in person, but who is prevented, by breaking their leg, from attending in person. He suggests that evidence of telephonic assistance will always be of limited weight and that it is likely to succeed only where the non-presence is involuntary, the claimant and the assistant would unhesitatingly say that actual presence would be preferable and that the telephone assistance is, at best, "fragile or not wholly successful". It remains the case then, that if the telephoned assistance is reliable and is sufficient for the claimant to achieve a reasonably normal level of daily activity it will not have been shown that anything more (i.e. actual assistance in person) is required. The case was returned to a new FTT for rehearing.

**p.645,** *annotation to Social Security (Disability Living Allowance) Regulations 1991 (SI 1991/2890) reg.12(1)(a) (physical disablement and physical condition)*

2.042    In *KS v SSWP* [2013] UKUT 390 (AAC) it was argued that the limitation of the higher rate of the mobility component to those conditions having a physical cause was overruled by the provisions of the Equality Act 2010, as being discriminatory on the grounds of mental disablement. The argument failed because the terms of that Act specify that nothing is unlawful if that action is required by the terms of legislation (see Sch.22 para.(1) of that Act).

**p.650,** *annotation to Social Security (Disability Living Allowance) Regulations 1991 (SI 1991/2890) reg.12 (1)(a)(ii) (virtually unable to walk)*

2.043    A good example of a tribunal leaping too readily to a conclusion that the claimant was not virtually unable to walk can be found in *JT v SSWP* [2013] UKUT 221 (AAC). There, evidence had been given that the claimant had recently been on holiday to Greece and that in doing so he had been able to walk to and from the aircraft at the airports on either end of his journeys. The FTT accepted this as showing that he was not "virtually unable to walk". The UT allowed an appeal on several grounds. First, the holiday in Greece was at a time after the decision against which he had appealed was made and no reason was given to show that, as evidence, it could be related to the earlier time (though to do so may not have been difficult). Secondly, no attempt had been made to examine the distance over which, the time in which, or the manner in which the claimant had accomplished this walk. Thirdly, it was likely that most, if not all, of the airport walking was done indoors—no attention had been given to the possible differences that might relate to walking out of doors. It is easy to see why the FTT might have been tempted to seize on what looked like clear evidence of walking ability, but it remains essential that the evidence is tested rationally and careful reasons given for the conclusions that are drawn.

**p.657,** *annotation to Social Security (Disability Living Allowance) Regulations 1991 (SI 1991/2890) reg.12(1)(a)(iii) (exertion and danger to life or serious risk to health)*

2.044    The decision in *CDLA/3941/2005* has been disagreed with by Judge Turnbull in *IP v SSWP* [2013] UKUT 235 (AAC). This is an important decision because it suggests a much more restricted interpretation of the sub-paragraph. In the earlier case Mr Commissioner Angus had suggested that the test to be applied was whether, without endangering life or health, the claimant could walk a distance that would be normal for a healthy person of her age. Judge Turnbull rejects this construction because it might be far too generous. It could result in claimants succeeding when they could walk far beyond, and in a far better manner, than claimants who failed the test under sub-para.(ii). It would mean that a claimant who could point to a serious endangerment to health would succeed, when someone whose walking was limited by pain would not, even though the former might walk much better. In his view this could not have been the intention that the legislation sought to express. This is to adopt a fairly extreme instance of purposive interpretation, but it may well be right.

Judge Turnbull points out that the sub-paragraphs in reg.12 (1) are made (under s.73(5) of the SSCBA 1992) to define the circumstances specified in s.73(1)(a) of that act—*viz* "unable to walk or virtually unable to do so". Sub-paragraph (i) simply repeats the phrase unable to walk; sub-paras (ii) and (iii) should therefore both be seen as expanding the meaning of "virtually unable to do so". This construction would mean that both of those sub-paragraphs were conditioned by the claimant being rendered virtually unable to walk by reason of his disability. In the present case, the claimant could walk for 10 or 12 minutes at a slow pace, even on a bad day, before her heart condition caused her to rest as a result of breathlessness. In the judge's view she was certainly not "virtually unable to walk" and her appeal failed.

Judge Turnbull also thought the result of adopting this construction would necessarily mean that the claimant in the case above should have failed—if she could walk 3 miles, even at risk to her knees, she was not virtually unable to walk. But need this be so? If the idea of virtual ability to walk were to include an element of what it was reasonable for the claimant to do (as earlier cases under this sub-paragraph have done), rather than a standard of what a person in good health might do, then it could be argued that the 3 miles a day that would have to be walked by the claimant in *CDLA/3941/2005* to get her children to and from school was a justifiable target, whereas more than a 10-minute walk by a middle-aged woman was not. But this seems to take decision makers and tribunals into difficult territory and an area of social judgment best avoided.

**p.667,** *amendment to Social Security (Disability Living Allowance) Regulations 1991 (SI 1991/2890) reg.12A (Hospitalisation in mobility component cases)*

In para.(1)(a), insert the words "in a hospital or similar institution under" at the beginning of that paragraph. **2.045**

**pp.730–731,** *amendment to Personal Independence Payment (Transitional Provisions) Regulations 2013 (SI 2013/387) reg.2 (Citation, commencement and interpretation)*

With effect from October 25, 2013, reg.2(2) of the Personal Independence Payment (Transitional Provisions) (Amendment) (No.2) Regulations 2013 (2013/2698) reg.2(2) amended this regulation in two respects. First, in para.(1), after the definition of "pay day", there was inserted the following new definition: **2.046**

""relevant date" means the date, specified by the Secretary of State in relation to any category of DLA entitled person, from which the

Secretary of State is satisfied that satisfactory arrangements will be in place to assess the entitlement of persons in that category to personal independence payment;";

Second, after para.(3), there was inserted the following new paragraph:

"(4) As soon as practicable after specifying a relevant date in relation to any category of DLA entitled person, the Secretary of State must publish, in such manner as the Secretary of State considers appropriate, information sufficient to enable any DLA entitled person to ascertain the relevant date, if any, which applies in their case.".

**p.732,** *amendments to the Personal Independence Payment (Transitional Provisions) Regulations 2013 (SI 2013/387) reg.3 (Invitations to persons entitled to disability living allowance to claim personal independence payment)*

2.047     With effect from October 6, 2013, reg.2(2) of the Personal Independence Payment (Transitional Provisions) (Amendment) Regulations 2013 (SI 2013/2231) amended this regulation so as to substitute the words "27th October 2013" for the words "6th October 2013" in paras (1), (3) and (5).

With effect from October 25, 2013, reg.2(3) of the Personal Independence Payment (Transitional Provisions) (Amendment) (No.2) Regulations 2013 (2013/2698) inserted the words "Subject to paragraphs (3A) and (4)," at the start of para.(3). The same amending regulations inserted after para.(3) the following new sub-paragraph:

"(3A) Paragraph (3) does not apply unless—
(a) the Secretary of State has specified a relevant date which applies in the case of the DLA entitled person, and
(b) that person reaches 16 on or after that relevant date."

The same amending regulations also inserted at the start of para.(5) the words "Subject to paragraph (5A)," and after para.(5) inserted the following new sub-paragraph:

"(5A) Paragraph (5) does not apply unless—
(a) the Secretary of State has specified a relevant date which applies in the case of the DLA entitled person, and
(b) that person notifies the Secretary of State of the change of circumstances on or after that relevant date."

**p.732,** *amendment to the Personal Independence Payment (Transitional Provisions) Regulations 2013 (SI 2013/387) reg.4 (Claims by persons entitled to disability living allowance for personal independence payment other than by invitation)*

2.048     With effect from October 6, 2013, reg.2(3) of the Personal Independence Payment (Transitional Provisions) (Amendment) Regulations 2013 (SI 2013/2231) substituted the words "28th October 2013" for the words "7th October 2013" in para.(2).

With effect from October 25, 2013, reg.2(4) of the Personal Independence Payment (Transitional Provisions) (Amendment) (No.2) Regulations 2013 (2013/2698) substituted the following new regulation for reg.4:

"**4.** A DLA entitled person who has not been sent a notification under regulation 3(1) may not make a claim for personal independence payment unless—
  (a) they were aged under 65 on 8th April 2013,
  (b) the Secretary of State has specified a relevant date which applies in their case, and
  (c) they make the claim on or after that relevant date.".

**p.733,** *amendment to Personal Independence Payment (Transitional Provisions) Regulations 2013 (SI 2013/387) reg.6 (Persons in the course of claiming disability living allowance not entitled to claim personal independence payment)*

With effect from October 6, 2013, reg.2(4) of the Personal Independence Payment (Transitional Provisions) (Amendment) Regulations 2013 (SI 2013/2231) substituted the words "28th October 2013" for the words "7th October 2013" in para.(1)(a).      2.049

**p.739,** *amendment of Personal Independence Payment (Transitional Provisions) Regulations 2013 (SI 2013/387) reg.18 (Extension of certain fixed term period awards of disability living allowance for persons reaching 16)*

With effect from October 6, 2013, reg.2(5) of the Personal Independence Payment (Transitional Provisions) (Amendment) Regulations 2013 (SI 2013/2231) substituted the words "27th October 2013" for the words "6th October 2013" in para.(1)(b).      2.050

**p.741,** *amendment of Personal Independence Payment (Transitional Provisions) Regulations 2013 (SI 2013/387) reg.22 (Extinguishment of right to claim disability living allowance)*

With effect from October 6, 2013, reg.2(6) of the Personal Independence Payment (Transitional Provisions) (Amendment) Regulations 2013 (SI 2013/2231) substituted the words "28th October 2013" for the words "7th October 2013" in para.(2).      2.051

With effect from October 25, 2013, reg.2(5) of the Personal Independence Payment (Transitional Provisions) (Amendment) (No.2) Regulations 2013 (2013/2698) omitted the words "before 28th October 2013," in para.(2).

**p.847,** *amendment of the Employment and Support Allowance Regulations 2008 (SI 2008/794) reg.1 (Citation and commencement)*

With effect from April 29, 2013, reg.37(1) and (2) of the Universal Credit (Consequential, Supplementary, Incidental and Miscellaneous      2.052

Provisions) Regulations 2013 (SI 2013/630) amended reg.1 by substituting the following for the heading:

"Citation, commencement, and application",

renumbering the existing text as para.(1) of the regulation and adding the following paragraph after the existing text:

"(2) These Regulations do not apply to a particular case on any day on which section 33(1)(b) of the 2012 Act (abolition of income-related employment and support allowance) is in force and applies in relation to that case."

**p.848,** *amendment of the Employment and Support Allowance Regulations 2008 (SI 2008/794) reg.2(1) (Interpretation—definition of 'attendance allowance')*

2.053　　With effect from October 29, 2013, reg.13(1) and (2)(a) of the Social Security (Miscellaneous Amendments) (No. 3) Regulations 2013 (SI 2013/2536) amended the definition of 'attendance allowance' in reg.2(1) by revoking paras (c) and (d).

**p.849,** *amendment of the Employment and Support Allowance Regulations 2008 (SI 2008/794) reg.2(1) (Interpretation—definition of 'contribution-based JSA')*

2.054　　With effect from April 29, 2013, reg.37(1) and (3)(a) of the Universal Credit (Consequential, Supplementary, Incidental and Miscellaneous Provisions) Regulations 2013 (SI 2013/630) amended reg.2(1) by adding the following definition after the definition of 'confinement':

"'contribution-based jobseeker's allowance' means an allowance under the Jobseekers Act as amended by the provisions of Part 1 of Schedule 14 to the 2012 Act that remove references to an income-based allowance, and a contribution-based allowance under the Jobseekers Act as that Act has effect apart from those provisions;"

**p.849,** *amendment of the Employment and Support Allowance Regulations 2008 (SI 2008/794) reg.2(1) (Interpretation—definition of 'councillor')*

2.055　　With effect from October 29, 2013, reg.13(1) and (2)(b) of the Social Security (Miscellaneous Amendments) (No. 3) Regulations 2013 (SI 2013/2536) amended the definition of 'councillor' in reg.2(1) by adding the words 'a county borough council,' after the words 'county council,' in para.(a).

**pp.849–850,** *amendment of the Employment and Support Allowance Regulations 2008 (SI 2008/794) reg.2(1) (Interpretation—definition of 'councillor's allowance')*

2.056　　With effect from October 29, 2013, reg.13(1) and (2)(c) of the Social Security (Miscellaneous Amendments) (No. 3) Regulations 2013 (SI

2013/2536) amended the definition of 'councillor's allowance' in reg.2(1) to read as follows:

"'councillor's allowance' means—
  (a) in England [ ... ], an allowance under or by virtue of—
      (i) section 173 or 177 of the Local Government Act 1972; or
      (ii) a scheme made by virtue of section 18 of the Local Government and Housing Act 1989, other than such an allowance as is mentioned in section 173(4) of the Local Government Act 1972; or
  (b) in Scotland, an allowance or remuneration under or by virtue of—
      (i) a scheme made by virtue of section 18 of the Local Government and Housing Act 1989; or
      (ii) [section 11] of the Local Governance (Scotland) Act 2004;
  [(c) in Wales, an allowance under or by virtue of a scheme made by virtue of section 18 of the Local Government and Housing Act 1989 other than such an allowance as is mentioned in section 173(4) of the Local Government Act 1972;"

**p.851,** *amendment of the Employment and Support Allowance Regulations 2008 (SI 2008/794) reg.2(1) (Interpretation—definition of 'enactment')*

With effect from October 29, 2013, reg.13(1) and (2)(d) of the Social Security (Miscellaneous Amendments) (No. 3) Regulations 2013 (SI 2013/2536) amended the definition of 'enactment' in reg.2(1) to read as follows:

2.057

"'enactment' includes an enactment comprised in, or in an instrument made under, an Act of the Scottish Parliament [or the National Assembly for Wales];"

**p.851,** *amendment of the Employment and Support Allowance Regulations 2008 (SI 2008/794) reg.2(1) (Interpretation—Definition of 'the Employment Skills and Enterprise Scheme')*

With effect from February 12, 2013 at 6.45 pm, reg.15(a) of the Jobseeker's Allowance (Schemes for Assisting Persons to Obtain Employment) Regulations 2013 (SI 2013/276) amended reg.1(2) by revoking the definition of "the Employment Skills and Enterprise Scheme".

2.058

**p.854,** *amendment of the Employment and Support Allowance Regulations 2008 (SI 2008/794) reg.2(1) (Interpretation—definition of 'new style ESA')*

With effect from April 29, 2013, reg.37(1) and (3)(b) of the Universal Credit (Consequential, Supplementary, Incidental and Miscellaneous

2.059

Provisions) Regulations 2013 (SI 2013/630) amended reg.2(1) by adding the following definition after the definition of 'New Deal options':

> "'new style ESA' means an allowance under Part 1 of the Act as amended by the provisions of Schedule 3, and Part 1 of Schedule 14, to the 2012 Act that remove references to an income-related allowance;"

**p.856–857,** *amendment of the Employment and Support Allowance Regulations 2008 (SI 2008/794) reg.2(1) (Interpretation—definition of 'relevant infection or contamination')*

2.060    With effect from October 29, 2013, reg.13(1) and (2)(e) of the Social Security (Miscellaneous Amendments) (No. 3) Regulations 2013 (SI 2013/2536) revoked the definition of 'relevant infection or contamination' in reg.2(1).

**p.857,** *amendment of the Employment and Support Allowance Regulations 2008 (SI 2008/794) reg.2(1) (Interpretation—definition of 'service user group')*

2.061    With effect from April 1, 2013, reg.11 and Sch.2, Pt 1, para.116(1) and (2) of the National Treatment Agency (Abolition) and the Health and Social Care Act 2012 (Consequential, Transitional and Saving Provisions) Order 2013. (SI 2013/235) added the following paragraphs after para.(f) in the definition of 'service user group' in reg.2(1):

> "(fa)   the National Institute for Health and Care Excellence in consequence of a function under Part 8 of the Health and Social Care Act 2012,
> (fb)    a clinical commissioning group in consequence of a function under section 14Z2 of the National Health Service Act 2006,
> (fc)    the National Health Service Commissioning Board in consequence of a function under section 13Q of the National Health Service Act 2006,".

With effect from October 29, 2013, reg.13(1) and (2)(f) of the Social Security (Miscellaneous Amendments) (No. 3) Regulations 2013 (SI 2013/2536) revoked the definition of 'service user group' in reg.2(1).

**p.858,** *amendment of the Employment and Support Allowance Regulations 2008 (SI 2008/794) reg.2(1) (Interpretation—definition of 'universal credit')*

2.062    With effect from April 29, 2013, reg.37(1) and (3)(c) of the Universal Credit (Consequential, Supplementary, Incidental and Miscellaneous Provisions) Regulations 2013 (SI 2013/630) amended reg.2(1) by adding the following definition after the definition of 'training allowance':

> "'universal credit' means universal credit under Part 1 of the 2012 Act;"

**p.860,** *amendment of the Employment and Support Allowance Regulations 2008 (SI 2008/794) reg.2 (Interpretation)*

With effect from October 29, 2013, reg.13(1) and (3) of the Social Security (Miscellaneous Amendments) (No. 3) Regulations 2013 (SI 2013/2536) amended reg.2 by adding the following paragraph after para.(7):   **2.063**

"(8) References in these Regulations to a person or claimant participating as a service user are to—
   (a) a person who is being consulted by or on behalf of—
        (i) a body which has a statutory duty to provide services in the field of health, social care or social housing; or
        (ii) a body which conducts research or undertakes monitoring for the purpose of planning or improving such services,
        in their capacity as a user, potential user, carer of a user or person otherwise affected by the provision of those services; or
   (b) the carer of a person consulted under sub-paragraph (a)."

**p.862,** *amendment to the Employment and Support Allowance Regulations 2008 (SI 2008/794) reg.4 (the end of the assessment phase)*

With effect from October 29, 2013, reg.13(4) of the Social Security (Miscellaneous Amendments) (No. 3) Regulations 2013 (SI 2013/2536) amended reg.4 to read:   **2.064**

"**The end of the assessment phase**

4.—(1) Subject to [paragraphs (2) and (3)] and regulation 5, the assessment phase in relation to a claimant ends on the last day of a period of 13 weeks beginning on the first day of the assessment phase as determined under section 24(2)(a) of the Act.
   [(2) Where paragraph (3) applies, the assessment phase is to end when it is determined whether the claimant has limited capability for work.
   (3) This paragraph applies where, at the end of the 13 week period referred to in paragraph (1)—
   (a) the claimant has not been assessed in accordance with a limited capability for work assessment; and
   (b) the claimant has not been treated as having limited capability for work in accordance with regulations 20, 25, 26, 29 or 33(2) (persons to be treated as having limited capability for work).]".

**p.863,** *annotation to the Employment and Support Allowance Regulations 2008 (SI 2008/794) reg.4 (the end of the assessment phase)*

Given the reformulation of the regulation (see update to p.862, above), "para.(2)" in line 10 should be replaced by "para.(3)". In addition, for "reg.6" in the last line substitute "regs 5(4) and 147A".   **2.065**

In *SSWP v NC (ESA)* [2013] UKUT 0477 (AAC), Judge Bano held that, despite poor wording, the effect of the then reg.4(2) (now reg.4(2), (3)) was that "subject to exceptions in cases involving appeals, the assessment phase lasts until the end of the three month period, or until a determination that a claimant has (or is to be treated as having) limited capability for work, whichever is the later" (para.9).

**p.863–864,** *amendment to the Employment and Support Allowance Regulations 2008 (SI 2008/794) reg.5 (the assessment phase—previous claimants)*

2.066    With effect from October 29, 2013, reg.13(5) of the Social Security (Miscellaneous Amendments) (No. 3) Regulations 2013 (SI 2013/2536) amended reg.5 to read:

### "The assessment phase—previous claimants

**5.**—(1) Where the circumstances in paragraph (2) apply in relation to a claimant the assessment phase—

(a) begins on the first day of the period for which the claimant was previously entitled to an employment and support allowance; and

(b) subject to [paragraphs (3), (3A) and (4)], ends on the day when the sum of the period for which the claimant was previously entitled to an employment and support allowance and the period for which the claimant is currently entitled to such an allowance is 13 weeks.

(2) The circumstances are that—

(a)  (i) the claimant's current period of limited capability for work is to be treated as a continuation of an earlier period of limited capability for work under regulation 145(1) . . . ,

(ii) the claimant was entitled to an employment and support allowance in the earlier period of limited capability for work;

(iii) the assessment phase had not ended in the previous period for which the claimant was entitled to an employment and support allowance; and

(iv) the period for which the claimant was previously entitled was no more than 13 weeks; or

(b)  (i) the claimant's current period of limited capability for work is to be treated as a continuation of an earlier period of limited capability for work under regulation 145(1),

(ii) the claimant was entitled to an employment and support allowance in the earlier period of limited capability for work,

(iii) the previous period of limited capability for work was terminated by virtue of a determination that the claimant did not have limited capability for work,

(iv) the period for which the claimant was previously entitled was no more than 13 weeks, and

(v) a determination is made in relation to the current period of limited capability for work that the claimant has or is

    treated as having limited capability for work, other than
    under regulation 30; or

  (c)  (i) the claimant's current period of limited capability for work
      is to be treated as a continuation of an earlier period of
      limited capability for work under regulation 145(1),

     (ii) the claimant was entitled to an employment and support
       allowance in the earlier period of limited capability for
       work,

   (iii) in relation to the previous award of an employment and
       support allowance, a determination was made that the
       claimant had limited capability for work or was treated as
       having limited capability for work, other than under regula-
       tion 30, and

   (iv) the period for which the claimant was previously entitled
       was no more than 13 weeks.

  [(3) Where paragraph (3A) applies, the assessment phase is to end
when it is determined whether the claimant has limited capability for
work.

  (3A) This paragraph applies where on the day referred to in paragraph (1)(b)—

  (a) the claimant has not been assessed in accordance with a limited
    capability for work assessment; and

  (b) the claimant has not been treated as having limited capability
    for work in accordance with regulations 20, 25, 26, 29 or 33(2)
    (persons to be treated as having limited capability for work).]

  (4) Where a person has made and is pursuing an appeal against a
decision of the Secretary of State that embodies a determination that
the claimant does not have limited capability for work—

  (a) [paragraphs (3) and (3A) do] not apply; and

  (b) paragraph (1) does not apply to any period of limited capability
    for work to which regulation 147A(2) applies until a determina-
    tion of limited capability for work has been made following the
    determination of the appeal by the First-tier Tribunal."

**pp.871–872,** *amendment to the Employment and Support Allowance
Regulations 2008 (SI 2008/794) reg.9 (condition relating to
youth—claimants aged 20 or over but under 25)*

With effect from October 29, 2013, reg.13(6) of the Social Security   2.067
(Miscellaneous Amendments) (No. 3) Regulations 2013 (SI 2013/2536)
amended reg.9(5)(a) to replace "Technician" with Technology" and
reg.9(5)(b) to replace "Technical" with "Technology".

**pp.883–884,** *amendments to the Employment and Support Allowance
Regulations 2008 (SI 2008/794) reg.19 (determination of limited capability
for work)*

With effect from October 29, 2013, reg.13(7) of the Social Security   2.068
(Miscellaneous Amendments) (No. 3) Regulations 2013 (SI 2013/2536)
amended reg.19(3) to read:

"(3) Subject to paragraph (6), for the purposes of Part 1 of the Act a claimant has limited capability for work if, by adding the points listed in column (3) of Schedule 2 against [each descriptor] listed in that Schedule [which applies in the claimant's case], the claimant obtains a total score of at least—

    (a) 15 points whether singly or by a combination of descriptors specified in Part 1 of that Schedule;

    (b) 15 points whether singly or by a combination of descriptors specified in Part 2 of that Schedule; or

    (c) 15 points by a combination of descriptors specified in Parts 1 and 2 of that Schedule."

From that date the amending provision also inserted "or" at the end of para.(5)(c)(i). It also amended para.(6) to read:

"(6) Where more than one descriptor specified for an activity [applies] to a claimant, only the descriptor with the highest score in respect of each activity which applies is to be counted."

**pp.886–888,** *annotation to the Employment and Support Allowance Regulations 2008 (SI 2008/794) reg.19(2) and (5)*

2.069    *JG v SSWP (ESA)* [2013] UKUT 037 (AAC) is now reported as [2013] AACR 23.

**pp.889–890,** *amendments to the Employment and Support Allowance Regulations 2008 (SI 2008/794) reg.20 (certain claimants to be treated as having limited capability for work)*

2.070    With effect from October 29, 2013, reg.13(8) of the Social Security (Miscellaneous Amendments) (No. 3) Regulations 2013 (SI 2013/2536) amended reg.20 to read:

**"Certain claimants to be treated as having limited capability for work**

**20.**—[(1)] A claimant is to be treated as having limited capability for work if—

    (a) the claimant is terminally ill;

    (b) the claimant is—

        (i) receiving treatment for cancer by way of chemotherapy or radiotherapy;

        (ii) likely to receive such treatment within six months after the date of the determination of capability for work; or

        (iii) recovering from such treatment,

    and the Secretary of State is satisfied that the claimant should be treated as having limited capability for work];

    (c) the claimant is—

        (i) excluded or abstains from work [ . . . ] pursuant to a request or notice in writing lawfully made [or given] under an enactment; or

    (ii) otherwise prevented from working pursuant to an enact-
       ment, by reason of it being known or reasonably suspected
       that the claimant is infected or contaminated by, or has
       been in contact with a case of, a relevant infection or
       contamination;
(d) in the case of a pregnant woman, there is a serious risk of
    damage to her health or to the health of her unborn child if she
    does not refrain from work;
(e) in the case of a pregnant woman, she—
    (i) is within the maternity allowance period [(which has the
       meaning it has in section 35(2) of the Contributions and
       Benefits Act)]; and
    (ii) is entitled to a maternity allowance under section 35(1) of
       the Contributions and Benefits Act;
(f) in the case of a pregnant woman whose expected or actual date
    of confinement has been certified in accordance with the Medi-
    cal Evidence Regulations, on any day in the period—
    (i) beginning with the first date of the 6th week before the
       expected week of her confinement or the actual date of her
       confinement, whichever is earlier; and
    (ii) ending on the 14th day after the actual date of her con-
       finement,
    if she would have no entitlement to a maternity allowance or
    statutory maternity pay were she to make a claim in respect of
    that period.
(g) [the claimant meets] any of the descriptors at paragraph 15 or
    16 of Schedule 3 [in accordance with regulation 34(2), (3) and
    (6) where applicable].

[(2) In this regulation, "relevant infection or contamination"
means—
(a) in England and Wales—
    (i) any incidence or spread of infection or contamination,
       within the meaning of section 45A(3) of the Public Health
       (Control of Disease) Act 1984 in respect of which regula-
       tions are made under Part 2A of that Act (public health
       protection) for the purpose of preventing, protecting
       against, controlling or providing a public health response
       to, such incidence or spread; or
    (ii) tuberculosis or any infectious disease to which regulation 9
       of the Public Health (Aircraft) Regulations 1979 (powers
       in respect of persons leaving aircraft) applies or to which
       regulation 10 of the Public Health (Ships) Regulations
       1979 (powers in respect of certain persons on ships)
       applies; and
(b) in Scotland, any—
    (i) infectious disease within the meaning of section 1(5) of the
       Public Health etc (Scotland) Act 2008, or exposure to an
       organism causing that disease; or

(ii) contamination within the meaning of section 1(5) of that Act, or exposure to a contaminant,

to which sections 56 to 58 of that Act (compensation) apply.]"

**p.891,** *amendment to the Employment and Support Allowance Regulations 2008 (SI 2008/794) reg.21(2) (information required for determining capability for work)*

2.071     With effect from October 29, 2013, reg.13(9) of the Social Security (Miscellaneous Amendments) (No. 3) Regulations 2013 (SI 2013/2536) amended reg.21(2) to read:

"(2) Where the Secretary of State is satisfied that there is sufficient information to determine whether a claimant has limited capability for work without the information specified in paragraph (1)(b), that information [must] not be required for the purposes of making the determination."

**pp.891–892,** *annotation to the Employment and Support Allowance Regulations 2008 (SI 2008/794) reg.21 (information required for determining capability for work)*

2.072     The impact on claimants with mental health problems (MHP) of the information collecting and assessment process administered by Atos Healthcare, the medical services provider for the DWP, remains the subject of challenge by way of the Upper Tribunal's judicial review jurisdiction, as constituting disability discrimination under the Equality Act 2010. The decision of a three judge tribunal in favour of the applicants in *MM & DM v SSWP* [2013] UKUT 0259 was appealed to the Court of Appeal by the Secretary of State.

On December 4, 2013, that Court rejected the appeal as to several matters and upheld it as to another in *Secretary of State for Work and Pensions v The Queen on the application of MM and DM (as respondents) and MIND, the National Autistic Society, Rethink Mental Illness and the Equality and Human Rights Commission (as interveners)* [2013] EWCA Civ 1565. The Court held that the Upper Tribunal was correct in holding that it had jurisdiction to deal with the matter of discrimination contrary to the Equality Act 2010 by way of judicial review, and that the applicants and the interveners had the requisite standing to maintain the application for judicial review. The Court also found that the Upper Tribunal's declaration that the information and examination process caused substantial disadvantage to claimants with mental health problems (and was thus discriminatory) was not erroneous in law nor, in the light of the evidence, was it perverse or irrational. However, the Court held that the Upper Tribunal had misunderstood the scope of its powers and should not have directed the Secretary of State to carry out an investigation or assessment within a specified time to see how the "Evidence Seeking Recommendation" (see below) could be implemented. Rather it was for the applicants to advance a reasonable adjustment proposal, leaving "the Secretary of State to adduce such evidence and advance such arguments as he thinks appropriate in order to discharge the burden now falling on him" of showing that such adjustment cannot reasonably be made (para.83). That matter will now be the subject of a renewed hearing before the Upper Tribunal on remedies.

The "Evidence Seeking Recommendation" was a less rigorous one than the proposal that in every case involving a mental health patient the decision-maker should always be required to seek further medical evidence (FME) before a decision was reached thus in many cases obviating the need for the ESA50 questionnaire and/or the face to face interview, both of which substantially disadvantaged mental health patients. The Upper Tribunal had rejected that as unduly onerous. Instead, the "Evidence Seeking Recommendation", seen by the Upper Tribunal as a prima facie "reasonable adjustment", proposes that "the decision-maker should at lest be required to consider obtaining FME in the case of MHP claimants and if FME was not sought, should explain why it was thought to be unnecessary" (para.2).

It should be noted that the need for this change was also supported as part of the independent review undertaken by Professor Harrington (see para.40 of his third report, cited in para.21 of the Court of Appeal judgment).

**p.892,** *amendment to the Employment and Support Allowance Regulations 2008 (SI 2008/794) reg.22 (failure to provide information in relation to limited capability for work)*

With effect from October 29, 2013, reg.13(10) of the Social Security (Miscellaneous Amendments) (No. 3) Regulations 2013 (SI 2013/2536) amended reg.22(2) to read:  2.073

> "(2) Paragraph (1) does not apply unless—
> [(a)  the claimant was sent a further request at least three weeks after the date of the first request;] and
> (b)  [ . . . ] at least 1 week has passed since the further request was sent."

**p.892,** *annotation to the Employment and Support Allowance Regulations 2008 (SI 2008/794) reg.22 (failure to provide information in relation to limited capability for work)*

Consequent on the change to the text of reg.22 noted in the previous update, the second sentence of the annotation should now read:  2.074

> "This can only happen, however, if a further request for information was sent at least three weeks after the first and at least one week has gone by since the second request was sent."

In *CT v SSWP (ESA)* [2013] UKUT 0414 (AAC), Judge Ward stressed the need for very careful appraisal of the evidence to determine exactly when requests and reminders were sent and their exact nature. He held that while a tribunal could properly conclude from an Atos computer print out that a document had been generated and would in due course be sent to an appropriate address, "the print out can do no more than indicate that some step had been taken in relation to the document in question" (para.9); it cannot support an argument that the document was sent out that day, since practices show that it may take some days before despatch in the ordinary course of business. In order to conclude that a document has been received, a decision-maker or tribunal should make enquiry as to whether it has been returned undelivered to the sender (paras 14, 15).

**p.893,** *amendment to the Employment and Support Allowance Regulations 2008 (SI 2008/794) reg.23 (claimant may be called for a medical examination to determine whether the claimant has limited capability for work)*

2.075    With effect from October 29, 2013, reg.13(11) of the Social Security (Miscellaneous Amendments) (No. 3) Regulations 2013 (SI 2013/2536) amended reg.22(2) and substituted a new para.(3) to read as follows:

"[(2) Subject to paragraph (3), where a claimant fails without good cause to attend for or to submit to an examination [mentioned] in paragraph (1), the claimant is to be treated as not having limited capability for work.
[(3) Paragraph (2) does not apply unless—
(a) written notice of the date, time and place for the examination was sent to the claimant at least seven days in advance; or
(b) that claimant agreed to accept a shorter period of notice whether given in writing or otherwise.]"

**p.893,** *annotation to the Employment and Support Allowance Regulations 2008 (SI 2008/794) reg.23 (claimant may be called for a medical examination to determine whether the claimant has limited capability for work)*

2.076    Consequent on the change to the text of reg.23 noted in the previous update, the first line of the third paragraph of the annotation should now read:

"Note that proper written notice means written notice of the date, time and place of".

**pp.893–895,** *annotation to the Employment and Support Allowance Regulations 2008 (SI 2008/794) reg 23 (claimant may be called for a medical examination to determine whether the claimant has limited capability for work)*

2.077    See update to pp.891–892, above, on the ongoing judicial review challenge under the Equality Act 2010 with respect to this aspect of the decision-making process.

**p.897,** *amendment to the Employment and Support Allowance Regulations 2008 (SI 2008/794) reg.26 (claimants receiving certain regular treatment)*

With effect from October 29, 2013, reg.13(12) of the Social Security 2.078 (Miscellaneous Amendments) (No. 3) Regulations 2013 (SI 2013/2536) amended reg.26(1) to read:

"(1) Subject to paragraph (2), a claimant receiving—
(a) regular weekly treatment by way of haemodialysis for chronic renal failure;
(b) treatment by way of plasmapheresis . . . ; or
(c) regular weekly treatment by way of total parenteral nutrition for gross impairment of enteric function,
is to be treated as having limited capability for work during any week in which that claimant is engaged in [receiving] that treatment or has a day of recovery from that treatment."

**p.900,** *amendment to the Employment and Support Allowance Regulations 2008 (SI 2008/794) reg.29 (exceptional circumstances)*

With effect from October 29, 2013, reg.13(13) of the Social Security 2.079 (Miscellaneous Amendments) (No. 3) Regulations 2013 (SI 2013/2536) amended reg.29 by adding after para.(3) a new para.(4) to read:

"(4) In this regulation "medical evidence" means—
(a) evidence from a health care professional approved by the Secretary of State; and
(b) evidence (if any) from any health care professional or a hospital or similar Institution,
or such part of such evidence as constitutes the most reliable evidence available in the circumstances."

**p.902,** *annotation to the Employment and Support Allowance Regulations 2008 (SI 2008/794) reg.29 (exceptional circumstances)*

In *GC v SSWP (ESA)* [2013] UKUT 0271 (AAC), the claimant 2.080 sought to rely on medical evidence issued after the Secretary of State had made his decision, on the evidence then before him, that the claimant's disease (bladder cancer) was controlled. Judge Jacobs considered reg.29 in the context of SSA 1998 s.12(8)(b) (an appeal tribunal shall not take into account any circumstances not obtaining at the time when the decision appealed against was made). He held that this was not the same situation as that in *R(DLA) 2 & 3/01* where later evidence could properly be adduced to show the circumstances prevailing at the date of decision:

"Regulation 29(1)(a)(i) is different. It does not refer to the claimant having a disease that is uncontrolled or uncontrollable. It refers to the need for *medical evidence* that that is so. In applying section 12(8)(b), the relevant circumstance is the existence of the evidence of the state of the claimant's condition. In Mr C's case, the evidence that his cancer had returned and required surgery did not exist until after the

Secretary of State made the decision under appeal. In such a case, it makes no sense to say that later evidence shows that there was evidence at the time of the decision. Such talk is entirely inconsistent with the requirements of section 29(1)(a), as it renders the requirement for contemporaneous evidence redundant" (para.12).

**pp.906–907,** *amendment to the Employment and Support Allowance Regulations 2008 (SI 2008/794) reg.30 (conditions for treating a claimant as having limited capability for work until a determination about limited capability for work has been made)*

2.081   With effect from October 29, 2013, reg.13(14) of the Social Security (Miscellaneous Amendments) (No. 3) Regulations 2013 (SI 2013/2536) amended reg.30 to read:

**"Conditions for treating a claimant as having limited capability for work until a determination about limited capability for work has been made**

**30.**—(1) A claimant is, if the conditions set out in paragraph (2) are met, to be treated as having limited capability for work until such time as it is determined—

(a) whether or not the claimant has limited capability for work;

(b) whether or not the claimant is to be treated as having limited capability for work otherwise than in accordance with this regulation; or

(c) whether the claimant falls to be treated as not having limited capability for work in accordance with regulation 22 (failure to provide information in relation to limited capability for work) or 23 (failure to attend a medical examination to determine limited capability for work).

(2) The conditions are—

(a) that the claimant provides evidence of limited capability for work in accordance with the Medical Evidence Regulations; and

(b) that it has not, within the 6 months preceding the date of claim [for employment and support allowance], been determined, in relation to the claimant's entitlement to any benefit, allowance or advantage which is dependent on the claimant having limited capability for work, that the claimant does not have limited capability for work or is to be treated as not having limited capability for work under regulation 22 or 23 [unless paragraph (4) applies]; or

(c) [*Omitted*]

(3) Paragraph (2)(b) does not apply where a claimant has made and is pursuing an appeal against a decision that embodies a determination that the claimant does not have limited capability for work and that appeal has not yet been determined by the First-tier Tribunal.

[(4) This paragraph applies where—

(a) the claimant is suffering from some specific disease or bodily or mental disablement from which the claimant was not suffering at the time of that determination;

(b) a disease or bodily or mental disablement from which the claimant was suffering at the time of that determination has significantly worsened; or

(c) in the case of a claimant who was treated as not having limited capability for work under regulation 22 (failure to provide information), the claimant has since provided the information requested under that regulation.]"

**p.908,** *annotation to Employment and Support Allowance Regulations 2008 (SI 2008/794) reg.30 (conditions for treating a claimant as having limited capability for work until a determination about limited capability for work has been made)*

Consequent upon the amendment noted in the immediately preceding update, the paragraph beginning "Para.(2)(c) prevents" should be deleted. 2.082

**p.909,** *amendment to the Employment and Support Allowance Regulations 2008 (SI 2008/794) reg.32 (certain claimants to be treated as not having limited capability for work)*

With effect from October 29, 2013, reg.13(15) of the Social Security (Miscellaneous Amendments) (No. 3) Regulations 2013 (SI 2013/2536) amended reg.32(1) by deleting "for Defence". This means that any Secretary of State is legally empowered to record days as ones of sickness absence. The annotation should be amended accordingly. 2.083

**p.910,** *amendment to the Employment and Support Allowance Regulations 2008 (SI 2008/794) reg.32A (claimants to be treated as not having limited capability for work at the end of the period covered by medical evidence)*

With effect from October 29, 2013, reg.13(16) of the Social Security (Miscellaneous Amendments) (No. 3) Regulations 2013 (SI 2013/2536) amended reg.32A(1) by deleting from line two the word "then". 2.084

**pp.911–912,** *amendment to the Employment and Support Allowance Regulations 2008 (SI 2008/794) reg.34 (determination of limited capability for work-related activity)*

With effect from October 29, 2013, reg.13(17) of the Social Security (Miscellaneous Amendments) (No. 3) Regulations 2013 (SI 2013/2536) amended reg.34 to read: 2.085

**"Determination of limited capability for work-related activity**

**34.**—(1) For the purposes of Part 1 of the Act, where, by reason of a claimant's physical or mental condition, at least one of the descriptors set out in Schedule 3 applies to the claimant, the [claimant has limited] capability for work-related activity [ . . . ] and the limitation [must] be such that it is not reasonable to require that claimant to undertake such activity.

(2) A descriptor applies to a claimant if that descriptor applies to the claimant for the majority of the time or, as the case may be, on the majority of the occasions on which the claimant undertakes or attempts to undertake the activity described by that descriptor.

(3) In determining whether a descriptor applies to the claimant, the claimant is to be assessed as if—

(a) the claimant were fitted with or wearing any prosthesis with which the claimant is normally fitted or normally wears; or, as the case may be,

(b) wearing or using any aid or appliance which is normally, or could reasonably be expected to be, worn or used.

(3A) [*Omitted.*]

(4) Where a determination has been made about whether a claimant—

(a) has limited capability for work-related activity;

(b) is to be treated as having limited capability for work-related activity; or

(c) is to be treated as not having limited capability for work-related activity,

the Secretary of State may, if paragraph (5) applies, determine afresh whether the claimant has or is to be treated as having limited capability for work-related activity.

(5) This paragraph applies where—

(a) the Secretary of State wishes to determine whether there has been a relevant change of circumstances in relation to the claimant's physical or mental condition;

(b) the Secretary of State wishes to determine whether the previous determination about limited capability for work-related activity or about treating the claimant as having or as not having limited capability for work-related activity, was made in ignorance of, or was based on a mistake as to, some material fact; or

(c) at least 3 months have passed since the date of the previous determination about limited capability for work-related activity or about treating the claimant as having or as not having limited capability for work-related activity.

[(6) In assessing the extent of a claimant's capability to perform any activity listed in Schedule 3, it is a condition that the claimant's incapability to perform the action arises—

(a) in respect of descriptors 1 to 8, 15(a), 15(b), 16(a) and 16(b)—

(i) from a specific bodily disease or disablement; or

(ii) as a direct result of treatment provided by a registered medical practitioner for a specific physical disease or disablement; or

(b) in respect of descriptors 9 to 14, 15(c), 15(d), 16(c) and 16(d)—

(i) from a specific mental illness or disablement; or

(ii) as a direct result of treatment provided by a registered medical practitioner for a specific mental illness or disablement.]"

**p.913,** *annotation to the Employment and Support Allowance Regulations 2008 (SI 2008/794) reg.34(2) (determination of limited capability for work-related activity)*

Regulation 34(2), dealing with when a descriptor applies to a claimant, remains unchanged by the amendment considered in the immediately preceding update. Its interrelationship with descriptors in Sch.3 deploying differing wording on periodicity ("at least once a week" [activity/descriptor 8], "always" [activity/descriptor 13], "on a daily basis" [activity/descriptor 14],) has been explored in a number of cases. 2.086

In *KB v SSWP (ESA)* [2013] UKUT 0152 (AAC), Judge Parker considered the relationship between this wording (the requisite of "always") and the stipulation in reg.34(2) that "a descriptor applies to a claimant if that descriptor applies to the claimant for the majority of the time or, as the case may be, on the majority of the occasions on which the claimant undertakes or attempts to undertake the activity described by that descriptor". Having looked at definitions of "always" in the Concise Oxford Dictionary, Judge Parker concluded that neither this activity and descriptor, nor its counterpart in Activity 16 of Sch.2 set out an "all or nothing test". Rather "always" here "means 'repeatedly' or 'persistent' or 'often'". A "majority" may be constituted by events which happen only on 50.1 per cent of the possible occasions, but a greater frequency is required by the use of the word "always". It is a question of degree, but a fact finding tribunal is eminently suited to applying these subtle nuances of difference in a common sense way. It suffices to say in the present case, that because a claimant attends one tribunal hearing, and his GP accepts that he comes to the surgery very occasionally, does not necessarily entail the conclusion, as the tribunal clearly considered that it did, that it 'cannot be said that engagement in social contact is always precluded'" (para.14).

Judge Fordham took much the same approach in *CH v SSWP (ESA)* [2013] UKUT 0207 (AAC) (para.8).

In *LM v SSWP (ESA)* [2013] UKUT 0552 (AAC) (see update to p.1076), however, Judge Mark agreed that "always" meant repeatedly or "persistent" but considered it did not mean "often" or "for the majority of the time".

In *WT v SSWP (ESA)* [2013] UKUT 0556 (AAC), Judge Ward was more definitive than Judge Parker on the relationship between reg.34(2) and activity/descriptor 14, stating that:

"the terminology of the descriptor in question excludes the application of regulation 34 (2), in that it cannot apply to qualify the meaning of the words 'on a daily basis' to mean 'the majority of the time' or, 'on the majority of occasions that the claimant undertakes or tries to undertake the activity', which would in logic lead to satisfaction of the test if it was satisfied on more than half of the days or attempts. That would drive a coach and horses through the descriptor, rendering the inclusion of any reference to the word 'daily' pointless. That cannot be what was intended. Regulation 34(2) does not apply to a schedule 3 descriptor where the 'majority of the time' approach would be inconsistent with the actual wording of the descriptor" (para.36).

**pp.915–916,** *annotation to the Employment and Support Allowance Regulations 2008 (SI 2008/794) reg.35 (certain claimants to be treated as having limited capability for work-related activity)*

2.087    How to deal with the practical difficulties pose for tribunals by the decisions in *AH* (now reported as [2013] AACR 32), *MN* (to be reported as [2014] AACR 6) and *ML* (now reported as [2013] AACR 33) has produced divergent views from Upper Tribunal judges. Those difficulties relate to avoiding the need for adjournments clogging up the adjudication system in a context in which the decision appealed against will have been made *before* the claimant has had an initial consultation with an adviser on appropriate work-related activity and in which there is generally no representative of the Secretary of State present at First-tier Tribunals to be questioned as to what activity might be appropriate.

In *AK v SSWP (ESA)* [2013] UKUT 0435 (AAC), Judge White thought many difficulties could be obviated in appeals where it was clear that reg.35(2) would be at issue

"if the submission to the tribunal provided some examples of typical types of work-related activity. That would give tribunals something beyond speculation to work with. If it was plainly the case that the appellant could undertake some of those activities safely, then the conditions in regulation 35(2) would not be met. If the examples were carefully considered, I suspect the circumstances presented by most claimants could be judged without the need for either speculation or an adjournment" (para.14).

He further thought that where no evidence was available, there was "nothing inappropriate in a tribunal indicating some typical examples of work-related activity that are within their knowledge and showing that a claimant can safely undertake those activities" (para.18).

Judge Ward and Judge Wright, however, have rejected that latter approach, seeing it as "looking at matters from the wrong end of the telescope". Judge Ward was not convinced it was the appropriate approach (*MT v SSWP (ESA)* [2013] UKUT 0545 (AAC)). Judge Wright in *DH v SSWP (ESA)* [2013] UKUT (ESA) 0573 (AAC) went further and specifically directed the tribunal to which he remitted the case that Judge White's decision was not to be followed (para.22). Instead Judge Wright endorsed the two options for tribunals advanced by Judge Ward in both *MT* and in *HS v SSWP (ESA)* [2013] UKUT 0591 (AAC). In *MT*, Judge Ward saw the two options as resulting in subtly different legal outcomes:

"The FTT could make a decision that in the absence of specific evidence of what would be required of this particular appellant by way of engagement in work related activity the Secretary of State has not shown that, at the date of the decision and appeal, they did not have limited capability for work-related activities. The provisions of regulation 35(2)(b) then apply. The Secretary of State could supersede that decision under regulation 6(2) of the Social Security and Child Support Decisions and Appeals Regulations 1999, the grounds being either a change of circumstances under 6(2)(a)(i) or error of material fact, 6(2)(c)(i), or, after a three-month period under regulation 35(5) of the Employment and Support Allowance Regulations. Either decision would provoke an appeal, in which an issue will again be as to what work-related activities can be accomplished without substantial risk. Under rule 24(2)(e) of the Tribunal Procedure (First-tier Tribunal)(Social Entitlement Chamber) Rules 2008 the Secretary of State must in that appeal set out his opposition to the appellant's case, stating the grounds. (*MN v Secretary of State for Work and Pensions* [2013] UKUT 262 (AAC).)

There are advantages in this approach for appellants over that of adjourning. The current legal proceedings are concluded, generally of itself a relief. If the Secretary of State decides to supersede there is the protection of the appeals process, but he may not choose to supersede the tribunal decision; the way through to engagement in work related activities may be negotiated with the skills and good sense of an adviser without the element of compulsion that can cause considerable stress, particularly to those who must have significant functional impairment having been already found to have limited capability for work. In the words of Lords Neuberger and Toulson delivering the judgement of the court in *R on the application of Reilly and another -v- Secretary Of State for Work and Pensions 2013 UKSC 68 at paragraph 64*, (in the context of those without any limitations as to their capacity to work) "For the individual, the discontinuance or threat of discontinuance of jobseeker's allowance may self-evidently cause significant misery and suffering.

The alternative is really the obverse of that, and deals with what I see as the problem which may arise from the approach set out in [*AK v SSWP (ESA)* [2013] UKUT 0435 (AAC)]. The tribunal could make a decision stating in terms what work-related activities would not result in a substantial risk to the health of the appellant, also stating that more onerous commitments would be likely to result in substantial risk to the health of the appellant, or where relevant, of any other person. That differs from the decision of the FTT in this case, where the basis of their finding was that the appellant would only be asked to perform non-onerous activities, and that she could do. Would that decision, with such 'conditional' findings, bind the Secretary of State? It would be [a] tribunal decision that contained specific findings of fact which the Secretary of State would need to make a fresh decision to overcome. This would be a supersession decision as above, and would carry rights of appeal; once again there would be an onus on the Secretary of State to provide information as set out previously.

For practical purposes following the appeal I would envisage a tribunal decision framed in those terms as carrying weight in the same way that, I understand, occurs where on appeal to an FTT the decision is that there is not limited capability for work, but some points are scored. The findings of the FTT in relation to specific descriptors being applicable are taken into account by the job centre in the drafting of the job seeker's agreement and in relation to the expectation to apply for specific jobs. It would seem reasonable for the findings of a tribunal as to which work-related activities or types of work-related activity an appellant could be expected to engage in without a substantial risk to their health or the health of others to be similarly acknowledged." (paras 30–32.)

**p.917,** *amendment to the Employment and Support Allowance Regulations 2008 (SI 2008/794) reg.36 (information required for determining limited capability for work)*

2.088    With effect from October 29, 2013, reg.13(18) of the Social Security (Miscellaneous Amendments) (No. 3) Regulations 2013 (SI 2013/2536) amended reg.36(2) to read:

"(2) Where the Secretary of State is satisfied that there is sufficient information to determine whether a claimant has limited capability for work-related activity without the information specified in paragraph (1)(a), that information [must] not be required for the purposes of making the determination."

**pp.917–918,** *amendment to the Employment and Support Allowance Regulations 2008 (SI 2008/794) reg.37 (failure to provide information in relation to work-related activity)*

2.089    With effect from October 29, 2013, reg.13(19) of the Social Security (Miscellaneous Amendments) (No. 3) Regulations 2013 (SI 2013/2536) amended reg.37(2) to read:

"(2) Paragraph (1) does not apply unless—
[(a)   the claimant was sent a further request at least three weeks after the date of the first request; and]
(b)    [ . . . ] at least 1 week has passed since the further request was sent."

**p.918,** *annotation to the Employment and Support Allowance Regulations 2008 (SI 2008/794) reg.37 (failure to provide information in relation to work-related activity)*

2.090    Consequent upon the amendment in the immediately preceding update, in the fourth and fifth lines delete "at least four weeks have passed since the claimant was first sent the request for information,".

**p.918,** *amendment to the Employment and Support Allowance Regulations 2008 (SI 2008/794) reg.38 (claimant must be called for medical examination to determine whether the claimant has limited capability for work-related activity")*

With effect from October 29, 2013, reg.13(20) of the Social Security (Miscellaneous Amendments) (No. 3) Regulations 2013 (SI 2013/2536) amended reg.38(2) and substituted a new para.(3) to read:   2.091

"(2) Subject to paragraph (3), where a claimant fails without good cause to attend for or to submit to an examination [mentioned] in paragraph (1), the claimant is to be treated as not having limited capability for work-related activity.

[(3) Paragraph (2) does not apply unless—

(a) written notice of the date, time and place for the examination was sent to the claimant at least seven days in advance; or

(b) the claimant agreed to accept a shorter period of notice whether given in writing or otherwise.]"

**pp.919–920,** *amendment to the Employment and Support Allowance Regulations 2008 (SI 2008/794) reg.40 (a claimant who works to be treated as not entitled to an employment and support allowance)*

With effect from October 29, 2013, reg.13(21) of the Social Security (Miscellaneous Amendments) (No. 3) Regulations 2013 (SI 2013/2536) amended reg.40(2)(d) to read:   2.092

"(d) duties undertaken in caring for another person who is accommodated with the claimant by virtue of arrangements made under any of the provisions referred to in paragraphs 28 or 29 of Schedule 8 (sums to be disregarded in the calculation of income other than earnings) [or] where the claimant is in receipt of any payment specified in those paragraphs;".

**pp.921–922,** *annotation to the Employment and Support Allowance Regulations 2008 (SI 2008/794) reg.40 (a claimant who works to be treated as not entitled to an employment and support allowance)*

Consequent on the amendment noted in the immediately preceding update, head (iv) of the annotation to "Complete Relief" (para.(2)) should now read:   2.093

"work as a foster parent or other specified carer in respect of someone accommodated in one's home or where the claimant is in receipt of any payment specified in Sch.8, paras.28, 29;".

**p.926,** *amendment of the Employment and Support Allowance Regulations 2008 (SI 2008/794) reg.43(1)(e) (Circumstances under which partners of claimants entitled to an income-related allowance are not to be treated as engaged in remunerative work)*

With effect from October 29, 2013, reg.13(1) and (22) of the Social Security (Miscellaneous Amendments) (No. 3) Regulations 2013 (SI   2.094

2013/2536) amended reg.43(1)(e) by substituting the following head for heads (i)–(iii):

> "(i) a part-time fire-fighter employed by a fire and rescue authority under the Fire and Rescue Services Act 2004 or by the Scottish Fire and Rescue Service established under section 1A of the Fire (Scotland) Act 2005;"

**p.928,** *amendment to the Employment and Support Allowance Regulations 2008 (SI 2008/794) reg.45 (exempt work)*

2.095   With effect from October 29, 2013, reg.13(23) of the Social Security (Miscellaneous Amendments) (No. 3) Regulations 2013 (SI 2013/2536) amended reg.45(4) by substituting for para.(4)(b) and (c) a new para. (4)(b) to read:

> "(b) is done by a claimant who has or is treated as having limited capability for work-related activity."

The amending provision also inserted from that date after para.(4), a new para.(4A) to read:

> "(4A) For the purposes of paragraph (4)(a), a period of specified work begins on the first day on which any specified work is undertaken and continues for a period of 52 weeks, whether or not any further specified work is undertaken during that period."

**p.939,** *amendment to the Employment and Support Allowance Regulations 2008 (SI 2008/794) reg.63(5) (reduction of employment and support allowance)*

2.096   With effect from April 29, 2013, reg.37(1), (4) of the Universal Credit (Consequential, Supplementary, Incidental and Miscellaneous Provisions) Regulations 2013 (SI 2013/630) amended reg.63(5) to read:

> "(5) For the purposes of determining the amount of any income-related allowance payable, a claimant is to be treated as receiving the amount of any contributory allowance [including new style ESA] which would have been payable but for any reduction made in accordance with this regulation [or section 11J of the Act respectively]."

**p.950,** *amendment of the Employment and Support Allowance Regulations 2008 (SI 2008/794) reg.70(4)(f) (Special cases: supplemental—persons from abroad)*

2.097   With effect from July 1, 2013, reg.7 of the Social Security (Croatia) Amendment Regulations 2013 (SI 2013/1474) amended reg.70(4)(f) to read as follows:

> "(f) a person who is treated as a worker for the purpose of the definition of 'qualified person' in regulation 6(1) of the Immigra-

tion (European Economic Area) Regulations 2006 pursuant to—

(i) regulation 6 of the Accession (Immigration and Worker Authorisation) Regulations 2006 (right of residence of a Bulgarian or Romanian who is an 'accession State national subject to worker authorisation'), or

(ii) regulation 5 of the Accession of Croatia (Immigration and Worker Authorisation) Regulations 2013 (right of residence of a Croatian who is an 'accession State national subject to worker authorisation');"

**p.950,** *amendment of the Employment and Support Allowance Regulations 2008 (SI 2008/794) reg.70(4) (Special cases: supplemental—persons from abroad)*

With effect from October 29, 2013, reg.13(1) and (24) of the Social **2.098** Security (Miscellaneous Amendments) (No. 3) Regulations 2013 (SI 2013/2536) amended reg.70(4) by substituting the following for sub-para.(h):

"(h) a person who has been granted leave or who is deemed to have been granted leave outside the rules made under section 3(2) of the Immigration Act 1971 where that leave is—

(i) discretionary leave to enter or remain in the United Kingdom;

(ii) leave to remain under the Destitution Domestic Violence concession; or

(iii) leave deemed to have been granted by virtue of regulation 3 of the Displaced Persons (Temporary Protection) Regulations 2005;"

and by adding the word 'or' at the end of sub-para.(i) and revoking sub-paras (k) and (l).

**p.951,** *modification of the Employment and Support Allowance Regulations 2008 (SI 2008/794) reg.70(4) (Special cases: supplemental—persons from abroad)*

Insert the following immediately before the heading "Definition": **2.098A**

*"Modification*

Reg.70(4) is modified by Sch.1, para.10A of the Employment and Support Allowance (Transitional Provisions, Housing Benefit and Council Tax Benefit) (Existing Awards) (No. 2) Regulations 2010 (SI 2010/1907) (as amended) for the purposes specified in reg.6(1). For details of the modification, see the text of those Regulations, below."

**p.955,** *amendment to the Employment and Support Allowance Regulations 2008 (SI 2008/794) reg.76 (deduction for councillor's allowance)*

2.099    With effect from October 29, 2013, reg.13(25) of the Social Security (Miscellaneous Amendments) (No. 3) Regulations 2013 (SI 2013/2536) amended reg.76(1) to read:

> "(1) Where the net amount of councillor's allowance to which a claimant is entitled in respect of any week exceeds 16 x National Minimum Wage, subject to paragraph (3), an amount equal to the excess is to be deducted from the amount of a contributory allowance to which that [claimant] is entitled in respect of that week, and only the balance remaining (if any) is to be payable."

**p.968,** *amendment to the Employment and Support Allowance Regulations 2008 (SI 2008/794) reg.93(2) (Date on which income is treated as paid)*

2.100    With effect from April 29, 2013, reg.37(5) of the Universal Credit (Consequential, Supplementary, Incidental and Miscellaneous Provisions) Regulations 2013 (SI 2013/630) substituted the words "severe disablement allowance or universal credit" for the words "or severe disablement allowance", and the words "on any day" for the words "the day of the benefit week", in reg.93(2).

**pp.971–972,** *amendment to the Employment and Support Allowance Regulations 2008 (SI 2008/794) reg.95 (Earnings of employed earners)*

2.101    With effect from October 29, 2013, reg.13(26)(a) of the Social Security (Miscellaneous Amendments) (No. 3) Regulations 2013 (SI 2013/2536) substituted the words "claimant participating as a service user" for the words "claimant's participation in a service user group" in reg.95(2)(f).
From the same date, reg.13(26)(b) of the same Regulations substituted "(f)" for "(e)" in reg.95(4)(b).

**p.981,** *amendment to the Employment and Support Allowance Regulations 2008 (SI 2008/794) reg.104 (Calculation of income other than earnings)*

2.102    With effect from October 29, 2013, reg.13(27) of the Social Security (Miscellaneous Amendments) (No. 3) Regulations 2013 (SI 2013/2536) added the following new paragraphs after para.(9) in reg.104:

> "(10) Where a claimant is a member of a couple and the claimant's partner is receiving a contributory allowance, and that benefit has been reduced under regulation 63 or section 11J of the Act, the amount of the benefit to be taken into account is the amount as if it had not been so reduced.
> (11) Where a claimant is a husband or wife by virtue of a polygamous marriage and the other party to the marriage or any spouse

additional to the marriage is receiving a contributory allowance, and that benefit has been reduced under regulation 63 or section 11J of the Act, the amount of the benefit to be taken into account is the amount as if it had not been so reduced."

**p.981,** *annotation to the Employment and Support Allowance Regulations 2008 (SI 2008/794) reg.104*

Paragraphs (10) and (11) have been added to reg.104 for the purposes   2.103
of consistency with other regulations (e.g. see reg.40(6) of the Income Support (General) Regulations 1987).

**p.984,** *amendment to the Employment and Support Allowance Regulations 2008 (SI 2008/794) reg.106(9) (Notional income—deprivation and income on application)*

With effect from October 29, 2013, reg.13(28) of the Social Security   2.104
(Miscellaneous Amendments) (No. 3) Regulations 2013 (SI 2013/2536) substituted the words "claimant participating as a service user" for the words "claimant's participation in a service user group" in reg.106(9).

**p.986,** *amendment to the Employment and Support Allowance Regulations 2008 (SI 2008/794) reg.107(8) (Notional income—income due to be paid or income paid to or in respect of a third party)*

With effect from October 29, 2013, reg.13(29) of the Social Security   2.105
(Miscellaneous Amendments) (No. 3) Regulations 2013 (SI 2013/2536) substituted the words "claimant participating as a service user" for the words "claimant's participation in a service user group" in reg.107(8).

**p.988,** *amendment to the Employment and Support Allowance Regulations 2008 (SI 2008/794) reg.108(5) (Notional income—other income)*

With effect from October 29, 2013, reg.13(30) of the Social Security   2.106
(Miscellaneous Amendments) (No. 3) Regulations 2013 (SI 2013/2536) substituted the words "claimant participating as a service user" for the words "claimant's participation in a service user group" in reg.108(5).

**p.1025,** *amendment to the Employment and Support Allowance Regulations 2008 (SI 2008/794) reg.147A(5A) (Claimants appealing a decision)*

With effect from October 28, 2013, reg.7(2) of the Social Security,   2.107
Child Support, Vaccine Damage and Other Payments (Decisions and Appeals) (Amendment) Regulations 2013 (SI 2013/2380) omitted the word "either", the word "or" at the end of sub-para.(a) and sub-para.(b) in reg.147A(5A).

**p.1029,** *annotation to the Employment and Support Allowance Regulations 2008 (SI 2008/794) reg.147A*

2.108    The amendment to para.(5A) of reg.147A is a consequence of the omission of reg.33 of the Social Security and Child Support (Decisions and Appeals) Regulations 1999 (SI 1999/991) with effect from October 28, 2013. Regulation 33 has been omitted as a result of the extension of "mandatory reconsideration" and "direct lodgement" of appeals to, inter alia, social security benefits that was introduced on October 28, 2013. See further the amendments to the Decisions and Appeals Regulations 1999 in the Updating Material to Vol.III of this series in Part IV of this Supplement.

**p.1047,** *amendment of the Employment and Support Allowance Regulations 2008 (SI 2008/794) reg.167(b) (Modification in the calculation of income)*

2.109    With effect from April 29, 2013, reg.37(1) and (6) of the Universal Credit (Consequential, Supplementary, Incidental and Miscellaneous Provisions) Regulations 2013 (SI 2013/630) amended reg.153(b) by inserting the words ", universal credit" after the words "income support".

**p.1047,** *amendment of the Employment and Support Allowance Regulations 2008 (SI 2008/794) reg 168 (Reduction in certain cases)*

2.110    With effect from October 29, 2013, reg.13(1) and (31) of the Social Security (Miscellaneous Amendments) (No. 3) Regulations 2013 (SI 2013/2536) substituted the following for reg.168:

"**Reduction in certain cases**

**168.**—(1) Where a disqualification is to be made in accordance with regulation 157 in respect of a part-week, the amount referred to in paragraph (2) is to be payable by way of an employment and support allowance in respect of that part-week.

(2) The amount mentioned in paragraph (1) is—

(a) one seventh of the employment and support allowance which would have been paid for the part-week if—

(i) there was no disqualification under regulation 157; and

(ii) it was not a part-week; multiplied by

(b) the number of days in the part-week in respect of which no disqualification is to be made in accordance with regulation 157."

**p.1050,** *amendment to the Employment and Support Allowance Regulations 2008 (SI 2008/794) Sch.2 para.1 descriptors (mobilising unaided etc.)*

2.111    With effect from October 29, 2013, reg.13(23) of the Social Security (Miscellaneous Amendments) (No. 3) Regulations 2013 (SI 2013/2536) amended the para.(1) descriptors to read:

| Descriptors | Points |
|---|---|
| 1(a) Cannot [unaided by another person] either: <br><br> (i) mobilise more than 50 metres on level ground without stopping in order to avoid significant discomfort or exhaustion; or <br><br> (ii) repeatedly mobilise 50 metres within a reasonable timescale because of significant discomfort or exhaustion. | 15 |
| (b) Cannot [unaided by another person] mount or descend two steps [...] even with the support of a handrail. | 9 |
| (c) Cannot [unaided by another person] either <br><br> (i) mobilise more than 100 metres on level ground without stopping in order to avoid significant discomfort or exhaustion; or | 9 |
| (ii) repeatedly mobilise 100 metres within a reasonable timescale because of significant discomfort or exhaustion. | |
| (d) Cannot [unaided by another person] either: <br><br> (i) mobilise more than 200 metres on level ground without stopping in order to avoid significant discomfort or exhaustion; or <br><br> (ii) repeatedly mobilise 200 metres within a reasonable timescale because of significant discomfort or exhaustion | 6 |
| (e) None of the above [applies]. | 0 |

**p.1051,** *amendment to the Employment and Support Allowance Regulations 2008 (SI 2008/794) Sch.2 para.5 descriptors (manual dexterity)*

With effect from October 29, 2013, reg.13(32) of the Social Security (Miscellaneous Amendments) (No. 3) Regulations 2013 (SI 2013/2536) substituted a new para.5(a) to read:  **2.112**

| Descriptors | Points |
|---|---|
| 5[(a) Cannot press a button (such as a telephone keypad) with either hand or cannot turn the pages of a book with either hand.] | 15 |

From the same date the amending provision amended para.5(c) to read:

| Descriptors | Points |
|---|---|
| (c) Cannot use a pen or pencil to make a meaningful mark [with either hand.] | 9 |

From that same date it amended para.5(e) to read:

| Descriptors | Points |
|---|---|
| (e) None of the above [applies]. | 0 |

**p.1051,** *amendment to the Employment and Support Allowance Regulations 2008 (SI 2008/794) Sch.2 para.7 descriptors (understanding communication etc)*

2.113    With effect from October 29, 2013, reg.13(32) of the Social Security (Miscellaneous Amendments) (No. 3) Regulations 2013 (SI 2013/2536) amended para.7(a) to read:

| Descriptors | Points |
|---|---|
| (a) Cannot understand a simple message [,such as the location of a fire escape,] due to sensory impairment [ . . . ]." | 15 |

From that same date it amended para.7(d) to read:

| Descriptors | Points |
|---|---|
| (d) None of the above [applies]. | 0 |

**p.1052,** *amendment to the Employment and Support Allowance Regulations 2008 (SI 2008/794) Sch.2 para.9 descriptors (absence or loss of control etc)*

2.114    With effect from October 29, 2013, reg.13(32) of the Social Security (Miscellaneous Amendments) (No. 3) Regulations 2013 (SI 2013/2536) amended para.9(c) to read:

| Descriptors | Points |
|---|---|
| (d) [Neither of the above applies]. | 0 |

**p.1053,** *amendment to the Employment and Support Allowance Regulations 2008 (SI 2008/794) Sch.2 para.12 descriptors (awareness of everyday hazards etc)*

With effect from October 29, 2013, reg.13(33) of the Social Security (Miscellaneous Amendments) (No. 3) Regulations 2013 (SI 2013/2536) amended para.12 (a), (b) and (c) to read:  2.115

| Descriptors | Points |
|---|---|
| (a) Reduced awareness of everyday hazards leads to a significant risk of: <br> (i) injury to self or others; or <br> (ii) damage to property or possessions <br> such that [the claimant requires] supervision for the majority of the time to maintain safety. | 15 |
| (b) Reduced awareness of everyday hazards leads to a significant risk of <br> (i) injury to self or others; or <br> (ii) damage to property or possessions <br> such that [the claimant requires] supervision for the majority of the time to maintain safety | 9 |
| (c) Reduced awareness of everyday hazards leads to a significant risk of: <br> (i) injury to self or others; or <br> (ii) damage to property or possessions <br> such that [the claimant occasionally requires] supervision to maintain safety. | 6 |

Fortunately this also affords an opportunity for us to correct the allocation of points in the Sch. mistakenly set out in the main volume where para.(b) had been reproduced twice.

**p.1053,** *amendment to the Employment and Support Allowance Regulations 2008 (SI 2008/794) Sch.2 para.13 descriptors (initiating and completing personal action etc)*

With effect from October 29, 2013, reg.13(33) of the Social Security (Miscellaneous Amendments) (No. 3) Regulations 2013 (SI 2013/2536) amended para.13(b), (c) and (d) to read:  2.116

| Descriptors | Points |
|---|:---:|
| (b) Cannot, due to impaired mental function, reliably initiate or complete at least 2 [sequential] personal actions for the majority of the time. | 9 |
| (c) Frequently cannot, due to impaired mental function, reliably initiate or complete at least 2 [sequential] personal actions. | 6 |
| (d) None of the above [applies]. | 0 |

**p.1054,** *amendment to the Employment and Support Allowance Regulations 2008 (SI 2008/794) Sch.2 para.16 descriptors (coping with social engagement due to cognitive impairment or mental disorder)*

2.117    With effect from October 29, 2013, reg.13(33) of the Social Security (Miscellaneous Amendments) (No. 3) Regulations 2013 (SI 2013/2536) amended para.16(a), (b), (c) and (d) to read:

| Descriptors | Points |
|---|:---:|
| (a) Engagement in social contact is always precluded due to difficulty relating to others or significant distress experienced by the [claimant]. | 15 |
| (b) Engagement in social contact with someone unfamiliar to the claimant is always precluded due to difficulty relating to others or significant distress experienced by the [claimant]. | 9 |
| (c) Engagement in social contact with someone unfamiliar to the claimant is not possible for the majority of the time due to difficulty relating to others or significant distress experienced by the [claimant]. | 6 |
| (d) None of the above [applies]. | 0 |

**pp.1055–1056,** *annotation to the Employment and Support Allowance Regulations 2008 (SI 2008/794) Sch.2 (a note on the background to the WCA and the new Schs 2 and 3 inserted on March 28, 2011) (correction of cross-reference)*

2.118    The previous version of the WCA is to be found in para.9.365 of the 2012/13 edition of this volume as updated by the 2012/13 Supplement.

**p.1060,** *annotation to the Employment and Support Allowance Regulations 2008 (SI 2008/794) Sch.2 (the reference to MM & DM v SSWP)*

2.119    See update to pp.891–892, above, on the ongoing judicial review challenge under the Equality Act 2010 with respect to aspects of the decision-making process.

**pp.1063–1064,** *annotation to the Employment and Support Allowance Regulations 2008 (SI 2008/794) Sch.2 (Approaching the Interpretation of the Schedule as a whole) (Evidence and attention to detail)*

In *SE v SSWP (ESA)* [2012] UKUT 469 (AAC), Judge Wright held  2.120
that with respect to a decision to supersede an award of benefit on the basis of a new work capability assessment, natural justice and the right to a fair trial under art.6(1) ECHR required that the Secretary of State make available to the tribunal the previous work capability assessment (ESA85). In *CA v SSWP (ESA)* [2013] UKUT 0442 (AAC), Judge Ward stated that it was likely to be an exceptional case in which a change in descriptors would exempt the Secretary of State from that duty, since a previous WCA assessment, particularly one close in time and where the condition in question is not said to be changing can prove of evidential value and assist the tribunal to assess the robustness of the latest assessment at issue, by giving a picture of the claimant's history and considering the descriptors thought by the previous HCP then to be relevant. It is ultimately for the tribunal what to make of that previous assessment.

Where the claimant has complained about an Atos examination and no response to that has been received by the tribunal, or any relevant Atos report is not before the tribunal, it is appropriate to consider whether to adjourn, but it does not follow that it must adjourn (*SA v SSWP (ESA)* [2013] UKUT 0616 (AAC), per Judge Mark):

"It needs to consider all the matters in issue in the complaint, the likelihood of their being resolved or at least further illuminated by the report, the relevance of the complaints to the matters before it and the likely relevance of any possible response by ATOS in addition to any other relevant matters. Having considered all relevant matters it needs to decide whether it was better to proceed or to adjourn in order to deal with the case fairly and justly in accordance with the overriding objective in rule 2 of the Tribunal Procedure (First-tier Tribunal) (SEC) Rules 2008 (see further *MA v SSWP* [2009] UKUT 221 (AAC)). It also needs to give reasons for its decision.

If, for example, the only complaint is that the reasoning in the report is irrational, it seems to me that there would be no need for an adjournment. The question of rationality could be considered by the tribunal without the views of ATOS on the question. Other complaints, for example as to rudeness, may also have no impact on the matters that the tribunal needs to address. Complaints that relate to the accuracy of factual statements in the report, on the other hand, or as to the failure of the disability analyst to read what should have been read, may or may not result in relevant findings by ATOS. For example, the analyst may be asked to comment and may concede certain issues or provide explanations as to disputed matters in the report" (paras 10, 11).

**pp.1065–1068,** *annotation to the Employment and Support Allowance Regulations 2008 (SI 2008/794) Sch.2 (Approaching the Interpretation of the Schedule as a whole) (the LCWA is not a snapshot—the need for an approach characterized by "reasonableness")*

2.121     In *AS v SSWP (ESA)* [2013] UKUT 0587 (AAC), Judge Wikeley held that the Court of Appeal decision in *Charlton v SSWP* [2009] EWCA Civ 42 (reported as *R(IB) 2/09*), which in the context of ESA Regulations 2008, reg.29 required an examination of the work required, does not assist in interpreting the Sch.2 descriptors (para.17). He then considered in some depth the relationship between Sch.2 and the work context, stating that he accepted as correctly made a concession by the Secretary of State's representative:

> "that the various activities in Schedule 2 have 'a connection with the workplace', albeit that the descriptors are not concerned with any one specific working environment and do not bring in wider questions of employability. This concession properly reflects the direction of policy travel as embodied in legislative change in this area. The first clue is in the change of name; Parliament has approved the shift from the 'personal capability assessment' in the incapacity benefit scheme to the 'work capability assessment' under the ESA regime. The second clue lies in the drafting of the various activities and individual descriptors, and in particular the amendments which took effect on March 28, 2011 (see further the Explanatory Memorandum to the draft 2011 Regulations, sent to the Social Security Advisory Committee on 13 August 2010). Thus the first three activities in the original Schedule 2 to the ESA Regulations—walking, standing and sitting, bending or kneeling—were seen as providing a high degree of overlap for e.g. wheelchair users, so providing an inaccurate assessment of an individual's true level of functional limitation in the workplace. This resulted in a radical re-writing of the first activity, transforming it from 'walking' to 'mobilising', the specific inclusion of the 'work station' test in the second activity (standing and sitting) and the abolition of the third activity (bending or kneeling) as being both an unnecessary and undesirable requirement in the modern workplace.
>
> It follows that the activities and descriptors in Schedule 2 do not exist in some sort of artificial or parallel universe, entirely divorced from the real world of work. They have to be applied on their own terms, but understood against the backdrop of the modern workplace. In deciding whether a particular descriptor is met, decision makers and tribunals may therefore find it helpful to consider the claimant's ability to undertake the activity in question in a range of different working contexts. However, claimants will not be awarded a defined descriptor simply because they can show that it would apply to them if they were employed to do a particular job in a specific type of working environment.
>
> This is entirely consistent with the well-established principle that decision makers and tribunals must consider whether a claimant can perform a particular activity with a reasonable degree of repetition,

sometimes referred to as 'reasonable regularity' principle. This principle applies to the ESA scheme just as it did to the previous incapacity benefit regime. As Upper Tribunal Judge Turnbull has explained, 'if the effect of performing the activity is likely to be to disable the claimant from performing it for a substantial period, that will need to be taken into account' (*see AF v Secretary of State for Work and Pensions (ESA)* [2011] UKUT 61 at paragraph 11, approved and followed in *SAG v Department for Social Development (ESA)* [2012] AACR 6). Judge Nicholas Paines QC has described the principle in similar terms: 'it is implicit in this that a description set out in a descriptor will not fit a claimant who can only perform the relevant task exceptionally or infrequently' (*AG v Secretary of State for Work and Pensions (ESA)* [2013] UKUT 077 (at paragraph 18)).

Within the legislative scheme as a whole, this principle only makes sense in the context of the needs of a modern workplace and the level of activity that an employer attuned to the requirements of disability discrimination law can reasonably expect. Plainly, the test is not about a high-pressure working environment, e.g. a call-centre with demanding targets or a factory production line with a fast-moving conveyor belt. Equally, however, the test is not about what the person can do in their own home and entirely in their own time and at their own pace, subject to no external constraints or pressures whatsoever. If reasonable regularity is judged by the latter criterion, then the test has ceased to be a test of 'whether a claimant's capability for work is limited by the claimant's physical or mental condition' within regulation 19(1) of the ESA Regulations" (paras 18–21).

**p.1069,** *annotation to the Employment and Support Allowance Regulations 2008 (SI 2008/794) Sch.2 Activity 1: mobilising unaided by another person with or without a walking stick, manual wheelchair or other aid if such aid is normally, or could reasonably be, worn or used:*

On wheelchair or other aids, the question is whether the wheelchair or other aid "could reasonably be worn or used" or "is normally worn or used". The meaning and context of this continues to trouble Upper Tribunal Judges. As Judge Ramsay noted in *NT v SSWP (ESA)* [2013] UKUT 0360 (AAC), Judge Gamble's decision in *M* has been widely cited and approved (see, for example, *AB v SSWP (ESA)*, decision CE 4267 2012, para.12; and *BG v SSWP (ESA)* [2013] UKUT 0504, paras 14 and 15, both noted below). She doubted whether it reflected legislative intention, but rightly said that:

"Where legislation fails to make its meaning clear, judges and other decision makers in applying the principles of statutory interpretation may, without error, end up with divergent ideas on the application of the legislative test" (para.11).

She seemed to prefer a focus on usability in the workday setting (the workplace level surface rather than indoors at home), as opposed to "therapeutic considerations", but conceded that whether the wheelchair

2.122

could be kept at home ready for use for trips elsewhere had also to be involved.

Judge Gray's disagreement with Judge Gamble (and implicitly with Judge Ramsay on the relevance of a place at home to keep a wheelchair?) is more fundamental. In *TB* v *SSWP (ESA)* [2013] UKUT 0408 (AAC), Judge Gray preferred and followed Commissioner Stockman and the line of authority on a functional approach set out in *MG*, thus eschewing consideration of "personal circumstances such as living in an unsuitable building". Judge Gray also followed Commissioner Stockman in concluding that it was difficult to envisage that a wheelchair could reasonably be used without the claimant having been referred by clinicians for a wheelchair assessment. Such a referral was not, however, conclusive of whether a wheelchair could in fact reasonably be used by the particular claimant.

As Judge Williams noted in *AR* v *SSWP (ESA)* [2013] UKUT 0417 (AAC)—a "lead" decision which he applied in *PL* v *SSWP (ESA)* [2013] UKUT 0448 (AAC) and in *MI* v *SSWP (ESA)* [2013] UKUT 0447 (AAC)—all the decisions have common ground in that they see the mobilisation test as an actual rather than hypothetical test. For him, the central approach should be "if the claimant had a manual wheelchair could he or she reasonably use it". He firmly rejected the broadening of the test to look at matters such as whether the claimant could afford to buy one. But even on this functional approach, it is not purely a matter of whether, when in the wheelchair, the claimant can mobilise. Reasonable use of a wheelchair involves several aspects of functional ability aside from the lower limbs. While there is no longer a "rising from sitting" activity in Sch.2, one must nonetheless consider it in the context of whether a wheelchair can reasonably be used. On a functional analysis, "can a claimant reasonably be expected to use a wheelchair (including getting into and out of it) without the aid of another person if he or she cannot reasonably be expected to handle the wheelchair whilst preparing to get into it, or after getting out of it" (para.35)? Unfortunately the standard forms (ESA50 and ESA85) do not deal with such issues because they are not dealt with elsewhere in the Schedules.

In contrast, Judge Mark favoured the much broader approach taken by Judge Gamble in *M*, commenting in *BG* v *SSWP (ESA)* [2013] UKUT 0504 (AAC):

> "The context of the work capability for work test is an attempt to assess who is going to be able to undertake work of some sort. For that being able to mobilise in fact rather than in theory is important. It does not make sense to say that somebody has or does not have limited capacity for work based on a hypothetical ability to mobilise with an aid that he or she does not have and cannot for practical reasons obtain and use. I disagree therefore with Judge Williams that the test is a freestanding one independent of the question whether the claimant can in fact [reasonably] be expected to have access to a wheelchair on a daily basis. It is not a notional test or thought experiment such as the cooking test in DLA where it is immaterial whether a person needs to cook or not or has the equipment or not.

The test in my judgment is whether the aid, the wheelchair, can reasonably be used by this claimant in his daily life. The use includes not merely mobilising once for any particular distance, but being able repeatedly to mobilise and to do so not just on one day but over a period of time. A claimant cannot reasonably use a wheelchair without having access to one, and I do not see how his ability to store one and to get to and from it can be disregarded in determining whether he can reasonably be expected to use it, in the same way as his ability to get in and out of it unaided would be relevant. It is even possible that inability to afford a wheelchair may be relevant, although it is would not normally be so given their relative cheapness and their availability from the NHS and charities where reasonably required." (paras 14, 15.)

Similarly, Judge White in *AB v SSWP (ESA)*, decision CE 4267 2012 agreed with Judge Gamble that "reasonableness" demanded:

"a broad exercise of in relation to a variety of factors. These will in my view always include (a) whether the use of the aid or wheelchair has been suggested or recommended (or indeed not recommended) by health care professionals, and why; (b) whether the claimant's health is such that he or she could use a walking stick or other aid or propel a manual wheelchair; (c) whether the claimant has access to a walking stick, or wheelchair, or other walking aid; and (d) whether, in the case of the use of a wheelchair, the claimant's living environment makes the use of a manual wheelchair practically feasible. For example, the situation of a person living on the upper floor of a block of flats without a lift is very different from that of a person living in a bungalow without any steps leading to it" (para.12).

The matter of the proper approach is now pending before a three-judge panel in *CE/327/2013* and *CE/509/2013*.

**pp.1069–1070,** *annotation to the Employment and Support Allowance Regulations 2008 (SI 2008/794) Sch.2 Activity 1: mobilising unaided by another person with or without a walking stick, manual wheelchair or other aid if such aid is normally, or could reasonably be, worn or used: descriptors (a)(ii), (c)(ii) and (d)(ii): "repeatedly mobilise [X metres] within a reasonable timescale"*

In *AS v SSWP (ESA)* [2013] UKUT 0587 (AAC), Judge Wikeley   2.123
considered the meaning of this phrase, which he saw as a legislative variant on the case law principle of "reasonable regularity" (para.28). He regarded as an "excellent starting point" Judge Jacob's decision in *AH v SSWP (ESA)* [2013] UKUT 0118 (AAC) (noted fully in the annotation to Sch.3 activity/descriptor 1) (para.9.398). From that case, he took two points. First of all, the need, when considering the "reasonable regularity" principle to focus on the particular wording of the descriptors so that in this context the use of "repeatedly in descriptors (a)(ii), (c)(ii) and (d)(ii) meant that the principle did not apply to limb (i) of each of those descriptors (para.27). Secondly, he took the point that it was important "where the legislative text contains irreducible terms, [to

apply] the statutory language without any gloss" (para.29). Like Judge Jacobs, he took the view that it was not for the Upper Tribunal to proffer a precise definition of these terms, but considered that in this case the tribunal's findings went beyond the bounds envisaged by case law. The provisions of the Schedule had to be construed "against the background of a working environment" (see update to pp.1065–1068, above). He continued:

> "What might well be a reasonable timescale for the Appellant at home would not necessarily be a reasonable timescale in the workplace. The consequence of the tribunal's approach was to rob the word 'repeatedly' of any real meaning, as the tribunal's findings would equally well meet a statutory test predicated on the activity in question being performed only 'occasionally . . . in the course of a day'. Whilst I am not prepared to draw a precise line, I am satisfied that on any reasonable analysis this tribunal's conclusion was the wrong side of the line. The ability to perform a function in a working environment 'repeatedly . . . within a reasonable timescale' must be something more than "occasionally . . . in the course of a day" (para.32).

**p.1070,** *annotation to the Employment and Support Allowance Regulations 2008 (SI 2008/794) Sch.2 Activity 2: standing and sitting*

2.124    *MC v SSWP (ESA)* [2012 UKUT 324 (AAC) is reported as [2013] AACR 13.

**p.1071,** *annotation to the Employment and Support Allowance Regulations 2008 (SI 2008/794) Sch.2 Activity 5 (manual dexterity), descriptor (d) (cannot use a suitable keyboard or mouse)*

2.125    In *CL v SSWP (ESA)* [2013] UKUT 0434 (AAC), Judge Mark thought that inability to use either is enough to score points. He approved Judge May's approach in *DW,* following *Moyna,* on the need to take a broad view on whether a claimant could or could not satisfy the descriptor, stating that there are no absolutes by reference to which "can" and "cannot" are to be defined. The fact that a claimant could use a mouse or keyboard to a limited extent does not mean that s/he can use it in the way it was intended to be used. He disagreed with this commentator's view in the annotation that the reformulation of the descriptor jarred with Judge May's approach, with the Judge himself being able to use a conventional keyboard with one hand, but did, however, accept that only being able to use one hand was more difficult, would be slower and that, on a conventional keyboard, combinations of three keys (typically control, alt and delete—often used for logging on and security or recovery purposes—would not be possible on a conventional keyboard. The principle of "reasonable regularity" may also have relevance (see *KE v Department for Social Development (ESA)* [2013] NI Com 59, a decision of Chief Commissioner Mullan) on the previous wording of the descriptor). Since the descriptor now refers to a suitable keyboard or mouse, it is submitted that for a tribunal properly to decide on this descriptor it needs evidence on the nature of the keyboard or mouse envisaged.

**p.1072,** *annotation to the Employment and Support Allowance Regulations 2008 (SI 2008/794) Sch.2 Activity 9 (Absence or loss of control whilst conscious leading to extensive evacuation of the bowel and/or bladder, other than enuresis (bed-wetting), despite the wearing or use of any aids or adaptations which are normally, or could reasonably be, worn or used)*

In *LB v SSWP (ESA)* [2013] UKUT 0352 (AAC), Judge Mark   2.126
considered the use of aids or adaptations. He thought that the DWP
guidance to decision-makers in Memo DMG 24/12, issued after Judge
Levenson's decision in *RP v SSWP* [2011] UKUT (ESA) 449 (AAC)
(noted in the annotation to reg.19(4)) (see para.9.49), embodied a non-
exhaustive set of useful matters to be considered in cases, but stressed, as
does the guidance itself, that those set out are not the only factors which
may be relevant. Judge Mark summarised the relevant parts of the
guidance thus:

"In relation to those physical descriptors which specifically refer to the
use of aids, including continence, it observes that decision makers
should apply the test in a way that displays consistency between the
work capability assessment as a whole and the assessment of each
descriptor in particular (para.6). It goes on to state that the decision
maker should establish whether the claimant normally uses an aid or
appliance, and if not, whether the use of it has been prescribed or
advised. If a claimant does not have an aid or appliance which they
have been prescribed or advised to use, the decision maker should
establish whether it would help the claimant, why they are not using
one and whether the explanation is reasonable.

The guidance goes on to state that the decision maker must consider
all the circumstances in deciding whether it would be reasonable to
assess the claimant as using an aid that they have not been prescribed
or that they have not been advised to use. Factors identified include
whether (1) the claimant possesses the aid or appliance; (2) the
claimant was given specific medical advice about managing their condition, and it is reasonable for them to continue to follow that advice;
(3) the claimant would be advised to use an aid or appliance if they
raised it with the appropriate authority such as a GP or occupational
therapist; (4) if it is medically reasonable for them to use an aid or
appliance; (5) the health condition or disability is likely to be of short
duration; (6) an aid or appliance is widely available; (7) an aid or
appliance is affordable in the claimant's circumstances; (8) the claimant is able to use and store the aid or appliance; and (9) the claimant
is unable to use an aid or appliance due to their physical or mental
health condition" (paras 11, 12).

He noted that the HCP had not carried out the recommended enquiries. Nor had the tribunal done so. It had referred to the claimant's urine
well which he kept in his car as "an aid which he used". But this failed
to address the fact it was only of use in the car and even there did not
always prove adequate because he could not get to it in time or was not
in a suitably quiet place to use it. It could not reasonably be expected to
be used in non-private places (para.20). As regards the possible use of

283

pads—which the claimant did not use because he felt shame at the continence problem at his age—Judge Ward stressed that while they could deal with post-urinary dribbling (which does not count for scoring purposes anyway), he was less clear how they could deal adequately with extensive evacuation of the bladder. Moreover—as an additional factor not mentioned in the DWP guidance—the tribunal should consider whether their use might actually exacerbate the problem of "accidents" where the claimant could reach a toilet in time "because they might increase the time required for the claimant to prepare himself to urinate" (para.22).

**pp.1073–1074,** *annotation to the Employment and Support Allowance Regulations 2008 (SI 2008/794) Sch.2 Activity 10: consciousness during waking moments: descriptor (a) "At least once a week, has an involuntary episode of lost or altered consciousness resulting in significantly disrupted awareness or concentration."*

2.127    In *JG v SSWP (ESA)* [2013] UKUT 0496 (AAC), Judge Mark considered the case of a claimant whose drowsiness was a direct side effect of his Parkinson's medication. Applying ESA Regulations 2008 reg.19(5)(c), it arose as a direct result of treatment by a medical practitioner for that disease. As tiredness induced by medication, it was thus distinguishable from the "natural tiredness" considered by Judge Jacobs in *AB v SSWP (ESA)* [2012 UKUT 151 (AAC). As regards Judge Jacob's comments on "natural tiredness" in that case, Judge Ward agreed that in general it was something one can control and cannot in the context of descriptor (a) be described as "involuntary", but stated further that:

"[i]t would not, however, be true of somebody suffering from narcolepsy, nor would it be true of somebody who has been administered a sedative designed to cause them to fall asleep, or which has that consequence. There will be occasions when the tiredness or drowsiness is so extreme that voluntary control is lost. Whether there are occasions when the claimant's medication results in such occasions, and if so, how frequently this occurs, is a matter for the tribunal to determine. . . . [T]he descriptor clearly refers both to lost and altered consciousness. Sleep is a form of lost consciousness just as much as a state induced by an epileptic fit. A person is not awake if they have lost consciousness and the reference to 'remaining conscious during waking moments' or, as here, 'consciousness during waking moments' is plainly concerned with involuntary loss of consciousness of any type. I can see no difference between losing consciousness due to narcolepsy and losing consciousness due to any other cause. . . . [D]rug induced drowsiness can, if severe enough, amount to or result in an involuntary episode of lost or altered consciousness resulting in significantly disrupted awareness or concentration. It is for the tribunal to investigate the cause, nature and extent of the problem and to determine whether there are occasions when the side effects of the claimant's medication have that effect on him, and if so, how frequently they occur" (paras 9–11).

In a Northern Ireland decision, *DM v Department for Social Development (ESA)* [2013] NI Com 17, following Judge Jacobs in *AB*, Commissioner Stockman considered that the "correct approach to the activity excludes considerations of periods of normal sleep. Falling asleep during the day does not equate to loss of consciousness" (para.24).

**p.1075,** *annotation to the Employment and Support Allowance Regulations 2008 (SI 2008/794) Sch.2 Activity 14: coping with change: descriptor (c): cannot cope with minor unplanned change . . . to the extent that overall, day to day life is made significantly more difficult*

In *GC v SSWP (ESA)* [2013] UKUT 0405 (AAC), Judge Ward considered:  **2.128**

"that both activity 14 . . . and activity 16 ('coping with social engagement' require an examination of what it is with which the person is unable to 'cope'. To 'cope' is a word of general application. Its significance in the present context is well expressed by a definition given in the Oxford English Dictionary (Online Edition) of 'To manage, deal (competently) with, a situation or problem. It seems to me that a variety of human behaviours and responses may be indicative of a failure to 'cope' in such a sense. Among them may be stress reactions and discomfort sufficient to require the intervention of another in circumstances where such intervention would not normally be expected" (para.6).

In mental health descriptor cases the context of a particular piece of evidence can be very important (see *PD v SSWP (ESA)* [2012] UKUT 255 (AAC)). In this case work-related stress had been the reason the claimant left his previous job as a driver. Being required to change his planned-out driving route part way through a shift, caused him stress, made him bad-tempered, such that he had to leave that job. The decision reflects Judge Ward's important reminder that different people have different abilities to cope with change. On the evidence Judge Ward found the claimant's ability to cope with change very low and that he satisfied descriptor (c) and had limited capability for work. He could not, however, satisfy the more stringent descriptor in Sch.3.

**p.1075,** *annotation to the Employment and Support Allowance Regulations 2008 (SI 2008/794) Sch.2 Activity 15; Getting about: descriptor (c): Is unable to get to a specified place with which the claimant is unfamiliar without being accompanied by another person.*

As Judge Mark said in *LM v SSWP (ESA)* [2013] UKUT 0552 (AAC), evidence that a claimant had gone unaccompanied to familiar places and accompanied to an unfamiliar one where she was trembling and sweating cannot support a finding that she could go unaccompanied to an unfamiliar place. The tribunal had thus erred in law.  **2.129**

**p.1076,** *annotation to the Employment and Support Allowance Regulations 2008 (SI 2008/794) Sch.2 Activity 16 (coping with social engagement due to cognitive impairment or mental disorder)*

2.130    See Judge Ward's comments on the meaning of "cope" in *GC v SSWP (ESA)* [2013] UKUT 0405 (AAC), in the update to p.1075 (Activity 14), above.

In *LM v SSWP (ESA)* [2013] UKUT 0552 (AAC), Judge Mark considered that descriptor (b) is satisfied if for the majority of the time, social engagement is always precluded (paras 12, 13). As regards descriptors (a) and (b) he could not read "always" as "often" or "for the majority of the time" (the term in descriptor (c)), but rather as "persistently or repeatedly". To say otherwise would have the odd result that a claimant could not satisfy descriptors (a) and (b) but, because of ESA Regulations 2008, reg.34(2) would satisfy descriptor 13 in Sch.3 (see para.15). Judge Mark continued:

> "the tribunal is required to form an overall picture of the claimant's ability to engage in social conduct over a period and it does not appear to me that occasional very limited engagement in such conduct need prevent a tribunal concluding that overall the claimant is always unable to do so. To take an extreme example, a person in a coma who surfaces occasionally and is able to engage briefly during that period with familiar and unfamiliar persons before lapsing into unconsciousness should nevertfeless be found in this context always to be unable to engage in social contact" (para.16).

He awarded the claimant points under descriptor (b).

The precise scope of "social" has troubled Upper Tribunal Judges. In *KB v SSWP (ESA)* [2013] UKUT 0152 (AAC), noted in the annotation to Sch.3, activity and descriptor 13 (see para.9.399), as regards "social engagement" and "social contact", Judge Parker, accepting the approach advanced by the Secretary of State's representative, thought that "social" was "a simple reference to relations with other human beings" carrying no connotations of "leisure, pleasure or mutuality", so that a tribunal could properly look at evidence about business visits or contacts with professionals, as well as with friends, relatives and strangers. It was not tied to contact in an informal setting (see paras 15–17). Judge Ward disagreed with this in *AR v SSWP (ESA)* [2013] UKUT 0446 (AAC). It rendered "social" virtually otiose, placing the focus purely on "engagement with others". It also jarred with the ordinary meaning of the word in the Concise Oxford Dictionary, a meaning Judge Ward thought closer to the legislator's intention. Looking at the legislative history, he considered that the difficulties faced by those with autistic spectrum disorder were very much in mind. Material from the National Autism Society showed the difficulties faced in understanding the rules on social contact and distinguishing a "true friend" from a "pretend friend". Accordingly, in Judge Ward's view:

> "social contact in this sense is not the same as contact for business or professional purposes. If one goes to a medical examination, or a tribunal hearing, the rules are firmly established by the process and/or

the person conducting it, and are typically clearly defined, often in writing. If the person being examined or whose case it is does not respond in a way that a person without disability might, the person conducting it may because of their professional responsibilities be expected within generous limits to accommodate the non-conforming response and certainly not, as it were, to take a poorer view of, or attempt to avoid further contact with, the person because of it. That is precisely what is lacking in the social sphere, where people are free to interact on their own terms and to accept the behaviour of another or to reject it, and largely do so on the basis of the sort of unwritten rules to which the National Autism Society guidance makes reference, an inability to respect which could, in the words of the descriptor, be an indication of 'difficulty relating to others'" (para.18).

In *LM v SSWP (ESA)* [2013] UKUT 0552 (AAC), Judge Mark cited this paragraph and gave it qualified support, stating that he agreed that:

"merely attending a medical examination or tribunal hearing does not establish an ability to engage in social contact, but it does not follow that in the course of that examination or hearing the party will not demonstrate an ability to respond appropriately and engage in limited social contact despite the distress that the meeting is causing and that such contact causes. The fact that a person is not so far along the autistic spectrum as to be wholly unable to engage in social contact does not mean that a person might not experience significant distress if required to engage in such contact. A tribunal needs to assess the ability to engage in social contact, which can be in any context, the extent to which a person has the capacity so to engage, the distress it causes when engagement occurs and the impact of that distress on the ability so to engage" (para.18).

In *AP v SSWP (ESA)* [2013] UKUT 0293 (AAC), Judge Turnbull considered descriptor (c). He accepted that:

"difficulty, from a mental point of view, in simply getting alone to the destination does not fall to be taken into account under activity 16 (unless the difficulty getting there is itself due to problems with engaging in social contact (e.g. on public transport)). In other words, a claimant does not qualify for points under activity 16(c) merely because he could not put himself in most of the situations where he might engage in social contact with someone unfamiliar, because he could not leave the house unaccompanied in order to do so" (para. 11).

"The difficulty with others" aspect of the descriptor envisaged the situation in which it is the need to engage with others which caused the problem. In contrast, however, the alternative—"significant distress experienced by the individual"—did not, in his view,

"require that it is the need to interact with others which per se causes the distress. . . . the wording is satisfied whatever the immediate cause of the distress may be, provided that it is due to cognitive impairment or mental disorder, and that it is sufficiently severe and occurs on sufficient occasions to prevent the claimant engaging with others 'for the majority of the time.'

Thus, if the effect of having to leave his home unaccompanied, or to enter unfamiliar buildings, is to cause distress which prevents the claimant then being able to engage with someone unfamiliar, . . . 16(c) could apply, even if the claimant would have been perfectly capable of engaging with that unfamiliar person if he had been accompanied by friend or family, or if he had been in familiar surroundings.

Thus, the Claimant in the present case was not in my judgment prevented from satisfying 16(c) merely because it was not the process of interacting with unfamiliar persons per se which caused her difficulty" (paras 12–14).

**p.1076,** *annotation to the Employment and Support Allowance Regulations 2008 (SI 2008/794) Sch.2 Activity 17 (appropriateness of behavior with other people, due to cognitive impairment or mental disorder)*

2.131     As regards descriptor (a), in *WT v SSWP (ESA)* [2013] UKUT 0556 (AAC), Judge Ward considered the meaning of "on a daily basis". While this was a decision dealing with identical wording in Sch.3, activity/descriptor 14, Judge Ward also applied it to descriptor (a), its "mirror descriptor". Rather than merely deploy a dictionary definition, he took the "mischief" approach to interpretation and reasoned thus:

"The mischief that the descriptor must be intended to remedy is the creation of an unsafe or otherwise unacceptable work environment for co-workers. The way in which the avoidance of that is accomplished is to exclude from the workplace those who, due to their mental health condition exhibit certain behaviour. If on virtually every day that they were at work they displayed such behaviour, would the fact that there were very rare days on which they did not prevent them from falling within the meaning of the descriptor? To answer 'yes' to that question would not be to address the mischief. The descriptor must, then, be interpreted more widely than literally every day.

I fortify myself in this view because the ordinary meaning of the words 'on a daily basis' seem to me to connote a lesser test than 'every day'. The phrase is not confined to events which happen literally every day. Someone might be said to read a particular newspaper on a daily basis even though there were periods when they did not, such as where they were abroad on holiday when it was not available. Walking the dog on a daily basis is an activity which may be interrupted by the ill-health of either dog or walker, but a short break would not change the very regular nature of the activity or make that description inapt.

The words 'on a daily basis', then, in the context of schedule 3 descriptor 14, and its mirror descriptor under schedule 2, [para.] 17 (a), means certainly more than for the majority of the time, that being the regulation 34(2) test, and must mean more than frequently, that being the test of periodicity in [para.]17(b), but it does not mean literally every day or even on every working day. The essence is of this being an enduring position; one which is happening regularly, constantly or continually. It is for the tribunal to find the facts as to the frequency of the behaviour set out in the descriptor, and then apply this approach to those facts with their usual common sense" (paras 40–42).

As regards descriptor (c), in *KE v SSWP (ESA)* [2013] UKUT 0370 (AAC), Judge Williams noted that "the incidence [of disinhibited behaviour] is at a lower level of occurrence but at a higher level of intensity than the previous test, although the underlying issue manifested by these forms of conduct is the same" (para.17). It now attracts three more points than its predecessor (9 rather than 6). The claimant had several times been required to leave the Jobcentre because of abusive and insulting things he said rather than did, "a classic form of disinhibited behaviour". As regards the criterion "unreasonable in any workplace, Judge Williams thought a Jobcentre unlikely to "apply a lower test than an employer would be expected to apply" (para.18).

**p.1077,** *amendment to the Employment and Support Allowance Regulations 2008 (SI 2008/794) Sch.3 para 5 descriptor (manual dexterity)*

With effect from October 29, 2013, reg.13(33) of the Social Security (Miscellaneous Amendments) (No. 3) Regulations 2013 (SI 2013/2536) amended the para.5 descriptor to read:   2.132

| Descriptors |
|---|
| Cannot press a button (such as a telephone keypad) with either hand or cannot turn the pages of a book with either hand. |

**p.1077,** *amendment to the Employment and Support Allowance Regulations 2008 (SI 2008/794) Sch.3 para.7 descriptor (understanding communication etc)*

With effect from October 29, 2013, reg.13(33) of the Social Security (Miscellaneous Amendments) (No. 3) Regulations 2013 (SI 2013/2536) amended the para.7 descriptor to read:   2.133

| Descriptors |
| --- |
| Cannot understand a simple message [,such as the location of a fire escape] due to sensory impairment [ . . . ] . |

**p.1077,** *amendment to the Employment and Support Allowance Regulations 2008 (SI 2008/794) Sch.3 para.10 descriptor (awareness of hazard)*

2.134     With effect from October 29, 2013, reg.13(33) of the Social Security (Miscellaneous Amendments) (No. 3) Regulations 2013 (SI 2013/2536) amended the para.10 descriptor to read:

| Descriptors |
| --- |
| Reduced awareness of everyday hazards, due to cognitive impairment or mental disorder, leads to a significant risk of: <br><br>(a) injury to self or others; or <br><br>(b) damage to property or possessions <br><br>such that [the claimant requires] supervision for the majority of the time to maintain safety. |

**p.1078,** *amendment to the Employment and Support Allowance Regulations 2008 (SI 2008/794) Sch.3 para.13 descriptor (coping with social engagement due to cognitive impairment or mental disorder)*

2.135     With effect from October 29, 2013, reg.13(33) of the Social Security (Miscellaneous Amendments) (No. 3) Regulations 2013 (SI 2013/2536) amended the para.13 descriptor to read:

| Descriptors |
| --- |
| Engagement in social contact is always precluded due to difficulty relating to others or significant distress experienced by the [claimant]. |

**p.1078,** *amendment to the Employment and Support Allowance Regulations 2008 (SI 2008/794) Sch.3 para.15 descriptors (conveying food or drink to the mouth)*

2.136     With effect from October 29, 2013, reg.13(33) of the Social Security (Miscellaneous Amendments) (No. 3) Regulations 2013 (SI 2013/2536) amended the para.15(b) descriptor to read:

| Descriptors |
|---|
| (b) Cannot convey food or drink to the claimant's own mouth without repeatedly [stopping or] experiencing breathlessness or severe discomfort; |

**p.1080,** *annotation to the Employment and Support Allowance Regulations 2008 (SI 2008/794) Sch.3*

*CD v SSWP (ESA)* [2012[ UKUT (AAC) 289 is now reported as [2013] AACR 12.　　　　2.137

**pp.1081–1082,** *annotation to the Employment and Support Allowance Regulations 2008 (SI 2008/794) Sch.3 para.1 (mobilising unaided . . . repeatedly . . . within a reasonable timescale)*

In *AS v SSWP (ESA)* [2013] UKUT 0587 (AAC), Judge Wikeley saw　2.138 *AH* (now reported, see below) as an "excellent starting point" for interpretation, and applied it to the case before him. See update to pp.1069–1070, above. On the need to interpret both Schedules against the background of a working environment, see that update and the update to pp.1065–1068, above.

*AH v SSWP (ESA)* [2013] UKUT 118 (AAC) is reported as [2013] AACR 32.

**p.1083,** *annotation to the Employment and Support Allowance Regulations 2008 (SI 2008/794) Sch.3 para.13 activity "coping with social engagement due to cognitive impairment or mental disorder"; descriptor "engagement in social contact is always precluded due to difficulty relating to others or significant distress experienced by the individual"*

See update to p.1076 (activity 16) for: Judge Ward's disagreement　2.139 with Judge Parker's interpretation of "social"; and Judge Mark's narrower view that "always" did not mean "often".

**p.1083,** *new annotation to the Employment and Support Allowance Regulations 2008 (SI 2008/794) Sch.3 para.14 activity: Appropriateness of behaviour with other people, due to cognitive impairment or mental disorder: descriptor: Has, on a daily basis, uncontrollable episodes of aggressive or disinhibited behaviour that would be unreasonable in any workplace.*

In *WT v SSWP (ESA)* [2013] UKUT 0556 (AAC), Judge Ward　2.140 considered the meaning of "on a daily basis". Rather than merely deploy a dictionary definition, he took the "mischief" approach to interpretation and reasoned thus:

"The mischief that the descriptor must be intended to remedy is the creation of an unsafe or otherwise unacceptable work environment for

291

co-workers. The way in which the avoidance of that is accomplished is to exclude from the workplace those who, due to their mental health condition exhibit certain behaviour. If on virtually every day that they were at work they displayed such behaviour, would the fact that there were very rare days on which they did not prevent them from falling within the meaning of the descriptor? To answer 'yes' to that question would not be to address the mischief. The descriptor must, then, be interpreted more widely than literally every day.

I fortify myself in this view because the ordinary meaning of the words 'on a daily basis' seem to me to connote a lesser test than 'every day'. The phrase is not confined to events which happen literally every day. Someone might be said to read a particular newspaper on a daily basis even though there were periods when they did not, such as where they were abroad on holiday when it was not available. Walking the dog on a daily basis is an activity which may be interrupted by the ill-health of either dog or walker, but a short break would not change the very regular nature of the activity or make that description inapt.

The words 'on a daily basis', then, in the context of schedule 3 descriptor 14, and its mirror descriptor under schedule 2, [para.]17 (a), means certainly more than for the majority of the time, that being the regulation 34 (2) test, and must mean more than frequently, that being the test of periodicity in [para.]17(b), but it does not mean literally every day or even on every working day. The essence is of this being an enduring position; one which is happening regularly, constantly or continually. It is for the tribunal to find the facts as to the frequency of the behaviour set out in the descriptor, and then apply this approach to those facts with their usual common sense" (paras 40–42).

**p.1090,** *correction to the Employment and Support Allowance Regulations 2008 (SI 2008/794) Sch.4, Pt 4, para.13 (Amounts—the components —support component)*

2.140A    Replace "£38.40" with "£34.80",

**p.1094,** *amendment of the Employment and Support Allowance Regulations 2008 (SI 2008/794) Sch.5 (Special cases)*

2.141    With effect from October 29, 2013, reg.13(1) and (31) of the Social Security (Miscellaneous Amendments) (No. 3) Regulations 2013 (SI 2013/2536) amended column 1 of Sch.5, Pt 2, para.13 to read as follows:

"**Patients**

13. Subject to paragraph 12, a single claimant who has been a patient for a continuous period of more than 52 weeks or, where the claimant is one of a couple, [each] member of the couple has been a patient for a continuous period of more than 52 weeks."

**p.1095,** *amendment to the Employment and Support Allowance Regulations 2008 (SI 2008/794) Sch.6 (Housing Costs) para.1(3)*

With effect from April 29, 2013, reg.37(7)(a) of the Universal Credit 2.142 (Consequential, Supplementary, Incidental and Miscellaneous Provisions) Regulations 2013 (SI 2013/630) omitted the word "or" after head (c) in para.1(3) and inserted the following new head after head (d):

"; or
   (e)  who is entitled to an award of universal credit the calculation of which includes an amount under regulation 27(1) of the Universal Credit Regulations 2013 in respect of the fact that that person has limited capability for work or limited capability for work and work-related activity, or would include such an amount but for regulation 27(4) or 29(4) of those Regulations;".

**pp.1111–1112,** *amendment to the Employment and Support Allowance Regulations 2008 (SI 2008/794) Sch.6 (Housing Costs) para.19*

With effect from April 29, 2013, reg.37(7)(b)(i) of the Universal 2.143 Credit (Consequential, Supplementary, Incidental and Miscellaneous Provisions) Regulations 2013 (SI 2013/630) omitted the word "or" after sub-para.(7)(g) of para.19 and inserted the following after sub-para. (7)(h):

"or
  (ha)  if the non-dependant is aged less than 25 and is entitled to an award of universal credit which is calculated on the basis that the non-dependant does not have any earned income;".

From the same date, reg.37(7)(b)(ii) of the same Regulations inserted the following new sub-paragraph after sub-para.(7) in para.19:

"(7A) For the purposes of sub-paragraph (7)(ha), "earned income" has the meaning given in regulation 52 of the Universal Credit Regulations 2013."

With effect from October 29, 2013, reg.13(36) of the Social Security (Miscellaneous Amendments) (No. 3) Regulations 2013 (SI 2013/2536) renamed para.19(7)(i) as para.19(7ZA) and in para.19(7ZA) substituted the words "For the purposes of sub-paragraph (7)(b)" for the words "in sub-paragraph (b)".

**pp.1114–1116,** *annotation to the Employment and Support Allowance Regulations 2008 (SI 2008/794) Sch.6 para.1(3)*

Paragraph 1(3) defines who is a "disabled person" for the purposes of 2.144 Sch.6. From April 29, 2013, following the commencement of universal credit, this includes a person whose award of universal credit contains a limited capability for work element or a limited capability for work and work-related activity element, or, in the case of a limited capability for work element, would do so but for the fact that the person satisfies the conditions for a carer element, or, in the case of joint claimants, would do so but for the fact that only one limited capability for work (or limited capability for work and work-related activity) element can be included even if both joint claimants meet the conditions for such an element (or elements).

**pp.1114–1116,** *annotation to the Employment and Support Allowance Regulations 2008 (SI 2008/794) Sch.6 para.19*

2.145    Paragraph 19(7) of Sch.6 lists those non-dependants in respect of whom no deduction from a claimant's housing costs is to be made. From April 29, 2013, following the commencement of universal credit, a person aged less than 25, who is entitled to an award of universal credit which is calculated on the basis that he does not have any earned income, is added to the list in para.19(7). On the meaning of "earned income" for the purposes of universal credit, see reg.52 of the Universal Credit Regulations and the notes to that regulation in Vol.V of this series.

**p.1120,** *amendment to the Employment and Support Allowance Regulations 2008 (SI 2008/794) Sch.8 (Sums to be disregarded in the calculation of income other than earnings) para.2A*

2.146    With effect from October 29, 2013, reg.13(37) of the Social Security (Miscellaneous Amendments) (No. 3) Regulations 2013 (SI 2013/2536) substituted the words "claimant participating as a service user" for the words "claimant's participation in a service user group" in para.2A.

**p.1121,** *amendment to the Employment and Support Allowance Regulations 2008 (SI 2008/794) Sch.8 (Sums to be disregarded in the calculation of income other than earnings) para.9*

2.147    With effect from April 29, 2013, reg.37(8) of the Universal Credit (Consequential, Supplementary, Incidental and Miscellaneous Provisions) Regulations 2013 (SI 2013/630) inserted the words ", universal credit" after the words "income support" in para.9(b).

**p.1125,** *amendment to the Employment and Support Allowance Regulations 2008 (SI 2008/794) Sch.8 (Sums to be disregarded in the calculation of income other than earnings) para.29*

2.148    With effect from April 1, 2013, art.11 of, and para.116(3)(a) of Part 1 of Sch.2 to, the National Treatment Agency (Abolition) and the Health and Social Care Act 2012 (Consequential, Transitional and Saving Provisions) Order 2013 (SI 2013/235) inserted the following new sub-paragraphs after sub-para.(d) in para.29:

"(da)  a clinical commissioning group;
(db)   the National Health Service Commissioning Board; or".

From the same date, art.11 of, and para.116(3)(b) of Part 1 of Sch.2 to, the same Regulations omitted sub-para.(e) in para.29, together with the word "or" following it.

**p.1134,** *amendment to the Employment and Support Allowance Regulations 2008 (SI 2008/794) Sch.9 (Capital to be disregarded) para.11*

With effect from April 29, 2013, reg.37(9)(a) of the Universal Credit **2.149** (Consequential, Supplementary, Incidental and Miscellaneous Provisions) Regulations 2013 (SI 2013/630) inserted the words ", universal credit" after the words "income-based jobseeker's allowance" in para. 11(1)(b).

From the same date, reg.37(9)(b) of the same Regulations inserted the words ", universal credit" after the words "income support" in para. 11(3)(a) and (b).

From the same date, reg.37(9)(c) of the same Regulations omitted the word "or" after para.11(3)(b)(ii) and inserted the following after para. 11(3)(b)(iii):

"; or
    (iv) in a case where universal credit is awarded to the claimant and another person as joint claimants, either the claimant or the other person, or both of them, received the relevant sum".

**p.1142,** *annotation to the Employment and Support Allowance Regulations 2008 (SI 2008/794) Sch.9 para.11*

The effect of the amendments to para.11 of Sch.9 made by reg.37(9) **2.150** of the Universal Credit (Consequential, Supplementary, Incidental and Miscellaneous Provisions) Regulations 2013 (SI 2013/630) with effect from April 29, 2013 is to add universal credit to the list of benefits, arrears, or any concessionary payment made to compensate for arrears due to non-payment of which, are disregarded under para.11.

**pp.1301–1302,** *annotation to the Social Security (Industrial Injuries) (Prescribed Diseases) Regulations 1985 (SI 1985/967) Sch.1 PD A14 (Osteoarthritis of the knee) (coal miners and related occupations) (carpet fitters and other layers of non-concrete floors)*

*GV v SSWP (II)* [2012] UKUT 208 (AAC) is now reported as [2013] **2.151** AACR 3.

**p.1346,** *amendment to the Vaccine Damage Regulations 1979 (SI 1979/432) reg.11 (decisions reversing earlier decisions made by the Secretary of State or appeal tribunals)*

With effect from October 28, 2013, reg.2(1) and (2) of the Social **2.152** Security, Child Support, Vaccine Damage and Other Payments (Decisions and Appeals) (Amendment) Regulations 2013 (SI 2013/2380) amended reg.11(2)(b) to read:

"(b) where the application is in respect of a decision of the Secretary of State, the application is made [at any time after notification of that decision was given but before a decision of an appeal tribunal has been made]; or".

**p.1347,** *amendment to the Vaccine Damage Regulations 1979 (SI 1979/432): insertion of a new reg.11A*

2.153 With effect from October 28, 2013, reg.2(1) and (3) of the Social Security, Child Support, Vaccine Damage and Other Payments (Decisions and Appeals) (Amendment) Regulations 2013 (SI 2013/2380) inserted after reg.11 a new reg.11A to read:

**"Consideration of reversal before appeal**

**11A.**—(1) This regulation applies in a case where—
 (a) the claimant's address is not in Northern Ireland;
 (b) the Secretary of State gives a person written notice of a decision; and
 (c) that notice includes a statement to the effect that there is a right of appeal to the First-tier Tribunal in relation to the decision only if the Secretary of State has considered an application for a reversal of the decision.

(2) In a case to which this regulation applies, a person has a right of appeal under section 4 of the Act in relation to the decision only if the Secretary of State has considered whether to reverse the decision under section 3A of the Act.

(3) The notice referred to in paragraph (1) must inform the person that, where the notice does not include a statement of the reasons for the decision, he may, within one month of the date of the notice, request that the Secretary of State provide him with written reasons.

(4) Where written reasons are requested under paragraph (3), the Secretary of State must provide them within 14 days of receipt of the request or as soon as practicable afterwards.

(5) Where, as the result of paragraph (2), there is no right of appeal against a decision, the Secretary of State may treat any purported appeal as an application for a reversal of the decision under section 3A of the Act."

# PART III

# UPDATING MATERIAL
# VOLUME II

# INCOME SUPPORT, JOBSEEKER'S ALLOWANCE, STATE PENSION CREDIT AND THE SOCIAL FUND

Commentary by

**Penny Wood**

**Richard Poynter**

**Nick Wikeley**

**David Bonner**

---

**Important preliminary note**

In this Part, "'Pathfinder' amendment or repeal" means one that applies only to those cases and areas in which "Pathfinder" pilots are operational. On this see the new Vol.V, *Universal Credit*, Part 4 dealing with transition and the key Welfare Reform Act 2012 Commencement Orders. These make the amendments operational from various dates on or after April 29, 2013.

**p.31,** *"Pathfinder" amendment to the Jobseekers Act 1995 s.1 (the jobseeker's allowance)*

With effect from various dates on or after April 29, 2013, ss.44(1), (2),   **3.001**
49(1), (2), 147 and Sch.14 Pt I of the Welfare Reform Act 2012
amended s.1 to read:

**"The jobseeker's allowance.**

1.—(1) An allowance, to be known as a jobseeker's allowance, shall be
payable in accordance with the provisions of this Act.
    (2) Subject to the provisions of this Act, a claimant is entitled to a
jobseeker's allowance if he–
    (a) [ . . . ]
    (b) has [accepted a claimant commitment];
    (c) [ . . . ]
    (d) satisfies the conditions set out in section 2;
    (e) is not engaged in remunerative work;
    (f) does not have limited capability for work;
    (g) is not receiving relevant education;
    (h) is under pensionable age; and
    (i) is in Great Britain.
    [(2A) . . .
    (2B) . . .
    (2C) . . .
    (2D) . . . .]
    (3) A jobseeker's allowance is payable in respect of a week.
    (4) [ . . . ]."

**pp.38–39,** *amendment to the Jobseekers Act 1995 s.2 (the contribution-based conditions)*

With effect from April 29, 2013, s.31 and Sch.2, para.35, of the   **3.002**
Welfare Reform Act 2012 amended s.2(3C) by inserting, before sub-
para.(a), a new sub-para.(za) to read:

    "(za) universal credit,".

**pp.38–39,** *"Pathfinder" amendment to the Jobseekers Act 1995 s.2 (the contribution-based conditions)*

With effect from various dates on or after April 29, 2013, s.147 and   **3.003**
Sch.14, Pt I of the Welfare Reform Act 2012 amended s.2(3C)(d) to
read:

    "(d) a [ . . . ] jobseeker's allowance, and".

**pp.38–39,** *modifications of the Jobseekers Act 1995 s.2 (the contribution-based conditions) with respect to share fisherman*

With effect from various dates after April 29, 2013, reg.69 of the   **3.004**
Jobseeker's Allowance Regulations 2013 (SI 2013/378) modified s.2 by

(a) inserting after "Class 1 contributions" in each place they appear the words "or special Class 2 contributions, and (b) inserting in subs.(4) after the definition of "relevant benefit year" the following definition:

"'special Class 2 contributions' means any Class 2 contributions paid by a share fisherman at the rate applicable to share fishermen in accordance with regulation 125(c) of the Social Security (Contributions) Regulations 2001.".

**pp.38–39,** *modifications of the Jobseekers Act 1995 s.2 (the contribution-based conditions) with respect to volunteer development workers*

3.005    With effect from various dates after April 29, 2013, reg.75 of the Jobseeker's Allowance Regulations 2013 (SI 2013/378) modified s.2 by inserting after "Class 1 contributions" in each place the occur the words "or Class 2 contributions under Case G of Part 9 of the Social Security (Contributions) Regulations 2001".

**pp.44–47,** *"Pathfinder" repeal of the Jobseekers Act 1995 ss.3 (the income-based conditions), 3A (the conditions for claims by joint-claim couples) and 3B (joint-claim couples: the nominated member)*

3.006    With effect from various dates on or after April 29, 2013, s.147 and Sch.14, Part I of the Welfare Reform Act 2012 repealed ss.3, 3A and 3B.

**pp.47–49,** *"Pathfinder" amendments to the Jobseekers Act 1995 s.4 (amount payable by way of jobseeker's allowance)*

3.007    With effect from various dates on or after April 29, 2013, s.147 and Sch.14, Part I of the Welfare Reform Act 2012 amended s.4 to read:

### "Amount payable by way of a jobseeker's allowance

4.—(1) In the case of a [ . . . ] jobseeker's allowance, the amount payable in respect of a claimant ("his personal rate") shall be calculated by—
   (a) determining the age-related amount applicable to him; and
   (b) making prescribed deductions in respect of earnings, pension payments, PPF payments and FAS payments.
(2) The age-related amount applicable to a claimant, for the purposes of subsection (1)(a), shall be determined in accordance with regulations.
   (3) [ . . . ].
   (3A) [ . . . ].
(4) Except in prescribed circumstances, a jobseeker's allowance shall not be payable where the amount otherwise payable would be less than a prescribed minimum.
(5) The applicable amount shall be such amount or the aggregate of such amounts as may be determined in accordance with regulations.
   (6)–(11A) *Repealed.*"

**pp.50–52,** *"Pathfinder" repeal of the Jobseekers Act 1995 s.4A (amount payable in respect of joint-claim couple)*

With effect from various dates on or after April 29, 2013, s.147 and    3.008
Sch.14, Part I of the Welfare Reform Act 2012 repealed s.4A.

**p.52,** *"Pathfinder" amendment to the Jobseekers Act 1995 s.5 (duration of a contribution-based jobseeker's allowance)*

With effect from various dates on or after April 29, 2013, s.147 and    3.009
Sch.14, Part I of the Welfare Reform Act 2012 amended s.5 to delete the
words "contribution-based" from the heading to the section and from
subss.(1), (2) and (3).

**pp.58–74,** *"Pathfinder" substitution of the Jobseekers Act 1995 ss.6–10 (dealing with "Jobseeking"), replacing them with new ss.6–6L (work-related requirements)*

With effect from various dates on or after April 29, 2013, s.49(1), (3)    3.010
of the Welfare Reform Act 2012 substituted for ss.6–10 and the italic
heading "Jobseeking" preceding them, new ss.6–6L to read:

*"Work-related requirements*

**Work-related requirements**

**6.**—(1) The following provisions of this Act provide for the Secretary
of State to impose work-related requirements with which claimants
must comply for the purposes of this Act.

(2) In this Act "work-related requirement" means—

(a) a work-focused interview requirement (see section 6B);

(b) a work preparation requirement (see section 6C);

(c) a work search requirement (see section 6D);

(d) a work availability requirement (see section 6E).

**Claimant commitment**

**6A.**—(1) A claimant commitment is a record of a claimant's responsibilities in relation to an award of a jobseeker's allowance.

(2) A claimant commitment is to be prepared by the Secretary of
State and may be reviewed and updated as the Secretary of State
thinks fit.

(3) A claimant commitment is to be in such form as the Secretary of
State thinks fit.

(4) A claimant commitment is to include—

(a) a record of the requirements that the claimant must comply
with under this Act (or such of them as the Secretary of State
considers it appropriate to include),

(b) any prescribed information, and

(c) any other information the Secretary of State considers it appropriate to include.

(5) For the purposes of this Act a claimant accepts a claimant commitment if, and only if, the claimant accepts the most up-to-date version of it in such manner as may be prescribed.

## Work-focused interview requirement

**6B.**—(1) In this Act a "work-focused interview requirement" is a requirement that a claimant participate in one or more work-focused interviews as specified by the Secretary of State.

(2) A work-focused interview is an interview for prescribed purposes relating to work or work preparation.

(3) The purposes which may be prescribed under subsection (2) include in particular that of making it more likely in the opinion of the Secretary of State that the claimant will obtain paid work (or more paid work or better-paid work).

(4) The Secretary of State may specify how, when and where a work-focused interview is to take place.

## Work preparation requirement

**6C.**—(1) In this Act a "work preparation requirement" is a requirement that a claimant take particular action specified by the Secretary of State for the purpose of making it more likely in the opinion of the Secretary of State that the claimant will obtain paid work (or more paid work or better-paid work).

(2) The Secretary of State may under subsection (1) specify the time to be devoted to any particular action.

(3) Action which may be specified under subsection (1) includes in particular—

(a) attending a skills assessment;
(b) improving personal presentation;
(c) participating in training;
(d) participating in an employment programme;
(e) undertaking work experience or a work placement;
(f) developing a business plan;
(g) any action prescribed for the purpose in subsection (1).

## Work search requirement

**6D.**—(1) In this Part a "work search requirement" is a requirement that a claimant take—

(a) all reasonable action, and
(b) any particular action specified by the Secretary of State, for the purpose of obtaining paid work (or more paid work or better-paid work).

(2) The Secretary of State may under subsection (1)(b) specify the time to be devoted to any particular action.

(3) Action which may be specified under subsection (1)(b) includes in particular—

(a) carrying out work searches;

(b) making applications;

(c) creating and maintaining an online profile;

(d) registering with an employment agency;

(e) seeking references;

(f) any other action prescribed for the purpose in subsection (1).

(4) Regulations may impose limitations on a work search requirement by reference to the work to which it relates; and the Secretary of State may in any particular case specify further such limitations on such a requirement.

(5) A limitation under subsection (4) may in particular be by reference to—

(a) work of a particular nature,

(b) work with a particular level of remuneration,

(c) work in particular locations, or

(d) work available for a certain number of hours per week or at particular times, and may be indefinite or for a particular period.

## Work availability requirement

**6E.**—(1) In this Act a "work availability requirement" is a requirement that a claimant be available for work.

(2) For the purposes of this section "available for work" means able and willing immediately to take up paid work (or more paid work or better-paid work).

(3) Regulations may impose limitations on a work availability requirement by reference to the work to which it relates; and the Secretary of State may in any particular case specify further such limitations on such a requirement.

(4) A limitation under subsection (3) may in particular be by reference to—

(a) work of a particular nature,

(b) work with a particular level of remuneration,

(c) work in particular locations, or

(d) work available for a certain number of hours per week or at particular times, and may be indefinite or for a particular period.

(5) Regulations may for the purposes of subsection (2) define what is meant by able and willing immediately to take up work.

## Imposition of work-related requirements

**6F.**—(1) The Secretary of State must, except in prescribed circumstances, impose on a claimant—

(a) a work search requirement, and

(b) a work availability requirement.

(2) The Secretary of State may, subject to this Act, impose either or both of the following on a claimant—

(a) a work-focused interview requirement;

(b) a work preparation requirement.

## Connected requirements

**6G.**—(1) The Secretary of State may require a claimant to participate in an interview for any purpose relating to—

(a) the imposition of a work-related requirement on the claimant;

(b) verifying the claimant's compliance with a work-related requirement;

(c) assisting the claimant to comply with a work-related requirement.

(2) The Secretary of State may specify how, when and where such an interview is to take place.

(3) The Secretary of State may, for the purpose of verifying the claimant's compliance with a work-related requirement, require a claimant to—

(a) provide to the Secretary of State information and evidence specified by the Secretary of State in a manner so specified;

(b) confirm compliance in a manner so specified.

(4) The Secretary of State may require a claimant to report to the Secretary of State any specified changes in their circumstances which are relevant to—

(a) the imposition of work-related requirements on the claimant;

(b) the claimant's compliance with a work-related requirement.

## Imposition of work-related and connected requirements: supplementary

**6H.**—(1) Regulations may make provision—

(a) where the Secretary of State may impose a requirement under the preceding provisions of this Act, as to when the requirement must or must not be imposed;

(b) where the Secretary of State may specify any action to be taken in relation to a requirement under the preceding provisions of this Act, as to what action must or must not be specified;

(c) where the Secretary of State may specify any other matter in relation to a such requirement, as to what must or must not be specified in respect of that matter.

(2) Where the Secretary of State may impose a work-focused interview requirement, or specify a particular action under section 6C(1) or 6D(1)(b), the Secretary of State must have regard to such matters as may be prescribed.

(3) Where the Secretary of State may impose a requirement under the preceding provisions of this Act, or specify any action to be taken in relation to such a requirement, the Secretary of State may revoke or change what has been imposed or specified.

(4) Notification of a requirement imposed under the preceding provisions of this Act (or any change to or revocation of such a requirement) is, if not included in the claimant commitment, to be in such manner as the Secretary of State may determine.

(5) Regulations must make provision to secure that, in prescribed circumstances, where a claimant has recently been a victim of domestic violence—

(a) a requirement imposed on the claimant under the preceding provisions of this Act ceases to have effect for a period of 13 weeks, and

(b) the Secretary of State may not impose any other requirement on the claimant during that period.

(6) For the purposes of subsection (5)—

(a) "domestic violence" has such meaning as may be prescribed;

(b) "victim of domestic violence" means a person on or against whom domestic violence is inflicted or threatened (and regulations under subsection (5) may prescribe circumstances in which a person is to be treated as being or not being a victim of domestic violence);

(c) a person has recently been a victim of domestic violence if a prescribed period has not expired since the violence was inflicted or threatened.

### Compliance with work-related and connected requirements

**6I.** Regulations may make provision as to circumstances in which a claimant is to be treated as having—

(a) complied with or not complied with any requirement imposed under the preceding provisions of this Act or any aspect of such a requirement, or

(b) taken or not taken any particular action specified by the Secretary of State in relation to such a requirement.

### Higher-level sanctions

**6J.**—(1) The amount of an award of jobseeker's allowance is to be reduced in accordance with this section in the event of a failure by a claimant which is sanctionable under this section.

(2) It is a failure sanctionable under this section if a claimant—

(a) fails for no good reason to comply with a requirement imposed by the Secretary of State under a work preparation requirement to undertake a work placement of a prescribed description;

(b) fails for no good reason to comply with a requirement imposed by the Secretary of State under a work search requirement to apply for a particular vacancy for paid work;

(c) fails for no good reason to comply with a work availability requirement by not taking up an offer of paid work;

(d) by reason of misconduct, or voluntarily and for no good reason, ceases paid work or loses pay.

(3) It is a failure sanctionable under this section if, at any time before making the claim by reference to which the award is made, the claimant—

(a) for no good reason failed to take up an offer of paid work, or

(b) by reason of misconduct, or voluntarily and for no good reason, ceased paid work or lost pay.

(4) For the purposes of subsections (2) and (3) regulations may provide—

(a) for circumstances in which ceasing to work or losing pay is to be treated as occurring or not occurring by reason of misconduct or voluntarily;

(b) for loss of pay below a prescribed level to be disregarded.

(5) Regulations are to specify—

(a) the amount of a reduction under this section;

(b) the period for which such a reduction has effect, not exceeding three years in relation to any failure sanctionable under this section.

(6) Regulations under subsection (5)(b) may in particular provide for the period of a reduction to depend on either or both of the following—

(a) the number of failures by the claimant sanctionable under this section;

(b) the period between such failures.

(7) Regulations may provide—

(a) for cases in which no reduction is to be made under this section;

(b) for a reduction under this section made in relation to an award that is terminated to be applied to any new award made within a prescribed period of the termination;

(c) for the termination or suspension of a reduction under this section.

**Other sanctions**

**6K.**—(1) The amount of an award of a jobseeker's allowance is to be reduced in accordance with this section in the event of a failure by a claimant which is sanctionable under this section.

(2) It is a failure sanctionable under this section if a claimant—

(a) fails for no good reason to comply with a work-related requirement;

(b) fails for no good reason to comply with a requirement under section 6G.

(3) But a failure by a claimant is not sanctionable under this section if it is also a failure sanctionable under section 6J.

(4) Regulations must specify—

(a) the amount of a reduction under this section;

(b) the period for which such a reduction has effect.

(5) Regulations under subsection (4)(b) may provide that a reduction under this section in relation to any failure is to have effect for—

(a) a period continuing until the claimant meets a compliance condition specified by the Secretary of State,

(b) a fixed period not exceeding 26 weeks which is—

(i) specified in the regulations, or

(ii) determined in any case by the Secretary of State, or

(c) a combination of both.

(6) In subsection (5)(a) "compliance condition" means—

(a) a condition that the failure ceases, or

(b) a condition relating to future compliance with a work-related requirement or a requirement under section 6G.

(7) A compliance condition specified under subsection (5)(a) may be—

(a) revoked or varied by the Secretary of State;

(b) notified to the claimant in such manner as the Secretary of State may determine.

(8) A period fixed under subsection (5)(b) may in particular depend on either or both the following—

(a) the number of failures by the claimant sanctionable under this section;

(b) the period between such failures.

(9) Regulations may provide—

(a) for cases in which no reduction is to be made under this section;

(b) for a reduction under this section made in relation to an award that is terminated to be applied to any new award made within a prescribed period of the termination;

(c) for the termination or suspension of a reduction under this section.

## Delegation and contracting out

**6L.**—(1) The functions of the Secretary of State under sections 6 to 6I may be exercised by, or by the employees of, such person as the Secretary of State may authorise for the purpose (an "authorised person").

(2) An authorisation given by virtue of this section may authorise the exercise of a function—

(a) wholly or to a limited extent;

(b) generally or in particular cases or areas;

(c) unconditionally or subject to conditions.

(3) An authorisation under this section—

(a) may specify its duration;

(b) may be varied or revoked at any time by the Secretary of State;

(c) does not prevent the Secretary of State or another person from exercising the function to which the authorisation relates.

(4) Anything done or omitted to be done by or in relation to an authorised person (or an employee of that person) in, or in connection with, the exercise or purported exercise of the function concerned is to be treated for all purposes as done or omitted to be done by or in relation to the Secretary of State or (as the case may be) an officer of the Secretary of State.

(5) Subsection (4) does not apply—

(a) for the purposes of so much of any contract made between the authorised person and the Secretary of State as relates to the exercise of the function, or

(b) for the purposes of any criminal proceedings brought in respect of anything done or omitted to be done by the authorised person (or an employee of that person).

(6) Where—

(a) the authorisation of an authorised person is revoked, and

(b) at the time of the revocation so much of any contract made between the authorised person and the Secretary of State as relates to the exercise of the function is subsisting, the authorised person is entitled to treat the contract as repudiated by the Secretary of State (and not as frustrated by reason of the revocation)."

For "new style JSA", the labour market conditions (jobseekers agreement; availability for work; and actively seeking work) are replaced by various "work related requirements", failure to comply with which can lead to sanctions: higher level sanctions, medium-level sanctions or lower level sanctions, resulting in reduction of JSA in the most extreme case for up to three years. See further the Jobseeker's Allowance Regulations 2013 (SI 2013/378), Pts 2 and 3 in the "New Legislation" section (Part I) of this Supplement. The relevant requirements now are:

(a) a work-focused interview requirement (see section 6B);

(b) a work preparation requirement (see section 6C);

(c) a work search requirement (see section 6D);

(d) a work availability requirement (see section 6E).

As regards "higher level sanctions" in s.6J, see the annotations to Jobseekers Act 1995, s.19 with respect to terms such as "misconduct", "voluntarily and for no good reason", "failure to apply".

**pp.75–76,** *"Pathfinder" amendment to the Jobseekers Act 1995 s.13 (Income and capital: income-based jobseeker's allowance)*

3.010A    With effect from various dates on or after April 29, 2013, s.147 of, and Sch.14, Part I to, the Welfare Reform Act 2012 repealed s.13.

**pp.83–89,** *"Pathfinder" repeal of the Jobseekers Act 1995 ss.15 (effect on other claimants), 15A (trade disputes: joint-claim couples), 16 (severe hardship) and 17 (reduced payments)*

3.011    With effect from various dates on or after April 29, 2013, s.147 and Sch.14, Pt I of the Welfare Reform Act repealed ss.15–17.

**pp.89–90,** *"Pathfinder" repeal of the Jobseekers Act 1995 s.17A (schemes for assisting persons to obtain employment: "work for your benefit" schemes etc.)*

3.012    With effect from various dates on or after April 29, 2013, s.147 Sch.14, Pt I of the Welfare Reform Act amended s.17A(10) by repealing the definition of "claimant", and then s.147 and Sch.1, Part 4 repealed the whole section insofar as not already repealed.

**p.91,** *"Pathfinder" repeal of the Jobseekers Act 1995 s.17B (section 17A: supplemental)*

With effect from various dates on or after April 29, 2013, s.147 and Sch.14, Pt 4 of the Welfare Reform Act repealed s.17A.     3.013

**pp.92–112,** *"Pathfinder" repeal of the Jobseekers Act 1995 ss.19 (higher level sanctions), 19A (other sanctions), 19B (claimants ceasing to be available for employment etc.), 19C (hardship payments)*

With effect from various dates on or after April 29, 2013, s.147 and Sch.14, Pt 4 of the Welfare Reform Act repealed these sections. In "Pathfinder" cases in the relevant districts, new ss.6–6L thus govern the matter of sanctions in respect of work-related requirements such as ceasing paid work or losing pay through misconduct, or voluntarily leaving without good reason, or failing without good reason to comply with a work-related requirement. See further, update to pp.58–74, above.     3.014

**p.112,** *amendment to the Jobseekers Act 1995 s.19C (Hardship Payments)*

It would appear on closer examination that this section is probably not in force. Although Welfare Reform Act 2012 s.46 (inserting ss.19–19C) was originally brought into force by art.2(6) of the Welfare Reform Act 2012 (Commencement No. 2) Order (SI 2012/1246) as from October 14, 2012, art.2(6) was revoked by art.2(7) of the Welfare Reform Act 2012 (Commencement No. 4) Order 2012 (SI 2012/2530). Although art.2(2)(a) of the No. 4 Order indeed brought Welfare Reform Act 2012 s.46(1) into force on October 22, 2012, its commencement was limited to the "purposes of the substitution of sections 19 to 19B of the Jobseekers Act 1995", thus, on a strict reading, suggesting that s.19C was not included. The text of the "Blue Books", however, also incorporates s.19C as in force, as did Westlaw, and the Explanatory Notes to the Welfare Reform Bill which became the 2012 Act clearly envisaged that ss.19–19C would be in force until transfer to universal credit was completely rolled out. Since s.19C only confers rule-making powers, the issue of whether it is in force may well not arise before tribunals, and the section itself has been repealed as regards "Pathfinder" cases in relevant areas. See update to pp.92–112, above.     3.015

**pp.112–113,** *"Pathfinder" amendments to the Jobseekers Act 1995 s.20 (exemptions from section 19 and 19A)*

With effect from various dates on or after April 29, 2013, s.147 and Sch.14, Pt 4 of the Welfare Reform Act repealed s.20(1)–(3), (7) and (8).     3.016

**pp.115–116,** *"Pathfinder" repeal of the Jobseekers Act 1995 s.20E (contracting out)*

3.017    With effect from various dates on or after April 29, 2013, s.147 and Sch.14, Pt 4 of the Welfare Reform Act repealed s.20E. In "Pathfinder" cases in relevant areas the matter of contracting out various functions with respect to JSA is instead dealt with by new s.6L. See update to pp.58–74, above.

**p.117,** *"Pathfinder" amendment to the Jobseekers Act 1995 s.23 (Recovery of sums in respect of maintenance)*

3.017A    With effect from various dates on or after April 29, 2013, s.147 of, and Sch.14, Part I to, the Welfare Reform Act 2012 repealed s.23.

**pp.118–119,** *"Pathfinder" amendment to the Jobseekers Act 1995 s.26 (The back to work bonus)*

3.017B    With effect from various dates on or after April 29, 2013, s.147 of, and Sch.14, Part I to, the Welfare Reform Act 2012 repealed s.26.

**p.121,** *"Pathfinder" amendment to the Jobseekers Act 1995 s.35(1) (Interpretation—definition of "claimant")*

3.017C    With effect from various dates on or after April 29, 2013 s.147 and Sch.14, Pt 1 of the Welfare Reform Act 2012 amended the definition of "claimant" in s.35(1) by repealing the words from "except" to the end.

**p.121,** *"Pathfinder" amendment to the Jobseekers Act 1995 s.35(1) (Interpretation—definition of "contribution-based jobseeker's allowance")*

3.017D    With effect from various dates on or after April 29, 2013 s.147 and Sch.14, Pt 1 of the Welfare Reform Act 2012 repealed the definition of "contribution-based jobseeker's allowance" in s.35(1).

**p.122,** *"Pathfinder" amendment to the Jobseekers Act 1995 s.35(1) (Interpretation—definition of "income-based jobseeker's allowance")*

3.017E    With effect from various dates on or after April 29, 2013 s.147 and Sch.14, Pt 1 of the Welfare Reform Act 2012 repealed the definition of "income-based jobseeker's allowance" in s.35(1).

**p.122,** *"Pathfinder" amendment to the Jobseekers Act 1995 s.35(1) (Interpretation—definition of "income-related employment and support allowance")*

3.017F    With effect from various dates on or after April 29, 2013 s.147 and Sch.14 Pt 1 of the Welfare Reform Act 2012 repealed the definition of "income-related employment and support allowance" in s.35(1).

**p.122,** *"Pathfinder" amendment to the Jobseekers Act 1995 s.35(1) (Interpretation—definitions of "joint-claim couple" and "joint claim jobseeker's allowance")*

With effect from various dates on or after April 29, 2013 s.147 and Sch.14 Pt 1 of the Welfare Reform Act 2012 repealed the definitions of "joint-claim couple" and "joint-claim jobseeker's allowance" in s.35(1).    **3.017G**

**p.122,** *"Pathfinder" amendment to the Jobseekers Act 1995 s.35(1) (Interpretation—definition of "the nominated member")*

With effect from various dates on or after April 29, 2013 s.147 and Sch.14, Pt 1 of the Welfare Reform Act 2012 repealed the definition of "the nominated member" in s.35(1).    **3.017H**

**p.130,** *amendment to the Jobseekers Act 1995 Sch.1 para.2 (limited capability for work)*

With effect from April 29, 2013, reg.10 of the Universal Credit (Consequential, Supplementary, Incidental and Miscellaneous Provisions) Regulations 2013. (SI 2013/630) amended para.2 to read:    **3.018**

"**2.**—(1) The question whether a person has, or does not have, limited capability for work shall be determined, for the purposes of this Act, in accordance with the provisions of Part 1 of the Welfare Reform Act 2007 (employment and support allowance)[or Part 1 of the Welfare Reform Act 2012 (universal credit) as the Secretary of State considers appropriate in the person's case].

(2) References in Part 1 of the Welfare Reform Act 2007 to the purposes of that Part shall be construed, where the provisions of that Part have effect for the purposes of this Act, as references to the purposes of this Act.

[(3) References in Part 1 of the Welfare Reform Act 2012 to the purposes of that Part are to be construed, where the provisions of that Part have effect for the purposes of this Act, as references to the purposes of this Act.]"

**p.130,** *"Pathfinder" amendment to the Jobseekers Act 1995 Sch.1 para.6 (employment protection sums)*

With effect from various dates on or after April 29, 2013, s.147 and Sch.14, Pt I of the Welfare Reform Act amended para.6(1) by deleting the words "contribution-based".    **3.019**

**pp.131–132,** *"Pathfinder" repeals of the Jobseekers Act 1995 Sch.1 paras 8, 8A, 9 (dealing with "exemptions") and 10 (claims yet to be determined and suspended payments)*

With effect from various dates on or after April 29, 2013, s.147 and Sch.14, Pt1 of the Welfare Reform Act deleted paras 8, 8A (repealed also    **3.020** by Sch.1, Part 4), 9, 9A, 9B, 9C, 9D and 10. In "Pathfinder" cases in relevant areas, the matter of exemption from "work-related requirements is dealt with by new ss.6–6L and the JSA Regs 2013. See update to pp.58–74, above, and the JSA Regs 2013 in the "New Legislation" section of this Supplement.

**p.133,** *"Pathfinder" amendment to the Jobseekers Act 1995 Sch.1 para.11 (presence in and absence from Great Britain))*

3.021    With effect from various dates on or after April 29, 2013, s.147 and Sch.14, Pt I of the Welfare Reform Act amended para.11(1) by deleting the words "contribution-based".

**pp.133–134,** *"Pathfinder" amendment to the Jobseekers Act 1995 Sch.1 para.16 (employment on ships etc.)*

3.022    With effect from various dates on or after April 29, 2013, s.147 and Sch.14, Pt I of the Welfare Reform Act amended para.16(1) and 16(2)(d) by deleting from them the words "contribution-based".

**p.134,** *"Pathfinder" amendment to the Jobseekers Act 1995 Sch.1 para.18 (Benefits Acts purposes)*

3.023    With effect from various dates on or after April 29, 2013, s.147 Sch.14, Pt I of the Welfare Reform Act amended para.18 by deleting sub-paras (b) and (c).

**p.143,** *annotation to State Pension Credit Act 2002 s.1 (entitlement)*

3.024    In *NB v Secretary of State for Work and Pensions (SPC)* [2013] UKUT 266 (AAC), an overpayment appeal, Judge Wright held that living on a British registered boat outside UK territorial waters was not "in Great Britain" for the purpose of s.1(2)(a) (following *R(IS) 8/06*). However, the claimant will have been in Great Britain for any period that he was either on land in the United Kingdom or on his boat when in UK waters, and the tribunal erred in law in not enquiring into this aspect. Remitting the appeal to a new tribunal, the Judge directed it to consider whether the temporary absence rule applied for any period (which provides that a claimant will continue to be entitled to SPC for 13 weeks while not in Great Britain if the period of absence is unlikely to exceed 52 weeks and he continues to satisfy the other conditions of entitlement; see reg.3).

**pp.175–176,** *annotation to the Age-Related Payments Act 2004*

3.025    Add the following paragraph:

"More recently, the power under s.7 of the Act has been used to make payments to people who bought a with-profits annuity from the Equitable Life Assurance Society on or before 31 August 1992, and were alive and aged over 60 on 20 March 2013. Such people are not eligible for compensation under the main Equitable Life Payments Scheme.

Under the Transfer of Functions (Age-Related Payments) Order 2013 (SI 2013/1442), the function of the Secretary of State under s.7 is exercisable concurrently with the Treasury, in so far as it relates to such payments and a consequential amendment was made to the section to reflect that transfer. The payments themselves (£5,000 for each 'qualifying Equitable Life annuitant' and an additional £5,000 for each such annuitant who was in receipt of SPC on November 1, 2013) are authorised by the Age-Related Payments Regulations 2013 (SI 2013/2980).

Payments to a limited class the policy-holders of a particular mutual Society cannot be described as part of the social security system (even though they are said to be made in recognition of 'the particular financial pressures this particular group are under' rather than as compensation for maladministration (see the Explanatory Memorandum to SI 2013/2980). For that reason, the text of the Order and the Regulations (and the amendment to s.7 made by the former) have not been reproduced in this Supplement. Note, however, that—by reg.5 of SI 2013/2980 and s.6 of the Act—no account is to be taken when considering a person's entitlement to benefit under an enactment relating to social security (irrespective of the name or nature of the benefit), or to a tax credit."

**p.181,** *annotation to the Child Support Act 1991 s.43 (Recovery of child support maintenance by deduction from benefit)*

From November 25, 2013, the deduction from benefit where maintenance liability has been assessed under the 2012 scheme has been increased from £5 to £7. This increased rate does not apply to cases assessed under the 1993 or 2003 schemes.    3.026

**p.197,** *amendment of the Income Support (General) Regulations 1987 (SI 1987/1967) reg.2(1) (Interpretation—definition of "contribution-based jobseeker's allowance")*

With effect from April 29, 2013, reg.28(1) and (2)(a) of the Universal Credit (Consequential, Supplementary, Incidental and Miscellaneous Provisions) Regulations 2013 (SI 2013/630) amended reg.2(1) by inserting the following definition immediately after the definition of "the Contributions and Benefits Act":    3.027

"'contribution-based jobseeker's allowance' means an allowance under the Jobseekers Act 1995 as amended by the provisions of Part 1 of Schedule 14 to the 2012 Act that remove references to an income-based allowance, and a contribution-based allowance under the Jobseekers Act 1995 as that Act has effect apart from those provisions;"

**p.197,** *amendment of the Income Support (General) Regulations 1987 (SI 1987/1967) reg.2(1) (Interpretation—definition of "contributory employment and support allowance")*

With effect from April 29, 2013, reg.28(1) and (2)(b) of the Universal Credit (Consequential, Supplementary, Incidental and Miscellaneous    3.028

313

Provisions) Regulations 2013 (SI 2013/630) substituted the following definition for the definition of "contributory employment and support allowance" in reg.2(1):

"'contributory employment and support allowance' means an allowance under Part 1 of the Welfare Reform Act as amended by the provisions of Schedule 3, and Part 1 of Schedule 14, to the 2012 Act that remove references to an income-related allowance, and a contributory allowance under Part 1 of the Welfare Reform Act as that Part has effect apart from those provisions;"

**p.198,** *amendment of the Income Support (General) Regulations 1987 (SI 1987/1967) reg.2(1) (Interpretation—definition of 'enactment')*

3.029    With effect from October 29, 2013, reg.4(1) and (2) of the Social Security (Miscellaneous Amendments) (No. 3) Regulations 2013 (SI 2013/2536) amended the definition of 'enactment' in reg.2(1) to read as follows:

"'enactment' includes an enactment comprised in, or in an instrument made under, an Act of the Scottish Parliament [or the National Assembly for Wales];"

**p.202,** *amendment of the Income Support (General) Regulations 1987 (SI 1987/1967), reg.2(1) (Interpretation—definition of "service user group")*

3.030    With effect from April 1, 2013, reg.11 and Sch.2, Pt 1, para.10(1) and (2) of the National Treatment Agency (Abolition) and the Health and Social Care Act 2012 (Consequential, Transitional and Saving Provisions) Order 2013. (SI 2013/235) added the following paragraphs after para.(f) in the definition of "service user group" in reg.2(1):

"(fa)    the National Institute for Health and Care Excellence in consequence of a function under Part 8 of the Health and Social Care Act 2012,

(fb)    a clinical commissioning group in consequence of a function under section 14Z2 of the National Health Service Act 2006,

(fc)    the National Health Service Commissioning Board in consequence of a function under section 13Q of the National Health Service Act 2006,".

**p.204,** *amendment of the Income Support (General) Regulations 1987 (SI 1987/1967) reg.2(1) (Interpretation—definition of "universal credit")*

3.031    With effect from April 29, 2013, reg.28(1) and (2)(c) of the Universal Credit (Consequential, Supplementary, Incidental and Miscellaneous Provisions) Regulations 2013 (SI 2013/630) amended reg.2(1) by inserting the following definition immediately after the definition of 'training allowance':

"'universal credit' means universal credit under Part 1 of the 2012 Act;"

**p.236,** *amendment to the Income Support (General) Regulations 1987 (SI 1987/1967) reg.4ZA (Prescribed categories of person)*

With effect from October 29, 2013, reg.4(3) of the Social Security **3.032**
(Miscellaneous Amendments) (No. 3) Regulations 2013 (SI 2013/2536)
omitted para.(3)(a) and the word "or" immediately following it in
reg.4ZA.

**p.240,** *annotation to the Income Support (General) Regulations 1987 (SI 1987/1967) reg.4ZA(3)(a)*

Under reg.2(1) of, and para.1 of the Schedule to, the Social Security **3.033**
(Immigration and Asylum) Consequential Amendments Regulations
2000 (SI 2000/636), s.115 of the Immigration and Asylum Act 1999
(which excludes "persons subject to immigration control" from certain
benefits) did not apply to people whose leave to enter or remain in the
United Kingdom was subject to the condition that they did not have
recourse to public funds and who had previously supported themselves
without such recourse, but who found themselves temporarily without
money because remittances from abroad had been interrupted. They
were eligible for income-related benefits for a maximum of 42 days
during any one period of leave (and social fund payments). Paragraph 1
of the Schedule to the 2000 Regulations has been abolished with effect
from October 29, 2013 by reg.9(3) of the Social Security (Miscellaneous
Amendments) (No. 3) Regulations 2013 (SI 2013/2536)—according to
the Explanatory Memorandum that accompanies those Regulations on
the basis that this provision is rarely used because people could use credit
cards, etc. to tide them over. Hence the omission of reg.4ZA(3)(a) with
effect from October 29, 2013 (and of the other income-related benefit
provisions that involved entitlement under para.1 of the Schedule to the
2000 Regulations).

**pp.265–266,** *amendment to the Income Support (General) Regulations 1987 (SI 1987/1967) reg.13(2) (Circumstances in which persons in relevant education may be entitled to income support)*

With effect from June 24, 2013, art.17(1) of, and para.12(2) of Sch.1, **3.034**
Part 2 to, the Children's Hearings (Scotland) Act 2011 (Consequential
and Transitional Provisions and Savings) Order 2013 (SI 2013/1465)
inserted the words ", or by virtue of any order or warrant made under the
Children's Hearings (Scotland) Act 2011," after the words "(promotion
of children's welfare by local authorities and by children's hearings etc.)"
in reg.13(2)(dd).

With effect from October 29, 2013, reg.4(4) of the Social Security
(Miscellaneous Amendments) (No. 3) Regulations 2013 (SI 2013/2536)
omitted sub-para.(bc) and the word "or" immediately following it in
reg.13(2).

**p.270,** *annotation to the Income Support (General) Regulations 1987 (SI 1987/1967) reg.13(2)(bc)*

Regulation 13(2)(bc) has been omitted with effect from October 29, **3.035**
2013 due to the abolition of para.1 of the Schedule to the Social Security

(Immigration and Asylum) Consequential Amendments Regulations 2000 (SI 2000/636). See further the note to reg.4ZA of the Income Support (General) Regulations 1987, above.

**p.273,** *amendment of the Income Support (General) Regulations 1987 (SI 1987/1967) reg.14(2) (Persons of a prescribed description)*

3.036  With effect from April 29, 2013, reg.28(1) and (3) of the Universal Credit (Consequential, Supplementary, Incidental and Miscellaneous Provisions) Regulations 2013 (SI 2013/630) amended reg.2(1) by revoking the word "or" between sub-paras (c) and (d) and inserting the following words at the end of sub-para.(d):

> "; or
> (e) entitled to universal credit"

**p.298,** *amendment of the Income Support (General) Regulations 1987 (SI 1987/1967) reg.21AA(4)(f) (Special cases: supplemental—persons from abroad)*

3.037  With effect from July 1, 2013, reg.2 of the Social Security (Croatia) Amendment Regulations 2013 (SI 2013/1474) amended reg.21AA(4)(f) to read as follows:

> "(f) a person who is treated as a worker for the purpose of the definition of "qualified person" in regulation 6(1) of the Immigration (European Economic Area) Regulations 2006 pursuant to—
>> (i) regulation 6 of the Accession (Immigration and Worker Authorisation) Regulations 2006 (right of residence of a Bulgarian or Romanian who is an 'accession State national subject to worker authorisation'), or
>> (ii) regulation 5 of the Accession of Croatia (Immigration and Worker Authorisation) Regulations 2013 (right of residence of a Croatian who is an 'accession State national subject to worker authorisation');"

**p.298,** *amendment of the Income Support (General) Regulations 1987 (SI 1987/1967) reg.21AA(4) (Special cases: supplemental—persons from abroad)*

3.038  With effect from October 29, 2013, reg.4(1) and (5) of the Social Security (Miscellaneous Amendments) (No. 3) Regulations 2013 (SI 2013/2536) amended reg.21AA(4) by substituting the following for sub-para.(h):

> "(h) a person who has been granted leave or who is deemed to have been granted leave outside the rules made under section 3(2) of the Immigration Act 1971(11) where that leave is—

    (i) discretionary leave to enter or remain in the United Kingdom;

   (ii) leave to remain under the Destitution Domestic Violence concession; or

  (iii) leave deemed to have been granted by virtue of regulation 3 of the Displaced Persons (Temporary Protection) Regulations 2005;"

and by adding the word "or" at the end of sub-para.(hh) and revoking sub-paras (j) and (k).

**p.303,** *annotation to the Income Support (General) Regulations 1987 (SI 1987/1967), reg.21AA (Special cases: supplemental—persons from abroad-Who are EEA nationals?)*

Croatia acceded to the European Union on July 1, 2013. During a 3.039 transitional period that will currently end on June 30, 2018, the rights of Croatian nationals to reside in the United Kingdom as workers and workseekers are subject to the scheme of worker authorisation established by the Accession of Croatia (Immigration and Worker Authorisation) Regulations 2013 (SI 2013/1460): see Pt I of this Supplement. The equivalent restrictions on the rights of Bulgarian and Croatian nationals under the Accession (Immigration and Worker Authorisation) Regulations 2006 came to an end on December 31, 2013.

**p.305,** *annotation to the Income Support (General) Regulations 1987 (SI 1987/1967), reg.21AA (Special cases: supplemental—persons from abroad-Nationals of Turkey and Croatia)*

Croatia acceded to the European Union on July 1, 2013.       3.040

**p.309,** *annotation to the Income Support (General) Regulations 1987 (SI 1987/1967) reg 21AA (Special cases: supplemental—persons from abroad—The 2006 Regulations)*

With effect from January 1, 2014, reg.4 and Sch.1, para.8 of the 3.041 Immigration (European Economic Area) (Amendment) (No. 2) Regulations 2013 (SI 2013/3032) amended reg.13(4) of the Immigration (European Economic Area) Regulations 2006 (which is reproduced in the commentary to reg.21AA) to read as follows:

"(4) A person who otherwise satisfies the criteria in this regulation will not be entitled to reside in the United Kingdom under this regulation where the Secretary of State has made a decision under [—

    (a) regulation 19(3)(b), 20(1) or 20A(1); or

    (b) regulation 21B(2), where that decision was taken in the preceding twelve months.]"

**p.309,** *annotation to the Income Support (General) Regulations 1987 (SI 1987/1967) reg.21AA (Special cases: supplemental—persons from abroad—The 2006 Regulations)*

3.042     With effect from January 1, 2014, reg.4 and Sch.1, para.9 of the Immigration (European Economic Area) (Amendment) (No. 2) Regulations 2013 (SI 2013/3032) amended reg.14(5) of the Immigration (European Economic Area) Regulations 2006 (which is reproduced in the commentary to reg.21AA) to read as follows:

> "(5) A person who otherwise satisfies the criteria in this regulation will not be entitled to a right to reside in the United Kingdom under this regulation where the Secretary of State has made a decision under[—
> (a) regulation 19(3)(b), 20(1) or 20A(1); or
> (b) regulation 21B(2) (not including such a decision taken on the basis of regulation 21B(1)(a) or (b)), where that decision was taken in the preceding twelve months.]"

**pp.309–310,** *annotation to the Income Support (General) Regulations 1987 (SI 1987/1967) reg.21AA (Special cases: supplemental—persons from abroad—The 2006 Regulations)*

3.043     With effect from January 1, 2014, reg.4 and Sch.1, para.10 of the Immigration (European Economic Area) (Amendment) (No. 2) Regulations 2013 (SI 2013/3032) amended reg.15(3) of the Immigration (European Economic Area) Regulations 2006 (which is reproduced in the commentary to reg.21AA) to read as follows:

> "(3) A person who satisfies the criteria in this regulation will not be entitled to a permanent right to reside in the United Kingdom where the Secretary of State has made a decision under [—
> (a) regulation 19(3)(b), 20(1) or 20A(1); or
> (b) regulation 21B(2) (not including such a decision taken on the basis of regulation 21B(1)(a) or (b)), where that decision was taken in the preceding twelve months.]"

**pp.310–311,** *annotation to the Income Support (General) Regulations 1987 (SI 1987/1967) reg.21AA (Special cases: supplemental—persons from abroad-The 2006 Regulations)*

3.044     With effect from January 1, 2014, reg.4 and Sch.1, para.1 of the Immigration (European Economic Area) (Amendment) (No. 2) Regulations 2013 (SI 2013/3032) amended reg.15A(9) of the Immigration (European Economic Area) Regulations 2006 (which is reproduced in the commentary to reg.21AA) to read as follows:

> "(9) A person who otherwise satisfies the criteria in paragraph (2), (3), (4) [2, (4A)] or (5) will not be entitled to a derivative right to reside in the United Kingdom where the Secretary of State has made a decision under [—

(a) regulation 19(3)(b), 20(1) or 20A(1); or
(b) regulation 21B(2), where that decision was taken in the preceding twelve months.]"

**p.319,** *annotation to the Income Support (General) Regulations 1987 (SI 1987/1967) reg.21AA (Special cases: supplemental—persons from abroad-Extended right of residence—Qualified persons—Workers and workseekers/ jobseekers—Persons who retain the status of worker)*

With effect from January 1, 2014, reg.4 and Sch.1, para.3 of the Immigration (European Economic Area) (Amendment) (No. 2) Regulations 2013 (SI 2013/3032) amended reg.6 of the Immigration (European Economic Area) Regulations 2006 (which is reproduced in the commentary to reg.21AA) so that the provisions on the retention of worker status now read as follows: 3.045

"(2) Subject to [2 regulations 7A(4) and 7B(4)], a person who is no longer working shall not cease to be treated as a worker for the purpose of paragraph (1)(b) if—]
(a) he is temporarily unable to work as the result of an illness or accident;
[(b) he is in duly recorded involuntary unemployment after having been employed in the United Kingdom for at least one year, provided that he—
    (i) has registered as a jobseeker with the relevant employment office; and
    (ii) satisfies conditions A and B;
(ba) he is in duly recorded involuntary unemployment after having been employed in the United Kingdom for less than one year, provided that he—
    (i) has registered as a jobseeker with the relevant employment office; and
    (ii) satisfies conditions A and B;]
(c) he is involuntarily unemployed and has embarked on vocational training; or
(d) he has voluntarily ceased working and embarked on vocational training that is related to his previous employment.
[(2A) A person to whom paragraph (2)(ba) applies may only retain worker status for a maximum of six months.]
. . .
[(7) A person may not retain the status of a worker pursuant to paragraph (2)(b), or jobseeker pursuant to paragraph (1)(a), for longer than six months unless he can provide compelling evidence that he is continuing to seek employment and has a genuine chance of being engaged.]"

The references to "conditions A and B" in sub-paras (6) and (6a) are to the amended definition of "jobseeker" (see below).
The amendments to reg.6 (other than the substitution of the words "regulations 7A(4) and 7B(4)" for the words "regulation 7A(4)") are

subject to the transitional provision established by reg.6 and Sch.3 para.1, which is in the following terms:

**"Qualified person**

**1.** For the purposes of paragraph 3(b) to (e) of Schedule 1—
  (a) any period of employment in the United Kingdom before the coming into force of these Regulations is to be treated as a period of employment under regulation 6 of the 2006 Regulations as amended by these Regulations; and
  (b) any period—
      (i) of duly recorded involuntary unemployment; or
      (ii) during which a person was a jobseeker for the purposes of regulation 6(1)(a) of the 2006 Regulations,
      before the coming into force of these Regulations is to be disregarded."

**p.321,** *annotation to the Income Support (General) Regulations 1987 (SI 1987/1967) reg.21AA (Special cases: supplemental—persons from abroad-Extended right of residence—Qualified persons—Workers and workseekers/ jobseekers—Persons who retain the status of worker—Temporarily unable to work—Pregnancy—Opinion of the Advocate General in* Saint Prix v Secretary of State for Work and Pensions*)*

3.046   The opinion of Advocate General Wahl in *Saint Prix v Secretary of State for Work and Pensions* (Case C-507/12) was given on December 12, 2013. The Advocate General proposed that the questions referred by the Supreme Court should be answered as follows:

"Article 7(3)(a) of [the Directive], read in light of Article 45 TFEU, is to be interpreted as meaning that a woman who can be deemed temporarily unable to work because of the physical constraints of the late stages of pregnancy must retain the status of worker. The status of worker is retained until such time as it is reasonable for the woman in question to return to work, or to seek work, after the birth of her child. To ensure that the principle of non-discrimination on grounds of nationality is observed, that period cannot be shorter than the period provided for under the national legislation governing the period during which pregnant women are exempted from being available for work, or from having actively to seek work."

At the time of going to press, no date had been fixed for the delivery of the Court's judgment.

**p.325,** *annotation to the Income Support (General) Regulations 1987 (SI 1987/1967) reg.21AA (Special cases: supplemental—persons from abroad —Extended right of residence—Qualified persons—Workers and workseekers/jobseekers—"Workseekers" and "Jobseekers")*

3.047   With effect from January 1, 2014, reg.4 and Sch.1 para.3 of the Immigration (European Economic Area) (Amendment) (No. 2) Regulations 2013 (SI 2013/3032) amended the definition of "jobseeker" in reg.6(4) of the Immigration (European Economic Area) Regulations 2006 (to which reference is made in the commentary to reg.21AA) to read as follows:

"(4) For the purpose of paragraph (1)(a), a 'jobseeker' is a person who satisfies conditions A and B.

(5) Condition A is that the person—

(a) entered the United Kingdom in order to seek employment; or

(b) is present in the United Kingdom seeking employment, immediately after enjoying a right to reside pursuant to paragraph (1)(b) to (e) (disregarding any period during which worker status was retained pursuant to paragraph (2)(b) or (ba)).

(6) Condition B is that the person can provide evidence that he is seeking employment and has a genuine chance of being engaged.

(7) A person may not retain the status of a worker pursuant to paragraph (2)(b), or jobseeker pursuant to paragraph (1)(a), for longer than six months unless he can provide compelling evidence that he is continuing to seek employment and has a genuine chance of being engaged.]"

The amendments to reg.6 (other than the substitution of the words "regulations 7A(4) and 7B(4)" for the words "regulation 7A(4)") are subject to the transitional provision established by reg.6 and Sch.3 para.1, which is in the following terms:

## "Qualified person

1. For the purposes of paragraph 3(b) to (e) of Schedule 1—

(a) any period of employment in the United Kingdom before the coming into force of these Regulations is to be treated as a period of employment under regulation 6 of the 2006 Regulations as amended by these Regulations; and

(b) any period—

(i) of duly recorded involuntary unemployment; or

(ii) during which a person was a jobseeker for the purposes of regulation 6(1)(a) of the 2006 Regulations,

before the coming into force of these Regulations is to be disregarded."

**p.325,** *annotation to the Income Support (General) Regulations 1987 (SI 1987/1967), reg.21AA (Special cases: supplemental—persons from abroad-Qualified persons—Jobseekers—Decision in* Shabani v Secretary of State for the Home Department*)*

In *Shabani (EEA—jobseekers; nursery education)* [2013] UKUT 00315 (IAC) the Home Secretary conceded, following an interdepartmental consultation, that "it is accepted that someone who has come to the UK as a jobseeker, has obtained work, becomes unemployed, and then sought work again is a jobseeker within the meaning of the Directive and [regulation] 6(1)(a) of the EEA Regulations": see para.10 of the decision.   **3.048**

**p.329,** *annotation to the Income Support (General) Regulations 1987 (SI 1987/1967) reg.21AA (Special cases: supplemental—persons from abroad—Extended right of residence—Qualified persons—Self-sufficient persons—Decision of the ECJ in* Pensionsversicherungsanstalt v Peter Brey*)*

3.049      The decision of the ECJ in *Pensionsversicherungsanstalt v Peter Brey* (Case C-140/12) was given on September 19, 2013. The Court ruled that:

> "EU law—in particular, as it results from Article 7(1)(b), Article 8(4) and Article 24(1) and (2) of [the Directive]—must be interpreted as precluding national legislation, such as that at issue in the main proceedings, which, even as regards the period following the first three months of residence, automatically—whatever the circumstances —bars the grant of a benefit, such as the compensatory supplement [see the main work], to a national of another Member State who is not economically active, on the grounds that, despite having been issued with a certificate of residence, he does not meet the necessary require-ments for obtaining the legal right to reside on the territory of the first Member State for a period of longer than three months, since obtain-ing that right of residence is conditional upon that national having sufficient resources not to apply for the benefit."

**p.331,** *annotation to the Income Support (General) Regulations 1987 (SI 1987/1967), reg.21AA (Special cases: supplemental—persons from abroad-Qualified persons—Students)*

3.050      For details of educational establishments recognised by the Secretary of State, see s.216 of the Education Reform Act 1988 as amended, the Education (Recognised Bodies) (Scotland) Order 2007 (SSI 2007/557) as amended, the Education (Recognised Bodies) (Wales) Order 2012 (SI 2012/1260), the Education (Recognised Bodies) (England) Order 2013 (SI 2013/2992), the Education (Listed Bodies) (Scotland) Order 2007 (SSI 2007/558) as amended, the Education (Listed Bodies) (Wales) Order 2012 (SI 2012/1259), and the Education (Listed Bodies) (Eng-land) Order 2013 (SI 2013/2993).

**pp.331–333,** *annotation to the Income Support (General) Regulations 1987 (SI 1987/1967) reg.21AA (Special cases: supplemental—persons from abroad—Extended right of residence—Family members—Opinion of the Advocate General in* Minister voor Immigratie, Integratie en Asiel v O and S*)*

3.051      In *Minister voor Immigratie, Integratie en Asiel v O* (Case C-456/12) the Raad van State (the Netherlands Council of State) referred the following questions to the ECJ:

> "(1) Should [the Directive], as regards the conditions governing the right of residence of members of the family of a Union citizen who have third-country nationality, be applied by analogy, as in the judg-ments of the Court of Justice of the European Communities in Case

322

C-370/90 *Singh* . . . and in Case C-291/05 *Eind* . . . , where a Union citizen returns to the Member State of which he is a national after having resided in another Member State in the context of Article 21(1) [TFEU], and as the recipient of services within the meaning of Article 56 [TFEU]?

(2) If so, is there a requirement that the residence of the Union citizen in another Member State must have been of a certain minimum duration if, after the return of the Union citizen to the Member State of which he is a national, the member of his family who is a third-country national wishes to gain a right of residence in that Member State?

(3) If so, can that requirement then also be met if there was no question of continuous residence, but rather of a certain frequency of residence, such as during weekly residence at weekends or during regular visits?

(4) As a result of the time which elapsed between the return of the Union citizen to the Member State of which he is a national and the arrival of the family member from a third country in that Member State, in circumstances such as those of the present case, has there been a lapse of possible entitlement of the family member with third-country nationality to a right of residence derived from Union law?"

In *Minister voor Immigratie, Integratie en Asiel v S* (Case C-457/12), the Raad van State referred the following questions to the ECJ:

"(1) Can a member, having third-country nationality, of the family of a Union citizen who lives in the Member State of which he is a national but who works in another Member State for an employer established in that other Member State derive, in circumstances such as those of the present case, a right of residence from Union law?

(2) Can a member, having third-country nationality, of the family of a Union citizen who lives in the Member State of which he is a national but who, in the course of his work for an employer established in that same Member State, travels to and from another Member State derive, in circumstances such as those of the present case, a right of residence from Union law?"

The opinion of Advocate General Sharpston was given on December 12, 2013. She proposed that the questions referred by the Raad van State should be answered as follows:

"In Case C-456/12 *O*:

(1) [The Directive] does not apply directly to EU citizens returning to their Member State of nationality. However, the Member State of nationality may not give such EU citizens less favourable treatment than that owed to them as a matter of EU law in the Member State from which they moved to their Member State of nationality. As a result, [the Directive] indirectly sets out the minimum standard of treatment that a returning EU citizen and his family members must enjoy in the EU citizen's Member State of nationality.

(2) EU law does not require an EU citizen to have resided for any minimum period of time in another Member State in order for his third country national family members to claim a derived right of residence in the Member State of nationality to which the EU citizen then returns.

(3) An EU citizen exercises his right of residence in another Member State if he makes that Member State the place where the habitual centre of his interests lies. Provided that, when all relevant facts are taken into account, that test is satisfied, it is irrelevant in this context whether that EU citizen keeps another form of residence elsewhere or whether his physical presence in the Member State of residence is regularly or irregularly interrupted.

(4) Where time elapses between the return of the EU citizen to the Member State of which he is a national and the arrival of the third country national family member in that Member State, the family member's entitlement to a derived right of residence in that Member State does not lapse provided that the decision to join the EU citizen is taken in the exercise of their right to a family life.

In Case C-457/12 *S*:

Where an EU citizen residing in his Member State of nationality exercises rights of free movement in connection with his employment, the right of his third country national family members to reside in that State depends on the closeness of their family connection with the EU citizen and on the causal connection between the family's place of residence and the EU citizen's exercise of rights of free movement. In particular, the family member must enjoy a right of residence if denying that right would cause the EU citizen to seek alternative employment that would not involve the exercise of rights of free movement or would cause him to move to another Member State. It is irrelevant in that regard whether the EU citizen is a frontier worker or exercises his right of free movement in order to fulfil his contract of employment concluded with an employer based in his Member State of nationality and residence."

At the time of going to press no date had been fixed for the delivery of the court's judgment.

**pp.331–333,** *annotation to the Income Support (General) Regulations 1987 (SI 1987/1967), reg.21AA (Special cases: supplemental—persons from abroad—Family members—Dependency—Decision in* Entry Clearance Officer (Manila) v Lim *[2013] UKUT 437 (IAC))*

3.052    The status of dependency as a factual issue has been reemphasised by the decision of Immigration Appeal Chamber of the Upper Tribunal in *Lim (EEA—dependency)* [2013] UKUT 437 (IAC). In that case, the claimant was a Malaysian citizen who owned a three-bedroom house in Malaysia valued at £80,000 and a substantial lump sum in an Employers Provident Fund on which she was free to draw at any time. However, she chose not to draw on that fund or to sell her home and relied instead upon remittances from her daughter, who was married to an EEA national working in the United Kingdom. She applied for entry clearance as a family member of her son-in-law and was refused on the ground that she was not genuinely dependent on her daughter. The FTT allowed her appeal and that decision was confirmed by Judge Storey in the UT. He held (at paras 21–22) that:

> "the overriding principle established by the jurisprudence of the Court of Justice that dependency is a matter of fact and reasons are irrelevant
> . . .
>
> The only qualification that the Court of Justice has ever made to this principle is that there must not be an abuse of rights. Accordingly, subject only to there being no abuse of rights, the jurisprudence clearly allows for dependency of choice."

**p.344,** *annotation to the Income Support (General) Regulations 1987 (SI 1987/1967), reg.21AA (Special cases: supplemental—persons from abroad-Permanent right of residence—Continuity of residence—Decision in* Babajanov v SSHD *[2013] UKUT 513 (IAC))*

In *Babajanov (Continuity of residence—Immigration (EEA) Regulations 2006)* [2013] UKUT 00513 (IAC), a Two-Judge Panel of the Immigration Appeals Chamber of the Upper Tribunal held that the right of permanent residence under reg.15 of the Immigration (European Economic Area) Regulations 2006 is capable of being established whilst a national of a Member State or a family member of that national is outside the host country.   3.053

**pp.344–345,** *annotation to the Income Support (General) Regulations 1987 (SI 1987/1967), reg.21AA (Special cases: supplemental—persons from abroad-Permanent right of residence—Imprisonment—Opinion of Advocate General in* Onuekwere v Secretary of State for the Home Department *(Case C-378/12))*

The judgment on the ECJ in *Onuekwere v Secretary of State for the Home Department* (Case C-378/12) was delivered on January 16, 2014. The Court ruled that:   3.054

1.  Article 16(2) of [the Directive] must be interpreted as meaning that the periods of imprisonment in the host Member State of a third-country national, who is a family member of a Union citizen who has acquired the right of permanent residence in that Member State during those periods, cannot be taken into consideration in the context of the acquisition by that national of the right of permanent residence for the purposes of that provision.
2.  Article 16(2) and (3) of [the Directive] must be interpreted as meaning that the continuity of residence is interrupted by periods of imprisonment in the host Member State of a third country national who is a family member of a Union citizen who has

acquired the right of permanent residence in that Member State during those periods.

**p.351,** *annotation to the Income Support (General) Regulations 1987 (SI 1987/1967) reg.21AA (Special cases: supplemental—persons from abroad —Rights to reside of children in education and their principal carers:* Baumbast, Ibrahim and Teixeira—*Age at which the child's right under Art.10 of Regulation 492/2011 arises—Decision in* Shabani v Secretary of State for the Home Department*)*

3.055    In *Shabani (EEA—jobseekers; nursery education)* [2013] UKUT 00315 (IAC) the Home Secretary conceded, that the exclusion by reg.15A(6) of the 2006 Regulations of those in "nursery education" from the derived right of residence conferred by that section does not apply to those in reception class education within a primary school: see para.61 of the decision.

**p.353,** *annotation to the Income Support (General) Regulations 1987 (SI 1987/1967) reg.21AA (Special cases: supplemental—persons from abroad —Parents of British children:* Zambrano—*Decision in* JS v SSWP (IS)*)*

3.056    The claimant in *JS v SSWP (IS)* [2013] UKUT 490 (AAC) was granted permission to appeal to the CA on December 18, 2013 (*sub nom. Jamil Sanneh v SSWP*).

**p.354,** *annotation to the Income Support (General) Regulations 1987 (SI 1987/1967) reg.21AA (Special cases: supplemental—persons from abroad —Parents of British Children:* Zambrano—*Judgment of the ECJ in* Alopka, Mondoulou and Mondoulou v Ministre du Travail, de l'Emploi et de l'Immigration*)*

3.057    The decision of the ECJ in *Alopka, Mondoulou and Mondoulou v Ministre du Travail, de l'Emploi et de l'Immigration* (Case C-86/12) was given on September 19, 2013. The court ruled that:

> "In a situation such as that at issue in the main proceedings, Articles 20 TFEU and 21 TFEU must be interpreted as meaning that they do not preclude a Member State from refusing to allow a third-country national to reside in its territory, where that third-country national has sole responsibility for her minor children who are citizens of the European Union, and who have resided with her in that Member State since their birth, without possessing the nationality of that Member State and making use of their right to freedom of movement, in so far as those Union citizens do not satisfy the conditions set out in [the Directive], or such a refusal does not deprive those citizens of effective enjoyment of the substance of the rights conferred by virtue of the status of European Union citizenship, a matter which is to be determined by the referring court."

**p.355,** *annotation to the Income Support (General) Regulations 1987 (SI 1987/1967) reg.21AA (Special cases: supplemental—persons from abroad —The special position of A8 and A2 nationals—The A2 Regulations—New regulation 7B of the 2006 Regulations)*

Note that, with effect from January 1, 2014, Immigration (European 3.058 Economic Area) (Amendment) (No. 2) Regulations 2013 (SI 2013/3032) reg.4 and Sch.1, para.4. added a new reg.7B to the 2006 Regulations as follows:

### "Application of the EU2 Regulations

(1) This regulation applies to an EEA national who was an accession State national subject to worker authorisation before 1st January 2014.

(2) In this regulation—

'accession State national subject to worker authorisation' has the same meaning as in regulation 2 of the EU2 Regulations;

'the EU2 Regulations' means the Accession (Immigration and Worker Authorisation) Regulations 2006.

(3) Regulation 2(12) of the EU2 Regulations (accession State national subject to worker authorisation: legally working) has effect for the purposes of this regulation as it does for regulation 2(3) and (4) of the EU2 Regulations.

(4) In regulation 5(7)(c), where the worker is an accession State national subject to worker authorisation, periods of involuntary unemployment duly recorded by the relevant employment office must only be treated as periods of activity as a worker when the unemployment began on or after 1st January 2014.

(5) Regulation 6(2) applies to an accession State national subject to worker authorisation where the accession State national subject to worker authorisation became unable to work, became unemployed or ceased to work, as the case may be, on or after 1st January 2014.

(6) For the purposes of regulation 15, an accession State national subject to worker authorisation must be treated as having resided in accordance with these Regulations during any period before 1st January 2014 in which the accession State national subject to worker authorisation was legally working in the United Kingdom.

(7) An accession worker card issued to an accession State national subject to worker authorisation under regulation 11 of the EU2 Regulations before 1st January 2014 must be treated as if it were a registration certificate issued under these Regulations so long as it has not expired.".

**pp.357–360,** *annotation to the Income Support (General) Regulations 1987 (SI 1987/1967) reg.21AA (Special cases: supplemental—persons from abroad—Compatibility of the right to reside test with EU law—Decision in* Mirga v Secretary of State for Work and Pensions)

*Mirga v Secretary of State for Work and Pensions* [2012] EWCA Civ 3.059 1952 concerned a claim for income support by a pregnant 17-year-old

A8 national who had lived primarily in the United Kingdom since the age of 10 and had done some work but had not completed 12 months' registered work. The Court of Appeal stated that, since the House of Lords in *Zalewska* had upheld the proportionality of the Worker Registration Scheme in general, a challenge to it based on particular individual circumstances was excluded. The claimant has applied to the Supreme Court for permission to appeal.

**p.372,** *annotation to the Income Support (General) Regulations 1987 (SI 1987/1967) reg.21ZB (Treatment of refugees)*

3.060    The revocation of reg.21ZB on June 14, 2007 did not offend against EU law or infringe the ECHR. Article 28 of Directive 2004/83/EC (the "Qualification Directive") does not require the United Kingdom to provide income support to a refugee for the period prior to the decision recognising refugee status even once such a decision has been made, and if the removal of the backdating rule did discriminate against the appellant (pursuant to art.14 of the European Convention on Human Rights when read with art.1 of the First Protocol to that Convention) it is justified: see the decision of the Three-Judge Panel of the Upper Tribunal in *HB v Secretary of State for Work and Pensions (IS)* [2013] UKUT 433 (AAC).

**p.375,** *revocation of the Income Support (General) Regulations 1987 (SI 1987/1967) reg.22B (Period for which applicable amount is to be calculated where person not excluded from income support under section 115 of the Immigration and Asylum Act 1999)*

3.061    With effect from October 29, 2013, reg.4(1) and (5) of the Social Security (Miscellaneous Amendments) (No. 3) Regulations 2013 (SI 2013/2536) revoked reg.22B.

**p.396,** *amendment to the Income Support (General) Regulations 1987 (SI 1987/1967) reg.31(2) (Date on which income is treated as paid)*

3.062    With effect from April 29, 2013, reg.28(4) of the Universal Credit (Consequential, Supplementary, Incidental and Miscellaneous Provisions) Regulations 2013 (SI 2013/630) substituted the words ", employment and support allowance or universal credit" for the words "or employment and support allowance", and the words "on any day" for the words "on the day of the benefit week", in reg.31(2).

**pp.396–398,** *"Pathfinder" amendment to the Welfare Reform Act 2007, Sch.1, Part 2 (Income-related Allowance)*

3.062A    With effect from various dates on or after April 29, 2013, s.147 of, and Sch.14, Part I to, the Welfare Reform Act 2012 repealed Sch.1, Part 2.

**p.402,** *annotation to the Income Support (General) Regulations 1987 (SI 1987/1967) reg.32(6)*

In *MC v SSWP (IS)* [2013] UKUT 384 (AAC) the claimant worked   3.063
as a football steward every other week when the club played at home. He received a payment for two home cup matches which for reasons that were not entirely clear the tribunal treated as an exceptional payment outside the normal pattern. The claimant argued that the payment should be treated as part of his 52-week cycle of work for the club and that his earnings should be averaged over 52 weeks.

Judge Wright points out that reg.32(6) mirrors reg.5(2)(b) of the Income Support (General) Regulations 1987, albeit in the context of the income earned rather than hours of work. Thus in deciding whether the claimant did have a recognisable cycle of work, the case law under reg.5(2)(b), and the equivalent JSA provision, reg.51(2)(b), should be applied, in particular *R(JSA) 5/03*. In that case the Tribunal of Commissioners stated:

"22. In our view, the approach taken by decision-makers should be as follows. Where a contract of employment comes to an end at the beginning of what would be a period of absence from work even if the contract continued, the person should be taken still to be in employment if it is expected that he or she will resume in employment after that period, either because there is some express arrangement, though not necessarily an enforceable contract, or because it is reasonable to assume that a long standing practice of re-employment will continue."

Judge Wright remitted the appeal to a fresh tribunal for it to decide whether the claimant did have a recognisable cycle of work, having regard to the nature of his agreement with the football club to work as a steward, how the off-season was treated, and whether he had to reapply (and if so, how) for the job of steward each August. (There was also the question of how a period of time off that the claimant had had in 2011 had been dealt with.) The Secretary of State had accepted that reg.32(6) could apply in this case on the basis that the claimant's income had changed more than once and the new tribunal would therefore need to decide which (if either) of sub-paras (a) or (b) of reg.32(6) applied (if neither applied it would seem that reg.32(1) would have to apply to the individual payment).

**p.429,** *amendment to the Income Support (General) Regulations 1987 (SI 1987/1967) reg.40(6) (Calculation of income other than earnings)*

With effect from April 29, 2013, reg.28(5) of the Universal Credit   3.064
(Consequential, Supplementary, Incidental and Miscellaneous Provisions) Regulations 2013 (SI 2013/630) inserted the words "or section 11J of the Welfare Reform Act as the case may be" after the words "Employment and Support Allowance Regulations" in reg.40(6)(c).

**p.550,** *amendment of the Income Support (General) Regulations 1987 (SI 1987/1967) reg.75(b) (Modifications in the calculation of income)*

3.065    With effect from April 29, 2013, reg.28(1) and (6) of the Universal Credit (Consequential, Supplementary, Incidental and Miscellaneous Provisions) Regulations 2013 (SI 2013/630) amended reg.75(b) by substituting the words "employment and support allowance or universal credit" for the words "or employment and support allowance".

**p.553,** *amendment to the Income Support (General) Regulations 1987 (SI 1987/1967) Sch.1B (Prescribed Categories of Person) para.2*

3.066    With effect from June 24, 2013, art.17(1) of, and para.12(3) of Sch.1, Part 2 to, the Children's Hearings (Scotland) Act 2011 (Consequential and Transitional Provisions and Savings) Order 2013 (SI 2013/1465) substituted the following paragraph for para.2 of Sch.1B:

"**2.** A single claimant or a lone parent with whom a child is placed—
   (a)  by a local authority or voluntary organisation within the meaning of the Children Act 1989;
   (b)  by a local authority or voluntary organisation within the meaning of the Children (Scotland) Act 1995;
   (c)  by virtue of any order or warrant made under the Children's Hearings (Scotland) Act 2011."

**p.601,** *amendment to the Income Support (General) Regulations 1987 (SI 1987/1967) Sch.3 (Housing Costs) para.1(3)*

3.067    With effect from April 29, 2013, reg.28(7)(a) of the Universal Credit (Consequential, Supplementary, Incidental and Miscellaneous Provisions) Regulations 2013 (SI 2013/630) inserted the following new head after head (d) in para.1(3):

"; or
   (e)  who is entitled to an award of universal credit the calculation of which includes an amount under regulation 27(1) of the Universal Credit Regulations 2013 in respect of the fact that he has limited capability for work or limited capability for work and work-related activity, or would include such an amount but for regulation 27(4) or 29(4) of those Regulations".

**p.617,** *amendment to the Income Support (General) Regulations 1987 (SI 1987/1967) Sch.3 (Housing Costs) para.18*

3.068    With effect from April 29, 2013, reg.28(7)(b)(i) of the Universal Credit (Consequential, Supplementary, Incidental and Miscellaneous Provisions) Regulations 2013 (SI 2013/630) inserted the following new head after head (i) in sub-para.(7) of para.18:

"(j)  if he is aged less than 25 and is entitled to an award of universal credit where the award is calculated on the basis that he does not have any earned income".

From the same date, reg.28(7)(b)(ii) of the same Regulations inserted the following new sub-paragraph after sub-para.(8) in para.18:

"(9) For the purposes of sub-paragraph (7)(j), "earned income" has the meaning given in regulation 52 of the Universal Credit Regulations 2013."

**p.629,** *annotation to the Income Support (General) Regulations 1987 (SI 1987/1967) Sch.3 para.1(3)*

Paragraph 1(3) defines who is a "disabled person" for the purposes of Sch.3. From April 29, 2013, following the commencement of universal credit, this includes a person whose award of universal credit contains a limited capability for work element or a limited capability for work and work-related activity element, or, in the case of a limited capability for work element, would do so but for the fact that the person satisfies the conditions for a carer element, or, in the case of joint claimants, would do so but for the fact that only one limited capability for work (or limited capability for work and work-related activity) element can be included even if both joint claimants meet the conditions for such an element (or elements).

3.069

**pp.631 and 634–635,** *annotation to the Income Support (General) Regulations 1987 (SI 1987/1967) Sch.3 para.3(1) and (10)–(12)*

*LES v Horsham District Council (HB)* [2013] UKUT 494 (AAC), a case on reg.7(1), (13) and (16)–(17) of the Housing Benefit Regulations 2006 (the equivalent of para.3(1) and (10)–(12)), applies para.19 of *R(H) 9/05* in holding that where a claimant is temporarily absent from the dwelling that she normally occupies as her home, she can only be treated as continuing to occupy that dwelling as her home if, and so long as, one of the provisions in reg.7 relating to temporary absences applies, but not otherwise.

3.070

**pp.635–637,** *annotation to the Income Support (General) Regulations 1987 (SI 1987/1967) Sch.3 para.3(11)–(12), "Absences for certain reasons"*

In *Obrey & Ors v Secretary of State for Work and Pensions* [2013] EWCA Civ 1584, a case on reg.7(16)–(17) of the Housing Benefit Regulations 2006 (the equivalent of para.3(11)–(12)), the claimants had been detained in hospital under s.3 of the Mental Health Act 1983 for more than 52 weeks. They contended that the 52 weeks' rule for the payment of housing benefit in reg.7(16)(c)(ii) and (17) unlawfully discriminated against them as mental health patients, and in particular as mental health patients detained under s.3, because detained mental health patients are more likely than other hospital patients to be resident in hospital for more than 52 weeks. The Court of Appeal, however, confirmed the decision of Judge Lloyd-Davies in *SSWP and Warwick DC v WO, JS and JS (CTB)* [2012] UKUT 489 (AAC) that, although the 52 weeks' rule did indirectly discriminate against the mentally ill in breach of art.14,

3.071

read with art.1, Prot.1, ECHR, the discrimination was justified as it did not meet the "manifestly without reasonable foundation" test (see *Humphreys v Revenue and Customs Commissioners* [2012] UKSC 18). The Court of Appeal found that there was no error of law in the Upper Tribunal's decision, emphasising that:

> "18. . . . the question whether the indirectly discriminatory effect of a particular rule in the benefits system because it does not distinguish between mental patients and other patients in hospital, is, or is not, 'manifestly without reasonable foundation' is . . . precisely the kind of issue that is best left for evaluation and judgment by a specialist appellate tribunal with a particular expertise in the field of social security law. . . . "

**pp.641–643,** *annotation to the Income Support (General) Regulations 1987 (SI 1987/1967) Sch.3 para.4(9)*

3.072    In *MA v SSWP (SPC)* [2013] UKUT 593 (AAC) the claimant, who was in receipt of state pension credit, his wife and daughter (all of whom fell within the definition of "disabled person" in para.1(2) of Sch.II to the State Pension Credit Regulations 2002) had lived with their son in his house for 22 months before taking out a loan to purchase their home. Judge Gray held that this was too long a gap for the property in which they had lived before moving to their son's property to be the comparator property for the purposes of para.5(10) of Sch.II to the State Pension Credit Regulations 2002 (the equivalent of para.4(9)), although she did state that it was not helpful to quantify the required level of linkage to a comparator property in terms of weeks or months. The accommodation in the son's property was physically much the same as in the new property and the new property was in the same street as the son's house. Although the move meant that the claimant, his wife and daughter were not living in someone else's house on a grace and favour basis, this did not render the accommodation "more suited to the special needs of a disabled person", as the psychological benefits of a move to a home of one's own are not restricted to disabled people but are universal. The consequence was that the claimant did not fall within para.5(10) of Sch.II and so he was not entitled to housing costs as part of his state pension credit. Judge Gray accepted that the claimant's move to his son's home had originally been intended to be only on a temporary basis but considered that "matters in fact moved on". It is suggested that in other circumstances a temporary move to an intermediate property may not preclude the application of para.4(9), depending of course on the facts.

**pp.675–676,** *annotation to the Income Support (General) Regulations 1987 (SI 1987/1967) Sch.3 para.18*

3.073    Paragraph 18(7) of Sch.3 lists those non-dependants in respect of whom no deduction from a claimant's housing costs is to be made. From April 29, 2013, following the commencement of universal credit, a person aged less than 25, who is entitled to an award of universal credit which is calculated on the basis that he does not have any earned income, is added to the list in para.18(7). On the meaning of "earned income" for the purposes of universal credit, see reg.52 of the Universal Credit Regulations and the notes to that regulation in Vol.V of this series.

**pp.686–687,** *amendment to the Income Support (General) Regulations 1987 (SI 1987/1967) Sch.8 (Sums to be disregarded in the calculation of earnings) para.7*

With effect from October 29, 2013, reg.4(7) of the Social Security 3.074 (Miscellaneous Amendments) (No. 3) Regulations 2013 (SI 2013/2536) omitted sub-paras (1)(a), (1)(aa) and (1)(ab) in para.7 and inserted the following new sub-para.(1)(a) before sub-para.(1)(b):

> "(a) a part-time fire-fighter employed by a fire and rescue authority under the Fire and Rescue Services Act 2004 or by the Scottish Fire and Rescue Service established under section 1A of the Fire (Scotland) Act 2005;".

**p.692,** *annotation to the Income Support (General) Regulations 1987 (SI 1987/1967) Sch.8 para.7(1)*

According to the Explanatory Memorandum that accompanies the 3.075 Social Security (Miscellaneous Amendments) (No. 3) Regulations 2013 (SI 2013/2536), the amendments to para.7(1) have been made to reflect the policy intention that it applies to part-time fire-fighters who live in Scotland but are employed by a fire and rescue authority in England and Wales (and those who live in England or Wales but are employed by the Scottish Fire and Rescue Service), as well as those who live and are employed as part-time fire-fighters in the same country.

**p.694,** *amendment to the Income Support (General) Regulations 1987 (SI 1987/1967) Sch.9 (Sums to be disregarded in the calculation of income other than earnings) para.7*

With effect from April 29, 2013, reg.28(8) of the Universal Credit 3.076 (Consequential, Supplementary, Incidental and Miscellaneous Provisions) Regulations 2013 (SI 2013/630) omitted the word "or" after sub-para.(c) in para.7 and inserted after sub-para.(d):

> "; or
> (e) universal credit".

**p.698,** *amendment to the Income Support (General) Regulations 1987 (SI 1987/1967) Sch.9 (Sums to be disregarded in the calculation of income other than earnings) para.27*

With effect from April 1, 2013, art.11 of, and para.10(3)(a) of Part 1 3.077 of Sch.2 to, the National Treatment Agency (Abolition) and the Health and Social Care Act 2012 (Consequential, Transitional and Saving Provisions) Order 2013 (SI 2013/235) inserted the following new sub-paras after sub-para.(d) in para.27:

"(da)  a clinical commissioning group established under section 14D of the National Health Service Act 2006;

(db)  the National Health Service Commissioning Board; or".

From the same date, art.11 of, and para.10(3)(b) of Part 1 of Sch.2 to, the same Regulations omitted sub-para.(e) in para.27, together with the word "or" following it.

**p.715,** *annotation to the Income Support (General) Regulations 1987 (SI 1987/1967) Sch.9 para.15*

3.078     *Lloyd v London Borough of Lewisham and Secretary of State for Work and Pensions* [2013] EWCA Civ 923 is reported as [2013] AACR 28.

**p.728,** *amendment to the Income Support (General) Regulations 1987 (SI 1987/1967) Sch.10 (Capital to be disregarded) para.7*

3.079     With effect from April 29, 2013, reg.28(9)(a) of the Universal Credit (Consequential, Supplementary, Incidental and Miscellaneous Provisions) Regulations 2013 (SI 2013/630) inserted after para.7(1)(d):

"；

(e)  universal credit".

From the same date, reg.28(9)(b)(i) of the same Regulations substituted the words ", an income-based jobseeker's allowance or universal credit" for the words "or of an income-based jobseeker's allowance" in both places in which they occur in para.7(3).
From the same date, reg.28(9)(b)(ii) of the same Regulations substituted the words "of any of" for the words "either of" in para.7(3)(a).
From the same date, reg.28(9)(b)(iii) of the same Regulations substituted the word "any" for the word "either" in para.7(3)(b).
From the same date, reg.28(9)(b)(iv) of the same Regulations inserted the following after para.7(3)(b)(iii):

"; or

(iv)  in a case where universal credit is awarded to the claimant and another person as joint claimants, either the claimant or the other person, or both of them, received the relevant sum".

**p.731,** *Income Support (General) Regulations 1987 (SI 1987/1967) Sch.10 (Capital to be disregarded) para.36*

3.080     Something has gone wrong with the text on p.731 and some stray lines have crept in. Paragraph 36 should read:

334

"[⁹36. Any payment in consequence of a reduction of [²⁰ [⁸⁶ ... ] council tax under section 13 [¹⁰² , 13A] or, as the case may be, section 80 of the Local Government Finance Act 1992 (reduction of liability for council tax)] but only for a period of 52 weeks from the date of the receipt of the payment.]"

**pp.747–748,** *annotation to the Income Support (General) Regulations 1987 (SI 1987/1967) Sch.10 para.7*

The effect of the amendments to para.7 of Sch.10 made by reg.28(9)  **3.081** of the Universal Credit (Consequential, Supplementary, Incidental and Miscellaneous Provisions) Regulations 2013 (SI 2013/630) with effect from April 29, 2013 is to add universal credit to the list of benefits, arrears, or any concessionary payment made to compensate for arrears due to non-payment of which, are disregarded under para.7.

*MK v SSWP (IS)* [2013] UKUT 629 (AAC) confirms that the disregard in para.7 only applies to the arrears of benefit that are paid and not to a sum equivalent to the arrears.

**p.799,** *annotation to the Social Security (Immigration and Asylum) Consequential Amendments Regulations 2000 (SI 2000/636) "Person subject to immigration control")*

Croatia acceded to the European Union on July 1, 2013. Croatian  **3.082** nationals are EU citizens and EEA nationals. They can therefore no longer be "persons subject to immigration control".

**pp.800–801,** *annotation to the Social Security (Immigration and Asylum) Consequential Amendments Regulations 2000 (SI 2000/636) (a person who has leave to enter or remain but subject to a condition that he does not have recourse to public funds)*

The former exception from the principle that a person who has leave  **3.083** to enter or remain but subject to a condition that he does not have recourse to public funds is excluded from benefit by s.115 of the Immigration and Asylum Act 1999 for those whose remittances from abroad had been disrupted (reg.2(1) and para.1 of Pt 1 of the Schedule) was abolished with effect from October 29, 2013, by reg.9(1) and (3) of the Social Security (Miscellaneous Amendments) (No. 3) Regulations 2013 (SI 2013/2536).

**p.803,** *annotation to the Social Security (Immigration and Asylum) Consequential Amendments Regulations 2000 (SI 2000/636) (The ECSMA agreement and the European Social Charter)*

Croatia acceded to the European Union on July 1, 2013. Croatian  **3.084** nationals are EU citizens and EEA nationals. They can therefore no longer be "persons subject to immigration control" and they have no need to rely on the exceptions created by para.4 of Pt 1 of the Schedule to the Regulations.

**p.805,** *amendment of the Social Security (Immigration and Asylum) Consequential Amendments Regulations 2000 (SI 2000/636) reg.1(3) (Citation, commencement and interpretation—definition of 'Universal credit')*

3.085    With effect from April 29, 2013, reg.31(1) and (2) of the Universal Credit (Consequential, Supplementary, Incidental and Miscellaneous Provisions) Regulations 2013 (SI 2013/630) amended reg.1(3) by adding the following definition after the definition of 'income-related employment and support allowance':

> ";
>
> 'universal credit' means universal credit under Part 1 of the Welfare Reform Act 2012"

**p.806,** *amendment of the Social Security (Immigration and Asylum) Consequential Amendments Regulations 2000 (SI 2000/636) reg.2 (Persons not excluded from specified benefits under section 115 of the Immigration and Asylum Act 1999)*

3.086    With effect from April 29, 2013, reg.31(1) and (3)(a) of the Universal Credit (Consequential, Supplementary, Incidental and Miscellaneous Provisions) Regulations 2013 (SI 2013/630) amended reg.2 by inserting the following paragraph after para.(1):

> "(1A) For the purposes of entitlement to universal credit, a person falling within a category or description of persons specified in paragraphs 2, 3 and 4 of Part I of the Schedule is a person to whom section 115 of the Act does not apply."

**p.807,** *amendment of the Social Security (Immigration and Asylum) Consequential Amendments Regulations 2000 (SI 2000/636) reg.2(5) (Persons not excluded from specified benefits under section 115 of the Immigration and Asylum Act 1999)*

3.087    With effect from April 29, 2013, reg.31(1) and (3)(b) of the Universal Credit (Consequential, Supplementary, Incidental and Miscellaneous Provisions) Regulations 2013 (SI 2013/630) amended reg.2(5) to read as follows:

> "(5) For the purposes of entitlement to [universal credit,] income support, [an income-based jobseeker's allowance under the Jobseekers Act 1995], an [income-related] employment and support allowance or a social fund payment under the Contributions and Benefits Act, as the case may be, a person who is an asylum seeker within the meaning of paragraph (4) of regulation 12 who has not ceased to be an asylum seeker by virtue of paragraph (5) of that regulation is a person to whom section 115 of the Act does not apply."

**p.807,** *revocation of the Social Security (Immigration and Asylum) Consequential Amendments Regulations 2000 (SI 2000/636) reg.2(8) (Persons not excluded from specified benefits under section 115 of the Immigration and Asylum Act 1999)*

With effect from October 29, 2013, reg.9(1) and (2) of the Social Security (Miscellaneous Amendments) (No. 3) Regulations 2013 (SI 2013/2536) amended reg.2 by revoking para.(8).  **3.088**

**p.809,** *amendment of the Schedule to the Social Security (Immigration and Asylum) Consequential Amendments Regulations 2000 (SI 2000/636) (Persons not excluded from specified benefits under section 115 of the Immigration and Asylum Act 1999)*

With effect from April 29, 2013, reg.31(1) and (3)(b) of the Universal Credit (Consequential, Supplementary, Incidental and Miscellaneous Provisions) Regulations 2013 (SI 2013/630) amended the heading to Part 1 of Schedule to read as follows:  **3.089**

"Persons not excluded under section 115 of the Immigration and Asylum Act from entitlement to [universal credit,] income-based job-seeker's allowance, income support, income- related employment and support allowance, a social fund payment, housing benefit or council tax benefit."

**pp.809–810,** *revocation of the Social Security (Immigration and Asylum) Consequential Amendments Regulations 2000 (SI 2000/636) Sch. Pt I para.1 (Persons not excluded from certain benefits under section 115 of the Immigration and Asylum Act 1999)*

With effect from October 29, 2013, reg.9(1) and (3) of the Social Security (Miscellaneous Amendments) (No. 3) Regulations 2013 (SI 2013/2536) amended Pt I of the Schedule by revoking para.1.  **3.090**

**p.810,** *amendment of the Schedule to the Social Security (Immigration and Asylum) Consequential Amendments Regulations 2000 (SI 2000/636) (Persons not excluded from certain benefits under section 115 of the Immigration and Asylum Act 1999)*

With effect from July 1, 2013, reg.8 of the Social Security (Croatia) Amendment Regulations 2013 (SI 2013/1474) amended para.1 of Pt II of the Schedule by adding the words "as modified or supplemented from time to time" after the words "on 17th March 1993".  **3.091**

**p.814,** *annotation to the Displaced Persons (Temporary Protection) Regulations 2005 (SI 2005/1379)*

Although the commentary is technically correct to state that the Regulations "do not remove the requirement to be habitually resident in the CTA in order to be entitled to IS, IBJSA, [IRESA] or SPC", that requirement is removed by reg.21AA(4)(h)(iii) of the Income Support  **3.092**

(General) Regulations 1987, reg.85A(4)(h)(iii) of the Jobseeker's Allowance Regulations, reg.70(4)(h)(iii) of the Employment and Support Allowance Regulations and reg.2(4)(h)(iii) of the State Pension Credit Regulations.

**p.822,** *amendment of the Accession (Immigration and Worker Authorisation) Regulations 2006 (SI 2006/3317) reg.7(2) (Issuing registration certificates and residence cards to nationals of Bulgaria and Romania and their family members during the accession period)*

3.093    With effect from January 1, 2014, reg.5 of, and Sch.3, para.2 to, the Immigration (European Economic Area) (Amendment) (No. 2) Regulations 2013 (SI 2013/3032) amended reg.7(2) by substituting the words "During the accession period, the Secretary" for the words "The Secretary".

**p.825,** *amendment of the Accession (Immigration and Worker Authorisation) Regulations 2006 (SI 2006/3317) reg.11(1) (Issuing an accession worker card etc)*

3.094    With effect from January 1, 2014, reg.5 of, and Sch.3, para.2 to, the Immigration (European Economic Area) (Amendment) (No. 2) Regulations 2013 (SI 2013/3032) amended reg.11(1) by substituting the words "During the accession period, subject" for the word "Subject".

**p.830,** *Amendment of the Community Charges (Deductions from Income Support) (No.2) Regulations 1990 (SI 1990/545) reg.1(2) (Citation, commencement and interpretation—definition of 'assessment period')*

3.095    With effect from April 29, 2013, regs 13 and 14(1) and (2) of the Fines, Council Tax and Community Charges (Deductions from Universal Credit and Other Benefits) Regulations 2013 (SI 2013/612) amended reg.1(2) by adding the following definition after the definition of "appropriate social security office":

"'assessment period' means the period prescribed by regulation 21 of the UC Regulations;"

**p.831,** *Amendment of the Community Charges (Deductions from Income Support) (No.2) Regulations 1990 (SI 1990/545) reg.1(2) (Citation, commencement and interpretation—definition of 'payments to third parties')*

3.096    With effect from April 29, 2013, regs 13 and 14(1) and (3) of the Fines, Council Tax and Community Charges (Deductions from Universal Credit and Other Benefits) Regulations 2013 (SI 2013/612) amended the definition of '"payments to third parties" in reg.1(2) to read as follows:

"'payments to third parties' means direct payments to third parties in accordance with Schedule 9 to the Social Security Claims and

Payments Regulations 1987, [or Schedule 6 to the UC etc. Claims and Payments Regulations,]"

**p.831,** *Amendment of the Community Charges (Deductions from Income Support) (No.2) Regulations 1990 (SI 1990/545) reg.1(2) (Citation, commencement and interpretation—definitions of 'the UC Regulations' 'the UC etc. Claims and Payments Regulations' and 'universal credit')*

With effect from April 29, 2013, regs 13 and 14(1) and (4) of the Fines, Council Tax and Community Charges (Deductions from Universal Credit and Other Benefits) Regulations 2013 (SI 2013/612) amended reg.1(2) by adding the following definitions after the definition of "tribunal":    3.097

"'the UC Regulations' means the Universal Credit Regulations 2013;

'the UC etc. Claims and Payments Regulations' means the Universal Credit, Personal Independence Payment, Jobseeker's Allowance and Employment and Support Allowance (Claims and Payments) Regulations 2013;

'universal credit' means universal credit under Part 1 of the Welfare Reform Act 2012;"

**p.832,** *Amendment of the Community Charges (Deductions from Income Support) (No.2) Regulations 1990 (SI 1990/545) reg.2 (Application for deductions from income support, state pension credit, jobseeker's allowance or employment and support allowance: England and Wales)*

With effect from April 29, 2013, regs 13 and 15 of the Fines, Council Tax and Community Charges (Deductions from Universal Credit and Other Benefits) Regulations 2013 (SI 2013/612) amended reg.2 by inserting the words "universal credit," after the words "income support," in the heading and on both occasions where the latter words occur in para.(1).    3.098

**pp.833–834,** *Amendment of the Community Charges (Deductions from Income Support) (No.2) Regulations 1990 (SI 1990/545) reg.3 (Deductions from debtor's income support, state pension credit or, jobseeker's allowance or employment and support allowance)*

With effect from April 29, 2013, regs 13 and 16 of the Fines, Council Tax and Community Charges (Deductions from Universal Credit and Other Benefits) Regulations 2013 (SI 2013/612) amended reg.3 by adding the words "universal credit," after the words "income support," in the heading; adding the following paragraphs after para.(1):    3.099

"(1A) Subject to paragraphs (1B), (1C) and (4A) and regulation 4, where the Secretary of State receives an application from an authority in respect of a debtor who is entitled to universal credit, the Secretary of State may deduct an amount from the universal credit payable to the debtor which is equal to 5 per cent. of the appropriate universal credit standard allowance and pay that sum to the authority towards satisfaction of any outstanding sum which is, or forms part of, the amount in respect of which the liability order was made.

(1B) No amount may be deducted under paragraph (1A) where it would reduce the amount of universal credit payable to the debtor to less than 1 penny.

(1C) For the purpose of paragraph (1A), where 5 per cent. of the appropriate universal credit standard allowance results in a fraction of a penny, that fraction is to be disregarded if it is less than half a penny and otherwise it is to be treated as a penny.

(1D) In paragraphs (1A) and (1C), 'appropriate universal credit standard allowance' means the appropriate universal credit standard allowance for the debtor for the assessment period in question under regulation 36 of the UC Regulations.";

and adding the following paragraph after para.(4):

"(4A) Before making a deduction under paragraph (1A), the Secretary of State must make any deduction which falls to be made in respect of a liability mentioned in paragraph 5(2)(a) to (c) of Schedule 6 to the UC etc. Claims and Payments Regulations.".

**p.835,** *Amendment of the Community Charges (Deductions from Income Support) (No.2) Regulations 1990 (SI 1990/545) reg.4 (Circumstances, time of making and termination of deductions)*

3.100      With effect from April 29, 2013, regs 11 and 17 of the Fines, Council Tax and Community Charges (Deductions from Universal Credit and Other Benefits) Regulations 2013 (SI 2013/612) amended reg.4 by substituting the words "regulation 3(1) or (2)" for the words "regulation 3" in para.(1)(a); adding the following paragraphs after para.(1):

"(1A) The Secretary of State may make deductions from universal credit under regulation 3(1A) only if—
(a) the debtor is entitled to universal credit throughout any assessment period; and
(b) no deductions are being made in respect of the debtor under any other application.";

and adding the words "universal credit," after the words "income support," each time the latter words occur in para.(2).

**p.837,** *Amendment of the Fines (Deductions from Income Support) Regulations 1992 (SI 1992/2182) reg.1(2) (Citation, commencement and interpretation—definition of 'the 2012 Act')*

3.101      With effect from April 29, 2013, regs 2 and 3(1) and (2) of the Fines, Council Tax and Community Charges (Deductions from Universal Credit and Other Benefits) Regulations 2013 (SI 2013/612) amended reg.1(2) by adding the following definition after the definition of "the 1998 Act":

"'the 2012 Act' means the Welfare Reform Act 2012;"

**p.837,** *Amendment of the Fines (Deductions from Income Support) Regulations 1992 (SI 1992/2182) reg.1(2) (Citation, commencement and interpretation—definition of 'assessment period')*

With effect from April 29, 2013, regs 2 and 3(1) and (3) of the Fines,    3.102
Council Tax and Community Charges (Deductions from Universal
Credit and Other Benefits) Regulations 2013 (SI 2013/612) amended
reg.1(2) by adding the following definition after the definition of
"application":

> "'assessment period' means the period prescribed by regulation 21 of
> the UC Regulations;"

**p.837,** *Amendment of the Fines (Deductions from Income Support) Regulations 1992 (SI 1992/2182) reg.1(2) (Citation, commencement and interpretation—definition of 'contribution-based jobseeker's allowance')*

With effect from April 29, 2013, regs 2 and 3(1) and (4) of the Fines,    3.103
Council Tax and Community Charges (Deductions from Universal
Credit and Other Benefits) Regulations 2013 (SI 2013/612) amended
the definition of "contribution-based jobseeker's allowance" in reg.1(2)
to read as follows:

> "'contribution-based jobseeker's allowance', except in a case to which
> paragraph (b) of the definition of income-based jobseeker's allow-
> ance applies, means a contribution-based jobseeker's allowance
> under Part I of the Jobseekers Act 1995 [as amended by the
> provisions of Part 1 of Schedule 14 to the 2012 Act that remove
> references to an income-based allowance or under Part 1 of the
> Jobseekers Act 1995 as it has effect apart from those amend-
> ments], but does not include any back to work bonus under
> section 26 of the Jobseekers Act which is paid as jobseeker's
> allowance;"

**p.837,** *Amendment of the Fines (Deductions from Income Support) Regulations 1992 (SI 1992/2182) reg.1(2) (Citation, commencement and interpretation—definition of 'contributory employment and support allowance')*

With effect from April 29, 2013, regs 2 and 3(1) and (5) of the Fines,    3.104
Council Tax and Community Charges (Deductions from Universal
Credit and Other Benefits) Regulations 2013 (SI 2013/612) amended
the definition of "contributory employment and support allowance" in
reg.1(2) to read as follows:

> "'contributory employment and support allowance' means a contribu-
> tory allowance under Part 1 of the Welfare Reform Act [as
> amended by the provisions of Schedule 3, and Part 1 of Schedule
> 14, to the 2012 Act that remove references to an income-related

allowance or under Part 1 of the Welfare Reform Act as it has effect apart from those amendments];"

**p.838,** *Amendment of the Fines (Deductions from Income Support) Regulations 1992 (SI 1992/2182) reg.1(2) (Citation, commencement and interpretation—definition of 'payments to third parties')*

3.105    With effect from April 29, 2013, regs 2 and 3(1) and (6) of the Fines, Council Tax and Community Charges (Deductions from Universal Credit and Other Benefits) Regulations 2013 (SI 2013/612) amended the definition of "payments to third parties" in reg.1(2) to read as follows:

> "'payments to third parties' means direct payments to third parties in accordance with Schedules 9 and 9A to the Claims and Payments Regulations, [Schedule 6 to the Universal Credit, Personal Independence Payment, Jobseeker's Allowance and Employment and Support Allowance (Claims and Payments) Regulations 2013,] regulation 2(4) of the Community Charges (Deductions from Income Support) (No.2) Regulations 1990 and regulation 2(4) of the Community Charges (Deductions from Income Support) (Scotland) Regulations 1989 and regulation 2 of the Council Tax (Deductions from Income Support) Regulations 1993;"

**p.838,** *Amendment of the Fines (Deductions from Income Support) Regulations 1992 (SI 1992/2182) reg.1(2) (Citation, commencement and interpretation—definitions of 'the UC Regulations' and 'universal credit')*

3.106    With effect from April 29, 2013, regs 2 and 3(1) and (7) of the Fines, Council Tax and Community Charges (Deductions from Universal Credit and Other Benefits) Regulations 2013 (SI 2013/612) amended reg.1(2) by adding the following definitions after the definition of "tribunal":

> "'the UC Regulations' means the Universal Credit Regulations 2013;
> 'universal credit' means universal credit under Part 1 of the 2012 Act;"

**p.839,** *Amendment of the Fines (Deductions from Income Support) Regulations 1992 (SI 1992/2182) reg.2 (Application for deductions from income support, state pension credit or, jobseeker's allowance or employment and support allowance)*

3.107    With effect from April 29, 2013, regs 2 and 4 of the Fines, Council Tax and Community Charges (Deductions from Universal Credit and Other Benefits) Regulations 2013 (SI 2013/612) amended reg.2 by inserting the words "universal credit," after the words "income support," in the heading and on both occasions where the latter words occur in para.(1).

**p.841,** *Amendment of the Fines (Deductions from Income Support) Regulations 1992 (SI 1992/2182) reg.4 (Deductions from offender's income support, state pension credit or, jobseeker's allowance)*

With effect from April 29, 2013, regs 2 and 5 of the Fines, Council Tax and Community Charges (Deductions from Universal Credit and Other Benefits) Regulations 2013 (SI 2013/612) amended reg.4 by adding the words "universal credit" after the words "income support," in the heading; adding the following paragraphs after para.(1):     3.108

"(1A) Subject to paragraphs (1C) and (1D) and regulation 7, where the Secretary of State receives an application from a court in respect of an offender who is entitled to universal credit, the Secretary of State may deduct from the universal credit payable to the offender an amount permitted by paragraph (1B) and pay that amount to the court towards satisfaction of the fine or the sum required to be paid by compensation order.

(1B) The amount that may be deducted under paragraph (1A) is any sum which is no less than 5 per cent. of the appropriate universal credit standard allowance for the offender for the assessment period in question under regulation 36 of the UC Regulations but no greater than £108.35.

(1C) No amount may be deducted under paragraph (1A) where it would reduce the amount of universal credit payable to the offender to less than 1 penny.

(1D) For the purpose of paragraph (1B), where 5 per cent. of the appropriate universal credit standard allowance results in a fraction of a penny, that fraction is to be disregarded if it is less than half a penny and otherwise it is to be treated as a penny.";

substituting the following paragraphs for para.(2):

"(2) Subject to paragraph (3) and regulation 7, where—
(a) the Secretary of State receives an application from a court in respect of an offender who is entitled to contribution-based jobseeker's allowance or contributory employment and support allowance; and
(b) the amount of that allowance payable, before any deduction under this paragraph, is 10 pence or more,
the Secretary of State may deduct a sum from that allowance, up to the appropriate maximum specified in paragraph (2A), and pay that sum to the court towards satisfaction of the fine or the sum required to be paid by compensation order.

(2A) The appropriate maximum is 40 per cent. of the appropriate age-related amount for the offender specified—
(a) where the offender is entitled to contribution-based jobseeker's allowance, in regulation 79 of the Jobseeker's Allowance Regulations 1996 or, as the case may be, regulation 49 of the Jobseeker's Allowance Regulations 2013;
(b) where the offender is entitled to contributory employment and support allowance, in paragraph 1(1) of Schedule 4 to the Employment and Support Allowance Regulations or, as the

case may be, regulation 62(1)(b) of the Employment and Support Allowance Regulations 2013.";

and revoking para.(4).

By reg.5(6) of SI 2013/612, the substitution of new paras (2) and (2A) for the former para.(2) does not have effect in respect of an application received by the Secretary of State from the court in respect of an offender before April 29, 2013.

**p.843,** *Amendment of the Fines (Deductions from Income Support) Regulations 1992 (SI 1992/2182) reg.7 (Circumstances, time of making and termination of deductions)*

3.109    With effect from April 29, 2013, regs 2 and 6 of the Fines, Council Tax and Community Charges (Deductions from Universal Credit and Other Benefits) Regulations 2013 (SI 2013/612) amended reg.7 by substituting the words "regulation 4(1) or (2)" for the words "regulation 4" in para.(1) and adding the following paragraphs after para.(1):

"(1A) The Secretary of State may make deductions from universal credit under regulation 4(1A) only if—
  (a) the offender is entitled to universal credit throughout any assessment period; and
  (b) no deductions are being made in respect of the offender under any other application.";

and by inserting the words, "universal credit," after the words, "income support," each time those words occur in paras (2)(b), (3), (4) and (6).

**p.846,** *Amendment of the Council Tax (Deductions from Income Support) Regulations 1993 (SI 1993/494) reg.1(2) (Interpretation—definition of 'the 2012 Act')*

3.110    With effect from April 29, 2013, regs 7 and 8(1) and (2) of the Fines, Council Tax and Community Charges (Deductions from Universal Credit and Other Benefits) Regulations 2013 (SI 2013/612) amended reg.1(2) by adding the following definition after the definition of "the 1998 Act":

"'the 2012 Act' means the Welfare Reform Act 2012;"

**p.847,** *Amendment of the Council Tax (Deductions from Income Support) Regulations 1993 (SI 1993/494) reg.1(2) (Citation, commencement and interpretation—definition of "assessment period")*

3.111    With effect from April 29, 2013, regs 7 and 8(1) and (3) of the Fines, Council Tax and Community Charges (Deductions from Universal Credit and Other Benefits) Regulations 2013 (SI 2013/612) amended reg.1(2) by adding the following definition after the definition of "application":

"'assessment period' means the period prescribed by regulation 21 of the UC Regulations;"

**p.847,** *Amendment of the Council Tax (Deductions from Income Support) Regulations 1993 (SI 1993/494) reg.1(2) (Citation, commencement and interpretation—definition of 'contribution-based jobseeker's allowance')*

With effect from April 29, 2013, regs 7 and 8(1) and (4) of the Fines,   3.112
Council Tax and Community Charges (Deductions from Universal Credit and Other Benefits) Regulations 2013 (SI 2013/612) amended the definition of "contribution-based jobseeker's allowance" in reg.1(2) to read as follows:

"'contribution-based jobseeker's allowance', except in a case to which paragraph (b) of the definition of income-based jobseeker's allowance applies, means a contribution-based jobseeker's allowance under Part I of the Jobseekers Act 1995 [as amended by the provisions of Part 1 of Schedule 14 to the 2012 Act that remove references to an income-based allowance or under Part 1 of the Jobseekers Act 1995 as it has effect apart from those amendments], but does not include any back to work bonus under section 26 of the Jobseekers Act which is paid as job-seeker's allowance;"

**p.847,** *Amendment of the Council Tax (Deductions from Income Support) Regulations 1993 (SI 1993/494) reg.1(2) (Citation, commencement and interpretation—definition of 'contributory employment and support allowance')*

With effect from April 29, 2013, regs 7 and 8(1) and (5) of the Fines,   3.113
Council Tax and Community Charges (Deductions from Universal Credit and Other Benefits) Regulations 2013 (SI 2013/612) amended the definition of "contributory employment and support allowance" in reg.1(2) to read as follows:

"'contributory employment and support allowance' means a contributory allowance under Part 1 of the Welfare Reform Act (employment and support allowance) [as amended by the provisions of Schedule 3, and Part 1 of Schedule 14, to the 2012 Act that remove references to an income-related allowance or under Part 1 of the Welfare Reform Act as it has effect apart from those amendments];"

**p.848,** *Amendment of the Council Tax (Deductions from Income Support) Regulations 1993 (SI 1993/494) reg.1(2) (Citation, commencement and interpretation—definitions of 'the UC Regulations' and 'universal credit')*

With effect from April 29, 2013, regs 7 and 8(1) and (6) of the Fines,   3.114
Council Tax and Community Charges (Deductions from Universal Credit and Other Benefits) Regulations 2013 (SI 2013/612) amended

reg.1(2) by adding the following definitions after the definition of "tribunal":

"'the UC Regulations' means the Universal Credit Regulations
2013;
'universal credit' means universal credit under P/art 1 of the 2012
Act;"

**p.849,** *Amendment of the Council Tax (Deductions from Income Support)
Regulations 1993 (SI 1993/494) reg.2 (Application for deductions from
income support, state pension credit, jobseeker's allowance or employment
and support allowance: England and Wales)*

3.115 With effect from April 29, 2013, regs 7 and 9 of the Fines, Council
Tax and Community Charges (Deductions from Universal Credit and
Other Benefits) Regulations 2013 (SI 2013/612) amended reg.2 by
inserting the words "universal credit," after the words "income support," in the heading and on both occasions where the latter words occur
in the regulation.

**p.849,** *Amendment of the Council Tax (Deductions from Income Support)
Regulations 1993 (SI 1993/494) reg.3 (Application for deductions from
income support, state pension credit, jobseeker's allowance or employment
and support allowance: Scotland)*

3.116 With effect from April 29, 2013, regs 7 and 10 of the Fines, Council
Tax and Community Charges (Deductions from Universal Credit and
Other Benefits) Regulations 2013 (SI 2013/612) amended reg.3 by
inserting the words "universal credit," after the words "income support," in the heading and on both occasions where the latter words occur
in the regulation.

**p.851,** *Amendment of the Council Tax (Deductions from Income Support)
Regulations 1993 (SI 1993/494) reg.5 (Deductions from debtor's income
support, state pension credit, jobseeker's allowance or employment and
support allowance)*

3.117 With effect from April 29, 2013, regs 7 and 11 of the Fines, Council
Tax and Community Charges (Deductions from Universal Credit and
Other Benefits) Regulations 2013 (SI 2013/612) amended reg.5 by
adding the words "universal credit," after the words "income support,"
in the heading; adding the following paragraphs after para.(1):

"(1A) Subject to paragraphs (1B) and (1C) and regulation 8, where
the Secretary of State receives an application from an authority in
respect of a debtor who is entitled to universal credit, the Secretary of
State may deduct from the universal credit payable to the debtor an
amount equal to 5 per cent. of the appropriate universal credit standard allowance and pay that sum to the authority towards satisfaction
of any outstanding sum which is, or forms part of, the amount in

346

respect of which the liability order was made or the summary warrant or decree was granted.

(1B) No amount may be deducted under paragraph (1A) where it would reduce the amount of universal credit payable to the debtor to less than 1 penny.

(1C) For the purpose of paragraph (1A), where 5 per cent. of the appropriate universal credit standard allowance results in a fraction of a penny, that fraction is to be disregarded if it is less than half a penny and otherwise it is to be treated as a penny.

(1D) In paragraphs (1A) and (1C), 'appropriate universal credit standard allowance' means the appropriate universal credit standard allowance for the debtor for the assessment period in question under regulation 36 of the UC Regulations.";

substituting the following paragraphs for para.(2):

"(2) Subject to regulation 8, where—
(a) the Secretary of State receives an application from an authority in respect of a debtor who is entitled to contribution-based jobseeker's allowance or contributory employment and support allowance; and
(b) the amount of that allowance payable, before any deduction under this paragraph, is 10 pence or more,

the Secretary of State may deduct a sum from that allowance, up to the appropriate maximum specified in paragraph (2A), and pay that sum to the authority towards satisfaction of any outstanding sum which is, or forms part of, the amount in respect of which the liability order was made or the summary warrant or decree was granted.

(2A) The appropriate maximum is 40 per cent. of the appropriate age-related amount for the debtor specified—
(a) where the debtor is entitled to contribution-based jobseeker's allowance, in regulation 79 of the Jobseeker's Allowance Regulations 1996 or, as the case may be, regulation 49 of the Jobseeker's Allowance Regulations 2013;
(b) where the debtor is entitled to contributory employment and support allowance, in paragraph 1(1) of Schedule 4 to the Employment and Support Allowance Regulations 2008 or, as the case may be, regulation 62(1)(b) of the Employment and Support Allowance Regulations 2013."

and revoking para.(3).

By reg.11(6) of SI 2013/612, the substitution of new paras (2) and (2A) for the former para.(2) does not have effect in respect of an application received by the Secretary of State before April 29, 2013.

**pp.852–853,** *Amendment of the Council Tax (Deductions from Income Support) Regulations 1993 (SI 1993/494) reg.8 (Circumstances, time of making and termination of deductions)*

With effect from April 29, 2013, regs 7 and 12 of the Fines, Council Tax and Community Charges (Deductions from Universal Credit and

**3.118**

347

Other Benefits) Regulations 2013 (SI 2013/612) amended reg.8 by substituting the words "regulation 5(1) or (2)" for the words "regulation 5" in para.(1); adding the following paragraphs after para.(1):

> "(1A) The Secretary of State may make deductions from universal credit under regulation 5(1A) only if—
>   (a) the debtor is entitled to universal credit throughout any assessment period;
>   (b) no deductions are being made in respect of the debtor under any other application; and
>   (c) no payments are being made under regulation 2 of the Community Charge (Deductions from Income Support)(Scotland) Regulations 1989 or regulation 2 of the Community Charge (Deductions from Income Support)(No.2) Regulations 1990.";

and adding the words "universal credit," after the words "income support," each time the latter words occur in paras (2), (3) and (5).

**p.865,** *amendment to the Children (Leaving Care) Social Security Benefits (Scotland) Regulations 2004 (SI 2004/747) reg.2(4) (Entitlement to benefits (Scotland))*

3.119  With effect from June 24, 2013, art.17(1) of, and para.20(a) of Sch.1, Part 2 to, the Children's Hearings (Scotland) Act 2011 (Consequential and Transitional Provisions and Savings) Order 2013 (SI 2013/1465) substituted the words "by giving effect to a compulsory supervision order and a requirement within that order of the type mentioned in section 83(2)(a) of the Children's Hearings (Scotland) Act 2011," for the words "in compliance with a direction made in a supervision requirement under section 70(3) of that Act," in reg.2(4)(b).

From the same date, art.17(1) of, and para.20(b) of Sch.1, Part 2 to, the same Order substituted the words "the Children (Scotland) Act 1995 or by giving effect to a requirement within a compulsory supervision order under the Children's Hearings (Scotland) Act 2011," for the words "that Act or in compliance with a direction made in a supervision requirement under that Act," in reg.2(4)(b).

**pp.867–868,** *amendment to the Child Support (Maintenance Calculations and Special Cases) Regulations 2000 (SI 2001/155) reg.4 (Flat rate)*

3.120  With effect from April 29, 2013, reg.43(3)(a) of the Universal Credit (Consequential, Supplementary, Incidental and Miscellaneous Provisions) Regulations 2013 (SI 2013/630) omitted the word "and" after sub-para.(c) in reg.4(2) and inserted the following after sub-para.(d):

> "; and
>   (e) universal credit under Part 1 of the Welfare Reform Act 2012, where the award of universal credit is calculated on the basis that the non-resident parent does not have any earned income".

From the same date, reg.43(3)(b) of the same regulations inserted the following new paragraph after para.(3) in reg.4:

> "(4) For the purposes of paragraph (2)(e) and regulation 5(d), "earned income" has the meaning given in regulation 52 of the Universal Credit Regulations 2013 (earned income)."

**p.879,** *amendment of the Jobseeker's Allowance Regulations 1996 (SI 1996/207) reg.1 (Citation, commencement and interpretation—definition of 'contributory employment and support allowance')*

With effect from April 29, 2013, reg.30(1) and (2)(a) of the Universal Credit (Consequential, Supplementary, Incidental and Miscellaneous Provisions) Regulations 2013 (SI 2013/630) amended the heading of reg.1 to read as follows: **3.121**

> "Citation, commencement, interpretation and application"

**p.879,** *amendment of the Jobseeker's Allowance Regulations 1996 (SI 1996/207) reg.1 (Citation, commencement and interpretation)*

With effect from April 29, 2013, reg.30(1) and (2)(b) of the Universal Credit (Consequential, Supplementary, Incidental and Miscellaneous Provisions) Regulations 2013 (SI 2013/630) amended reg.1 by inserting the following new paragraph after para.(2): **3.122**

> "(2A) These Regulations do not apply to a particular case on any day on which section 33(1)(a) of the 2012 Act (abolition of income-based jobseeker's allowance) is in force and applies in relation to that case."

**p.879,** *amendment of the Jobseeker's Allowance Regulations 1996 (SI 1996/207) reg.1(3) (Interpretation—definition of 'attendance allowance')*

With effect from October 29, 2013, reg.6(1) and (2)(a) of the Social Security (Miscellaneous Amendments) (No. 3) Regulations 2013 (SI 2013/2536) amended the definition of "attendance allowance" in reg.1(3) by revoking paras (c) and (d). **3.123**

**p.881,** *amendment of the Jobseeker's Allowance Regulations 1996 (SI 1996/207) reg.1(3) (Citation, commencement and interpretation—definition of 'contributory employment and support allowance')*

With effect from April 29, 2013, reg.30(1) and (2)(c)(i) of the Universal Credit (Consequential, Supplementary, Incidental and Miscellaneous Provisions) Regulations 2013 (SI 2013/630) amended reg.1(3) by inserting the following definition after the definition of "the Contributions Regulations": **3.124**

> "'contributory employment and support allowance' means an allowance under Part 1 of the Welfare Reform Act as amended by the provisions of Schedule 3, and Part 1 of Schedule 14, to the 2012

349

Act that remove references to an income-related allowance, and a contributory allowance under Part 1 of the Welfare Reform Act as that Part has effect apart from those provisions;"

**p.882,** *amendment of the Jobseeker's Allowance Regulations 1996 (SI 1996/207) reg.1(3) (Interpretation—definition of 'enactment')*

3.125 With effect from October 29, 2013, reg.6(1) and (2)(b) of the Social Security (Miscellaneous Amendments) (No. 3) Regulations 2013 (SI 2013/2536) amended the definition of 'enactment' in reg.1(3) to read as follows:

> "'enactment' includes an enactment comprised in, or in an instrument made under, an Act of the Scottish Parliament [or the National Assembly for Wales];"

**pp.888–889,** *amendment of the Jobseeker's Allowance Regulations 1996 (SI 1996/207) reg.1(3) (Citation, Commencement and Interpretation—definition of "service user group")*

3.126 With effect from April 1, 2013, reg.11 and Sch.2, Pt 1, para.27(1) and (2) of the National Treatment Agency (Abolition) and the Health and Social Care Act 2012 (Consequential, Transitional and Saving Provisions) Order 2013. (SI 2013/235) added the following paragraphs after para.(f) in the definition of "service user group" in reg.1(3):

> "(fa)  the National Institute for Health and Care Excellence in consequence of a function under Part 8 of the Health and Social Care Act 2012,
>
> (fb)   a clinical commissioning group in consequence of a function under section 14Z2 of the National Health Service Act 2006,
>
> (fc)   the National Health Service Commissioning Board in consequence of a function under section 13Q of the National Health Service Act 2006,".

**p.890,** *amendment of the Jobseeker's Allowance Regulations 1996 (SI 1996/207) reg.1(3) (Citation, commencement and interpretation—definition of 'universal credit')*

3.127 With effect from April 29, 2013, reg.30(1) and (2)(c)(ii) of the Universal Credit (Consequential, Supplementary, Incidental and Miscellaneous Provisions) Regulations 2013 (SI 2013/630) amended reg.1(3) by inserting the following definition after the definition of "training allowance":

> "'universal credit' means universal credit under Part 1 of the 2012 Act;"

**p.934,** *amendment to the Jobseeker's Allowance Regulations 1996 (SI 1996/207) reg.14A(10)*

3.128 With effect from October 29, 2013, reg.2 of the Jobseeker's Allowance (Domestic Violence)(Amendment) Regulations 2013 (SI 2013/2722) amended reg.14A(10) by substituting for the definition of "domestic violence" the following definitions:

> "'coercive behaviour' means an act of assault, humiliation or intimidation or other abuse that is used to harm, punish or frighten V;
> 'controlling behaviour' means an act designed to make V subordinate or dependent by isolating them from sources of support, exploiting their resources and capacities for personal gain, depriving them of the means needed for independence, resistance or escape or regulating their everyday behaviour;
> 'domestic violence' means any incident or pattern of incidents of controlling behaviour, coercive behaviour, violence or abuse including but not limited to—
>> (a) psychological abuse;
>> (b) physical abuse;
>> (c) sexual abuse;
>> (d) financial abuse; and
>> (e) emotional abuse;
> regardless of the gender or sexuality of V;".

**p.937,** *annotation to the Jobseeker's Allowance Regulations 1996 (SI 1996/207) reg.15 (circumstances in which a person is not to be regarded as available) (full-time students)*

Generally a full time student cannot be regarded as available for employment during the period of study, but paras (2)–(4) afford an exception for those responsible for a child or young person. In *MB v SSWP (JSA)* [2013] UKUT 0535 (AAC), Judge Wikeley considered their application to a lone parent mature student. Recognising that the FTT had been faced with a poor and unhelpful set of papers from the Jobcentre office concerned, he held that the tribunal had erred in law in not considering the application of the exemption. On the balance of probabilities he accepted the claimant's son as a qualifying young person in both the relevant summers so that the exemption applied and the claimant was entitled to JSA for each of the summers in question. 3.129

**p.974,** *amendment to the Jobseeker's Allowance Regulations 1996 (SI 1996/207), reg.45B (relaxation of the first set of conditions)*

With effect from October 29, 2013, reg.6(1), (4) of the Social Security (Miscellaneous Amendments)(No. 3) Regulations 2013 (SI 2013/2536) amended reg.45B(1) by deleting the word "also". 3.130

**p.992,** *amendment of the Jobseeker's Allowance Regulations 1996 (SI 1996/207) reg.53(d) (Persons treated as not engaged in remunerative work)*

With effect from October 29, 2013, reg.6(1) and (5) of the Social Security (Miscellaneous Amendments) (No. 3) Regulations 2013 (SI 2013/2536) amended reg.53(d) to read as follows: 3.131

> "(d) he is engaged in employment as—

[(i) a part-time fire-fighter employed by a fire and rescue authority under the Fire and Rescue Services Act 2004 or by the Scottish Fire and Rescue Service established under section 1A of the Fire (Scotland) Act 2005;]

(ii) an auxiliary coastguard in respect of coastal rescue activities;

(iii) a person engaged part-time in the manning or launching of a lifeboat;

(iv) a member of any territorial or reserve force prescribed in Part I of Schedule 6 to the Social Security (Contributions) Regulations 2001;"

**pp.996,** *amendment to the Jobseeker's Allowance Regulations 1996 (SI 1996/207) reg.55(1) (short periods of sickness)*

3.132    In reg.55(1)(b), for "adjudication officer" substitute "Secretary of State" (change effected from October 18, 1999 by Social Security Act 1998 (Commencement No. 11, and Savings and Consequential and Transitional Provisions) Order 1999 (SI 1999/2860) Sch.12, para.2.

**p.996,** *amendment to the Jobseeker's Allowance Regulations 1996 (SI 1996/207) reg.55(4) (Short periods of sickness)*

3.133    With effect from October 29, 2013, reg.6(6) of the Social Security (Miscellaneous Amendments) (No. 3) Regulations 2013 (SI 2013/2536) substituted the following paragraph for para.(4) of reg.55:

"(4) The preceding provisions of this regulation do not apply to any person where the first day in respect of which they are unable to work falls within eight weeks beginning with the day the person ceased to be entitled to statutory sick pay."

**p.1025,** *annotation to the Jobseeker's Allowance Regulations 1996 (SI 1996/207) reg.70A (cases in which no reduction is to be made under section 19 or 19A)*

3.134    Failure to comply with reg.23 (attendance) or reg.23A (attendance by a joint claim couple) can only be subject to a reduction under s.19A(2)(a) of the Jobseekers Act 1995 if the claimant failing to participate fails within five days to show good reason for the failure. Any reduction imposed before the end of that five-day period will be invalid. See Judge Wikeley's decision in *DL v SSWP (JSA)* [2013] UKUT 0295 (AAC) on the similarly structured but now revoked reg.7(1) of the Jobseeker' Allowance (Employment, Skills and Enterprise Scheme) Regulations 2011 (SI 2011/917).

**p.1032,** *amendment of the Jobseeker's Allowance Regulations 1996 (SI 1996/207) reg.76(2) (Persons of a prescribed description)*

3.135    With effect from April 29, 2013, reg.30(1) and (3) of the Universal Credit (Consequential, Supplementary, Incidental and Miscellaneous

Provisions) Regulations 2013 (SI 2013/630) amended Universal reg.76(2) by inserting the following words at the end of sub-para.(e):

'; or
  (f)  entitled to universal credit'

**p.1038,** *amendment to the Jobseeker's Allowance Regulations 1996 (SI 1996/207) reg.79 (weekly amounts of contribution-based jobseeker's allowance)*

With effect from October 29, 2013, reg.6(1), (6) of the Social Security    3.136
(Miscellaneous Amendments)(No. 3) Regulations 2013 (SI 2013/2536) amended reg.79(1) by replacing sub-paras (a) and (b) with a single sub-paragraph to read:

"(a)  in the case of a person who has not attained the age of 25, £56.80 per week;".

**p.1040,** *correction to the Jobseeker's Allowance Regulations 1996 (SI 1996/207) reg.81(1) (payments by way of pensions)*

In para.(1) replace "benefit week" with "week".    3.137

**pp.1047–1048,** *amendment of Jobseeker's Allowance Regulations 1996 (SI 1996/207) reg.85A(2) (Special cases: supplemental—persons from abroad)*

With effect from January 1, 2014, reg.2 of the Jobseeker's Allowance    3.138
(Habitual Residence) Amendment Regulations 2013 (SI 2013/3196) amended reg.85A by substituting the following paragraph for para.(2):

"(2) No claimant shall be treated as habitually resident in the United Kingdom, the Channel Islands, the Isle of Man or the Republic of Ireland unless—
  (a)  the claimant has been living in any of those places for the past three months; and
  (b)  the claimant has a right to reside in any of those places, other than a right to reside which falls within paragraph (3)."

Regulation 3 of SI 2013/3196 contains a savings provision under which the above amendment does not apply in relation to a claim for a jobseeker's allowance which is made or treated as made before January 1, 2014.

**p.1048,** *amendment of the Jobseeker's Allowance Regulations 1996 (SI 1996/207) reg.85A(4)(f) (Special cases: supplemental—persons from abroad)*

With effect from July 1, 2013, reg.3 of the Social Security (Croatia)    3.139
Amendment Regulations 2013 (SI 2013/1474) amended reg.85A(4)(f) to read as follows:

"(f) a person who is treated as a worker for the purpose of the definition of "qualified person" in regulation 6(1) of the Immigration (European Economic Area) Regulations 2006 pursuant to—

    (i) regulation 6 of the Accession (Immigration and Worker Authorisation) Regulations 2006 (right of residence of a Bulgarian or Romanian who is an 'accession State national subject to worker authorisation'), or

    (ii) regulation 5 of the Accession of Croatia (Immigration and Worker Authorisation) Regulations 2013 (right of residence of a Croatian who is an 'accession State national subject to worker authorisation');"

**pp.1048–1049,** *amendment of the Jobseeker's Allowance Regulations 1996 (SI 1996/207) reg.85A(4) (Special cases: supplemental—persons from abroad)*

3.140     With effect from October 29, 2013, reg.6(1) and (8) of the Social Security (Miscellaneous Amendments) (No. 3) Regulations 2013 (SI 2013/2536) amended reg.21AA(4) by substituting the following for sub-para.(h):

"(h) a person who has been granted leave or who is deemed to have been granted leave outside the rules made under section 3(2) of the Immigration Act 1971 where that leave is—

    (i) discretionary leave to enter or remain in the United Kingdom;

    (ii) leave to remain under the Destitution Domestic Violence concession; or

    (iii) leave deemed to have been granted by virtue of regulation 3 of the Displaced Persons (Temporary Protection) Regulations 2005;"

and by adding the word 'or' at the end of sub-para.(hh) and revoking sub-paras (j) and (k).

**pp.1059–1061,** *amendment to the Jobseeker's Allowance Regulations 1996 (SI 1996/207) reg.94 (Calculation of earnings derived from employed earner's employment and income other than earnings)*

3.141     With effect from October 29, 2013, reg.6(9)(a) of the Social Security (Miscellaneous Amendments) (No. 3) Regulations 2013 (SI 2013/2536) substituted the following new sub-paragraph for sub-para.(b) in reg.94(2):

"(b) in any other case, a period equal to such number of weeks as is equal to the number obtained by applying the formula—

$$\frac{E}{J+D}$$

where—

E is the amount of net earnings, or in the case of income which does not consist of earnings, the amount of that income less any amount paid by way of tax on that income which is disregarded under paragraph 1 of Schedule 7 (sums to be disregarded in the calculation of income other than earnings);

J is the amount of jobseeker's allowance which would be payable had the payment not been made;

D is an amount equal to the total of the sums which would fall to be disregarded from that payment under Schedule 6 and Schedule 6A (sums to be disregarded in the calculation of earnings) or, as the case may be, any paragraph of Schedule 7 other than paragraph 1 of that Schedule, as is appropriate in the claimant's case,".

From the same date, reg.6(9)(b) of the same Regulations inserted the following new paragraph after para.(10) in reg.94:

"(11) For the purposes of the number obtained as referred to in paragraph (2)(b), any fraction is to be treated as a corresponding fraction of a week.".

**p.1062,** *annotation to the Jobseeker's Allowance Regulations 1996 (SI 1996/207) reg.94*

Regulation 94(2)(b) has been rewritten and a new para.(11) has been added to reg.94 so that it matches the equivalent rule for "new-style JSA" (see reg.54(2)(c) and (13) of the Jobseeker's Allowance Regulations 2013 (SI 2013/378) in Part I of this Supplement) but the substance of the provision remains the same.    3.142

**p.1064,** *amendment to the Jobseeker's Allowance Regulations 1996 (SI 1996/207) reg.96(2) (Date on which income is treated as paid)*

With effect from April 29, 2013, reg.30(4) of the Universal Credit (Consequential, Supplementary, Incidental and Miscellaneous Provisions) Regulations 2013 (SI 2013/630) substituted the words ", employment and support allowance or universal credit" for the words "or employment and support allowance", and the words "on any day" for the words "on the day of the benefit week", in reg.96(2).    3.143

**p.1067,** *amendment to the Jobseeker's Allowance Regulations 1996 (SI 1996/207) reg.98(1) (Earnings of employed earners)*

With effect from October 29, 2013, reg.6(10) of the Social Security (Miscellaneous Amendments) (No. 3) Regulations 2013 (SI 2013/2536) substituted "131 or 132" for "131 and 132" in reg.98(1)(f).    3.144

**pp.1071–1073,** *amendment to the Jobseeker's Allowance Regulations 1996 (SI 1996/207) reg.101 (Calculation of net profit of self-employed earners)*

With effect from October 29, 2013, reg.6(11) of the Social Security (Miscellaneous Amendments) (No. 3) Regulations 2013 (SI 2013/2536)    3.145

substituted the words "national insurance contributions" for the words "social security contributions" in paras (1)(b)(i), (4)(b)(ii) and (10)(a)(ii) of reg.101.

**pp.1073–1074,** *amendment to the Jobseeker's Allowance Regulations 1996 (SI 1996/207) reg.102 (Deduction of tax and contributions for self-employed earners)*

3.146    With effect from October 29, 2013, reg.6(12) of the Social Security (Miscellaneous Amendments) (No. 3) Regulations 2013 (SI 2013/2536) substituted the following new reg.102:

### "Deduction of tax and contributions for self-employed earners

**102.**—(1) Subject to paragraph (2), the amount to be deducted in respect of income tax under regulation 101(1)(b)(i), (4)(b)(i) or (10)(a)(i) (calculation of net profit of self-employed earners) is to be calculated—

(a) on the basis of the amount of chargeable income; and

(b) as if that income were assessable to income tax at the basic rate of tax less only the personal allowance to which the claimant is entitled under sections 35 and 38 to 40 of the Income Tax Act 2007 (personal reliefs) as is appropriate to their circumstances.

(2) If the period determined under regulation 95 is less than a year, the earnings to which the basic rate of tax is to be applied and the amount of the personal allowance deductible under paragraph (1) is to be calculated on a pro rata basis.

(3) Subject to paragraph (4), the amount to be deducted in respect of national insurance contributions under regulation 101(1)(b)(i), (4)(b)(ii) or (10)(a)(ii) is to be the total of—

(a) the amount of Class 2 contributions payable under section 11(1) or, as the case may be, 11(3) of the Benefits Act at the rate applicable at the date of claim except where the claimant's chargeable income is less than the amount specified in section 11(4) of that Act (small earnings exception) for the tax year in which the date of claim falls; and

(b) the amount of Class 4 contributions (if any) which would be payable under section 15 of that Act (Class 4 contributions recoverable under the Income Tax Acts) at the percentage rate applicable at the date of claim on so much of the chargeable income as exceeds the lower limit but does not exceed the upper limit of profits and gains applicable for the tax year in which the date of claim falls.

(4) If the period determined under regulation 95 is less than a year—

(a) the amount specified for the tax year referred to in paragraph (3)(a) is to be reduced pro rata; and

(b) the limits referred to in paragraph (3)(b) are to be reduced pro rata.

(5) In this regulation "chargeable income" means—

(a) except where sub-paragraph (b) applies, the earnings derived from the employment less any expenses deducted under regulation 101(4)(a) or, as the case may be, (5); and

(b) in the case of employment as a child minder, one-third of the earnings of that employment.".

**p.1074,** *annotation to the Jobseeker's Allowance Regulations 1996 (SI 1996/207) reg.102*

Regulation 102 has been rewritten so that it matches the equivalent 3.147 rule for "new-style JSA" (see reg.62 of the Jobseeker's Allowance Regulations 2013 (SI 2013/378) in Part I of this Supplement) but the substance of the provision remains the same.

**p.1080,** *amendment to the Jobseeker's Allowance Regulations 1996 (SI 1996/207) reg.103(5B) (Calculation of income other than earnings)*

With effect from April 29, 2013, reg.30(5) of the Universal Credit 3.148 (Consequential, Supplementary, Incidental and Miscellaneous Provisions) Regulations 2013 (SI 2013/630) inserted the words "or section 11J of the Welfare Reform Act as the case may be" after the words "Employment and Support Allowance Regulations" in reg.103(5B).

**p.1148,** *amendment of the Jobseeker's Allowance Regulations 1996 (SI 1996/207) reg.153(b) (Modification in the calculation of income)*

With effect from April 29, 2013, reg.30(1) and (6) of the Universal 3.149 Credit (Consequential, Supplementary, Incidental and Miscellaneous Provisions) Regulations 2013 (SI 2013/630) amended reg.153(b) by inserting the words ", universal credit" after the words "the Benefits Act".

**p.1176,** *amendment to the Jobseeker's Allowance Regulations 1996 (SI 1996/207) Sch.2 (Housing Costs) para.1(3)*

With effect from April 29, 2013, reg.30(7)(a) of the Universal Credit 3.150 (Consequential, Supplementary, Incidental and Miscellaneous Provisions) Regulations 2013 (SI 2013/630) inserted the following new head after head (e) in para.1(3):

"; or

(f) who is entitled to an award of universal credit the calculation of which includes an amount under regulation 27(1) of the Universal Credit Regulations 2013 in respect of the fact that he has limited capability for work or limited capability for work and work-related activity, or would include such an amount but for regulation 27(4) or 29(4) of those Regulations".

**pp.1191–1192,** *amendment to the Jobseeker's Allowance Regulations 1996 (SI 1996/207) Sch.2 (Housing Costs) para.17*

3.151     With effect from April 29, 2013, reg.30(7)(b)(i) of the Universal Credit (Consequential, Supplementary, Incidental and Miscellaneous Provisions) Regulations 2013 (SI 2013/630) inserted the following new head after head (i) in sub-para.(7) of para.17:

"or
(j)   if he is aged less than 25 and is entitled to an award of universal credit which is calculated on the basis that he does not have any earned income".

From the same date, reg.30(7)(b)(ii) of the same Regulations inserted the following new sub-paragraph after sub-para.(8) in para.17:

"(9) For the purposes of sub-paragraph (7)(j), "earned income" has the meaning given in regulation 52 of the Universal Credit Regulations 2013."

**p.1196,** *annotation to the Jobseeker's Allowance Regulations 1996 (SI 1996/207) Sch.2*

3.152     On the amendments to paras 1(3) and 17 of Sch.2 made by the Universal Credit (Consequential, Supplementary, Incidental and Miscellaneous Provisions) Regulations 2013 (SI 2013/630) with effect from April 29, 2013, see the note to the amendments to paras 1(3) and 18 of Sch.3 to the Income Support (General) Regulations 1987, above.

**p.1208,** *amendment to the Jobseeker's Allowance Regulations 1996 (SI 1996/207) Sch.6 (Sums to be disregarded in the calculation of earnings) para.9*

3.153     With effect from October 29, 2013, reg.6(14) of the Social Security (Miscellaneous Amendments) (No. 3) Regulations 2013 (SI 2013/2536) omitted sub-paras (1)(a), (1)(aa) and (1)(ab) in para.9 and inserted the following new sub-para.(1)(a) before sub-para.(1)(b):

"(a)  a part-time fire-fighter employed by a fire and rescue authority under the Fire and Rescue Services Act 2004 or by the Scottish Fire and Rescue Service established under section 1A of the Fire (Scotland) Act 2005;".

**p.1212,** *annotation to the Jobseeker's Allowance Regulations 1996 (SI 1996/207) Sch.6 para.9*

3.154     See the note to the amendment to para.7 of Sch.8 to the Income Support (General) Regulations 1987 above.

**p.1216,** *amendment to the Jobseeker's Allowance Regulations 1996 (SI 1996/207) Sch.7 (Sums to be disregarded in the calculation of income other than earnings) para.8*

With effect from April 29, 2013, reg.30(8) of the Universal Credit **3.155** (Consequential, Supplementary, Incidental and Miscellaneous Provisions) Regulations 2013 (SI 2013/630) omitted the word "or" after sub-para.(c) in para.8 and inserted after sub-para.(d):

"; or
    (e) universal credit".

**p.1220,** *amendment to the Jobseeker's Allowance Regulations 1996 (SI 1996/207) Sch.7 (Sums to be disregarded in the calculation of income other than earnings) para.28*

With effect from April 1, 2013, art.11 of, and para.27(3)(a) of Part 1 **3.156** of Sch.2 to, the National Treatment Agency (Abolition) and the Health and Social Care Act 2012 (Consequential, Transitional and Saving Provisions) Order 2013 (SI 2013/235) inserted the following new sub-paragraphs after sub-para.(d) in para.28:

"(da)  a clinical commissioning group established under section 14D of the National Health Service Act 2006;
(db)  the National Health Service Commissioning Board; or".

From the same date, art.11 of, and para.27(3)(b) of Part 1 of Sch.2 to, the same Regulations omitted sub-para.(e) in para.28, together with the word "or" following it.

**pp.1232–1233,** *amendment to the Jobseeker's Allowance Regulations 1996 (SI 1996/207) Sch.8 (Capital to be disregarded) para.12*

With effect from April 29, 2013, reg.30(9) of the Universal Credit **3.157** (Consequential, Supplementary, Incidental and Miscellaneous Provisions) Regulations 2013 (SI 2013/630) inserted the words ", universal credit" after the words "working tax credit" in para.12(1)(b).

**pp.1256–1257,** *amendments to the Jobseeker's Allowance (Schemes for Assisting Persons to Obtain Employment) Regulations 2013 (SI 2013/276) reg.3 (schemes for assisting persons to obtain employment)*

With effect from November 5, 2013, reg.2 of the Jobseeker's Allow- **3.158** ance (Schemes for Assisting Persons to Obtain Employment) (Amendment) Regulations 2013 (SI 2013/2584) amended reg.3 by inserting after para.(8) new paras (8A) and (8B) to read:

"(8A) Community Work Placements is a scheme lasting up to 30 weeks, designed to assist a claimant who requires further support in order to obtain and sustain employment, in which participants undertake work placements for the benefit of the community and work-related activity.

(8B) (a) Traineeships is a scheme for a claimant who has limited educational qualifications and work history and meets the age criteria in sub-paragraph (b). The scheme consists of a government-funded course which, for a period of up to 6 months, provides the claimant with work preparation training, a work experience placement and, where required, English and Maths tuition.

      (b) The age criteria are that on the first day of the course the claimant must be—

          (i) aged between 16 and 23 years; or

          (ii) subject to a Learning Difficulty Assessment and aged between 16 and 24 years."

From the same date the amending regulation also inserted into para.(9) before the definition of self-employment, a new definition to read:

"'Learning Difficulty Assessment' has the same meaning as in section 139A of the Learning and Skills Act 2000."

**pp.1265–1270,** *amendment to State Pension Credit Regulations 2002 (SI 2002/1792) reg.1(2) (citation, commencement and interpretation)*

3.159     With effect from October 29, 2013, reg.10(2) of the Social Security (Miscellaneous Amendments) (No. 3) Regulations 2013 (SI 2013/2536) amended the definition of "attendance allowance" so as to omit paragraphs (c) and (d); and inserted "or the National Assembly for Wales" in the definition of "enactment" after "Parliament".

With effect from April 29, 2013, reg.33(2) of the Universal Credit (Consequential, Supplementary, Incidental and Miscellaneous Provisions) Regulations 2013 (SI 2013/630) inserted the following new definitions after the definitions of "close relative", "the Health Service (Wales) Act" and "the Skipton Fund" respectively:

"'contribution-based jobseeker's allowance' means an allowance under the Jobseekers Act 1995 as amended by the provisions of Part 1 of Schedule 14 to the 2012 Act that remove references to an income-based allowance, and a contribution-based allowance under the Jobseekers Act 1995 as that Act has effect apart from those provisions;";

"'income-based jobseeker's allowance' means an income-based allowance under the Jobseekers Act 1995;";

"'universal credit' means universal credit under Part 1 of the 2012 Act;".

In addition, the same amending Regulations substituted for the definition of "contributory employment and support allowance" the following:

"'contributory employment and support allowance' means an allowance under Part 1 of the Welfare Reform Act as amended by the provisions of Schedule 3, and Part 1 of Schedule 14, to the 2012 Act that remove references to an income-related allowance, and a contributory allowance under Part 1 of the Welfare Reform Act as that Part has effect apart from those provisions;".

**pp.1273–1274,** *amendment to State Pension Credit Regulations 2002 (SI 2002/1792) reg.2 (persons not in Great Britain)*

With effect from July 1, 2013, reg.4(2) of the Social Security (Croatia) Amendment Regulations 2013 (SI 2013/1474) substituted for reg.2(3)(f) the following sub-paragraph: **3.160**

"(f) a person who is treated as a worker for the purpose of the definition of 'qualified person' in regulation 6(1) of the Immigration (European Economic Area) Regulations 2006 pursuant to—
  (i) regulation 6 of the Accession (Immigration and Worker Authorisation) Regulations 2006 (right of residence of a Bulgarian or Romanian who is an "accession State national subject to worker authorisation"), or
  (ii) regulation 5 of the Accession of Croatia (Immigration and Worker Authorisation) Regulations 2013 (right of residence of a Croatian who is an 'accession State national subject to worker authorisation');"

With effect from October 29, 2013, reg.10(3) of the Social Security (Miscellaneous Amendments) (No. 3) Regulations 2013 (SI 2013/2536) substituted a new sub-para.(h):

"(h) a person who has been granted leave or who is deemed to have been granted leave outside the rules made under section 3(2) of the Immigration Act 1971 (where that leave is—
  (i) discretionary leave to enter or remain in the United Kingdom;
  (ii) leave to remain under the Destitution Domestic Violence concession; or
  (iii) leave deemed to have been granted by virtue of regulation 3 of the Displaced Persons (Temporary Protection) Regulations 2005;"

The same amending regulation added "or" at the end of sub-para.(hh) and omitted sub-paras (j) and (k).

**pp.1279–1280,** *annotation to State Pension Credit Regulations 2002 (SI 2002/1792) reg.5 (persons treated as being or not being members of the same household)*

On the meaning of a "person subject to immigration control" within sub-para.(1)(h), see *OO v Secretary of State for Work and Pensions (SPC)* [2013] UKUT 335 (AAC). A spouse who falls within that definition is not treated as part of the claimant's household for SPC purposes, i.e. when calculating the claimant's applicable amount or income. The tribunal in this case had failed to distinguish between a spouse being "sponsored" for immigration purposes and a person being subject to a **3.161** sponsorship undertaking (under immigration law, written sponsorship undertakings cannot apply to a spouse). The claimant's statement on his SPC claim form that his wife was sponsored to be in the United Kingdom was accurate (he had not stated that he had signed a written undertaking). The DWP, which had wrongly assumed that his wife was a person subject to immigration control (rather than having been given indefinite leave to remain, as in fact was the case), had failed to make proper enquiries as to her true immigration status. The resulting overpayment was, therefore, due to official error and was not recoverable. The entitlement decision was remitted to a new tribunal for detailed findings on the claimant's means which were required to determine his entitlement to SPC.

**p.1283,** *amendment to State Pension Credit Regulations 2002 (SI 2002/1792) reg.9 (qualifying income for the purposes of savings credits)*

3.162     With effect from April 29, 2013, reg.33(3) of the Universal Credit (Consequential, Supplementary, Incidental and Miscellaneous Provisions) Regulations 2013 (SI 2013/630) omitted "within the meaning of section 1(4) of the Jobseekers Act 1995" in para.(c).

**p.1289,** *amendment to State Pension Credit Regulations 2002 (SI 2002/1792) reg.13A (part-weeks)*

3.163     With effect from April 29, 2013, reg.33(4) of the Universal Credit (Consequential, Supplementary, Incidental and Miscellaneous Provisions) Regulations 2013 (SI 2013/630) inserted "universal credit," before "income support" in para.(1)(a).

**pp.1289–1290,** *amendment to State Pension Credit Regulations 2002 (SI 2002/1792) reg.13B (date on which benefits are treated as paid)*

3.164     With effect from April 29, 2013, reg.33(5) of the Universal Credit (Consequential, Supplementary, Incidental and Miscellaneous Provisions) Regulations 2013 (SI 2013/630) omitted "within the meaning of section 1(4) of the Jobseekers Act 1995" in para.(1)(d).

**p.1319,** *amendment to State Pension Credit Regulations 2002 (SI 2002/1792) Sch.II para.1 (housing costs)*

3.165     With effect from April 29, 2013, reg.33(6)(a) of the Universal Credit (Consequential, Supplementary, Incidental and Miscellaneous Provisions) Regulations 2013 (SI 2013/630) inserted after sub-para.(ee) in para.1(2)(a)(iii), the following:

    "; or
      (ff)  is entitled to an award of universal credit the calculation of which includes an amount under regulation 27(1) of the Universal Credit Regulations 2013 in respect of the fact that he has limited capability for work or limited capability for work

and work-related activity, or would include such an amount but for regulation 27(4) or 29(4) of those Regulations".

**p.1331,** *amendment to State Pension Credit Regulations 2002 (SI 2002/1792) Sch.II para.14 (persons residing with the claimant)*

With effect from April 29, 2013, reg.33(6)(b) of the Universal Credit 3.166 (Consequential, Supplementary, Incidental and Miscellaneous Provisions) Regulations 2013 (SI 2013/630) inserted after sub-para.(7)(g) the following:

"; or
   (h) if he is aged less than 25 and is entitled to an award of universal credit which is calculated on the basis that he does not have any earned income";

and inserted after sub-para.(8), the following:

"(9) For the purposes of sub-paragraph (7)(h), 'earned income' has the meaning given in regulation 52 of the Universal Credit Regulations 2013.".

**p.1333,** *annotation to State Pension Credit Regulations 2002 (SI 2002/1792) Sch.II para.5 (housing costs not met)*

For a useful discussion of the authorities, and confirmation that the 3.167 test under para.(10) is that "the satisfaction of the 'more suited' test requires some demonstration as to what the special needs are, and how the new accommodation caters better for them", see *MAA v Secretary of State for Work and Pensions* [2013] UKUT 593 (AAC) (at paras 31–44).

**p.1335,** *annotation to State Pension Credit Regulations 2002 (SI 2002/1792) Sch.II para.13 (other housing costs)*

The case law on the treatment of eligible service charges was con- 3.168 sidered further in *DL v Secretary of State for Work and Pensions* [2013] AACR 22; [2013] UKUT 29 (AAC). This review of the authorities confirmed that charges for maintenance, repairs, cleaning, and utility charges for communal areas and gardens are eligible (CIS/1459/1995); charges for reserve fund contributions for accommodation costs are eligible (CPC/968/2005 and CIS/667/2002); staffing costs fairly attributable to the provision of adequate accommodation based on what the staff actually do in the particular development or similar developments are eligible (R(PC) 1/07 and CPC/977/2007); and other administrative costs, which cannot be neatly categorised, should be apportioned in the same ratio as eligible and non-eligible charges in the rest of the budget (R(PC) 1/07 and CPC/968/2005), rather than in the same ratio as eligible and non-eligible charges in the staff costs budget only (as held in R(IS) 2/07).

**p.1345,** *amendment to State Pension Credit Regulations 2002 (SI 2002/1792) Sch.II Part 1 (capital disregarded for the purpose of calculating income)*

3.169    With effect from April 29, 2013, reg.33(7) of the Universal Credit (Consequential, Supplementary, Incidental and Miscellaneous Provisions) Regulations 2013 (SI 2013/630) inserted after para.20(2)(o) the following:

> ";
>
> (p) universal credit";

and omitted "or" after para.20A(2)(h) and inserted after sub-para.(i) the following:

> "or (j) paragraph 17 of Schedule 10 to the Universal Credit Regulations 2013;".

The reference to "paragraph 17" in new sub-para.(j) was then corrected to read "paragraph 18" with effect from October 29, 2013 by reg.10(4) of the Social Security (Miscellaneous Amendments) (No. 3) Regulations 2013 (SI 2013/2536).

**p.1350,** *amendment to State Pension Credit Regulations 2002 (SI 2002/1792) Sch.VI (sums disregarded from claimant's earnings)*

3.170    With effect from October 29, 2013, reg.10(5) of the Social Security (Miscellaneous Amendments) (No. 3) Regulations 2013 (SI 2013/2536) omitted paras (a), (aa) and (ab) in paragraph 2(2) and inserted before para.(b) a new para.(a) as follows:

> "(a) a part-time fire-fighter employed by a fire and rescue authority under the Fire and Rescue Services Act 2004 or by the Scottish Fire and Rescue Service established under section 1A of the Fire (Scotland) Act 2005;".

**p.1355,** *amendment of the Social Fund Cold Weather Payments (General) Regulations 1988 (SI 1988/1724) reg 1(2) (Citation, commencement and interpretation—definition of "the 2012 Act")*

3.171    With effect from November 1, 2013, reg.2(1) and (2)(a) of the Social Fund Cold Weather Payments (General) Regulations 1988 (SI 2013/248) amended reg.1(2) by inserting the following definition immediately before the definition of "the Act":

> "'the 2012 Act' means the Welfare Reform Act 2012;"

**p.1355,** *amendment of the Social Fund Cold Weather Payments (General) Regulations 1988 (SI 1988/1724) reg.1(2) (Citation, commencement and interpretation—definition of "claimant")*

3.172    With effect from November 1, 2013, reg.2(1) and (2)(b) of the Social Fund Cold Weather Payments (General) Regulations 1988 (SI

2013/248) amended the definition of "claimant" in reg.1(2) to read as follows:

> "'claimant' means a person who is claiming or has claimed income support, state pension credit, income-based jobseeker's allowance [, income-related employment and support allowance or universal credit]."

**p.1356,** *amendment of the Social Fund Cold Weather Payments (General) Regulations 1988 (SI 1988/1724) reg.1(2) (Citation, commencement and interpretation—definition of "universal credit")*

With effect from November 1, 2013, reg.2(1) and (2)(c) of the Social Fund Cold Weather Payments (General) Regulations 1988 (SI 2013/248) amended reg.1(2) by inserting the following definition immediately after the definition of "station": **3.173**

> "'universal credit' means universal credit under Part 1 of the 2012 Act;".

**p.1358,** *amendment of the Social Fund Cold Weather Payments (General) Regulations 1988 (SI 1988/1724) reg.1A(2) (Prescribed description of persons)*

With effect from November 1, 2013, reg.2(1) and (3) of the Social Fund Cold Weather Payments (General) Regulations 1988 (SI 2013/248) amended reg.1A(2), by revoking the word "or" between sub-paras (c) and (d) and inserting the following words at the end of sub-para.(d): **3.174**

> "; or
>    (e) universal credit."

**p.1358,** *amendment of the Social Fund Cold Weather Payments (General) Regulations 1988 (SI 1988/1724) reg.1A(3) (Prescribed description of persons)*

With effect from November 1, 2013, reg.2(1) and (4) of the Social Fund Cold Weather Payments (General) Regulations 1988 (SI 2013/248) amended reg.1A(3), by substituting the words "(c), (d) or (e)" for the words "(c) or (d)", revoking the word "or" between sub-paras (d) and (e) and inserting the following words at the end of sub-para.(e): **3.175**

> "; or
>    (f) where P has been awarded universal credit—
>       (i) the award includes an amount under section 10(2) of the 2012 Act (child or qualifying young person who is disabled); or
>       (ii) the award includes an amount under section 12(1) of the 2012 Act in respect of the needs or circumstances specified in section 12(2)(a) or (b) (limited capability for work or

limited capability for work and work-related activity) or would do so if it did not include an amount in respect of the needs or circumstances specified in section 12(2)(c) (caring responsibilities for a severely disabled person)."

**p.1358,** *amendment of the Social Fund Cold Weather Payments (General) Regulations 1988 (SI 1988/1724) reg.1A (Prescribed description of persons)*

3.176    With effect from November 1, 2013, reg.2(1) and (5) of the Social Fund Cold Weather Payments (General) Regulations 1988 (SI 2013/248) amended reg.1A, by adding the following paragraph after para.(4):

"(4A) In relation to a person who has been awarded universal credit, the third condition applies as if paragraph (4)(d) were omitted."

**p.1359,** *amendment of the Social Fund Cold Weather Payments (General) Regulations 1988 (SI 1988/1724) reg.1A (Prescribed description of persons)*

3.177    With effect from November 1, 2013, reg.2(1) and (6) of the Social Fund Cold Weather Payments (General) Regulations 1988 (SI 2013/248) amended reg.1A, by adding the following paragraphs after para.(6):

"(6) The fourth condition, which applies only where the person has been awarded universal credit and their award of universal credit does not include an amount under section 10(2) of the 2012 Act (child or qualifying young person who is disabled) is that—
(a) in a case where a cold weather payment is payable in relation to a recorded period of cold weather as mentioned in regulation 2(1)(a)(i), the person was not in employment or gainful self-employment on any day during that period; or
(b) in a case where a cold weather payment is payable in relation to a forecasted period of weather as mentioned in regulation 2(1)(a)(ii), the person is not in employment or gainful self-employment on the day when the Meteorological Office supplies the Department for Work and Pensions with the forecast.
(7) For the purpose of paragraph (6)—
(a) 'employment' means employment under a contract of service, or in an office, including an elective office;
(b) a person is in gainful self-employment where—
  (i) they are carrying on a trade, profession or vocation as their main employment;
  (ii) their earnings from that trade, profession or vocation are treated as self-employed earnings for the purpose of regulations made under section 8(3) of the 2012 Act; and
  (iii) the trade, profession or vocation is organised, developed, regular and carried on in expectation of profit."

**pp.1359–1360,** *annotation to Social Fund Cold Weather Payments (General) Regulations 1988 (SI 1988/1724) reg.1A (Prescribed description of persons)*

Replace the General Note in the main work with the following: **3.178**

"Regulation 1A sets out the four conditions which a claimant must satisfy in order to receive a cold weather payment. The second, third and fourth conditions do not apply to all claimants. However, where they apply, the conditions are cumulative so failure to satisfy any of them means that no cold weather payment can be made.

The first condition is that the claimant must actually have been awarded (i.e. an underlying entitlement will not suffice) SPC, IS, income-based JSA income-related ESA, or universal credit for at least one day in the relevant (forecasted or recorded) period of cold weather.

The second condition is that, unless the claimant has been awarded SPC, then—for that day—either:

- his or her family must include a child under five; or
- the claimant has an award of child tax credit which includes an individual element for a disabled, or severely disabled, child or qualifying young person.
- (if the claimant has been awarded IS or income-based JSA) his or her applicable amount must include one of the pensioner or disability premiums; or
- (if the claimant has been awarded income-related ESA) his or her applicable amount must include either one of the pensioner or disability premiums or the work-related activity component or the support component; or
- (if the claimant has been awarded universal credit) the award includes either the disabled child addition (i.e. the additional amount of the child element payable for a child or qualifying young person who is disabled); or the LCW element or the LCWRA element; or would include the LCW element if it did not include the carer element (see Vol.V). Those who qualify on the basis that their award includes the LCW element or the LCWRA element must also satisfy the fourth condition.

The third condition applies to claimants who do not have a child under five in their family and who do not have an award of child tax credit which includes one of the individual elements specified above. It is that the claimant does not reside in a care home or independent hospital (as defined in each case in para.(5)) or (for claimants who are not in receipt of universal credit: see para.(4A)) in an Abbeyfield Home or accommodation provided under the specified provisions of the Polish Resettlement Act 1947.

The fourth condition applies to claimants who have an award of universal credit that does not include the disabled child addition (i.e. those who have limited capability for work or work-related activity (see above). It is that the claimant is not in gainful employment or self-

367

employment (as defined in para.(7)) during the period of cold weather
in respect of which the cold weather payment is payable.

Since no claim for a cold weather payment is possible, the decision
maker will identify qualifying claimants from Departmental records
and make a payment automatically."

**pp.1363–1366,** *amendment of the Social Fund Cold Weather Payments*
*(General) Regulations 1988 (SI 1988/1724) Sch.1 (Identification of*
*stations and postcode districts)*

3.179     With effect from November 1, 2013, reg.2(1) of the Social Fund Cold
Weather Payments (General) Amendment (No.2) Regulations 2013 (SI
2013/2538) substituted the following schedule for Sch.1:

"Regulation 2(1)(a),(2) and 2(1A)

SCHEDULE 1

IDENTIFICATION OF STATIONS AND POSTCODE DISTRICTS

| Column (1) | Column (2) |
|---|---|
| *Meteorological Office Station* | *Postcode Districts* |
| 1. Aberporth | SA35–48, SA64–65. |
| 2. Aboyne | AB30–34, AB38, AB51–55, DD8–9. |
| 3. Albemarle | DH1–7, DH9, DL4–5, DL14–17, NE1–13, NE15–18, NE20–21, NE23, NE25–46, SR1–7, TS21, TS28–29. |
| 4. Andrewsfield | CB1–5, CB10–11, CB21–25, CM1–9, CM11–24, CM77, CO9, RM4, SG8–11. |
| 5. Auchincruive | DG9, KA1–26, KA28–30, PA20. |
| 6. Aultbea | IV21–22, IV26. |
| 7. Aviemore | AB37, IV13, PH19–26. |
| 8. Bainbridge | BD23–24, DL8, DL11–13. |
| 9. Bedford | MK1–19, MK40–46, NN1–16, NN29, PE19, SG 5–7, SG15–19. |
| 10. Bingley | BB4, BB8–12, BB18, BD1–22, BL0, BL7–8, HD3, HD7–9, HX1–7, LS21, LS29, OL1–5, OL11–16, S36. |
| 11. Bishopton | G1–5, G11–15, G20–23, G31–34, G40–46, G51–53, G60–62, G64, G66, G69, G71–78, G81–84, ML1–5, PA1–19, PA21–27, PA32. |
| 12. Boscombe Down | BA12, RG28, SO20–23, SP1–5, SP7, SP9–11. |
| 13. Boulmer | NE22, NE24, NE61–70. |

| Column (1) | Column (2) |
|---|---|
| *Meteorological Office Station* | *Postcode districts* |
| 14. Braemar | AB35–36, PH10–11, PH18. |
| 15. Brize Norton | OX1–6, OX8, OX10–14, OX18, OX20, OX25–29, OX33, OX44, SN7. |
| 16. Capel Curig | LL24–25, LL41. |
| 17. Cardinham (Bodmin) | PL13–18, PL22–35, TR9. |
| 18. Carlisle | CA1–8, DG12, DG16. |
| 19. Cassley | IV27–28, KW11, KW13. |
| 20. Charlwood | BN5–6, BN44, GU5–6, ME6, ME14–20, RH1–20, TN1–20, TN22, TN27. |
| 21. Charterhall | NE71, TD1–6, TD8, TD10–15. |
| 22. Chivenor | EX23, EX31–34, EX39. |
| 23. Coleshill | B1–21, B23–38, B40, B42–50, B60–80, B90–98, CV1–12, CV21–23, CV31–35, CV37, CV47, DY1–14, LE10, WS1–15, WV1–16. |
| 24. Crosby | CH41–49, CH60–66, FY1–8, L1–40, PR1–5, PR8–9, PR25–26. |
| 25. Culdrose | TR1–8, TR10–20, TR26–27. |
| 26. Dunkeswell Aerodrome | DT6–8, EX1–5, EX8–15, EX24, TA21. |
| 27. Dunstaffnage | PA30–31, PA34–35, PA37–38, PA62–65, PA67–75, PA80. |
| 28. Dyce | AB10–16, AB21–25, AB39, AB41–43. |
| 29. Edinburgh Gogarbank | EH1–42, EH47–49, EH51–55, FK1–7, FK9–10, KY3, KY11–12. |
| 30. Eskdalemuir | DG3–4, DG10–11, DG13–14, ML12, TD7, TD9. |
| 31. Filton | BS1–11, BS13–16, BS20–24, BS29–32, BS34–37, BS39–41, BS48–49, GL11–13, NP16, NP26. |
| 32. Fylingdales | YO13, YO18, YO21–22, YO62. |
| 33. Gravesend | BR5–8, CM0, DA1–18, ME1–5, ME7–8, RM1–3, RM5–20, SS0–17. |
| 34. Hawarden Airport | CH1–8, LL11–14, SY14. |
| 35. Heathrow | BR1–4, CR0, CR2–9, E1–18, EC1–4, EN1–5, EN7–11, HA0–9, IG1–11, KT1–24, N1–22, NW1–11, SE1–28, SL0, SL3, SM1–7, SW1–20, TW1–20, UB1–11, W1–14, WC1–2, WD1–2. |

| *Column (1)* | *Column (2)* |
|---|---|
| *Meteorological Office Station* | *Postcode districts* |
| 36. Hereford-Credenhill | GL1–6, GL10, GL14–20, GL50–53, HR1–9, NP7–8, NP15, NP25, SY8, WR1–11, WR13–15. |
| 37. Herstmonceux, West End | BN7–8, BN20–24, BN26–27, TN21, TN31–40. |
| 38. High Wycombe | HP5–23, HP27, OX9, OX39, OX49, RG9, SL7–9. |
| 39. Hurn (Bournemouth Airport) | BH1–25, BH31, DT1–2, DT11, SP6. |
| 40. Isle of Portland | DT3–5. |
| 41. Keele | CW1–3, CW5, CW12, ST1–8, ST11–12, ST14–21. |
| 42. Kinloss | AB44–45, AB56, IV1–3, IV5, IV7–12, IV15–20, IV30–32, IV36. |
| 43. Kirkwall | KW15–17. |
| 44. Lake Vyrnwy | LL20–21, LL23, SY10, SY15–17, SY19, SY21–22. |
| 45. Leconfield | DN14, HU1–20, YO11–12, YO14–17, YO25. |
| 46. Leek | DE4, DE45, S32–33, SK13, SK17, SK22–23, ST9–10, ST13. |
| 47. Lerwick | ZE1–3. |
| 48. Leuchars | DD1–7, DD10–11, KY1–2, KY6–10, KY15–16, PH12, PH14. |
| 49. Linton on Ouse | DL1–3, DL6–7, DL9–10, HG1–5, LS1–20, LS22–28, TS9, TS15–16, YO1, YO7–8, YO10, YO19, YO23–24, YO26, YO30–32, YO41–43, YO51, YO60–61. |
| 50. Liscombe | EX16, EX35–36, TA22, TA24. |
| 51. Little Rissington | CV36, GL54–56, OX7, OX15–17, WR12. |
| 52. Loch Glascarnoch | IV4, IV6, IV14, IV23–24, IV63. |
| 53. Loftus | SR8, TS1–8, TS10–14, TS17–20, TS22–27. |
| 54. Lusa | IV40–49, IV51–56, PH36, PH38–41. |
| 55. Lyneham | BA1–3, BA11, BA13–15, GL7–9, RG17, SN1–6, SN8–16, SN25–26. |
| 56. Machrihanish | KA27, PA28–29, PA41–49, PA60. |
| 57. Manston | CT1–21, ME9–13, TN23–26, TN28–30. |
| 58. Marham | CB6–7, IP24–28, PE12–14, PE30–38. |

| Column (1) | Column (2) |
|---|---|
| *Meteorological Office Station* | *Postcode districts* |
| 59. Mona | LL33–34, LL42–49, LL51–78. |
| 60. North Wyke | EX6–7, EX17–22, EX37–38, PL19–21,TQ1–6, TQ9–14. |
| 61. Norwich Airport | NR1–35. |
| 62. Nottingham Watnall | CV13, DE1–3, DE5–7, DE11–15, DE21–24, DE55–56, DE65, DE72–75, LE1–9, LE11–14, LE16–19, LE65, LE67, NG1–22, NG25, NG31–34. |
| 63. Pembrey Sands | SA1–8, SA14–18, SA31–34, SA61–63, SA66–73. |
| 64. Plymouth | PL1–12, TQ7–8. |
| 65. Redesdale | CA9, DH8, NE19, NE47–49. |
| 66. Rhyl | LL15–19, LL22, LL26–32. |
| 67. Rostherne | BL1–6, BL9, CW4, CW6–11, M1–9, M11–35, M38, M40–41, M43–46, M50, M90, OL6–10, PR7, SK1–12, SK14–16, WA1–16, WN1–8. |
| 68. Rothamsted | AL1–10, EN6, HP1–4, LU1–7, SG1–4, SG12–14, WD3–7, WD17–19, WD23–25. |
| 69. St. Athan | CF3, CF5, CF10–11, CF14–15, CF23–24, CF31–36, CF61–64, CF71–72, NP10, NP18–20, SA10–13. |
| 70. St. Bees Head | CA13–15, CA18–28. |
| 71. Salsburgh | EH43–46, G65, G67–68, ML6–11. |
| 72. Scilly, St. Mary's | TR21–25. |
| 73. Sennybridge | LD1–8, SA19–20, SY7, SY9, SY18. |
| 74. Shap | CA10–12, CA16–17, LA8–10, LA21–23. |
| 75. Shawbury | SY1–6, SY11–13, TF1–13. |
| 76. Sheffield | DN1–8, DN11–12, HD1–2, HD4–6, S1–14, S17–18, S20–21, S25–26, S35, S40–45, S60–66, S70–75, S80–81, WF1–17. |
| 77. South Farnborough | GU1–4, GU7–35, GU46–47, GU51–52, RG1–2, RG4–8, RG10, RG12, RG14, RG18–27, RG29–31, RG40–42, RG45, SL1–2, SL4–6, SO24. |
| 78. Stonyhurst | BB1–3, BB5–7, LA2, LA6–7, PR6. |
| 79. Stornoway Airport | HS1–9. |

| Column (1) | Column (2) |
|---|---|
| *Meteorological Office Station* | *Postcode districts* |
| 80. Strathallan | FK8, FK11–19, G63, KY4–5, KY13–14, PH1–7, PH13. |
| 81. Thorney Island | BN1–3, BN9–18, BN25, BN41–43, BN45, PO1–22, PO30–41, SO14–19, SO30–32, SO40–43, SO45, SO50–53. |
| 82. Threave | DG1–2, DG5–8. |
| 83. Tiree | PA61, PA66, PA76–78, PH42–44. |
| 84. Trawsgoed | LL35–40, SY20, SY23–25. |
| 85. Tredegar | CF37–48, CF81–83, NP4, NP11–13, NP22–24, NP44, SA9. |
| 86. Tulloch Bridge | FK20–21, PA33, PA36, PA40, PH8–9, PH15–17, PH30–35, PH37, PH49–50. |
| 87. Waddington | DN9–10, DN13, DN15–22, DN31–41, LN1–13, NG23–24, PE10–11, PE20–25. |
| 88. Walney Island | LA1, LA3–5, LA11–20. |
| 89. Wattisham | CB8–9, CO1–8, CO10–16, IP1–23, IP29–33. |
| 90. Wick Airport | IV25, KW1–3, KW5–10, KW12, KW14. |
| 91. Wittering | LE15, NN17–18, PE1–9, PE15–17, PE26–29. |
| 92. Yeovilton | BA4–10, BA16, BA20–22, BS25–28, DT9–10, SP8, TA1–20, TA23." |

"

**p.1367,** *amendment of the Social Fund Cold Weather Payments (General) Regulations 1988 (SI 1988/1724) Sch.2 (Specified alternative stations)*

**3.180**   With effect from November 1, 2013, reg.2(2) of the Social Fund Cold Weather Payments (General) Amendment (No.2) Regulations 2013 (SI 2013/2538) substituted the following schedule for Sch.2:

"Regulation 2(1A) (a) and 2(1B)(a)

SCHEDULE 2

SPECIFIED ALTERNATIVE STATIONS

| Column (1) | Column (2) |
|---|---|
| *Meteorological Office Station* | *Specified Alternative Station* |
| Aberporth | Pembrey Sands |

| Column (1) | Column (2) |
|---|---|
| *Meteorological Office Station* | *Specified Alternative Station* |
| Boulmer | Albemarle |
| Braemar | Aboyne |
| Capel Curig | Lake Vyrnwy |
| Cardinham (Bodmin) | North Wyke |
| Carlisle | Keswick |
| Charlwood | Kenley Airfield |
| Coleshill | Pershore College |
| Crosby | Rhyl |
| Culdrose | Scilly St. Marys |
| Dunstaffnage | Lusa |
| Edinburgh Gogarbank | Strathallan |
| Eskdalemuir | Redesdale |
| Filton | St. Athan |
| Gravesend | Kenley Airfield |
| Heathrow | Gravesend |
| Hereford-Credenhill | Pershore College |
| High Wycombe | Rothamsted |
| Hurn (Bournemouth Airport) | Swanage |
| Keele | Shawbury |
| Kinloss | Lossiemouth |
| Leconfield | Linton on Ouse |
| Linton on Ouse | Bramham |
| Liscombe | North Wyke |
| Mona | Rhyl |
| North Wyke | Okehampton |
| Rhyl | Crosby |
| Rostherne | Keele |
| St. Athan | Mumbles |

| Column (1) | Column (2) |
|---|---|
| *Meteorological Office Station* | *Specified Alternative Station* |
| St. Bees Head | Threave |
| Sennybridge | Tredegar |
| Shap | Keswick |
| Sheffield | Nottingham - Watnall |
| Thorney Island | Solent |
| Threave | Dundrennan |
| Tiree | Lusa |
| Trawsgoed | Aberporth |
| Tulloch Bridge | Aviemore." |

**p.1371,** *amendment of the Social Fund Winter Fuel Payment Regulations 2000 (SI 2000/729) reg.2 (Social fund winter fuel payments)*

**3.181**     With effect from September 16, 2013, reg.2 of the Social Fund Winter Fuel Payment (Amendment) Regulations 2013 (SI 2013/1509) amended reg.2 to read as follows:

"2.—(1) Subject to paragraphs (2) [to (4)] and regulation 3 of these Regulations, and regulation 36(2) of the Social Security (Claims and Payments) Regulations 1987, the Secretary of State shall pay to a person who—
  [(a) in respect of any day falling within the qualifying week is—
         (i) ordinarily resident in Great Britain; or
        (ii) habitually resident in Switzerland or an EEA state other than the United Kingdom; and]
   (b) in or before the qualifying week has attained the qualifying age for state pension credit, a winter fuel payment of—
         (i) £200 unless he is in residential care or head (ii)(aa) applies; or
        (ii) £100 if state pension credit, an income-based jobseeker's allowance or an income-related employment and support allowance has not been, nor falls to be, paid to him in respect of the qualifying week and he is—
              (aa) in that week living with a person to whom a payment under these Regulations has been, or falls to be, made in respect of the winter following the qualifying week; or
              (bb) in residential care.
   (2) Where such a person has attained the age of 80 in or before the qualifying week—
   (a) in paragraph (1)(i), for the sum of £200 there shall be substituted the sum of £300; and

(b) in paragraph (1)(ii), for the sum of £100 there shall be substituted the sum of £200, except that—

(i) where he is in that week living with a person to whom a payment under these Regulations has been, or falls to be, made in respect of the winter following that week who has also attained the age of 80 in or before that week, or

(ii) where he is in residential care, there shall be substituted the sum of £150.

(3) Where such a person has not attained the age of 80 in or before the qualifying week but he is a partner of and living with a person who has done so, in paragraph (1)(i) for the sum of £200 there shall be substituted the sum of £300.

[(4) A person does not qualify for a winter fuel payment by virtue of falling within paragraph (2)(a)(ii) above unless—

(a) they are a person to whom Council Regulation (EC) No 1408/71 on the application of social security schemes to employed persons, to self-employed persons and to members of their families moving within the Community, or Regulation (EC) No 883/2004 of the European Parliament and of the Council on the coordination of social security systems, applies; and

(b) they are able to demonstrate a genuine and sufficient link to the United Kingdom social security system.]"

**p.1372,** *annotation to the Social Fund Winter Fuel Payment Regulations 2000 (SI 2000/729) reg.2 (Social fund winter fuel payments)*

Replace the first four paragraphs of the annotation with the following:  **3.182**

"Regulation 2 sets out the conditions of entitlement to a winter fuel payment. A person qualifies if:

(a) he or she is either ordinarily resident in Great Britain, or habitually resident in an EEA state (other than the UK) or Switzerland, for at least one day in the qualifying week (*i.e.*, the week commencing on the third Monday in September (see reg.1(2)).

For the winter of 2012/2013, the qualifying week ran from Monday, September 17 to Sunday, September 23, 2012, for the winter of 2013/2014 it ran from Monday, September 16 to Sunday, September 22, 2013, and for the winter of 2014/2015 it will run from Monday, September 15 to Sunday, September 21, 2014.

(b) he attains the qualifying age for state pension credit before the end of the qualifying week. The progressive increase in state pension age for women born after April 5, 1950 (to which the qualifying age for state pension credit is linked) means that, for the winter of 2012/2013, the claimant must have been born on or before July 5, 1951; for the winter of 2013/2014 s/he must have been born on or before January 5, 1952; and for the winter of 2014/2015 s/he will have to have been born on or before July

1952. Those born after those dates do not reach the qualifying age until—at the earliest—6 November in each of those years".

Replace the final paragraph of the annotation with the following:

"From September 16, 2013 para.(4) provides that claimants who qualify by being habitually resident in Switzerland, or in an EEA state other than the United Kingdom—rather than on the basis that they are ordinarily resident in the United Kingdom—must also fall within the personal scope of Regulation 1408/71 (EEC) or of Regulation (EC) 883/2004 and have a "genuine and sufficient link to the United Kingdom social security system": see, further the commentary to the latter regulation in Vol.III of the main work as updated below."

**p.1374,** *amendment of the Social Fund Winter Fuel Payment Regulations 2000 (SI 2000/729) reg.3 (Persons not entitled to a social fund winter fuel payment)*

**3.183** With effect from September 16, 2013, reg.2 of the Social Fund Winter Fuel Payment (Amendment) Regulations 2013 (SI 2013/1509) amended reg.3 by adding the following paragraph after para.(2):

"(3) No person is entitled to a winter fuel payment for the winter of 1997 to 1998, 1998 to 1999 or 1999 to 2000 unless they have made a claim for such a payment on or before 31st March 2014."

**p.1375,** *annotation to the Social Fund Winter Fuel Payment Regulations 2000 (SI 2000/729) reg.3 (Persons not entitled to a social fund winter fuel payment)*

**3.184** Add the following at the end of the annotation:

"The final time limit for claiming a winter fuel payment for the winters of 1997/1998, 1998/1999 and 1999/2000 is March 31, 2014 (see para.(3))."

**p.1397,** *annotation to the Social Fund Maternity and Funeral Expenses (General) Regulations 2005 (SI 2005/3061) reg.7(6) (Funeral payments: entitlement—Time limit)*

**3.185** The three-month time limit begins to run on the day after the funeral and ends on the day three months later that corresponds to the day of the month on which the funeral took place: see *SSWP v SC (SF)* [2013] UKUT 607 (AAC) in which the funeral took place on July 26, 2011 and the time limit ended on October 26, 2011 so that a claim made on October 27, 2011 was out of time.

# PART IV

# UPDATING MATERIAL
## VOLUME III

# ADMINISTRATION, ADJUDICATION AND THE EUROPEAN DIMENSION

Commentary by

**Mark Rowland**

**Robin White**

**p.15,** *amendment to Social Security Administration Act 1992 s.1*
*(Entitlement to benefit dependent on claim)*

Subsections (3) and(4) now read as follows: 4.001

"(3) Where a person purports to make a claim for benefit on behalf
of another—
[¹ (za) for personal independence payment by virtue of section 82 of
the Welfare Reform Act 2012; or]
(a) for an attendance allowance by virtue of section 66(1) of the
Contributions and Benefits Act; [¹ . . . ]
that other shall be regarded for the purposes of this section as making
the claim, notwithstanding that it is made without his knowledge or
authority.
(4) In this section and section 2 below "benefit" means—
[² (za) universal credit;]
(a) benefit as defined in section 122 of the Contributions and
Benefits Act;
[³ (aa) a jobseeker's allowance;]
[⁴ (ab) state pension credit;]
[⁵ (ac) an employment and support allowance,]
[¹ (ad) personal independence payment.]
(b) any income-related benefit."

AMENDMENTS

1. Welfare Reform Act 2012 Sch.9 para.8 (April 8, 2013).
2. Welfare Reform Act 2012 Sch.2 para.4 (February 25, 2013 for regulation
making purposes only).
3. Jobseekers Act 1995 Sch.2 para.38 (April 22, 1996).
4. State Pension Credit Act 2002 Sch.1 para.2 (April 7, 2003).
5. Welfare Reform Act 2007 Sch.3 para.10 (October 27, 2008).

**p.53,** *repeals of parts of Social Security Administration Act 1992 s.71*
*(Overpayments—general)*

With effect from April 29, 2013, the Welfare Reform Act 2012 (Com- 4.002
mencement No. 8 and Savings and Transitional Provisions) Order 2013
(SI 2013/358) art.5(4) brings into force provisions of the Welfare
Reform Act 2012 repealing subs.(10A) and (10B), as well as (11)(aa)
and (11)(ac). However art.5(6) provides that the benefits referred to in
subs.(11)(aa) and (11)(ac) "remain benefits to which section 71 of the
1992 Act applies to the extent that those benefits have been claimed
before 29th April 2013."

**p.53,** *annotation to Social Security Administration Act 1992 s.71*
*(Overpayments—general)*

*Requirement for revision or supersession as a precondition for recovery*

*SS v SSWP (JSA)* [2013] UKUT 233 (AAC) contains some useful 4.003
observations of dealing with cases where the Secretary of State's decision-making is arguably incoherent in that there is inconsistency of

decision-making resulting in considerable lack of clarity as to whether there has been a proper revision or supersession of the entitlement decision.

*Causation* (paras 1.147 to 1.149)

*SSWP v SS (SPC)* [2013] UKUT 272 (AAC) considers when the chain of causation is broken, and how a tribunal should proceed when an argument on this issue arises in the course of the hearing. The judge rules that it will be a breach of natural justice to fail to adjourn a hearing to enable the Secretary of State to respond to arguments that the chain of causation has been broken (para.6). Whether and when the chain of causation is broken is a question of fact, but a failure to respond immediately to information arising from a Generalised Matching Service Scan will not necessarily result in a break in the chain of causation (see especially para.15). The case includes a review of some earlier case-law.

*The amount of the overpayment which is recoverable* (paras 1.150–1.154)

For the proper approach to whether arrears in respect of a period of suspension may be set off against an overpayment in respect of an earlier period, see *MR v SSWP (IS)* [2013] UKUT 588 (AAC).

**p.106,** *insertion of s.71ZB into Social Security Administration Act 1992*

4.004    With effect from April 29, 2013, the Welfare Reform Act 2012 (Commencement No. 8 and Savings and Transitional Provisions) Order 2013 (SI 2013/358), art.5(2) brings into force provisions of the Welfare Reform Act 2012 which insert new ss.71ZB (to a limited extent), 71ZF, 71ZG and 71ZH into the Administration Act as follows:

"*Recovery of benefit payments*

### Recovery of overpayments of certain benefits

**71ZB.**—(1) The Secretary of State may recover any amount of the following paid in excess of entitlement—
    (a) universal credit,
    (b) jobseeker's allowance,
    (c) employment and support allowance,
    (d) *not yet in force*
    (2) An amount recoverable under this section is recoverable from—
    (a) the person to whom it was paid, or
    (b) such other person (in addition to or instead of the person to whom it was paid) as may be prescribed.
    (3) An amount paid in pursuance of a determination is not recoverable under this section unless the determination has been—
    (a) reversed or varied on an appeal, or

    (b) revised or superseded under section 9 or section 10 of the Social
       Security Act 1998,
except where regulations otherwise provide.

    (4) Regulations may provide that amounts recoverable under this
section are to be calculated or estimated in a prescribed manner.

    (5) Where an amount of universal credit is paid for the sole reason
that a payment by way of prescribed income is made after the date
which is the prescribed date for payment of that income, that amount
is for the purposes of this section paid in excess of entitlement.

    (6) In the case of a benefit referred to in subsection (1) which is
awarded to persons jointly, an amount paid to one of those persons
may for the purposes of this section be regarded as paid to the
other.

    (7) An amount recoverable under this section may (without preju-
dice to any other means of recovery) be recovered—
    (a) by deduction from benefit (section 71ZC);
    (b) by deduction from earnings (section 71ZD);
    (c) through the courts etc (section 71ZE);
    (d) *not yet in force.*

## Adjustment of benefit

**71ZF.** Regulations may for the purpose of the recovery of the amounts
recoverable under section 71ZB make provision—
    (a) for treating any amount paid to a person under an award which
       it is subsequently determined was not payable—
        (i) as properly paid, or
        (ii) as paid on account of a payment which it is determined
           should be or should have been made,
    and for reducing or withholding arrears payable by virtue of the
    subsequent determination;
    (b) for treating any amount paid to one person in respect of another
       as properly paid for any period for which it is not payable in
       cases where in consequence of a subsequent determination—
        (i) the other person is entitled to a payment for that period,
          or
        (ii) a third person is entitled in priority to the payee to a
          payment for that period in respect of the other person,
    and by reducing or withholding any arrears payable for that
    period by virtue of the subsequent determination.

## Recovery of payments on account

**71ZG.**—(1) The Secretary of State may recover any amount paid
under section 5(1)(r) (payments on account).

    (2) An amount recoverable under this section is recoverable
from—
    (a) the person to whom it was paid, or

(b) such other person (in addition to or instead of the person to whom it was paid) as may be prescribed.

(3) Regulations may provide that amounts recoverable under this section are to be calculated or estimated in a prescribed manner.

(4) in the case of a payment on account of a benefit which is awarded to persons jointly, an amount paid to one of those persons may for then purposes of this section be regarded as paid to the other.

(5) section 71ZC, 71ZD and 71ZE apply in relation to amounts recoverable under this section as to amounts recoverable under section 71ZB.

### Recovery of hardship payments etc

**71ZH.**—(1) The Secretary of State may recover any amount paid by way of—

(a) a payment under section 28 of the Welfare Reform Act 2012 (universal credit hardship payments) which is recoverable under that section,

(b) *payment under section 19C of the Jobseeker's Act 1995 (jobseeker's allowance hardship payments) which is recoverable under that section,*

(c) a payment of a jobseeker's allowance under paragraph 8 or 8A of Schedule 1 to that Act (exemptions), where the allowance is payable at a prescribed rate under paragraph 9 of that Schedule and is recoverable under that paragraph,

(d) a payment of a jobseeker's allowance under paragraph 10 of that Schedule (claims yet to be determined etc) which is recoverable under that paragraph, or

(e) a payment which is recoverable under section 6B(5A)(d) or (7)(d), 7(2A)(d) or (4)(d), 8(3)(aa), (4)(d) or 9(2A)(d) of the Social Security Fraud Act 2001.

(2) An amount recoverable under this section is recoverable from—

(a) the person to whom it was paid, or

(b) such other person (in addition to or instead of the person to whom it was paid) as may be prescribed.

(3) Regulations may provide that amount recoverable under this section are to be calculated or estimated in a prescribed manner.

(4) Where universal credit or a jobseeker's allowance is claimed by persons jointly, an amount paid to one claimant may for the purposes of this section be regarded as paid to the other.

(5) Sections 71ZC to 71ZF apply in relation to amounts recoverable under this section as to amounts recoverable under section 71ZB."

GENERAL NOTE

The significance of the words in italics in s.71ZH(1)(b) is that this paragraph is repealed with effect from April 29, 2013, but is maintained in force for certain purposes: see the Welfare Reform Act 2012 (Commencement No. 9 and Transitional and Transitory Provisions and Commencement No. 8 and Savings and Transitional Provisions (Amendment)) Order 2013 (SI 2013/983) art.7(1)(e).

**p.111,** *annotation to the Social Security Administration Act 1992 s.74 (Income support and other payments)*

In *PT v SSWP (JSA)* [2013] UKUT 372 (AAC), the judge explained    4.005
that s.74(2) "is concerned with cases where a claimant in receipt of an income-related benefit is entitled to arrears of another benefit (or other payment from public funds) that would have fallen to be taken into account as income and so would have reduced entitlement to the income-related benefit had it been paid at the correct time." (para.10). It does not cover the situation of a person where an error in the Department has resulted in a failure to recoup overpaid jobseeker's allowance from arrears of an employment and support allowance. The only way such a sum could be recouped was through the operation of reg.5 of the Social Security (Payments on account etc) Regulations 1988. Because s.74(2) did not apply, s.74(4) could not apply to justify recovery under s.74.

**p.115,** *amendment to the Social Security Administration Act 1992 s.74A (Payment of benefit where maintenance payments collected by Secretary of State)*

With effect from April 29, 2013, the Welfare Reform Act 2012 (Com-    4.006
mencement No. 9 and Transitional and Transitory Provisions and Commencement No. 8 and Savings and Transitional Provisions (Amendment)) Order 2013 (SI 2013/983), art.3(1)(b) brings into force provisions of the Welfare Reform Act 2012 amending s.74A(7) by inserting the words "universal credit," before the words "income support".

**p.116,** *amendment to the Social Security Act 1992 s.78 (Recovery of social fund awards)*

With effect from April 29, 2013, the Welfare Reform Act 2012 (Com-    4.007
mencement No. 8 and Savings and Transitional Provisions) Order 2013 (SI 2013/358) art.5(5) brings into force provisions of the Welfare Reform Act 2012 amending s.78(6)(d) by inserting the words "universal credit" after the word "receiving".

**p.120,** *amendment to the Social Security Administration Act 1992 s.105 (Failure to maintain—general)*

With effect from April 29, 2013, the Welfare Reform Act 2012 (Com-    4.008
mencement No. 9 and Transitional and Transitory Provisions and Commencement No. 8 and Savings and Transitional Provisions (Amendment)) Order 2013 (SI 2013/983), art.3(1)(b) brings into force

provisions of the Welfare Reform Act 2012 amending s.105(1)(b) by inserting the words "universal credit," after the word "neglect".

**p.121,** *amendment to the Social Security Administration Act 1992 s.106 (Recovery of expenditure on benefit from person liable for maintenance)*

4.009    With effect from April 29, 2013, the Welfare Reform Act 2012 (Commencement No. 9 and Transitional and Transitory Provisions and Commencement No. 8 and Savings and Transitional Provisions (Amendment)) Order 2013 (SI 2013/983), art.3(1)(b) brings into force provisions of the Welfare Reform Act 2012 amending subs.(1), (2), (3), and (4)(a) and (b) by inserting the words "or universal credit" after the words "income support".

**p.122,** *amendment to the Social Security Administration Act 1992 s.108 (Reduction of expenditure on income support: certain maintenance orders to be enforceable by the Secretary of State)*

4.010    With effect from April 29, 2013, the Welfare Reform Act 2012 (Commencement No. 9 and Transitional and Transitory Provisions and Commencement No. 8 and Savings and Transitional Provisions (Amendment)) Order 2013 (SI 2013/983) art.3(1)(b) brings into force provisions of the Welfare Reform Act 2012 amending s.108(1)(a) by inserting the words "or universal credit" after the words "income support".

**p.124,** *amendment to the Social Security Administration Act 1992 s.109 (Diversion of arrested earnings to Secretary of State—Scotland)*

4.011    With effect from April 29, 2013, the Welfare Reform Act 2012 (Commencement No. 9 and Transitional and Transitory Provisions and Commencement No. 8 and Savings and Transitional Provisions (Amendment)) Order 2013 (SI 2013/983), art.3(1)(b) brings into force provisions of the Welfare Reform Act 2012 amending s.109(1) by inserting the words "universal credit" after the words "in receipt of" in both places where the words occur.

**p.126,** *amendment to the Social Security Administration Act 1992 s.109B (Power to require information)*

4.012    With effect from June 17, 2013 (for the purpose of making regulations) and from October 1, 2013 (for all other purposes), the Welfare Reform Act 2012 (Commencement No. 10) Order 2013 (SI 2013/1250) art.3 brings into force provisions of the Welfare Reform Act 2012 amending s.109B(2) as follows:

   (a) by inserting the following paragraph after paragraph (i):

      "(ia) a person of a prescribed description;"

   (b) in paragraph (j), by substituting "(ia)" in place of "(i)".

**p.132,** *inclusion of additional provisions of the Social Security Administration Act 1992 ss.110ZA to 115D*

The following provisions of the Administration Act are relevant to    4.013
tribunals and are added to material reproduced in Vol.III:

**"[¹ Class 1, 1A, 1B or 2 contributions: powers to call for documents etc]**

**110ZA**—(1) Section 20 of the Taxes Management Act 1970 (power to call for documents etc) applies (with sections 20B and 20BB) in relation to a person's liability to pay relevant contributions as it applies in relation to a person's tax liability (but subject to the modifications provided by subsection (2)).

Those sections apply as if—
 (a) the references to the taxpayer, a taxpayer or a class of taxpayers were to the person, a person or a class of persons required to pay relevant contributions,
 (b) the references to an inspector were to an officer of the Inland Revenue,
 (c) the references to any provision of the Taxes Acts were to any provision of this Act or the Contributions and Benefits Act relating to relevant contributions,
 (d) the references to the assessment or collection of tax were to the assessment of liability for, and payment of, relevant contributions,
 (e) the reference to an appeal relating to tax were to an appeal relating to relevant contributions, and
 (f) the reference to believing that tax has been, or may have been, lost to the Crown were to believing that the Crown has, or may have, incurred a loss.
In this section "relevant contributions" means 1, Class 1A, Class 1B or Class 2 contributions.]

AMENDMENT

1. This section was substituted by the National Insurance and Statutory Payments Act 2004 (May 6, 2005).

*Sections 110A omitted*

**[¹ Power of local authority to require electronic access to information**

**110B.**—(1) Subject to section (2) below, where it appears to an authority administering housing benefit or council tax benefit—
 (a) that a person falling within section 109B(2A) keeps any electronic records,
 (b) that the records contain or are likely, from time to time, to contain information about any matter that is relevant for any one or more of the purposes mentioned in section 110A(2) above, and

385

(c) that facilities exist under which electronic access to those records is being provided, or is capable of being provided, by that person to other persons,

that authority may require that person to enter into arrangements under which authorised officers are allowed such access to those records.

(2) An authorised officer—

(a) shall be entitled to obtain information in accordance with arrangements entered into under subsection (1) above only if his authorisation states that his authorisation applies for the purposes of that subsection; and

(b) shall not seek to obtain any information in accordance with any such arrangements other than information which–

  (i) relates to a particular person; and

  (ii) could be the subject of any such requirement under section 109B above as may be imposed in exercise of the powers conferred by section 110A(8) above.

(3) The matters that may be included in the arrangements that a person is required to enter into under subsection (1) above may include—

(a) requirements as to the electronic access to records that is to be made available to authorised officers;

(b) requirements as to the keeping of records of the use that is made of the arrangements;

(c) requirements restricting the disclosure of information about the use that is made of the arrangements; and

(d) such other incidental requirements as the authority in question considers appropriate in connection with allowing access to records to authorised officers.

(4) An authorised officer who is allowed access in accordance with any arrangements entered into under subsection (1) above shall be entitled to make copies of, and to take extracts from, any records containing information which he is entitled to make the subject of a requirement such as is mentioned in subsection (2)(b) above.

(5) An authority administering housing benefit or council tax benefit shall not—

(a) require any person to enter into arrangements for allowing authorised officers to have electronic access to any records; or

(b) otherwise than in pursuance of a requirement under this section, enter into any arrangements with a person specified in section 109B(2A) above for allowing anyone acting on behalf of the authority for purposes connected with any benefit to have electronic access to any private information contained in any records,

except with the consent of the Secretary of State and subject to any conditions imposed by the Secretary of State by the provisions of the consent.

(6) A consent for the purposes of subsection (5) may be given in relation to a particular case, or in relation to any case that falls within a particular description of cases.

(7) In this section "private information", in relation to an authority administering housing benefit or council tax benefit, means any information held by a person who is not entitled to disclose it to that authority except in compliance with a requirement imposed by the authority in exercise of their statutory powers.]

AMENDMENT

1. This section was inserted by the Social Security Fraud Act 2001 s.2(2) (April 30, 2002).

*Sections 111–112 omitted.*

## [¹ **Breach of regulations**

**113.**—(1) Regulations and schemes under any of the [² legislation to which this section applies] may provide that any person who contravenes, or fails to comply with, any provision contained in regulations made under [² that legislation]—
  (a) in the case of a provision relating to contributions, shall be liable to a penalty;
  (b) in any other case, shall be guilty of an offence under [² any enactment contained in the legislation in question].
  [³ (1A) The legislation to which this section applies is–
  (a) the relevant social security legislation; and
  (b) the enactments specified in section 121DA(1) so far as relating to contributions, [⁴ . . . ].]
(2) Any regulations or scheme making such provision as is mentioned in subsection (1)(a) above shall—
  (a) prescribe the amount or rate of penalty, or provide for how it is to be ascertained;
  (b) provide for the penalty to be imposed by the [⁵ Inland Revenue]—
    (i) within six years after the date on which the penalty is incurred; or
    (ii) where the amount of the penalty is to be ascertained by reference to the amount of any contributions payable, at any later time within three years after the final determination of the amount of those contributions;
  (c) provide for determining the date on which, for the purposes of paragraph (b) above, the penalty is incurred;
  (d) prescribe the means by which the penalty is to be enforced; and
  (e) provide for enabling the [¹Inland Revenue], in [¹their] discretion, to mitigate or to remit any such penalty, or to stay or to compound any proceedings for a penalty.
(3) *Omitted*
(4) Any provision contained in regulations which authorises statutory sick pay or statutory maternity pay to be set off against secondary Class 1 contributions is not a provision relating to contributions for the purposes of this section.]

AMENDMENTS

1. This section substituted by the Social Security Act 1998 s.60 (March 4 1999).
2. Child Support, Pensions and Social Security Act 2000 s.67 (November 1 2000).
3. Social Security Contributions (Transfer of Functions etc.) Act 1999 Sch.⁵ para.5 (April 6, 1999).
4. National Insurance and Statutory Payments Act 2004 s.9 (April 6 2005).
5. Social Security Contributions (Transfer of Functions etc) Act 1999 Sch.⁵ para.5 (April 6, 1999).

*Sections 113A to 115 omitted*

## [¹ Penalty as an alternative to prosecution

**115A**—(1) This section applies where an overpayment is recoverable from a person by, or due from a person to, the Secretary of State [¹ . . . ] under or by virtue of section [³ 71ZB] [² . . . ] above and i appears to the Secretary of State [² . . . ] that
  (a) the making of the overpayment was attributable to an act o: omission on the part of that person; and
  (b) there are grounds for instituting against him proceedings for ar offence (under this Act or any other enactment) relating to the overpayment.
[⁴ (1A) This section also applies where—
  (a) it appears to the Secretary of State [² . . . ] that there are grounds for instituting proceedings against a person for ar offence (under this Act of any other enactment) relating to ar act or omission on the part of that person in relation to any benefit, and
  (b) if an overpayment attributable to that act or omission had beer made, the overpayment would have been recoverable from the person by, or due from the person to, the Secretary of State [¹ . . . ] under or by virtue of section 71, 71ZB, [² . . . above.]
(2) The Secretary of State [² . . . ] may give the person a writter notice—
  (a) stating that he may be invited to agree to pay a penalty and that if he does so in the manner specified by the Secretary of State [¹ . . . ], no [⁴ proceedings referred to in subsection (1) or (1A² above] will be instituted against him; and
  (b) containing such information relating to the operation of thi: section as may be prescribed.
[⁵ (3) The amount of the penalty in a case falling within subsectior (1) is 50% of the amount of the overpayment (rounded down to the nearest whole penny), subject to—
  (a) a minimum amount of £350, and
  (b) a maximum amount of £2000.
(3A) The amount of the penalty in the case falling within subsectior (1A) is £350.

(3B) The Secretary of State may by order amend—

(a) the percentage for the time being specified in subsection (3);

(b) any figure for the time being specified in subsection (3)(a) or (b) of (3A).]

(4) If the person agrees in the specified manner to pay the penalty—

(a) the amount of the penalty shall be recoverable by the same methods as those by which the overpayment is [⁴ or would have been] recoverable; and

(b) no proceedings will be instituted against him for an offence (under this Act or any other enactment) relating to the overpayment [⁴ or to the act or omission referred to in subsection (1A)(a).]

(5) The person may withdraw his agreement to pay the penalty by notifying the Secretary of State [² . . . ] in the manner specified by the Secretary of State [² . . . ], at any time during the period of [⁴ 14] days beginning with the day on which he agrees to pay it; and if he does so—

(a) so much of the penalty as has already been recovered shall be repaid; and

(b) subsection (4)(b) above shall not apply.

(6) [⁵ In a case referred to in subsection (1A)(a)] where, after the person has agreed to pay the penalty, the amount of the overpayment is revised on a review or appeal or in accordance with regulations—

(a) so much of the penalty as has already been recovered shall be repaid; and

(b) subsection (4)(b) above shall no longer apply by reason of the agreement;

but if a new agreement is made under this section in relation to the revised overpayment, the amount already recovered by way of penalty, to the extent that it does not exceed the amount of the new penalty, may be treated as recovered under the new agreement instead of being repaid.

(7A) [² . . . ]

(8) In this section "overpayment" means—

(a) a payment which should not have been made;

(b) a sum which the Secretary of State should have received;

(c) an amount of benefit paid in excess of entitlement; or

(d) an amount equal to an excess of benefit allowed;

and the reference in subsection (1)(a) [⁴ or (1A)(b)] above to the making of the overpayment is to the making of the payment, the failure to receive the sum, the payment of benefit in excess of entitlement or the allowing of an excess of benefit.

AMENDMENTS

1. This section inserted by the Social Security Administration (Fraud) Act 1997 (December 18, 1997).

2. Welfare Reform Act 2012 Sch.14 (April 1, 2013).

3. Welfare Reform Act 2012 s.105(3) (April 29, 2013).
4. Welfare Reform Act 2012 ss.113–115 (May 8, 2012).

*Section 115B omitted.*

[¹ *Civil penalties*

### Incorrect statements

**115C.**—(1) This section applies where—
- (a) a person negligently makes an incorrect statement or representation, or negligently gives incorrect information or evidence—
  - (i) in or in connection with acclaim for a relevant social security benefit, or
  - (ii) in connection with an award of a relevant social security benefit,
- (b) the person fails to take reasonable steps to correct the error,
- (c) the error results in the making of an overpayment, and
- (d) the person has not been charged with an offence or cautioned, or been given a notice under section 115A, in respect of the overpayment.

(2) A penalty of a prescribed amount may be imposed by the appropriate authority—
- (a) in any case, on the person,
- (b) in a case where the person ("A") is making, or has made, a claim for the benefit for a period jointly with another ("B"), on B instead of A.
- (c) The error results in the making of an overpayment, and
- (d) the person has not been charged with an offence or cautioned, or been given a notice under section 115A, in respect of the overpayment.

(3) Subsection (2)(b) does not apply if B was not, and could not reasonably be expected to have been, aware that A had negligently made the incorrect statement or representation or given the incorrect information or evidence.

(4) A penalty imposed under subsection (2) is recoverable by the appropriate authority from the person on whom it is imposed.

(5) Sections 71ZC, 71ZD and 71ZE apply in relation to amounts recoverable by the appropriate authority under subsection (4) as to amounts recoverable by the Secretary of State under section 71ZB (and, where the appropriate authority is not the Secretary of State, those sections so apply as if references to the Secretary of State were to that authority).

(6) In this section and section 115D—"appropriate authority" means—
- (a) the Secretary of State, or
- (b) an authority which administers housing benefit or council tax benefit;

"overpayment" has the meaning given in section 115A(8), and the reference to the making of an overpayment is to be construed in accordance with that provision;

"relevant social security benefit" has the meaning given in section 121DA(7).]

AMENDMENTS

1. This provision inserted by Welfare Reform Act 2012 s.116 (May 10, 2012).

## [¹ Failure to disclose information

**115D.**—(1) A penalty of a prescribed amount may be imposed on a person by the appropriate authority where—

(a) the person, without reasonable excuse, fails to provide information or evidence in accordance with requirements imposed on the person by the appropriate authority in connection with a claim for, or an award of, a relevant social security benefit,

(b) the failure results in the making of an overpayment, and

(c) the person has not been charged with an offence or cautioned, or been given a notice under section 115A, in respect of the overpayment.

(2) A penalty of a prescribed amount may be imposed on a person by the appropriate authority where—

(a) the person, without reasonable excuse, fails to notify the appropriate authority of a relevant change of circumstances in accordance with requirements imposed on the person under relevant social security legislation,

(b) the failure results in the making of an overpayment, and

(c) the person has not been charged with an offence or cautioned, or been given a notice under section 115A, in respect of the overpayment.

(3) Where a person is making, or has made, a claim for a benefit for a period jointly with another, and both of them fail as mentioned in subsection (1) or (2), only one penalty may be imposed in respect of the same overpayment.

(4) A penalty imposed under subsection (1) or (2) is recoverable by the appropriate authority from the person on whom it is imposed.

(5) Sections 71ZC, 71ZD and 71ZE apply in relation to amounts recoverable by the appropriate authority under subsection (4) as to amounts recoverable by the Secretary of State under section 71ZB (and, where the appropriate authority is not the Secretary of State, those sections so apply as if references to the Secretary of State were to that authority).

(6) In this section "relevant change of circumstances, in relation to a person, means a change of circumstances which affects any entitlement of the person to any benefit or other payment or advantage under any provision of the relevant social security legislation.]

AMENDMENTS

1. This provision inserted by Welfare Reform Act 2012 s.116 (May 10, 2012)."

**p.132,** *amendment to Social Security Administration Act 1992 s.124*
*(Provisions relating to age, death and marriage)*

4.014    With effect from April 29, 2013, the Welfare Reform Act 2012 (Commencement No. 9 and Transitional and Transitory Provisions and Commencement No. 8 and Savings and Transitional Provisions (Amendment)) Order 2013 (SI 2013/983) art.3(1)(b) brings into force provisions of the Welfare Reform Act 2012 amending s.124 as follows:
(a)  s.124(1)(ac) is amended by repealing the final "and".
(b)  a new s.124(1)(ad) is added as follows

"(ad) of the provisions of Part 1 of the Welfare Reform Act 2012;"

**p.135,** *amendment to Social Security Administration Act 1992 s.125*
*(Regulations as to notification of death)*

4.015    With effect from April 29, 2013, the Welfare Reform Act 2012 (Commencement No. 9 and Transitional and Transitory Provisions and Commencement No. 8 and Savings and Transitional Provisions (Amendment)) Order 2013 (SI 2013/983), art.3(1)(b) brings into force provisions of the Welfare Reform Act 2012 amending s.125(1) by inserting the words ", Part 1 of the Welfare Reform Act 2012" after the number "2007".

**p.135,** *amendment to Social Security Administration Act 1992 s.126*
*(Personal representatives to give information about the estate of a deceased person who was in receipt of income support or supplementary benefit)*

4.016    With effect from April 29, 2013, the Welfare Reform Act 2012 (Commencement No. 9 and Transitional and Transitory Provisions and Commencement No. 8 and Savings and Transitional Provisions (Amendment)) Order 2013 (SI 2013/983), art.3(1)(b) brings into force provisions of the Welfare Reform Act 2012 amending s.126(1) by inserting the words "universal credit" after the words "in receipt of".

**p.137,** *amendment to Social Security Administration Act 1992 s.130*
*(Duties of employers—statutory sick pay and claims for other benefits)*

4.017    With effect from April 29, 2013, the Welfare Reform Act 2012 (Commencement No. 9 and Transitional and Transitory Provisions and Commencement No. 8 and Savings and Transitional Provisions (Amendment)) Order 2013 (SI 2013/983), art.3(1)(b) brings into force provisions of the Welfare Reform Act 2012 amending s.130 by inserting before paragraph (a) of subsection (1) the following paragraph:

"(za) universal credit;"

**p.138,** *amendment to Social Security Administration Act 1992 s.132*
*(Duties of employers—statutory maternity pay and claims for other benefits*

With effect from April 29, 2013, the Welfare Reform Act 2012 (Com-    **4.018**
mencement No. 9 and Transitional and Transitory Provisions and Commencement No. 8 and Savings and Transitional Provisions
(Amendment)) Order 2013 (SI 2013/983) art.3(1)(b) brings into force
provisions of the Welfare Reform Act 2012 amending s.132 by inserting
before paragraph (a) of subsection (1) the following paragraph:

"(za) universal credit;"

**p.161,** *amendment to Social Security Administration Act 1992 s.179*
*(Reciprocal agreements with countries outside the United Kingdom)*

With effect from April 29, 2013, the Welfare Reform Act 2012 (Com-    **4.019**
mencement No. 9 and Transitional and Transitory Provisions and Commencement No. 8 and Savings and Transitional Provisions
(Amendment)) Order 2013 (SI 2013/983) art.3(1)(b) brings into force
provisions of the Welfare Reform Act 2012 amending s.179 as follows:
   (a) by inserting in s.179(3)(a) the words ", Part 1 of the Welfare
      Reform Act 2012" after the number "2007".
   (b) by inserting the following paragraph in s.179(4):

      "(ag) to Part 1 of the Welfare Reform Act 2012; and"

   (c) by inserting in s.179(5) the following paragraph before paragraph
      (a)"

      "(za) universal credit;".

**p.165,** *amendment to Social Security Administration Act 1992 s.187*
*(Certain benefit to be inalienable)*

With effect from April 29, 2013, the Welfare Reform Act 2012 (Com-    **4.020**
mencement No. 9 and Transitional and Transitory Provisions and Commencement No. 8 and Savings and Transitional Provisions
(Amendment)) Order 2013 (SI 2013/983), art.3(1)(b) brings into force
provisions of the Welfare Reform Act 2012 amending s.187(1) by inserting the following paragraph before para.(a):

"(za) universal credit;"

**pp.196–197,** *amendments to the Social Security (Recovery of Benefits)*
*Act 1997, s.11 (appeals against certificates of recoverable benefits)*

With effect from February 25, 2013, the Welfare Reform Act 2012    **4.020A**
s.102(6) and Sch.11, paras 9 and 10, inserted new subs.(2A) and (2B)
for regulation-making purpose. They took effect for all other purposes
from April 29, 2013:

   "(2A) Regulations may provide that, in such cases or circumstances
   as may be prescribed, an appeal may be made under this section only

if the Secretary of State has reviewed the certificate under section 10.

(2B) The regulations may in particular provide that that condition is met only where—

(a) the review by the Secretary of State was on an application,

(b) the Secretary of State considered issues of a specified description, or

(c) the review by the Secretary of State satisfied any other condition specified in the regulations."

In addition, the words "(or, where in accordance with regulations under subsection (2A) there is no right of appeal, any purported appeal)" are inserted after "any such appeal" in subs.(5).

Although these amendments were brought fully into force on April 29, 2013, the first regulations made under these powers did not come into force until October 28, 2013. These inserted reg.9ZB into, and substituted reg.29(6) of, the Social Security and Child Support (Decisions and Appeals) Regulations 1999 (see below). The effect is to require a person to seek a review of a decision before lodging an appeal, but to enable the Secretary of State to treat a purported appeal as an application for a review, and is consistent with the policy behind s.12(3A) to (3C) of the Social Security Act 1998 (see the main work).

**p.212,** *amendment to the Social Security (Recovery of Benefits) Act 1997, s.29 (general interpretation)*

4.020B    With effect from April 29, 2013, the Welfare Reform Act 2012 s.31 and Sch.2, paras 40 and 41, inserted "universal credit" after "means" in the definition of "benefit".

**p.212,** *amendments to the Social Security (Recovery of Benefits) Act 1997, s.30 (regulations and orders)*

4.020C    With effect from February 25, 2013 for regulation-making purposes, and from April 29, 2013 for all other purposes, the Welfare Reform Act 2012 s.102(6) and Sch.11, paras 9 and 11, s.30(2) inserted "11(2A) or" after "regulations under section" and also inserted a new subs.(2A)—

"(2A) A statutory instrument containing regulations under section 11(2A) may not be made unless a draft of the instrument has been laid before and approved by a resolution of each House of Parliament."

**p.212,** *amendment to the Social Security (Recovery of Benefits) Act 1997, Sch.2 (calculation of compensation payment)*

4.020D    With effect from April 29, 2013, the Welfare Reform Act 2012 s.31 and Sch.2, paras 40 and 42, inserted "Universal credit" at the top of the second column relating to compensation for earnings lost during the relevant period.

**pp.220–221,** *amendments to the Social Security Act 1998, s.2 (use of computers)*

With effect from April 29, 2013, the Welfare Reform Act 2012 s.31 and Sch.2 paras 43 and 44, repealed the final "or" at the end of subs.(2)(i) and inserted after para.(j)—     **4.020E**

"(k) Part 1 of the Welfare Reform Act 2012;"

**pp.223–224,** *amendments to the Social Security Act 1998, s.8 (decisions by Secretary of State)*

The amendments made by the Welfare Reform Act 2012 (see main work) became effective for all purposes from April 29, 2013.     **4.020F**

**pp.237–238,** *amendment to the Social Security Act 1998, s.12 (appeal to First-tier Tribunal)*

With effect from April 29, 2013, the Welfare Reform Act 2012 s.105(6) inserted ", 71ZB, 71ZG, 71ZH, " in subs.(4) after "71".     **4.020G**

**pp.238–257,** *annotation to the Social Security Act 1998, s.12 (appeal to First-tier Tribunal)*

*BMcD v DSD (DLA)* [2011] NICom 175, mentioned three times in the annotation, has been reported as [2013] AACR 29.     **4.020H**
Regulation 3ZA of the Social Security and Child Support (Decisions and Appeals) Regulations 1999 (see below) has now been made under subs.(3A), with effect from October 28, 2013.

**pp.279–281,** *amendment to the Social Security Act 1998, s.27 (restriction on entitlement in cases of error)*

The amendment to subs.(7) made by the Welfare Reform Act 2012 (see main work) became effective for all purposes from April 29, 2013.     **4.020I**

**p.283,** *Social Security Act 1998, s.28 (correction of errors and setting aside of decisions)*

*Erratum:* In subs.(3)(h), "2012" should appear after "Act".     **4.020J**

**p.288,** *Social Security Act 1998, ss.36 to 38 (social fund payments)*

These provisions have now all been repealed, subject to a saving provision.     **4.020K**

**pp.289–290,** *amendment to the Social Security Act 1998, s.39 (interpretation etc. of Chapter II)*

4.020L The additional definition of "claimant" inserted by the Welfare Reform Act 2012 (see main work) became effective for all purposes from April 29, 2013.

**p.293,** *partial repeal of Social Security Act 1998, s.79(8) (regulations and orders)*

4.020M Section 79(8) has been repealed with effect from April 1, 2013 in so far as it relates to council tax benefit, subject to a saving (Welfare Reform Act 2012 s.147 and Part 1 of Sch.14; Welfare Reform Act 2012 (Commencement No.8 and Savings and Transitional Provisions) Order 2013 (SI 2013/358), arts 8(c) and 9 and Sch.4).

**pp.295–296,** *amendment to the Social Security Act 1998, Sch.2 (decisions against which no appeal lies)*

4.020N With effect from April 29, 2013, the Welfare Reform Act 2012 s.31 and Sch.2, paras 50(1) and (2) amended para.6(b) by inserting at the end—

"or
(v) section 159D(1)(b) of that Act (universal credit)."

With effect from April 15, 2013, the Welfare Reform Act 2012 s.97(6) inserted a new para.8A—

*"Reduction on application of benefit cap*

**8A.** A decision to apply the benefit cap in accordance with regulations under section 96 of the Welfare Reform Act 2012."

**pp.297–298,** *amendment to the Social Security Act 1998, Sch.3 (decisions against which an appeal lies)*

4.020O With effect from April 29, 2013, the Welfare Reform Act 2012 s.105(7) inserted a new para.6B—

**"6B.** A decision as to the amount of payment recoverable under section 71ZB, 71ZG or 71ZH of the Administration Act."

Paragraph 6A, which is to be inserted by s.105(7) of the 2012 Act when housing credit is introduced for claimants of state pension credit, has not yet been brought into force.

**p.308,** *amendments to Welfare Reform and Pensions Act 1999 s.72 (Supply of information for certain purposes)*

4.021 With effect from April 29, 2013, reg.15 of the Universal Credit (Consequential Supplementary, Incidental and Miscellaneous Provisions)

Regulations 2013 (SI 2013/630) amended s.72(3) by adding the word "or" at the end of para.(c) and adding new para.(e) after para.(d) as follows:

"(e) Part 1 of the Welfare Reform Act 2012."

**p.315,** *annotation to the Social Security Fraud Act 2001, s.6B (loss of benefit in case of conviction, penalty or caution for benefit offence)*

Note that the words "or an authority which administers housing benefit or council tax benefit" in subs.(2)(b)(i) and the whole of subss.(6), (7), (9) and (10) have formally been repealed with effect from April 1, 2013 in so far as they apply to council tax benefit, subject to a saving (Welfare Reform Act 2012 s.147 and Part 1 of Sch.14; Welfare Reform Act 2012 (Commencement No.8 and Savings and Transitional Provisions) Order 2013 (SI 2013/358), arts 8(c) and 9 and Sch.4).   **4.021A**

**pp.321–322,** *annotation to the Social Security Fraud Act 2001, s.7 (loss of benefit for repeated benefit fraud)*

Note that the words "8 or" in subs.(10) and the whole of subss.(3), (4), (4B) and (5) have formally been repealed with effect from April 1, 2013 in so far as they apply to council tax benefit, subject to a saving (Welfare Reform Act 2012 s.147 and Part 1 of Sch.14; Welfare Reform Act 2012 (Commencement No.8 and Savings and Transitional Provisions) Order 2013 (SI 2013/358), arts 8(c) and 9 and Sch.4).   **4.021B**

**p.327,** *annotation to the Social Security Fraud Act 2001, s.9 (effect of offence on benefits for members of offender's family)*

Note that subss.(1)(a), (b), (bc), (c) and (d), (3), (4), (4B) and (5) have formally been repealed with effect from April 1, 2013 in so far as they apply to council tax benefit, subject to a saving (Welfare Reform Act 2012 s.147 and Part1 of Sch.14; Welfare Reform Act 2012 (Commencement No.8 and Savings and Transitional Provisions) Order 2013 (SI 2013/358), arts 8(c) and 9 and Sch.4).   **4.021C**

**p.365,** *amendments to the Social Security (Claims and Payments) Regulations 1987 (1987/1968) reg.2 (Interpretation)*

With effect from April 29, 2013, reg.29(2) of the Universal Credit (Consequential Supplementary, Incidental and Miscellaneous Provisions) Regulations 2013 (SI 2013/630) amended reg.2(1) by adding the following definition after the definition of "State Pension Credit":   **4.022**

"'universal credit' means universal credit under Part 1 of the Welfare Reform Act 2012;"

With effect from July 29, 2013, reg.2(2) of the Social Security (Miscellaneous Amendments) (No. 2) Regulations 2013 (SI 2013/1508) amended reg.2(1) by adding the following definition after the definition of "the 2002 Act":

"'the 2013 Regulations' means the Universal Credit, Personal Independence Payment, Jobseeker's Allowance and Employment and Support Allowance (Claims and Payments) Regulations 2013;"

**p.373,** *annotation to the Social Security (Claims and Payments) Regulations 1987 (1987/1968) reg.4 (Making a claim for benefit)*

*Paras (1A)—(1C) (paras 2.40 to 2.41)*

4.023    For a case addressing the proper approach to a case in which a person seeks to resurrect a claim for income support some considerable time after sending in a letter indicating an intention to claim income support, see *IJ v SSWP (IS)* [2013] UKUT 302 (AAC).

**p.392,** *annotation to the Social Security (Claims and Payments) Regulations 1987 (1987/1968) reg.4G (Making a claim for employment and support allowance by telephone)*

4.024    In *TR v SSWP (ESA)* [2013] UKUT 555 (AAC) the judge draws attention to the distinction between the provision of information (as required by this section) and the provision of information *and evidence,* which is required elsewhere in the regulations. The judge says that information "comprises facts" whereas evidence requires some documentary evidence to support those facts (para.7).

**p.394,** *amendments to the Social Security (Claims and Payments) Regulations 1987 (1987/1968) reg.5 (Amendment and withdrawal of claim)*

4.025    With effect from October 29, 2013, the Social Security (Miscellaneous Amendments) (No. 3) Regulations 2013 (SI 2013/2536) reg.5(2) substituted the following text for reg.5(1):

"5.—(1) A person who has made a claim for benefit may amend it at any time before a determination has been made on the claim by notice in writing received at an appropriate office, by telephone call to a telephone number specified by the Secretary of State or in such other manner as the Secretary of State may decide or accept.

(1A) Any claim amended in accordance with paragraph (1) may be treated as if it had been so amended in the first instance."

**p.395,** *annotation to the Social Security (Claims and Payments) Regulations 1987 (1987/1968) reg.6 (Date of claim)*

*Para. (1) (paras 2.71–2.72)*

4.026    For a decision on the proper approach where the Department contends that a claim form has not been received, see *SSWP v ZVR (CA)* [2013] UKUT 515 (AAC).

**p.431,** *amendments to the Social Security (Claims and Payments) Regulations 1987 (1987/1968) reg.16A (Date of entitlement under an award of state pension credit for the purpose of payability and effective date of change rate)*

With effect from April 29, 2013, reg.29(3) of the Universal Credit **4.027** (Consequential Supplementary, Incidental and Miscellaneous Provisions) Regulations 2013 (SI 2013/630) amended reg.16A(2) as follows:

(a) by inserting in para.(2)(a) the words "universal credit," after the words "income support,"

(b) by inserting in para.(2)(b) the words "or universal credit" after the words "income-based jobseeker's allowance".

**pp.487–488,** *amendments to the Social Security (Claims and Payments) Regulations 1987 (1987/1968) reg.43 (children)*

In subs.(6), for "district health authority" substitute "[² health author- **4.028** ity]" and for "[³ NHS Foundation Trust]" substitute "[⁴ NHS Foundation Trust]". The correct full text of subs.(7) should then read as follows:

"(7) For the purposes of this regulation—

[² . . . ]

[³ 'child' means a person under the age of 16;]

'child's father' and 'child's mother' include a person who is a child's father or mother by adoption or would be such a relative if an illegitimate child had been born legitimate;

[² 'health authority' means—

    (a) [⁵ . . . ]

    (b) in relation to Wales, a Health Authority established under section 8 of that Act; and

    (c) in relation to Scotland, a Health Board within the meaning of the National Health Service (Scotland) Act 1978;]

'hospital or similar institution' means any premises for the reception of and treatment of person suffering from any illness, including any mental disorder, or of persons suffering from physical disability, and any premises used for providing treatment during convalescence or for medical rehabilitation;

'local authority' means, in relation to England and Wales, a local authority as defined in the Local Government Act 1972 and, in relation to Scotland, a local authority as defined in the Local Government (Scotland) Act 1973;

'social services authority' means—

    (a) in relation to England and Wales, the social services committee established by a local authority under section 2 of the Local Authority Social Services Act 1970; and

> (b) in relation to Scotland, the social work committee established by a local authority under section 2 of the Social Work (Scotland) Act 1968."

AMENDMENTS

1. The Social Security (Claims and Payments) Amendment Regulations 1991 (SI 1991/2741) reg.21 (February 3, 1992).
2. The National Health Service Reform and Health Care Professions Act 2002 (Supplementary, Consequential etc. Provisions) Regulations 2002 (SI 2002/2469) reg.4 and Sch.1, Pt 2, para.44(b) (October 1, 2002).
3. The Social Security, Child Support and Tax Credits (Miscellaneous Amendments) Regulations 2005 (SI 2005/337) reg.7 (March 18, 2005).
4. The Health and Social Care (Community Health and Standards) Act 2003 (Supplementary and Consequential Provisions) (NHS Foundation Trusts) Order 2004 (SI 2004/696) art.3 and Sch.3 (March 11, 2004).
5. National Treatment Agency (Abolition) and the Health and Social Care Act 2012 (Consequential, Transitional and Saving Provisions) Order 2013 (SI 2013/235) art.11 and Sch.2, Pt 1, para.11 (April 1, 2013).

**p.501,** *amendments to the Social Security (Claims and Payments) Regulations 1987 (1987/1968) Sch.9 (Deductions from benefit and direct payment to third parties)*

4.029　　With effect from July 29, 2013, reg.2(3) of the Social Security (Miscellaneous Amendments) (No. 2) Regulations 2013 (SI 2013/1508) amended Sch.9 by inserting the following after para.7C(6):

> "(6A) The Secretary of State shall not make deductions from a benefit mentioned in sub-paragraph (2) where the borrower is in receipt of any benefit within the meaning of "eligible benefit" in paragraph 11(8) (eligible loans) of Schedule 6 (deductions from benefit and direct payment to third parties) to the 2013 Regulations unless the amount of benefit mentioned in that definition is insufficient to meet the deduction."

With effect from October 29, 2013, reg.5(3) of the Social Security (Miscellaneous Amendments) (No. 3) Regulations 2013 (SI 2013/2536) amended Sch.9 as follows:

(a) by substituting the following text for sub-para.(1)(b):

> "(b) in the case of income support, jobseeker's allowance or employment and support allowance, is made to person who is in accommodation provided under section 3(1) of, and Part 2 of the Schedule to, the Polish Resettlement Act 1947(2) (provision by the Secretary of State of accommodation in camps); or
>
> (c) in the case of state pension credit, is made to a person residing in—
>
>> (i) a care home as defined in regulation 1(2) of the State Pension Credit Regulations;

400

     (ii)  an independent hospital as defined in regulation 1(2) of those Regulations;

    (iii)  an establishment run by the Abbeyfield Society (including all bodies corporate or incorporate which are affiliated to the Society); or

    (iv)  accommodation provided under section 3(1) of, and Part 2 of the Schedule to, the Polish Resettlement Act 1947 where the person requires personal care,"

(b) by substituting the words "sub-paragraph (1)(c)(ii)" for the words "regulation 15(7)(d) of the State Pension Credit Regulations".

(c) by substituting ", (b) or (c)" for "or (b)".

**p.525,** *amendments to the Social Security (Claims and Payments) Regulations 1987 (1987/1968) Sch.9B (Deductions from benefit in respect of child support maintenance and payment to persons with care)*

With effect from July 29, 2013, the Social Security (Miscellaneous Amendments) (No. 2) Regulations 2013 (SI 2013/1508) reg.2(4) amended Sch.9B by inserting the following paragraph after para.2(2):    **4.030**

"(2A) Where paragraph 5 (flat rate maintenance) of Schedule 7 (deductions from benefit in respect of child support maintenance and payment to persons with care) to the 2013 Regulations applies, the Secretary of State shall not make deductions under paragraphs 5 and 6 of this Schedule, unless the amount of 'specified benefit' within the meaning of paragraph 1 of Schedule 7 to the 2013 Regulations is insufficient to meet the deduction under paragraph 5 of that Schedule."

**pp.561–564,** *annotation to the Social Security and Child Support (Decisions and Appeals) Regulations 1999, reg.1(3) (citation, commencement, application and interpretation)*

The definition of "official error" does not include errors of tribunals and, in any event, there is no power to revise a decision of a tribunal. Nor is there any power under reg.6 to supersede a decision of a tribunal on the ground of error of law. The consequence is that, where the Secretary of State makes the same official error in a number of cases and some claimants appeal unsuccessfully but others do not appeal, it is possible to revise the decisions in order to correct the error in those cases where claimants did not appeal but the error cannot be corrected retrospectively by the Secretary of State in the cases where the claimant did appeal. It was held in *ED v SSWP (DLA)* [2013] UKUT 583 (AAC) that there are sound reasons of principle why the Secretary of State's power to overturn a decision of a tribunal are limited and therefore, even where the error is a breach of EU law, this inability to correct a tribunal's error retrospectively is not itself contrary to EU law. It is always open to the claimant to make a new claim and it may be possible for there to be a further appeal in some cases, so as to correct the error from the date    **4.030A** that the earlier decision was effective, but that would have involved an impermissible extension of time in *ED*.

**p.566,** *amendments to the Social Security and Child Support (Decisions and Appeals) Regulations 1999, reg.3(1)(b) (revision of decisions)*

4.030B    With effect from October 28, 2013, the Social Security, Child Support, Vaccine Damage and Other Payments (Decisions and Appeals) (Amendment) Regulations 2013 (SI 2013/2380) reg.4(1) and (2)) inserted the words "paragraph (3)(b) of regulation 3ZA or" immediately before "paragraph (1)(b)" in both sub-para.(ii) and sub-para.(iii).

**pp.578–579,** *annotation to the Social Security and Child Support (Decisions and Appeals) Regulations 1999, reg.3(5) (revision of decisions)*

4.030C    In *AL v SSWP (IB)* [2013] UKUT 476 (AAC), the Upper Tribunal followed *JL v SSWP (DLA)* [2011] UKUT 293 (AAC); [2012] AACR 14, decided in relation to reg.7(2)(c), and held that a decision could not be revised under reg.3(5)(d) in respect of a period before September 24, 2007 which was when that subparagraph was first inserted.

**p.582,** *insertion of the Social Security and Child Support (Decisions and Appeals) Regulations 1999, reg.3ZA (consideration of revision before appeal)*

4.030D    With effect from October 28, 2013, the Social Security, Child Support, Vaccine Damage and Other Payments (Decisions and Appeals) (Amendment) Regulations 2013 (SI 2013/2380) reg.4(1) and (3) inserted a new reg.3ZA after reg.3—

### "Consideration of revision before appeal

**3ZA.** (1) This regulation applies in a case where—
  (a) the Secretary of State gives a person written notice of a decision under section 8 or 10 of the Act (whether as originally made or as revised under section 9 of that Act); and
  (b) that notice includes a statement to the effect that there is a right of appeal in relation to the decision only if the Secretary of State has considered an application for a revision of the decision.
  (2) In a case to which this regulation applies, a person has a right of appeal under section 12(2) of the Act in relation to the decision only if the Secretary of State has considered on an application whether to revise the decision under section 9 of the Act.
  (3) The notice referred to in paragraph (1) must inform the person—
  (a) of the time limit specified in regulation 3(1) or (3) for making an application for a revision; and
  (b) that, where the notice does not include a statement of the reasons for the decision ("written reasons"), he may, within one

month of the date of notification of the decision, request that the Secretary of State provide him with written reasons.

(4) Where written reasons are requested under paragraph (3)(b), the Secretary of State must provide them within 14 days of receipt of the request or as soon as practicable afterwards.

(5) Where, as the result of paragraph (2), there is no right of appeal against a decision, the Secretary of State may treat any purported appeal as an application for a revision under section 9 of the Act."

This regulation is made under s.12(3A) and (3B) of the Social Security Act 1998 (see the main work, Vol.III, p.237) and implements the policy of requiring claimants to seek reconsideration of decisions before they may appeal. Equivalent provision has already been made in reg.7 of the Universal Credit, Personal Independence Payment, Jobseeker's Allowance and Employment and Support Allowance (Decisions and Appeals) Regulations 2013 (see the main work, Vol.III, p.680). Like that provision, reg.3ZA enables the Secretary of State to require a person to apply for a review before exercising his or her right of appeal and it harks back to s.33 of the Social Security Administration Act 1992 which had the effect that an appeal relating to attendance allowance or disability living allowance could be brought only following a decision made under s.30 on review. Those provisions were repealed in 1999, when the 1998 Act came into force, and were not re-enacted, presumably because requiring a review in all cases created delay that was not justified by improved decision-making and a reduction in the number of appeals. This time, it is proposed that the review should be more intensive, involving telephoning the claimant to discuss the case, and thereby better elicit evidence that might otherwise not be elicited save at a hearing before the First-tier Tribunal and better explain the decision that has been made. The expectation is that this process of revising decisions before appeals are lodged will largely replace the revising of decisions under reg.3(4A) after appeals have been lodged. Consequently, in cases where there has been consideration of an application for a revision as required by this regulation, an appeal will be lodged with the First-tier Tribunal, rather than with the Secretary of State (see the supplementary annotation to r.22 of the Tribunal Procedure (First-tier Tribunal) (Social Entitlement Chamber) Rules 2008, below).

Paragraph (1) does not require the Secretary of State to issue a notice complying with subpara.(b) in all cases where the original decision has not already been the subject of reconsideration, although it is expected that he will initially. Its terms enable the Secretary of State to decide that certain classes of decision, or even individual decisions, should be appealable without the claimant first being obliged to seek reconsideration. Whether he issues a notice complying with subpara.(b) is a matter within his discretion. The regulation does not expressly forbid the Secretary of State from issuing a notice complying with subpara.(b) when a decision in respect of which such a notice has already been issued has been revised, but Memo DMG 20/13 makes it clear that the policy intention is that: "Once a decision has been subjected to mandatory reconsideration, further dispute rights are not dependent upon a further mandatory reconsideration". The notice issued with the revised decision in those circumstances should be the "notice of the result of mandatory reconsideration", which should be issued in duplicate so that, if the claimant wishes to appeal, he or she can send one copy to the First-tier Tribunal as required by r.22(4)(a)(i) of the Tribunal Procedure (First-tier Tribunal) (Social Entitlement Chamber) Rules 2008 (see the main work, Vol.III, p.1545).

Where a notice complying with para.(1)(b) is issued, it is para.(2) that operates to restrict the right of appeal. It is to be noted that it does not say under what paragraph of reg.3 any application for revision should be made, although para.(3)(a) clearly anticipates applications being made under reg.3(1) or (3). There are time limits for making applications under those provisions and, although time may be extended by the Secretary of State under reg.4, there is no right of appeal against a refusal to extend time and it is doubtful that the Secretary of State can be said to have "considered . . . whether to revise the decision" if he has refused to extend the time for applying for the revision. However, an application under reg.3(5)(a), for instance, does not need to be made within any specific time. If a claimant is refused an extension of time for making an application under reg.3(1) but makes an unsuccessful application under reg.3(5)(a), it may be arguable that the terms of para.(2) of this regulation are satisfied and he or she may appeal against the original decision.

If written reasons are provided following a request under para.(3)(b), the usual one-month time limit for applying for a revision under reg.3(1) is automatically extended (see reg.3(1)(b)(ii) and (iii), as amended by the 2013 Regulations (see above)), but there is no equivalent extension of time in relation to applications under reg.3(3) (relating to social fund payments for maternity or funeral expenses), despite what para.(3) of this regulation might suggest. Therefore, if a claimant has delayed applying for a revision of a decision in respect of a payment for maternity of funeral expenses and in consequence the usual one-month time limit has passed, he or she must rely on the Secretary of State exercising his discretionary power to extend time under reg.4.

Paragraph (5) enables the Secretary of State to treat a purported appeal as an application for revision. This would appear to apply whether the appeal is lodged with the Secretary of State in error or whether it is lodged with the First-tier Tribunal and then copied to the Secretary of State, although in the latter case the date of the application for revision is likely to be taken to be the date the appeal was received by the Secretary of State rather than when it was received by the First-tier Tribunal. Note that para.(5) applies only where there is no right of appeal. It will therefore not apply where the original decision was made before October 28, 2013 or was for any other reason not accompanied by a notice of the type mentioned in para.(1). In such a case, the Secretary of State will still be entitled to consider revising the decision under reg.3(4A) but the appeal will have been valid so that the Secretary of State will be obliged to send a response to the appeal to the First-tier Tribunal if the original decision is not revised in the claimant's favour.

**p.582,** *insertion of the Social Security and Child Support (Decisions and Appeals) Regulations 1999, reg.3B (consideration of revision before appeal in relation to certain child support decisions)*

With effect from October 28, 2013, the Social Security, Child Support, Vaccine Damage and Other Payments (Decisions and Appeals) (Amendment) Regulations 2013 (SI 2013/2380) reg.4(1) and (4) inserted a new reg.3B after reg.3A. This makes, for certain child support decisions, provision equivalent to reg.3ZA (see above). As it applies only to child support cases, it need not be set out here.   4.030E

**pp.582–583,** *amendments to the Social Security and Child Support (Decisions and Appeals) Regulations 1999, reg.4 (late application for a revision)*

With effect from October 28, 2013, the Social Security, Child Support, Vaccine Damage and Other Payments (Decisions and Appeals) (Amendment) Regulations 2013 (SI 2013/2380), reg.4(1) and (5) made three amendments to reg.4. In para.(3)(b), after "in accordance with" there is inserted "regulation 3ZA(3)(b) or". At the end of para.(4)(b) there is inserted ", except in a case to which regulation 3ZA or 3B applies." In para.(6), after "extension of time" there is inserted ", except in a case to which regulation 3ZA or 3B applies,".   4.030F

The third of those amendments disapplies the stringent conditions of reg.4(6) in cases where a claimant's right of appeal depends on an application for revision being admitted and considered.

The second of those amendments is ambiguous and the full stop after the inserted word "applies" is plainly an error, since para.(4)(b) is followed by subpara.(4)(c). Paragraph 4(4) peviously read—

"(4) An application for an extension of time shall not be granted unless the applicant satisfies the Secretary of State 85 that—
(a) it is reasonable to grant the application;
(b) the application for revision has merit; and
(c) special circumstances are relevant to the application and as a result of those special circumstances it was not practicable for the application to be made within the time limit specified in regulation 3 or 3A."

If the full stop at the end of the inserted words was intended to be a comma, the amendment was clearly intended to follow the word "and" and so has the effect of disapplying para.(4)(c) where reg.3ZA or 3B applies. However, if no punctuation mark was intended, the amendment presumably precedes the semicolon and so disapplies para.(4)(b). Comparison with reg.6(5) of the Universal Credit, Personal Independence Payment, Jobseeker's Allowance and Employment and Support Allowance (Decisions and Appeals) Regulations 2013 (see the main work, Vol.III, p.679) suggests that the second of those constructions is the right one and that is clearly what the author of the Departmental guidance in DMG Memo 20/13 understood the position to be since he or she refers to the test of "special circumstances" still being applicable.

The guidance also says that "Applicants are *not* expected to show unexpected or exceptional circumstances" and that an extension of time should be allowed "where the person is able to explain why their application for a revision is late and is reasonable". At first sight, that might seem inconsistent with the language of para.(4)(c). However, that is not necessarily so and the approach appears justified in the light of *R(S) 3/79* and *R(I) 1/90*, in which it was held that reasonable ignorance of the law or a reasonable mistake as to the law could make it not "practicable" to take action. (In the earlier of those cases, reference was made to *Dedman v British Building and Engineering Appliances Ltd* [1974] ICR 53 and *Wall's Meat Co Ltd v Khan* [1979] ICR 52, but it was suggested that, in the social security context, one should focus only on the reasonableness of any ignorance or mistake on the part of the claimant in the light of any advice he or she received or should have sought, even if an advisor's ignorance or mistake was not reasonable.) On the other hand, if the approach taken in those cases is correct, it perhaps weakens the impact of para.(6) where it is not disapplied, since para.(6)(a) provides that ignorance of, or a mistake as to, the law is not relevant to whether it is "reasonable to grant the application" (the para.(4)(a) issue) which is of doubtful effect if such ignorance or mistake is relevant to whether there are "special circumstances" (the para.(4)(c) issue).

**pp.598–601,** *annotation to the Social Security and Child Support (Decisions and Appeals) Regulations 1999, reg.6(2)(g) and (r) (supersession of decisions)*

4.030G
A Tribunal of Commissioners in Northern Ireland, having analysed several incapacity benefit cases (most of which are mentioned in the annotation to reg.6(2)(g) in the main work), had reached a conclusion similar to that reached in *ST v SSWP (ESA)* [2012] UKUT 469 (AAC), mentioned in the annotation to reg.6(2)(r) in the main work, about the duty of the Secretary of State to provide the First-tier Tribunal with reports arising from earlier assessments where they were relevant and to inform the First-tier Tribunal of reports that were possibly relevant. The Tribunal of Commissioners considered that the Department for Social Development should list details of all previous assessment determinations within the current claim, which the Department had said "should be straightforward in most cases . . . from computer records", but that the assessment need only be provided "in a limited class of case, where there is an assertion that there has been no change in the claimant's condition, and where the evidence associated with the previous adjudication history is relevant to that submission or, for example, where the claimant's medical condition, and the evidence associated with the previous adjudication history assists in the assessment of the claimant's overall capacity" (*JC v DSD (IB)* [2011] NICom 177).

In *AM v SSWP (ESA)* [2013] UKUT 458 (AAC), the judge expressed reservations about what was said in *ST.* In any event, *AM* was a "conversion" case so that the tests applied in the earlier assessments were different from those to be applied in the current assessment. In those circumstances, it was held that the First-tier Tribunal was entitled to conclude that it had enough evidence upon which to determine the appeal without obtaining the reports from previous assessments. Thus, *AM* and *ST* are not necessarily inconsistent since it can be said that the earlier reports in *AM* were unlikely to be relevant.

**pp.623–624,** *amendment to the Social Security and Child Support (Decisions and Appeals) Regulations 1999, reg.9ZA (review of certificates)*

With effect from October 28, 2013, the Social Security, Child Support, Vaccine Damage and Other Payments (Decisions and Appeals) (Amendment) Regulations 2013 (SI 2013/2380), reg.4(1) and (10)(a) omitted the words "and 33" in reg.9ZA(2), save where notice of the certificate of recoverable benefits or recoverable lump sum payments was posted to the appellant's last known address before October 28, 2013 (see reg.8(1) and (3) of the 2013 Regulations).  **4.030H**

**p.624,** *insertion of the Social Security and Child Support (Decisions and Appeals) Regulations 1999, reg.9ZB (consideration of review before appeal)*

With effect from October 28, 2013, the Social Security, Child Support, Vaccine Damage and Other Payments (Decisions and Appeals) (Amendment) Regulations 2013 (SI 2013/2380), reg.4(1) and (6) inserted a new reg.9ZB after reg.9ZA—  **4.030I**

**"Consideration of review before appeal**

**9ZB.** (1) This regulation applies in a case where—
  (a) the Secretary of State has issued a certificate of recoverable benefits or certificate of recoverable lump sum payments; and
  (b) that certificate is accompanied by a notice to the effect that there is a right of appeal in relation to the certificate only if the Secretary of State has considered an application for review of the certificate.
  (2) In a case to which this regulation applies, a person has a right of appeal under section 11 of the 1997 Act against the certificate only if the Secretary of State has considered an application for review of the certificate under section 10 of that Act.".

This makes, for appeals under the Social Security (Recovery of Benefits) Act 1997, provision equivalent to reg.3ZA(1) and (2) (see above). It is made under the new subss.(2A) and (2B) inserted into s.11 of the 1997 Act by the Welfare Reform Act 2012 (see above). For the power to treat a purported appeal as an application for review where there is no right of appeal as a result of this provision, see the new reg.29(6) (see below).

**p.642,** *amendment to the Social Security and Child Support (Decisions and Appeals) Regulations 1999, reg.25 (other persons with a right of appeal)*

With effect from October 28, 2013, the Social Security, Child Support, Vaccine Damage and Other Payments (Decisions and Appeals)  **4.030J**

(Amendment) Regulations 2013 (SI 2013/2380), reg.4(1) and (7) inserted after "section 12(2)" the words ", but subject to regulation 3ZA,".

**p.643,** *amendment to the Social Security and Child Support (Decisions and Appeals) Regulations 1999, reg.26 (decisions against which an appeal lies)*

4.030K    With effect from October 28, 2013, the Social Security, Child Support, Vaccine Damage and Other Payments (Decisions and Appeals) (Amendment) Regulations 2013 (SI 2013/2380) reg.4(1) and (8)) inserted the words "Subject to regulation 3ZA," at the beginning of reg.26.

**p.646,** *amendments to the Social Security and Child Support (Decisions and Appeals) Regulations 1999, reg.29 (further particulars required relating to certificate of recoverable benefits or, as the case may be, recoverable lump sum payments appeals)*

4.030L    With effect from October 28, 2013, the Social Security, Child Support, Vaccine Damage and Other Payments (Decisions and Appeals) (Amendment) Regulations 2013 (SI 2013/2380) reg.4(1) and (10)(b) omitted paras (3) to (5), save where notice of the certificate of recoverable benefits or recoverable lump sum payments was posted to the appellant's last known address before October 28, 2013 (see reg.8(1) and (3) of the 2013 Regulations).    Regulation 4(1) and (9) of the 2013 Regulations substituted para.(6) with effect from the same date—

"(6) The Secretary of State may treat any—
(a) purported appeal (where, as the result of regulation 9ZB(2) (consideration of review before appeal), there is no right of appeal);
(b) appeal relating to the certificate of recoverable benefits; or
(c) appeal relating to the certificate of recoverable lump sum payments,
as an application for review under section 10 of the 1997 Act."

As para.(6) will be the sole surviving paragraph of reg.29 when the saving in respect of paras (3) to (5) ceases to apply, the heading of the regulation will then be anachronistic.

**pp.649–650,** *revocation of the of Social Security and Child Support (Decisions and Appeals) Regulations 1999, reg.32 (late appeals)*

4.030M    With effect from October 28, 2013, the Social Security, Child Support, Vaccine Damage and Other Payments (Decisions and Appeals) (Amendment) Regulations 2013 (SI 2013/2380), reg.4(1) and (10)(c) omitted reg.32, save where notice of the Secretary of State's decision was posted to the appellant's last known address before October 28, 2013 (see reg.8(1) and (3) of the 2013 Regulations). Regulation 32 has become unnecessary and, indeed, is arguably unnecessary even in the cases for which it remains in effect (see the annotation on p.650 of the main work).

**pp.651–652,** *revocation of the Social Security and Child Support (Decisions and Appeals) Regulations 1999, reg.33 (notice of appeal)*

With effect from October 28, 2013, the Social Security, Child Support, Vaccine Damage and Other Payments (Decisions and Appeals) (Amendment) Regulations 2013 (SI 2013/2380) reg.4(1) and (10)(d) omitted reg.33, save where notice of the Secretary of State's decision was posted to the appellant's last known address before October 28, 2013 (see reg.8 of the 2013 Regulations). This is because appeals against decisions made on or after October 28, 2013 are lodged with the First-tier Tribunal under r.22 of the Tribunal Procedure (First-tier Tribunal) (Social Entitlement Chamber) Rules 2008 (see the supplementary annotation to that rule, below). 4.030N

**pp.653–654,** *revocation of the Social Security and Child Support (Decisions and Appeals) Regulations 1999, reg.34 (death of a party to an appeal)*

With effect from October 28, 2013, the Social Security, Child Support, Vaccine Damage and Other Payments (Decisions and Appeals) (Amendment) Regulations 2013 (SI 2013/2380) reg.4(1) and (10)(e) omitted reg.34, save where notice of the Secretary of State's decision was posted to the appellant's last known address before October 28, 2013 (see reg.8(1) and (3) of the 2013 Regulations) and save also for the purpose of reg.8 of the Personal Injuries (NHS Charges) (Reviews and Appeals) (Scotland) Regulations 2006 (SSI 2006/593) (see reg.8(2) of the 2013 Regulations). This Scottish statutory instrument makes procedural provision for appeals referred to appeal tribunals by Scottish Ministers under s.158 of the Health and Social Care (Community Health and Standards) Act 2003 and applies a number of otherwise revoked regulations in Part V of the 1999 Regulations for those purposes. As recorded in the annotation to ss.59–67 of the Social Security Act 1998 (see the main work, Vol.III, pp.222–223), the appeal tribunals are those constituted under that Act, which remain in existence solely for the purpose of appeals in Scotland under the 2003 Act. If there were in fact any such appeals, the Scottish Parliament might perhaps legislate to redirect the appeals to another tribunal or court. 4.030O

The revocation of reg.34 may leave a lacuna that has not been filled by Tribunal Procedure Rules. Although there seems to be no reason why there should not be an appointment under reg.30(1) of the Social Security (Claims and Payments) Regulations 1987 (see the main work, Vol.III, p.461) after an appeal relating to a claim for benefit has been lodged, in other cases where an appointment could previously have been made under reg.34 it is likely that an appeal will have to be abated until someone has been appointed to administer the deceased's estate.

**pp.669–670,** *amendment to the Social Security and Child Support (Decisions and Appeals) Regulations 1999, Sch.3C (date from which change of circumstances takes effect where claimant entitled to employment and support allowance)*

**4.030P** With effect from October 29, 2013, the Social Security (Miscellaneous Amendments) (No.3) Regulations 2013 (SI 2013/2536), reg.8 inserted after para.3(e) of Sch.3C—

"(f) regulation 9 of the Social Security (Disability Living Allowance) Regulations 1991 (persons in care homes) applies, or ceases to apply, to the claimant for a period of less than one week; or
(g) regulations under section 85(1) of the Welfare Reform Act 2012 (care home residents) apply, or cease to apply, to the claimant for a period of less than one week.".

**pp.764–766,** *amendments to the Social Security (Loss of Benefit) Regulations 2001, reg.1 (citation, commencement and interpretation)*

**4.030Q** With effect from April, 29 2013, the Social Security (Loss of Benefit)(Amendment) Regulations 2013 (SI 2013/385) regs 2 and 3(d), (e) and (g) inserted new definitions into reg.1(2) as follows—
After the definition of "the Jobseeker's Allowance Regulations" insert—

""the UC Regulations" means the Universal Credit Regulations 2013;
"assessment period" has the same meaning as in the UC Regulations;".

After the definition of "disqualification period" insert—

""income-based jobseeker's allowance" means an income-based allowance under the Jobseekers Act as it has effect apart from the amendments made by Part 1 of Schedule 14 to the 2012 Act (to remove references to an income-based allowance);
"income-related employment and support allowance" means an income-related allowance under the Part 1 of the 2007 Act as it has effect apart from the amendments made by Schedule 3 and Part 1 of Schedule 14 to the 2012 Act (to remove references to an income-related allowance);
"joint claimant" means each of joint claimants as defined in section 40 of the 2012 Act;".

After the definition of "relevant authority" add—

""universal credit" means the benefit payable under Part 1 of the 2012 Act.".

**pp.766–767,** *amendments to the Social Security (Loss of Benefit) Regulations 2001, reg.1A (disqualification period: section 6B(11) of the Act)*

With effect from April 29, 2013, the Social Security (Loss of Bene-   **4.030R** fit)(Amendment) Regulations 2013 (SI 2013/385) regs 2 and 4(3), (6) and (7) amended para.(2)(a) by adding "or universal credit" at the end and inserting new paras (6A) and (6B)—

"(6A) Paragraph (6B) applies where, on the determination day, the offender or, as the case may be, the offender's family member is in receipt of universal credit.
(6B) Where this paragraph applies, DQ-day is—
(a) if the first day after the end of the period of 28 days beginning with the determination day is the first day of an assessment period, that day;
(b) if the first day after the end of the period of 28 days beginning with the determination day is not the first day of an assessment period, the first day of the next assessment period after that day.".

Also, para.(7)(a) is amended by inserting "or (6A)" after "paragraph (2)" and para.(7)(b) is amended by substituting "those paragraphs" for "that paragraph" and inserting "or (6B)" after "paragraph (3)".

**pp.767–768,** *amendments to the Social Security (Loss of Benefit) Regulations 2001, reg.2 (disqualification period: section 7(6) of the Act)*

With effect from April 29, 2013, the Social Security (Loss of Bene-   **4.030S** fit)(Amendment) Regulations 2013 (SI 2013/385), regs 2 and 5(3), (5)(b) and (6) amended para.(2)(a) by adding "or universal credit" at the end, amended para.(6)(c) by inserting "universal credit," at the beginning and inserted new paras (6A) and (6B)"

"(6A) Paragraph (6B) applies where on the determination day, the offender or, as the case may be, the offender's family member is in receipt of universal credit.
(6B) Where this paragraph applies, DQ-day is—
(a) if the first day after the end of the period of 28 days beginning with the determination day is the first day of an assessment period, that day;
(b) if the first day after the end of the period of 28 days beginning with the determination day is not the first day of an assessment period, the first day of the next assessment period after that day.".

**p.771,** *insertion of the Social Security (Loss of Benefit) Regulations 2001, reg.3ZB (reduction of universal credit)*

With effect from April 29, 2013, the Social Security (Loss of Bene-   **4.030T** fit)(Amendment) Regulations 2013 (SI 2013/385) regs 2 and 9 inserted a new reg.3ZB after reg.3ZA—

411

## "Reduction of universal credit

**3ZB.**—(1) Any payment of universal credit which falls to be made to an offender or an offender's family member ("O") in respect of an assessment period wholly or partly within a disqualification period is to be reduced in accordance with paragraph (2) or (5).

(2) Except where paragraph (5) applies and subject to paragraphs (6) and (7), the amount of the reduction is to be calculated by multiplying the daily reduction rate by the number of days in the assessment period or, if lower, the number of days in the assessment period to which the reduction is to relate.

(3) The daily reduction rate for the purposes of paragraph (2) is, unless paragraph (4) applies, an amount equal to the amount of the standard allowance applicable to the award multiplied by 12 and divided by 365.

(4) The daily reduction rate for the purposes of paragraph (2) is 40 per cent. of the rate calculated in accordance with paragraph (3) if, at the end of the assessment period—

  (a) O, or where O is a joint claimant, the other joint claimant ("J"), falls within section 19 of the 2012 Act (claimant subject no work-related requirements) by virtue of—

    (i) subsection (2)(c) of that section (responsible carer for a child under the age of 1), or

    (ii) regulation 89(1)(c), (d) or (f) of the UC Regulations (adopter, claimants within 11 weeks before, or 15 weeks after, confinement or responsible foster parent of a child under the age of 1); or

  (b) O or, as the case may be, O or J, falls within section 20 of the 2012 Act (claimant subject to work-focused interview only).

(5) Where the disqualification period ends during an assessment period, the amount of the reduction for that assessment period is to be calculated by multiplying the daily reduction rate under paragraph (3) or, as the case may be, paragraph (4) by the number of days in that assessment period which are within the disqualification period.

(6) The amount of the daily reduction rate in paragraphs (3) and (4) is to be rounded down to the nearest 10 pence.

(7) The amount of the reduction under paragraph (2) in respect of any assessment period must not exceed the amount of the standard allowance which is applicable to O in respect of that period.

(8) Where the rate of universal credit payable to O or as the case may be, to O and J, changes, the rules set out above for a reduction in the universal credit payable are to be applied to the new rate and any adjustment to the reduction is to take effect from the first day of the first assessment period to start after the date of the change.

(9) In the case of joint claimants—

  (a) each joint claimant is considered individually for the purpose of determining the rate applicable under paragraph (3) or (4); and

  (b) half of any applicable rate is applied to each joint claimant accordingly.

(10) In this regulation, "standard allowance" means the allowance of that name, the amount of which is set out in regulation 36 of the UC Regulations.".

**p.784,** *insertion of the Social Security (Loss of Benefit) Regulations 2001, Part 4B (hardship: universal credit)*

With effect from April 29, 2013, the Social Security (Loss of Bene-  4.030U
fit)(Amendment) Regulations 2013 (SI 2013/385) regs 2 and 14 inserted a new Part 4B after Part 4A—

"PART 4B

HARDSHIP: UNIVERSAL CREDIT

**Payment of universal credit to specified persons**

**16D.**—(1) Subject to regulation 16E, universal credit is payable in accordance with the following provisions of this Part to an offender or an offender's family member ("O") or where O is a joint claimant, to O and the other joint claimant ("J"), where the Secretary of State is satisfied that they are in hardship.

(2) For the purposes of paragraph (1), O or, as the case may be, O and J must be considered as being in hardship only where—
  (a) they meet the conditions for entitlement to universal credit;
  (b) they cannot meet their immediate and most basic and essential needs, specified in paragraph (3), or the immediate and most basic and essential needs of a child or qualifying young person for whom O is, or O and J are, responsible only because the amount of their award has been reduced under—
    (i) section 26 or 27 of the 2012 Act by the daily reduction rate determined in accordance with regulation 111 of the UC Regulations; or
    (ii) regulation 3ZB above by the daily reduction rate determined in accordance with paragraph (3) or (4) of that regulation;
  (c) they have made every effort to access alternative sources of support to meet, or partially meet, such needs; and
  (d) they have made every effort to cease to incur any expenditure which does not relate to such needs.

(3) The needs referred to in paragraph (2) are—
  (a) accommodation;
  (b) heating;
  (c) food;
  (d) hygiene.

(4) In paragraph (2)(b), "child" and "qualifying young person" have the same meaning as in Part 1 of the 2012 Act and whether or not O is, or O and J are, responsible for a child or qualifying young person

413

is to be determined in accordance with regulation 4 of the UC Regulations.

### Requirements for payments under regulation 16D(1)

**16E.** The Secretary of State must not make a payment under regulation 16D(1) unless—

(a) O completes and submits or, as the case may be, O and J complete and submit, an application in a form approved for the purpose by the Secretary of State, or in such other form as the Secretary of State accepts as sufficient, in such manner as the Secretary of State determines;

(b) O furnishes or, as the case may be, O and J furnish, such information or evidence relating to the matters specified in regulation 16D(2)(b) to (d) as the Secretary of State may require, in such manner as the Secretary of State determines; and

(c) O accepts or, as the case may be O and J accept, that any such payments that are paid are recoverable and may be recovered in accordance with section 71ZH of the Administration Act, except in such cases as the Secretary of State determines otherwise.

### Period in respect of which payments under regulation 16D(1) are to be made

**16F.** A payment under regulation 16D(1) is to be made in respect of—

(a) a period which—
  (i) begins with the date on which the application under regulation 16E(a) is submitted or, if later, the date on which all of the conditions in regulation 16D(2) are met; and
  (ii) ends with the day before the date on which O's, or as the case may be, O and J's next full payment of universal credit for an assessment period is due to be made (or would be made but for a reduction under regulation 3ZB); or

(b) where the period calculated in accordance with paragraph (a) is 7 days or less, that period plus a further period ending with the day referred to in paragraph (a)(ii) or, if sooner, the last day in respect of which O's, or as the case may be, O and J's award is reduced in accordance with regulation 3ZB.

### The amount of payments under regulation 16D(1)

**16G.** The amount of a payment under regulation 16D(1) for each day in respect of which such a payment is to be is made is to be determined in accordance with the formula—

$$60\% \text{ of } \left( \frac{A \times 12}{365} \right)$$

where A is equal to the amount of the reduction in the amount of O's award or, as the case may be, the amount of O and J's award, calculated under regulation 3ZB for the assessment period preceding the assessment period in which an application is submitted under regulation 16E(a).

### Recoverability of payments made under regulation 16D(1)

**16H.** Payments made under regulation 16D(1) are recoverable by virtue of section 71ZH of the Administration Act as if they were hardship payments under regulation 116 of the UC Regulations and for this purpose, regulation 119 of those Regulations applies to payments under regulation 16D(1) as it applies to such hardship payments.".

**p.786,** *amendments to the Social Security (Medical Evidence) Regulations 1976 (SI 1976/615) reg.1 (Citation, commencement and interpretation)*

With effect from April 29, 2013, the Universal Credit (Consequential Supplementary, Incidental and Miscellaneous Provisions) Regulations 2013 (SI 2013/630) reg.24 amended reg.1 as follows:  4.031
(a) by substituting the following definitions for those currently in the regulation:

> "'limited capability for work' has the meaning—
> (a) for the purposes of employment and support allowance, given in section 1(4) of the Welfare Reform Act 2007; and
> (b) for the purposes of universal credit, given in section 37 of the Welfare Reform Act 2012;"
> "'limited capability for work assessment' means the assessment of whether a person has limited capability for work—
> (a) for the purposes of old style ESA, under Part 5 of the Employment and Support Allowance Regulations;
> (b) for the purposes of new style ESA, under Part 4 of the Employment and Support Allowance Regulations 2013;
> (c) for the purposes of universal credit, under Part 5 of the Universal Credit Regulations 2013;"

(b) by adding after para.(4):

> "(5) For the purposes of the definition of 'limited capability for work assessment' in paragraph (2)—
> (a) 'old style ESA' means an allowance under Part 1 of the Welfare Reform Act 2007 as that Part has effect apart from the amendments made by Schedule 3, and Part 1 of Schedule 14, to the Welfare Reform Act 2012 that remove references to an income-related allowance; and
> (b) 'new style ESA' means an allowance under Part 1 of the Welfare Reform Act 2007 as amended by the provisions

of Schedule 3, and Part 1 of Schedule 14, to the Welfare Reform Act 2012 that remove references to an income-related allowance."

**p.793,** *amendment to the Social Security (Medical Evidence) Regulations 1976 (SI 1976/615) Sch.2 (form of certificate)*

4.032  With effect from April 1, 2013, art.11 of, and para.6(3) of Part 1 of Sch.2 to, the National Treatment Agency (Abolition) and the Health and Social Care Act 2012 (Consequential, Transitional and Saving Provisions) Order 2013 (SI 2013/235) substituted "(unless the form has been stamped, in Wales, by the Local Health Board in whose medical performers list you are included or, in Scotland," for the words from "if the form" to "(or, in Scotland," in Part 2 of Sch.2 (form of certificate).

**p.798,** *additional provisions of the Social Security (Overpayments and Recovery) Regulations 2013 (SI 2013/384) brought into force*

4.033  With effect from April 29, 2013, the Social Security (Overpayments and Recovery) Regulations 2013 (SI 2013/384) reg.1 brings Parts 2 to 5 of the regulations into effect. The new provisions are as follows:

"PART 2

RECOVERABILITY

**Recoverable amounts**

3.—(1) In these Regulations, "recoverable amount" means—
   (a) subject to regulations 7 to 9, the amount of any overpayment; and
   (b) any other amount recoverable under any provision of the Act specified in paragraph (2).
(2) Those provisions are(12)—
   (a) section 71ZE(3) (costs of court action etc.);
   (b) section 71ZG (recovery of payments on account);
   (c) section 71ZH (recovery of hardship payments);
   (d) section 115B(4) (recovery of penalties imposed as an alternative to prosecution);
   (e) section 115C(4) (recovery of civil penalties for incorrect statements); and
   (f) section 115D(4) (recovery of civil penalties for failure to disclose information).

## Persons from whom an overpayment may be recovered

**4.**—(1) The following paragraphs apply for determining the person from whom an overpayment is recoverable in the circumstances specified in those paragraphs.

(2) Where the payee is a person appointed under regulation 57 of the UC etc. Claims and Payments Regulations or a person to whom the Secretary of State has directed that payment be made in accordance with regulation 58 of those Regulations, then the overpayment is recoverable from the claimant in addition to the payee.

(3) Where the payee is a person to whom universal credit, jobseeker's allowance or employment and support allowance has been paid pursuant to Schedule 6 to the UC etc. Claims and Payments Regulations (payments to third parties), then, to the extent that the amount paid does not exceed the amount payable to the payee under that Schedule, the overpayment is recoverable from the claimant instead of the payee.

(4) Paragraphs (5) to (7) apply only in relation to overpayments of housing costs.

(5) Where the Secretary of State is satisfied that an overpayment occurred in consequence of any change of dwelling occupied by the claimant as their home, then if the claimant and the payee are not the same person, the overpayment is recoverable from the claimant in addition to the payee.

(6) Where the Secretary of State is satisfied that an overpayment occurred in consequence of a misrepresentation, or a failure to disclose a material fact (in either case, whether fraudulent or otherwise), by any person ("M"), then, if M and the payee are not the same person, the overpayment is recoverable from M instead of the payee.

(7) Where the Secretary of State is satisfied that an overpayment occurred for a reason other than that mentioned in paragraph (5) or (6), then, except where paragraph (2) or (8) applies in relation to the overpayment, if the claimant and the payee are not the same person, the overpayment is recoverable from the claimant instead of the payee.

(8) This paragraph applies where the overpayment occurred due to the amount of the payment exceeding the amount of housing costs for which the claimant is liable.

(9) In this regulation, "payee" means the person to whom the overpayment has been paid.

## Circumstances in which a determination need not be reversed, varied, revised or superseded prior to recovery

**5.** Section 71ZB(3) of the Act (recoverability of an overpayment dependent on reversal, variation, revision or supersession) does not apply where the circumstances of the overpayment do not provide a basis for the decision pursuant to which the payment was made to be revised under section 9 of the Social Security Act 1998(**13**) or super-seded under section 10 of that Act.

PART 3

PREVENTION OF DUPLICATION OF PAYMENTS

**Duplication and prescribed income**

**6.**—(1) The income prescribed for the purpose of section 71ZB(5) of the Act (duplication of payments: universal credit) is any income which falls to be taken into account in accordance with Chapters 2 and 3 of Part 6 of the UC Regulations.

(2) The date prescribed for the payment of income for the purpose of that subsection is—

    (a) where the payment of income is made in respect of a specific day or period, that day or the first day of that period;

    (b) where the payment of income is not so made, the day or first day of the period to which it is fairly attributable.

PART 4

CALCULATION OF RECOVERABLE AMOUNT OF AN OVERPAYMENT

**Diminution of capital**

**7.**—(1) Paragraph (2) applies where—

    (a) there is an overpayment of universal credit which occurred as a consequence of an error relating to the amount of a person's capital; and

    (b) the overpayment period is 3 months or more.

(2) Where this paragraph applies, the Secretary of State must, for the purpose only of calculating the recoverable amount of that over-payment—

    (a) at the end of the first 3 months of the overpayment period, treat the amount of that capital as having been reduced by the amount of universal credit overpaid during those 3 months;

    (b) at the end of each subsequent period of 3 months, if any, of the overpayment period, treat the amount of that capital as having been further reduced by the amount of universal credit overpaid during the immediately preceding 3 months.

(3) Capital is not to be treated as reduced over any period other than 3 months in any circumstances other than those for which paragraph (2) provides.

418

**Sums to be deducted**

**8.**—(1) In calculating the recoverable amount of an overpayment of jobseeker's allowance or employment and support allowance, the Secretary of State must deduct the amounts specified in paragraphs (2) and (3).

(2) Any amount which has been offset under regulation 16.

(3) Any additional amount of universal credit which was not payable to the claimant or their partner under the original or any other determination but which should have been determined to be payable in respect of all or part of the overpayment period to the claimant, or to the claimant and their partner jointly—

   (a)  on the basis of the claim for universal credit as presented to the Secretary of State;

   (b)  on the basis of that claim as it would have appeared if any change of circumstances, except a change of the dwelling which the claimant occupies as their home, had been notified at the time that change occurred;

   (c)  where the overpayment arose by virtue of a misrepresentation or a failure to disclose a material fact, on the basis that that misrepresentation or failure had been remedied prior to the award being made; or

   (d)  where the overpayment arose by virtue of an error made by, or on behalf of, the Secretary of State, on the basis that that error had not been made.

**Sums to be deducted: change of dwelling**

**9.**—(1) This regulation applies where an overpayment of housing costs has occurred in the following circumstances—

   (a)  the claimant has moved from the dwelling previously occupied as their home ('dwelling A') to another dwelling which they occupy as their home ('dwelling B');

   (b)  they have been awarded housing costs in respect of dwelling A to which they are not entitled because they are no longer occupying or treated as occupying dwelling A as their home; and

   (c)  housing costs are payable to the same person in respect of the claimant's occupation of dwelling B as it was paid to in respect of dwelling A.

(2) In calculating the recoverable amount of the overpayment, the Secretary of State may, at his or her discretion, deduct an amount equal to the claimant's entitlement to housing costs for the assessment period in respect of dwelling B for the number of assessment periods equal to the number of assessment periods during which the claimant was overpaid housing costs in respect of dwelling A.

(3) Where a sum has been deducted under paragraph (2), an equivalent sum is to be treated as having been paid in respect of the claimant's entitlement to housing costs in respect of dwelling B for the number of assessment periods equal to the number of assessment periods during which the claimant was overpaid housing costs in respect of dwelling A.

PART 5

THE PROCESS OF RECOVERY

## Recovery by deduction from benefits

**10.**—(1) Subject to regulations 11 to 14, the Secretary of State may recover a recoverable amount from a liable person by deduction from the benefits specified in paragraph (2) which are payable to them.

(2) Those benefits are—

(a) benefits under Parts 2 to 5 of the Social Security Contributions and Benefits Act 1992;

(b) universal credit;

(c) jobseeker's allowance;

(d) employment and support allowance;

(e) state pension credit payable under the State Pension Credit Act 2002; and

(f) personal independence payment payable under Part 4 of the 2012 Act.

## Recovery by deduction from universal credit

**11.**—(1) The following paragraphs apply where the recoverable amount falls to be recovered by deduction from universal credit payable to the liable person.

(2) Subject to paragraphs (5) to (9), regulation 10 is to apply to the amount of universal credit to which the liable person is presently entitled to the extent that there may be recovered in any one assessment period—

(a) in a case to which paragraph (3) applies, an amount equivalent to not more than [¹ 40 per cent.] of the appropriate universal credit standard allowance;

(b) in a case to which paragraph (4) applies but paragraph (3) does not apply, an amount equivalent to not more than [¹ 25 per cent.] of that allowance; and

(c) in any other case, an amount equivalent to not more than [¹ 15 per cent.] of that allowance.

(3) This paragraph applies where deductions from universal credit are made to recover from the liable person—

(a) the whole or part of an overpayment in respect of which the liable person has—

(i) been found guilty of an offence whether under statute or otherwise;

(ii) made an admission after caution of deception or fraud for the purpose of obtaining benefit under the Act or a tax credit under the Tax Credits Act 2002; or

(iii) agreed to pay a penalty under section 115A of the Act (penalty as an alternative to prosecution) and the agreement has not been withdrawn; or

(b) a payment which is recoverable by virtue of section 71ZH of the Act (hardship payments).

(4) This paragraph applies where amounts are deducted from earned income in an award of universal credit by virtue of regulation 22(1)(b) of the UC Regulations (adjustment to take account of income and amount of earnings disregarded).

(5) Paragraph (2) is subject to paragraphs 4 and 5 of Schedule 6 to the UC etc. Claims and Payments Regulations (payments to third parties).

[¹ (6) For the purpose of paragraph (2), where the relevant percentage of the appropriate universal credit standard allowance results in a fraction of a penny, that fraction is to be disregarded if it is less than half a penny and otherwise it is to be treated as a penny.]

(7) No deduction made under paragraph (2) is to be applied so as to reduce the universal credit in respect of an assessment period to less than 1 penny.

(8) The limitations in paragraph (2) do not apply where the deduction falls to be made from any payment of arrears of universal credit other than any arrears caused by the operation of regulation 46 of the Universal Credit, Personal Independence Payment, Jobseeker's Allowance and Employment and Support Allowance (Decisions and Appeals) Regulations 2013 (making of payments which have been suspended).

(9) The limitations in paragraph (2) do not apply where—

(a) the recoverable amount is an overpayment of housing costs; and

(b) the person from whom that amount falls to be recovered is not the claimant.

(10) In this regulation and in regulation 14, 'admission after caution' means—

(a) in England and Wales, an admission after a caution has been administered in accordance with a Code issued under the Police and Criminal Evidence Act 1984;

(b) in Scotland, admission after a caution has been administered, such admission being duly witnessed by two persons.

(11) In paragraph (2), 'the appropriate universal credit standard allowance' means the appropriate universal credit standard allowance included in the award of universal credit made to the liable person, or to the liable person and their partner as joint claimants, by virtue of regulation 36 of the UC Regulations."

AMENDMENTS

1. The Social Security (Miscellaneous Amendments) (No. 2) Regulations 2013 (SI 2013/1508) reg.5 (July 29, 2013).

## Recovery by deduction from jobseeker's allowance

**12.**—(1) The following paragraphs apply where the recoverable amount falls to be recovered by deduction from jobseeker's allowance payable to the liable person.

(2) Subject to paragraphs (3) and (4), regulation 10 is to apply to the amount of a jobseeker's allowance to which the liable person is presently entitled to the extent that there may be recovered in respect of any benefit week an amount equivalent to 40 per cent. of the age-related amount applicable to the liable person as specified in regulation 49 of the Jobseeker's Allowance Regulations 2013(**19**).

(3) Paragraph (2) is subject to paragraphs 4 and 5 of Schedule 6 to the UC etc. Claims and Payments Regulations (payments to third parties).

(4) Where the amount deductible under paragraph (2) is not a multiple of five pence, it is to be rounded up to the next higher such multiple.

(5) In paragraph (2), 'benefit week' has the same meaning as in regulation 2(1) of the Jobseeker's Allowance Regulations 2013.

## Recovery by deduction from employment and support allowance

**13.**—(1) The following paragraphs apply where the recoverable amount falls to be recovered by deduction from employment and support allowance payable to the liable person.

(2) Subject to paragraphs (3) and (4), regulation 10 is to apply to the amount of an employment and support allowance to which the liable person is presently entitled to the extent that there may be recovered in respect of any one benefit week an amount equivalent to 40 per cent. of the age-related amount applicable to the liable person as specified in regulation 62(1)(b) of the Employment and Support Allowance Regulations 2013(**20**).

(3) Paragraph (2) is subject to paragraphs 4 and 5 of Schedule 6 to the UC etc. Claims and Payments Regulations (payments to third parties).

(4) Where the amount deductible under paragraph (2) is not a multiple of five pence, it is to be rounded up to the next higher such multiple.

(5) In paragraph (2), 'benefit week' has the same meaning as in regulation 2 of the Employment and Support Allowance Regulations 2013.

## Recovery by deduction from state pension credit

**14.**—(1) The following paragraphs apply where the recoverable amount falls to be recovered by deduction from state pension credit payable to the liable person.

(2) Subject to paragraphs (4) and (5), regulation 10 is to apply to the amount of state pension credit to which the liable person is presently entitled to the extent that there may be recovered in any one benefit week—

    (a) in a case to which paragraph (3) applies, an amount equivalent to not more than 5 times 5 per cent. of the standard allowance for a single person aged 25 or over under regulation 36 of the UC Regulations; and

(b) in any other case, an amount equivalent to not more than 3 times 5 per cent. of that allowance.

(3) This paragraph applies where deductions from state pension credit are made to recover from the liable person—

(a) the whole or part of an overpayment in respect of which the liable person has—

    (i) been found guilty of an offence whether under statute or otherwise;

    (ii) made an admission after caution of deception or fraud for the purpose of obtaining universal credit, jobseeker's allowance or employment and support allowance; or

    (iii) agreed to pay a penalty under section 115A of the Act (penalty as an alternative to prosecution) and the agreement has not been withdrawn; or

(b) a payment which is recoverable by virtue of section 71ZH of the Act (hardship payments).

(4) Where the amount deductible under paragraph (2) is not a multiple of five pence, it is to be rounded up to the next higher such multiple.

(5) No deduction made under paragraph (2) is to be applied so as to reduce the state pension credit in respect of a benefit week to less than 10 pence.

(6) In this regulation, 'benefit week' has the same meaning as in regulation 2(1) of the State Pension Credit Regulations 2002(21).

## Restrictions on recovery of rent and consequent notifications

**15.**—(1) Paragraph (2) applies where, pursuant to section 71ZC(2)(b) of the Act, an amount of housing costs has been, or falls to be, recovered by deduction from benefit paid to a person ("the landlord") to discharge (in whole or in part) an obligation owed to the landlord by the person on whose behalf the recoverable amount was paid ("the tenant").

(2) Where, in respect of the overpayment of that amount, the landlord has—

(a) been found guilty of an offence whether under statute or otherwise; or

(b) agreed to pay a penalty under section 115A of the Act (penalty as an alternative to prosecution) and the agreement has not been withdrawn,

that obligation is to be taken to be discharged by the amount of the deduction.

(3) In any case to which paragraph (2) applies or will apply when recovery is made, the Secretary of State must notify both the landlord and the tenant—

(a) that the overpayment that it has recovered or that the Secretary of State has determined to recover ("that sum") is, or will be, one to which paragraph (2) applies; and

(b) that the landlord has no right in relation to that sum against the tenant, and that the tenant's obligation to the landlord is to be taken to be discharged by the amount so recovered.

## Offsetting

**16.**—(1) Paragraph (2) applies where a person has been paid a sum of benefit under a decision ('the original decision') which is subsequently—

(a) revised or further revised;

(b) superseded or further superseded; or

(c) set aside on an appeal.

(2) Any universal credit, jobseeker's allowance or employment and support allowance paid in respect of a period covered by the subsequent decision is to be offset against arrears of entitlement to benefit under that decision and, except to the extent that the universal credit, jobseeker's allowance or employment and support allowance exceeds the arrears, is to be treated as properly paid on account of them.

(3) Where an amount has been deducted under regulation 8 or 9 (sums to be deducted in calculating recoverable overpayments), an equivalent sum is to be offset against any arrears of entitlement under the subsequent decision except to the extent that the sum exceeds the arrears and is to be treated as properly paid on account of them.

(4) No amount may be offset under paragraph (2) which is an overpayment.

(5) In this regulation, "subsequent decision" means the decision referred to in paragraph (1)(a), (b) or (c) which was taken in relation to the original decision."

**p.812,** *amendments to the Social Security (Payments on Account etc) Regulations 1988 (SI 1988/664) reg.1 (Citation, commencement and interpretation)*

4.034    With effect from April 29, 2013, the Social Security (Overpayment and Recovery) Regulations 2013 (SI 2013/384) reg.31(1)(d) to (g) adds the following new definitions to reg.1:

(a) insert after the definition of "disabled person's tax credit":

"'employment and support allowance' means, for the purposes of Parts 3 to 6, employment and support allowance under Part 1 of the 2007 Act as that Part has effect apart from the amendments made by Schedule 3, and Part 1 of Schedule 14, to the 2012 Act that remove references to an income-related allowance;"

(b) insert after the definition of "Income Support Regulations":

"'jobseeker's allowance' means, for the purposes of Parts 3 to 6, jobseeker's allowance under the 1995 Act as that Act has effect apart from the amendments made by Part 1 of Schedule 14 to the 2012 Act that remove references to an income-based allowance;"

(c) insert after the definition of "Jobseeker's Allowance Regulations":

"'personal independence payment' means the allowance under
Part 4 of the 2012 Act;"
(d) insert after the definition of "tax credit":
"'universal credit' means universal credit under Part 1 of the 2012
Act;"

**p.814,** *amendments to the Social Security (Payments on Account etc)*
*Regulations 1988 (SI 1988/664) reg.5 (Offsetting prior payment against*
*subsequent award)*

With effect from April 29, 2013, reg.31(3) of the Social Security   4.035
(Overpayment and Recovery) Regulations 2013 (SI 2013/384) amended
reg.5(2) by inserting the words "or, as the case may be, universal credit"
after the words "another benefit".

**p.819,** *amendments to the Social Security (Payments on Account etc)*
*Regulations 1988 (SI 1988/664) reg.8 (Duplication and prescribed*
*payments)*

With effect from April 29, 2013, reg.31(4) of the Social Security   4.036
(Overpayment and Recovery Regulations 2013 (SI 2013/384) amended
reg.8 as follows:
   (a) by inserting after para.(1)(a):

   "(aa) any personal independence payment;"

   (b) by inserting the words "universal credit," after the words "income
   support,".

**p.821,** *amendments to the Social Security (Payments on Account etc)*
*Regulations 1988 (SI 1988/664) reg.11 (Recovery of overpayments by*
*automated or other direct credit transfer)*

With effect from April 29, 2013, reg.31(5) of the Social Security   4.037
(Overpayment and Recovery) Regulations 2013 (SI 2013/384) inserted
new para.(1A) at the beginning of reg.11 as follows:

   "(A1) This regulation applies only in respect of payments to which
   section 71 of the Administration Act applies."

**p.827,** *amendment to the Social Security (Payments on Account etc)*
*Regulations 1988 (SI 1988/664) reg.15 (Recovery by deduction from*
*benefits)*

With effect from April 29, 2013, reg.31(7)(b) of the Social Security   4.038
(Overpayment and Recovery) Regulations 2013 (SI 2013/384) inserted
the following paragraph after para.(2)(g):

   "(h) universal credit."

**p.828,** *amendment to the Social Security (Payments on Account etc) Regulations 1988 (SI 1988/664) reg.16 (Limitations on deductions from prescribed benefits)*

4.039　　With effect from April 29, 2013, Sch.3, para.2 of the Universal Credit, Personal Independence Payment, Jobseeker's Allowance and Employment and Support Allowance (Claims and Payments) Regulations 2013 (SI 2013/380) amended reg.16(6) by omitting the words ", and any increase" to the end of the paragraph.

**p.840,** *amendments to the Social Security (Payments on Account of Benefit) Regulations 2013 (SI 2013/383) reg.3 (Definition of "benefit")*

4.040　　With effect from July 29, 2013, reg.7(2) of the Social Security (Miscellaneous Amendments) (No. 2) Regulations 2013 (SI 2013/1508) amended reg.3(1)(f) by substituting the words ", disability living allowance and guardian's allowance" for the words "and disability living allowance".

**p.905,** *amendments to the Child Benefit and Guardian's Allowance (Administration) Regulations 2003 (SI 2003/492) reg.19 (Persons who may elect to have child benefit paid weekly)*

4.041　　With effect from April 29, 2013, reg.81 of the Universal Credit (Consequential Supplementary, Incidental and Miscellaneous Provisions) Regulations 2013 (SI 2013/630), amended reg.19(1)(b) by adding new para.(v) as follows:

> "(v) universal credit under Part 1 of the Welfare Reform Act 2012"

**p.921,** *amendments to the Child Benefit and Guardian's Allowance (Administrative Arrangements) Regulations 2003 (SI 2003/494) reg.5 (Recording, verification and holding, and forwarding, of claims etc. received by relevant authorities)*

4.042　　With effect from April 29, 2013, reg.82 of the Universal Credit (Consequential Supplementary, Incidental and Miscellaneous Provisions) Regulations 2013 (SI 2013/630), amended reg.5(8) by adding new para.(c) as follows:

> "(c) universal credit under Part 1 of the Welfare Reform Act 2012"

**pp.948–949,** *annotation to the Child Benefit and Guardian's Allowance (Decisions and Appeals) Regulations 1999, reg.28 (time within which an appeal is to be brought)*

4.042A　　Rule 5(3)(aa) of the Tribunal Procedure (First-tier Tribunal) (Social Entitlement Chamber) Rules 2008, inserted with effect from November

1, 2013 (see below), empowers the First-tier Tribunal to extend the time for appealing by up to a year.

**p.988,** *annotation to Treaty on the Function of the European Union art.20*

In *SSWP v JS (IS)* [2013] UKUT 490 (AAC) the Judge applied *O and S* in deciding that a Gambian national with a daughter who was a United Kingdom national (and so a citizen of the Union) did not have a right to reside as the primary carer of a citizen of the Union for the purposes of a claim to income support. This was because the evidence, in the form of the continued presence of the child and her mother in the United Kingdom, showed that the refusal of income support would not have the result that the child would cease to enjoy the rights of a citizen of the Union. The Court of Appeal has given permission to appeal in this case under the title *Sanneh v Secretary of State for Work and Pensions*.    4.042B

**p.989,** *annotation to Treaty on the Functioning of the European Union art.21*

The Commission has at long last initiated proceedings before the Court of Justice arguing that the "right to reside" test as an additional condition to habitual residence constitutes unlawful discrimination under the EU rules on the coordination of social security systems: see Press Release IP/13/475 of May 30, 2013. The case number is understood to be Case C-640/13 *Commission v United Kingdom*.    4.043

**p.1039,** *annotation to Regulation (EU) No 492/2011 art.10*

Both the AAC decisions and the judgment of the Court of Justice on the references made in the cases of *SSWP v LC (IS)* [2011] UKUT 108 (AAC) and *SSWP v MP (IS)* [2011] UKUT 109 (AAC) are reported as [2013] AACR 6.    4.044

In *Shabani v Secretary of State for the Home Department* [2013] UKUT 315 (IAC) the Secretary of State for the Home Department conceded that the primary carer of a child of a Union citizen who has been employed in the host Member State is entitled to a derivative right of residence once that child has entered into reception class education. The Secretary of State also indicated that the definition of "education" was to be reviewed.

**p.1050,** *annotation to Directive 2004/38/EC art.2 (definitions)*

In *Case C-423/12 Reyes v Migrationsverket*, Judgment of January 16, 2014, the Court of Justice has ruled that art.2(2)(c) must be interpreted as meaning that a Member State cannot require a direct descendant who is 21 years old or older to show that he or she has tried unsuccessfully to secure employment or subsistence in the Member State or country of origin in order to qualify as a dependant. Nor is the dependant precluded from seeking to obtain employment in the Member State to which he or she moves as a dependant.    4.044A

**p.1058,** *annotation to Directive 2004/38/EC art. 7 (Right of residence for more than three months)*

*Retaining the status of worker or self-employed person: illness or accident: art. 7(1)(a)* (paras 3.217–3.219)

4.045    *Shabani v Secretary of State for the Home Department* [2013] UKUT 315 (IAC) confirms that a woman who has left the labour market in order to look after her children does not retain her status as a worker: *SSWP v Dias* [2009] EWCA Civ 807 applied.

The Advocate General has delivered his Opinion (on December 12, 2013) in Case C-507/12 *Jessy Saint Prix v SSWP*—the reference from the Supreme Court. The Advocate General proposes that the answer the Court should deliver is that the Citizenship Directive, read in the light of art.45 TFEU:

> "is to be interpreted as meaning that a woman who can be deemed temporarily unable to work because of the physical constraints of the late stages of pregnancy must retain the status of worker. The status of worker is retained until such time as it is reasonable for the woman in question to return to work, or to seek work, after the birth of her child. To ensure that the principle of non-discrimination on grounds of nationality is observed, that period cannot be shorter than the period provided for under the national legislation governing the period during which pregnant women are exempted from being available for work, or from having actively to seek work."

*A burden on the social assistance system* (para.3.225)

In Case C-140/12 *Pensionversicherungsanstalt v Brey*, Judgment of September 19, 2013, the Court of Justice addresses the relationship between Regulation 883/2004 and the Citizenship Directive and the entitlement of those who are not economically active to be self-sufficient in order to have a right to reside for more than three months.

The Court ruled that the definition of social assistance was not the same in both instruments. It had been argued that any benefit falling within Regulation 883/2004 (even special non-contributory benefits) could not constitute social assistance for the purposes of the Citizenship Directive. The Court rejects this proposition. The concept of social assistance for the purposes of the Citizenship Directive is defined by reference to the purpose of the benefit (paras 60–62 of the Judgment). However, the Court immediately goes on to say:

> "63. Consequently, the fact that a national of another Member State who is not economically active may be eligible, in light of his low pension, to receive [social assistance] could be an indication that that national does not have sufficient resources to avoid becoming an unreasonable burden on the social assistance system of the host Member State for the purposes of Article 7(1)(b) of Directive 2004/38 . . .
> .

64. However, the competent national authorities cannot draw such conclusions without first carrying out an overall assessment of the specific burden which granting that benefit would place on the national social assistance system as a whole, by reference to the personal circumstances characterizing the individual situation of the person concerned."

This means that it is not compatible with EU law to have a blanket rule. The Court ruled that there must always be an assessment of the burden an individual claim would place on the social security system which takes account of such factors as the length of residence, the amount and regularity of any income, the amount of benefit and the period for which it is available, and the overall personal circumstances of the claimant. This was a case in which the claimant was seeking a top up benefit because of his low pension income. The Court said:

"78. . . . . In addition, in order to ascertain more precisely the extent of the burden which [the] grant [of social assistance] would place on the national social assistance system, it may be relevant . . . to determine the proportion of the beneficiaries of that benefit who are Union citizens in receipt of a retirement pension in another Member State."

The requirement for the measure to be proportionate would not be satisfied unless such an individualised assessment was undertaken.

There is a useful and detailed analysis of the implications of the *Brey* judgment in *VP v SSWP (ESA)* [2014] UKUT 32 (AAC). This decision also considers what constitutes self-sufficiency and "comprehensive sickness insurance cover". The decision discusses the practical problems of determining retrospectively whether a person was self-sufficient in considering whether permanent residence has been achieved.

**p.1093,** *Regulation 883/2004*

General note

The United Kingdom's challenge to the legal base of the Decision extending the operation of Regulation 883/2004 to the three EEA countries and to Switzerland has been rejected by the Court of Justice: Case C-431/11 *United Kingdom v Council* Judgment of September 26, 2013.    4.046

**p.1101,** *annotation to Regulation (EC) No 883/2004 art.1*

In Joined Cases C-216/12 and C-217/12 *Caisse nationale des prestations familiales v Hiddal and Bernand* Judgment of September 19, 2013, the Court has ruled that a parental leave allowance constitutes a family benefit under Regulation 1408/71. Since the definition of "family benefit" is, if anything, wider under Regulation 883/2004, such an allowance almost certainly constitutes a family benefit under Regulation 883/2004. There is certainly nothing in the Court's reasoning to suggest otherwise.    4.047

In Case C-177/12 *Caisse nationale des prestations familiales v Lachleb* Judgment of October 24, 2012, the Court ruled that a "child bonus" (which appears to be a form of tax credit) constituted a family benefit under Regulation 1408/71. It would also almost certainly constitute a family benefit under Regulation 883/2004.

**p.1107,** *annotation to Regulation (EC) No 883/2004 art.3*

4.048    In two linked appeals, *SSWP v JG (RP)* [2013] UKUT 300 (AAC), and *SSWP v JG (IS)* [2013] UKUT 298 (AAC), the judge ruled that the requirement to show a genuine and sufficient connection with the United Kingdom established in the *Lucy Stewart* case should be applied in the context of the benefit being claimed. In the cases before him, the judge decided that there was a genuine and sufficient connection in relation to the claim for a Category D retirement pension, but not for winter fuel payments. The claimant had lived in the United Kingdom only for modest periods some time ago, but was in receipt of a partial Category A retirement pension. His residence in both Gibraltar and the Isle of Man was relevant. The Secretary of State is understood to be seeking permission from the Court of Appeal to appeal against the retirement pension decision.

**p.1116,** *annotation to Regulation (EC) No 883/2004 art.8*

4.049    The appeal against *SSWP v LT (DLA)* [2012] UKUT 282 (AAC) has been dismissed by the Court of Appeal (*SSWP v Linda Tolley (deceased)* [2013] EWCA Civ 1471). Both the AAC and Court of Appeal decisions are reported as [2014] AACR 10. The Court of Appeal has refused permission to appeal to the Supreme Court, but it is understood that the Secretary of State has renewed the application before the Supreme Court.

**p.1190,** *annotation to Regulation (EC) No 883/2004 art.87*

4.050    In *SSWP v PW (CA)* [2013] UKUT 200 (AAC), the judge ruled that the transitional provision in art.87(8):

> "applies to preserve entitlement that has already been established. If so, it allows that entitlement to continue for no longer than 10 years. It does not, on my understanding, allow a claimant to rely on it in order to establish entitlement from a date after Regulation 883/2004 came into force. That is the only interpretation that is consistent with the nature of a transitional provision. If it allowed a claimant to make a claim and rely on Regulation 1408/71 for ten years, it would effectively postpone the replacement of that Regulation by Regulation 883/2004 and have the effect that two Regulations were fully in force simultaneously. Neither of those results is impossible, but they are so unlikely and unusual that a clear and express provision would be needed to produce that outcome. There is no such provision." (para.5)

**p.1320,** *annotation to Directive 79/7/EC art.4*

*Issues arising under the Gender Recognition Act 2004* (paras 3.626–3.628)

In *MB v SSWP (RP)* [2013] UKUT 290 (AAC) the judge rules that   4.051
the requirement in s.4 of the Gender Recognition Act 2004 not to be
married in order to get a full gender recognition certificate does not
breach the requirement of equal treatment in art.4 of the Directive.

**p.1345,** *annotation to Human Rights Act 1998 s.4 (Declaration of
incompatibility)*

Judge Wikeley has followed *SH v SSWP (JSA)* [2011] UKUT 428   4.052
(AAC) in *AB v SSWP (JSA)* [2013] UKUT 288 (AAC). He found that
tribunal did not err in law when it found that the claimant could not
succeed before it in an argument that the abatement rule under which
occupational pension payments were taken into account in determining
entitlement to contribution-based jobseeker's allowance constituted
indirect discrimination which could not be justified.

**p.1368,** *annotation to Human Rights Act 1998 Sch.1 art.4 ECHR
(Prohibition of slavery and forced labour)*

The fourth issue determined by the Supreme Court in *R (on the*   4.053
*application of Reilly and another) v SSWP* [2013] UKSC 68 was whether
the conditionality requirements for entitlement to jobseeker's allowance
involving participation in work or work-related activity constituted force
labour under art.4. The Supreme Court after consideration of the key
Strasbourg authorities concluded that they did not.

**p.1395,** *annotation to Human Rights Act 1998 Sch.1 art.14 ECHR
(Prohibition of discrimination)*

*Is the difference of treatment capable of objective and reasonable justification*
(paras 4.129–4.131)

The Court of Appeal in *Obrey, Snodgrass and Shadforth v SSWP*   4.054
[2013] EWCA Civ 1584 has dismissed the appeal against the decision in
*SSWP and Warwick DC v OB, JS and JS (CTB)* [2012] UKUT 489
(AAC) which held that the provisions of the housing benefit legislation
which causes entitlement to cease after persons have been in hospital for
52 weeks, though indirectly discriminatory in respect of those with a
mental illness, was capable of objective justification since the "bright
line" provision was a policy matter not "manifestly without reasonable
foundation."

**pp.1424–1441,** *annotation to the Tribunals, Courts and Enforcement Act
2007, s.3 (the First-tier Tribunal and the Upper Tribunal)*

An appeal against *R.(RS) v First-tier Tribunal (CIC)* [2012] UKUT   4.055
205 (AAC) was allowed in *R.(RS) v First-tier Tribunal* [2013] EWCA

Civ 1040; [2013] AACR 34 but the point that the Upper Tribunal had made about relying on the police officer's opinion on a matter strictly beyond his expertise was not challenged and was accepted as a reason why the case still had to be remitted to the First-tier Tribunal.

A statutory declaration is generally to be given more weight than a simple written statement, but the First-tier Tribunal went too far in stating that such a declaration should be accepted unless there was "the strongest possible evidence" to the contrary (*SA v SSWP (BB)* [2013] UKUT 436 (AAC)).

The circumstances in which it is appropriate to draw adverse inferences from the failure of a party to provide evidence have recently been considered by Lord Sumption in *Prest v Petrodel Resources Ltd* [2013] UKSC 34; [2013] 2 AC 415 at [44] and [45] and by King J. in *M v M (No.2 financial remedy: resulting trusts)* [2013] EWHC 2534 (Fam) at [195] to [204]. Although the principles in these family law cases may be most relevant in child support cases in the First-tier Tribunal, they may by extension also be relevant in other cases where a court or tribunal exercises something of an inquisitorial jurisdiction. Lord Sumption, having set out a passage from Lord Diplock's speech in *British Railways Board v Herrington* [1972] AC 877, 930–931, said—

> "44. . . . . The courts have tended to recoil from some of the fiercer parts of this statement, which appear to convert open-ended speculation into findings of fact. There must be a reasonable basis for some hypothesis in the evidence or the inherent probabilities, before a court can draw useful inferences from a party's failure to rebut it. For my part I would adopt, with a modification which I shall come to, the more balanced view expressed by Lord Lowry with the support of the rest of the committee in *R v Inland Revenue Commissioners, Ex p TC Coombs & Co* [1991] 2 AC 283, 300:
>
>> 'In our legal system generally, the silence of one party in face of the other party's evidence may convert that evidence into proof in relation to matters which are, or are likely to be, within the knowledge of the silent party and about which that party could be expected to give evidence. Thus, depending on the circumstances, a prima facie case may become a strong or even an overwhelming case. But, if the silent party's failure to give evidence (or to give the necessary evidence) can be credibly explained, even if not entirely justified, the effect of his silence in favour of the other party may be either reduced or nullified.'
>
> Cf. *Wisniewski v Central Manchester Health Authority* [1998] PIQR 324, 340.
>
> 45. The modification to which I have referred concerns the drawing of adverse inferences in claims for ancillary financial relief in matrimonial proceedings, which have some important distinctive features. There is a public interest in the proper maintenance of the wife by her former husband, especially (but not only) where the interests of the children are engaged. Partly for that reason, the proceedings although in form adversarial have a substantial inquisitorial element. The family finances will commonly have been the responsibility of the husband,

432

so that although technically a claimant, the wife is in reality dependent on the disclosure and evidence of the husband to ascertain the extent of her proper claim. The concept of the burden of proof, which has always been one of the main factors inhibiting the drawing of adverse inferences from the absence of evidence or disclosure, cannot be applied in the same way to proceedings of this kind as it is in ordinary civil litigation. These considerations are not a licence to engage in pure speculation. But judges exercising family jurisdiction are entitled to draw on their experience and to take notice of the inherent probabilities when deciding what an uncommunicative husband is likely to be concealing. I refer to the husband because the husband is usually the economically dominant party, but of course the same applies to the economically dominant spouse whoever it is."

**p.1441,** *insertion of the Tribunals, Courts and Enforcement Act 2007, s.6A (certain judges who are also judges of the First-tier Tribunal)*

By s.21 of, and paras 6 and 9 of Sch.14 to, the Crime and Courts Act 2013, a new s.6A is inserted, providing that certain fee-paid judges in the courts are to be judges of the First-tier Tribunal so that they may be deployed as such if necessary. 4.056

**pp.1441–1442,** *amendment to the Tribunals, Courts and Enforcement Act 2007, s.7 (chambers: jurisdiction and Presidents)*

With effect from October 1, 2013, the Crime and Courts Act 2013, s.20 and Sch.13, paras 42 and 43 substituted "Senior President of Tribunals" for "Lord Chancellor" in subs.(7). 4.057

**p.1443,** *amendment to the Tribunals, Courts and Enforcement Act 2007, s.8 (Senior President of Tribunals: power to delegate)*

With effect from October 1, 2013, the Crime and Courts Act 2013, s.20 and Sch.13, paras 42 and 44 inserted a new subs.(1A)— 4.058

"(1A) A function under paragraph 1(1) or 2(1) of Schedule 2 may be delegated under subsection (1) only to a Chamber President of a chamber of the Upper Tribunal."

Also, in subs.(2), for "under section 7(9)" there is substituted—

"under any of the following—
section 7(7);
section 7(9);
paragraph 2(1) of Schedule 3;
paragraph 7(1) of Schedule 3;
paragraph 2 of Schedule 4;
paragraph 5(1) and (3) of Schedule 4;
paragraph 5(5) to (8) of Schedule 4;
paragraph 5A(2)(a) of Schedule 4;
paragraph 5A(3)(a) of Schedule 4."

These amendments are related to the transfer of powers to appoint certain judges and members in tribunals from the Lord Chancellor to the Senior President of Tribunals. There does not seem to have been any amendment to para.4 of Sch.4 to the 2007 Act expressly to prevent a Chamber President from further delegating a function mentioned in subs.(1A) if it is delegated to him or her, but any such further delegation would presumably be regarded as inconsistent with subs.(1A).

**pp.1450–1460,** *annotation to the Tribunals, Courts and Enforcement Act 2007 s.11 (right of appeal to Upper Tribunal)*

4.058A    It is normally a breach of the rules of natural justice for a member of a tribunal to absent himself or herself while a witness is giving oral evidence and later to return to participate in the decision, but there is no breach where a party agreed to that procedure and the agreement is voluntary, informed and unequivocal. Moreover, in the absence of any evidence to the contrary, a tribunal is entitled to rely on the agreement of a properly qualified advocate without checking that his or her client also agreed. See *R. (Hill) v Institute of Chartered Accountants in England and Wales* [2013] EWCA Civ 555; [2014] 1 W.L.R. 86. The Court considered that there had been no breach of the rules of natural justice, rather than that there had been a breach but that it had been waived, because there had been agreement in advance. Its decision rested partly on Mr Hill himself not having had second thoughts during a six-week adjournment following the irregularity but that appears to have been regarded as confirming that he had indeed given voluntary and informed consent to the procedure in advance, having been present and having raised no objection at the time. Note that the advocate in that case was a solicitor. *CSDLA/444/2002,* mentioned in the main work, Vol.III, p.1456, suggests that a different approach might be taken where there is a lay representative.

**pp.1460–1463,** *annotation to the Tribunals, Courts and Enforcement Act 2007, s.12 (proceedings on appeal to Upper Tribunal)*

4.059    In *ZB v SSWP (CSM)* [2013] UKUT 367 (AAC), it was said that, although a person who had been barred from taking part in proceedings in the First-tier Tribunal was entitled to appeal to the Upper Tribunal against the decision in those proceedings, the fact that he or she had been so barred might have a bearing on how the Upper Tribunal would exercise its power under s.12(2)(a) to refuse to set aside a decision of the First-tier Tribunal notwithstanding that it has found that the making of the decision involved an error of law. In that case, the Upper Tribunal found that the appellant had not suffered any significant injustice as a result of the First-tier Tribunal's failure to provide a fuller statement of reasons and it declined to set aside the decision.

Where a case has been remitted to the First-tier Tribunal, the First-tier Tribunal is not entitled to decide that the Upper Tribunal had no jurisdiction to give the decision and on that ground refuse to rehear the case. In *Nesbitt's Application* [2013] NIQB 111, the High Court in

Northern Ireland quashed a decision of the President of appeal tribunals who refused to rehear a case that had been remitted by the Chief Social Security Commissioner with a direction that it be reheard. The President had taken the view that the Chief Commissioner had had no jurisdiction to hear the case because the claimant had validly withdrawn his appeal, even though the Chief Commissioner had expressly determined, following an extensive analysis, that the case had not been withdrawn. Treacy J. held that: "Even if the Commissioner had no jurisdiction, it still would not have been open to the [President] to simply reject it and in effect overturn the Commissioner's decision himself. . . . In the absence of adjudication by a court of appropriate jurisdiction on the Commissioner's jurisdiction to hear the appeal his decision remains extant and binding on the [President] regardless of the President's view as to its legality."

There may be cases where fairness requires a decision to be set aside and the relative expertise of the First-tier Tribunal may make it appropriate for the Upper Tribunal to remit the case rather than decide it itself but where a complete rehearing before a different panel is undesirable and unnecessary. This may be the case where a witness would otherwise have to give evidence again on matters in respect of which previous findings have not been challenged or vitiated by the error of law found by the First-tier Tribunal. In such a case, the Upper Tribunal may decide to direct that the decision be re-made by the same members who previously decided the case, in effect requiring them to address the issue they had previous failed to consider or to give the reasons they had previously failed to give (*Shah v NHS England* [2013] UKUT 538 (AAC)). This will seldom be appropriate or necessary in the social security context, where hearings are generally short and oral evidence from witnesses other than the parties is rare.

*AB v SSWP (JSA)* [2013] UKUT 288 (AAC) was another case where the Upper Tribunal considered it unnecessary to consider arguments under the Human Rights Act 1998 because it had no power to make a declaration of incompatibility but, unlike in *SH v SSWP (JSA)* [2011] UKUT 428 (AAC), mentioned in the main work, the judge declined to grant permission to appeal, taking the view that, although the case undoubtedly raised a point of principle, it was best left to the Court of Appeal to decide whether it raised an *important* point of principle or some other compelling reason to hear the appeal (see the annotation to s.13(6) and (7) in the main work).

**pp.1463–1465,** *amendment to the Tribunals, Courts and Enforcement Act 2007, s.13 (right to appeal to Court of Appeal etc.)*

With effect from July 15, 2013, the Crime and Courts Act 2013 s.23 **4.060** inserted a new subs.(6A)—

"(6A) Rules of court may make provision for permission not to be granted on an application under subsection (4) to the Court of Session that falls within subsection (7) unless the court considers—

(a) that the proposed appeal would raise some important point of principle, or

(b) that there is some other compelling reason for the court to hear the appeal."

Rule 41.57 of the Rules of the Court of Session has been made under this power. It came into force on August 19, 2013 in respect only of applications for permission lodged from that date (Act of Sederunt (Rules of the Court of Session Amendment No. 5) (Miscellaneous) 2013 (SSI 2013/238), rr.1, 2 and 4). As mentioned in the annotation to subs.(6) and (7) in the main work, this brings the position in Scotland into line with that in England and Wales and Northern Ireland.

**p.1465–1469,** *annotation to the Tribunals, Courts and Enforcement Act 2007, s.13 (right to appeal to Court of Appeal etc.)*

4.061       The Court of Appeal has continued to try to discourage appeals from the Upper Tribunal, stressing the Upper Tribunal's expertise. In *R.(MM) v Secretary of State for Work and Pensions* [2013] EWCA Civ 1565, the Court of Appeal accepted that the Upper Tribunal (Administrative Appeals Chamber) did not have a special expertise in discrimination issues as far as interpretation of the legislation was concerned, but its judges were "specialists who are daily dealing with the practices in the social welfare field and are far better equipped than this court to analyse and assess the evidence relating to the particular difficulties which [mental health patients] may face in handling procedures" so that the court would be even more cautious than usual about overturning a finding which was one of mixed law and fact. Similarly, in *Obrey v Secretary of State for Work and Pensions* [2013] EWCA Civ 1584, it was said that "the question whether the indirectly discriminatory effect of a particular rule in the benefits system because it does not distinguish between mental patients and other patients in hospital is, or is not, 'manifestly without reasonable foundation' is very far from being an issue of 'constitutional significance'. On the contrary, it is precisely the kind of issue that is best left for evaluation and judgment by a specialist appellate tribunal with a particular expertise in the field of social security law." In that case, Sullivan L.J. referred to the judgment of Lord Hope in *R. (Jones) v First-tier Tribunal* [2013] UKSC 19; [2013] 2 W.L.R 1012; [2013] AACR 25, in which he said—

> "A pragmatic approach should be taken to the dividing line between law and fact, so that the expertise of tribunals at the first-tier and that of the Upper Tribunal can be used to best effect. An appeal court should not venture too readily into this area by classifying issues as issues of law which are really best left for determination by specialist appellate tribunals."

Moreover, although the Court of Appeal had said in *AP v (Trinidad and Tobago) v Secretary of State for the Home Department* [2011] EWCA Civ 551 (mentioned in the main work) that it was as adept as the Upper

Tribunal at identifying errors of law made by First-tier Tribunals, inadequacy of reasons was a rather special error of law and a decision of the Upper Tribunal that a determination by the First-tier Tribunal is inadequately reasoned would be treated with respect by the Court of Appeal (*PK (Congo) v Secretary of State for the Home Department* [2013] EWCA Civ 1500).

In *McGraddie v McGraddie* [2013] UKSC 58; [2013] 1 W.L.R. 2477, the Supreme Court reiterated the "long settled principle" that an appellate court should not interfere with a trial judge's conclusions on primary facts unless it was satisfied that he or she was plainly wrong, even where an appeal is not limited to a point of law. The Court also held that, although the relevant legal principles had long been settled, the failure by appellate courts to apply those principles correctly could raise a point of law of general public importance justifying an appeal to the Supreme Court. Presumably an appeal to an appellate court would similarly be justified if the Upper Tribunal were to fail to follow settled principles of law.

There is no right of appeal to the Court of Appeal against a decision of the Upper Tribunal to refuse permission to appeal to the Upper Tribunal because such a refusal of permission is an "excluded decision" (see s.13(8)(c)). The question then arises whether there is any right of appeal against a refusal to set aside, under r.43 of the Tribunal Procedure (Upper Tribunal) Rules 2008, such a refusal of permission. In *Samuda v Secretary of State for Work and Pensions* [2014] EWCA Civ 1, a two-judge Court of Appeal sat to consider an application for permission to appeal, presumably with a view to answering that question. Unfortunately, it seems to have understood that, in considering whether to set aside the refusal of permission, the Upper Tribunal was considering whether to review it under s.10. The Court therefore dismissed the application on the ground that there was no power to review an "excluded decision" (see s.10(1)) and that, in any event, any purported refusal to review would itself be an "excluded decision" under s.13(8)(d). However, r.43 is made under a rule-making power that is not related to s.10 (para.15(2) of Sch.5 to this Act) and it is suggested that the real question is simply whether s.13(8)(c) is to be construed as extending to any refusal to set aside a refusal of permission to appeal under r.43 (or a refusal to make a correction to a refusal of permission to appeal under r.42) in order to give full effect to the legislature's intention. That remains to be determined on another occasion.

As noted in the main work, Vol.III, p.1467, a refusal of permission to appeal may be challenged by way of judicial review. The "second appeal" approach taken in *R. (Cart) v Upper Tribunal (Public Law Project intervening)* [2011] UKSC 28; [2012] 1 A.C. 663; [2011] AACR 38 has been incorporated into the Civil Procedure Rules in England and Wales as a condition for the grant of permission to apply for judicial review of a decision of the Upper Tribunal refusing permission to appeal against a decision of the First-tier Tribunal (CPR r.54.7A(7)(b)). There is no right to renew before the Administrative Court such an application for judicial review where it has been refused on paper without an oral hearing.

**p.1475–1476,** *annotation to the Tribunals, Courts and Enforcement Act 2007, s.18 (limits of jurisdiction under section 15(1))*

4.062    The part of para.2 of the Practice Direction of October 29, 2008 set out in the annotation in the main work has been amended by inserting after "First-tier Tribunal" in para.(b) the words "(other than its Immigration and Asylum Chamber)". The amendment is included in a Practice Direction of August 21, 2013, revoking the Practice Direction of October 17, 2011 (mentioned in the annotation) and dealing comprehensively with judicial review in the Immigration and Asylum Chamber of the Upper Tribunal.

**p.1477,** *annotation to the Tribunals, Courts and Enforcement Act 2007, s.19 (transfer of judicial review applications from High Court)*

4.063    Section 22(1) and (3) of the Crime and Courts Act 2013 has made amendments to the 1981 and 1978 Acts mentioned in s.19 that are equivalent to those made to s.20 of this Act (see below), so as to remove the restriction on the High Court transferring immigration cases to the Upper Tribunal. These amendments are not relevant to social security cases but have led to substantial amendments to the Tribunal Procedure (Upper Tribunal) Rules 2008 (see below).

**p.1477,** *amendment to the Tribunals, Courts and Enforcement Act 2007, s.20 (transfer of judicial review applications from the Court of Session)*

4.064    By s.22(2) of the Crime and Courts Act 2013, amendments are made to s.20 with effect from November 1, 2013 so as to allow judicial review cases in immigration matters to be transferred to the Upper Tribunal. Section 22(1) and (3) of the 2013 Act made similar amendments to the relevant legislation in England and Wales and Northern Ireland. In subs.(1)(a), "and 2 are met, and" is substituted for ", 2 and 4 are met" and, in subs.(1)(b), "and 3" is substituted for ", 3 and 4". Also subss.(1)(aa) (including the "and" following it), (5) and (5A) are omitted. Subsections (1)(aa) and (5A) had been inserted by s.53 of the Borders, Citizenship and Immigration Act 2009 with effect from August 8, 2011 but were accidentally omitted from the main work. These amendments are not relevant to social security cases but have led to substantial amendments to the Tribunal Procedure (Upper Tribunal) Rules 2008 (see below).

**p.1501,** *annotation to the Transfer of Tribunal Functions Order 2008, Sch.4 (transitional provisions)*

4.065    Before November 3, 2008, the time for applying for leave to appeal to a Social Security Commissioner against a decision of an appeal tribunal could not be extended by more than 12 months. No such absolute limit applies to extensions of the time for appealing to the Upper Tribunal against a decision of the First-tier Tribunal. However, where the absolute time limit for appealing against a decision of an appeal tribunal under the old legislation had expired before November 3, 2008, it would give an impermissible retrospective effect to the new legislation to rely on para.4 of this Schedule to extend the time for appealing against that decision (*ED v SSWP (DLA)* [2013] UKUT 583 (AAC), following *LS v LB Lambeth* (HB) [2010] UKUT 461 (AAC); [2011] AACR 27).

**pp.1515–1516,** *amendment to the Tribunal Procedure (First-tier Tribunal) (Social Entitlement Chamber) Rules 2008, r.5 (case management powers)*

With effect from November 1, 2013, the Tribunal Procedure (Amend-   **4.066** ment No. 4) Rules 2013 (SI 2013/2067) rr.22 and 23, inserted into r.5(3)—

"(aa)  extend the time within which an appeal must be brought under regulation 28(1) of the Child Benefit and Guardian's Allowance (Decisions and Appeals) Regulations 2003;"

Originally, the power to extend the time limit in reg.28 of the 2003 Regulations was to be found in reg.29 but reg.29 now applies only in Northern Ireland and has done so since 2008, presumably on the assumption that time could be extended under r.5(3)(a). However, r.5(3)(a) applies only where the time limit is in "any rule, practice direction or direction" and not if it is in a regulation. This amendment fills the lacuna. Rules 22 and 23 have been amended (see below) so that time cannot be extended under r.5(3)(aa) by more than twelve months, as was previously the case under reg.29.

**pp.1516–1522,** *annotation to the Tribunal Procedure (First-tier Tribunal) (Social Entitlement Chamber) Rules 2008, r.5 (case management powers)*

In *DTM v Kettering BC (CTB)* [2013] UKUT 625 (AAC), it was held   **4.067** perverse to direct the claimant to inform the tribunal whether he wished his appeal to continue and, if so, whether he wished there to be a hearing, on pain of his case being struck out if he did not reply. The case could have been determined without his response.

Where there is an absolute time limit that cannot be extended under r.5(3)(a) or, now, (aa), it must nonetheless be read as being subject to the First-tier Tribunal's discretion so far as that is necessary to avoid a breach of Article 6 of the European Convention on Human Rights. However, the circumstances have to be exceptional and the appellant must personally have done everything possible to act within time before Article 6 requires the discretion to be exercised (*Adesina v Nursing and Midwifery Council* [2013] EWCA Civ 818; [2013] 1 W.L.R. 3156).

**pp.1526–1528,** *annotation to the Tribunal Procedure (First-tier Tribunal) (Social Entitlement Chamber) Rules 2008, r.8 (striking out a party's case)*

In *DTM v Kettering BC (CTB)* [2013] UKUT 625 (AAC), it was   **4.068** pointed out that, where a judge had issued a direction stating that a failure to comply with it "will lead to the striking out of the appeal without any further procedure under rule 8(1) of the Tribunal Procedure

(First-tier Tribunal (Social Entitlement Chamber) Rules 2008), the result of non-compliance was that the appeal was indeed struck out so that, in the absence of reinstatement under para.(5), the First-tier Tribunal no longer had jurisdiction to hear the appeal. Accordingly, it was held, the Upper Tribunal was bound to set aside the decision made without jurisdiction. The Upper Tribunal acknowledged that the First-tier Tribunal judge determining the purported appeal could have reinstated it but it did not consider whether it might therefore exercise its power under s.12(2)(a) of the Tribunals, Courts and Enforcement Act 2007 not to set aside the First-tier Tribunal's decision. However, since it considered that the First-tier Tribunal's decision was wrong in any event, that question did not really arise. What the Upper Tribunal did do was substitute its own decision, first reinstating the appeal against the local authority's decision and then allowing it.

The direction had actually been given because the claimant had not returned the enquiry form issued by the First-tier Tribunal and asking the claimant whether he wished to withdraw his appeal and, if not, whether he wished there to be an oral hearing. The direction had required the claimant to state within 14 days of the date of the direction whether he wished his appeal to continue. In fact, the direction was not posted to the claimant for a week and the claimant replied to the direction by returning the enquiry for so that it arrived nearly a week after the deadline. The Upper Tribunal said that it had been irrational to issue the direction at all because the failure to return the enquiry form did not prevent the First-tier Tribunal from determining the appeal and, indeed, the failure to return it would have entitled the First-tier Tribunal to determine the appeal without a hearing if it considered that not to be inappropriate (see r.27(1)). The inquisitorial role of the First-tier Tribunal and the overriding objective both pointed towards determining the appeal one way or another, rather than issuing a direction that included words having the effect that non-compliance would lead automatically to a striking it out.

In *ZB v SSWP (CSM)* [2013] UKUT 367 (AAC), it was held that a person barred under r.8(7) from taking further part in proceedings nonetheless does not lose the right to appeal and is therefore also entitled to a statement of reasons. However, the fact that a person has been barred from taking further part in the proceedings so that the First-tier Tribunal is entitled to determine issues against him or her summarily has a bearing on how much detail is required in the statement of reasons and on how the Upper Tribunal exercises its power under s.12(2)(a) of the Tribunals, Courts and Enforcement Act 2007 not to set aside the First-tier Tribunal's decision even if it is satisfied that it is wrong in law. Presumably, it might therefore also be a reason for refusing permission to appeal in a case notwithstanding that there is an arguable point of law. In *ZB* itself, the First-tier Tribunal had in fact largely explained its decision in the decision notice and, although the Upper Tribunal held that the First-tier Tribunal had erred in law in refusing to provide a fuller statement of reasons, the Upper Tribunal refused to set aside the First-tier Tribunal's decision because it considered it to be unlikely that the First-tier Tribunal had erred in its approach to the case and it was therefore not satisfied that the appellant had suffered any significant injustice.

**p.1541,** *annotation to the Tribunal Procedure (First-tier Tribunal) (Social Entitlement Chamber) Rules 2008 r.17 (withdrawal)*

The right to withdraw part of a case does not enable a claimant to prevent the First-tier Tribunal from adjudicating on part of a decision of the Secretary of State that is favourable to him or her (*AE v SSWP (ESA)* [2014] UKUT 5 (AAC)). This was on the basis that the claimant's "case" was that the unfavourable part of the Secretary of State's was wrong. In that instance, the Upper Tribunal held that the First-tier Tribunal was bound in law to consider the other part of the Secretary of State's decision but that would not usually be so. In any event, to the extent that support for part of a decision of the Secretary of State might be part of a claimant's case, withdrawal of that part of the case would be an invitation to adjudicate on the issue rather than the reverse. A challenge to part of a decision of a decision of the Secretary of State can clearly be withdrawn under this rule but the First-tier Tribunal would usually still have the power to consider that part of the decision if it thought it necessary to do so (see s.12(8)(a) of the Social Security Act 1998). Therefore, there may not be much point in formally withdrawing part of a case in the social security context. 4.068A

**pp.1542–1543,** *amendment to the Tribunal Procedure (First-tier Tribunal) (Social Entitlement Chamber) Rules 2008, r.19 (confidentiality in child support or child trust fund cases)*

With effect from November 1, 2013, the Tribunal Procedure (Amendment No. 4) Rules 2013 (SI 2013/2067), rr.22 and 24, replaced subparas (a) to (c) of r.19(2) as follows— 4.069

"(a)  in the notice of appeal or when notifying the Secretary of State or the Tribunal of any subsequent change of address; or
(b)  within 14 days after an enquiry is made by the recipient of the notice of appeal or the notification referred to in sub-paragraph (a)."

The rule has been reworded because notices of appeal against child support decisions made on or after October 28, 2013 are sent straight to the First-tier Tribunal rather than to the Secretary of State and so it will be the First-tier Tribunal rather than the Secretary of State who will be making the enquiry in those cases.

**pp.1544–1545,** *amendment to the Tribunal Procedure (First-tier Tribunal) (Social Entitlement Chamber) Rules 2008, r.22 (cases in which the notice of appeal is to be sent to the tribunal)*

With effect from November 1, 2013, the Tribunal Procedure (Amendment No. 4) Rules 2013 (SI 2013/2067) rr.22 and 25, inserted "or (aa)" after "rule 5(3)(a)" in both places where it occurs in r.22(6). 4.070

**p.1546,** *annotation to the Tribunal Procedure (First-tier Tribunal) (Social Entitlement Chamber) Rules 2008, r.22 (cases in which the notice of appeal is to be sent to the tribunal)*

4.071    All social security and child support decisions issued since October 28, 2013, except those made by HMRC or local authorities, have informed claimants that an appeal should be sent to the First-tier Tribunal rather than to the Secretary of State. From the same date, the Secretary of State for Work and Pensions has been empowered to issue a notice within the scope of para.(9) in all cases where he is the decision-maker and did not already have that power, so that the would-be appellant is bound to apply for a revision or equivalent reconsideration before exercising a right of appeal (see regs 3ZA, 3B and 9ZB of the Social Security and Child Support (Decisions and Appeals) Regulations 1999, reg.11A of the Vaccine Damage Payments Regulations 1979, reg.4B of the Mesothelioma Lump Sum Payments (Claims and Reconsiderations) Regulations 2008 and new provisions in child support legislation beyond the scope of this work). There is no provision for mandatory reconsideration in relation to the recovery of NHS charges, although appeals in those cases are now to be sent to the First-tier Tribunal.

**p.1547,** *amendment to the Tribunal Procedure (First-tier Tribunal) (Social Entitlement Chamber) Rules 2008, r.23 (cases in which the notice of appeal is to be sent to the decision maker)*

4.072    With effect from November 1, 2013, the Tribunal Procedure (Amendment No. 4) Rules 2013 (SI 2013/2067) rr.22 and 26, inserted "or (aa)" after "rule 5(3)(a)" in para.(8).

**pp.1551–1552,** *annotation to the Tribunal Procedure (First-tier Tribunal) (Social Entitlement Chamber) Rules 2008, r.24 (responses and replies)*

4.073    In *AM v SSWP (ESA)* [2013] UKUT 458 (AAC), the judge expressed reservations about what was said in *ST v SSWP (ESA)* [2012] UKUT 469 (AAC) (mentioned in the main work). In fact, *AM* was a "conversion" case so that the tests applied in the earlier assessments were different from those to be applied in the current assessment. In those circumstances, it was held that the First-tier Tribunal was entitled to conclude that it had enough evidence upon which to determine the appeal without obtaining the reports from previous assessments. *AM* and *ST* are therefore not necessarily inconsistent since it can be said that the earlier reports in *AM* were unlikely to be relevant.

A Tribunal of Commissioners in Northern Ireland had previously reached a conclusion similar to that reached in *ST*. The Tribunal of Commissioners considered that the Department for Social Development should list details of all previous assessment determinations within the current claim, which the Department had said "should be straightforward in most cases . . . from computer records", but that the assessment need only be provided "in a limited class of case, where there is an assertion that there has been no change in the claimant's condition, and where the evidence associated with the previous adjudication history is relevant to that submission or, for example, where the claimant's medical condition, and the evidence associated with the previous adjudication history assists in the assessment of the claimant's overall capacity" (*JC v DSD (IB)* [2011] NICom 177). This issue is likely to be considered by a three-judge panel in Great Britain early in 2014.

**pp.1555–1561,** *annotation to the Tribunal Procedure (First-tier Tribunal) (Social Entitlement Chamber) Rules 2008, r.27 (decision with or without a hearing)*

Procedural fairness may require a person to be offered an oral hearing where legislation does not provide an absolute right to one. Relevant factors were identified in *R.(Osborne) v Parole Board* [2013] UKSC 61; [2013] 3 W.L.R. 1020 of which the first, and perhaps the most relevant in the social security context, is "where facts which appear ... to be important are in dispute, or where a significant explanation or mitigation is advanced which needs to be heard orally in order fairly to determine its credibility". In *R.(AG) v First-tier Tribunal (CIC)* [2013] UKUT 357 (AAC), the Upper Tribunal held that it was not appropriate to challenge the honesty or integrity of a claimant where an oral hearing has been refused and that reasons for refusing a hearing need to refer to the specific facts of the case in issue and not just "a standard (or perhaps pro forma) list of reasons". In *R.(TG) v First-tier Tribunal (CIC)* [2013] UKUT 366 (AAC), the Upper Tribunal said that— 4.074

> "The particular factors in this case which should have prompted the First-tier Tribunal to offer the applicant the opportunity to have an oral hearing include the complexity of the factual background (including the applicant's complaints about the nature of the investigation, her very lengthy (if not always accurate) analysis of the case, her belief that the investigation was bungled, the police complaint investigation, and the continuing trouble between the two families) and the applicant's obvious difficulties in keeping to the most relevant matters when expressing herself in writing."

The words "extend a time limit" in r.27(5)(c) do not include "waive a time limit" (*JM v Advocate General for Scotland* [2013] CSOH 169).

**pp.1563–1565,** *annotation to the Tribunal Procedure (First-tier Tribunal) (Social Entitlement Chamber) Rules 2008, r.30 (public and private hearings)*

There are now fewer domiciliary hearings than formerly (see the supplementary annotation to r.31, below). 4.075

**pp.1566–1567,** *annotation to the Tribunal Procedure (First-tier Tribunal) (Social Entitlement Chamber) Rules 2008, r.31 (hearings in a party's absence)*

It was held in *KO v SSWP (ESA)* [2013] UKUT 544 (AAC) that there is a continuing duty to consider whether it is in the interests of 4.076

justice to proceed with a hearing in a party's absence so that, if in the course of considering a case in the absence of a party issues emerge that cannot really be dealt with fairly in the absence of the party, an initial decision to proceed in the parties absence may have to be reconsidered. The judge also made observations about the modern approach to domiciliary hearings:

> "The Secretary of State has referred to the decision of Judge Mark in *CI/4093/99*, where he said 'If in fact the claimant cannot reasonably be expected to come to the tribunal, then the tribunal must offer to come to the claimant.' That decision is now some 14 years old. Matters have moved on during that time in respect of the desirability of holding domiciliary hearings. It is rare that they are either appropriate or necessary. Enquiries may need to be made as to how an appellant attends other appointments, such as hospital visits. Few people are totally housebound, and it may be that an appellant can attend if transport is provided. If the issue has not become apparent prior to the date [of] the scheduled hearing those enquiries should be made as early as possible on that day in a telephone call to the appellant's home by the clerk at the venue as the case may be able to proceed as listed or later in the day if a taxi could be arranged, or an adjournment may be necessary so that a taxi could be provided on another occasion. If other methods of transport (such as a private ambulance) are under consideration, or if it is thought that the tribunal venue itself may be unsuitable and another venue, whether a hearing centre or a local community facility may be preferable, or, unusually that the issue of a domiciliary visit does arise, the tribunal will want to adjourn the case for the attention of the local District Tribunal Judge who will know about local options and facilities, and who may direct medical evidence as to the nature of the difficulties in order to assess suitability."

**pp.1570–1580,** *annotation to the Tribunal Procedure (First-tier Tribunal) (Social Entitlement Chamber) Rules 2008, r.34 (reasons for decision)*

4.077    A person who has been barred from further participation in proceedings under r.8(7) is nonetheless entitled to a statement of reasons for a decision if a request is made properly under this rule, although the fact that he or she has been barred may have a bearing on how detailed the reasoning need be because issues may be determined summarily against such a person (*ZB v SSWP (CSM)* [2013] UKUT 367 (AAC)).

**p.1593,** *annotation to the Tribunal Procedure (First-tier Tribunal) (Social Entitlement Chamber) Rules 2008, Sch.1 (time limits for providing notices of appeal)*

4.078    The first, fifth and sixth entries in this Schedule are less important than they were, now that the right of appeal in most cases where the Secretary of State for Work and Pensions is the respondent is conditional upon a person having first applied for a revision or equivalent reconsideration as a result of new regs 3ZA, 3B and 9ZB of the Social Security and

Child Support (Decisions and Appeals) Regulations 1999, new reg.11A of the Vaccine Damage Payments Regulations 1979, new reg.4B of the Mesothelioma Lump Sum Payments (Claims and Reconsiderations) Regulations 2008 and new provisions in child support legislation beyond the scope of this work. Where those new regulations have applied, the time for appealing is one month after the date on which the appellant was sent notice of the result of the mandatory reconsideration (see r.22(2)(d)(i)).

Rule 5(3)(aa) has now been inserted (see above) to enable the time for appealing in child benefit and guardian's allowance cases to be extended. Time limits in tax credit and child trust fund cases are in primary legislation and amendments to that legislation are required if a power to extend the time limits is to be conferred on the First-tier Tribunal.

**pp.1599–1600,** *amendments to the Tribunal Procedure (Upper Tribunal) Rules 2008, r.1 (citation, commencement, application and interpretation)*

With effect from November 1, 2013, the Tribunal Procedure (Amendment No. 4) Rules 2013 (SI 2013/2067) rr.2 and 4, inserted "Upper" before "Tribunal finally" in the definition of "party". In addition, the definition of "fresh claim proceedings" is omitted and a definition of "immigration judicial review proceedings" is inserted, but those amendments are not relevant to social security cases. 4.079

**pp.1608–1609,** *amendment to the Tribunal Procedure (Upper Tribunal) Rules 2008, r.8 (striking out a party's case)*

With effect from November 1, 2013, the Tribunal Procedure (Amendment No. 4) Rules 2013 (SI 2013/2067) rr.2 and 5 substituted a new r.8(1)(b) but this amendment is not relevant to social security cases. 4.080

**pp.1611–1613,** *amendment to the Tribunal Procedure (Upper Tribunal) Rules 2008, r.10 (orders for costs)*

With effect from November 1, 2013, the Tribunal Procedure (Amendment No. 4) Rules 2013 (SI 2013/2067) rr.2 and 6 inserted "Upper" before "Tribunal" in para.(10). 4.081

**pp.1614–1615,** *amendments to the Tribunal Procedure (Upper Tribunal) Rules 2008, r.11 (representatives)*

With effect from November 1, 2013, the Tribunal Procedure (Amendment No. 4) Rules 2013 (SI 2013/2067) rr.2 and 7 substituted "immigration judicial review" for "fresh claim" in paras (5A) and (5B), but those amendments are not relevant to social security cases. 4.082

**p.1617,** *amendment to the Tribunal Procedure (Upper Tribunal) Rules 2008, r.13 (sending and delivery of documents)*

With effect from November 1, 2013, the Tribunal Procedure (Amendment No. 4) Rules 2013 (SI 2013/2067) rr.2 and 8 inserted "Upper" before "Tribunal" in para.(7). 4.083

**pp.1628–1629,** *annotation to the Tribunal Procedure (Upper Tribunal) Rules 2008, r.21 (application to the Upper Tribunal for permission to appeal)*

4.084    In *ZN v LB Redbridge (HB)* [2013] UKUT 503 (AAC), the Upper Tribunal followed *MA v SSD* [2009] UKUT 57 (AAC), mentioned in the main work, in holding that the requirement under r.21(2) to obtain a decision of the First-tier Tribunal on an application for permission to appeal could be waived.

**pp.1636–1637,** *amendment to the Tribunal Procedure (Upper Tribunal) Rules 2008, r.28 (applications for permission to bring judicial review proceedings)*

4.085    With effect from November 1, 2013, the Tribunal Procedure (Amendment No. 4) Rules 2013 (SI 2013/2067) rr.2 and 10 substituted "immigration judicial review" for "fresh claim" in para.(8), but this amendment is not relevant to social security cases.

**p.1638,** *amendments to the Tribunal Procedure (Upper Tribunal) Rules 2008, r.29 (acknowledgement of service)*

4.086    With effect from November 1, 2013, the Tribunal Procedure (Amendment No. 4) Rules 2013 (SI 2013/2067) rr.2 and 12 substituted "immigration judicial review" for "fresh claim" in paras (1) (twice) and (2A), but those amendments are not relevant to social security cases.

**p.1639,** *amendments to the Tribunal Procedure (Upper Tribunal) Rules 2008, r.30 (decision on permission or summary dismissal)*

4.087    With effect from November 1, 2013, the Tribunal Procedure (Amendment No. 4) Rules 2013 (SI 2013/2067) rr.2 and 13 substituted "Subject to paragraph (4A), in" for "In" in para.(1), inserted a new para.4A and substituted "immigration judicial review" for "fresh claim" in para.(5), but those amendments are not relevant to social security cases.

**p.1642,** *amendments to the Tribunal Procedure (Upper Tribunal) Rules 2008, r.34 (decision with or without a hearing)*

4.088    With effect from November 1, 2013, the Tribunal Procedure (Amendment No. 4) Rules 2013 (SI 2013/2067) rr.2 and 14 substituted "paragraphs (2) and (3)" for "paragraph 2" in para.(1) and added new paras (3) and (4), but those amendments are not relevant to social security cases.

**p.1646,** *amendment to the Tribunal Procedure (Upper Tribunal) Rules 2008, r.39 (consent orders)*

4.089    With effect from November 1, 2013, the Tribunal Procedure (Amendment No. 4) Rules 2013 (SI 2013/2067) rr.2 and 15 inserted "Upper" before "Tribunal" in para.(2).

**p.1647,** *amendment to the Tribunal Procedure (Upper Tribunal) Rules 2008, r.40 (decisions)*

With effect from November 1, 2013, the Tribunal Procedure (Amend-  4.090
ment No. 4) Rules 2013 (SI 2013/2067) rr.2 and 16 inserted new paras
(1A) and (1B), but this amendment is not relevant to social security
cases.

**p.1649,** *amendment to the Tribunal Procedure (Upper Tribunal) Rules 2008, r.43 (setting aside a decision which disposes of proceedings)*

With effect from November 1, 2013, the Tribunal Procedure (Amend-  4.091
ment No. 4) Rules 2013 (SI 2013/2067) rr.2 and 17 inserted "Upper"
before "Tribunal" in para.(3).

**p.1650,** *annotation to the Tribunal Procedure (Upper Tribunal) Rules 2008, r.43 (setting aside a decision which disposes of proceedings)*

For the question whether there is a right of appeal against a refusal to  4.092
set aside a refusal of permission to appeal to the Upper Tribunal, see the
supplementary annotation to s.13 of the Tribunals, Courts and Enforcement Act 2007, above.

**pp.1650–1651,** *amendments to the Tribunal Procedure (Upper Tribunal) Rules 2008, r.44 (application for permission to appeal)*

With effect from November 1, 2013, the Tribunal Procedure (Amend-  4.093
ment No. 4) Rules 2013 (SI 2013/2067) rr.2 and 18 inserted "Upper"
before "Tribunal" in para.(7)(a). Also, "paragraphs (4A) and (4B)" is
substituted for "paragraph (4A) in para.(1), ",(3D) or (4C)" is substituted for "or (3D)" in para.(4) and new paras (4A), (4B) and (4C) are
substituted for para.(4A), but those amendments are not relevant to
social security cases.

**p.1652,** *amendments to the Tribunal Procedure (Upper Tribunal) Rules 2008, r.45 (Upper Tribunal's consideration of application for permission to appeal)*

With effect from November 1, 2013, the Tribunal Procedure (Amend-  4.094
ment No. 4) Rules 2013 (SI 2013/2067) rr.2 and 19 substituted "provide" for "send" in paras (3) and (4).

**p.1655,** *amendment to the Tribunal Procedure (Upper Tribunal) Rules 2008, r.48 (power to treat an application as a different type of application)*

With effect from November 1, 2013, the Tribunal Procedure (Amend-  4.095
ment No. 4) Rules 2013 (SI 2013/2067) rr.2 and 20 inserted "Upper"
before "Tribunal".

# PART V

# UPDATING MATERIAL
## VOLUME IV

## TAX CREDITS AND HMRC-ADMINISTERED SOCIAL SECURITY BENEFITS

Commentary by

**Nick Wikeley**

**David Williams**

**Ian Hooker**

**pp.31–32,** *annotation to Social Security Contributions and Benefits Act 1992 s.143 (Meaning of "person responsible for child or qualifying young person")*

The importance of focusing of the right question in deciding whether a child is living with the claimant is demonstrated in *SB v HMRC* [2013] UKUT 24 (AAC). The claimant, who was a Polish national, had come to this country together with her four-year-old daughter. Shortly after arrival, and when she was in employment, she claimed both Child Benefit and Child Tax Credit. The claimant was asked to provide documentary evidence of the fact that the child was attending school and was registered at a GP surgery. At first both benefits were refused because it would seem that the claimant had not provided that documentation. However, after appealing it seems that the documents were received by the section dealing with CTC and that claim was allowed. An electronic file dealing with that claim was stored on the HMRC computer system. But the child benefit appeal was rejected and an appeal to the FTT was also dismissed. At the tribunal hearing the claimant produced a letter from the school confirming attendance, but no GP documentation. The FTT regarded the school letter as deficient and the absence of the other as significant. In the UT Judge Wikeley is critical of the approach adopted both within HMRC and at the FTT. As he points out the sole question relevant was whether the child was "living with" her mother. No questions were asked that addressed that issue. The documents requested could be evidence of the child's existence, but, unless they recorded the child's address as being the same as that of the claimant, they really say nothing about the living arrangements. It does appear, however, that such evidence is all that is required by HMRC because on the basis of the documents that had been received the claim to CTC had been accepted. Judge Wikeley also points out that the existence of the CTC appeal was revealed on the papers relating to the claim for child benefit and he was assured by HMRC's representative that it would be easy for each section to access the information used by the other—as he puts it a lamentable failure by the left hand to know of what was done by the right. This is a prime example of what an FTT should have done in exercising its inquisitorial function. The appeal was allowed.

**p.67,** *amendments to Social Security Contributions and Benefits Act 1992, Part XIIZA (Ordinary and additional statutory paternity pay)*

The following sections should have been inserted in the main text at the foot of p.67 after s.171ZE and before s.171ZF:

#### "[¹ Entitlement to additional statutory paternity pay: birth

**171ZEA.**—(1) The Secretary of State may by regulations provide that, where all the conditions in subsection (2) are satisfied in relation to a person ("the claimant"), the claimant shall be entitled in accordance with the following provisions of this Part to payments to be known as "additional statutory paternity pay".

5.001

5.002

451

(2) Those conditions are—

(a) that the claimant satisfies prescribed conditions—

    (i) as to relationship with a child, and

    (ii) as to relationship with the child's mother;

(b) that the claimant has been in employed earner's employment with an employer for a continuous period of at least the prescribed length ending with a prescribed week;

(c) that the claimant's normal weekly earnings for a prescribed period ending with a prescribed week are not less than the lower earnings limit in force under section 5(1)(a) at the end of that week;

(d) if regulations so provide, that the claimant continues in employed earner's employment (whether or not with that employer) until a prescribed time;

(e) that the mother of the child by reference to whom the condition in paragraph (a) is satisfied became entitled, by reference to the birth of the child—

    (i) to a maternity allowance, or

    (ii) to statutory maternity pay;

(f) that the mother has, in relation to employment as an employed or self-employed earner, taken action that is treated by regulations as constituting for the purposes of this section her return to work;

(g) that the day on which the mother is treated as returning to work falls—

    (i) after the end of a prescribed period beginning with the birth of the child, but

    (ii) at a time when at least a prescribed part of her maternity allowance period or maternity pay period remains unexpired;

(h) that it is the claimant's intention to care for the child during a period beginning not later than a prescribed time.

(3) The regulations may—

(a) exclude the application of the conditions mentioned in paragraphs (f) and (g) of subsection (2) in cases where the child's mother has died, and

(b) provide that the condition mentioned in paragraph (e) of that subsection shall have effect with prescribed modifications in such cases.

(4) A person's entitlement to additional statutory paternity pay under this section shall not be affected by the birth of more than one child as a result of the same pregnancy.]

AMENDMENTS

1. Work and Families Act 2006 s.6 (March 3, 2010).

**[¹Entitlement to additional statutory paternity pay: adoption**

**171ZEB.**—(1) The Secretary of State may by regulations provide that, where all the conditions in subsection (2) are satisfied in relation to a person ("the claimant"), the claimant shall be entitled in accordance with the following provisions of this Part to payments to be known as "additional statutory paternity pay".

(2) Those conditions are—

(a) that the claimant satisfies prescribed conditions—

    (i) as to relationship with a child who has been placed for adoption under the law of any part of the United Kingdom, and

    (ii) as to relationship with a person with whom the child is so placed for adoption ("the adopter");

(b) that the claimant has been in employed earner's employment with an employer for a continuous period of at least the prescribed length ending with a prescribed week;

(c) that the claimant's normal weekly earnings for a prescribed period ending with a prescribed week are not less than the lower earnings limit in force under section 5(1)(a) at the end of that week;

(d) if regulations so provide, that the claimant continues to work in employed earner's employment (whether or not with that employer) until a prescribed time;

(e) that the adopter became entitled to statutory adoption pay by reference to the placement of the child for adoption;

(f) that the adopter has, in relation to employment as an employed or self-employed earner, taken action that is treated by regulations as constituting for the purposes of this section the adopter's return to work;

(g) that the day on which the adopter is treated as returning to work falls—

    (i) after the end of a prescribed period beginning with the placement of the child for adoption, but

    (ii) at a time when at least a prescribed part of the adopter's adoption pay period remains unexpired;

(h) that it is the claimant's intention to care for the child during a period beginning not later than a prescribed time.

(3) The regulations may—

(a) exclude the application of the conditions mentioned in paragraphs (f) and (g) of subsection (2) in cases where the adopter has died, and

(b) provide that the condition mentioned in paragraph (e) of that subsection shall have effect with prescribed modifications in such cases.

(4) A person may not elect to receive additional statutory paternity pay if he has elected in accordance with section 171ZL to receive statutory adoption pay.

(5) A person's entitlement to additional statutory paternity pay under this section shall not be affected by the placement for adoption of more than one child as part of the same arrangement.]

AMENDMENTS

1. Work and Families Act 2006 s.7 (March 3, 2010).

**[¹ Entitlement to additional statutory paternity pay: general]**

**171ZEC.**—(1) A person shall not be entitled to payments of additional statutory paternity pay in respect of any period unless—

    (a) he gives the person who will be liable to pay it notice of the date from which he expects the liability to pay him additional statutory paternity pay to begin and the date on which he expects that liability to end, and

    (b) the notice is given by such time as may be prescribed.

(2) The notice shall be in writing if the person who is liable to pay the additional statutory paternity pay so requests.

(3) The Secretary of State may by regulations—

    (a) provide that the conditions mentioned in subsection (2)(b) or (c) of section 171ZEA or 171ZEB shall have effect subject to prescribed modifications in such cases as may be prescribed;

    (b) provide that subsection (1) of this section shall not have effect, or shall have effect subject to prescribed modifications, in such cases as may be prescribed;

    (c) impose requirements about evidence of entitlement;

    (d) specify in what circumstances employment is to be treated as continuous for the purposes of section 171ZEA or 171ZEB;

    (e) provide that a person is to be treated for the purposes of section 171ZEA or 171ZEB as being employed for a continuous period of the length prescribed under that section where—

        (i) he has been employed by the same employer for a period of at least that length under two or more contracts of service, and

        (ii) those contracts were not continuous;

    (f) provide for amounts earned by a person under separate contracts of service with the same employer to be aggregated for the purposes of section 171ZEA or 171ZEB;

    (g) provide that—

        (i) the amount of a person's earnings for any period, or

        (ii) the amount of his earnings to be treated as comprised in any payment made to him or for his benefit,

shall be calculated or estimated for the purposes of section 171ZEA or 171ZEB in such manner and on such basis as may be prescribed and that for that purpose payments of a particular class or description made or falling to be made to or by a person shall, to such extent as may be prescribed, be disregarded or, as the case may be, be deducted from the amount of his earnings.]

AMENDMENTS

1. Work and Families Act 2006 s.8 (March 3, 2010).

**[¹ Liability to make payments of additional statutory paternity pay**

**171ZED.**—(1) The liability to make payments of additional statutory paternity pay under section 171ZEA or 171ZEB is a liability of any

454

person of whom the person entitled to the payments has been an employee as mentioned in subsection (2)(b) of that section.

(2) Regulations shall make provision as to a former employer's liability to pay additional statutory paternity pay to a person in any case where the former employee's contract of service with him has been brought to an end solely, or mainly, for the purpose of avoiding liability for additional statutory paternity pay or ordinary statutory paternity pay, or both.

(3) The Secretary of State may, with the concurrence of the Commissioners for Her Majesty's Revenue and Customs, by regulations specify circumstances in which, notwithstanding this section, liability to make payments of additional statutory paternity pay is to be a liability of the Commissioners.]

AMENDMENTS

1. Work and Families Act 2006 s.9 (March 3, 2010).

[¹ **Rate and period of pay: additional statutory paternity pay**]

171ZEE.—(1) Additional statutory paternity pay shall be payable at such fixed or earnings-related weekly rate as may be prescribed by regulations, which may prescribe different kinds of rate for different cases.

(2) Subject to the following provisions of this section, additional statutory paternity pay shall be payable in respect of a period ("the additional paternity pay period")—

    (a) beginning with such day as may (subject to subsection (3)) be determined in accordance with regulations, and

    (b) ending with—

        (i) the day on which the additional statutory pay period is ended by virtue of subsection (4) or (8), or

        (ii) such earlier day as the employee may choose in accordance with regulations.

(3) The first day of the additional paternity pay period must not be earlier than the day on which the child's mother or the person with whom the child is placed for adoption ("the mother or adopter") is treated for the purpose of section 171ZEA or 171ZEB as returning to work; but this subsection does not apply in a case where the mother or adopter has died.

(4) The additional paternity pay period—

    (a) shall not last longer than any prescribed number of weeks,

    (b) shall not continue after the end of the period of 12 months beginning with the relevant date, and

    (c) shall not continue after the end—

        (i) in a case falling within section 171ZEA, of the mother's maternity allowance period or maternity pay period, or

        (ii) in a case falling within section 171ZEB, of the adoption pay period of the person with whom the child is placed for adoption.

(5) In subsection (4)(b), "the relevant date" means—

(a) in the case of a person to whom the conditions in section 171ZEA(2) apply, the date of the child's birth (or, where more than one child is born as a result of the same pregnancy, the date of birth of the first child born as a result of the pregnancy), and

(b) in the case of a person to whom the conditions in section 171ZEB(2) apply, the date of the child's placement for adoption (or, where more than one child is placed for adoption as part of the same arrangement, the date of placement of the first child to be placed as part of the arrangement).

(6) Additional statutory paternity pay shall not be payable to a person in respect of a week if it is not his purpose at the beginning of the week to care for the child by reference to whom he satisfies the condition in sub-paragraph (i) of section 171ZEA(2)(a) or 171ZEB(2)(a).

(7) Except in such cases as may be prescribed, additional statutory paternity pay shall not be payable to a person in respect of a week during any part of which he works for any employer.

(8) Where subsection (6) or (7) prevents additional statutory paternity pay being payable to a person in respect of any week, the person's additional paternity pay period shall be taken to have ended at the end of the previous week.

(9) Where for any purpose of this Part of this Act or of regulations it is necessary to calculate the daily rate of additional statutory paternity pay, the amount payable by way of additional statutory paternity pay for that day shall be taken to be one seventh of the weekly rate.

(10) In this section "week" means a period of seven days beginning with the day of the week on which the additional paternity pay period began.]

AMENDMENTS

1. Work and Families Act 2006 s.10 (March 3, 2010)."

**p.115,** *annotation at para.1.227 to the Tax Credits Act 2002*

5.003      Statistics for take-up of tax credits in 2011–12 have been published by HMRC. They show a central estimate of take-up of working tax credit of 65 per cent but a continuing low take-up (33 per cent) by households with no children. Take-up of child tax credit remains high at 85 per cent claiming an estimated 93 per cent of total national entitlement.

**p.122,** *annotation to the Tax Credits Act 2002 s.3(5A) (claims)*

5.004      In *DG v HMRC (TC)* [2014] UKUT 0631 (AAC) Judge Wikeley emphasised that the statutory definition of a married couple is deliberately phrased in a different way to the standard social security definition. He also cautioned against adopting from family law the definition in the Matrimonial Causes Act 1973. He concluded on the facts of the case that a woman who was living both in the same house and in the same household as her husband was, nonetheless, separated from him for tax credit purposes. Consequently he upheld the wife's appeal against a First-tier Tribunal decision to the opposite effect. More generally he declined to follow the decision in *HMRC v TD (TC)* [2012] UKUT 230 (AAC) insofar as it took a contrary view. He also commented on HMRC guidance about any necessity for a separation between spouses to be formalised.

**p.123,** *annotation to the Tax Credits Act 2002 s.3 (claims)*

The reference to CTC/1629/2005 should read "CTC/1630/2005,   **5.005** reported as R(TC) 2/05)".

**p.141,** *annotation to the Tax Credits Act 2002 s.14 (initial decisions)*

*ZM and AB v HMRC (TC)* [2013] UKUT 547 (AAC) is the decision   **5.006** of the Upper Tribunal in a test case brought by the Child Poverty Action Group about the meaning of s.14. The case concerned a joint claim refused by HMRC because of a query about the identity of one of the couple. This turned in part on reg.5 of the Tax Credits (Claims and Notifications) Regulations 2002. HMRC argued that a decision whether a claim was properly made under that regulation was not subject to any statutory procedure.

Judge Ward accepted that argument with regard to UK domestic legislation but then turned to an argument based by CPAG on the Human Rights Act 1988 ss.3 and 6, and art.6 of the European Convention on Human Rights. It was not in dispute before him that determination of a claim for tax credits was a determination of the claimant's civil rights. That must follow from the decision of the Supreme Court in *Tomlinson and others v Birmingham City Council* [2010] UKSC 8. Judge Ward considered in detail whether the availability of judicial review was an art.6 compliant remedy for this kind of case. He decided that it was not, drawing support from the reasoning about the scope of judicial review of a First-tier Tribunal in the decision of Judge Turnbull in *SG v HMRC (TC)* [2011] UKUT 199 (AAC) and the decision of (then) Commissioner Levenson in *CTC/31/2006* (unreported) which he cites at some length. He concluded (at para.64) that he was required by the Human Rights Act 1998 to read s.14(1) as if it said:

> "On a claim for a tax credit or on what would constitute such a claim but for the Board's view that the person or one of the persons making the claim could not avail themselves of regulation 5(8) of the Tax Credits (Claims and Notifications) Regulations 2002 where that provision is in issue . . . "

Judge Ward noted that reg.5(8) had been introduced by amending regulations without any certificate of compliance with the 1998 Act and that it was not in contemplation when the 2002 Act was passed. He concluded that his approach was a proper approach to be taken as a matter of rights-compliant interpretation and was not in effect legislation.

While the judge carefully kept his focus on the specific issue in dispute, the strength of the arguments suggest that they might be applied to any other "decision" that is not regarded by HMRC as appealable save where (as with overpayments) there is clear legislative authority that the determination is not appealable.

**p.176,** *annotation to the Tax Credits Act 2002 s.38 (appeals)*

5.007     In *SH v HMRC and SC(TC)* [2013] UKUT 0297 (AAC) Judge Wikeley drew attention to the sensitivity of appeals involving the relationships of two separated parents to a child or children, particularly where there was a dispute between them about a child. Allowing an appeal, he gave careful directions to the First-tier Tribunal requiring anonymity for all aspects of the further hearing of the appeal by that tribunal.

**p.178,** *annotation to the Tax Credits Act 2002 s.39 (exercise of right of appeal)*

5.008     In a robust decision criticising both HMRC's submissions to a First-tier Tribunal and the failure of that tribunal to note their deficiencies, Judge Ward sets out in some detail in his decision in *AG v HMRC (TC)* [2013] UKUT 530 (AAC) the extent to which HMRC is required to provide a FTT with evidence about a tax credit appeal. The case concerned a claim by an appellant that he had provided information to HMRC about a change of circumstances. A FTT had directed HMRC to produce further details about the case. HMRC had produced nothing relevant and had failed to respond to part of the direction, but a second FTT ignored the failure and found against the appellant. In the UT, Judge Ward directed full disclosure. In response he was given details of the telephone conversations recorded by HMRC from its helpline. He rules that this should have been provided to the FTT, noting that the failure to do so was a breach of r.24(3) of the FTT's procedure rules. It followed that the decision of that tribunal was in error of law for failure to consider the full case. The judge helpfully scheduled to his decision part of an affidavit of evidence from HMRC about the evidence it records and how it is recorded.

See also the criticisms about the failure of HMRC to provide FTT hearings with full papers in the decisions of Judge Wikeley in *SH v HMRC (TC)* [2013] UKUT 297 (AAC) and Judge Turnbull in *JP v HMRC (TC)* [2013] UKUT 519 (AAC), where he commented that this was not the first time on which he had noted a reluctance of HMRC to put all potentially relevant documents before a FTT. In *TM v HMRC (TC)* [2013] UKUT 444 (AAC) Judge Wright set aside a FTT decision in a case where HMRC produced its submission only at the last minute to the tribunal. The appellant had not been given an adequate time to consider it as HMRC had not issued it to the appellant. The failure to issue to the appellant was a breach of the duty on HMRC under the tribunal procedure rules, unless a tribunal had expressly waived the requirement.

**p. 362,** *annotation to the Welfare Reform Act 2012*

Progress in introducing universal credit is slower than originally 5.009
planned, with only limited pilot schemes scheduled to be running as at
April 6, 2014. See further the new Vol.V in this series.

**p.377,** *amendment to the Working Tax Credit (Entitlement and Maximum
Rate) Regulations 2002 (SI 2002/2005) reg.2 (interpretation)*

With effect from April 29, 2013, reg.77(2) of the Universal Credit 5.010
(Consequential, Supplementary, Incidental and Miscellaneous Provisions) Regulations 2013 (SI 2013/630) inserted in para.(1), in the definition of "contributory employment and support allowance", and after
"Welfare Reform Act" the following:

"('the 2007 Act') as amended by the provisions of Schedule 3, and
Part 1 of Schedule 14, to the Welfare Reform Act 2012 that remove
references to an income-related allowance, and a contributory allowance under Part 1 of the 2007 Act as that Part has effect apart from
those provisions".

The same amending regulation inserted in para.(5)(a), after "2008",
the phrase "or regulation 86 of the Employment and Support Allowance
Regulations 2013".

**p.381,** *amendment to the Working Tax Credit (Entitlement and Maximum
Rate) Regulations 2002 (SI 2002/2005) reg.4 (entitlement to basic element
of working tax credit: qualifying remunerative work)*

With effect from August 5, 2013, reg.2 of the Working Tax Credit 5.011
(Entitlement and Maximum Rate) (Amendment) Regulations 2013 (SI
2013/1736) substituted "regulation 13(4) to (12)" for "regulation 13(4)
to (8)" in sub-para.(c)(i) of the Second condition, Third variation specified in para.(1).

**p.384,** *annotation to the Working Tax Credit (Entitlement and Maximum
Rate) Regulations 2002 (SI 2002/2005) reg.4 entitlement to basic element
of working tax credit)*

In CTC/3443/2012 the Upper Tribunal applied the decision of the 5.012
Court of Appeal in *R(IS) 22/95* to the appeal of a claimant arguing that
he was undertaking work for 30 hours a week. The judge emphasised
that this is a question of fact taking into account work necessary for a
particular employment and that the work must be undertaken in expectation of payment for that work.

**p.392,** *annotation to the Working Tax Credit (Entitlement and Maximum
Rate) Regulations 2002 (SI 2002/2005) reg.7D (ceasing to undertake
work or working for less than 16, 24 or 30 hours a week)*

See the note to reg.16 below about the relationship between this 5.013
regulation and reg.16.

**p.395,** *amendment to the Working Tax Credit (Entitlement and Maximum Rate) Regulations 2002 (SI 2002/2005) reg.9 (disability element and workers who are to be treated as at a disadvantage in getting a job)*

5.014    With effect from April 29, 2013, reg.77(3) of the Universal Credit (Consequential, Supplementary, Incidental and Miscellaneous Provisions) Regulations 2013 (SI 2013/630) inserted after para.(7) the following:

> "(7A) In paragraph (7)(b)(iv), the reference to contributory employment and support allowance is a reference to an allowance under Part 1 of the Welfare Reform Act 2007 ('the 2007 Act') as amended by the provisions of Schedule 3, and Part 1 of Schedule 14, to the Welfare Reform Act 2012 that remove references to an income-based allowance, and a contributory allowance under Part 1 of the 2007 Act as that Part has effect apart from those provisions."

**p.401,** *amendment to the Working Tax Credit (Entitlement and Maximum Rate) Regulations 2002 (SI 2002/2005) reg.13 (entitlement to child care element of working tax credit)*

5.015    With effect from August 5, 2013, reg.3(2) of the Working Tax Credit (Entitlement and Maximum Rate) (Amendment) Regulations 2013 (SI 2013/1736) substituted "paragraphs (5) to (12)" for "paragraphs (5) to (8)" in para.(4). Regulation 3(3) of the same amending Regulations substituted a new para.(5) as follows:

> "(5) The circumstances specified in this paragraph are where housing benefit is payable under Part 7 of the Contributions and Benefits Act to the other member or the other member's partner and the applicable amount of the person entitled to the benefit includes a disability premium on account of the other member's incapacity or regulation 28(1)(c) of the Housing Benefit Regulations 2006 (treatment of child care charges) applies in that person's case."

With effect from April 29, 2013, reg.77(4) of the Universal Credit (Consequential, Supplementary, Incidental and Miscellaneous Provisions) Regulations 2013 (SI 2013/630) inserted after para.(6) the following:

> "(6A) In paragraph (6)(h), the reference to contributory employment and support allowance is a reference to an allowance under Part 1 of the Welfare Reform Act 2007 ('the 2007 Act') as amended by the provisions of Schedule 3, and Part 1 of Schedule 14, to the Welfare Reform Act 2012 that remove references to an income-related allowance, and a contributory allowance under Part 1 of the 2007 Act as that Part has effect apart from those provisions."

With effect from August 5, 2013, reg.3(4) of the Working Tax Credit (Entitlement and Maximum Rate) (Amendment) Regulations 2013 (SI 2013/1736) inserted after para.(8) the following new paragraphs:

"(9) The circumstances specified in this paragraph are where, on 31st March 2013, council tax benefit was payable under Part 7 of the Contributions and Benefits Act (as then in force) to the other member or the other member's partner and the applicable amount of the person entitled to the benefit included a disability premium on account of the other member's incapacity.

(10) Paragraph (9) is subject to paragraphs (11) and (12).

(11) Paragraph (9) does not apply unless the other member of the couple was incapacitated (for the purposes of paragraph (1)(c)(i) and regulation 4(1) Second condition, Third variation (c)(i)) solely by virtue of that person or their partner having been in receipt, on 31st March 2013, of council tax benefit which included a disability premium on account of the other member's incapacity, and none of the other circumstances specified in paragraphs (5) to (8) applied on that date.

(12) If—

(a) the other member of the couple is incapacitated in the circumstances specified in paragraph (9), and

(b) the couple ceases to be entitled to working tax credit (for any reason) on or after 1st April 2013,

that member of the couple shall not be treated as incapacitated in the circumstances specified in paragraph (9) in relation to any subsequent claim.".

**p.405,** *annotation to Working Tax Credit (Entitlement and Maximum Rate) Regulations 2002 (SI 2002/2005) reg.12(2)(f)(entitlement to child care element of working tax credit)*

With effect from October 1, 2103, minor amendments are made to the Tax Credits (Approval of Child Care Providers) (Wales) Scheme 2007 by SI 2013/2237. They affect only the information powers under the Scheme and do not make any changes to entitlement. **5.016**

**p.409,** *annotation to Working Tax Credit (Entitlement and Maximum Rate) Regulations 2002 (SI 2002/2005) reg.16 (change of circumstances)*

In *HMRC v CB (TC)* [2013] UKUT 484 (AAC) the Upper Tribunal considered the interaction of reg.16 with reg.7D. The question in issue was the length of time for which entitlement to tax credits continued after a claimant who had been working 40 hours a week stopped working. The specific issue was the period for which the childcare element remained payable. There had been a timely notification of changes of circumstances. HMRC argued that the "run on" periods in regs 7D and 16 ran concurrently, while the appellant argued that they should be applied consecutively. Judge Ovey agreed with the appellant's arguments in part, noting that reg.13 determined the questions of entitlement to the childcare element and that reg.16 is concerned with actual changes only and with the date of any required recalculation. However, on the facts, this did not assist the appellant. **5.017**

**p.447,** *amendment to the Tax Credit (Definition and Calculation of Income) Regulations 2002 (SI 2002/2006) reg.7 (social security income)*

5.018    With effect from April 29, 2013, reg.78(2) of the Universal Credit (Consequential, Supplementary, Incidental and Miscellaneous Provisions) Regulations 2013 (SI 2013/630) inserted after "Jobseeker's Act 1995" in Table 3 in reg.7(3), in the entry in row 16, the following:

"as amended by the provisions of Part 1 of Schedule 14 to the Welfare Reform Act 2012 that remove references to an income-based allowance, and a contribution-based allowance under the Jobseekers Act 1995 as that Act has effect apart from those provisions".

**p.463,** *amendment to the Tax Credits (Definition and Calculation of Income) Regulations 2002 (SI 2002/2006) reg.17 (claimants providing services to other persons for less than full earnings)*

5.019    With effect from April 29, 2013, reg.78(3) of the Universal Credit (Consequential, Supplementary, Incidental and Miscellaneous Provisions) Regulations 2013 (SI 2013/630) substituted for para.7(2)(b)(i) the following:

"(i) in Great Britain, which is approved by the Secretary of State;".

**p.475,** *amendment to the Child Tax Credit Regulations 2002 (SI 2002/2007) reg.2 (interpretation)*

5.020    With effect from June 24, 2013, para.19(2) of Sch.1 to the Children's Hearings (Scotland) Act 2011 (Consequential and Transitional Provisions and Savings) Order 2013 (SI 2013/1465) inserted at the end of the definition of "looked after by a local authority" the following:

", and (in Scotland) includes a child in respect of which a child assessment order within the meaning of section 35 of the Children's Hearings (Scotland) Act 2011 has been made or a child protection order within the meaning of section 37 of that Act has been made."

**p.477,** *amendment to the Child Tax Credit Regulations 2002 (SI 2002/2007) reg.3 (circumstances in which a person is or is not responsible for a child or qualifying young person)*

5.021    With effect from June 24, 2013, para.19(3) of Sch.1 to the Children's Hearings (Scotland) Act 2011 (Consequential and Transitional Provisions and Savings) Order 2013 (SI 2013/1465) inserted after "Part II of the Children (Scotland) Act 1995" in reg.3(1), Rule 4.1, Case A, the following:

"by virtue of a requirement in a child assessment order within the meaning of section 35 of the Children's Hearings (Scotland) Act 2011, a child protection order within the meaning of section 37 of that Act, a compulsory supervision order within the meaning of section 83 of that Act or an interim compulsory supervision order within the meaning of section 86 of that Act,".

**p.480,** *annotation to the Child Tax Credits Regulations 2002 (SI 2002/2007) reg.3(1) (circumstances in which a person is or is not responsible for a child or qualifying young person)*

In *GJ v HMRC (TC)* [2013] UKUT 561 (AAC), Judge Wikeley 5.022 emphasised that the "normally living with" test bears its ordinary meaning and that the relevant facts take priority over the terms of a residence order stating what ought to be the case. Such cases are therefore essentially to be determined on the evidence before a tribunal about the actual arrangements within which a child normally lives at relevant times.

**p.484,** *amendment to the Child Tax Credit Regulations 2002 (SI 2002/2007) reg.5 (maximum age and prescribed conditions for a qualifying young person)*

With effect from April 29, 2013, reg.79 of the Universal Credit (Con- 5.023 sequential, Supplementary, Incidental and Miscellaneous Provisions) Regulations 2013 (SI 2013/630) substituted "," for the "or" after "Welfare Reform Act 2007" in para.(4)(c) and inserted "or universal credit under Part 1 of the Welfare Reform Act 2012" after "Jobseekers Act 1995".

**p.506,** *annotation to the Tax Credits (Claims and Notifications) Regulations 2002 (SI 2002/2014) reg.5 (manner in which claims to be made)*

See the note to s.14 of the 2002 Act, above against p.141, for a 5.024 decision on appeals against decisions under this regulation.

**p.519,** *annotation to the Tax Credits (Claims and Notifications) Regulations 2002 (SI 2002/2014) reg.21(requirement to notify change of circumstances)*

In *JL v HMRC (TC)* [2013] UKUT 325 (AAC) the Upper Tribunal 5.025 allowed an appeal concerning a job swap between a husband and wife. They were jointly claiming tax credits. At the start of the period the husband worked 16 hours a week. At the end of one week the husband stopped working at that work, and the wife took over, working the same hours and earning the same money. HMRC decided that this required the joint claim to stop and for a new claim to be made because there had been a change of circumstances within reg.21. The judge could identify no provision in reg.21(2) that applied to the couple as there was no change in the working pattern (one of the couple working 16 hours a week) and no change in entitlement. Consequently there was no relevant change of circumstances. The HMRC decisions, affirmed by the FTT, that the joint claim had ended with the change, and that no new award could be made until a new claim was made, were set aside and entitlement throughout the relevant period confirmed.

**pp.546–547**, *amendment to the Tax Credits (Administrative Arrangements) Regulations 2002 (SI 2002/3036) reg.5 (recording, verification and holding, and forwarding, of claims etc. received by relevant authorities)*

5.026    With effect from April 29, 2013, reg.80 of the Universal Credit (Consequential, Supplementary, Incidental and Miscellaneous Provisions) Regulations 2013 (SI 2013/630) removed the "or" between sub-paras 5(6)(a) and (b) and after sub-para.(b) inserted:

"; or
   (c) universal credit under Part 1 of the Welfare Reform Act 2012".

**p.567**, *annotation to the Tax Credits (Residence) Regulations 2003 (SI 2003/654) reg.3*

5.027    The Finance Act 2013 introduced a completely new and detailed tax regime for determining the residence and ordinary residence of individuals for income tax purposes, commencing for the tax year 2013–14, subject to transitional provisions. They therefore apply to income tax returns due for that and later years. The main change is one of approach. The former general case law led factual approach is replaced by two extremely detailed sets of rules applying two new sets of tests. The first is a statutory residence test (or, rather, a set of parallel tests) applied by s.218 of and Sch.45 to the 2013 Act. The other is the abolition of the test of ordinary residence entirely by s.219 of and Sch.46 to the 2013 Act, the concept being replaced by specific statutory tests, such as a three-year non-residence test for employees. The legislation deals in considerable detail with the new tests for all relevant aspects of income tax, including split year rules. As these have no direct effect on tax credits legislation to date, none of the detailed amendments to the income tax legislation have been included in this volume. The guidance about the former income tax treatment remains fully relevant to tax credits. Booklet IR20 has been kept on the HMRC website for reference although it has no current relevance to income tax. (For current income tax purposes it has been replaced by Guidance Notes, in particular RDR1 on *Residence, Domicile and the Remittance Basis*.)

**p.573**, *annotation to the Tax Credits (Official Error) Regulations 2003 (SI 2003/692) reg.3*

5.028    In *JP v HMRC (TC)* [2013] UKUT 519 (AAC), the Upper Tribunal considered reg.3 of the Regulations in a case where a DWP official assisted a claimant in making a tax credits claim but in doing so omitted a claim for the disability of the claimant's child. Judge Turnbull accepted as correct an HMRC concession that the actions of the DWP official were official actions. However, the error had led to the award decision under s.14 of the 2002 Act. That had been replaced by an entitlement decision under s.18. Following the decision in *CTC 262 2005*, the decision to be considered in the appeal was the s.18 decision, and the relevant question was whether the official error was the cause of that decision. On the facts, and applying a commonsense approach to causation as indicated in *R(Sier) v Cambridge CC HBRB* [2001] EWCA Civ 1523, it was decided that the original official error no longer operated to cause the error in the s.18 decision. The claimant had twice been warned to check the decision and had not done so.

**p.845,** *amendment to Child Trust Funds Regulations 2004 (SI 2004/1450) reg.2 (interpretation)*

With effect from August 5, 2013, reg.3(a) of the Child Trust Funds (Amendment No. 2) Regulations 2013 (SI 2013/1744) substituted in reg.2(1)(b) for the definitions of "EEA Agreement" and "EEA State" the following:    **5.029**

"'EEA Agreement' means the agreement on the European Economic Area signed at Oporto on 2nd May 1992, together with the Protocol adjusting that Agreement signed at Brussels on 17th March 1993, as modified or supplemented from time to time;
'EEA State', in relation to any time, means a state which at that time is a member State, or any other state which at that time is a party to the EEA Agreement;".

Regulation 3(b) of the same amending Regulations substituted "section 1005 of ITA 2007" for "section 841 of the Taxes Act" in the definition of "recognised stock exchange", while regulation 4 inserted after regulation 2(1) the following:

"(1A) In these Regulations—
(a) a 'bulk transfer of accounts' occurs where two or more accounts are transferred, without a break in the management of the accounts, by an account provider ('the transferor') direct to another account provider ('the transferee')—
   (i) pursuant to an agreement made between the transferor and the transferee where the transfers are not made pursuant to requests made by the person who is the registered contact in relation to the accounts transferred; or
   (ii) pursuant to an insurance business transfer scheme or a banking business transfer scheme under Part 7 (Control of Business Transfers) of FISMA 2000;
(b) a 'group transfer of accounts' occurs where a bulk transfer of accounts is made between account providers that are members of the same group of companies when the transfer occurs;
(c) two companies are members of the same group of companies if—
   (i) one is a 75% subsidiary of the other, or
   (ii) both are 75% subsidiaries of a third company.".

**p.862,** *amendment to Child Trust Funds Regulations 2004 (SI 2004/1450) reg.12 (qualifying investments for an account)*

5.030    With effect from August 5, 2013, reg.5 of the Child Trust Funds (Amendment No. 2) Regulations 2013 (SI 2013/1744) substituted "either officially listed on a recognised stock exchange or, in the European Economic Area, admitted to trading on a recognised stock exchange (see paragraph (3))" for the words "officially listed on a recognised stock exchange (see paragraph (3))" in para.(2)(a). The same amending Regulations inserted ", or the condition as to admission to trading in paragraph (2)(a)," before "if" in para.(3) and inserted "or admitted to such trading" before "within" and "or trading" before ", would be qualifying investments" in para.(3)(a).

**p.869,** *amendment to Child Trust Funds Regulations 2004 (SI 2004/1450) reg.14 (account provider—qualifications and Board's approval)*

5.031    With effect from September 1, 2013, reg.8 of the Financial Services Act 2012 (Consequential Amendments and Transitional Provisions) (No. 3) Order 2013 substituted "FISMA 2000" for "section 31(1)(a) of the Financial Services and Markets Act 2000" in para.(2)(d)(iia).

**p.874,** *amendment to Child Trust Funds Regulations 2004 (SI 2004/1450) reg.19 (account provider ceasing to act (or ceasing to accept Revenue allocated accounts)*

5.032    With effect from August 5, 2013, reg.6 of the Child Trust Funds (Amendment No. 2) Regulations 2013 (SI 2013/1744) substituted new regs 19 and 19A:

**"Account provider's intention to make a bulk transfer of accounts or to cease to act as an account provider**

**19.**—(1) An account provider must give notice to the Board if the account provider—
   (a)  intends to cease to act as an account provider; or
   (b)  intends to make a bulk transfer of accounts.
   (2) An account provider must give notice to the person who is the registered contact (or, if there is no registered contact, the named child) if the account provider—
   (a)  intends to cease to act as an account provider; or
   (b)  intends that the account will be one of the accounts transferred in a bulk transfer of accounts.
   (3) The notices described in paragraphs (1) and (2) must—
   (a)  specify whether the account provider—
      (i)  intends to cease to act as an account provider; or
      (ii)  intends to make a bulk transfer of accounts;
   (b)  where the notice specifies an intention to cease to act as an account provider—

  (i) specify the day on or after which the account provider intends to cease to act as an account provider; and

  (ii) be given no less than 30 days before that day;

(c) where the notice specifies an intention to make a bulk transfer of accounts—

  (i) specify the day on or after which the account provider intends to make the first transfer in the bulk transfer of accounts;

  (ii) be given no less than 30 days before that day; and

  (iii) advise the name and address of the person to whom the account provider intends to transfer accounts.

(4) The notice described in paragraph (2) must also—

(a) identify the account to which it relates;

(b) in the case of a notice under paragraph (2)(a), advise the registered contact of the right to transfer the account under regulation 21 and of his rights under regulation 20(3);

(c) in the case of a notice under paragraph (2)(b)—

  (i) advise the registered contact that the account may be transferred otherwise than in a bulk transfer of accounts, such that regulation 21 applies, if sufficient instructions are provided to enable the account provider to do so; and

  (ii) advise the day by which the account provider must receive sufficient instructions for the account to be transferred otherwise than in a bulk transfer of accounts.

(5) Where an account provider intends to make a bulk transfer of accounts in consequence of an intention to cease to act as an account provider, such intention may be specified in a single notice to the Board or to a registered contact (or, if there is no registered contact, the named child) (as appropriate, respectively) provided the requirements of paragraphs (3), (4)(a) and (c) are met.

### Account provider ceasing to accept Revenue allocated accounts

19A. A person shall give notice to the Board of his intention to cease to accept further Revenue allocated accounts under regulation 6, not less than 30 days before he so ceases."

**p.875,** *amendment to Child Trust Funds Regulations 2004 (SI 2004/1450) reg.20 (account provider ceasing to qualify)*

With effect from August 5, 2013, reg.7 of the Child Trust Funds (Amendment No. 2) Regulations 2013 (SI 2013/1744) substituted "19(2)(a)" for the reference to "19(1)" in para.(3)(a). 5.033

**p.875,** *amendment to Child Trust Funds Regulations 2004 (SI 2004/1450) reg.21 (transfer of accounts to other account providers)*

With effect from August 5, 2013, reg.8 of the Child Trust Funds (Amendment No. 2) Regulations 2013 (SI 2013/1744) omitted "or" 5.034

after "('the transferee')" in para.(1)(a), added "or" after "qualify as an account provider," in para.(1)(b), inserted after para.(1)(b).

> "(c) an account is transferred in a bulk transfer of accounts or in a group transfer of accounts,".

The same amending Regulations substituted "(3H)" for "(3A)" after para.(3) and inserted before that para.(3H) the following:

> "(3A) Paragraph (3) does not apply where an account is transferred in a bulk transfer of accounts.
>
> (3B) Where an account is transferred in a bulk transfer of accounts, a subscription to the account after the transfer may only be made if—
>
> (a) an application to the transferee in relation to the account in accordance with regulation 13 has been made; or
>
> (b) the subscription is permitted by virtue of paragraph (3C);
>
> and regulation 13(2) is then modified for the purposes of this paragraph as if the words 'applied for' were replaced with 'following the transfer'.
>
> (3C) A subscription to an account is permitted by this paragraph where—
>
> (a) the account has been transferred to the transferee in a bulk transfer of accounts pursuant to a scheme described in regulation 2(1A)(a)(ii) or pursuant to a transfer of the type described in regulation 2(1A)(b); and
>
> (b) the most recent application in accordance with regulation 13 relating to the transferred account made before its transfer is available to the transferee.
>
> (3D) For the purposes of paragraph (3C)(b), an application in accordance with regulation 13 as described in that paragraph is available to a transferee if paragraph (3E) or (3F) applies.
>
> (3E) This paragraph applies where the application described in paragraph (3C)(b) (or a copy of it) is held by the transferee.
>
> (3F) This paragraph applies where—
>
> (a) the application described in paragraph (3C)(b) (or a copy of it) is held by the transferor; and
>
> (b) the transferee can require the transferor to make it available to the transferee for any purpose necessary to ensure the transferee's compliance with these regulations.
>
> (3G) An account transferred in accordance with this regulation in a bulk transfer of accounts is an account opened pursuant to an application in accordance with regulation 13 for the purposes of these Regulations whether or not an application in accordance with regulation 13 as described in paragraph (3B)(a) is made."

**p.883,** *amendment to Child Trust Funds Regulations 2004 (SI 2004/1450) reg.31 (records to be kept by account provider)*

5.035    With effect from August 5, 2013, reg.9 of the Child Trust Funds (Amendment No. 2) Regulations 2013 (SI 2013/1744) inserted after para.(2) the following:

"(3) Where an account is transferred by an account provider ('the transferor') to another account provider ('the transferee') in a group transfer of accounts, any records (or copies of records) kept by the transferor in respect of the account at the time when it is transferred shall be treated for the purposes of this regulation as kept by the transferee for so long as sub-paragraphs (a), (b) and (c) of paragraph (4) apply.

(4) For the purposes of paragraph (3)—
   (a) this sub-paragraph applies as if the records described in paragraph (3) are kept by the transferor;
   (b) this sub-paragraph applies if the transferor and transferee are members of the same group of companies; and
   (c) this sub-paragraph applies if the transferee can require the transferor to make the records available to the transferee for any purpose necessary to ensure the transferee's compliance with these regulations."

**p.886,** *amendment to Child Trust Funds Regulations 2004 (SI 2004/1450) reg.33A (the Official Solicitor or Accountant of Court to be the person who has the authority to manage an account)*

With effect from June 24, 2013, para.21 of Sch.1 to the Children's Hearings (Scotland) Act 2011 (Consequential and Transitional Provisions and Savings) Order 2013 (SI 2013/1465) substituted in Condition 3 in para.(2) for "(or, in Scotland, a supervision requirement made with a condition regulating contact under section 70(5)(b) of the Children (Scotland) Act 1995 that the child shall have no contact with a person with parental responsibilities)" the following:    **5.036**

"(or, in Scotland, a compulsory supervision order or an interim compulsory supervision order is in force and contains a direction regulating contact to the effect that the child has no contact with a person who has parental responsibilities in relation to that child)";

The same amending Regulations inserted at the end of para.(2) the following:

"In this Condition—
   (a) 'compulsory supervision order' has the meaning given by section 83 of the Children's Hearings (Scotland) Act 2011;
   (b) 'interim compulsory supervision order' has the meaning given by section 86 of that Act; and
   (c) 'contact direction' means a measure mentioned in section 83(2)(g) of that Act and contained within a compulsory supervision order or an interim compulsory supervision order.".

**p.893,** *amendment to Child Trust Funds Regulations 2004 (SI 2004/1450) Sch. (stakeholder accounts)*

With effect from August 5, 2013, reg.10 of the Child Trust Funds (Amendment No. 2) Regulations 2013 (SI 2013/1744) inserted "or, in    **5.037** the European Economic Area, admitted to trading on a recognised stock exchange" in para.2(2)(a)(via) after "stock exchange;" and inserted "or, in the European Economic Area, admitted to trading on a recognised stock exchange" in para.2(6) in the definition of "equities" after "exchange".

# PART VI

# FORTHCOMING CHANGES AND
# UP-RATINGS OF BENEFITS

# FORTHCOMING CHANGES

This section aims to give users of Social Security Legislation 2013/14 some information on significant changes coming into force between January 1, 2014—the date to which this Supplement is up to date—and mid-April 2014, the date to which the 2014/15 edition will be up to date. The information here reflects our understanding of sources available to us as at January 1, 2014 and users should be aware that there will no doubt be further legislative amendment between then and mid-April 2014. This Part of the Supplement will at least enable users to access the relevant legislation (and usually accompanying Explanatory Notes prepared by the Department) on the Government Legislation website (*http:/ /www.legislation.gov.uk*) operated by the National Archives.

## STATUTES

### Welfare Benefits Up-rating Act 2013

The Welfare Benefits Up-rating Act 2013 (c.16) came into force on October 1, 2013 (see the Welfare Benefits Up-rating Act 2013 (Commencement) Order 2013 (SI 2013/2317), and so is included in Part I of this Supplement, although the actual changes to benefits and tax credits take effect for the financial years 2014–15 and 2015–16.

### Marriage (Same Sex Couples) Act 2013

The Marriage (Same Sex Couples) Act 2013 (c.30) enables same sex couples to marry, either in a civil ceremony or (subject to certain conditions) on religious premises. Part 5 of Sch.4 to the Act makes supplementary provision about a person's entitlement to state pension, based on a current or deceased spouse's or civil partner's National Insurance record, by amending SSCBA 1992. The relevant provisions are not yet in force.

### Mesothelioma Act 2014

The Mesothelioma Act 2014 (c.1), which received the Royal Assent on January 30, 2014, provides for a scheme for lump sum payments for victims of mesothelioma, building on the Pneumoconiosis etc (Workers' Compensation) Act 1979 and Part 4 of the Child Maintenance and Other Payments Act 2008. The 2014 Act is intended to tackle one of the problems caused by the disease's long latency period, namely that by the time symptoms appear the employer may well have gone out of business and it is also not possible to trace the insurance company carrying the relevant employers' liability insurance. The scheme is financed by way of a levy on the insurance industry. The Act itself does not establish a scheme, but empowers the Secretary of State to do so. The Act provides that any such scheme must include a right of appeal to the First-tier Tribunal. At the time of writing the draft Diffuse Mesothelioma Payment Scheme Regulations 2014 had been published, which require affirmative resolutions of both Houses of Parliament.

# REGULATIONS

## The Draft Tax Credits, Child Benefit and Guardian's Allowance Reviews and Appeals Order

The draft Tax Credits, Child Benefit and Guardian's Allowance Reviews and Appeals Order 2014 provides for compulsory reviews of HMRC decisions about tax credits, child benefit and guardian's allowance before an appeal may be made to the First-tier Tribunal or Northern Ireland equivalents. It therefore mirrors changes being made to mainstream social security benefits administered by the DWP. It also repeals and revokes the rules requiring notice of such appeals to be given, sent or delivered to HMRC. For tax credits, art.2 provides that an application within 30 days of notification of the decision triggers a review (or, if notification is dispensed with, within 30 days of the decision). This time is extendable by HMRC in special circumstances, where reasonable to do so, but only if an application is made within 12 months of the initial 30-day deadline.

## The Draft Tax Credits (Late Appeals) Order 2014

The draft Tax Credits (Late Appeals) Order 2014 makes provision in respect of appeals made under s.38 of Tax Credits Act 2002 which are made, in Great Britain, to the First-tier Tribunal. Article 2(2) makes provision in respect of late tax credits appeals that corresponds in substance to that previously provided by reg.5 (late appeals) of the Tax Credits (Appeals) (No. 2) Regulations 2002 (SI 2002/3196). Article 2(3) provides that the new s.39A validates any decision by HMRC to allow a late appeal made on or after April 1, 2013 and before this Order enters force.

# NEW BENEFIT RATES FROM APRIL 2014

**NEW BENEFIT RATES FROM APRIL 2014**

**(Benefits covered in Volume I)**

|  | April 2013 | April 2014 |
|---|---|---|
|  | £ pw | £ pw |
| *Disability benefits* |  |  |
| Attendance allowance |  |  |
| *higher rate* | 79.15 | 81.30 |
| *lower rate* | 53.00 | 54.45 |
| Disability living allowance |  |  |
| care component |  |  |
| *highest rate* | 79.15 | 81.30 |
| *middle rate* | 53.00 | 54.45 |
| *lowest rate* | 21.00 | 21.55 |
| mobility component |  |  |
| *higher rate* | 55.25 | 56.75 |
| *lower rate* | 21.00 | 21.55 |
| Personal independence payment |  |  |
| daily living component |  |  |
| *enhanced rate* | 79.15 | 81.30 |
| *standard rate* | 53.00 | 54.45 |
| mobility component |  |  |
| *enhanced rate* | 55.25 | 56.75 |
| *standard rate* | 21.00 | 21.55 |
| Carer's allowance | 59.75 | 61.35 |
| Severe disablement allowance |  |  |
| *basic rate* | 71.80 | 73.75 |
| *age related addition—higher rate* | 10.70 | 11.00 |
| *age related addition—middle rate* | 6.00 | 6.15 |
| *age related addition—lower rate* | 6.00 | 6.15 |

|  | April 2013 | April 2014 |
|---|---|---|
|  | £ pw | £ pw |

### Maternity benefits

| Maternity allowance<br>*standard rate* | 136.78 | 138.18 |
|---|---|---|

### Bereavement benefits and retirement pensions

|  | | |
|---|---|---|
| Widowed parent's allowance or widowed<br>mother's allowance | 108.30 | 110.20 |
| Bereavement allowance or widow's pension<br>*standard rate* | 108.30 | 110.20 |
| Retirement pension | | |
| *Category A* | 110.15 | 113.10 |
| *Category B (higher)* | 110.15 | 113.10 |
| *Category B (lower)* | 66.00 | 67.80 |
| *Category C* | 66.00 | 67.80 |
| *Category D* | 66.00 | 67.80 |

### Incapacity benefit

|  | | |
|---|---|---|
| Long-term incapacity benefit | | |
| *basic rate* | 101.35 | 104.10 |
| *increase for age—higher rate* | 10.70 | 11.00 |
| *increase for age—lower rate* | 6.00 | 6.15 |
| *invalidity allowance—higher rate* | 10.70 | 11.00 |
| *invalidity allowance—middle rate* | 6.00 | 6.15 |
| *invalidity allowance—lower rate* | 6.00 | 6.15 |
| Short-term incapacity benefit | | |
| *under pension age—higher rate* | 90.50 | 92.95 |
| *under pension age—lower rate* | 76.45 | 78.50 |
| *over pension age—higher rate* | 101.35 | 104.10 |
| *over pension age—lower rate* | 97.25 | 99.90 |

### Dependency increases

|  | | |
|---|---|---|
| Adult | | |
| carer's allowance | 35.15 | 36.30 |
| severe disablement allowance | 35.35 | 36.10 |
| retirement pension | 63.20 | 64.90 |
| long-term incapacity benefit | 58.85 | 60.45 |
| short-term incapacity benefit under pension age | 45.85 | 47.10 |
| short-term incapacity benefit over pension age | 56.65 | 58.20 |
| Child | 11.35[1] | 11.35[1] |

## New Benefit Rates from April 2014

|  | April 2013 £ pw | April 2014 £ pw |
|---|---|---|
| **Industrial injuries benefits** | | |
| Disablement benefit | | |
| *100%* | 161.60 | 166.00 |
| *90%* | 145.44 | 149.40 |
| *80%* | 129.28 | 132.80 |
| *70%* | 113.12 | 116.20 |
| *60%* | 96.96 | 99.60 |
| *50%* | 80.80 | 83.00 |
| *40%* | 64.64 | 66.40 |
| *30%* | 48.48 | 49.80 |
| *20%* | 32.32 | 33.20 |
| unemployability supplement | | |
| *basic rate* | 99.90 | 102.60 |
| *increase for adult dependant* | 58.85 | 60.45 |
| *increase for child dependant* | 11.35[1] | 11.35[1] |
| *increase for early incapacity—higher rate* | 20.70 | 31.25 |
| *increase for early incapacity—middle rate* | 13.30 | 13.70 |
| *increase for early incapacity—lower rate* | 6.65 | 6.85 |
| constant attendance allowance | | |
| *exceptional rate* | 129.40 | 132.80 |
| *intermediate rate* | 97.05 | 99.60 |
| *normal maximum rate* | 64.70 | 66.40 |
| *part-time rate* | 32.35 | 33.20 |
| exceptionally severe disablement allowance | 64.70 | 66.40 |
| Reduced earnings allowance | | |
| *maximum rate* | 64.64 | 66.40 |
| Death benefit | | |
| widow's pension | | |
| *higher rate* | 110.15 | 113.10 |
| *lower rate* | 33.05 | 33.93 |
| widower's pension | 110.15 | 113.10 |

Notes
1. These sums payable in respect of children are reduced if payable in respect of the only, elder or eldest child for whom child benefit is being paid (see reg.8 of the Social Security (Overlapping Benefits) Regulations 1979 on p.565 of Vol 1 of the main work ).

|  | April 2013 £ pw | April 2014 £ pw |
|---|---|---|
| **Employment and support allowance** | | |
| Contribution-based personal rates | | |
| assessment phase—*aged under 25* | 56.80 | 57.35 |
| *aged 25 or over* | 71.70 | 72.40 |
| main phase | 71.70 | 72.40 |
| Components | | |
| work-related activity | 28.45 | 28.75 |
| support | 34.80 | 35.75 |
| Income-based personal allowances | | |
| single person—*aged under 25* | 56.80 | 57.35 |
| *aged 25 or over* | 71.70 | 72.40 |
| lone parent—*aged under 18* | 56.80 | 57.35 |
| *aged 18 or over* | 71.70 | 72.40 |
| couple—*both aged under 18* | 56.80 | 57.35 |
| *both aged under 18, with a child* | 85.80 | 86.65 |
| *both aged under 18, (main phase)* | 71.70 | 72.40 |
| *both aged under 18, with a child (main phase)* | 112.55 | 113.70 |
| *one aged under 18, one aged 18 or over* | 112.55 | 113.70 |
| *both aged 18 or over* | 112.55 | 113.70 |
| Premiums | | |
| pensioner—*single person with no component* | 73.70 | 75.95 |
| *couple with no component* | 109.50 | 112.80 |
| enhanced disability—*single person* | 15.15 | 15.55 |
| *couple* | 21.75 | 22.30 |
| severe disability—*single person* | 59.50 | 61.10 |
| *couple (one qualifies)* | 59.50 | 61.10 |
| *couple (both qualify)* | 119.00 | 122.20 |
| carer | 33.30 | 34.20 |

# NEW BENEFIT RATES FROM APRIL 2014

## (Benefits covered in Volume II)

| | April 2013 £ pw | April 2014 £ pw |
|---|---|---|
| **Contribution-based jobseeker's allowance** | | |
| personal rates—*aged under 25* | 56.80 | 57.35 |
| *aged 25 or over* | 71.70 | 72.40 |
| **Income support and income-based jobseeker's allowance** | | |
| personal allowances | | |
| single person—*aged under 25* | 56.80 | 57.35 |
| *aged 25 or over* | 71.70 | 72.40 |
| lone parent—*aged under 18* | 56.80 | 57.35 |
| *aged 18 or over* | 71.70 | 72.40 |
| couple—*both aged under 18* | 56.80 | 57.35 |
| *both aged under 18, with a child* | 85.80 | 86.65 |
| *one aged under 18, one aged under 25* | 56.80 | 57.35 |
| *one aged under 18, one aged 25 or over* | 71.70 | 86.65 |
| *both aged 18 or over* | 112.55 | 113.70 |
| child | 65.62 | 66.33 |
| premiums | | |
| family—*ordinary* | 17.40 | 17.45 |
| *lone parent* | 17.40 | 17.45 |
| pensioner—*single person (JSA only)* | 73.70 | 75.95 |
| *couple* | 109.50 | 112.80 |
| disability—*single person* | 31.00 | 31.85 |
| *couple* | 44.20 | 45.40 |
| enhanced disability—*single person* | 15.15 | 15.55 |
| *couple* | 21.75 | 22.35 |
| *child* | 23.45 | 24.08 |
| severe disability—*single person* | 59.50 | 61.10 |
| *couple (one qualifies)* | 59.50 | 61.10 |
| *couple (both qualify)* | 119.00 | 122.20 |
| disabled child | 57.89 | 59.50 |
| carer | 33.30 | 34.20 |
| **Pension credit** | | |
| Standard minimum guarantee | | |
| single person | 145.40 | 148.35 |
| couple | 222.05 | 226.50 |

| | April 2013 £ pw | April 2014 £ pw |
|---|---|---|
| Additional amount for severe disability | | |
| single person | 59.50 | 61.10 |
| couple (one qualifies) | 59.50 | 61.10 |
| couple (both qualify) | 119.00 | 122.20 |
| Additional amount for carers | 33.30 | 34.20 |
| Savings credit threshold | | |
| single person | 115.30 | 120.35 |
| couple | 183.90 | 192.00 |
| Maximum savings credit | | |
| single person | 18.06 | 16.80 |
| couple | 22.89 | 20.70 |

# NEW TAX CREDIT AND BENEFIT RATES 2014–2015

## (Benefits covered in Volume IV)

| | 2013–14 | 2014–15 |
|---|---|---|
| | £ pw | £ pw |
| **Benefits in respect of children** | | |
| Child benefit | | |
| *only, elder or eldest child (couple)* | 20.30 | 20.50 |
| *each subsequent child* | 13.40 | 13.55 |
| Guardian's allowance | 15.90 | 16.35 |
| **Employer-paid benefits** | | |
| Standard rates | | |
| Statutory sick pay | 86.70 | 87.55 |
| Statutory maternity pay | 136.78 | 138.18 |
| Statutory paternity pay | 136.78 | 138.18 |
| Statutory adoption pay | 136.78 | 138.18 |
| Income threshold | 109.00 | 110.00 |

| | 2013–14 | 2014–15 |
|---|---|---|
| | £ pa | £ pa |
| **Working tax credit** | | |
| Basic element | 1,920 | 1,940 |
| Couple and lone parent element | 1,970 | 1,990 |
| 30 hour element | 790 | 800 |
| Disabled worker element | 2,855 | 2,935 |
| Severe disability element | 1,220 | 1,255 |
| Child care element | | |
| *maximum eligible cost for one child* | *175 pw* | *175 pw* |
| *maximum eligible cost for two or more children* | *300 pw* | *300 pw* |
| *per cent of eligible costs covered* | *70%* | *70%* |
| **Child tax credit** | | |
| Family element | 545 | 545 |
| Child element | 2,720 | 2,750 |
| Disabled child element | 3,015 | 3,100 |
| Severely disabled child element | 1,220 | 1,255 |
| **Tax credit income thresholds** | | |
| Income rise disregard | 5,000 | 5,000 |
| Income fall disregard | 2,500 | 2,500 |
| Income threshold | 6,420 | 6,420 |
| Income threshold for those entitled to child tax credit only | 15,910 | 16,010 |
| *Withdrawal rate* | *41%* | *41%* |

# NEW UNIVERSAL CREDIT RATES FROM APRIL 2014

## NEW UNIVERSAL CREDIT RATES FROM APRIL 2014

### (Benefits covered in Volume V)

| | April 2013 | April 2014 |
|---|---|---|
| | £ pw | £ pw |
| *Standard allowances* | | |
| Single claimant—*aged under 25* | 246.81 | 249.28 |
| *aged 25 or over* | 311.55 | 314.67 |
| Joint claimant—*both aged under 25* | 387.42 | 391.29 |
| *one or both aged 25 or over* | 489.06 | 493.95 |
| Child element—*first child* | 272.08 | 274.58 |
| *second/ subsequent child* | 226.67 | 229.17 |
| Disabled child addition—*lower rate* | 123.62 | 124.86 |
| *higher rate* | 352.92 | 362.92 |
| Limited Capability for Work element | 123.62 | 124.86 |
| Limited Capability for Work and Work-Related Activity element | 303.66 | 311.86 |
| Carer element | 144.70 | 148.61 |
| Childcare element—*maximum for one child* | 532.29 | 532.29 |
| *maximum for two or more children* | 912.50 | 912.50 |
| *Non-dependants' housing cost contributions* | 68.00 | 68.68 |
| *Work allowances* | | |
| Higher work allowance (no housing element) | | |
| Single claimant—*no dependent children* | 111.00 | 111.00 |
| *one or more children* | 734.00 | 734.00 |
| *limited capability for work* | 647.00 | 647.00 |
| Joint claimant—*no dependent children* | 111.00 | 111.00 |
| *one or more children* | 536.00 | 536.00 |
| *limited capability for work* | 647.00 | 647.00 |

## New Universal Credit Rates from April 2014

|  | April 2013 | April 2014 |
|---|---|---|
|  | £ pw | £ pw |
| Lower work allowance |  |  |
| Single claimant—*no dependent children* | 111.00 | 111.00 |
| *one or more children* | 263.00 | 263.00 |
| *limited capability for work* | 192.00 | 192.00 |
| Joint claimant—*no dependent children* | 111.00 | 111.00 |
| *one or more children* | 222.00 | 222.00 |
| *limited capability for work* | 192.00 | 192.00 |